Carving Exotic Fish

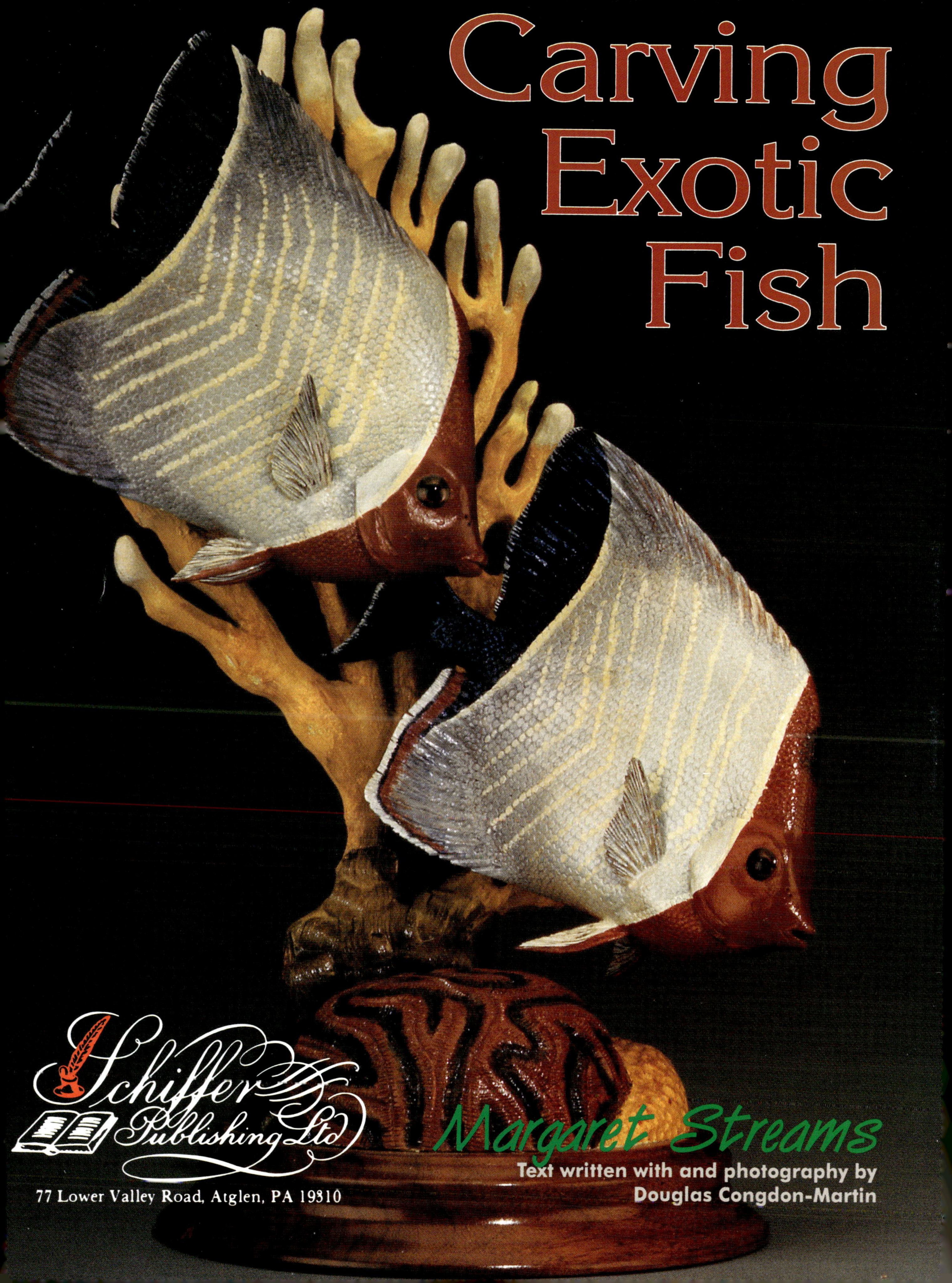

Margaret Streams

Text written with and photography by Douglas Congdon-Martin

Schiffer Publishing Ltd
77 Lower Valley Road, Atglen, PA 19310

Dedication

To William A. Sugden,
Father, Friend, and Fine Fisherman.
You taught me that with an idea, determination, and the right tools I could do great things.

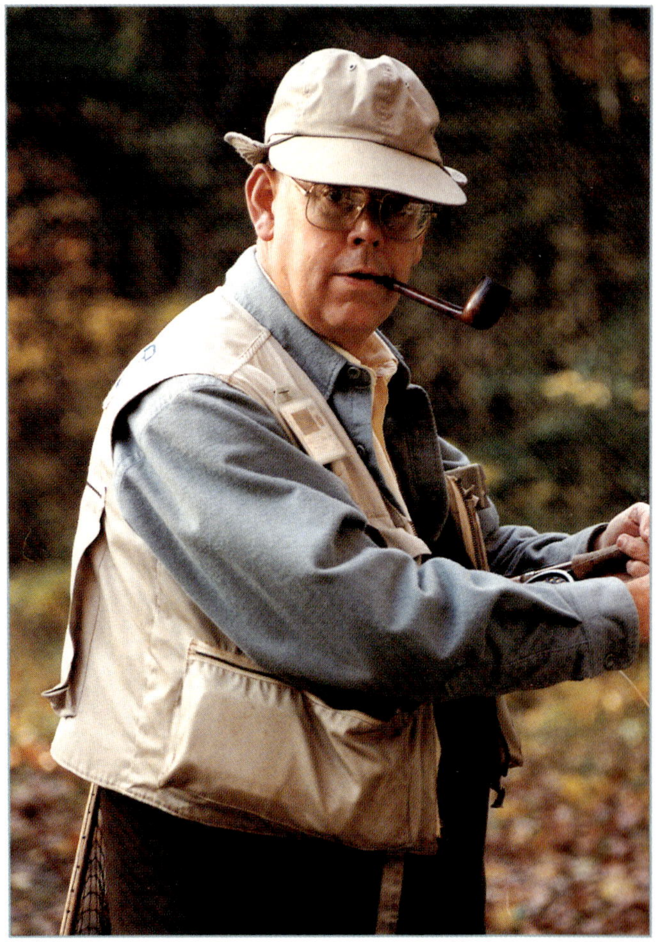

This book is meant only for personal home use and recreation. It is not intended for commercial applications or manufacturing purposes.

Printed in Hong Kong

ISBN: 0-88740-946-6

Book Design by Audrey L. Whiteside.

Library of Congress Cataloging-in-Publication Data

Streams, Margaret, 1967-
Carving exotic fish/Margaret Streams; text written with and photography by Douglas Congdon-Martin.
p.. cm.
ISBN 0-88740-946-6 (hardcover)
1. Wood-carving. 2. Fishes in art. I. Congdon-Martin, Douglas. II. Title.
TT199.7.S765 1996
731'.832--dc20 95-47998
CIP

Published by Schiffer Publishing, Ltd.
77 Lower Valley Road
Atglen, PA 19310
Please write for a free catalog.
This book may be purchased from the publisher.
Please include $2.95 postage.
Try your bookstore first.

We are interested in hearing from authors
with book ideas on related subjects.

Special Thanks

To my husband, Dale, and my family and friends for believing in me. To Douglas Congdon-Martin for his enthusiasm and expertise in the writing and photography of this book.

Contents

Preface 4
Introduction 5
Red Crane Crest
Patterns 6
Carving 9
Carving the Base 53
Painting 58
Fresh Water Angelfish *Pterophyllum scalare*
Pattern 67
Carving 70
Painting 110
Long-Nosed Butterfly *Forcipiger flavissimus*
Patterns 118
Carving 120
Painting 144
The Gallery 151

Acknowledgments

To Howard Suzuki and Mark Frazier for their advice, strong support, and encouragement in helping me "find my own style."
Also a special thanks to the many suppliers who assisted me with advice and a fine selection of products. As a special note, eyes may be ordered from Tohickon Glass Eyes, P.O. Box 15, 15 Geigel Hill Road, Erwinna, PA 18920

Preface

It was late spring of 1991 and we eagerly walked to a stream full of anticipation, our pockets bulging with hoagies, chips and sport drinks. She joked that it ought to be a good day because, at long last, she "jangled." She did, indeed, with enough retractable tools and paraphernalia to make a clinking sound as we walked. Taking our favorite places on a stretch of the Bushkill with an assortment of tied flies, we began our day. Within minutes, from the corner of my eye, I saw her rapidly exiting the stream. My first thought was to scold her for putting down the pool for other fishermen, but I realized she was gently cradling a Brookie. She laid it down on the streamside grass and rapidly photographed its brilliant colors. A fond look at the catch and the release, put me down as at no other time since a freshman in medical college. She was my daughter.

Margaret Streams, then Meg Sugden, came back to the nest after graduating from Penn State in Animal Production and a two year hiatus of getting her act together. Always a whittler, she carved animals to delight her roommates and friends, but at home she took my tools and began carving birds. I'll never forget the evening the cellar door opened and she entered our family room carrying a delicately carved miniature Avocet. It far surpassed my Ward Foundation entries of the 1970s, but no amount of praise could silence her protestations of failure at not being able to carve "like you, Dad."

Within weeks we attended a local carving show where she returned with a book of fish carving by Bob Berry. This began Meg's fish carving career. A life-like Rainbow Trout, a hungry Large Mouth Bass and a variety of salt water fish soon emerged from wood. Thus progressed Margaret's skills towards excellence. Several months later a move to her own apartment with her Golden Retriever, a horse of her own, a job with all the perks, and the fortuitous meeting of Dale Streams, DVM, soon turned her name to Margaret Streams.

I could go on and on, but basically Meg has been my fishing buddy, my pupil for too short a time, and now my mentor. Thanks to many kind and generous folks who have constructively criticized and encouraged her. Among them are the Effrems of Wood Carvers Supply, Mark Frazier of Kent, Ohio, and Dr. Howard Suzuki of Florida. My personal thanks to them for guiding Meg, who will always be at my side along "the streams that make glad the city of God."

William A. Sugden, M.D.
Buckingham, Pennsylvania
1995

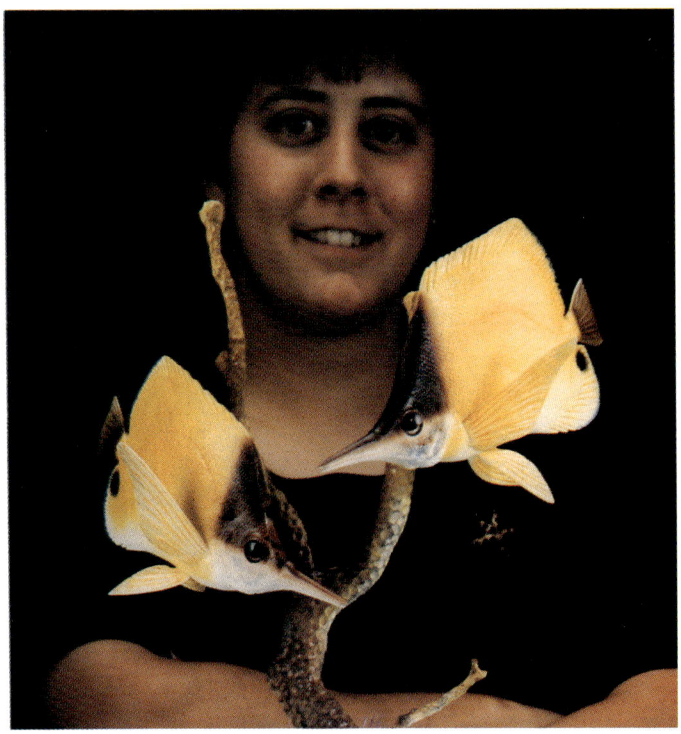

Introduction

Seventy percent of our earth's surface is covered by water and it is this abundant and diverse supply that makes our planet unique. There are few watery places that do not support at least a small number of fish, since they have adapted themselves to seemingly inhospitable environments. Habitats range from fast flowing streams and high mountain lakes, to tide pools and unlighted depths of the ocean, and to acidic waters and even temporary pools that contain no water at all for months at a time.

For most of our history these diverse waters have been impenetrable and unknown, as are the fish that inhabit them. Fish are fascinating creatures with whom we share our planet. In the past our knowledge of life in the watery worlds was limited to what we could catch. Now, developments in science and technology have made it possible for us to observe them in their own environments. Scuba, submersibles, and a vast interest in home aquariums are only a few advancements that allow for direct observation. Now we can determine the exact depth from which a fish came, how it changes through the seasons, mating and feeding behaviors, how fast it grew, and how long it lived. This form of direct observation that was alien in the past will help open new doors for the fish carver.

In this book, I am introducing three unique fish carving projects to the beginner and the experienced carver alike. The first is the Chinese Goldfish called the Red Crane Crest. It has been developed over many centuries and selected for unique traits. In short, it has been created and molded by human hands.

The second fish is the Freshwater Angelfish. Its natural habitat is in the acidic, murky waters of the Amazon. It has become, however, quite common in the home aquarium.

The third project is the Long-nosed Butterfly Fish. It is common in the Indo-Pacific region, and is notable for its unique feeding habits and colorings.

Each project is clearly illustrated with photographs and step-by-step descriptions of the techniques used. I use a combination of power tool carving, traditional carving, and woodburning to bring life, action, and emotion to the carvings.

I hope you enjoy the book and receive many hours of pleasure from it.

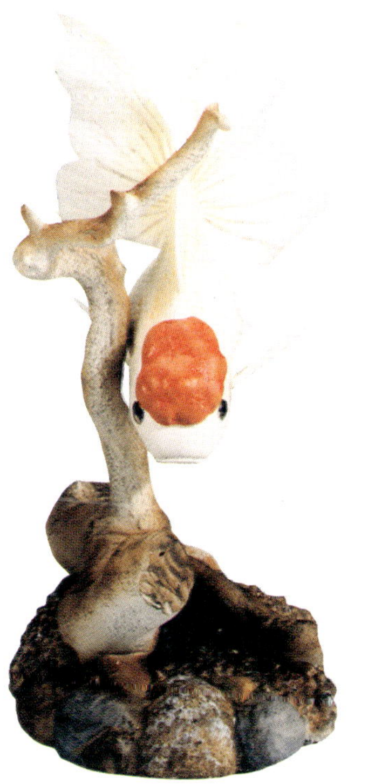

Red Crane Crest

CHARACTERISTICS

Head Varieties
- Flat
- Lion Head
- Goose Head
- Tiger Head
- High Head
- Frog Head

Eye Varieties
- Dragon
- Sky-Grazing
- Bubble
- Normal*

*Normal eyes have round pupils

Other Characteristics
- Velvet balls
- Reverse gills
- Smooth back
- Pearl Scales

Best Reference
Chinese Goldfish, Tetra Press

Chinese Goldfish Pattern
"Red Crane Crest"

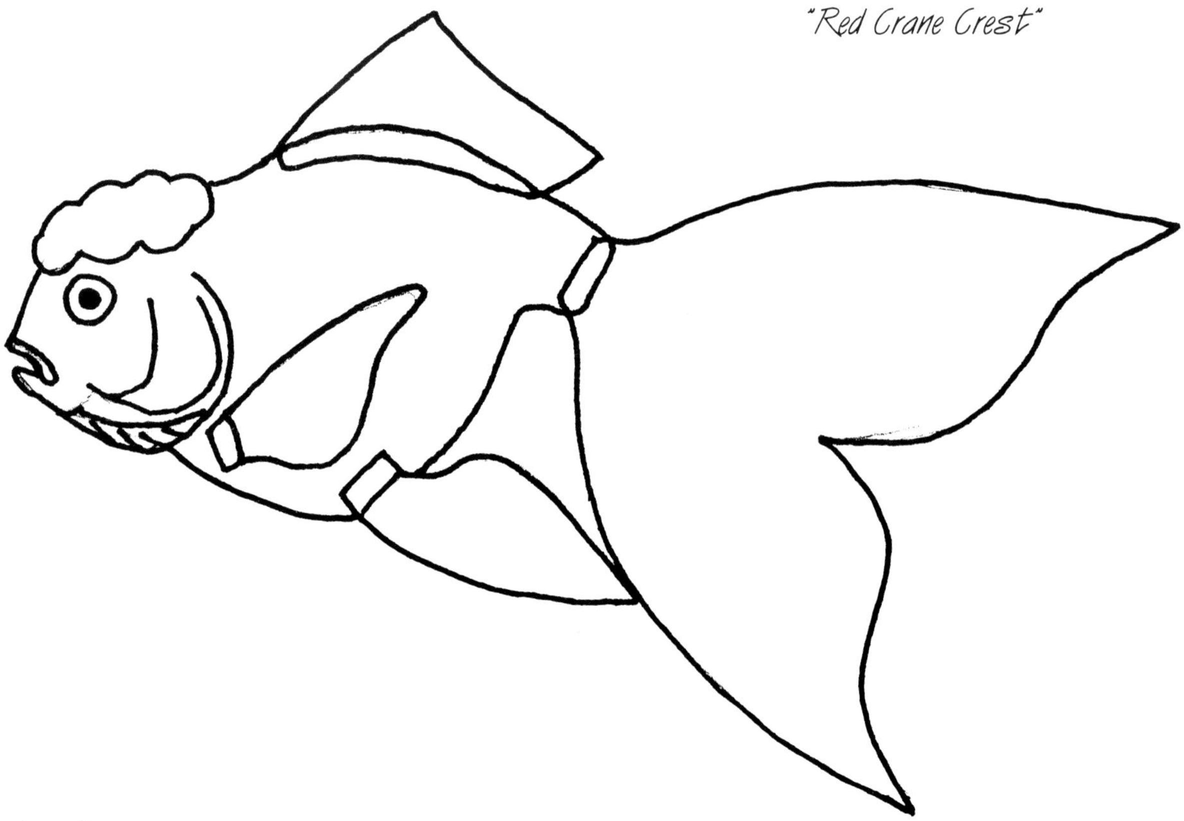

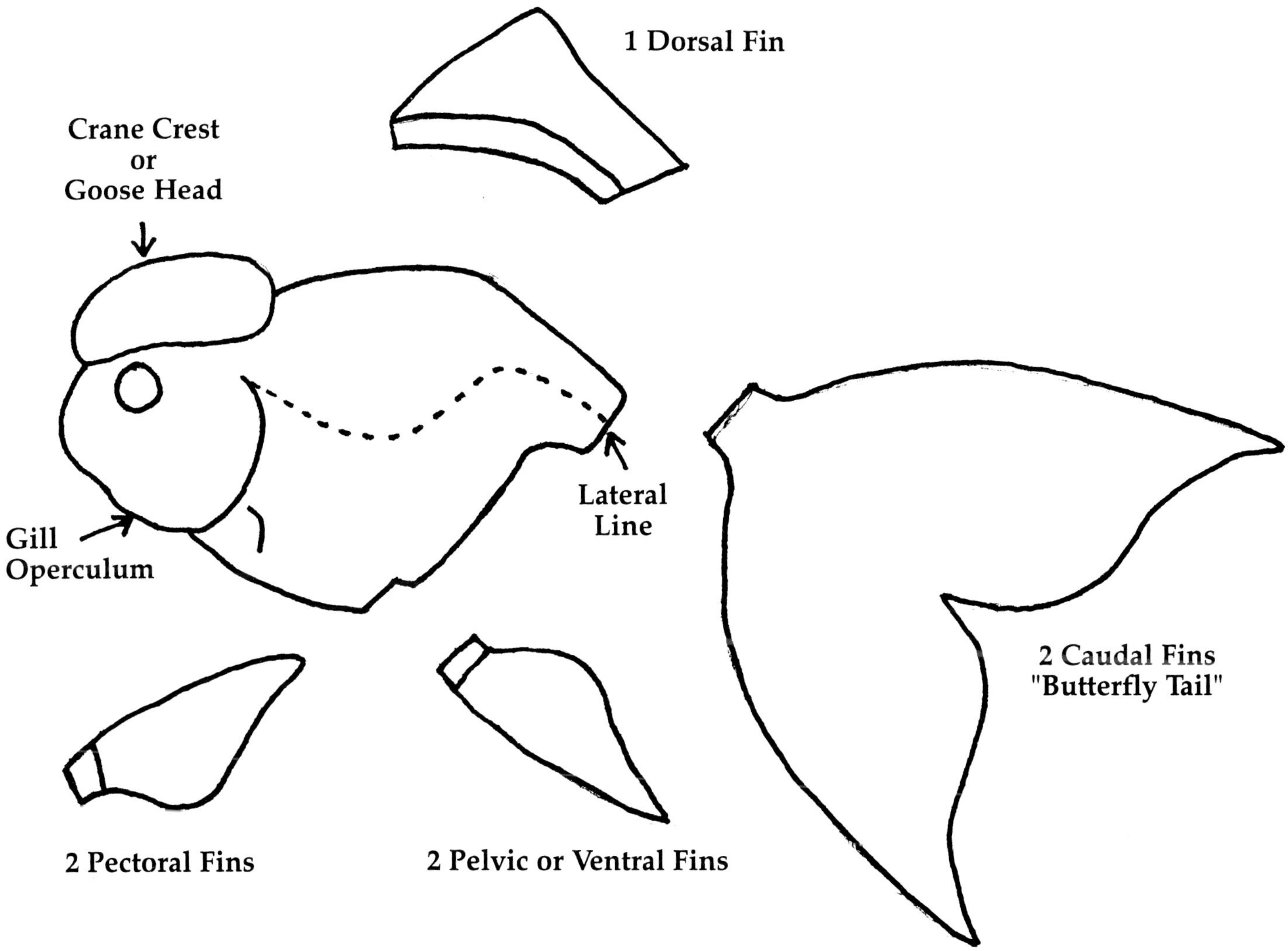
1 Dorsal Fin
Crane Crest
or
Goose Head
Lateral
Line
Gill
Operculum
2 Caudal Fins
"Butterfly Tail"
2 Pectoral Fins
2 Pelvic or Ventral Fins

Cross Sections

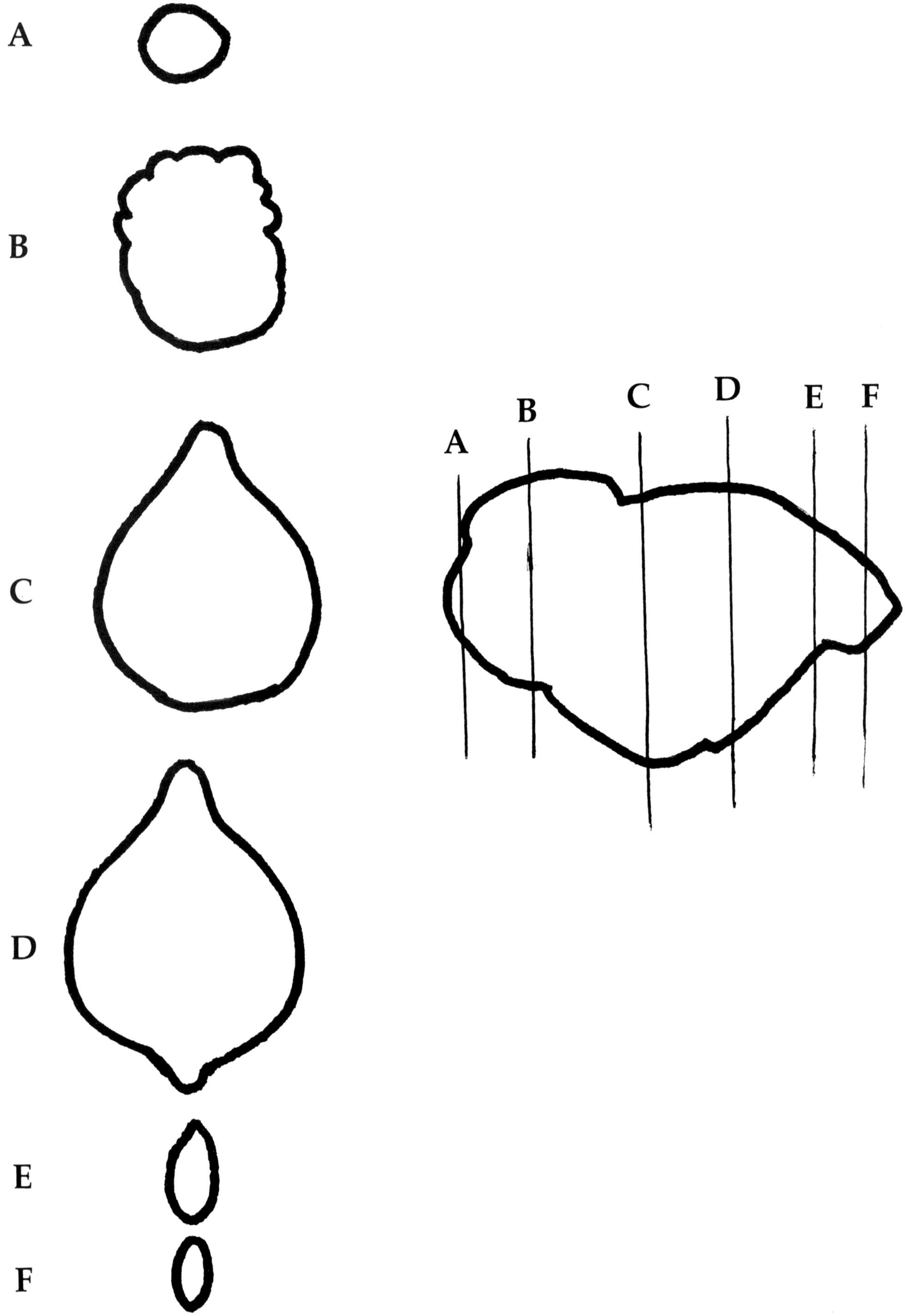

Carving the Red Crane Crest

Goldfish, "Flowers of the Water," are traditional Chinese ornamental fish. They come in many astonishing colors and elegant, graceful shapes. They have been domesticated since the southern Chinese Song Dynasty, 1127-1279. Their rich beauty makes it easy to see why they symbolize surplus in the Chinese New Year, offering years of happiness and satisfaction.

Their long course of breeding and selection has led to many varieties. One of the most precious is the Red Crest Crane. The name derives from the red bulge on its head and the swimming action which is reminiscent of a crane dancing. They were first bred in the Ming Dynasty, 1368-1644.

The basics of carving the Red Crane Crest may lead you to carving other goldfish varieties. From the list on page 6 you can see the possibilities.

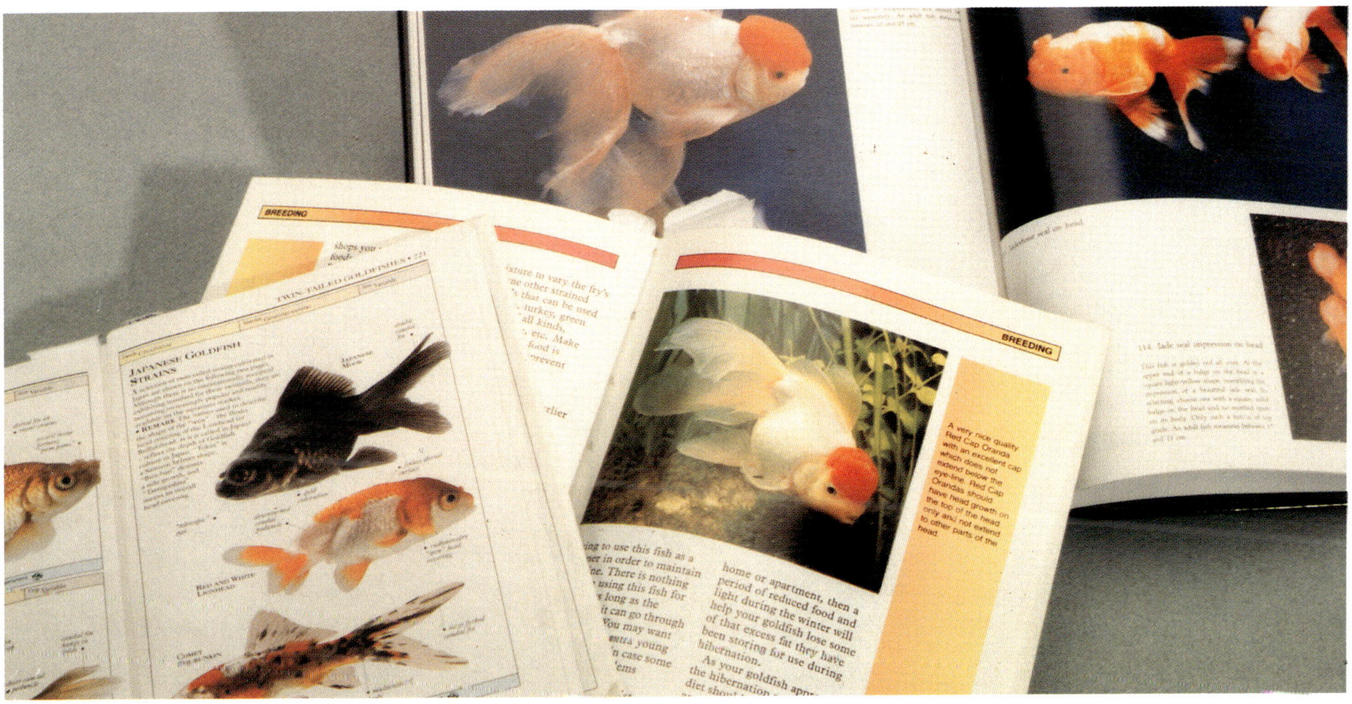

With exotics I use two forms of reference: books and live examples. I try to find as many sources as I can. I use these for reference during carving. Because they sometimes give a distorted view, I am careful about using them for patterns. Whenever possible I refer to dead specimens and anatomical references.

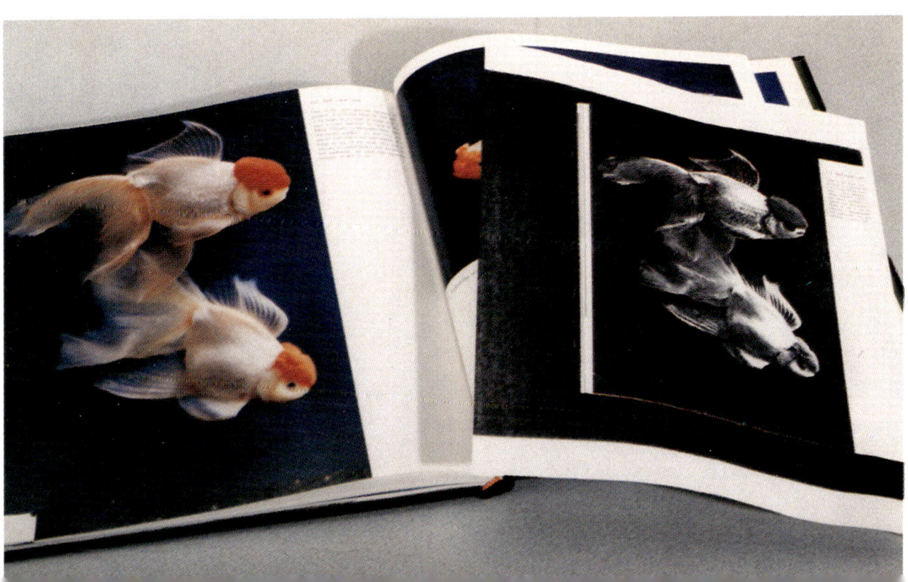

If I find a picture I like I photocopy it...

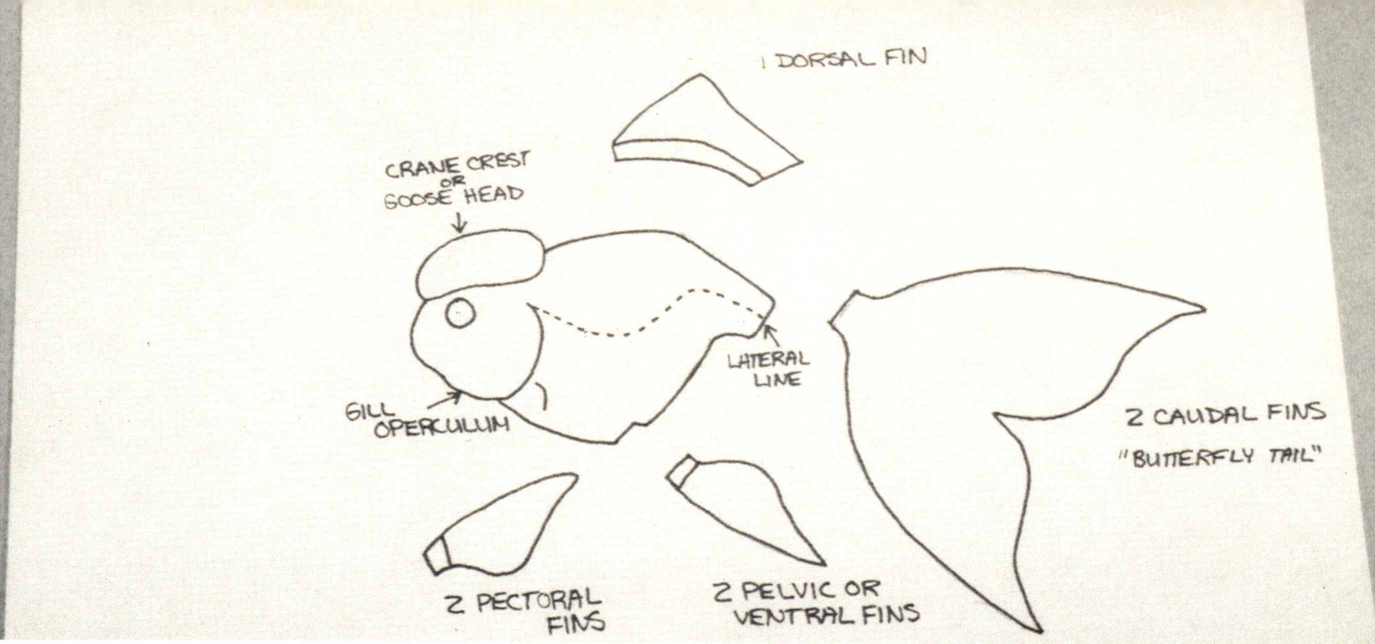

and trace it for the pattern.

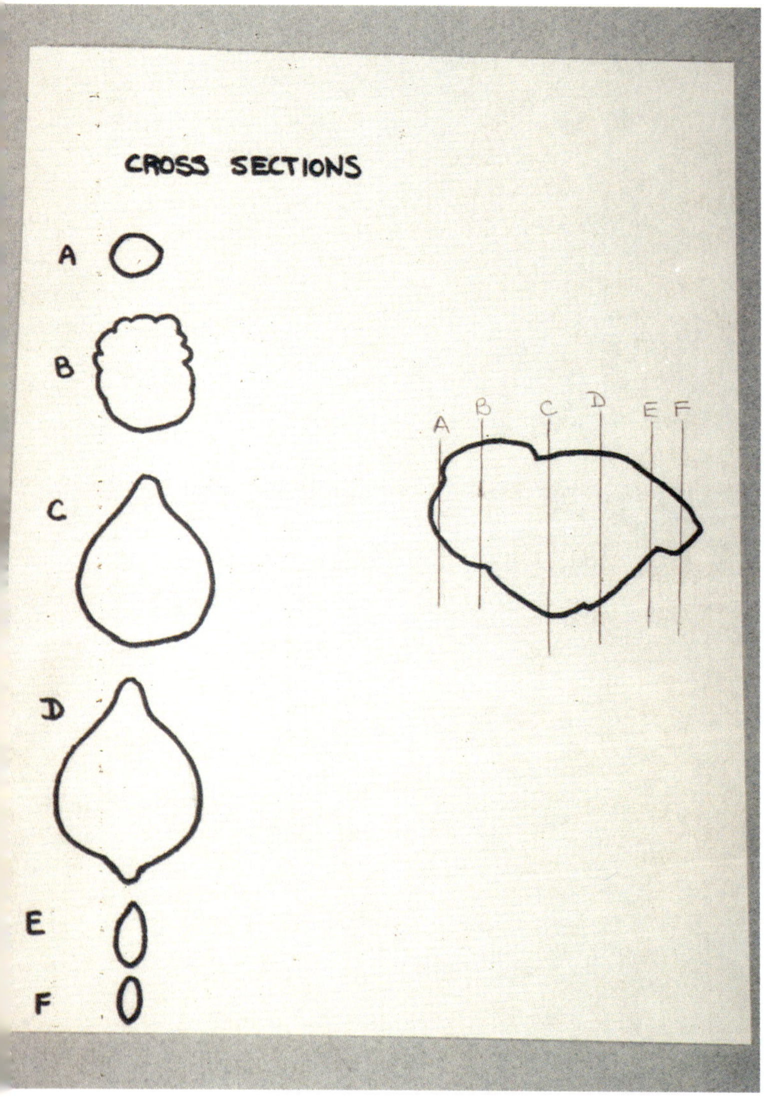

Working with a dead specimen allows me to draw the cross-sections. This research makes for much more realistic carving. I continue with research of the background of the fish, its history and its habitat.

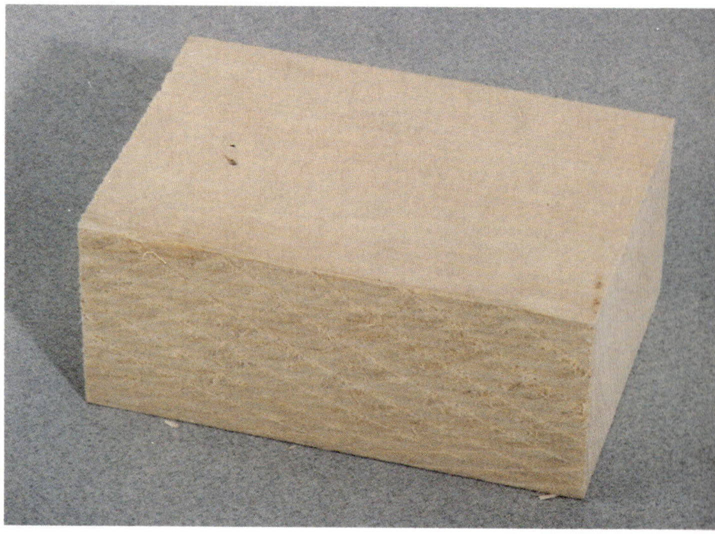

I use basswood for carving. I like to do a lot of hand carving, and basswood works well under the knife. The drawback is that with power tools it tends to lift fuzzies. Before finishing, careful sanding and sealing is necessary. The body block is 4.25" x 3" x 1.5".

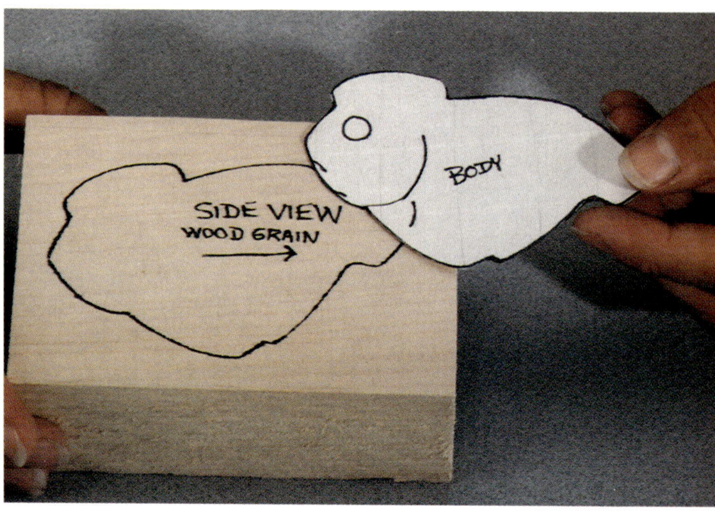

Lay the side pattern so the grain goes through the length.

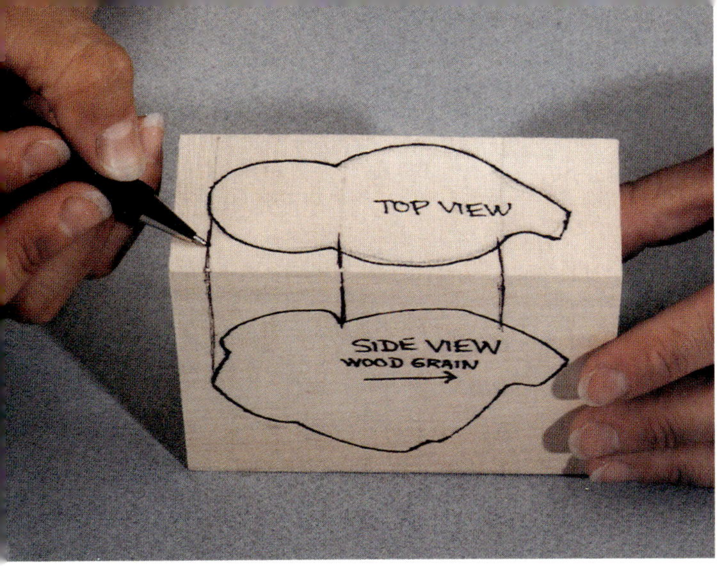

I carry major lines from the side view to the top: the front, the back of the head, and the back of the belly. Then I draw the top pattern by hand, making it larger than the final carving.

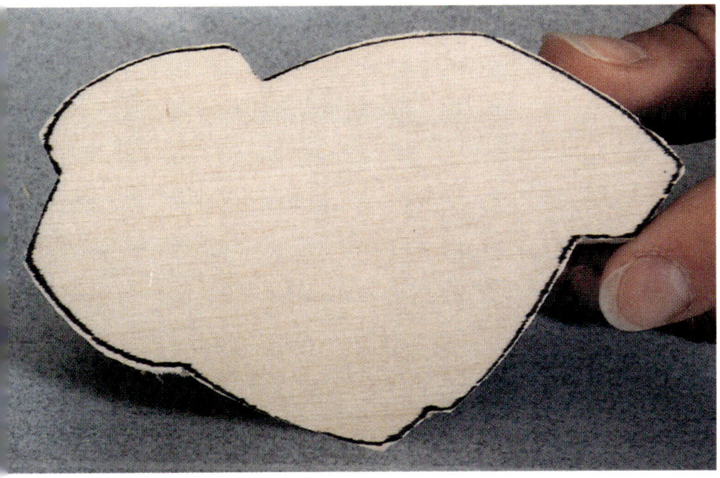

I cut the side pattern first...

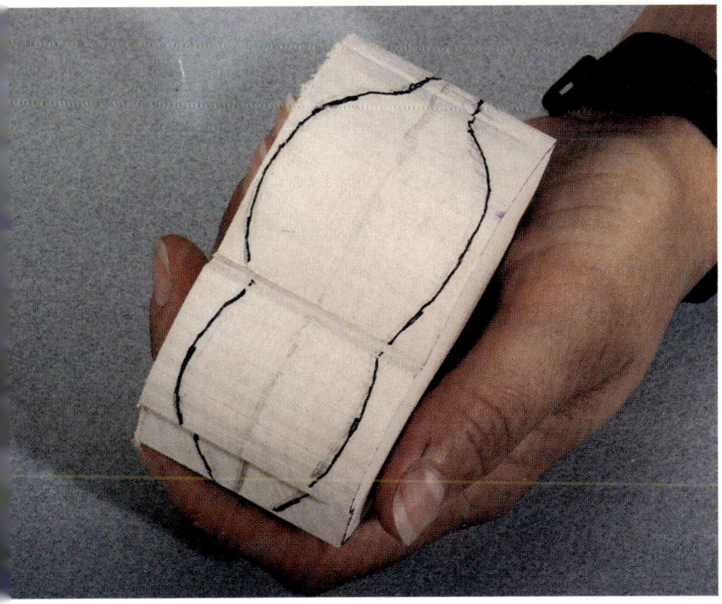

then redraw the top pattern.

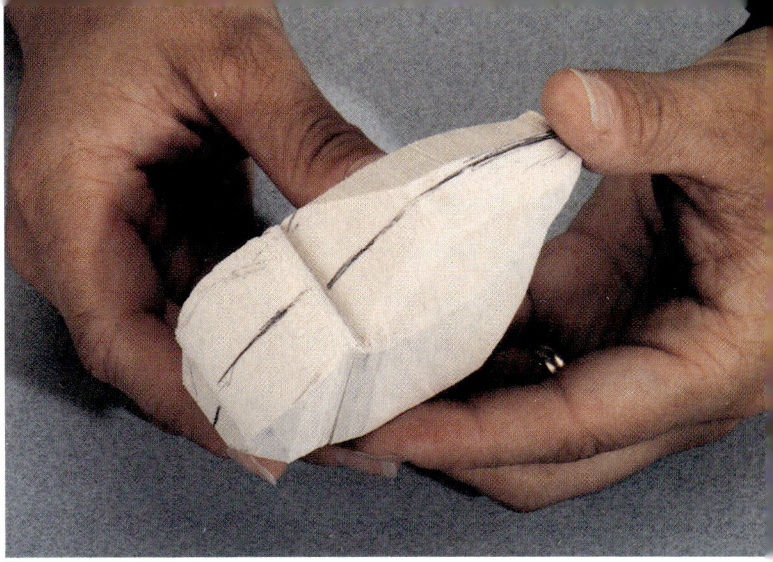

Next I cut the plane view on the bandsaw and knock off the corners by tilting the table.

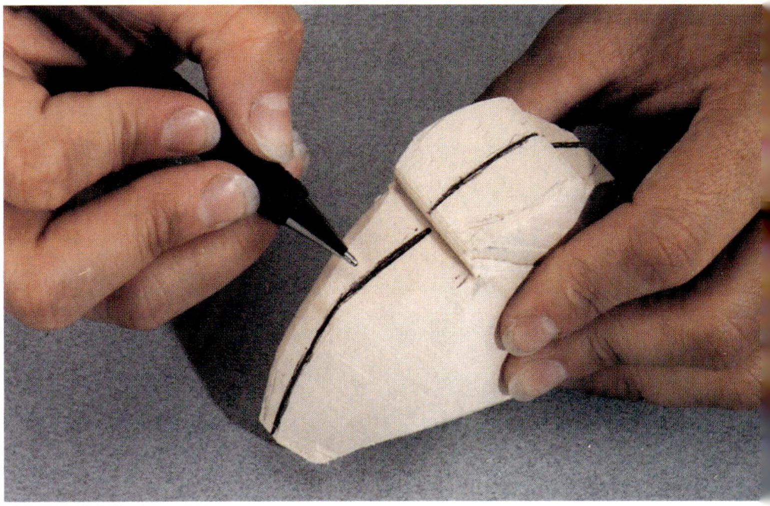

Establish the center line all around. This is a very important reference for your carving. I never cut into the center line until the final steps, when I am sanding.

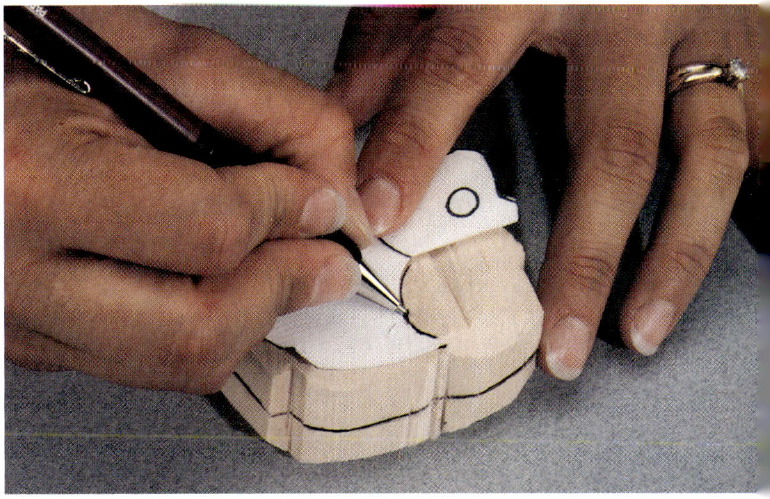

On the pattern I cut along the gill line. This allows me lift part of the pattern to draw in the line of the gill plate. Do it on both sides.

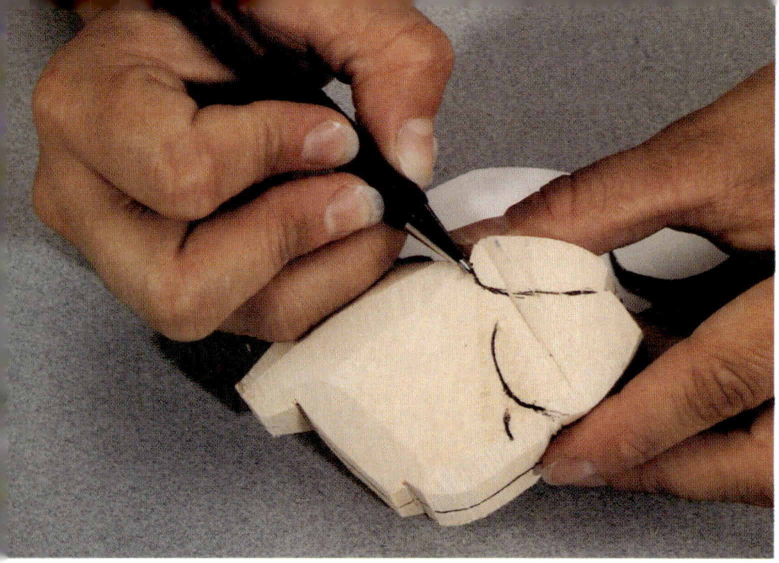

I draw the crest of the head by hand.

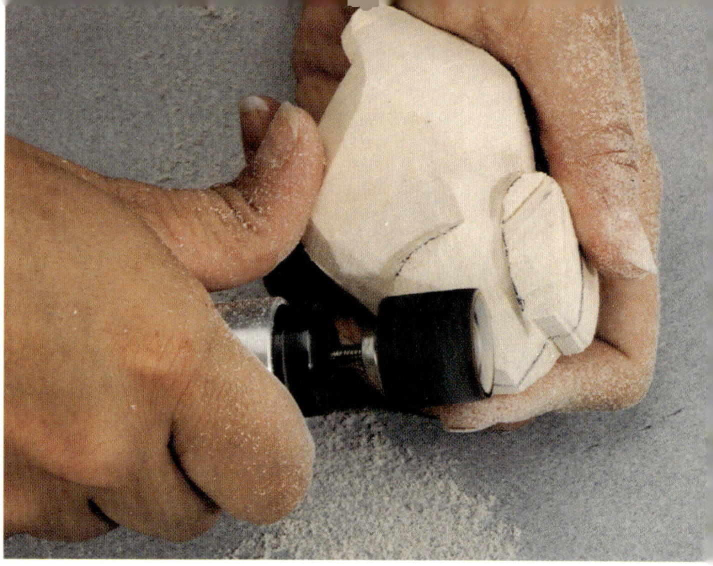

and blend the contour of the head back to the crest line.

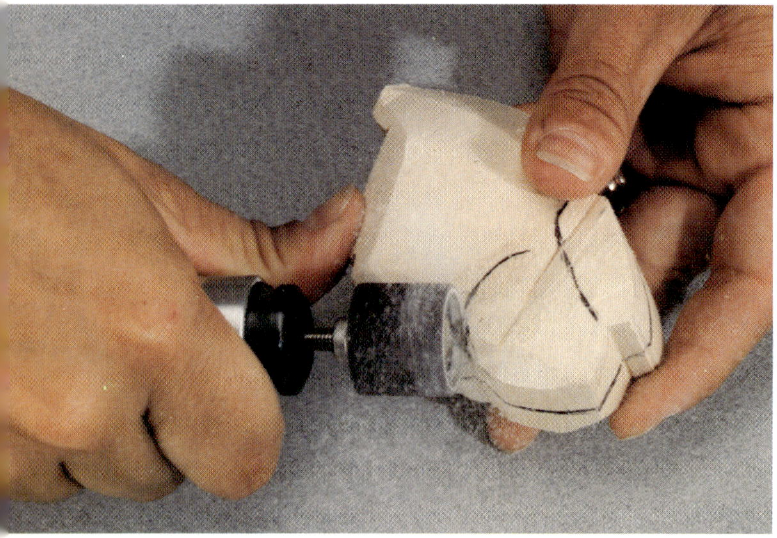

Use the edge of a coarse grit sanding drum to reduce the body behind the gill plate, establishing the line.

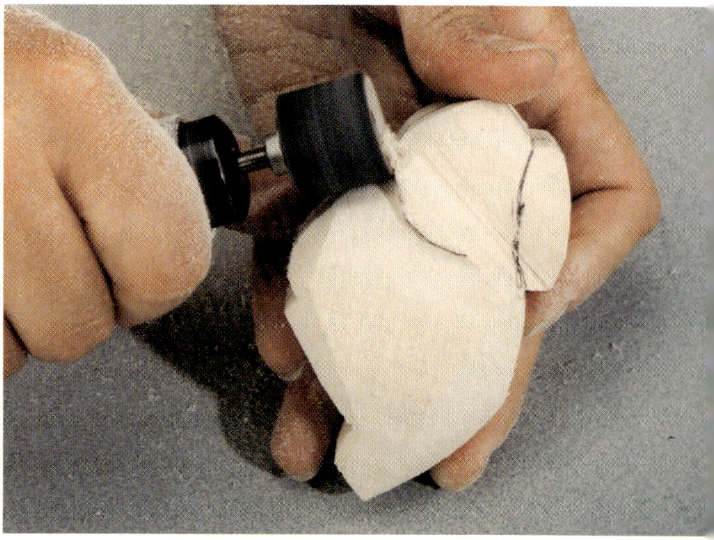

Repeat on the other side.

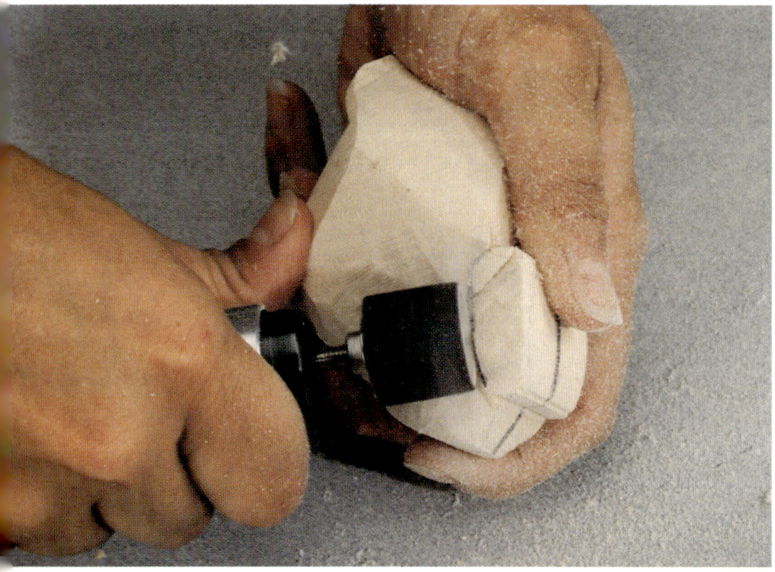

Do the same below the line of the crest...

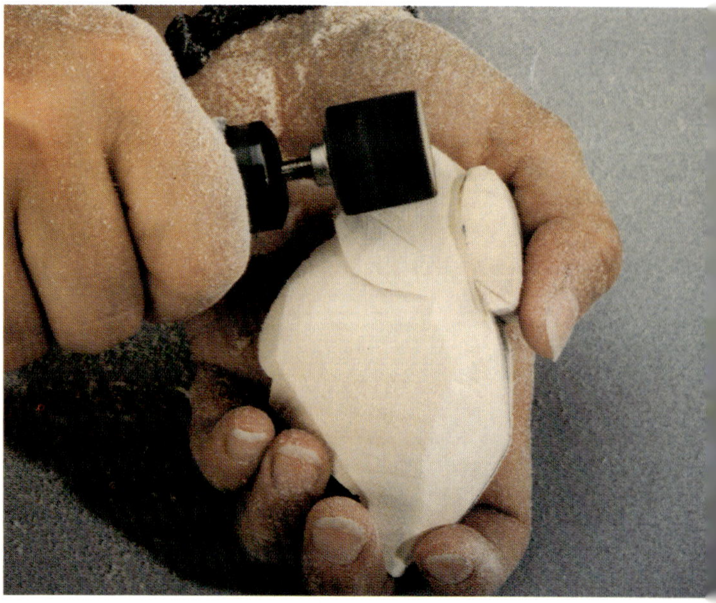

Thin the head.

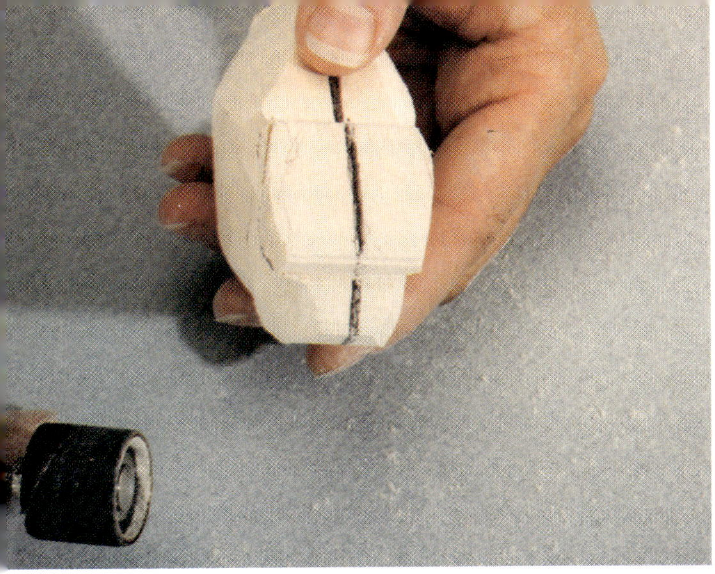

The result.

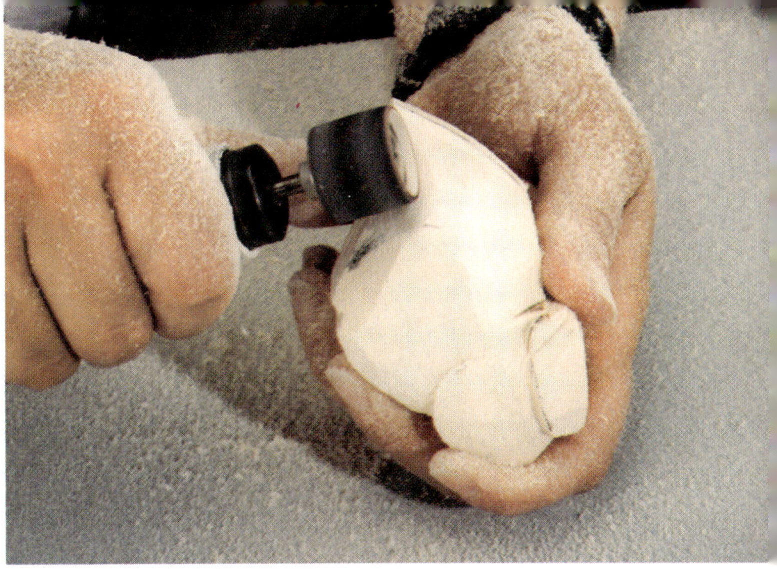

Thin the caudal peduncle.

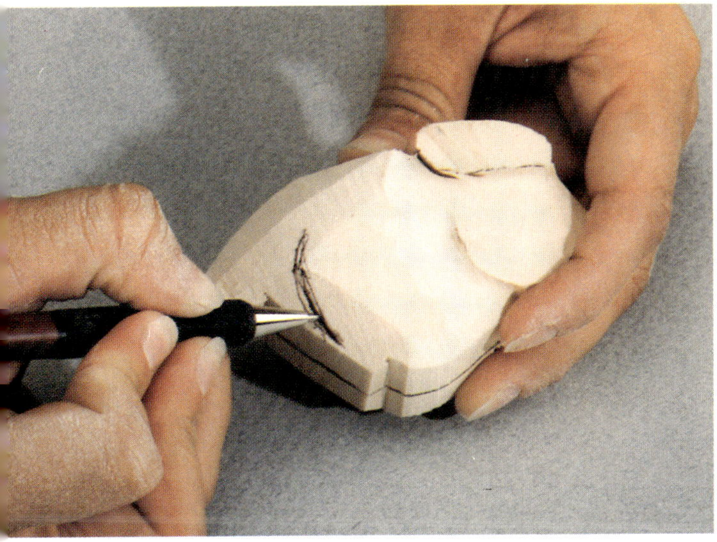

The belly continues up at this point, and the caudal peduncle and spine area thin down radically from here. The spine is ridge-like.

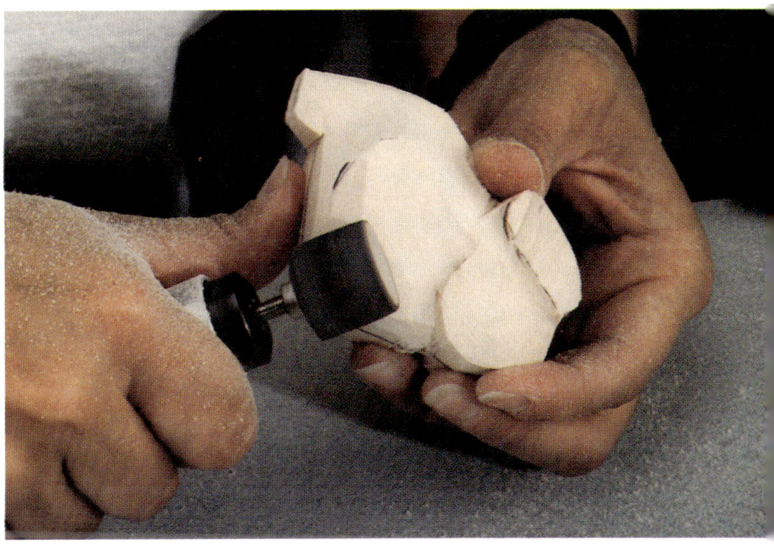

Round the belly.

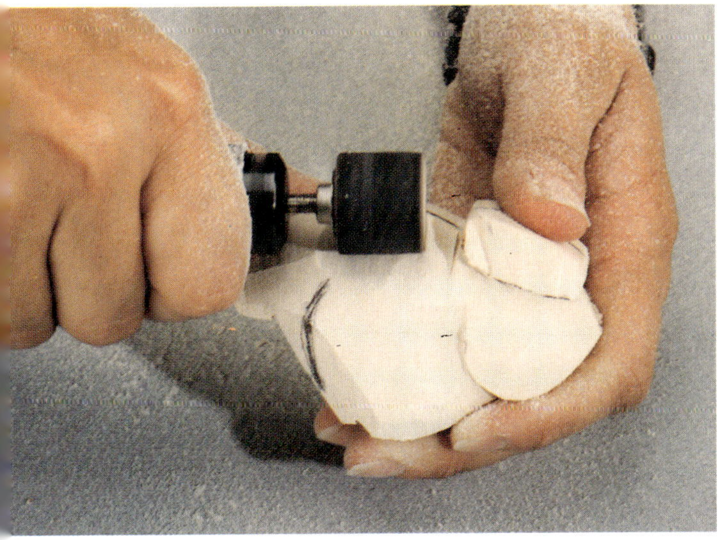

Thin the back along the spine.

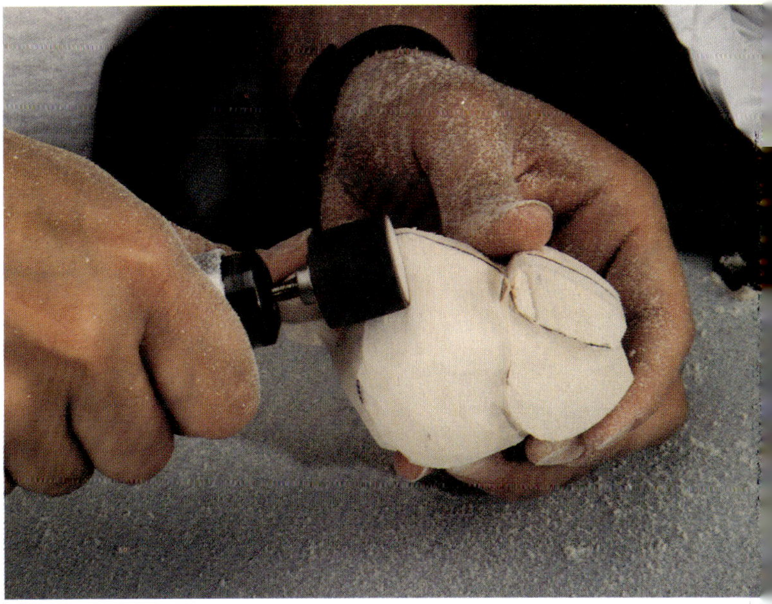

Blend where the belly and the back meet.

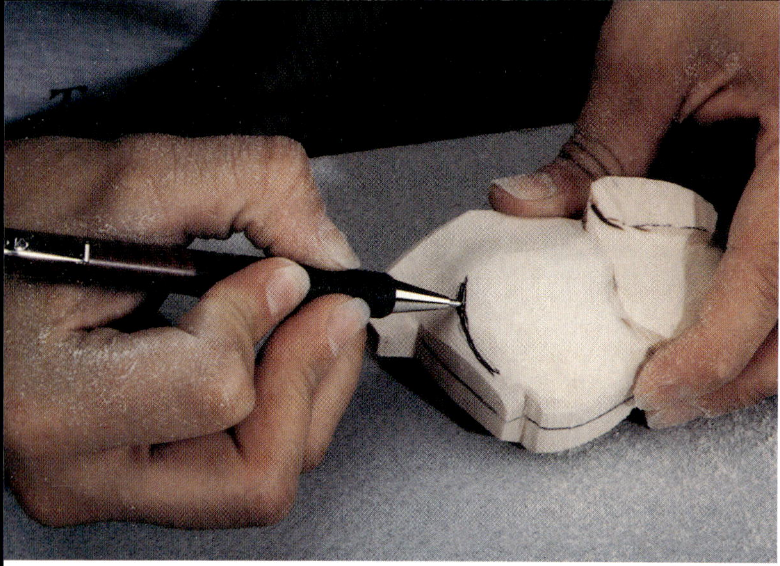

Redraw the belly line...

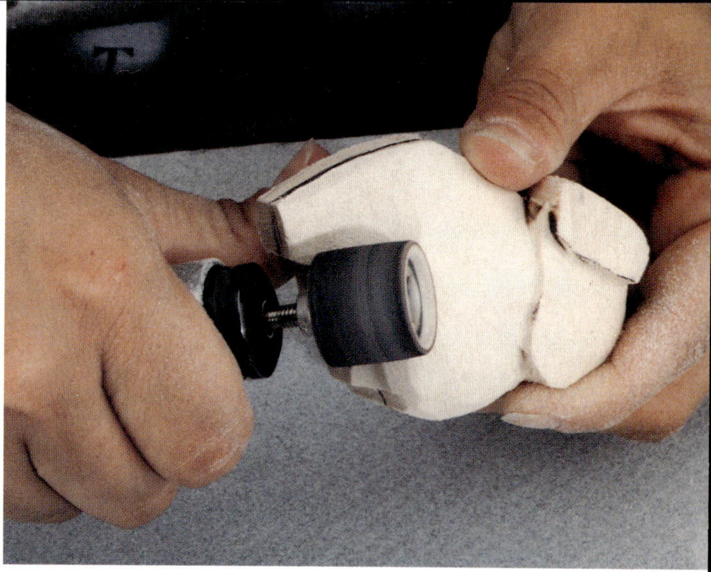

Blend the peduncle into the belly.

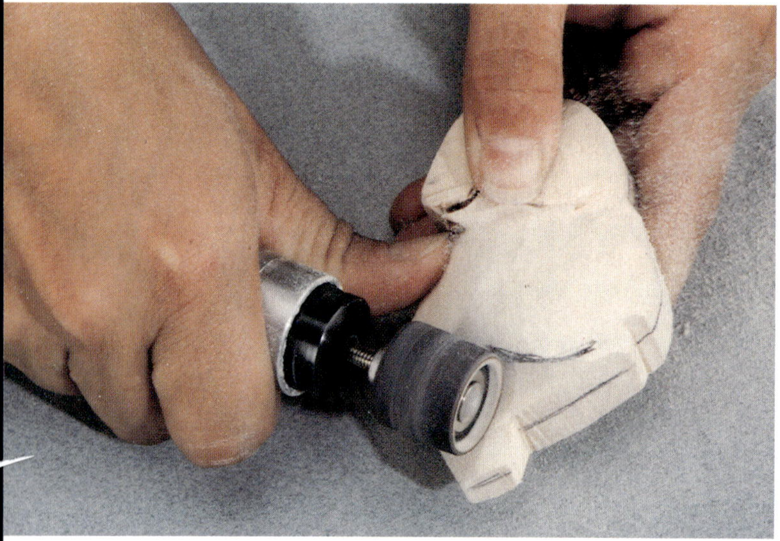

and run the side of the grinder along it to create a depression in the peduncle. This will create a ridge at the base of the anal fin.

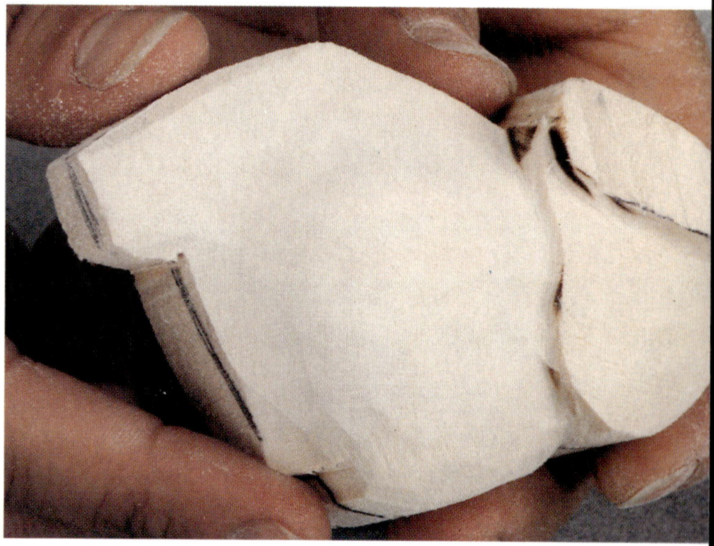

The result. Repeat on the other side.

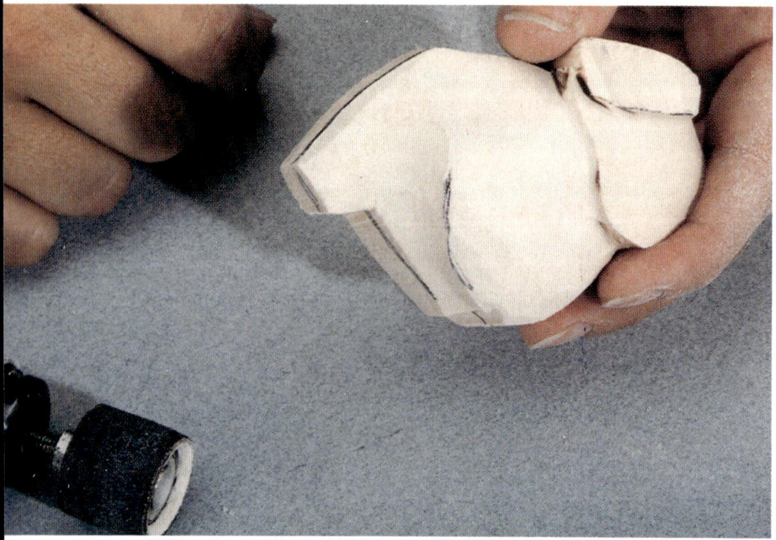

The result.

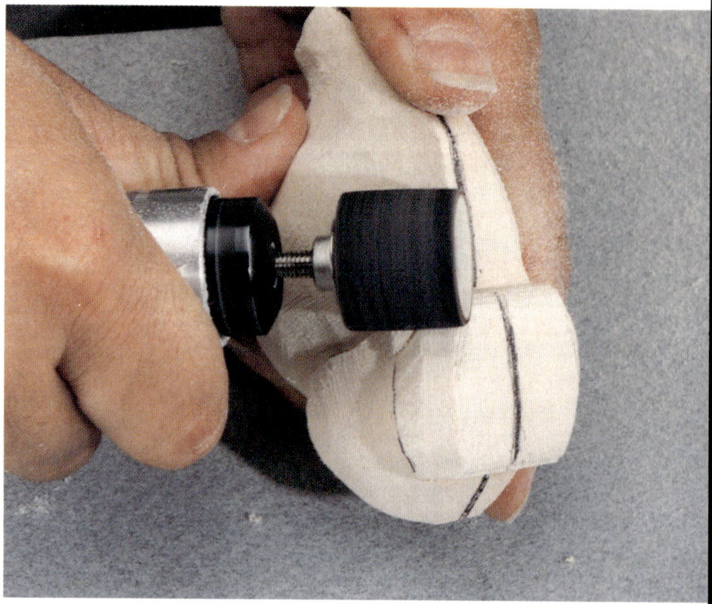

Round off the crest of the head.

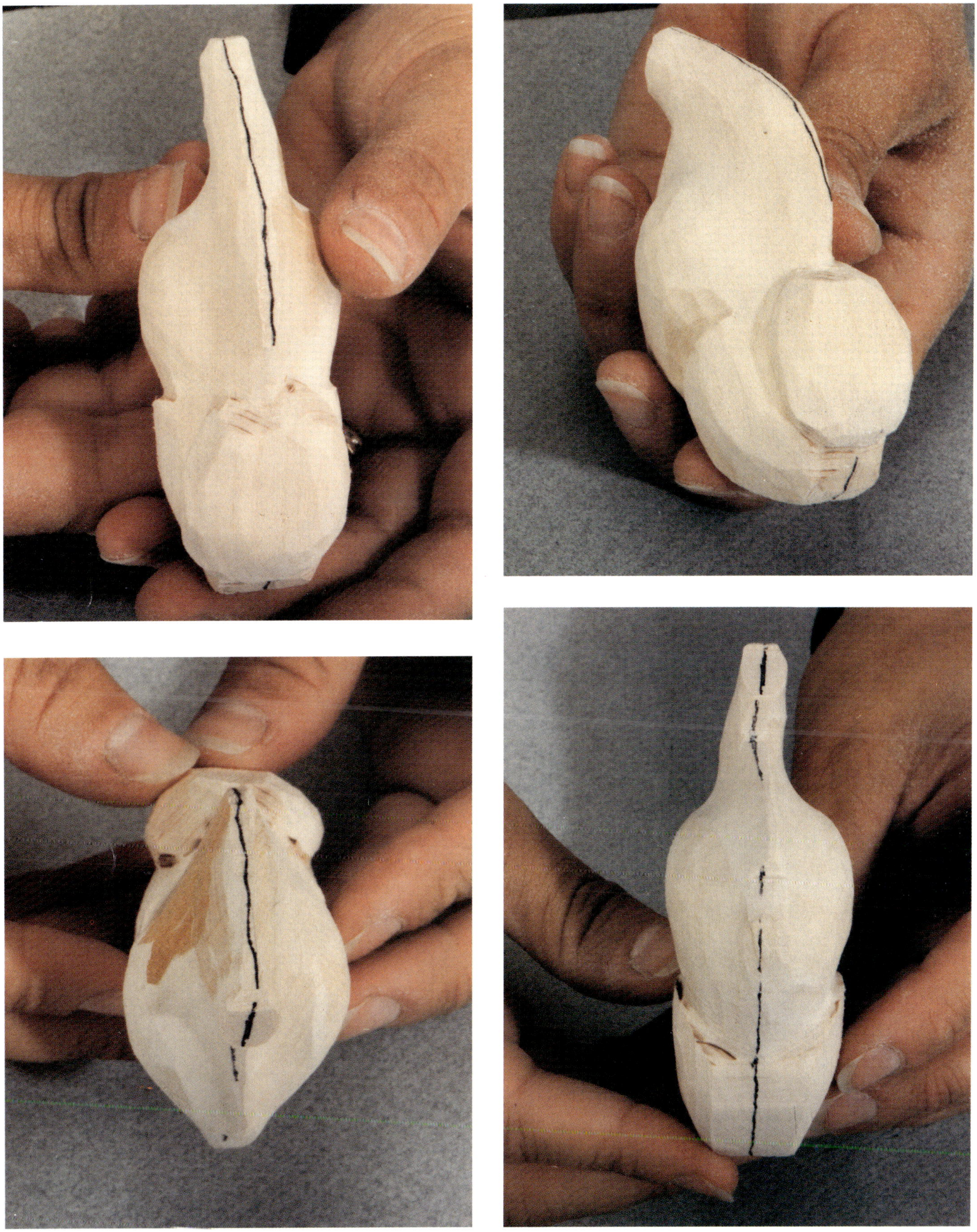

Progress.

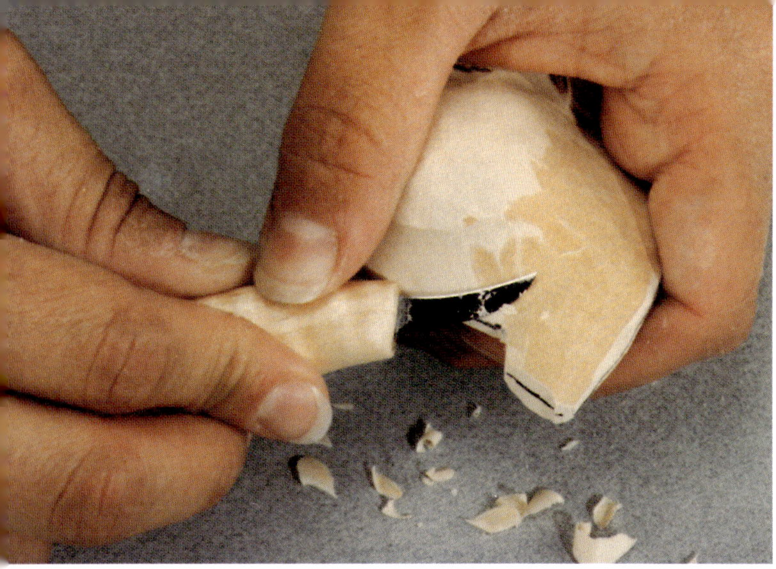

I switch to a knife for the most of the remaining carving. Continue smoothing the belly. Because the basic shape was set with the grinder, the key, now, is to take off enough to smooth it, but not enough to distort its shape.

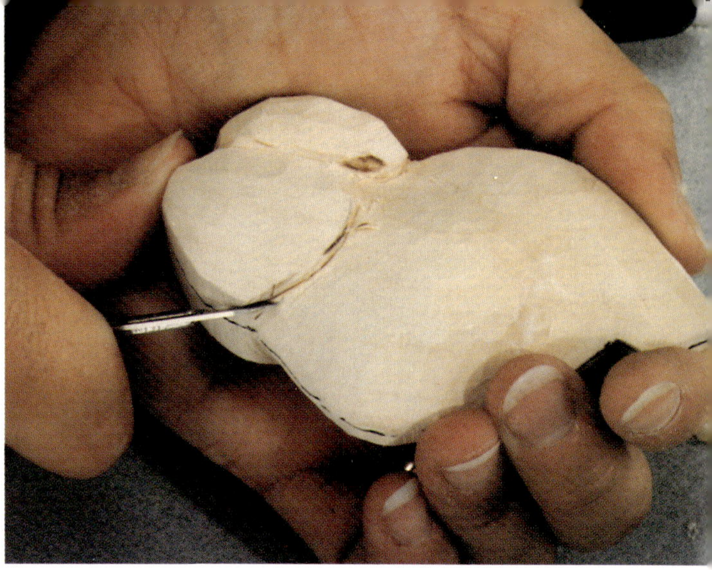

Make another stop at the back of the gill.

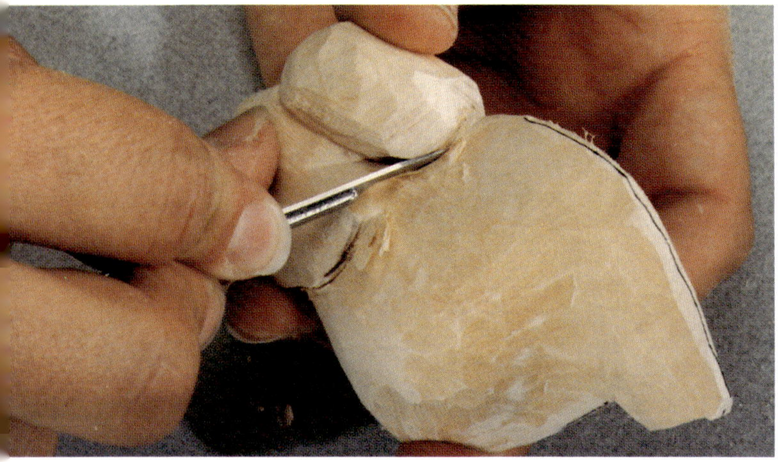

Make a stop cut at the border of the crest, beginning at the back...

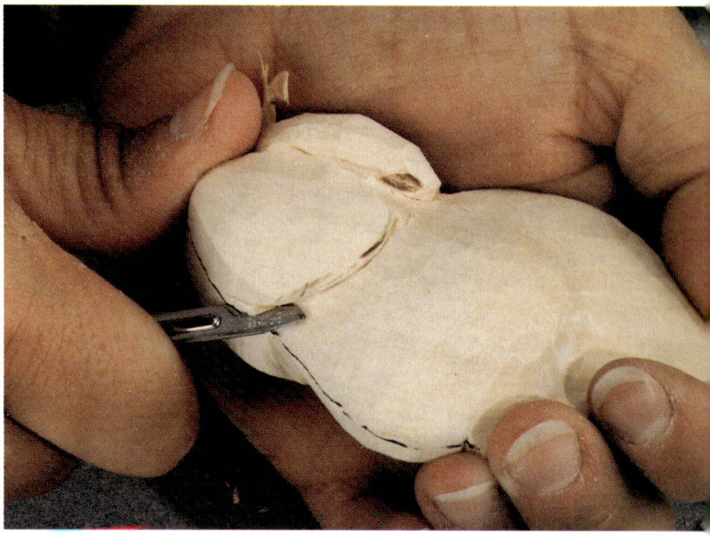

Cut back to the stop from the body. Notice that the thumb of my knife hand is protected by being hidden behind the head.

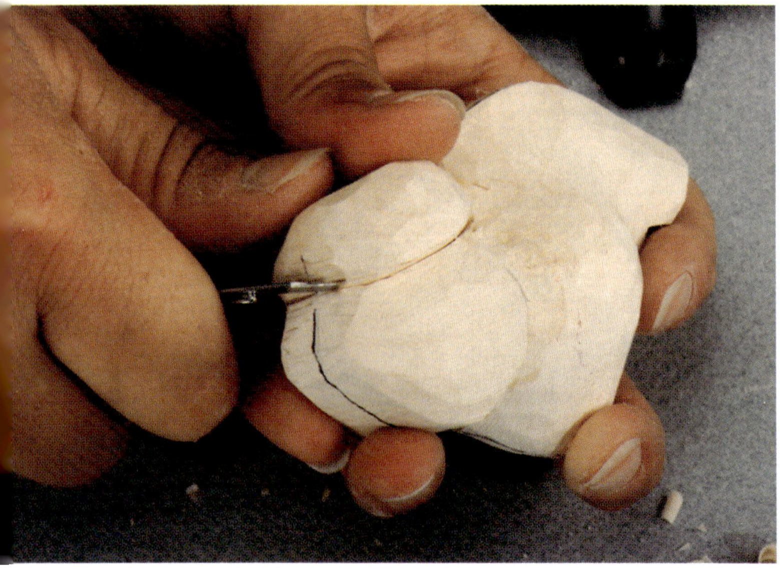

and working toward the front.

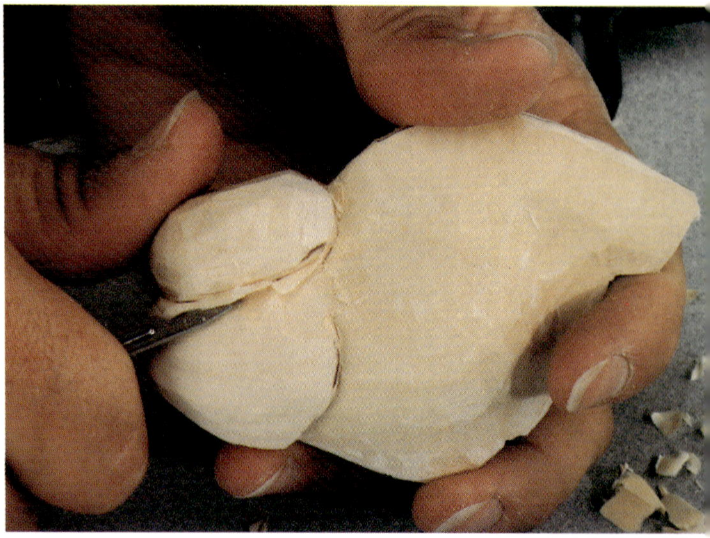

In the same way, cut back to the crest from the body and the head.

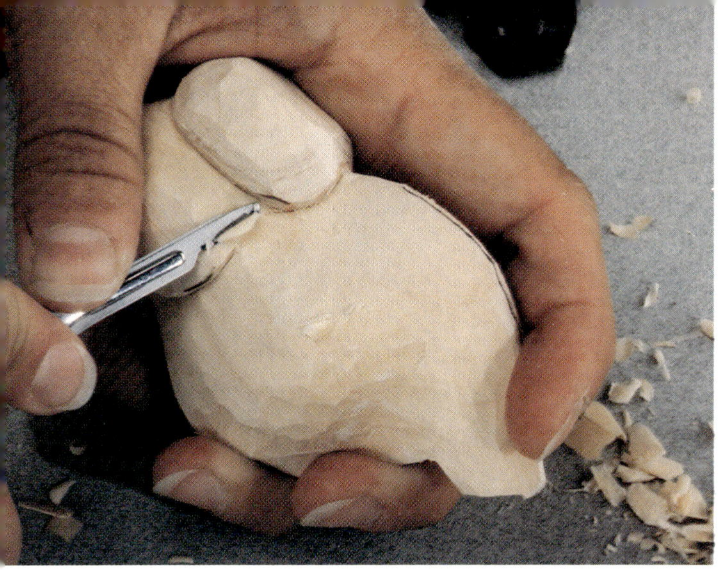

Smooth the transition from the head to the body above the gill.

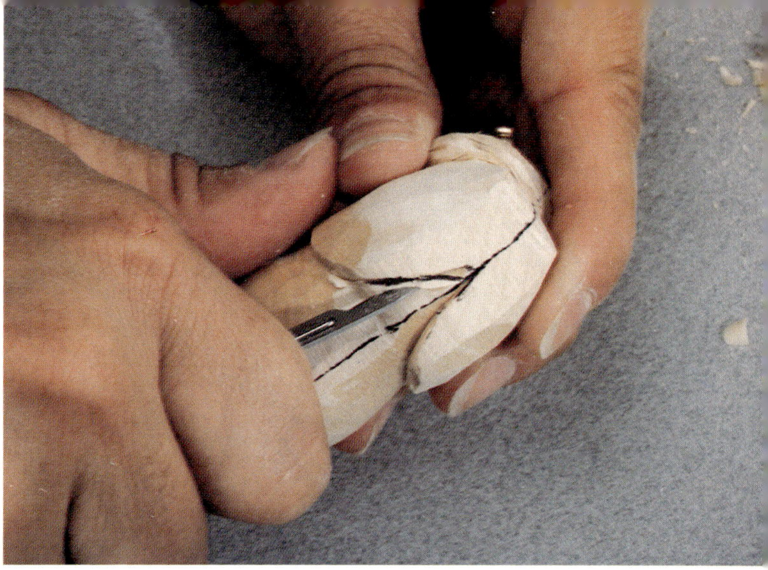

and slice back to it from between the gills.

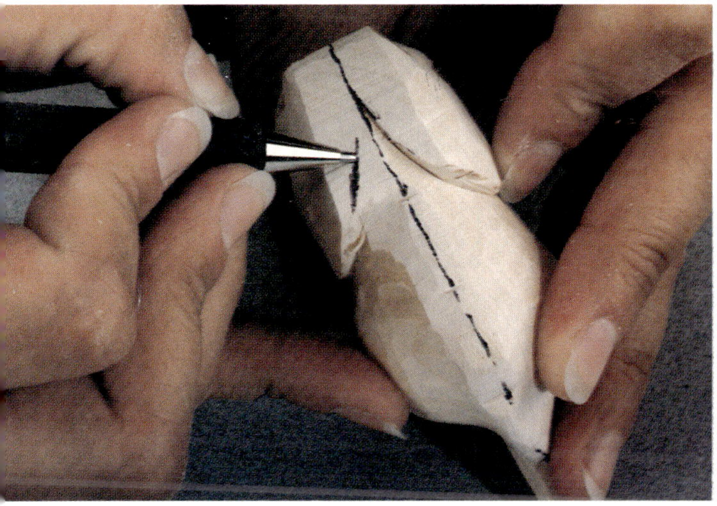

Establish the bottom of the gills so they meet at the center line.

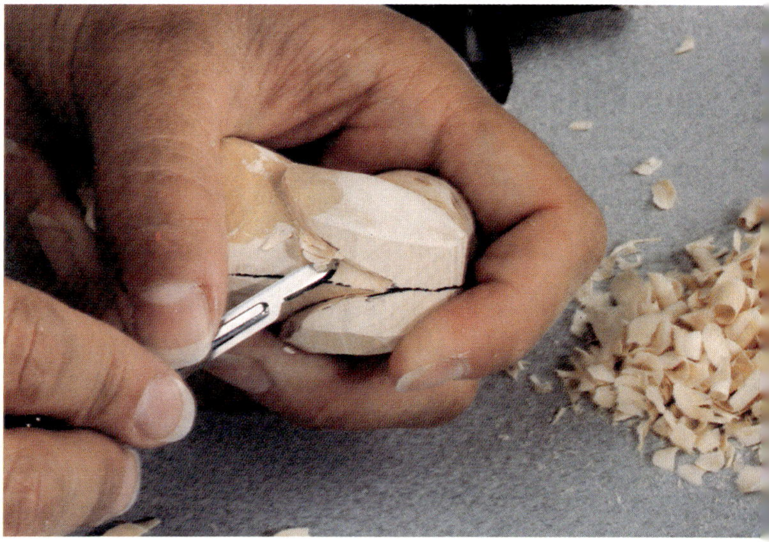

Clean the area between the lower gills.

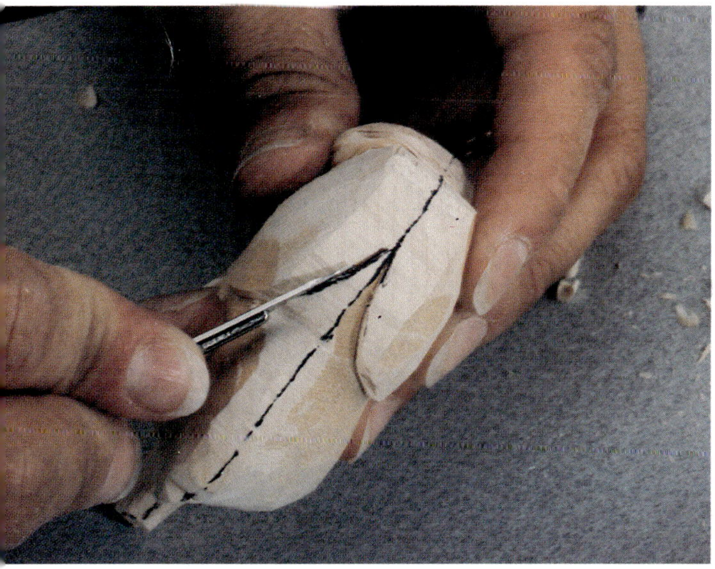

Make a stop cut in the line...

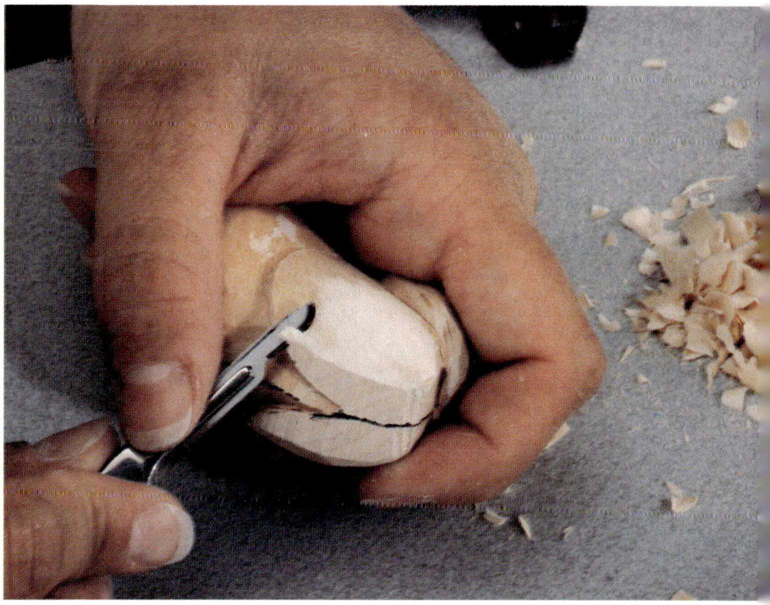

Round off the ridge at the mandible.

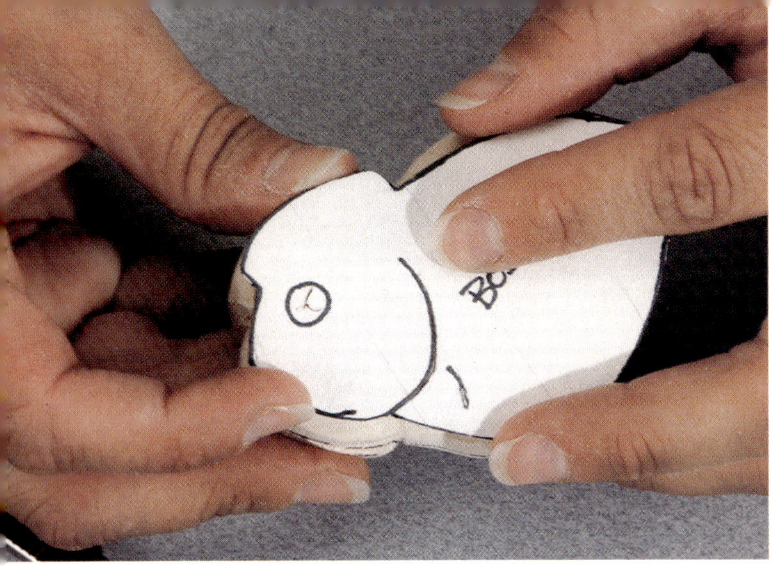

Lay the pattern over the carving again...

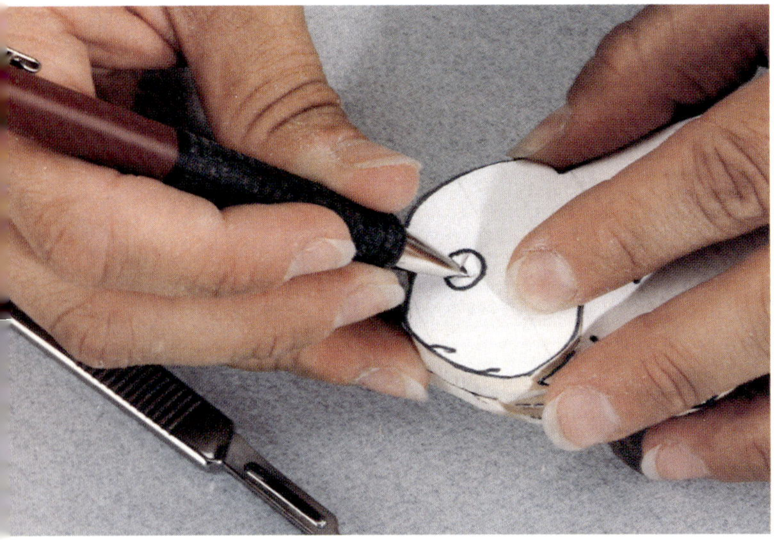

and mark the center of the eye through the pattern.

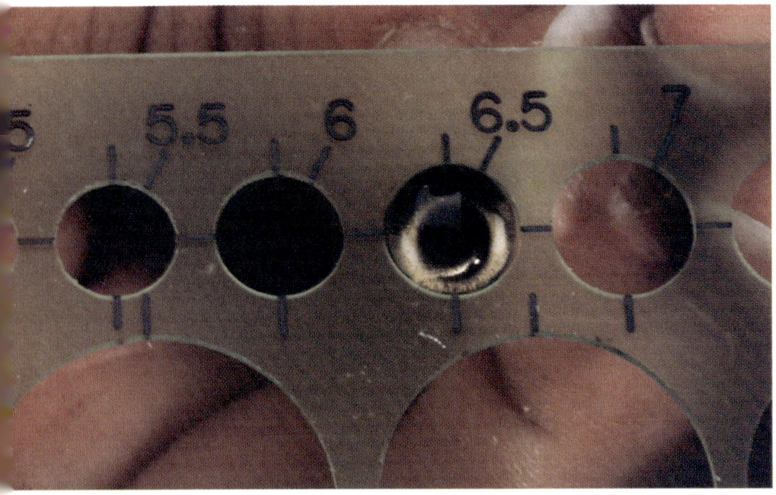

I use pre-painted Tohickon glass eyes. These are actually bird eyes. The gold fish is the only variety I know that does not have an ovoid pupil. It is round, so it is acceptable to use bird eyes. This eye is a 6.5mm.

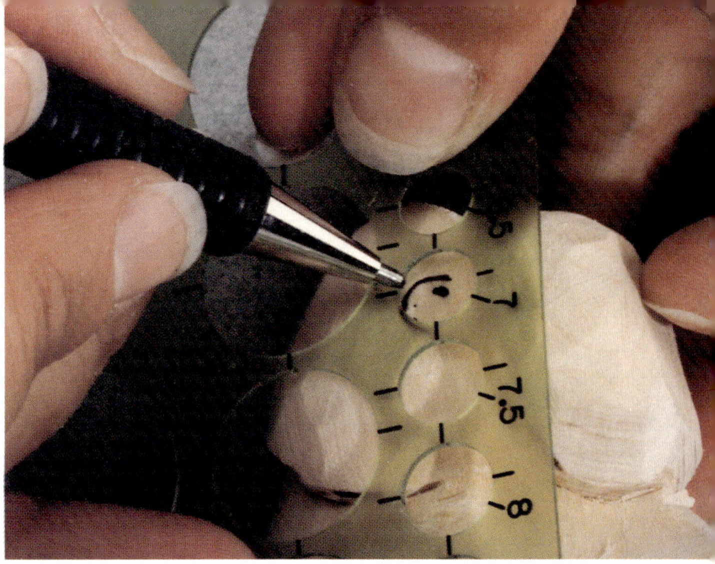

I draw eye holes using the next larger sized template, in this case 7mm. Align the template so it is centered, and draw the perimeter.

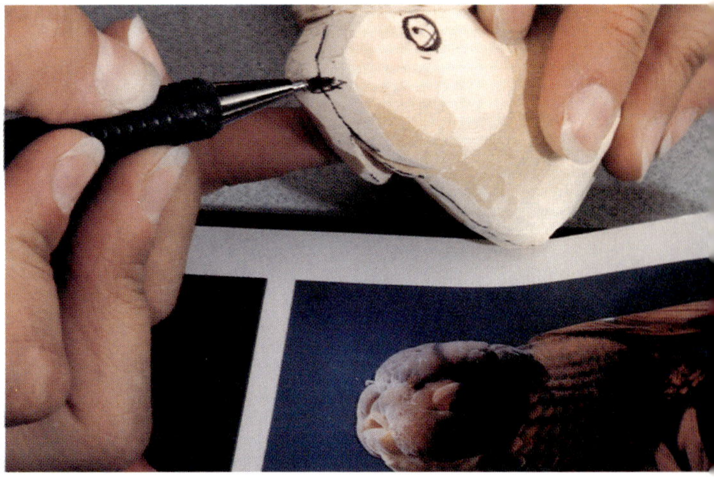

With the reference material handy, draw in the lips...

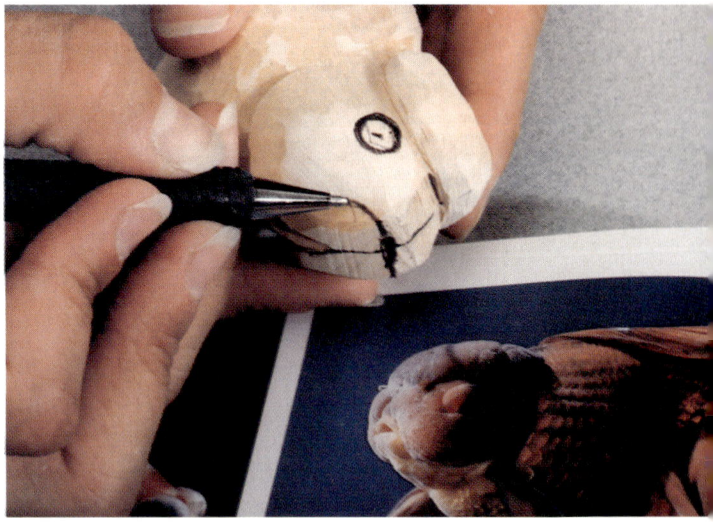

Carry the line around to the side. I end it before the beginning of the eye. Though the line is large, the mouth will be much smaller when it is finished.

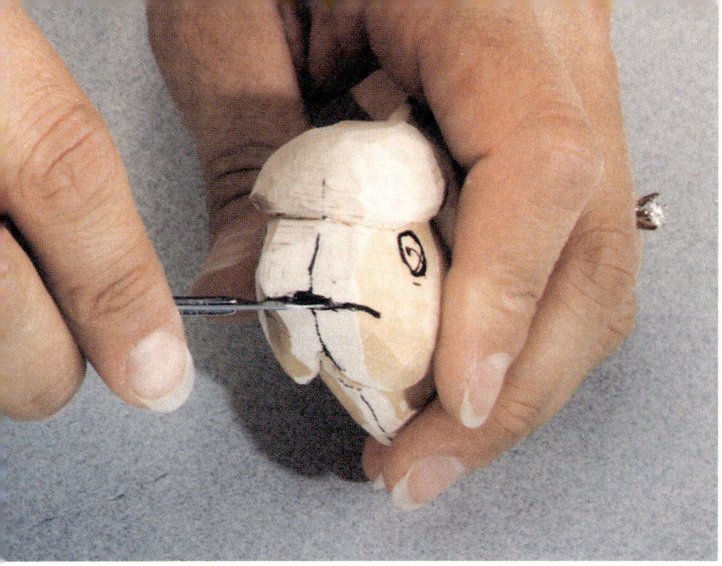

Make a stop cut in the line at the center.

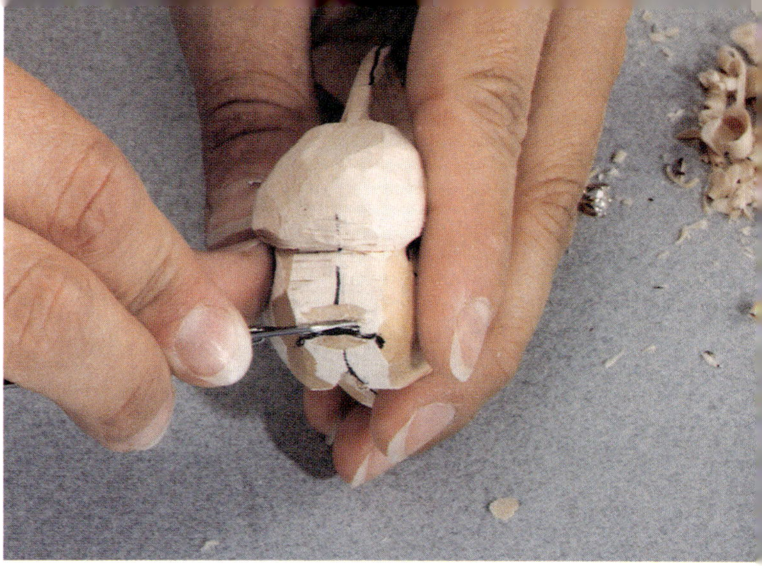

Cut a stop in the line...

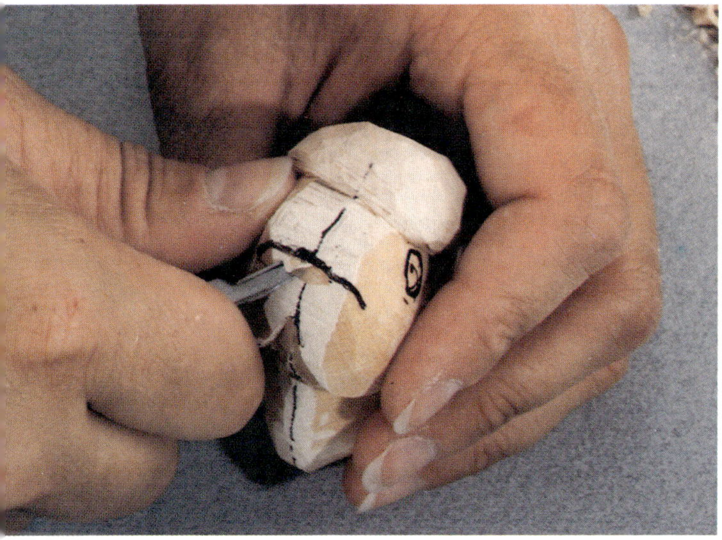

Cut back to it from below.

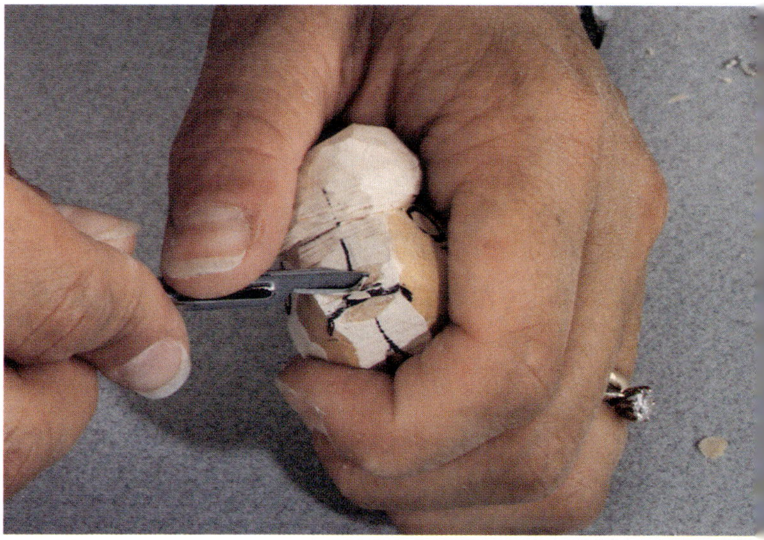

and carve back to it from above to establish the lip.

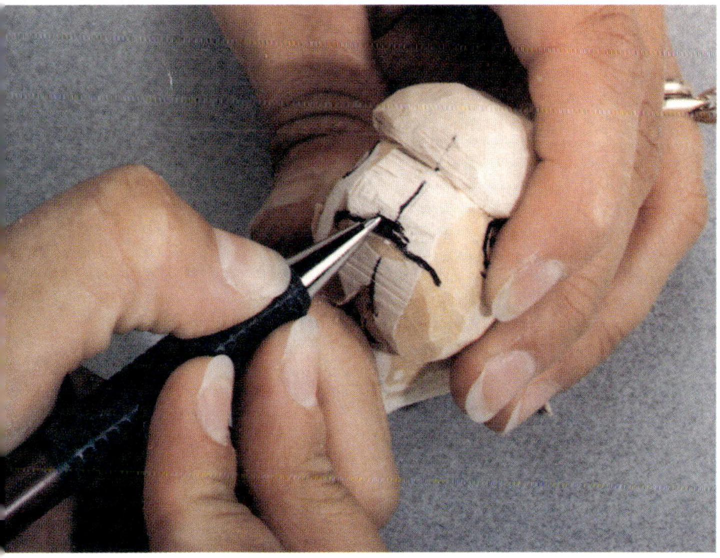

Establish a mark above the line to define the area of the lip that will **not** be carved for now.

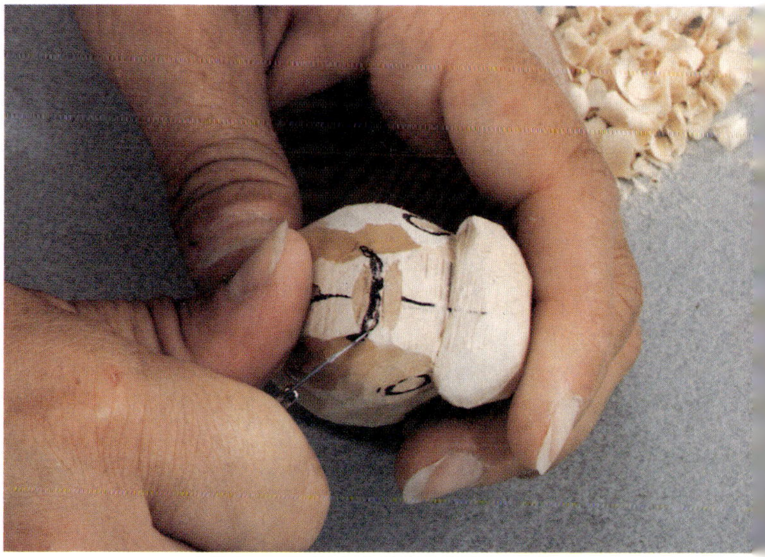

Continue the upper line of the lip, drooping it at the ends. Cut a stop in the line...

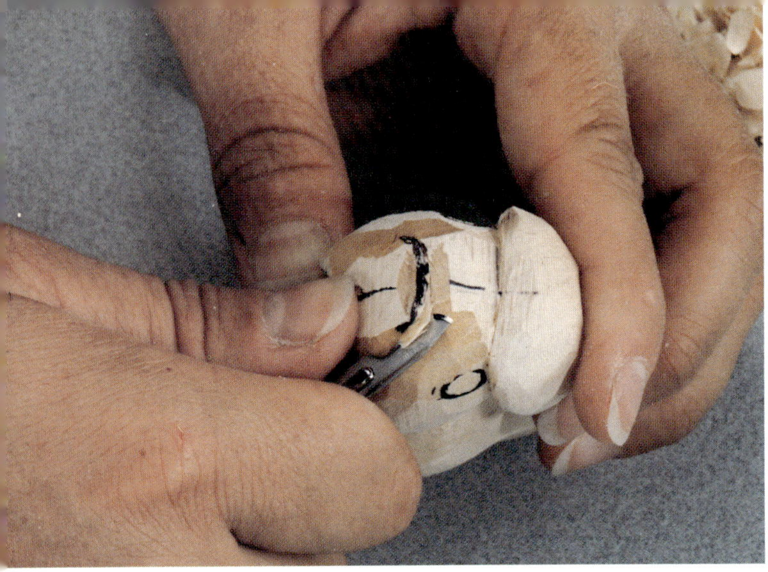

and carve back to it from above.

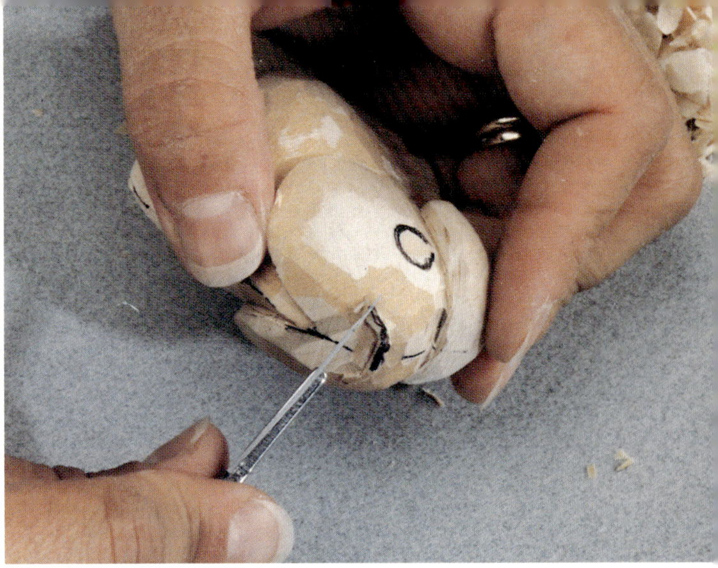

Establish the ends of the lips by making a stop...

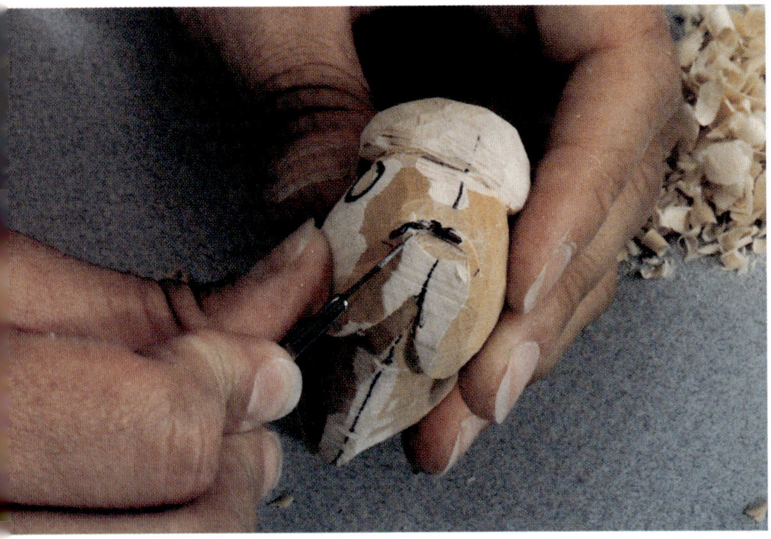

Cut the same drooping stop on the bottom edge of the lip.

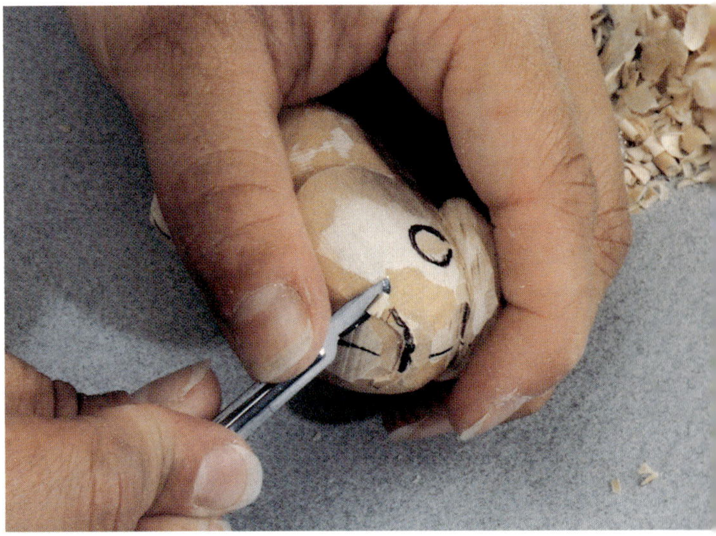

and cutting back to it from the face.

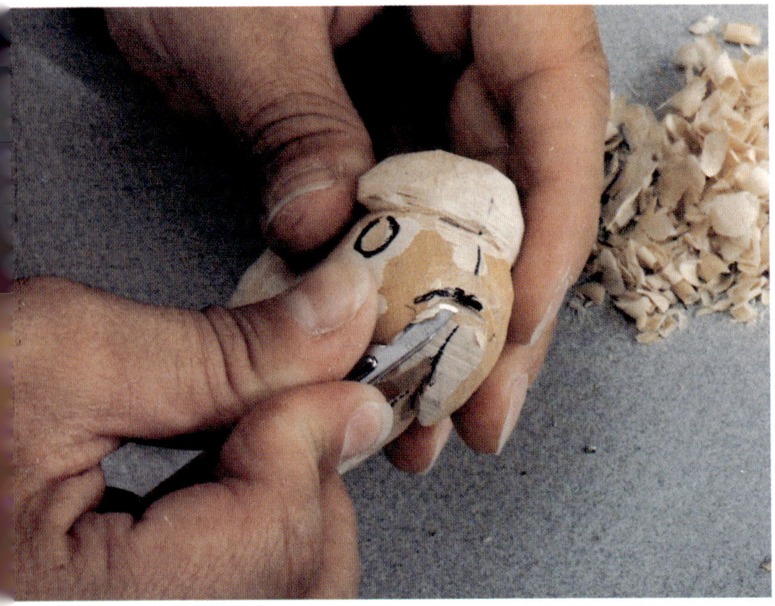

Cut back to it from below.

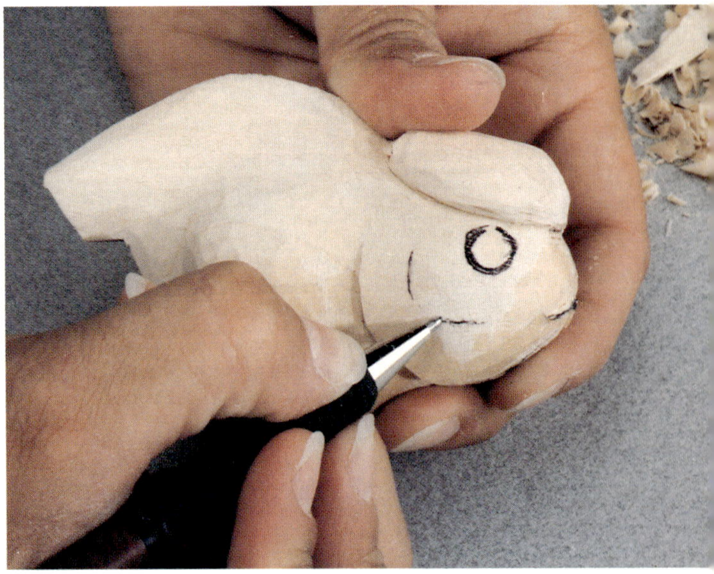

This gold fish has a puffiness under the eye, the preopercle. I draw the outside edge of it by hand, referring to the pattern.

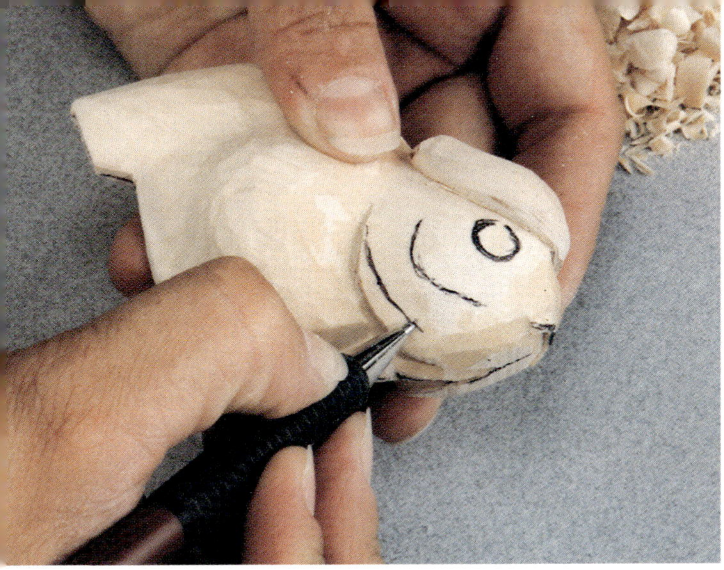

Draw in the line of the opercle in the gill.

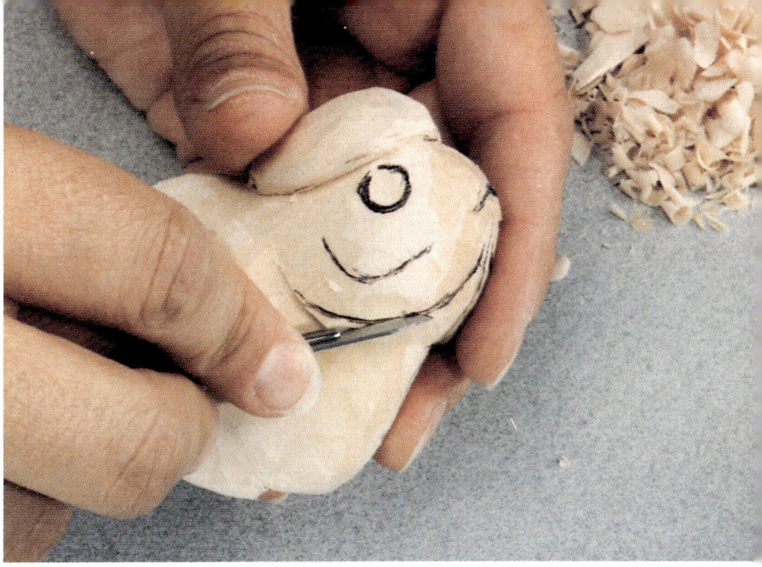

and the opercle.

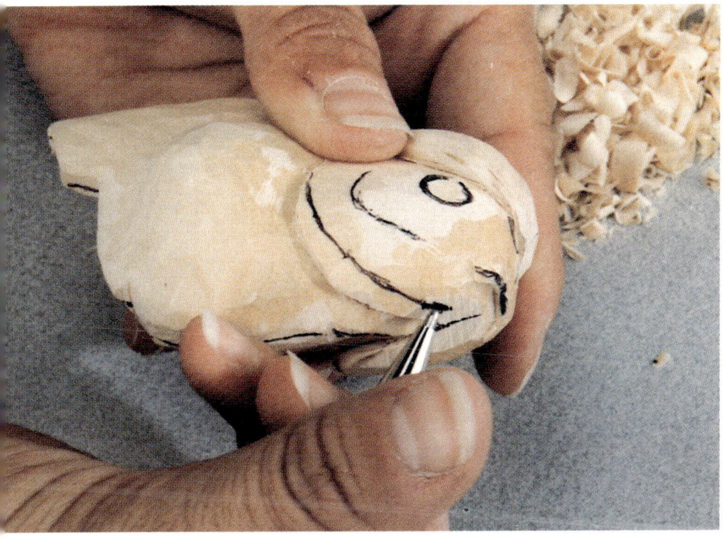

It continues into the lower jaw.

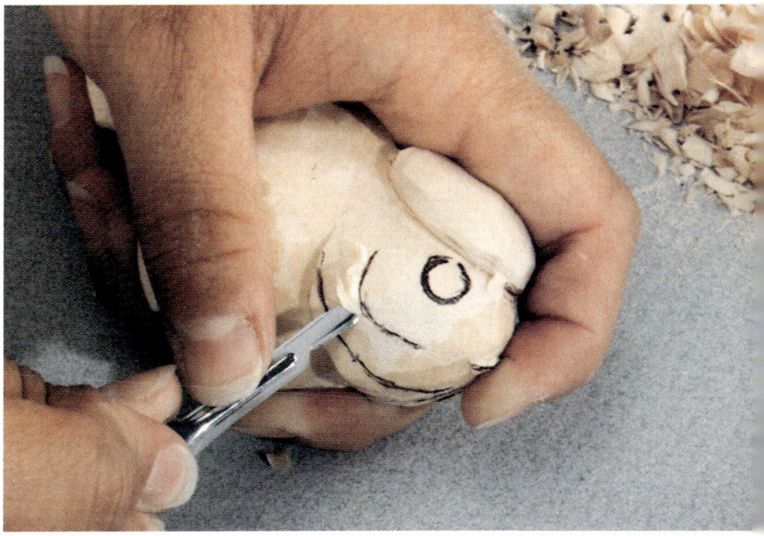

Cut back to the stops from below. At the preopercle line you have some artistic license. The deeper you go the puffier the area will be. There is no right or wrong here, as each individual fish varies considerably.

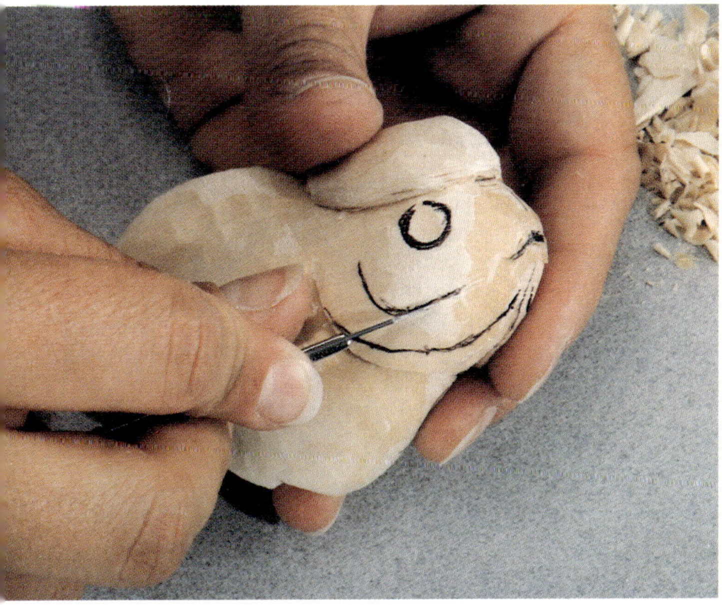

Cut a stop in the lines of the preopercle...

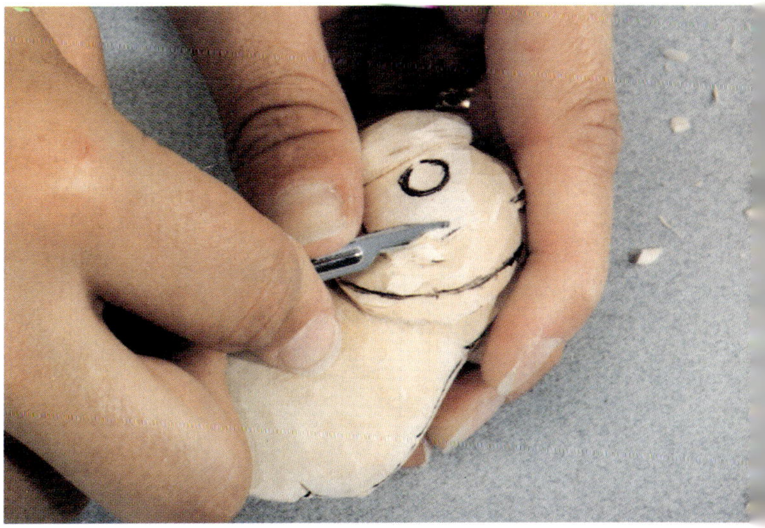

Once the ridge is established, cut down over it to round it.

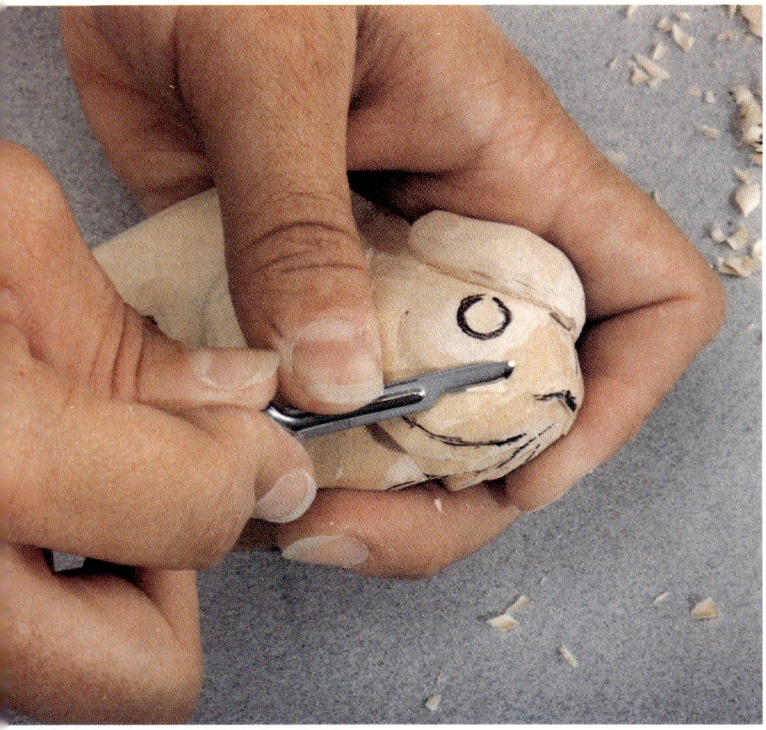

Smooth it off and cut a little dip toward the maxillary. I want to give the fish a kind of comical puffy look.

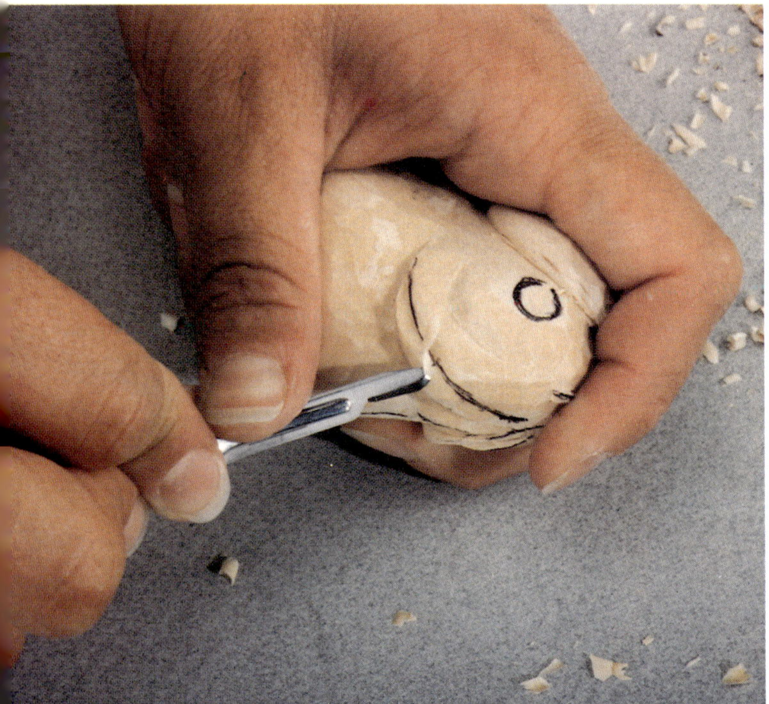

Slice along the stop in the opercle.

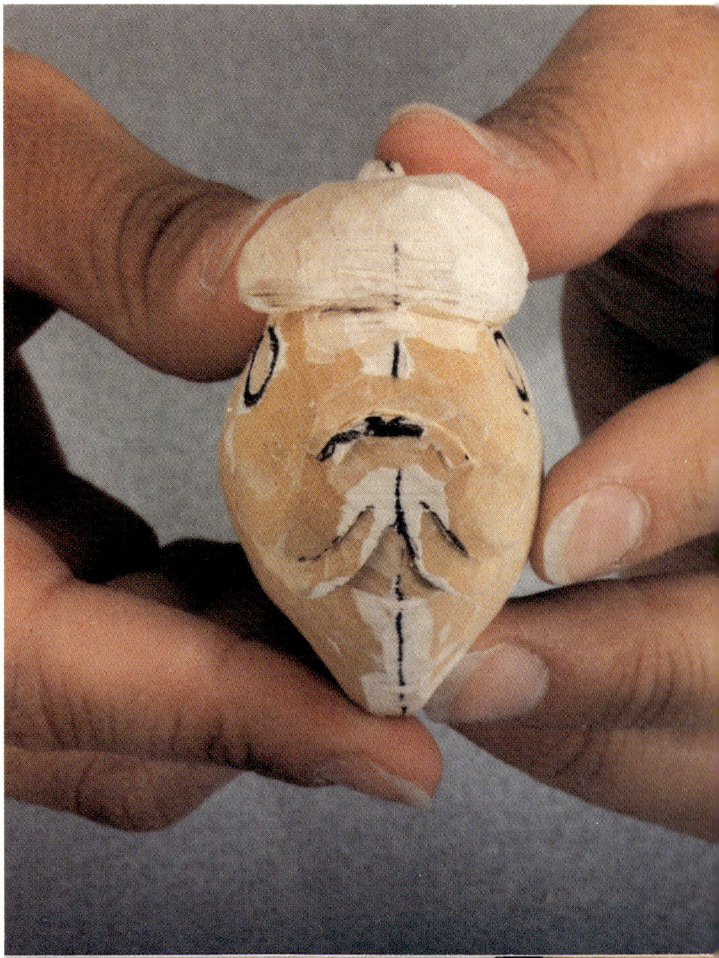

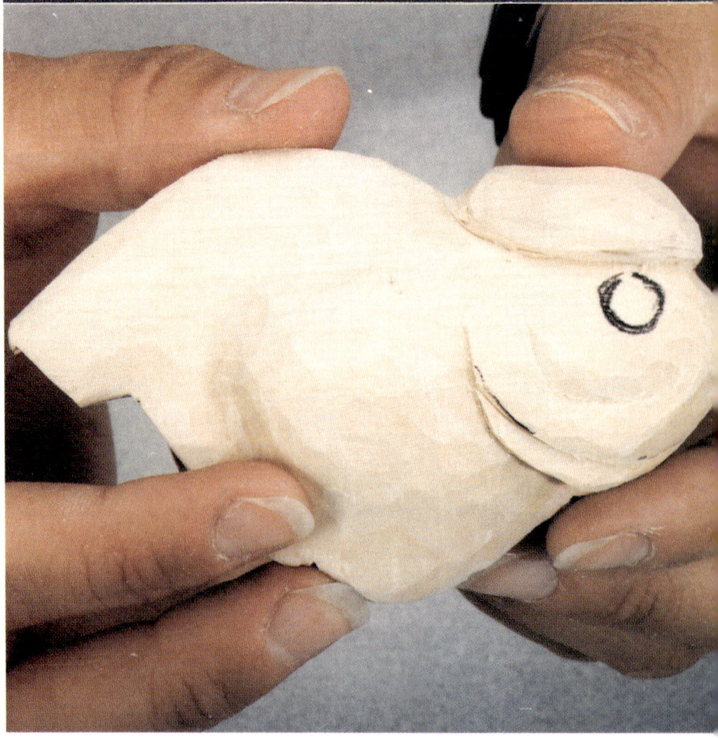

Progress.

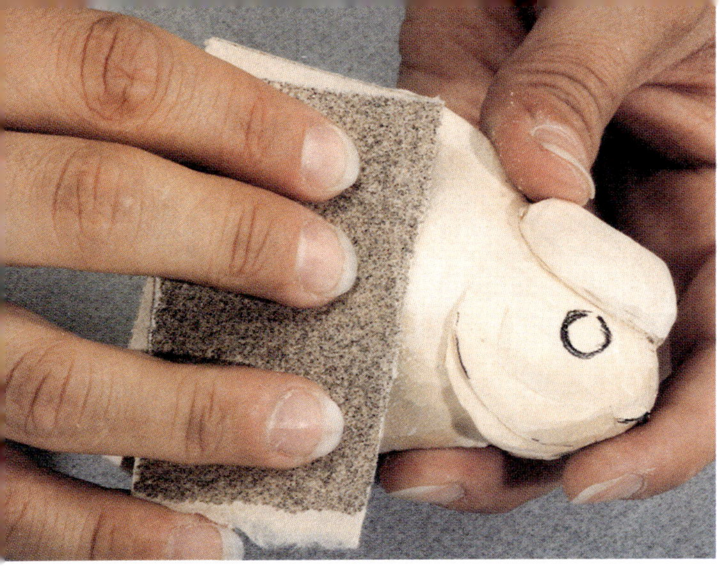

The body carving is finished. I rough sand it with 100 grit paper.

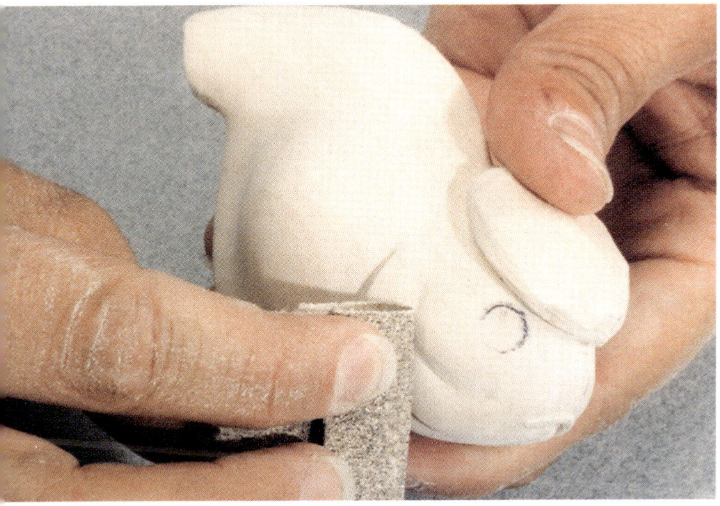

Some light shaping can be done as you sand. This finishes rounding out what I started with the knife.

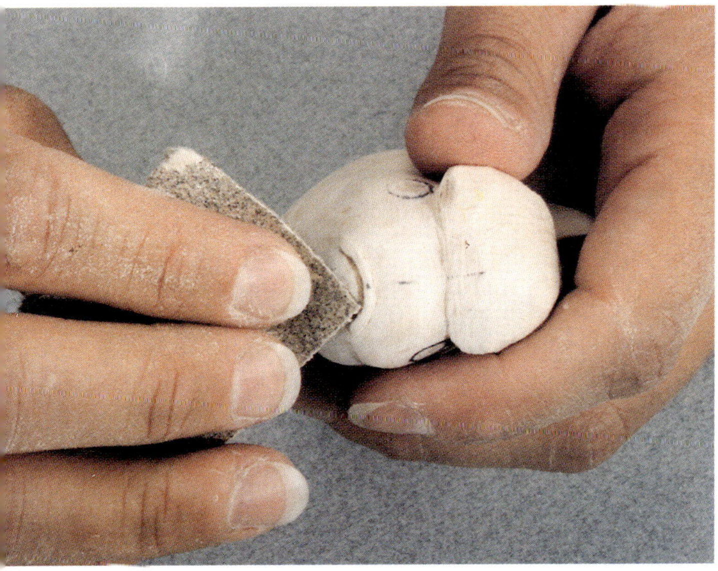

This is particularly helpful on the lips and the maxillary.

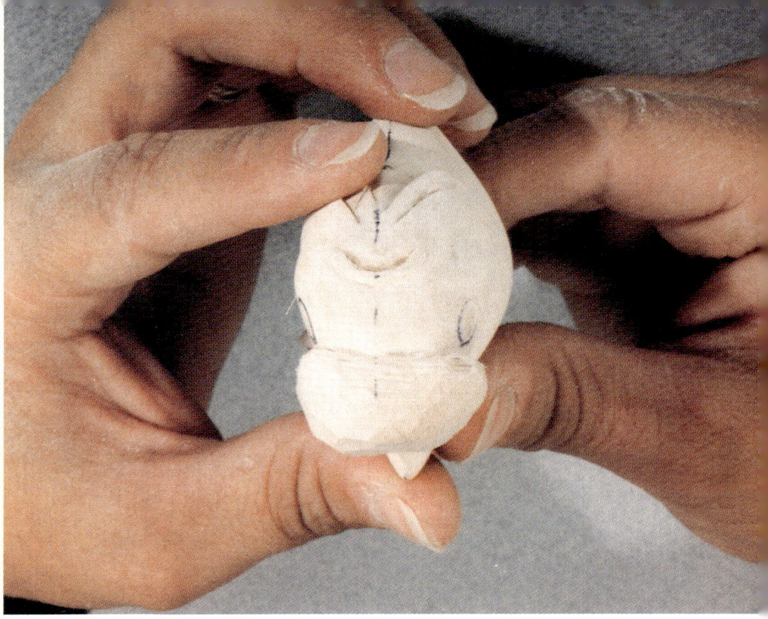

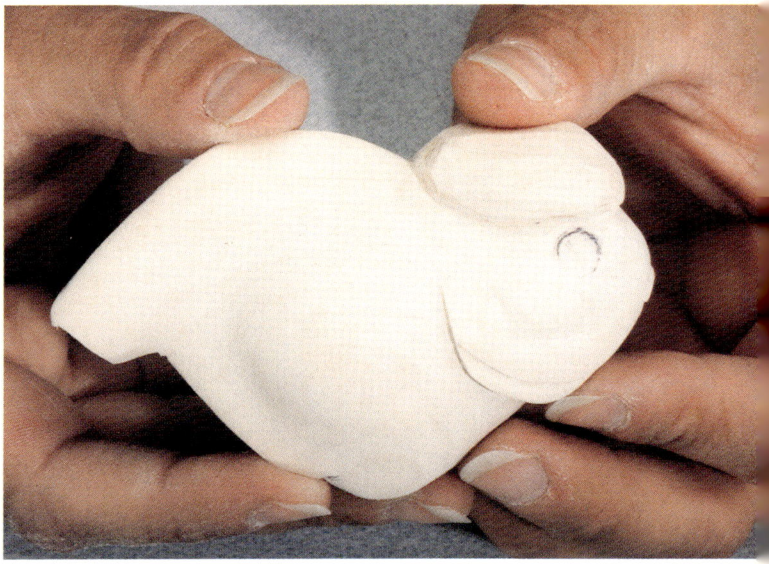

Progress.

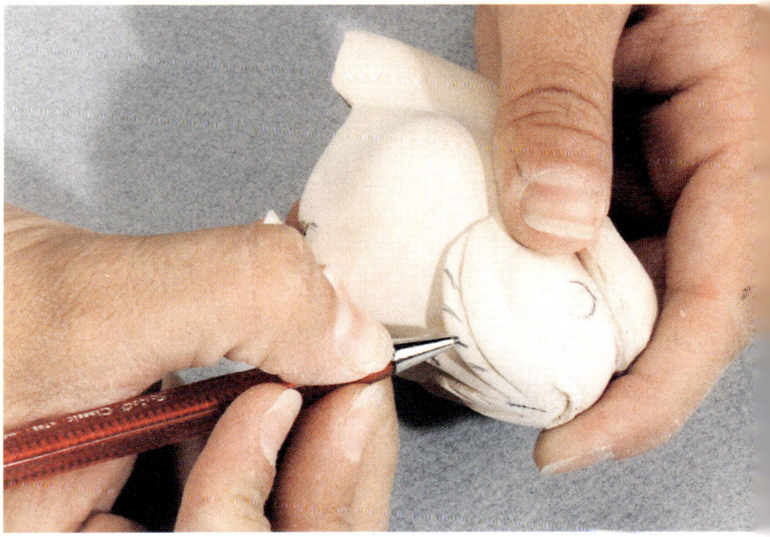

Draw in the branchiostegal rays. In a competition I would actually count the rays, but for artistic purposes I generally use fewer than the actual number.

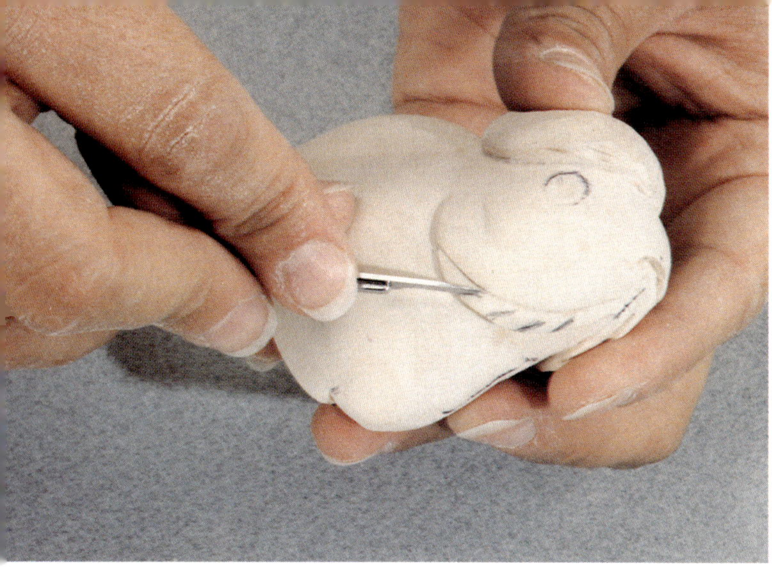

Cut a stop in each line.

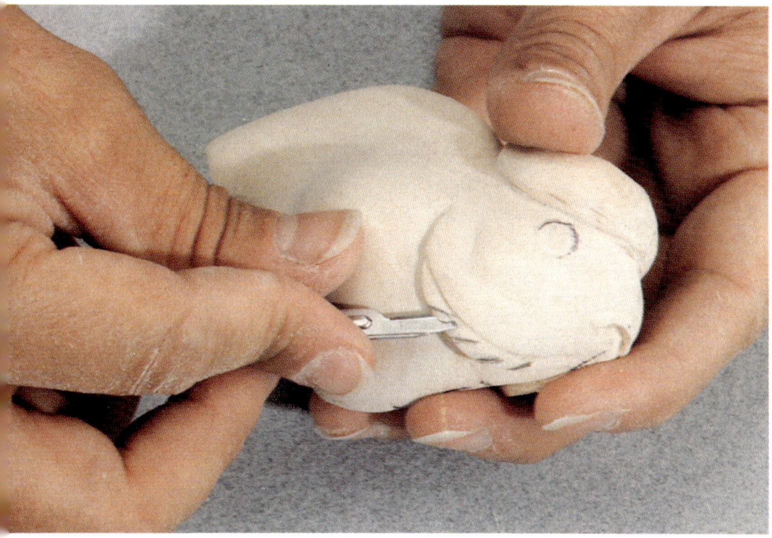

Cut back to the stop from the segment in front of it.

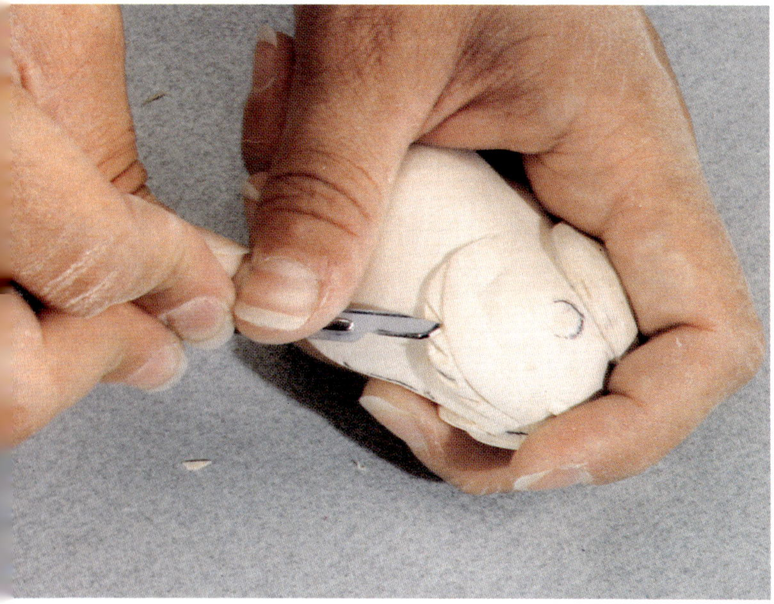

Blend the surfaces of the gill segments.

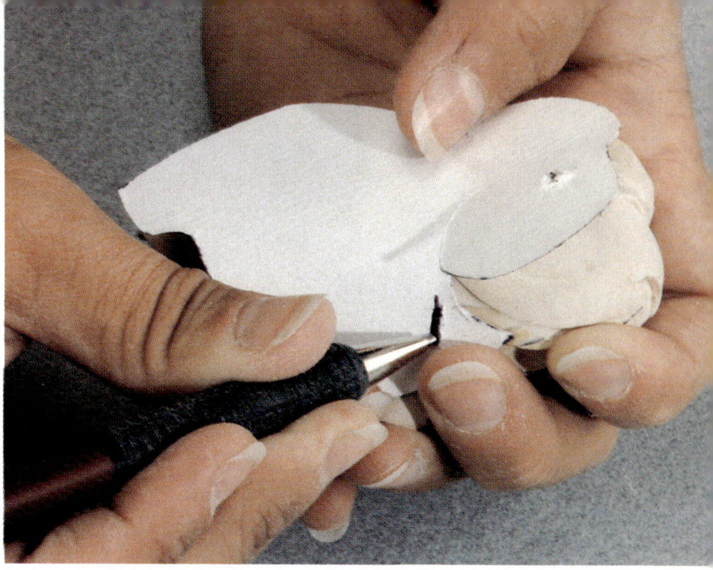

Cut a slit in the pattern on the line of the pectoral fin butt. Lay the pattern on the fish and draw the line through the slit.

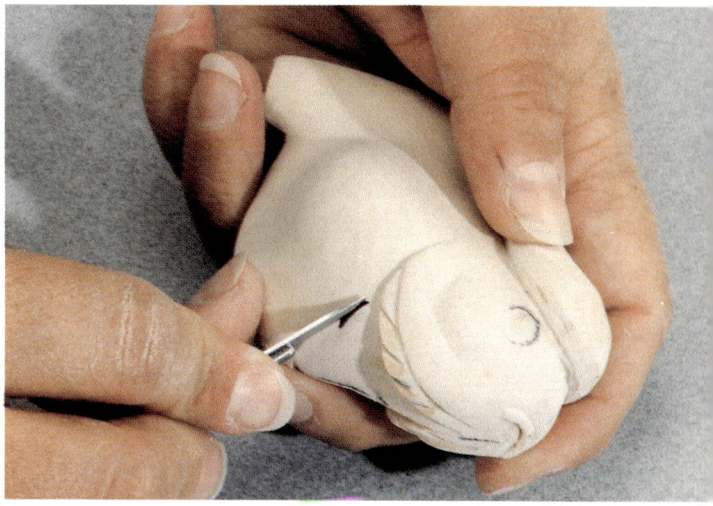

Cut a stop on the line...

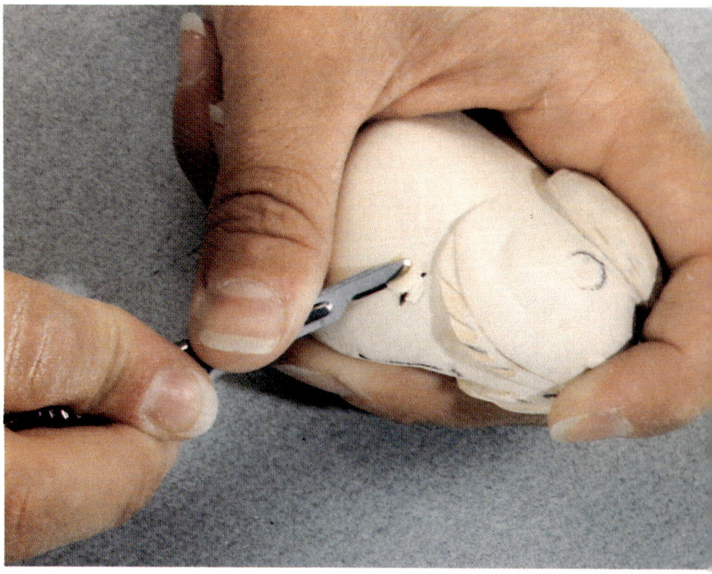

and thin the body back to the line. This keeps the fin away from the body.

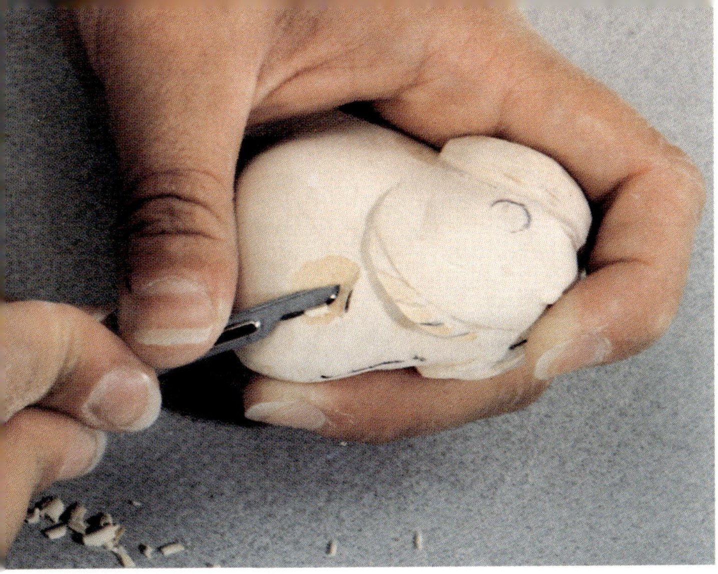

Taper the cut into the body.

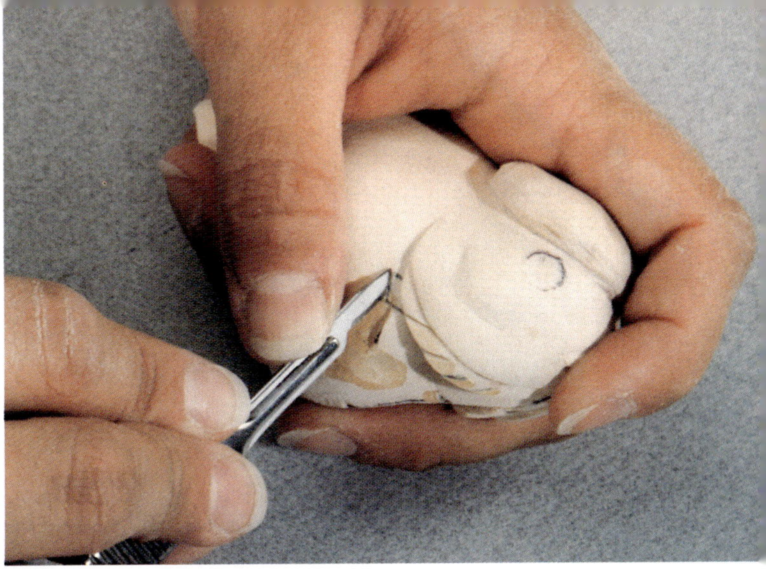

Cut stops on the three sides...

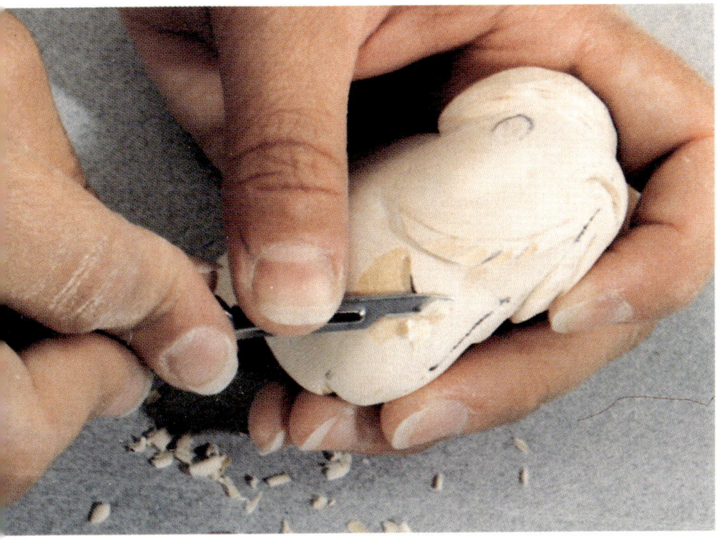

Relieve the area under the pectoral muscle with a scoop cut. This will make the muscle stand out more.

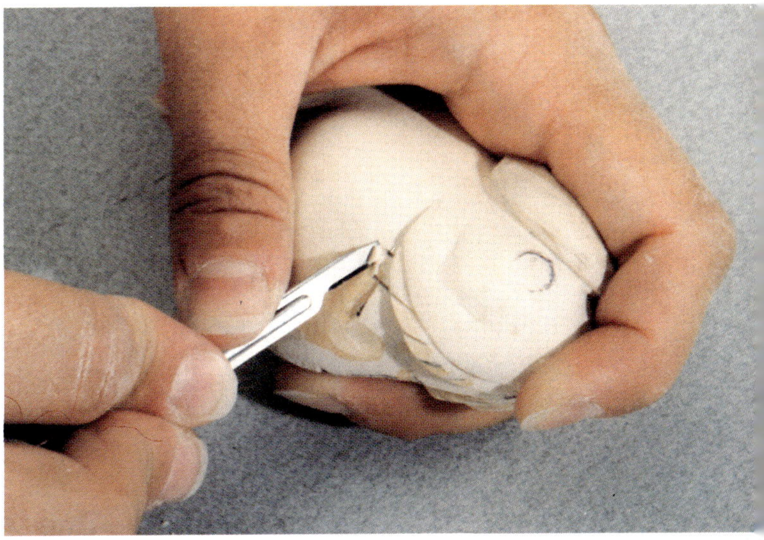

and carve back to them from the body.

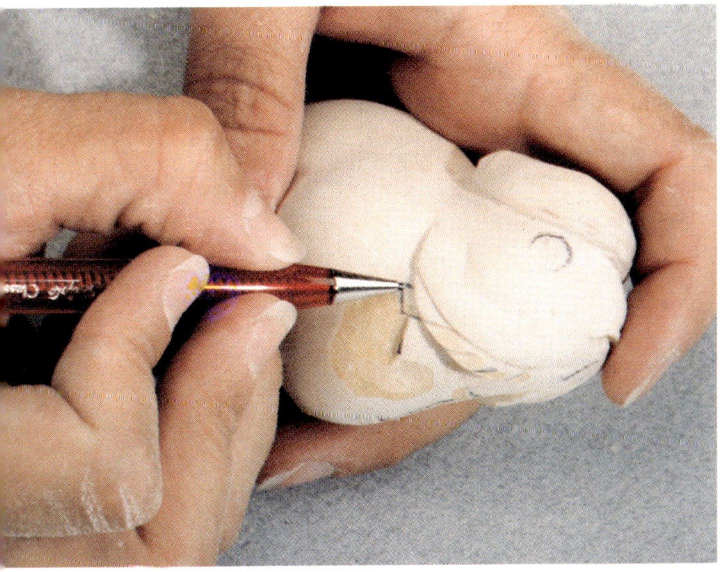

Draw in the cleithrum above the pectoral fin.

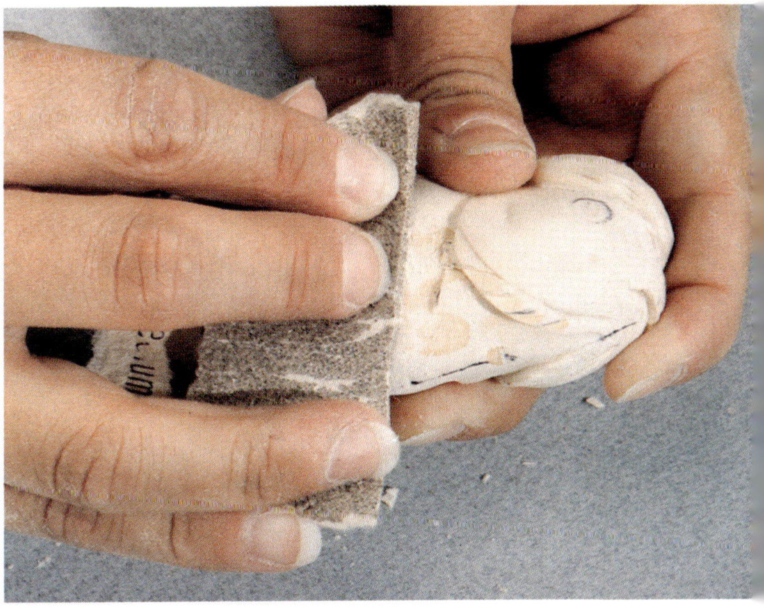

Sand the carved area with medium grit paper.

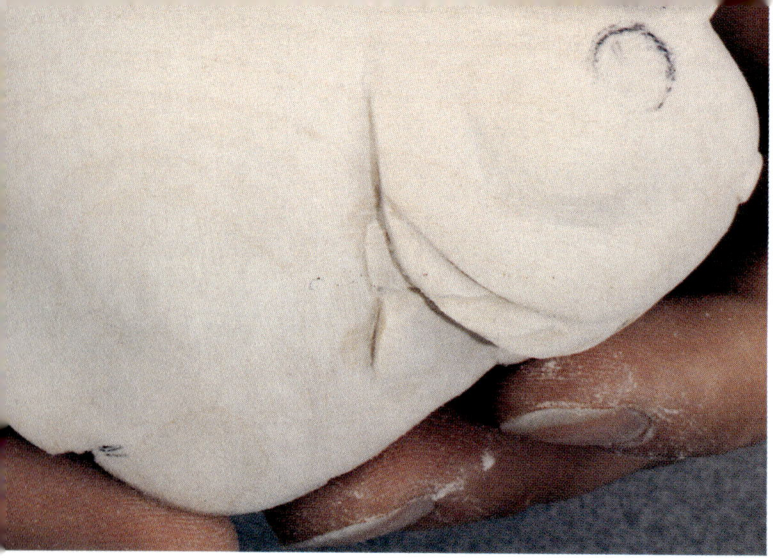

Progress.

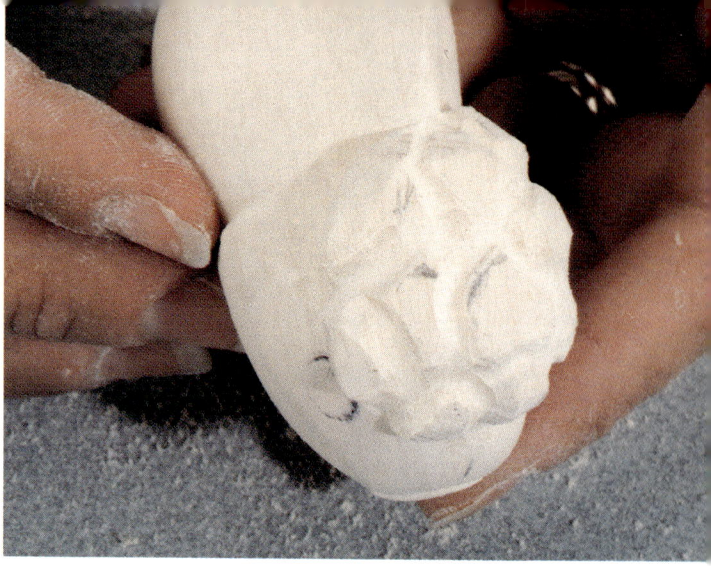

This is the roughed out, "brain" stage.

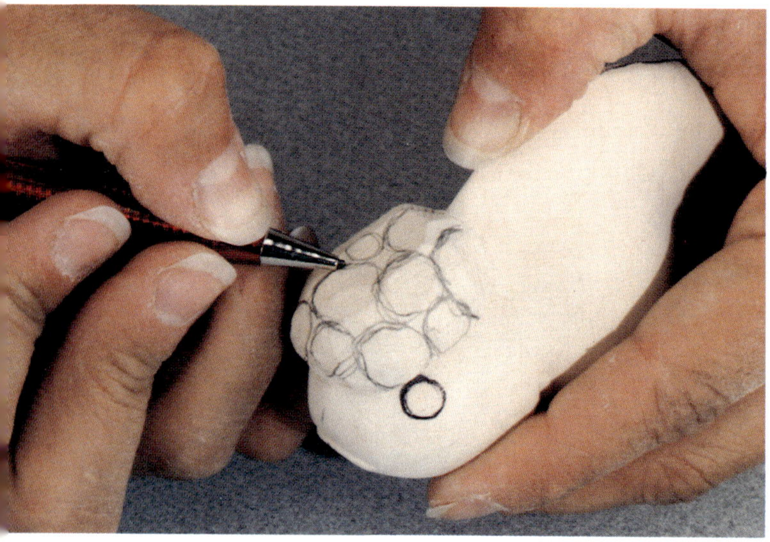

I return to the rotary tool to create the texture of the crest. Begin by drawing random circles on the crest.

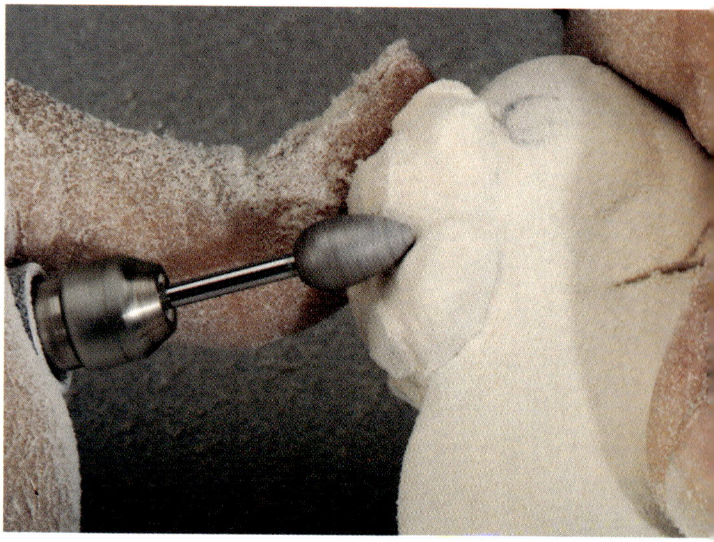

Using a lighter touch, round each bulge that you roughed out, blending them into distinct, but flowing lobes. The pear-shaped bit allows you to round and get into the crevices.

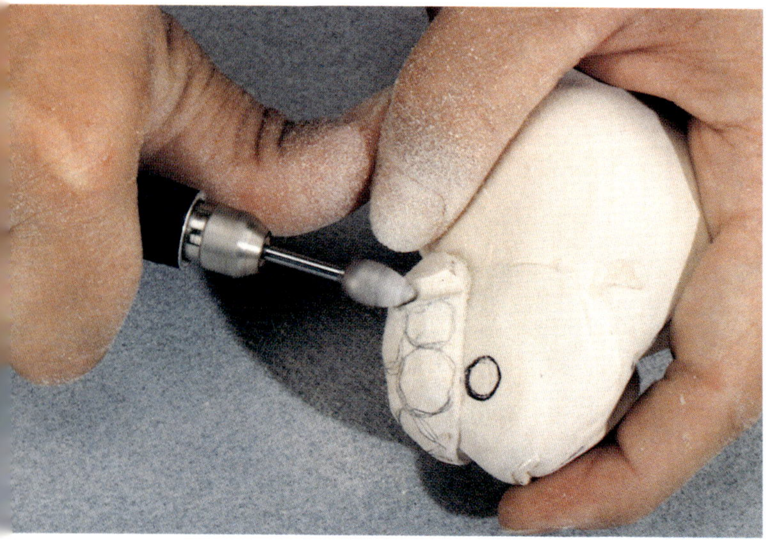

I use a pear-shape diamond point bit to carve the lines I've drawn.

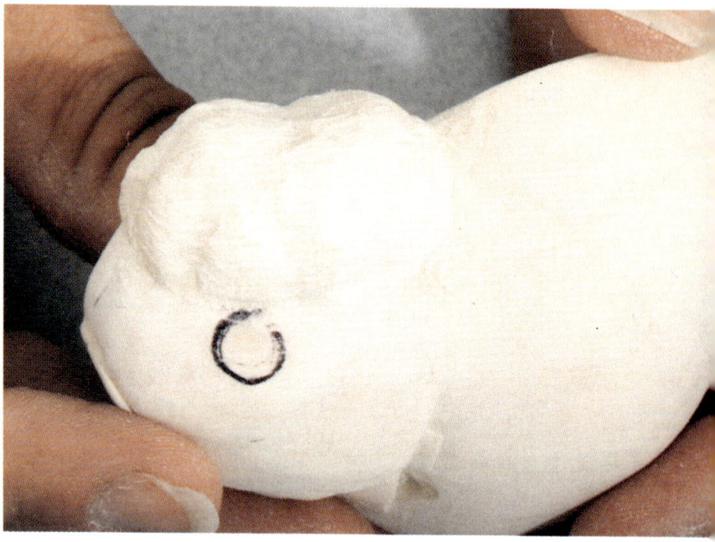

The result.

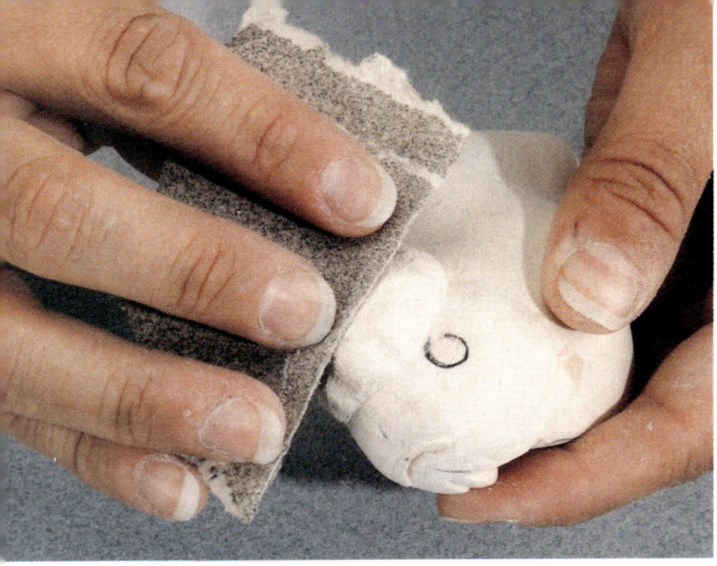

Sand it with medium grit paper.

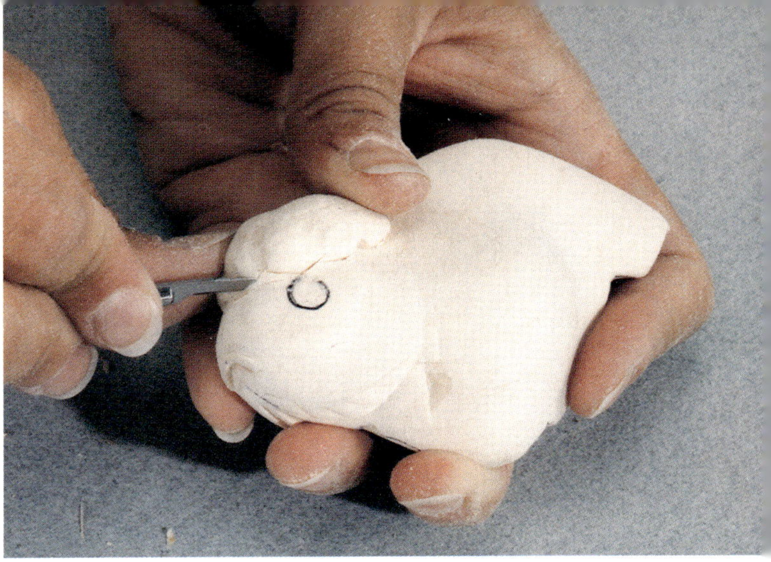

Go all the way around.

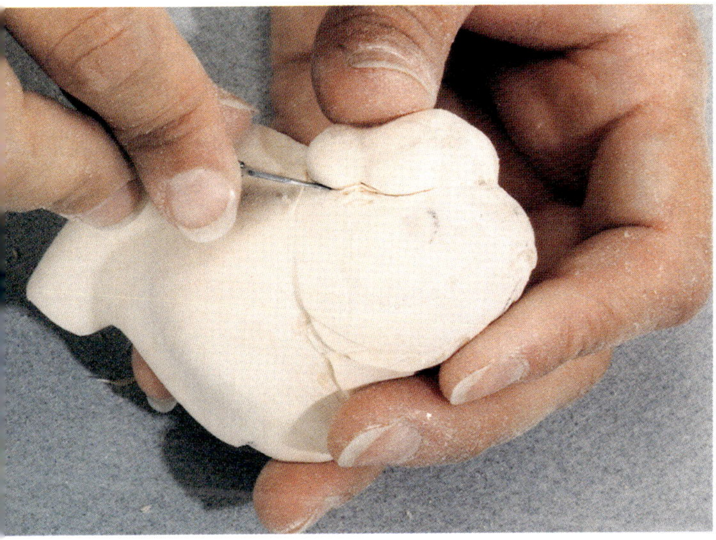

Make a stop around the bottom edge of the crest...

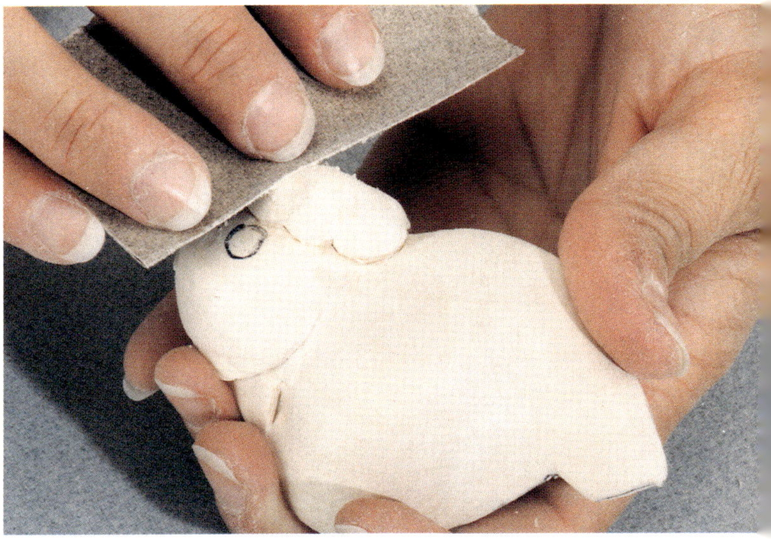

Lightly sand the whole fish with 150 grit paper. Fish have small indentations and bumps in nature, and I don't want to remove them by sanding. I just want to take off the burrs.

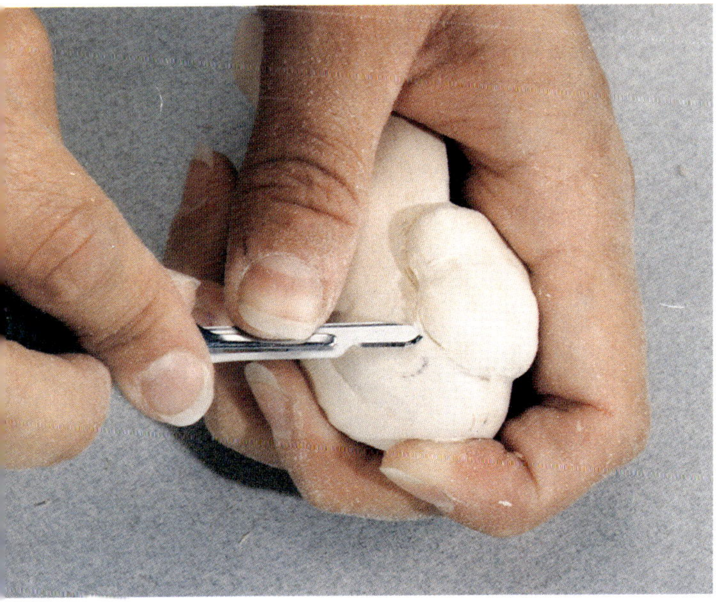

and trim back to it from the head.

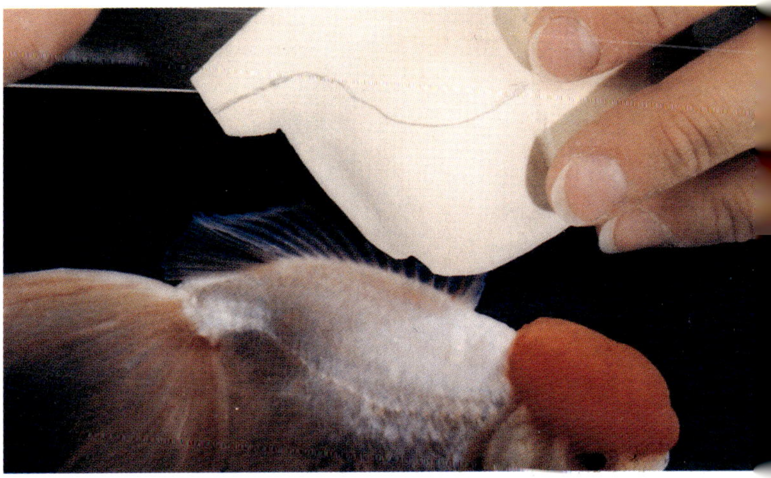

Checking your reference material, draw the lateral line. In most goldfish it dips down at the belly. Repeat on the other side.

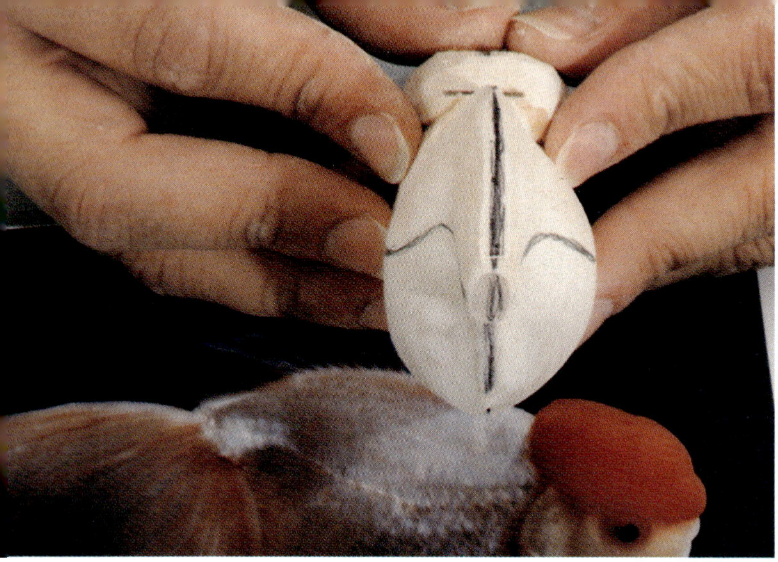

When both sides are drawn you can check that they are even by looking at the fish from the back.

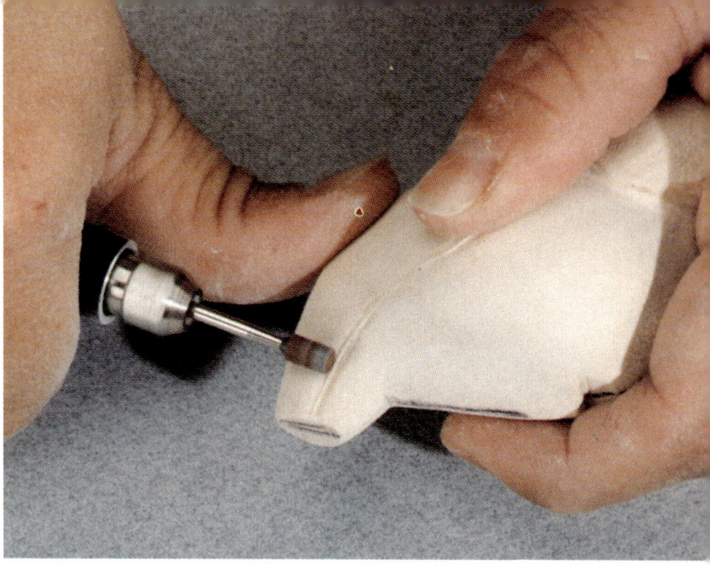

Turn the fish over and cut above the lateral line in the same way. Keep the line between as thin as you can get it.

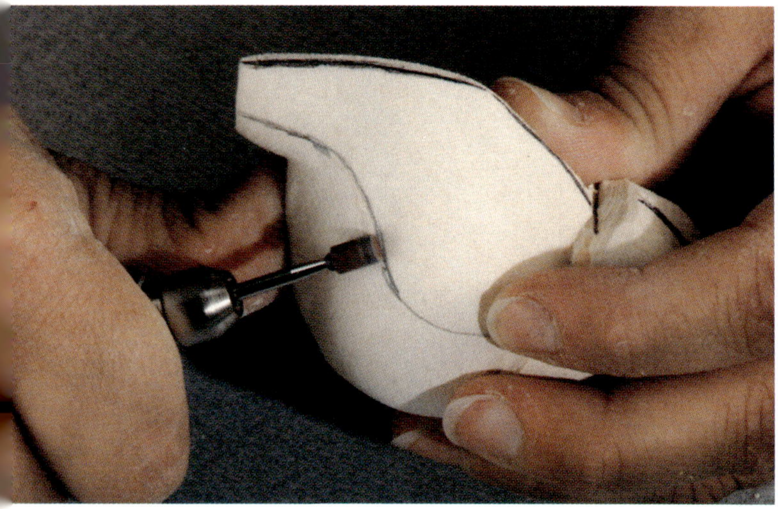

Switch to a medium grit, textured stone, cylinder bit in the rotary tool. To raise the lateral line use this tool to carve on each side of it. Begin just below the line and run the tool along the whole length.

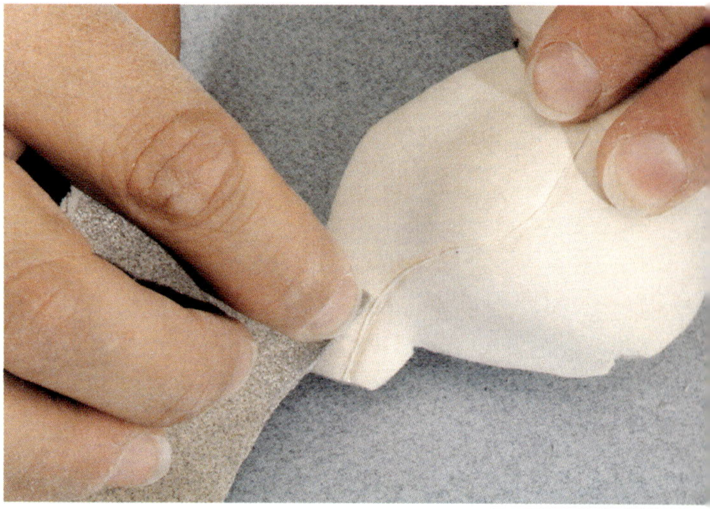

Sand as before, but even more carefully. It is really easy to sand away the lateral line.

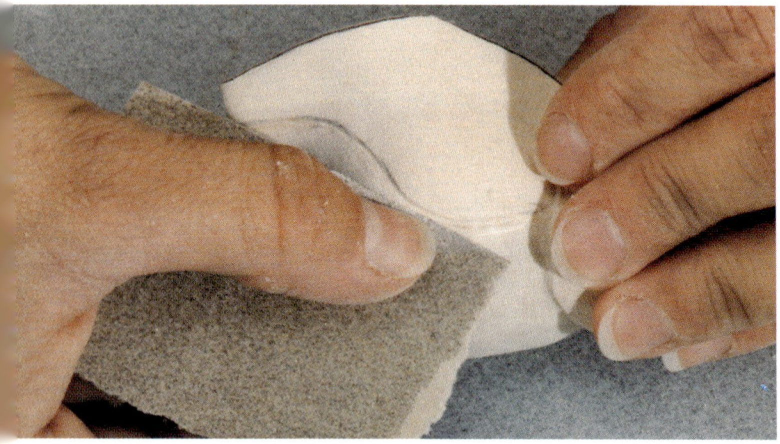

With the fine paper go over the work of the rotary tool. Blend the surface of the grind into the body and clean up any imperfections in the line.

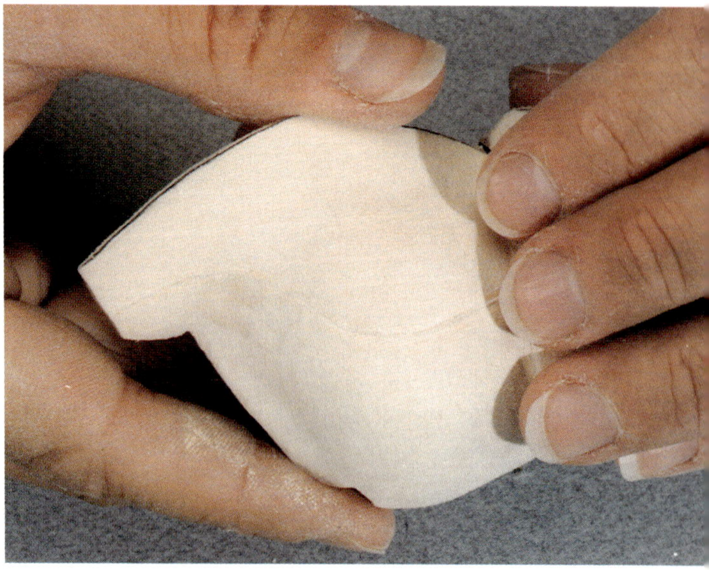

A slight, raised line between is what you are seeking.

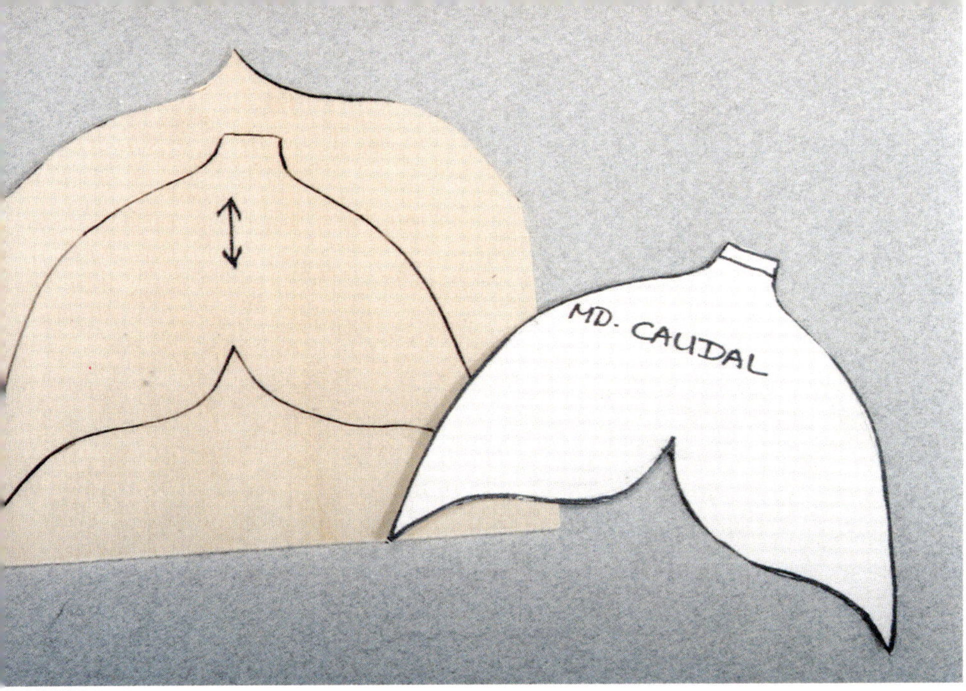

The goldfish has pectoral fins, ventral fins, anal fins, and a dorsal fin, as well as beautiful caudal fins. The caudal fins are formed from 1/32" basswood. This is hard to get, but sometimes you can find it at a hobby store that deals in models or doll houses. I've included a source in the introduction to this book. Lay the patterns out on the wood. You will need two pieces.

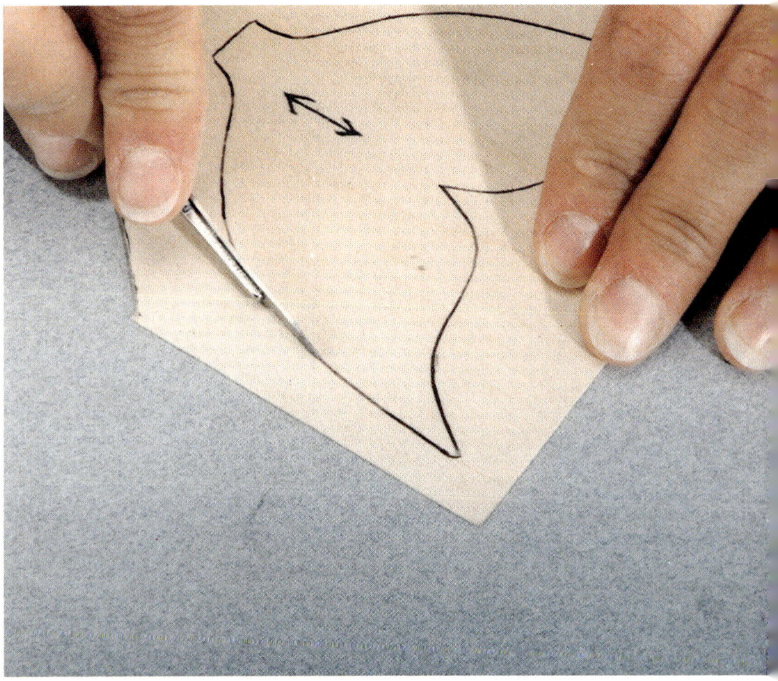

Because the wood is so thin, the tail can be cut with a knife.

The excess breaks right off.

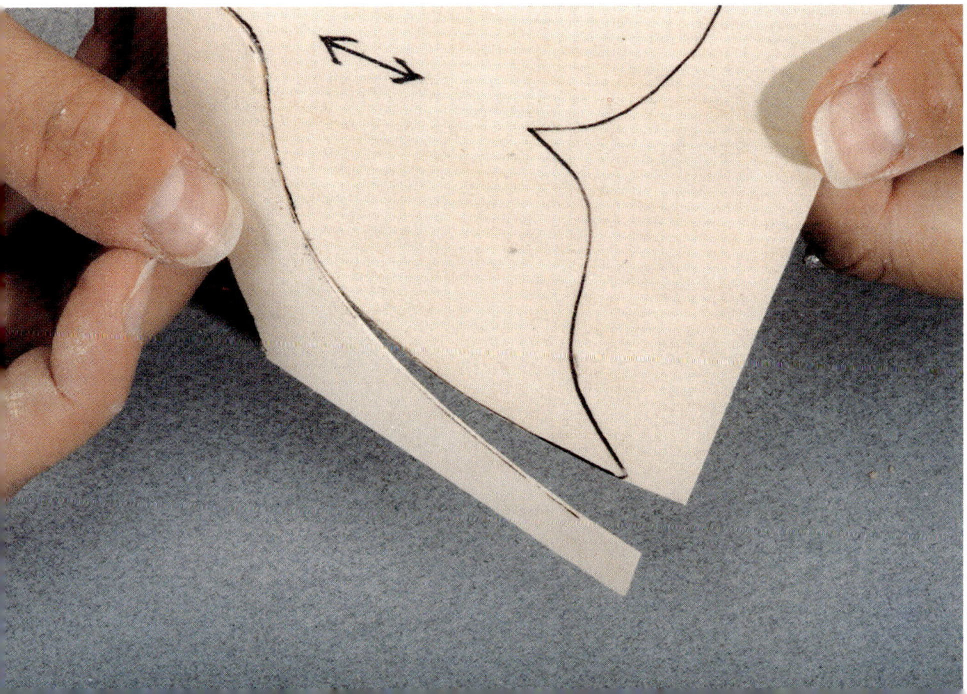

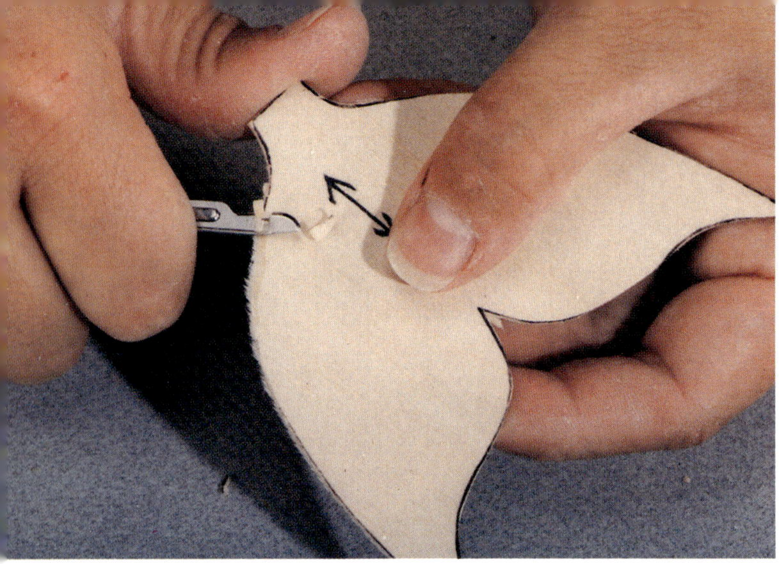

With a knife, shave the edges. Be careful of the grain. Sometimes you can get caught in it and split the fin. Shave all edges on both sides.

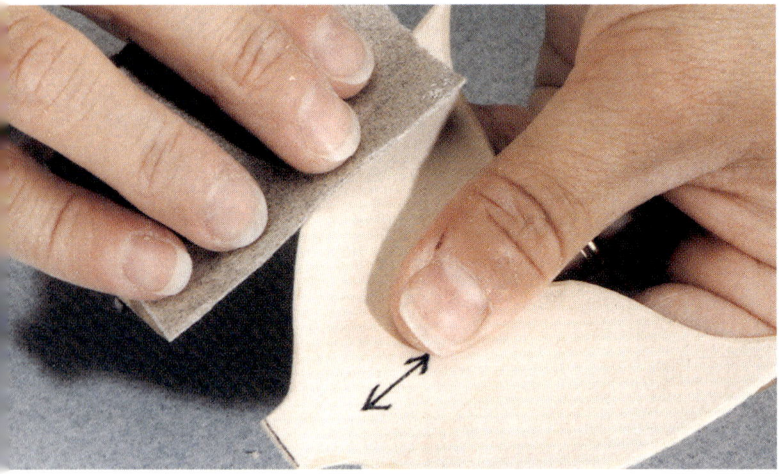

Sand the edges lightly with the fine sand paper.

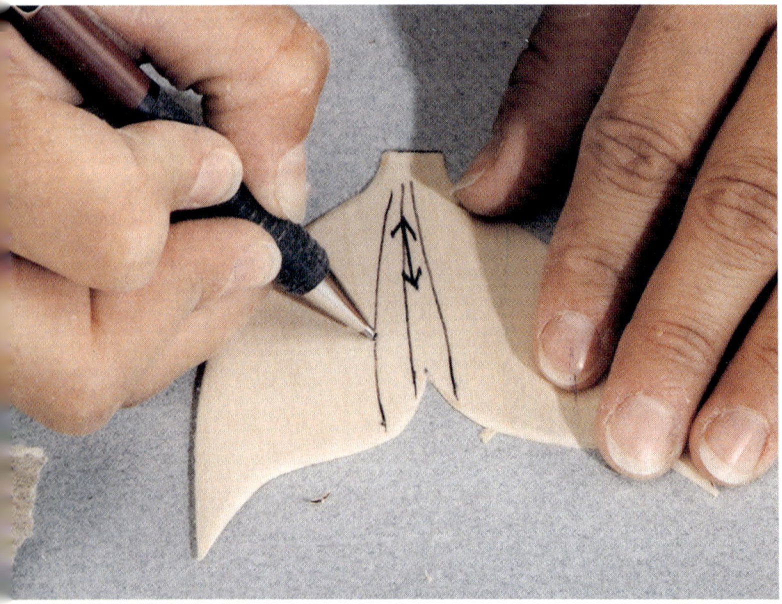

Working out from the center, draw in the fin rays.

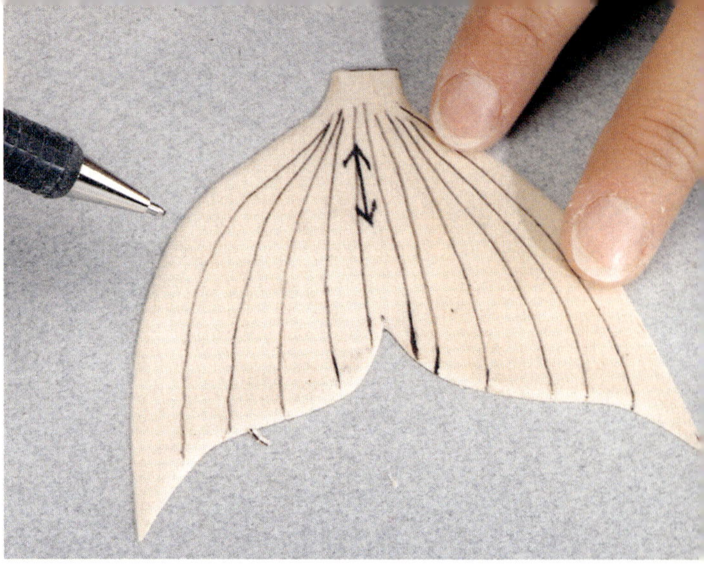

An exact number of rays is not necessary. I draw as many as look good, usually about 11 or 12.

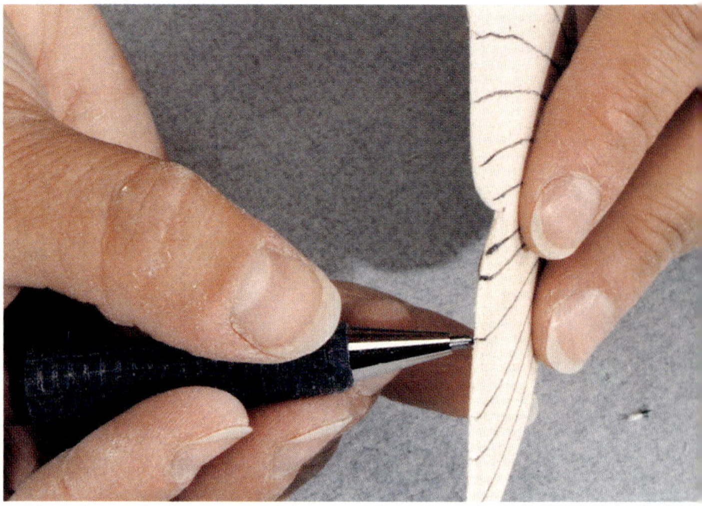

After one side is drawn, mark on the other side where the ray ends. When I gouge the line the wood becomes quite thin. These marks tell where **not** to carve on the other side. I carve to one side or the other of the mark.

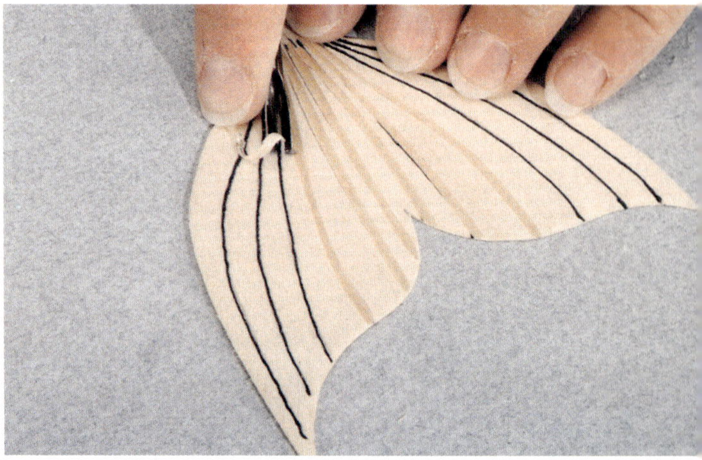

The rays are carved with a wide micro gouge. Place the fin on a surface and starting at the peduncle end, carve the rays out to the end of the fin.

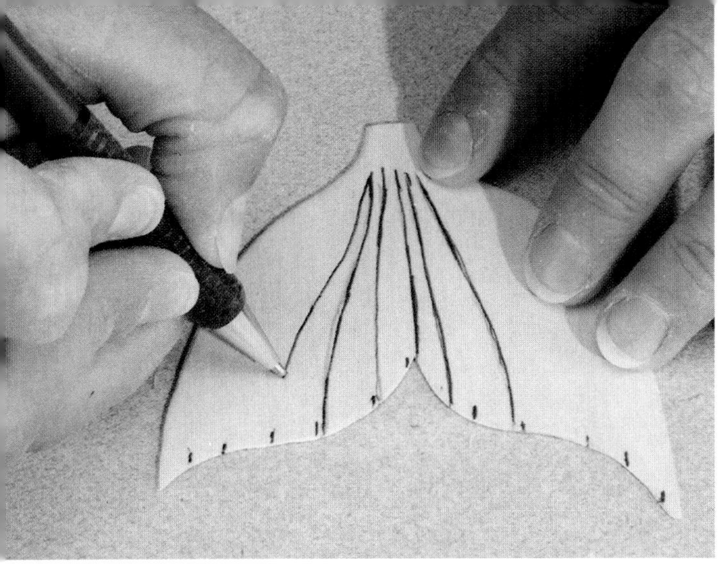

Turn the fin over and draw the rays so they don't end where they did on the other side. You can check yourself by holding the fin up to a bright light. You will see your original cuts, and be able to avoid any overlapping on this side.

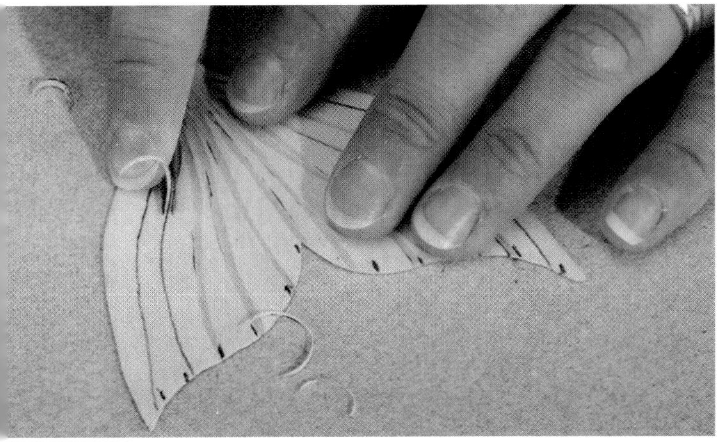

When the lines are correct, carve the rays on this side in the same way.

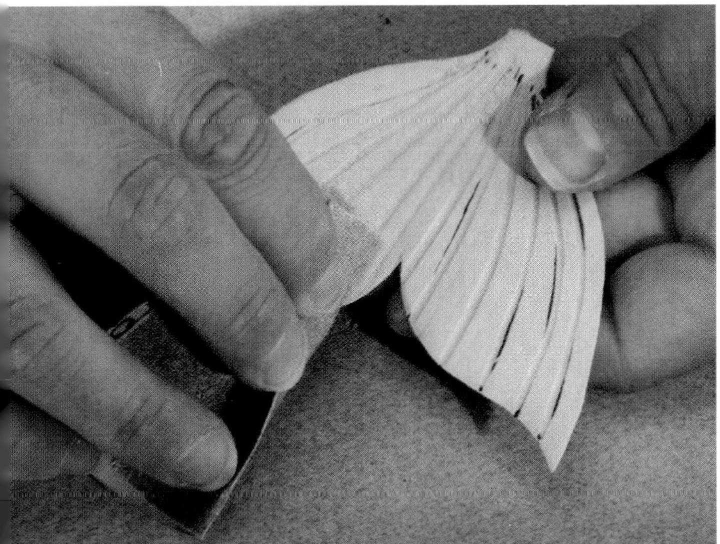

With a rolled piece of fine paper, lightly sand the grooves.

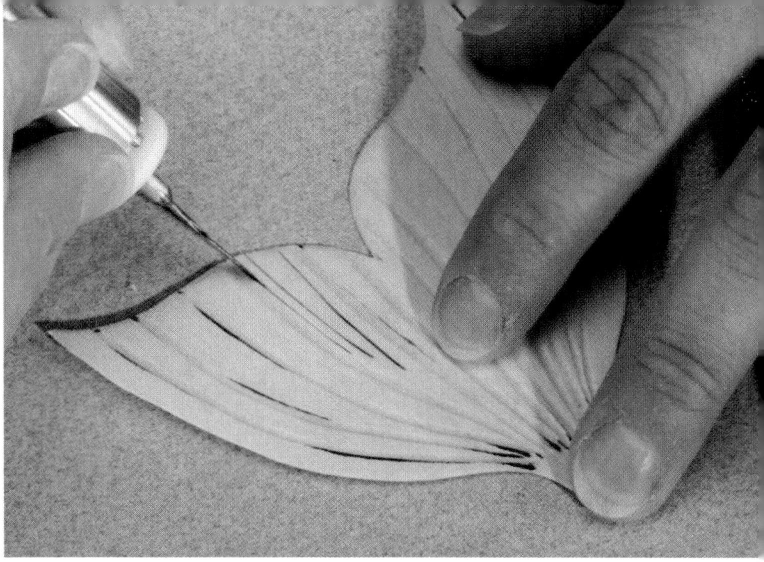

Use a burner with a straight edged tip to make the final rays. If you think of the fin as being divided into thirds from the peduncle to the trailing edge of the fin, start at the beginning of the second third, away from the caudal peduncle. Make a few rays going from there to the end. Be careful not to burn through the fin.

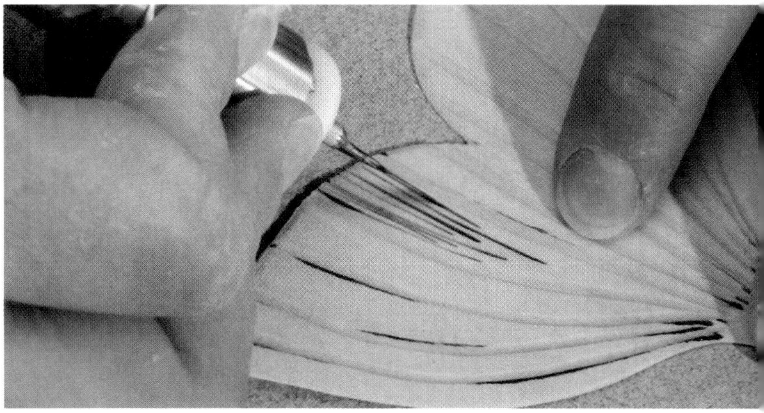

Between those rays, start closer to the edge and make some more.

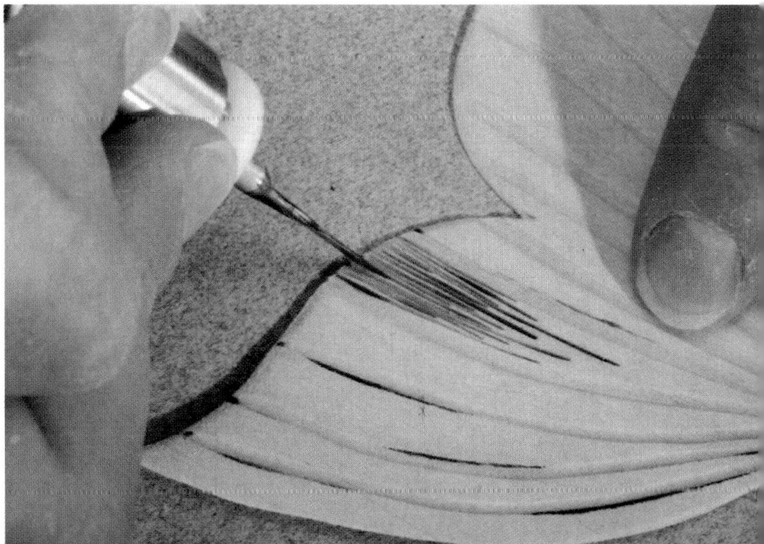

Make more lines in the final third...

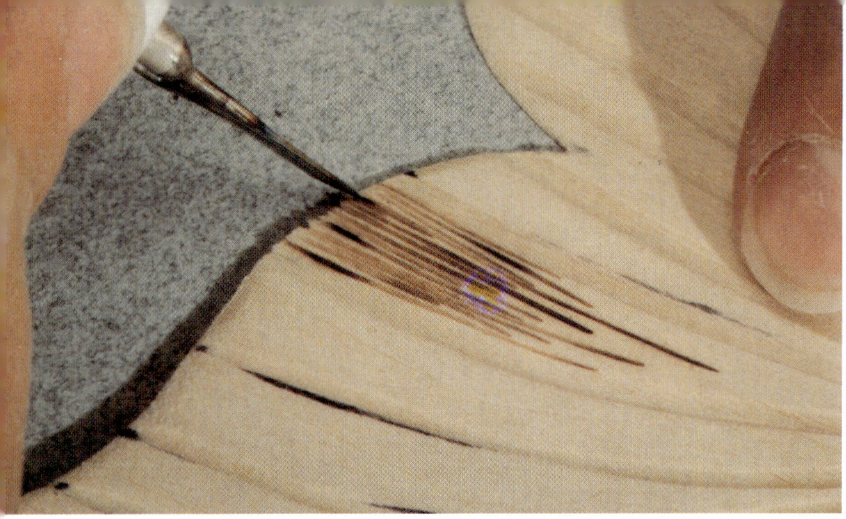

and still more along the edge.

The result is a random pattern with more lines at the edge and only a few running through the middle third of the tail. This burning process weakens an already weak caudal fin, s[o] be careful with it.

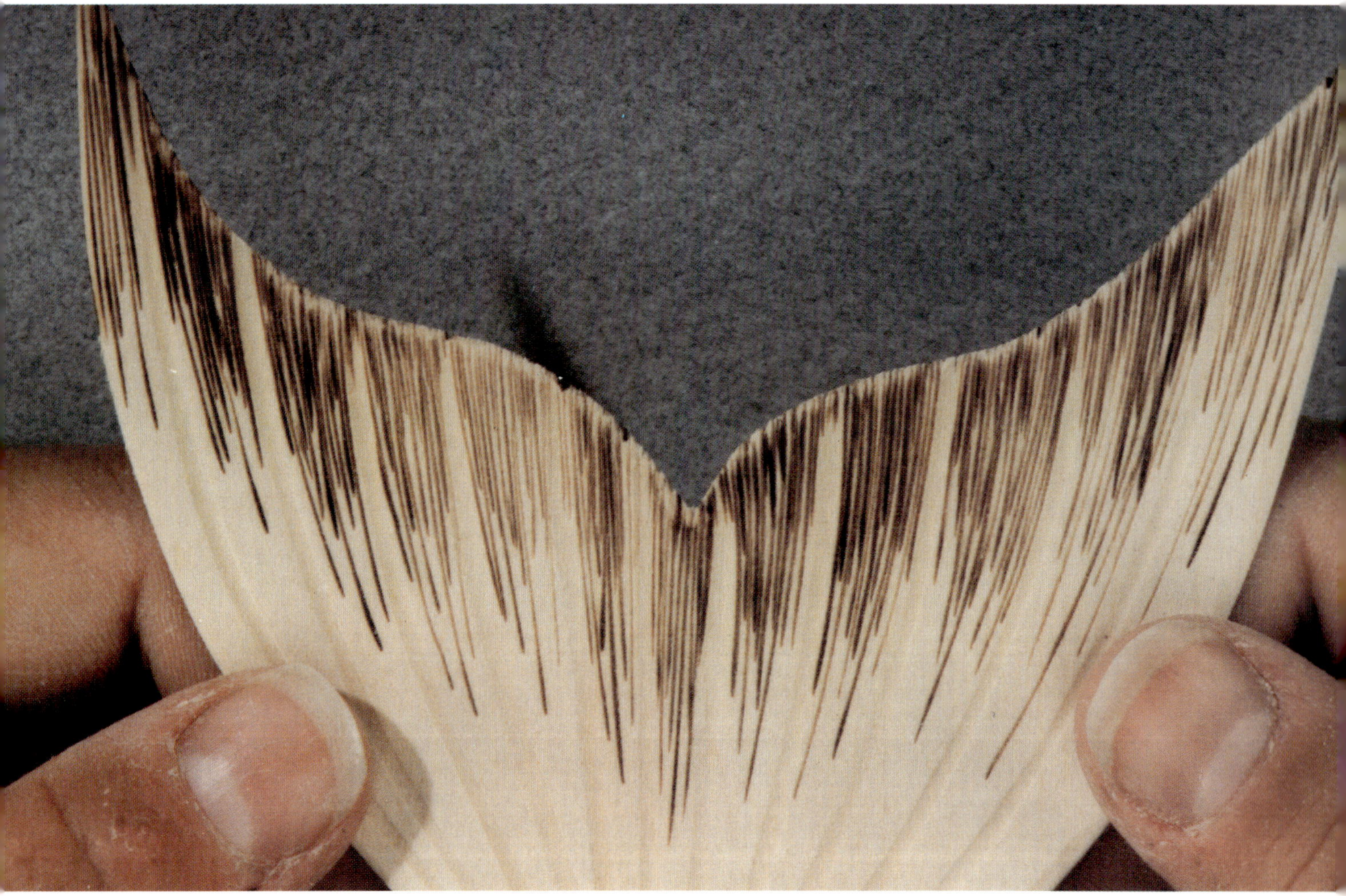

Place the fin in a sauce pan with about 1/2" of water. Place it on the stove and apply high heat. In about one minute remove the fin from the water.

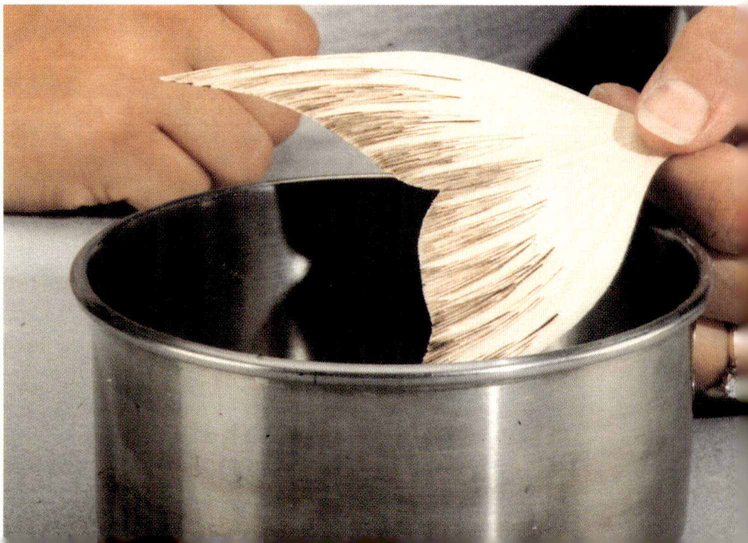

Immediately wrap the fin around a drinking glass, using pencils, paintbrushes, and anything else you want to create folds in the fin. Hold this assembly together with rubber bands and let it stand over night.

When it is dry it has the desired curl.

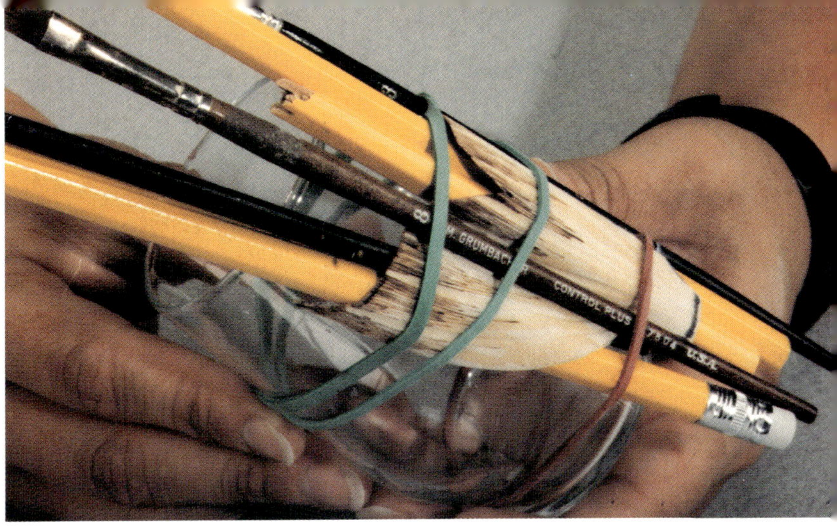

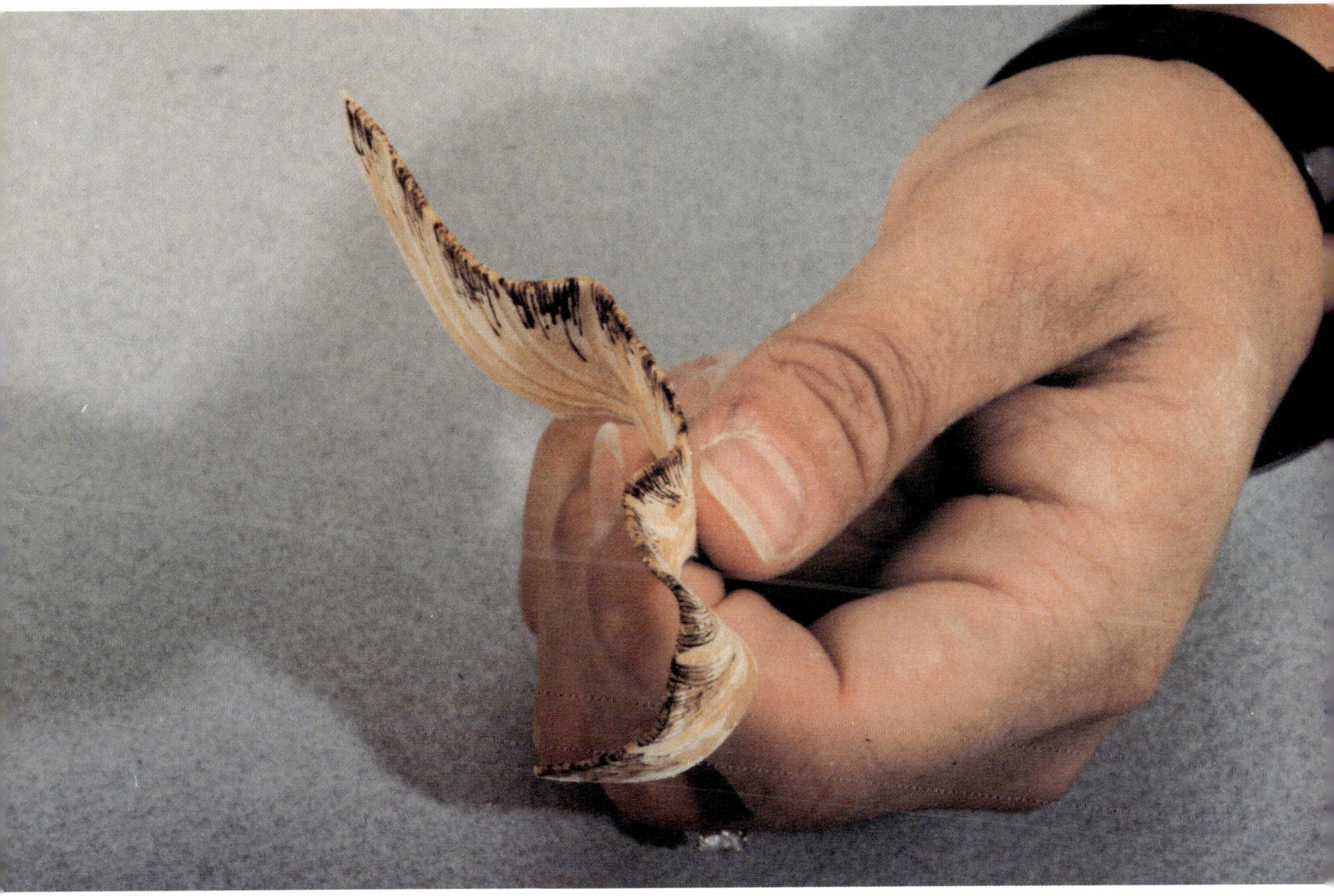

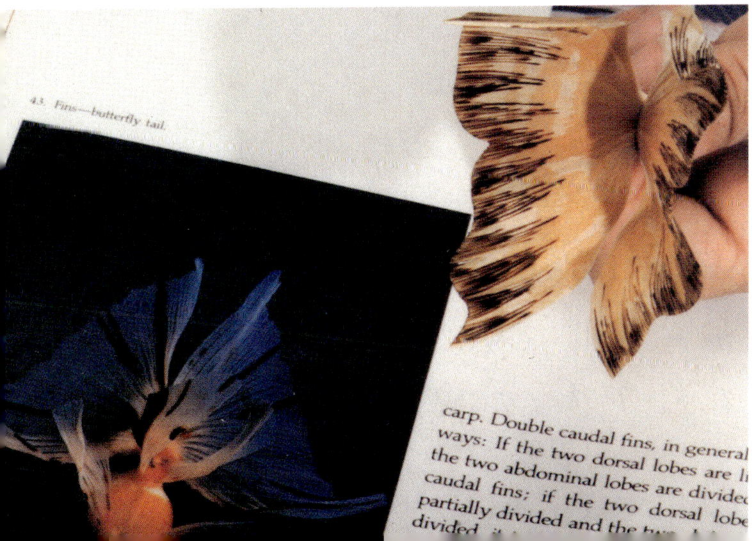

The fins go together like this at the base.

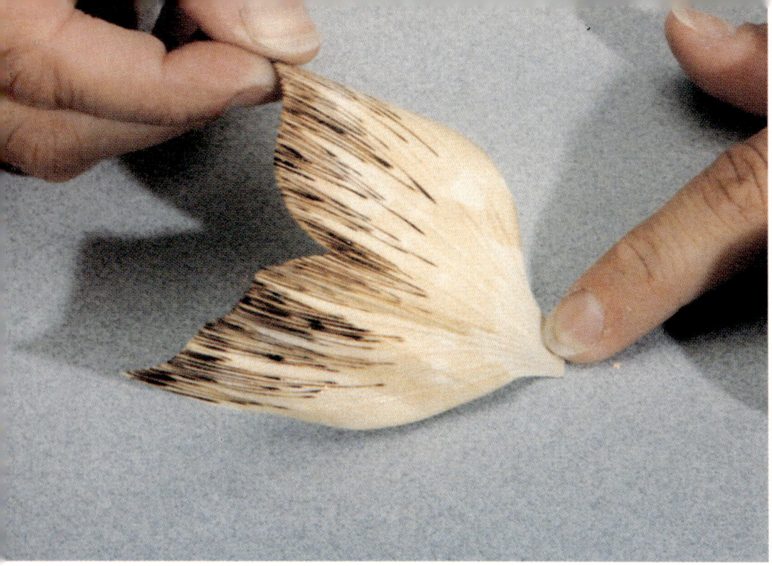

When the fin is wet I add a bend to the tab where they join by holding the tab down with my finger and bending up the fin.

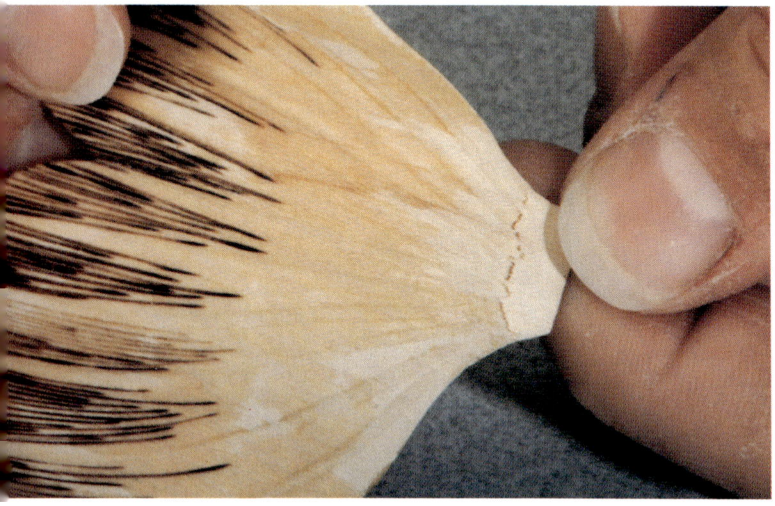

Because this goes against the grain it always results in a little break on the inside of the tab. This should not carry through to the other side. If it does you will need to start over. The break will be buried in the peduncle.

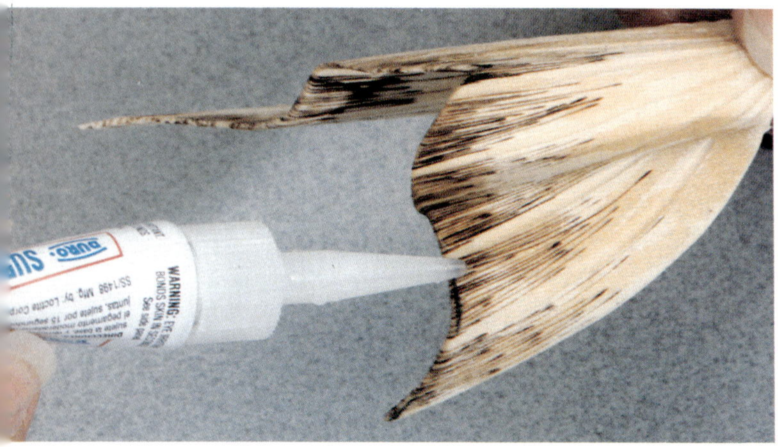

The caudal fin is very fragile. To strengthen it I add super glue to the whole thing. Begin by running it down the edge. Capillary action will carry it into the fin.

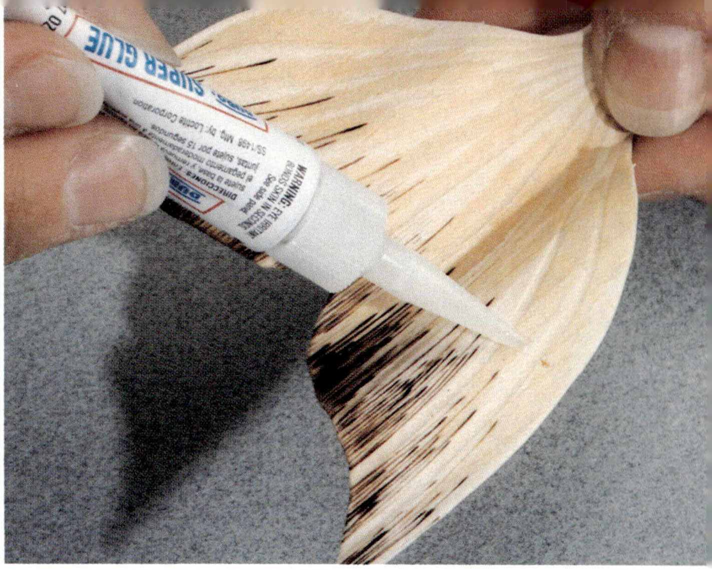

Then run the glue along each of the fin rays. Set the fin aside until you are ready for assembly.

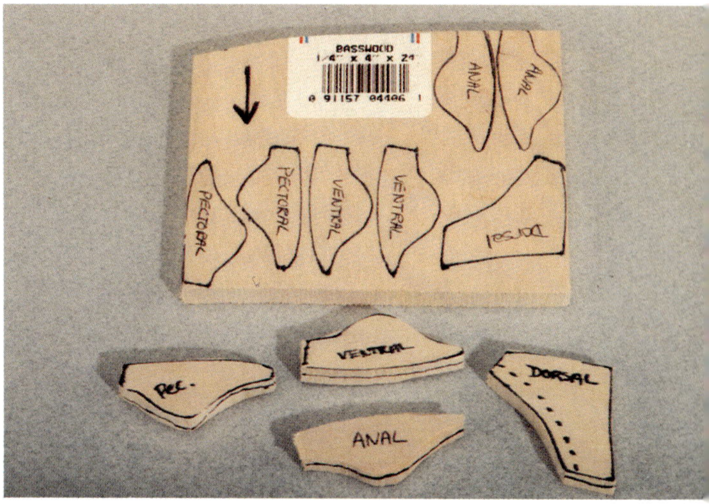

The remaining fins are cut out on the bandsaw.

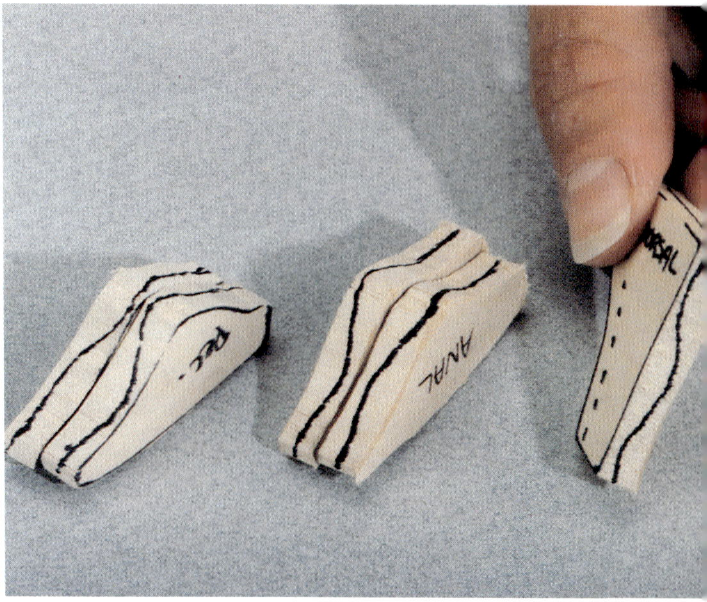

Draw a wavy center line that establishes the flow of the fin.

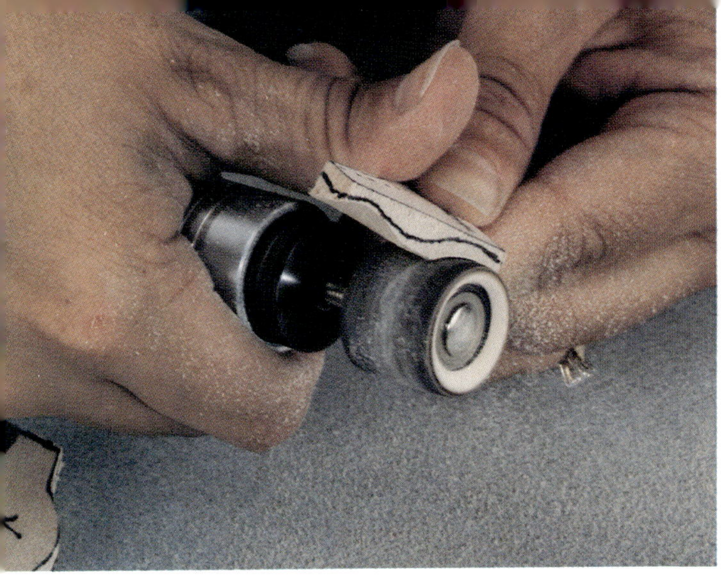

With the coarse sanding drum, carve one side of the fin, making the contour follow the line you drew.

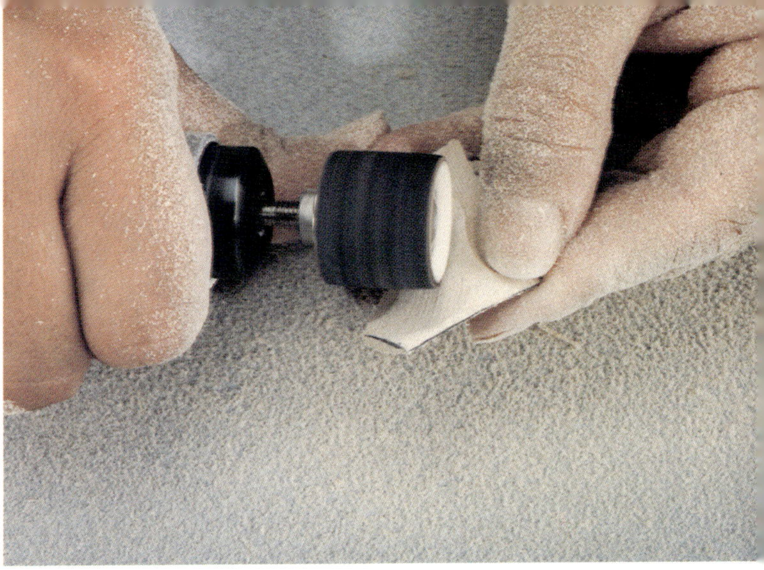

With the general shape determined, thin down the whole fin.

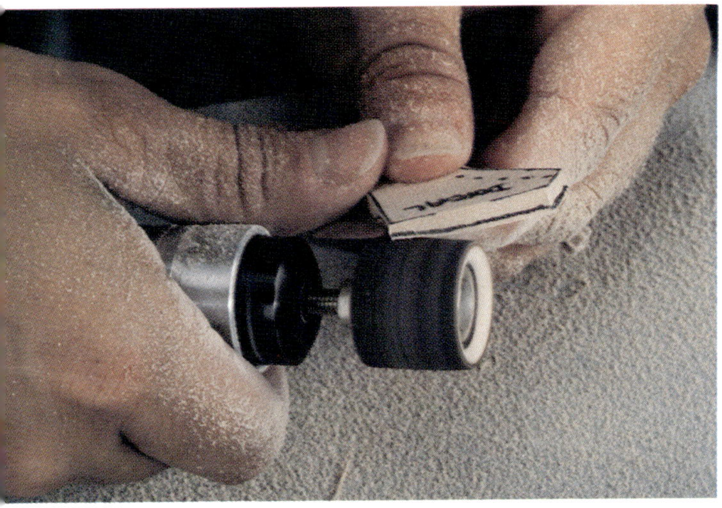

Taper the leading edge to the line.

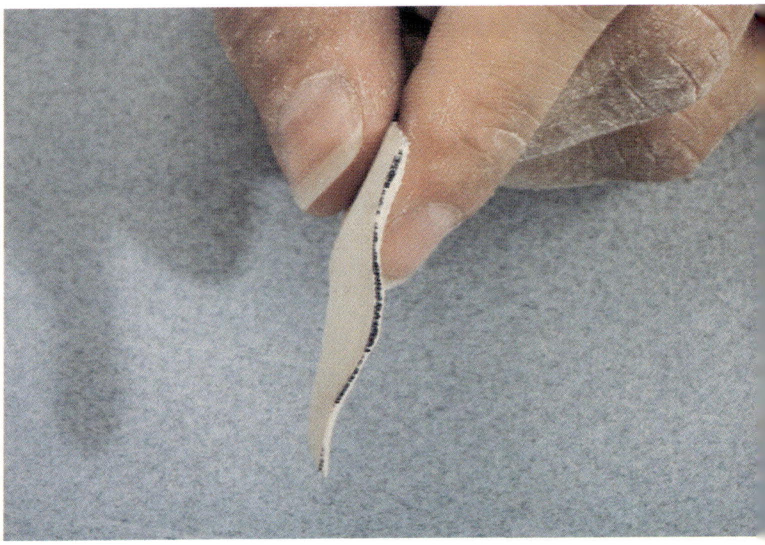

Even though it has been thinned considerably, the center line is still intact.

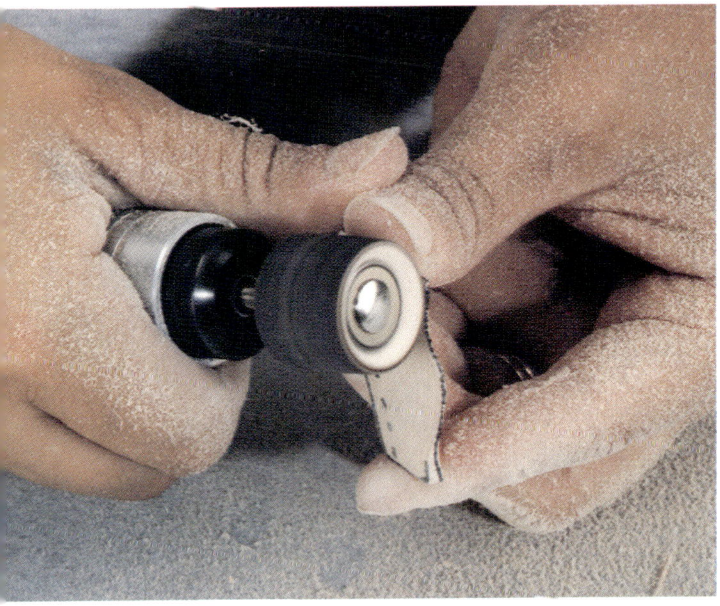

Shape the other side of the fin.

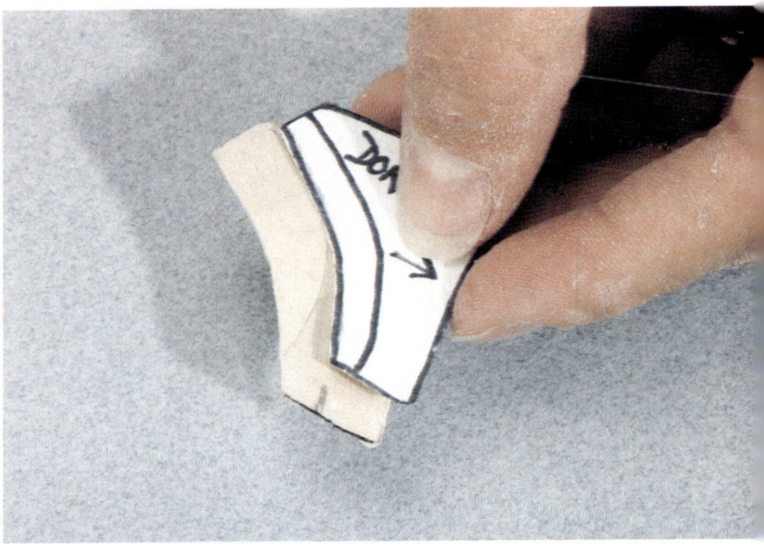

Refer to the pattern to set the curve that is the lower edge of the fin and the top of the tab.

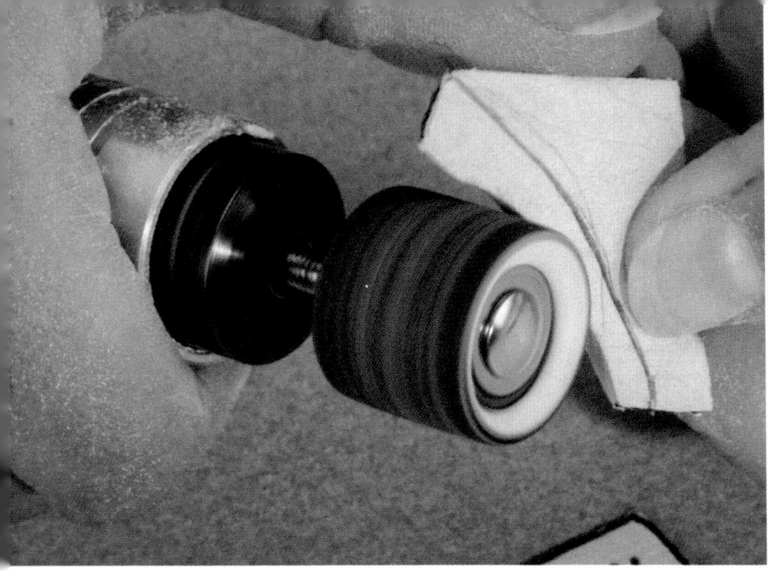

Reduce the tab so it is about 1/4" deep and parallel to the curve.

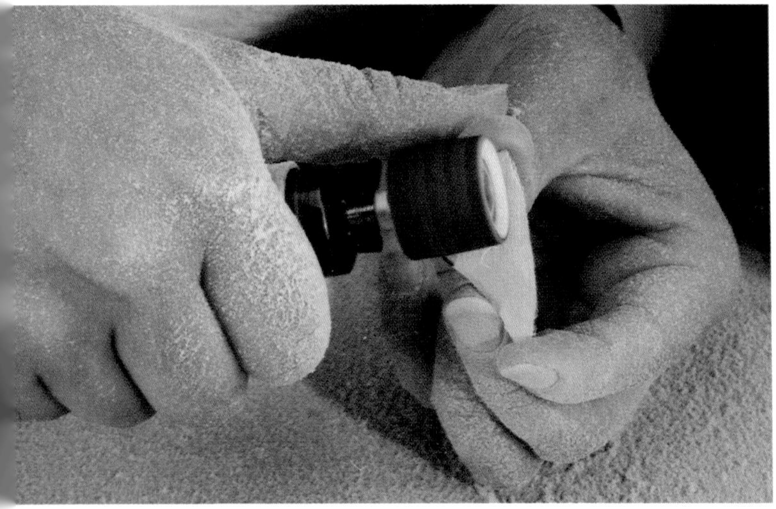

Do the other fins in the same way.

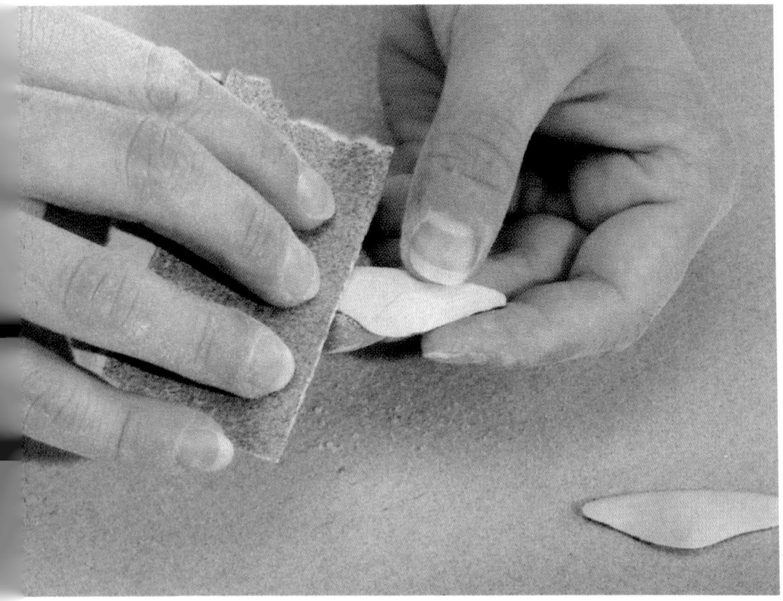

When they are finished, sand with the medium...

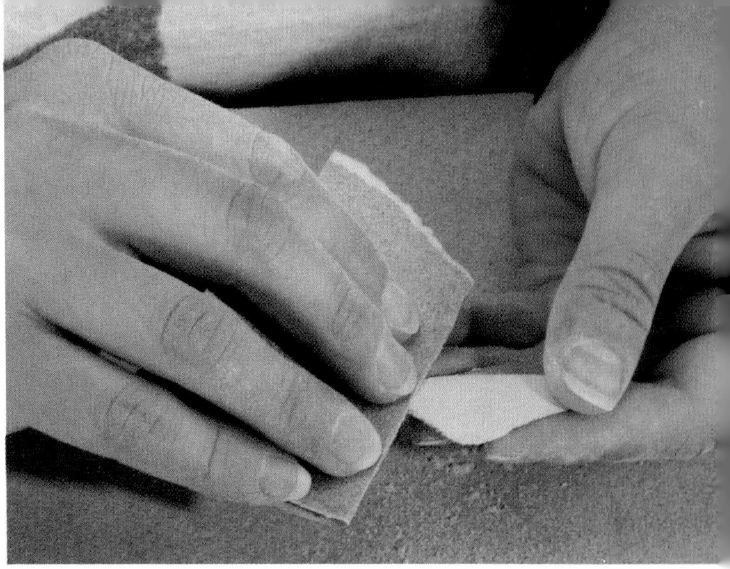

then fine papers.

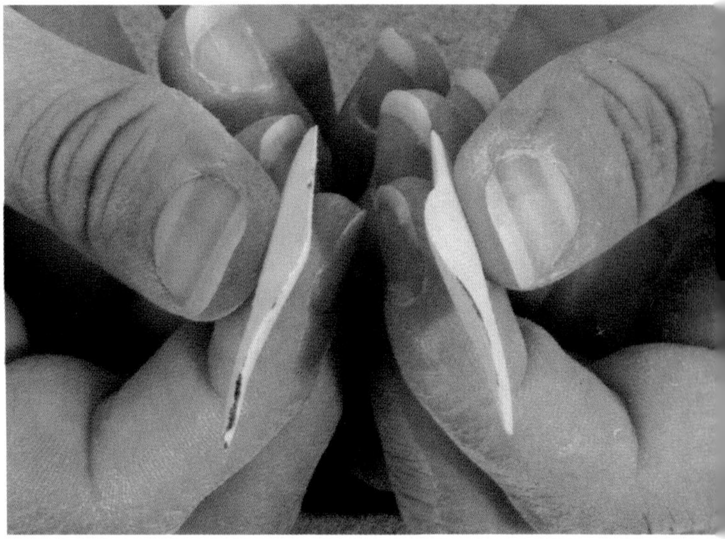

The results are fins that have an interesting flow, and are quite individualized.

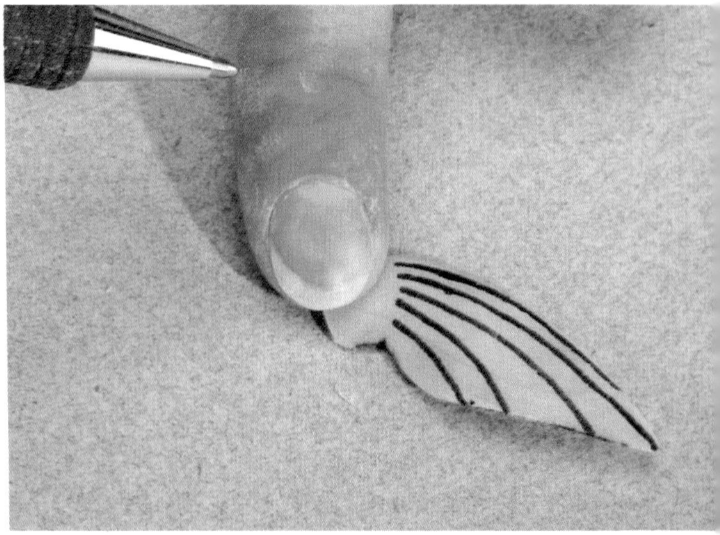

Draw in the fin rays. For competition you may wish to count them, but for artist's pieces it usually looks better with fewer.

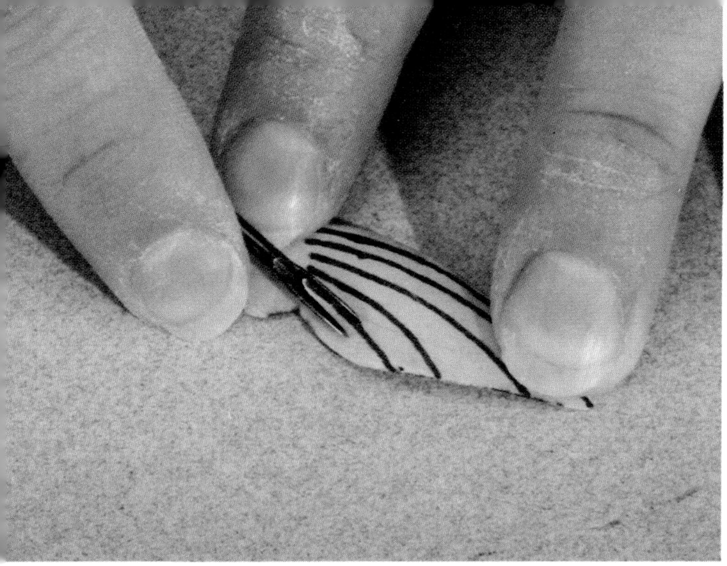

Use a small micro gouge to cut the rays.

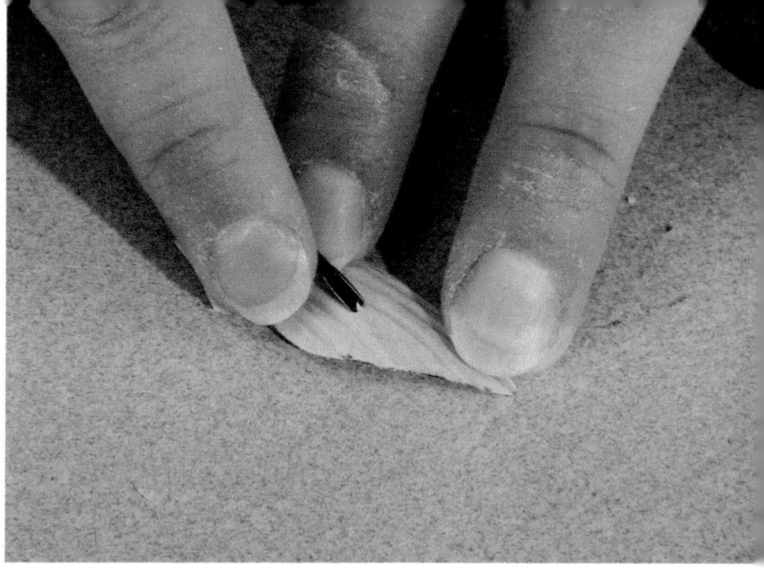

Use a small micro v-tool to work between the rays. Starting about half way down, run a line that...

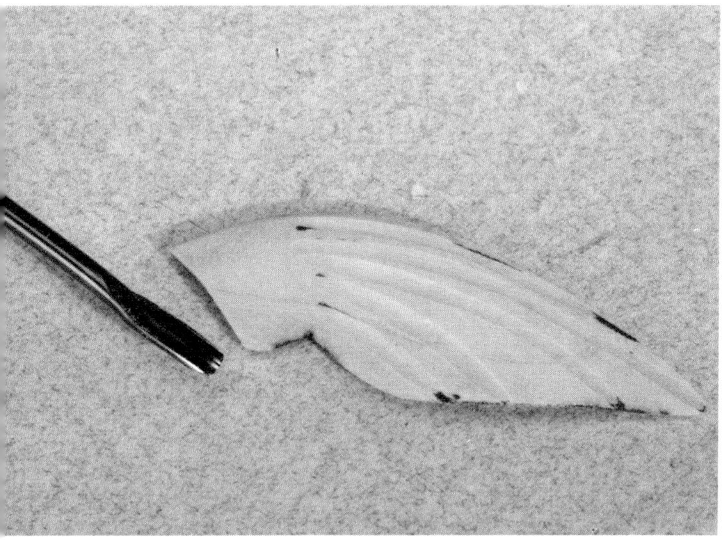

Progress.

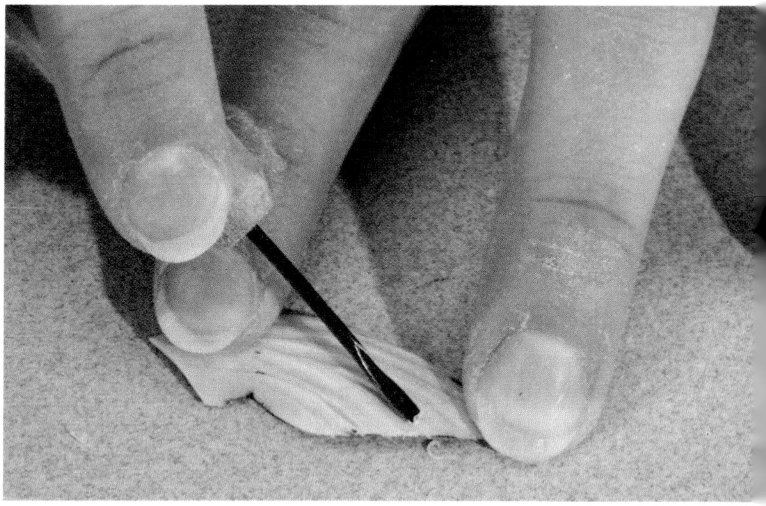

splits the ray in half.

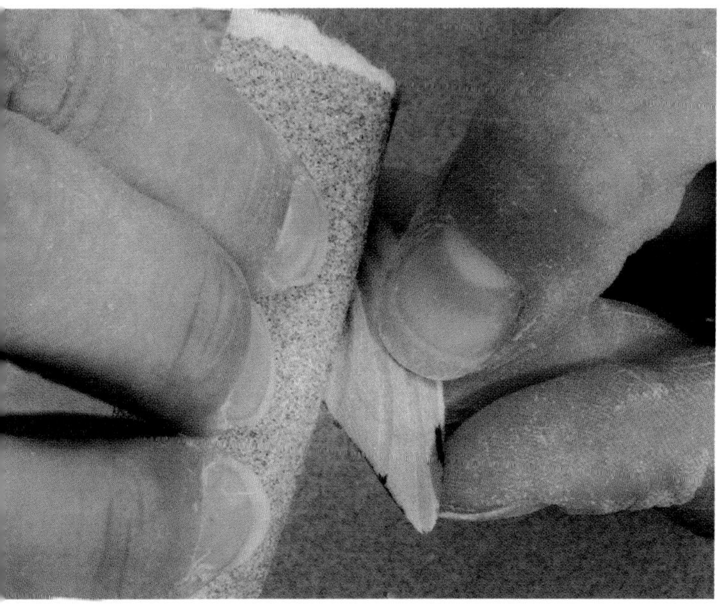

Sand the grooves.

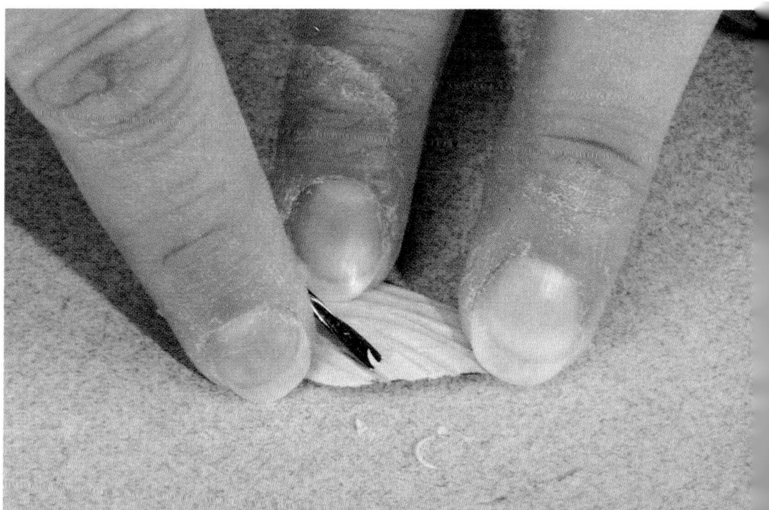

With the same tool, split the last quarter of the rays one more time.

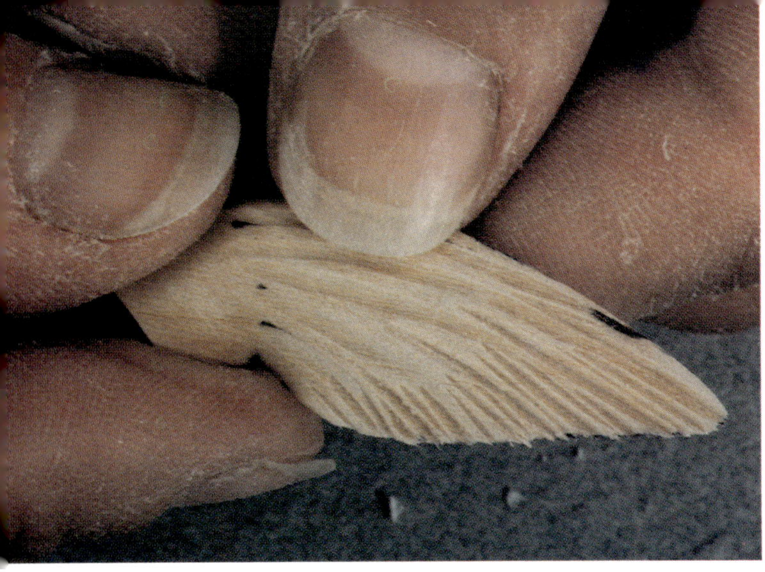

The result.

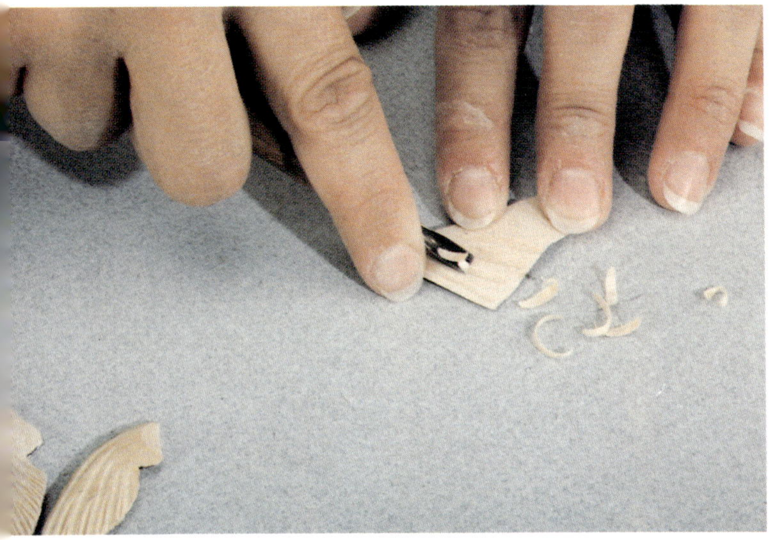

Repeat the process on all the fins.

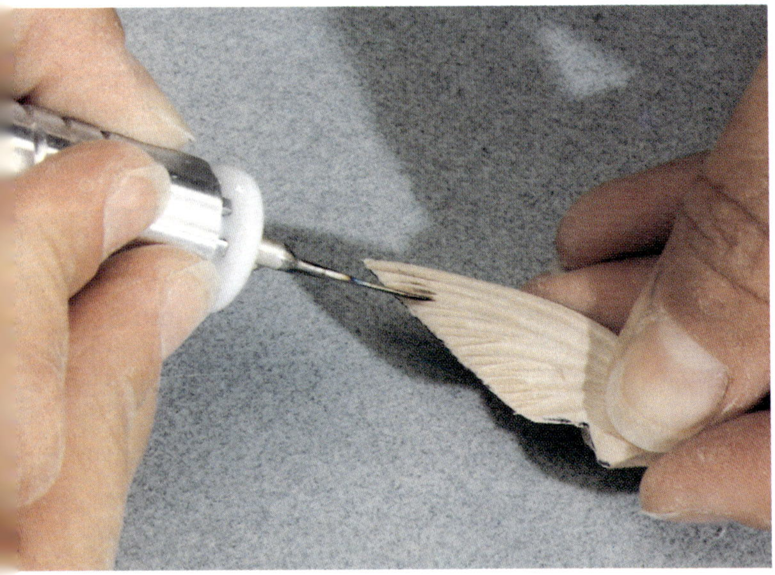

With a straight edge burner, go over the gouge cuts to remove any minor fuzzing.

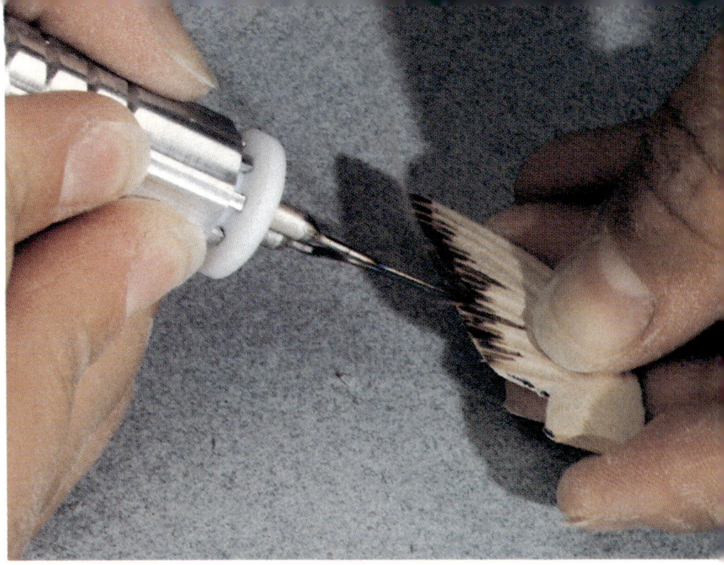

Then split some of the thicker rays again. Repeat on the other side and with other fins.

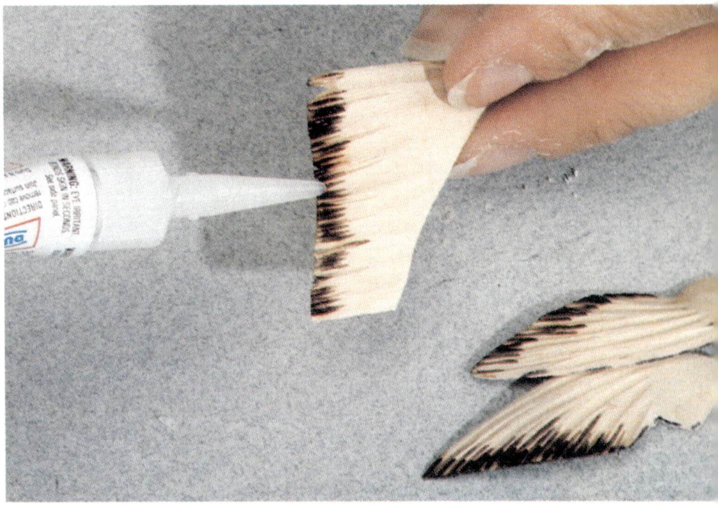

Apply a bead of super glue to the edge of the fins. Again, capillary action will pull it into the wood to give added strength.

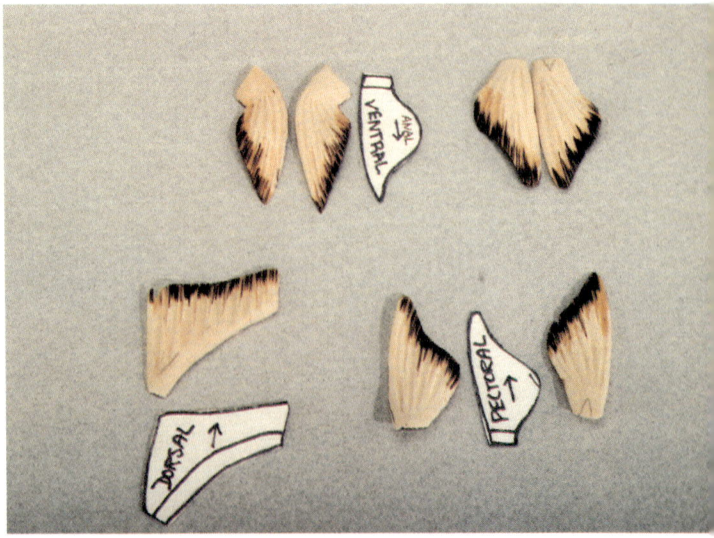

The fins are ready.

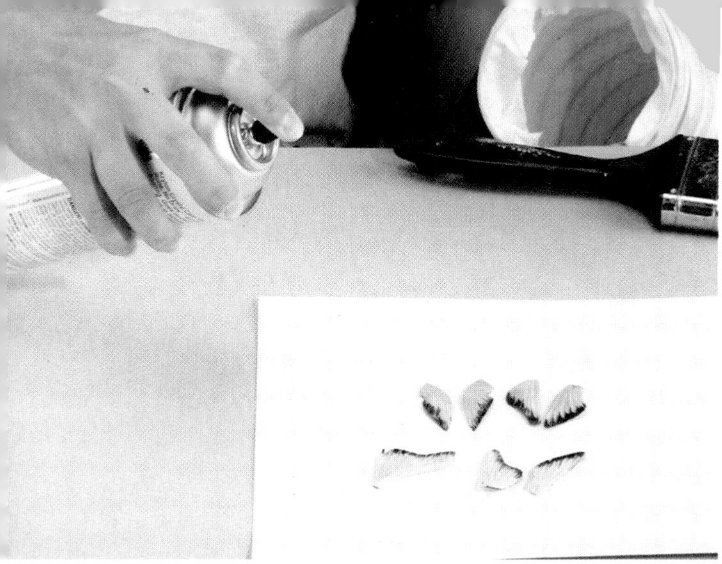

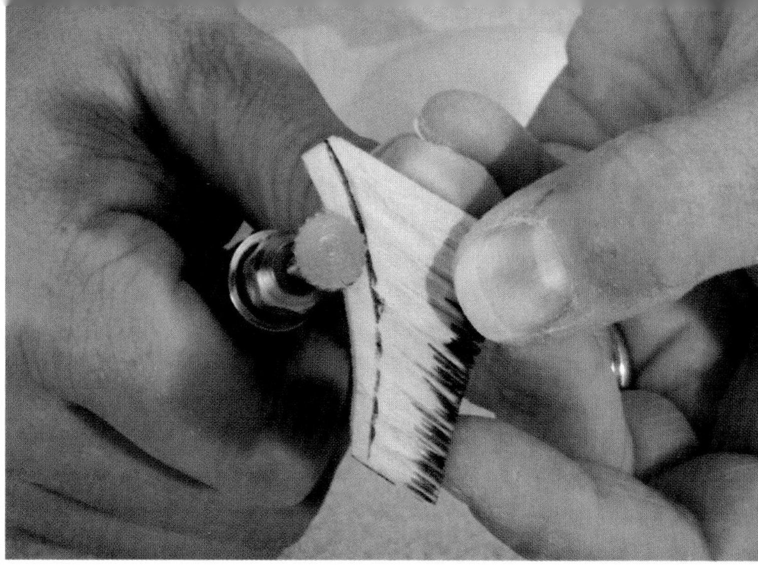

Spray with Krylon Clear Coat. This helps seal the wood for painting.

The steel cutter bit I use has a cutting radius of 1/8", which matches the depth of the tab.

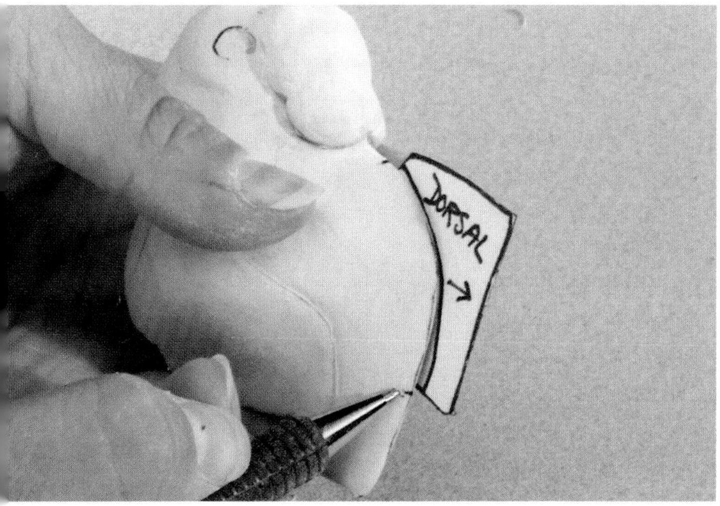

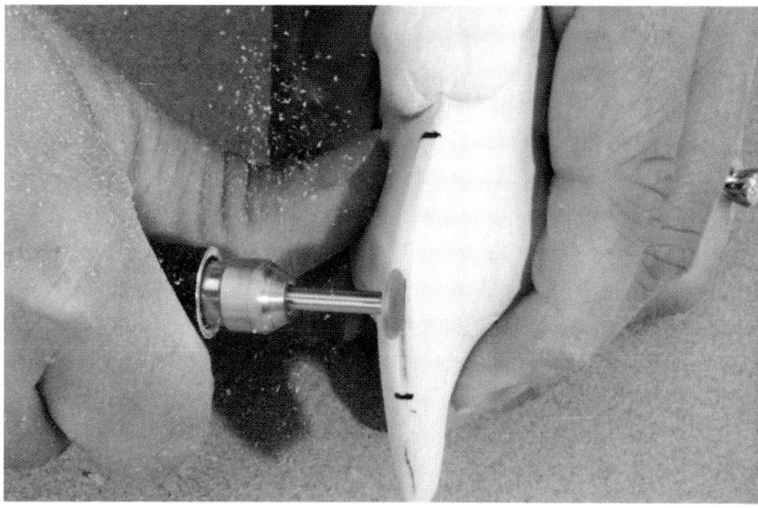

Hold the dorsal pattern to the body and mark the beginning and the end of the slot it will go into.

You don't want to make a mistake here or you may need to start all over again. Start lightly...

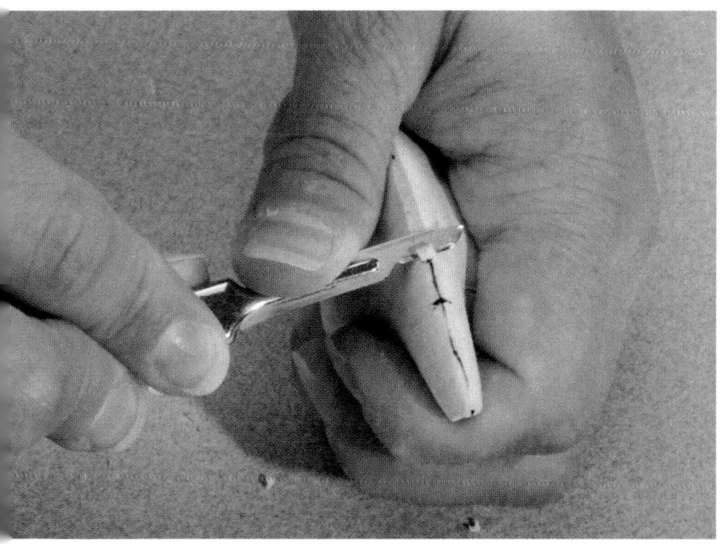

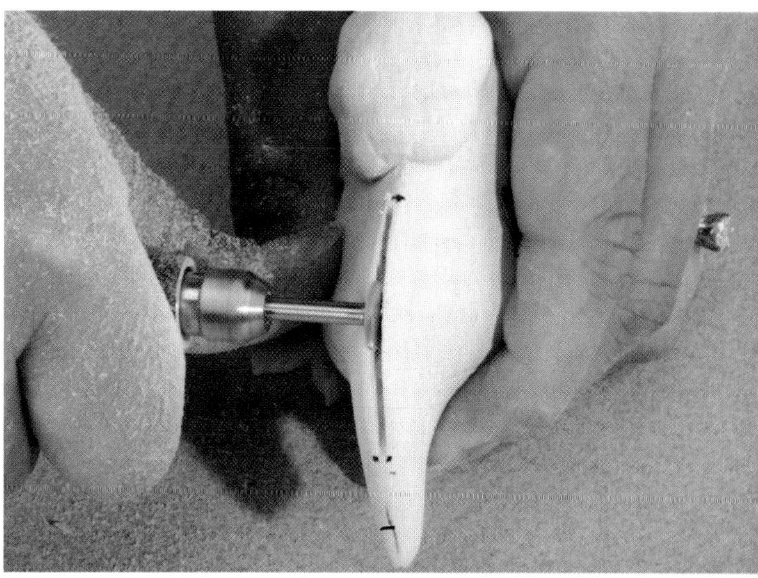

Slightly flatten the ridge of the back between the marks. You need a flat area for the cutting tool.

and go deeper.

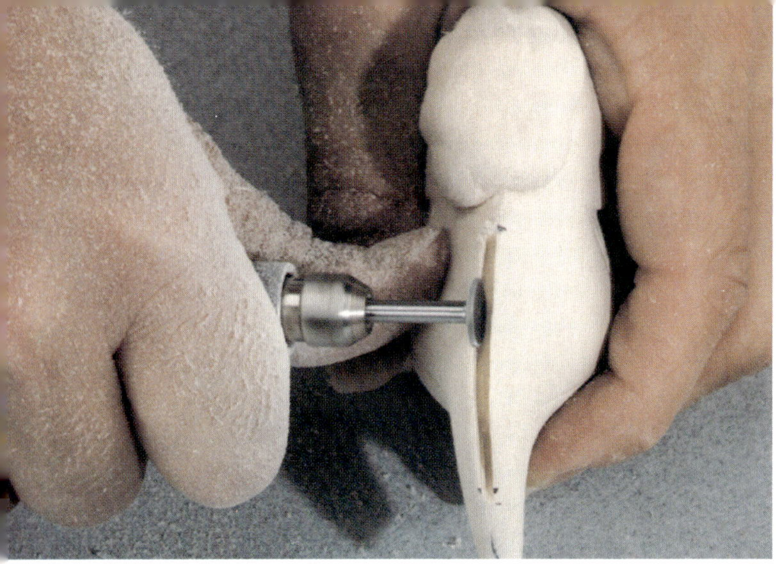

Make the slot wider by going along the edges.

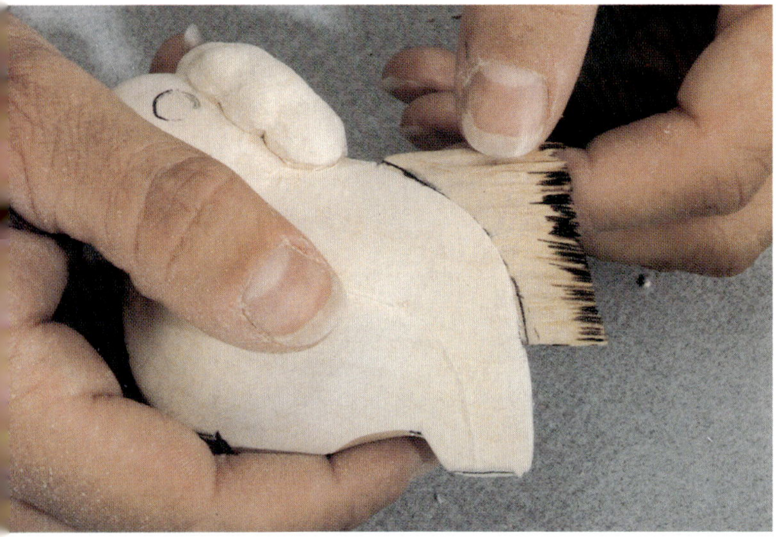

Check the fit. It is a little raised in the middle.

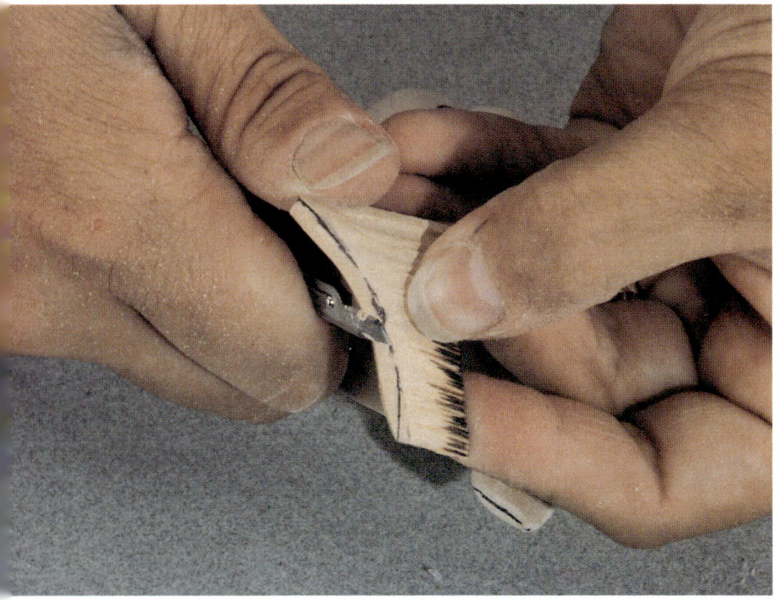

Make adjustments with a knife...

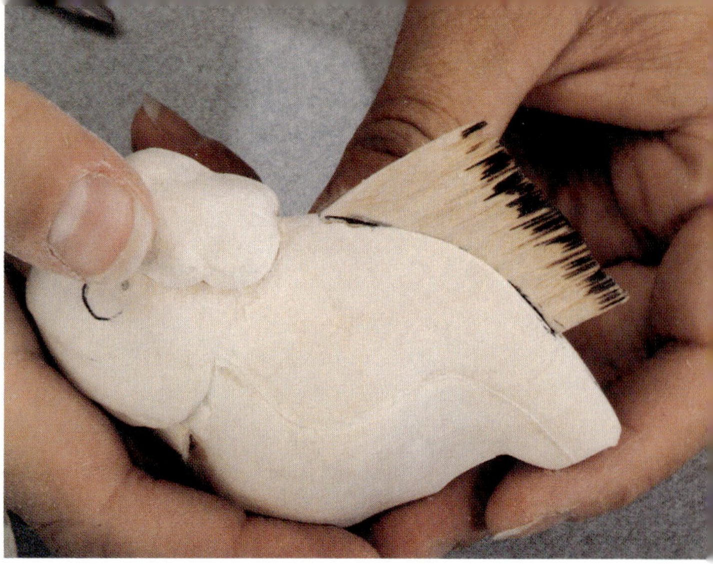

until it fits perfectly.

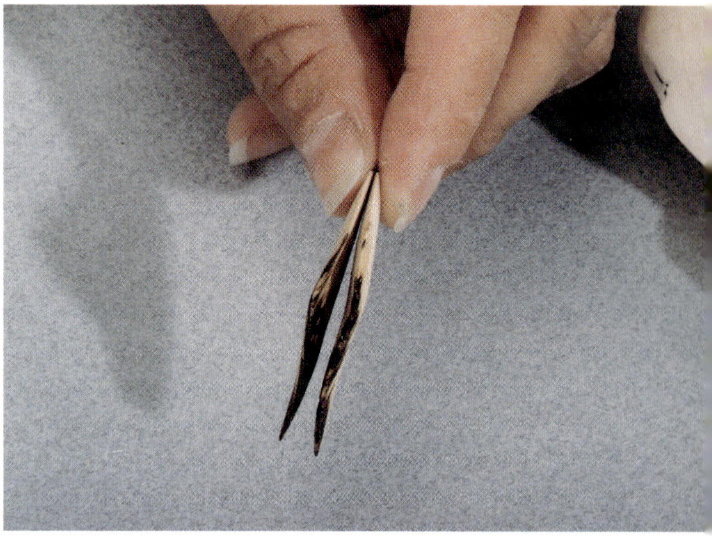

The anal fins are paired, so they are mounted in the same hole.

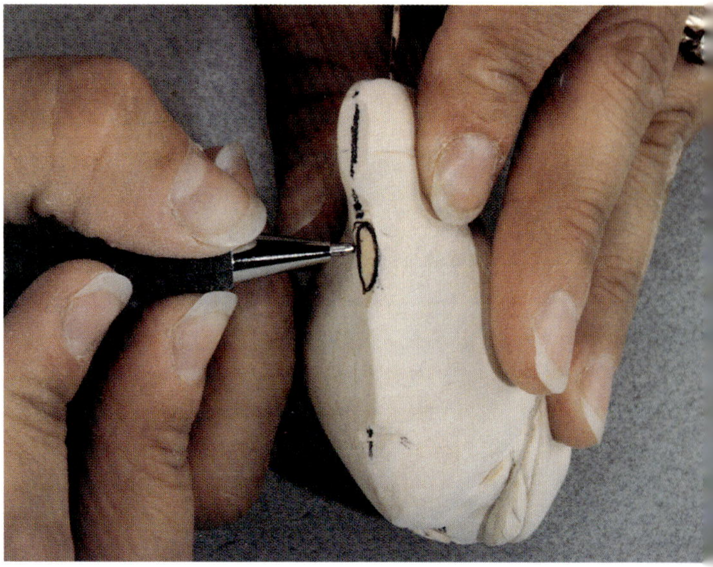

They go right under the caudal peduncle. Draw the hole.

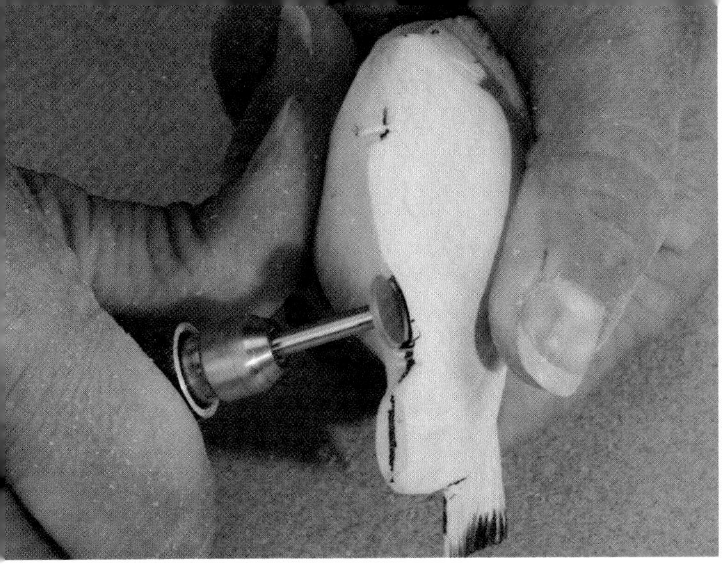

Make the hole using the same cutting tool.

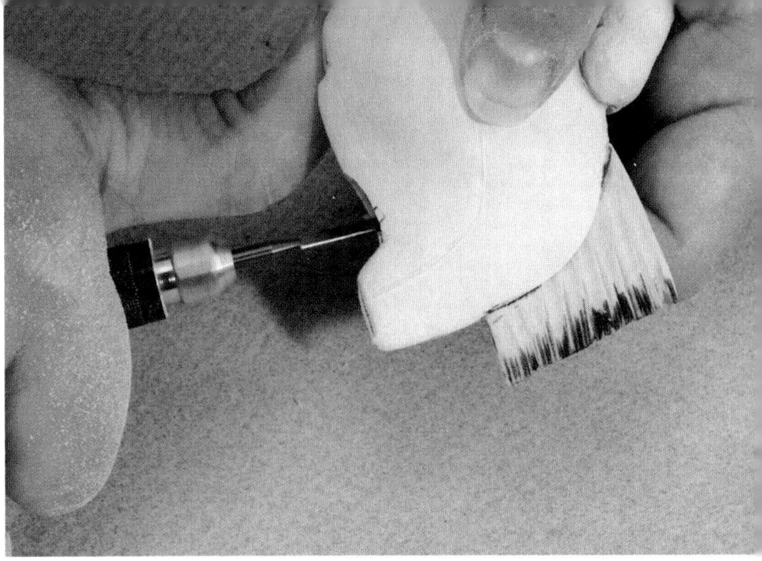

To go deeper I'm switching to a long shank carbide burr. This long thin bit will deepen the socket as I need it.

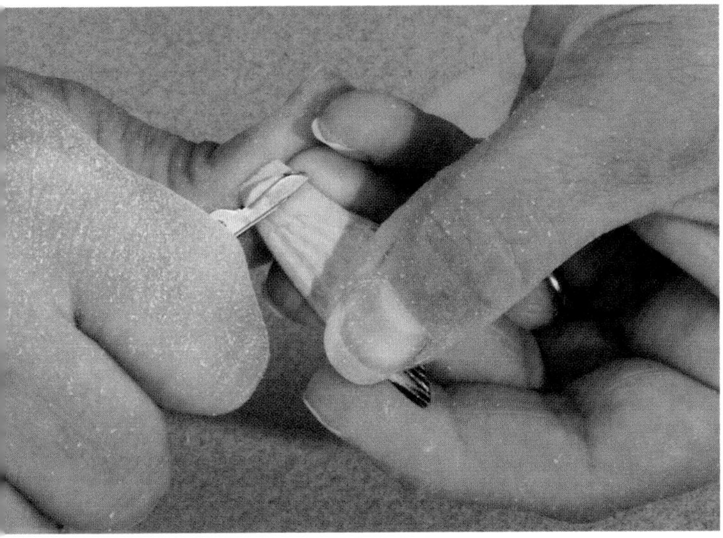

You may need to thin the fins to fit in the hole.

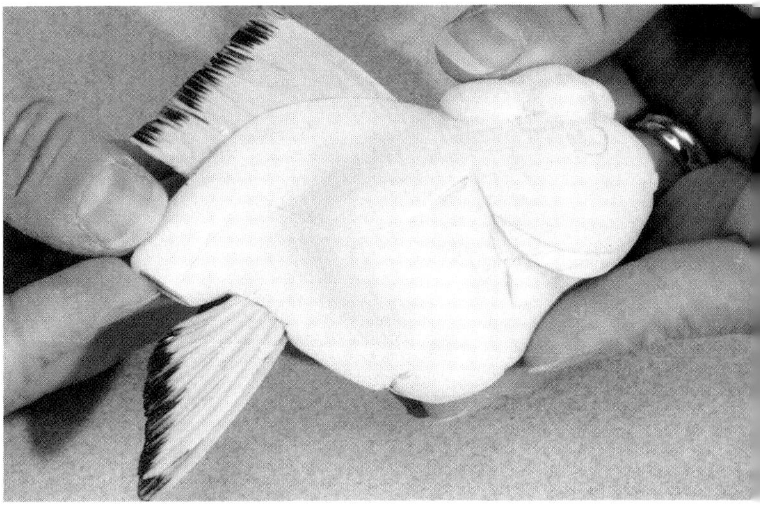

This works much better.

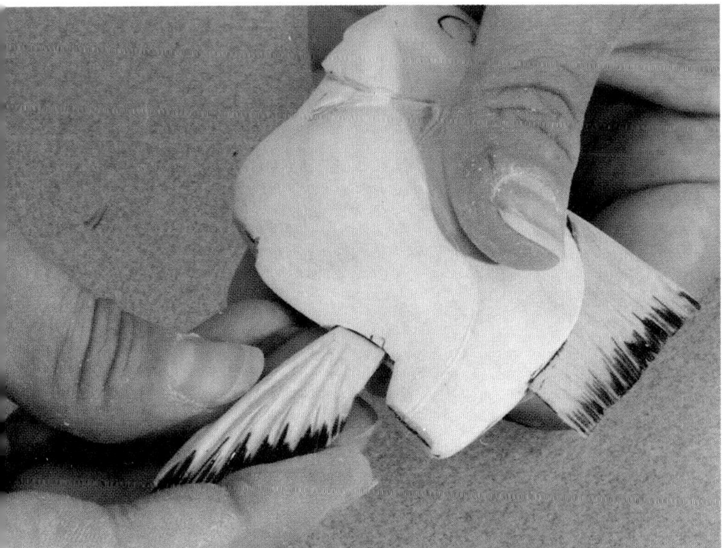

A test fit shows me that I need more depth to make them sturdier.

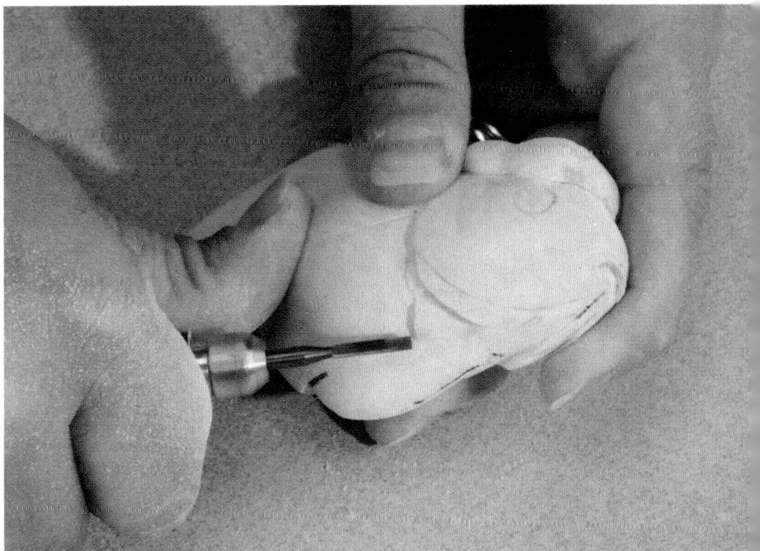

With the same tool make the hole for the pectoral fin. Start by deepening the recess...

then form the socket.

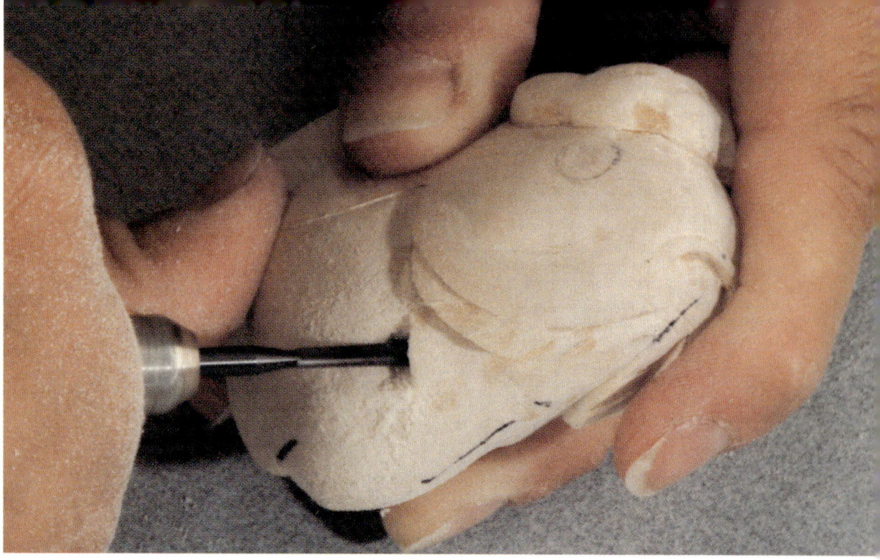

Test the fit and adjust. Repeat on the other side.

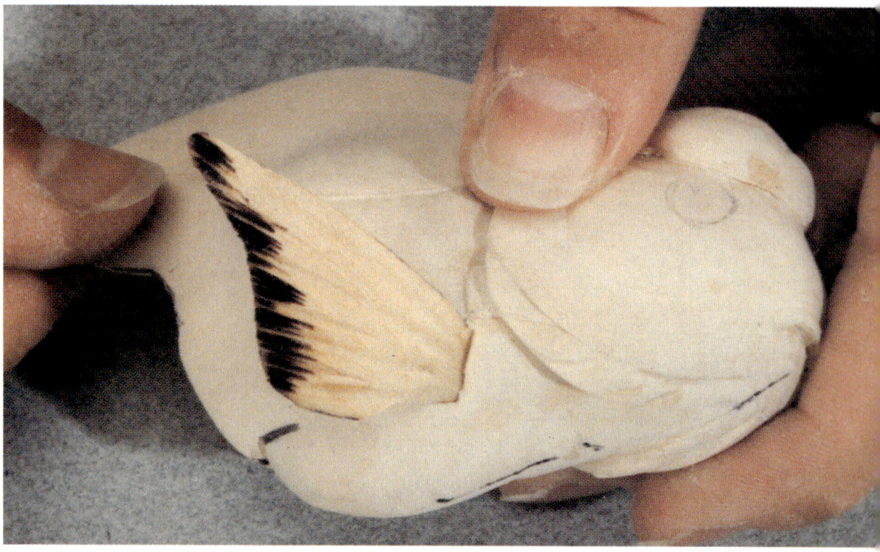

The pectoral fins flare back, as you can see here.

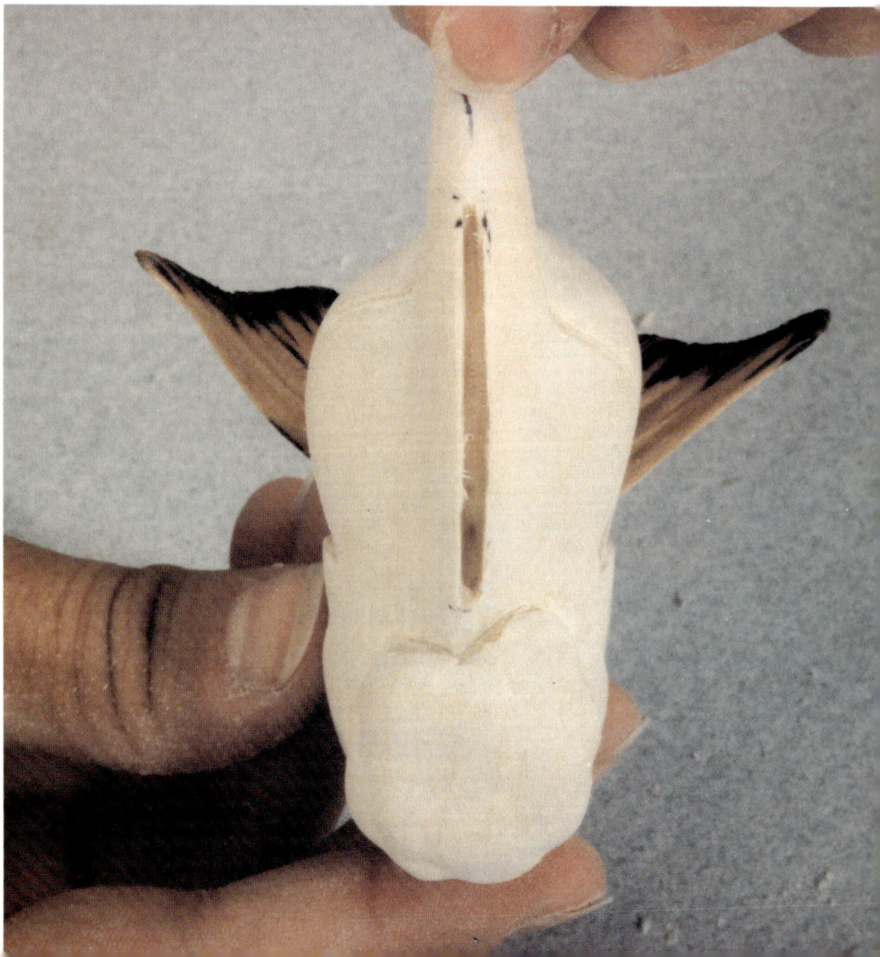

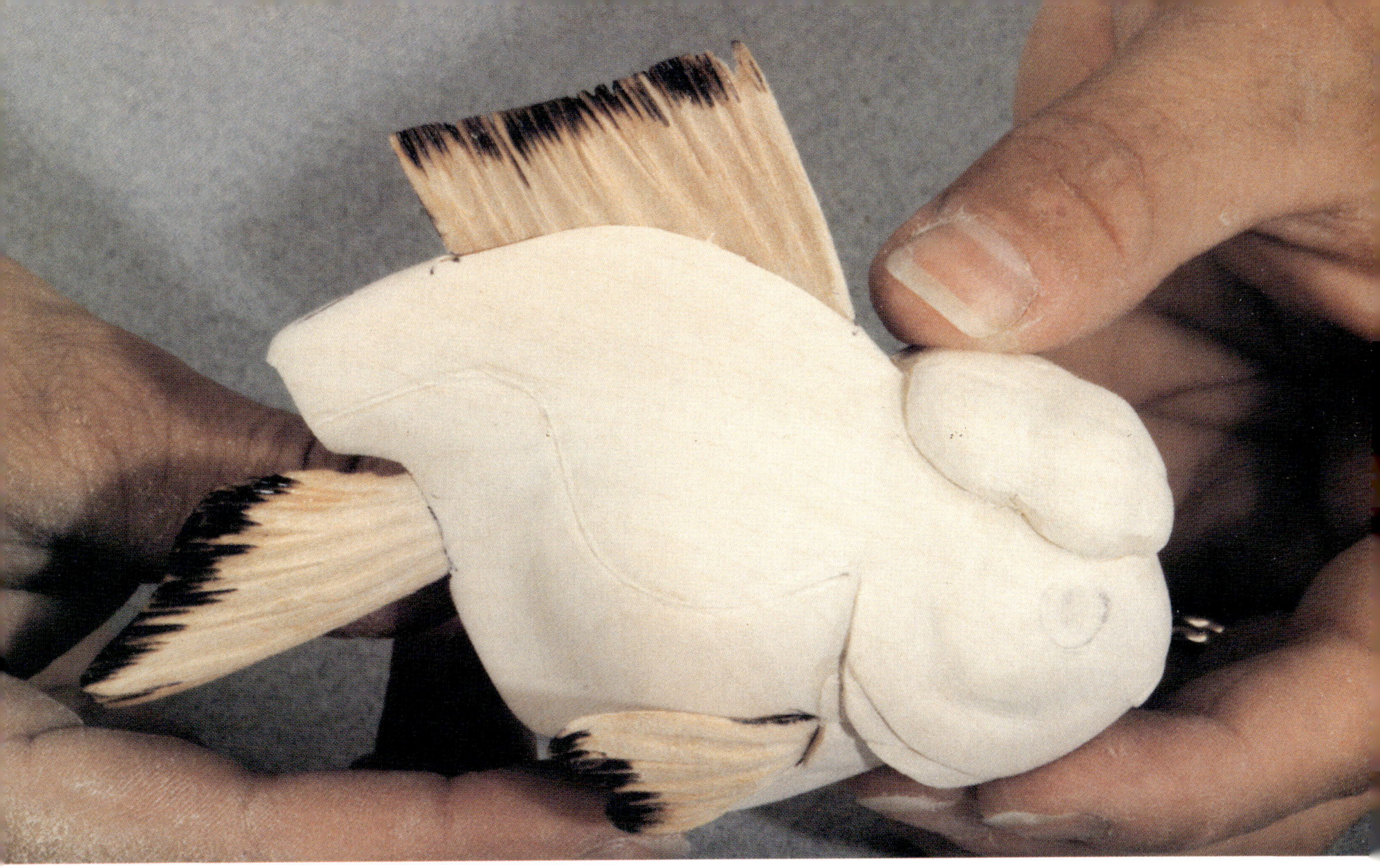

Progress.

Next, the ventral fins go above the notch in the belly. Score the lines with a gouge to help guide the rotary bit.

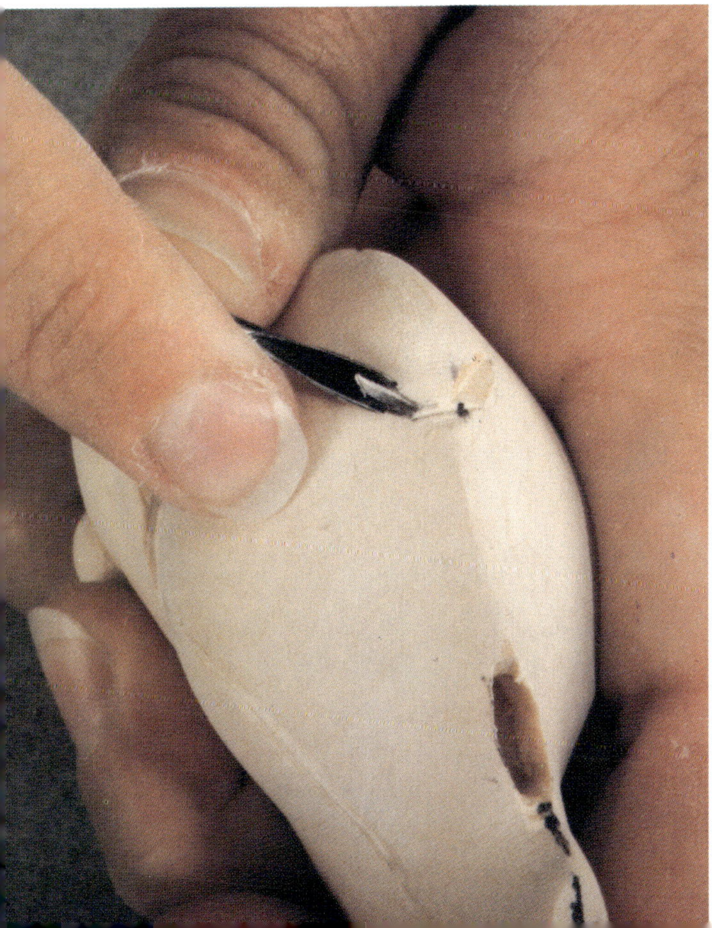

I switch back to the steel cutter for control.

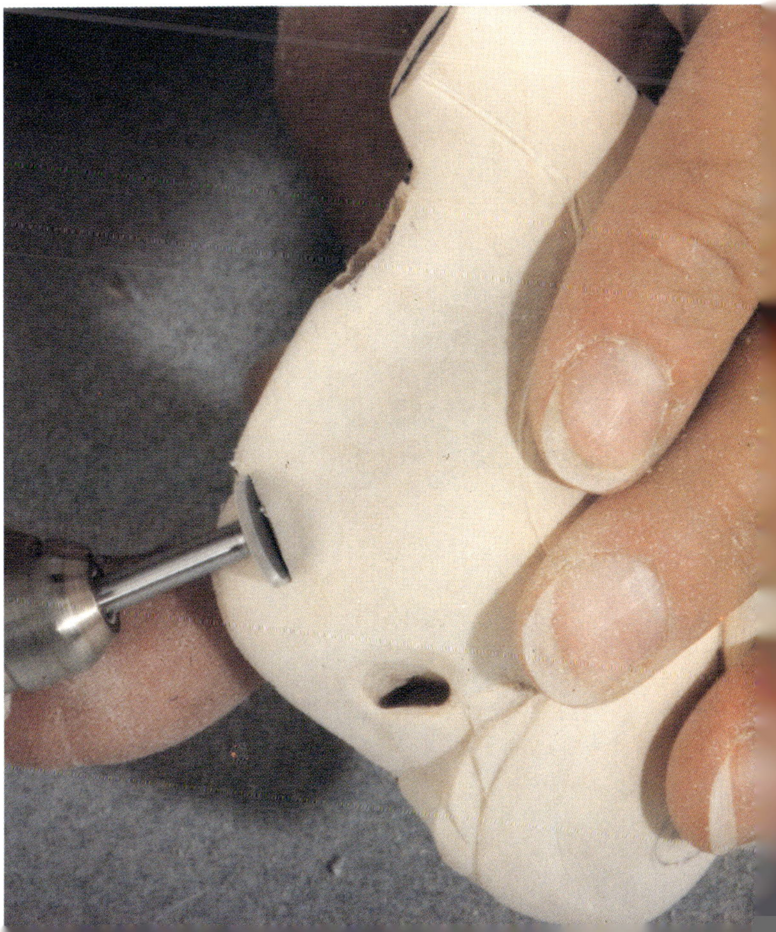

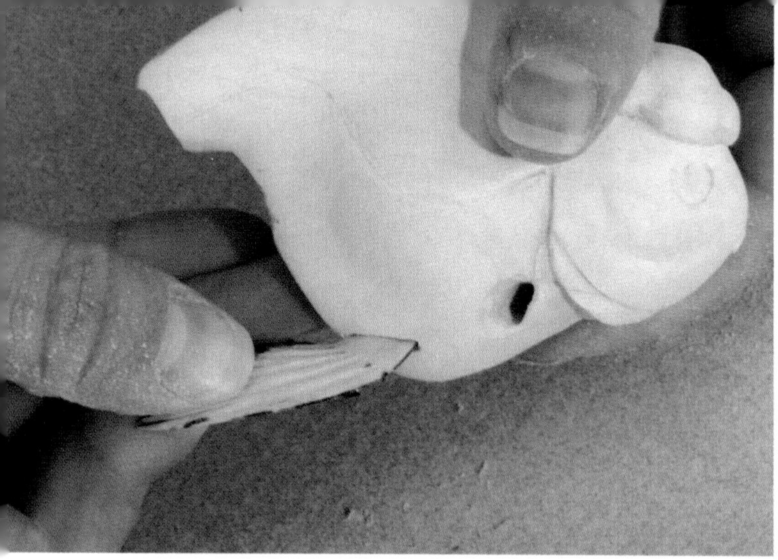

The slot it makes, however is not deep enough...

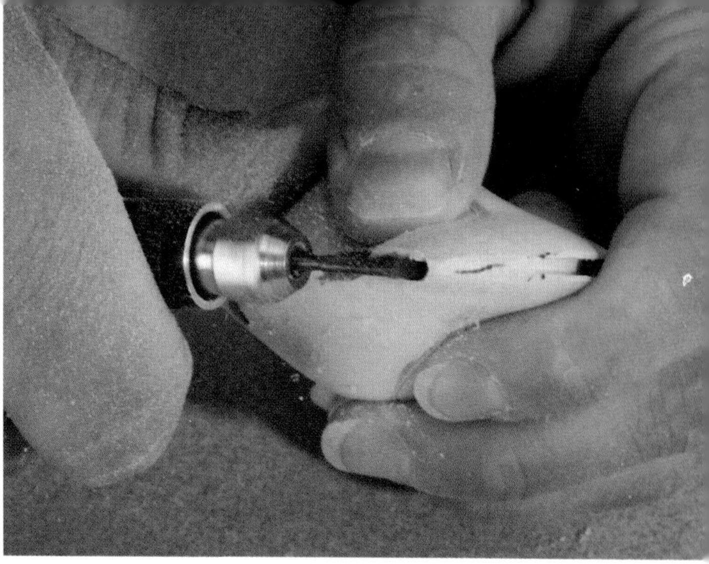

Make the socket for the caudal fins with the carbide burr.

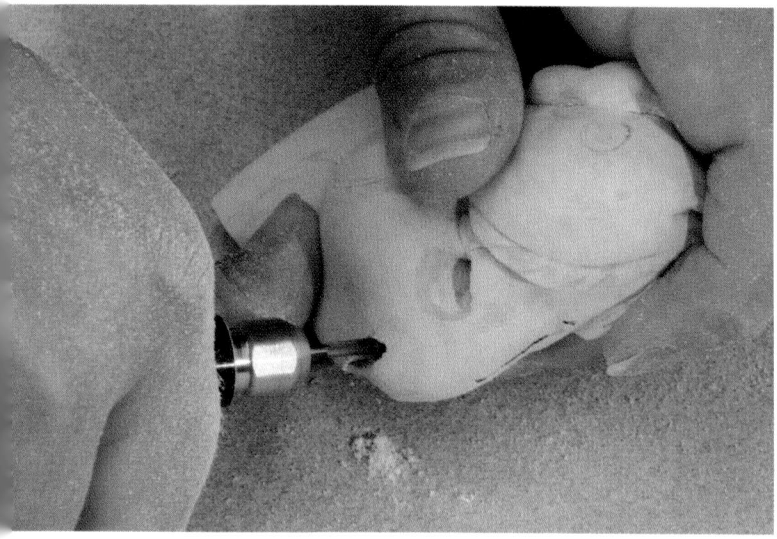

so I use the carbide burr to finish it up.

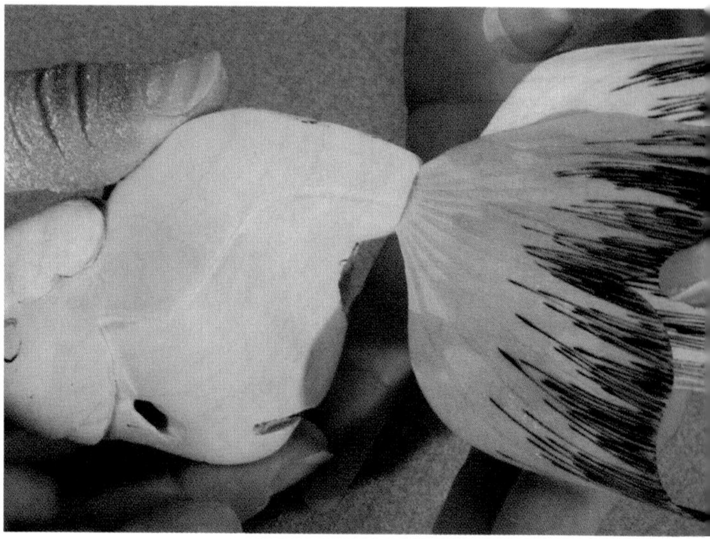

Both fins go in the same hole.

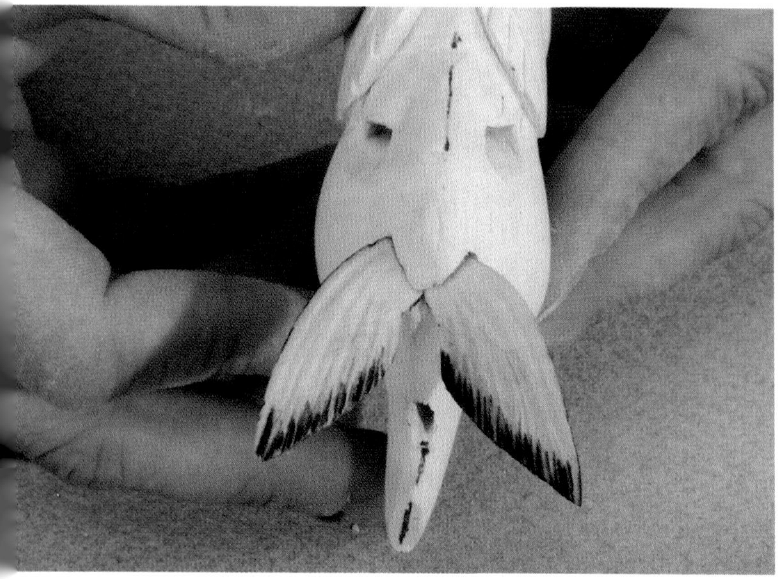

This is a better fit. When the hole gets a little too big, as it is here, I fill it later.

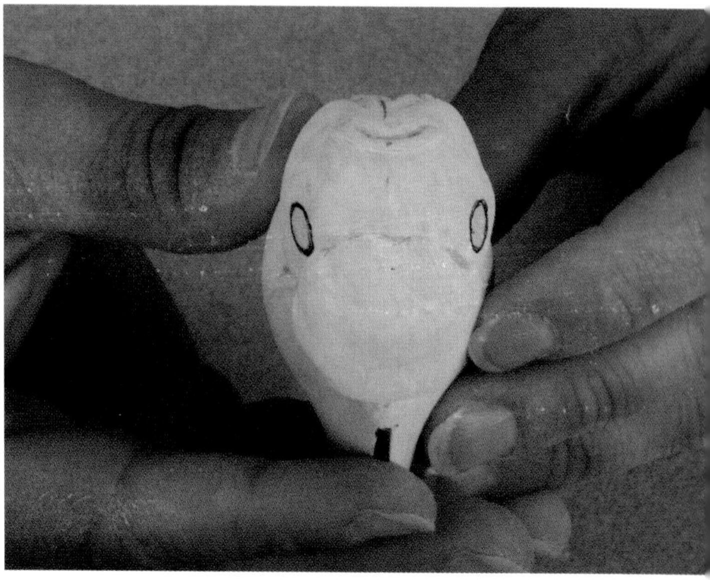

Begin the eyes by checking the alignment. I look straight on from the top to get a good perspective.

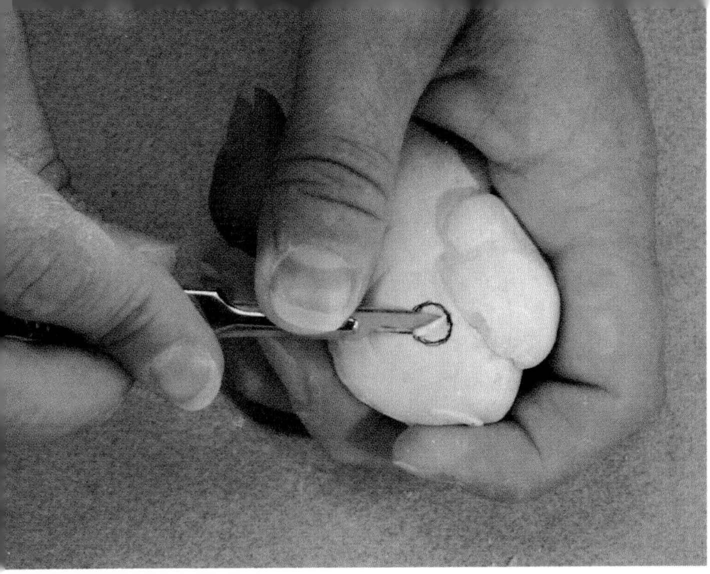

Carve a little of the eye to give guidance to the cutting burr.

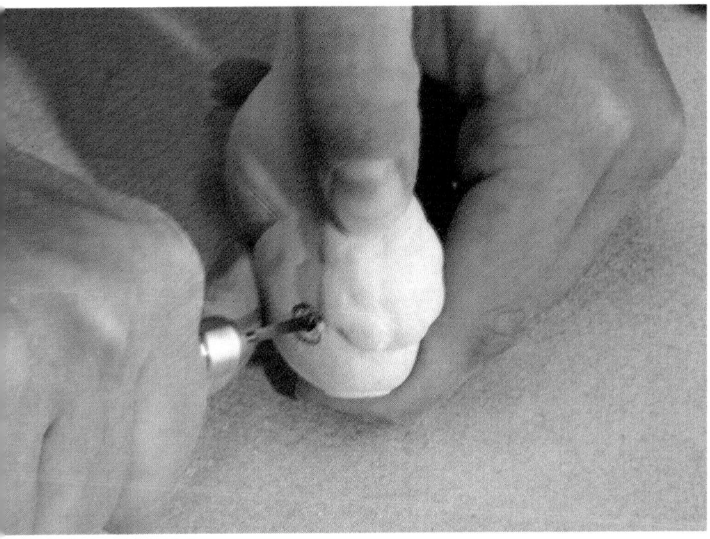

Cut a hole deep enough for the eye, in this case about 1/8".

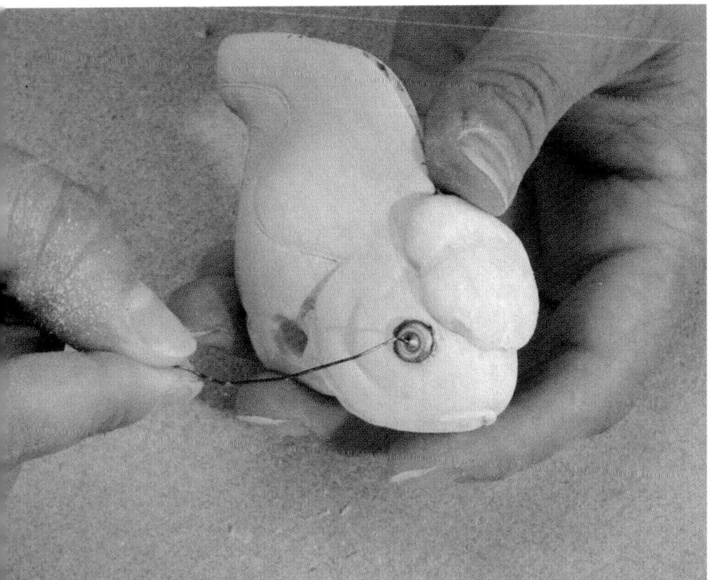

Test the fit with the glass eye. I still have further to go.

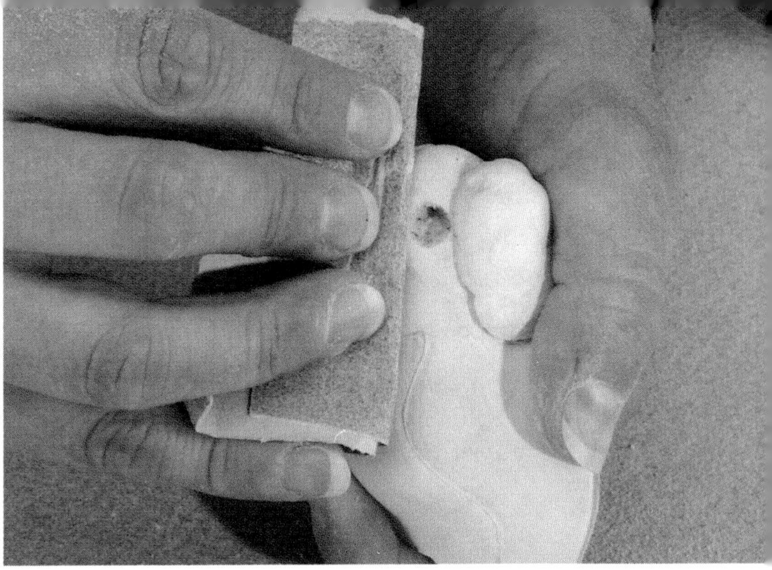

Lightly sand the socket.

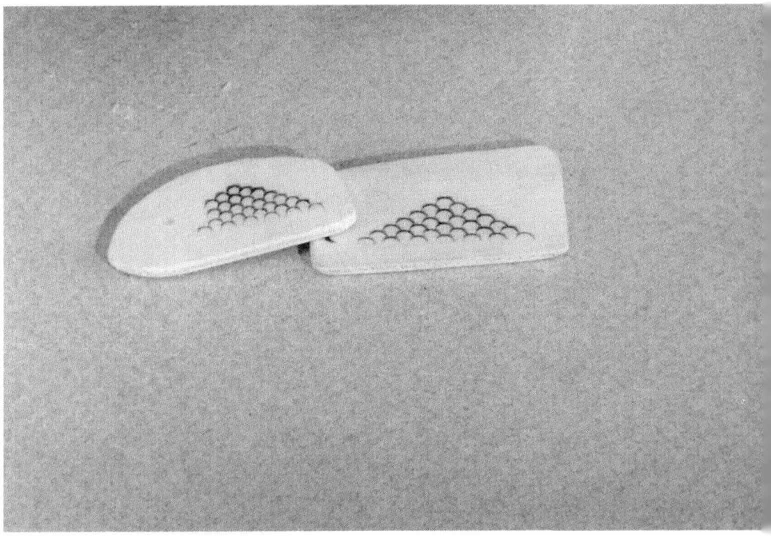

The scaling is done with two sizes of scale burning tips. You can see the difference in the result. Some fish have scales on the face and some don't, so it is important to know your subject. This fish does not.

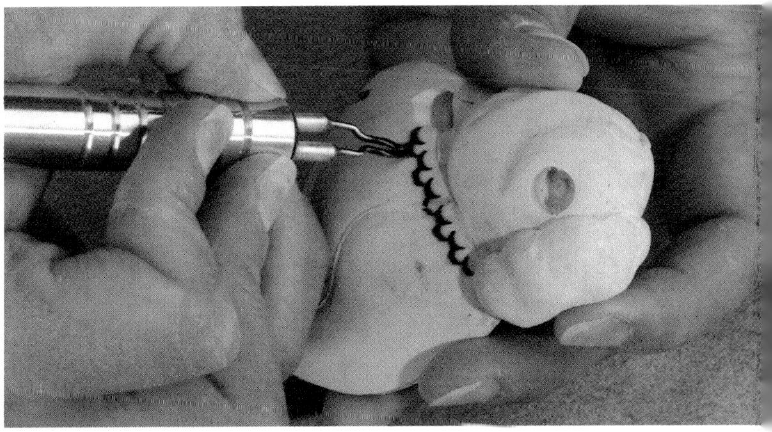

Begin with the large scales behind the head. Go right over the lateral line. The burning action is pushing down, then dragging back. This allows the trailing edge of the scale to be felt.

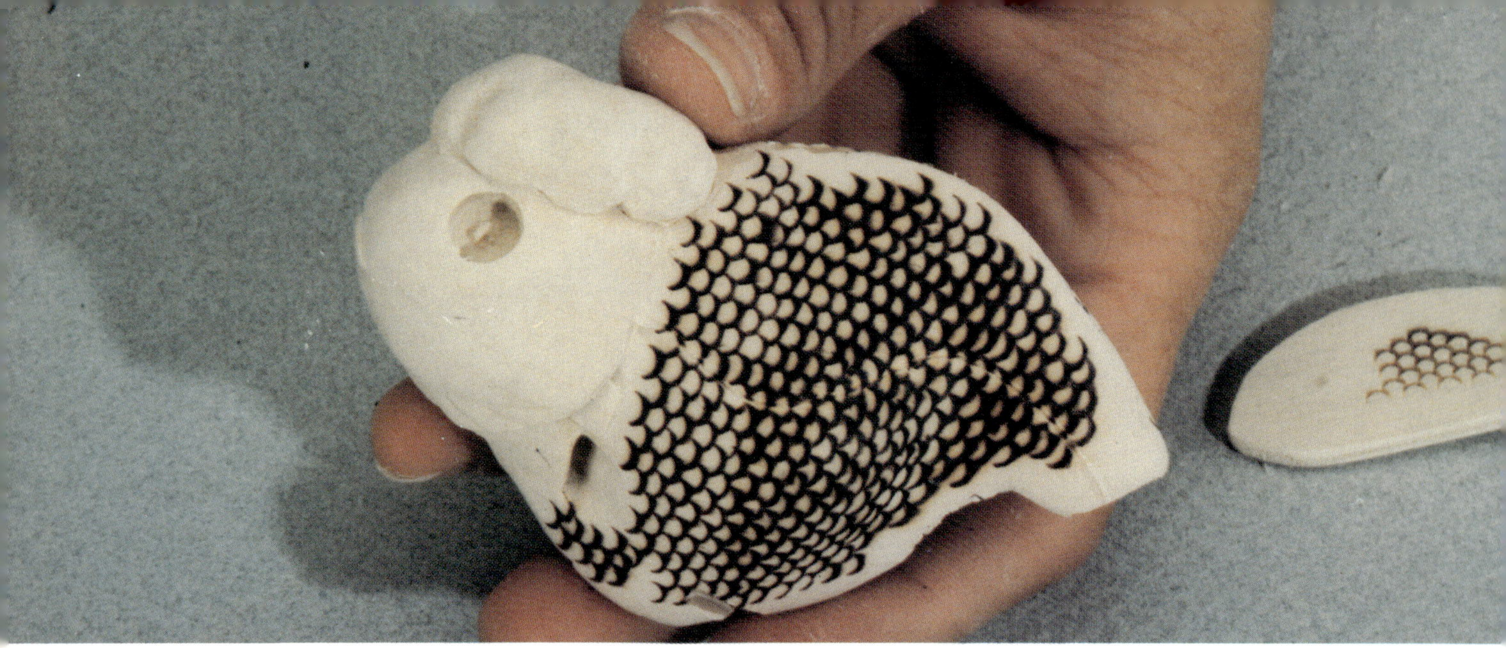

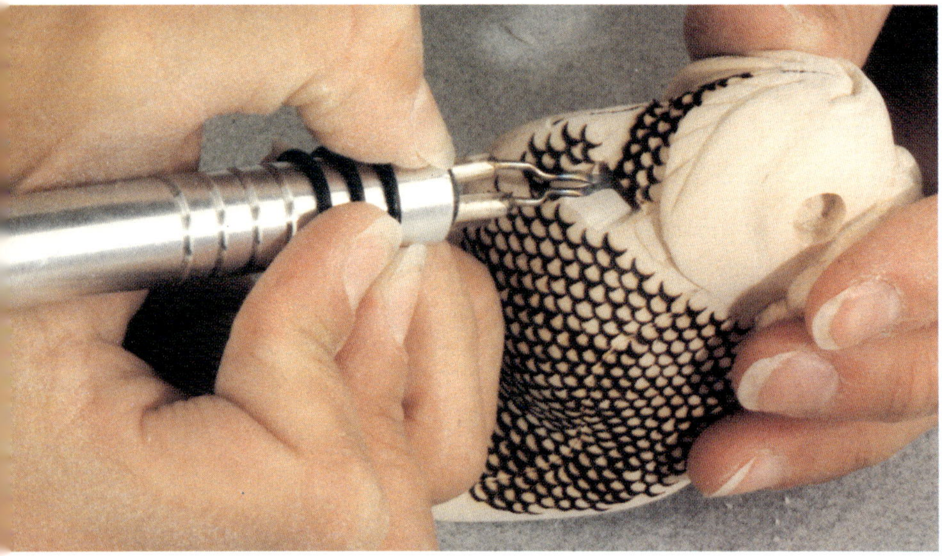

The larger scales cover the sides...

and the smaller scales go in the surrounding areas.

The scales applied.

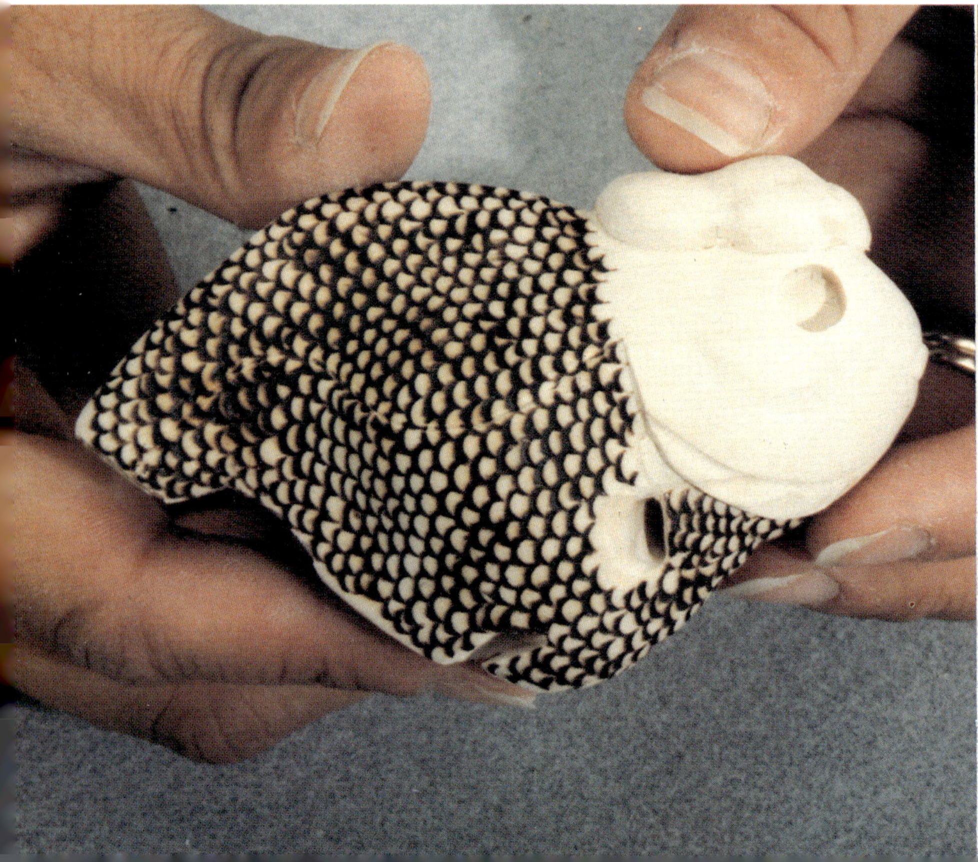

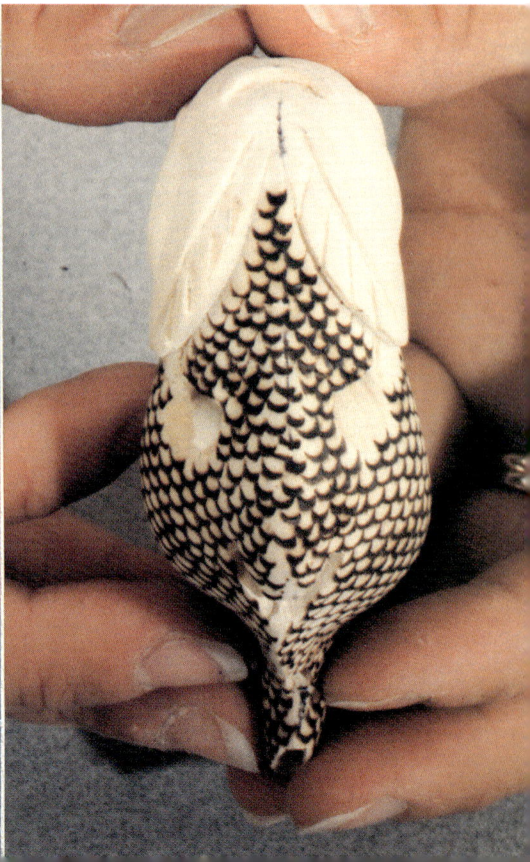

To join the fins, I use Tuf-Carve™ putty. The paste mixes in 10-to-1 ration with the hardening agent. It sets quickly, so only mix small amounts at a time. Mix the two parts thoroughly together.

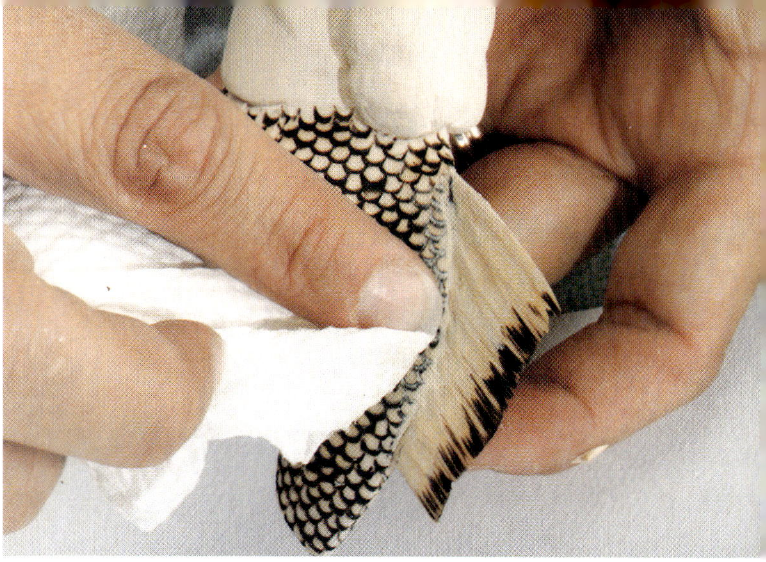

Smooth and clean the surrounding area with a paper towel before it sets.

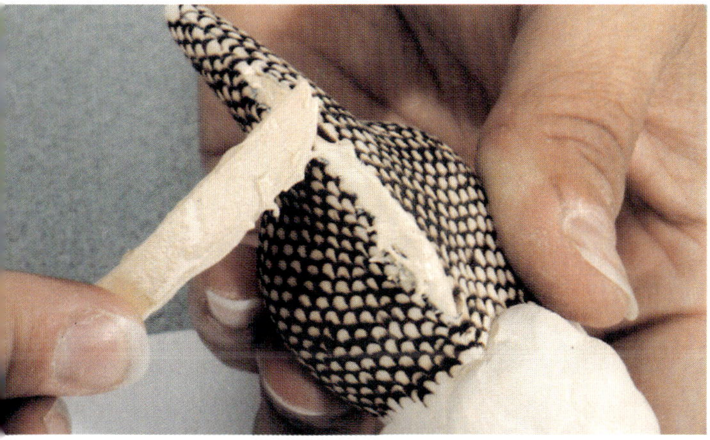

Fill the socket with the mixture.

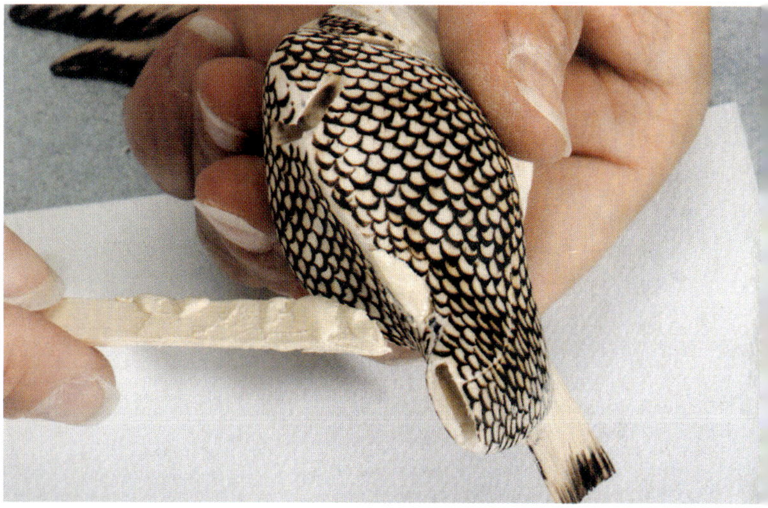

Continue with the other fins. This is the anal fins' socket.

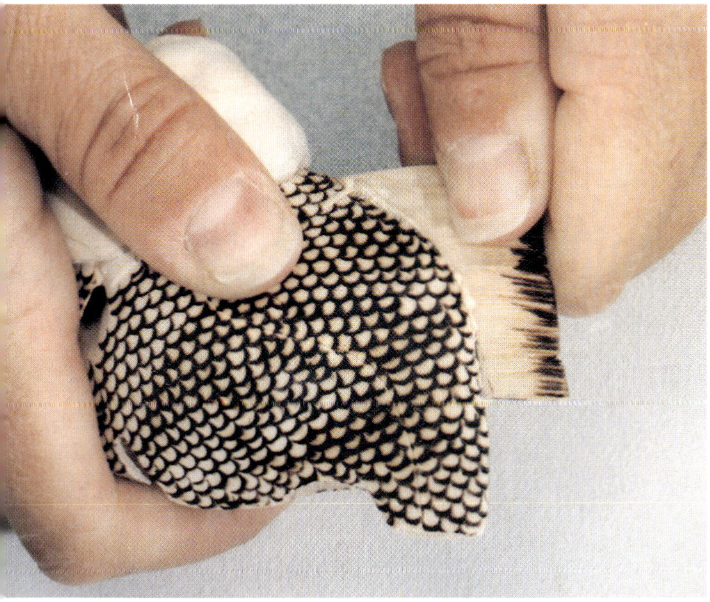

Push the fin in place.

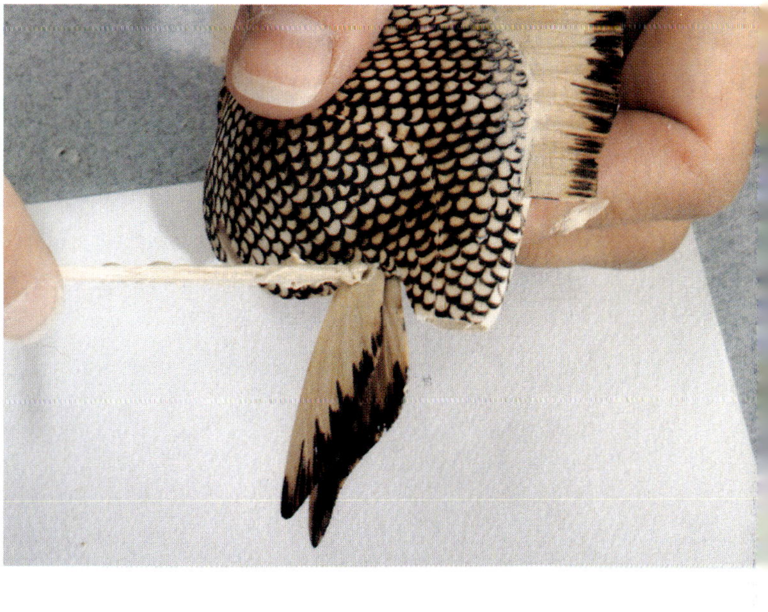

Set the fins in place and fill any gaps with the mixture. A moistened finger helps blend the areas.

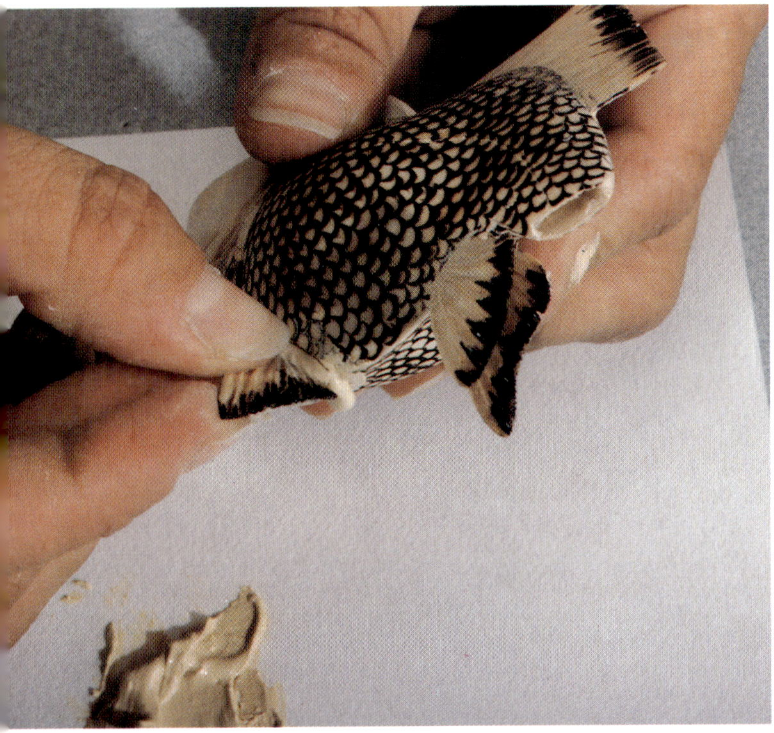

Set the ventral fins in the same way...

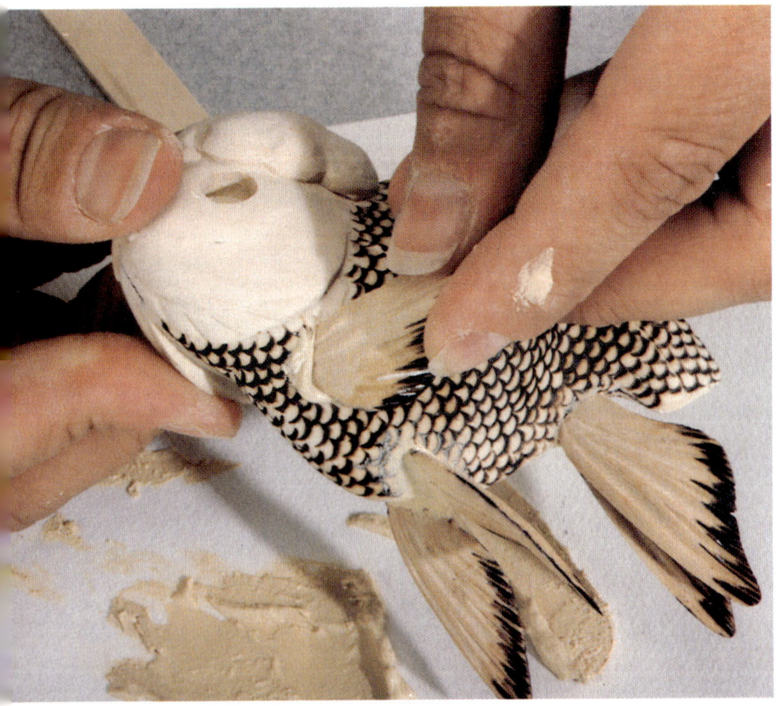

and the pectoral fins.

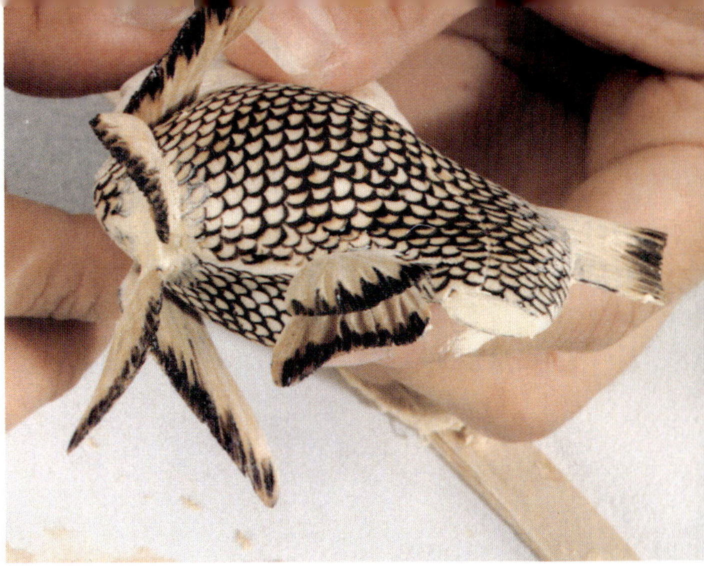

Before working on the tail, be sure the anal fins are set-up.

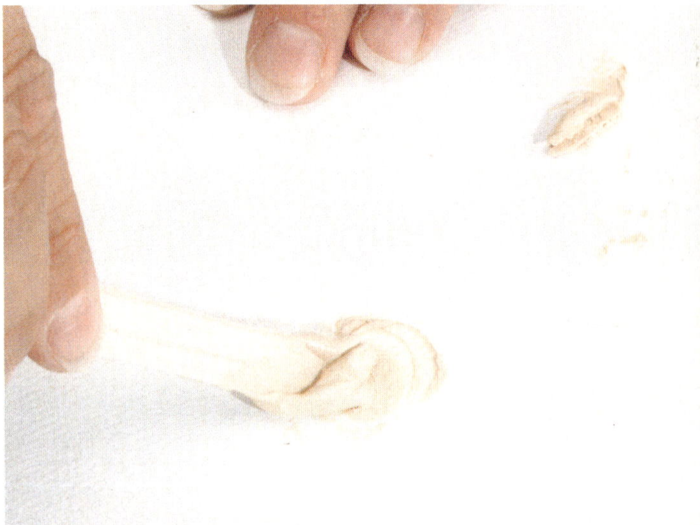

If the mixture begins to harden, make up another batch.

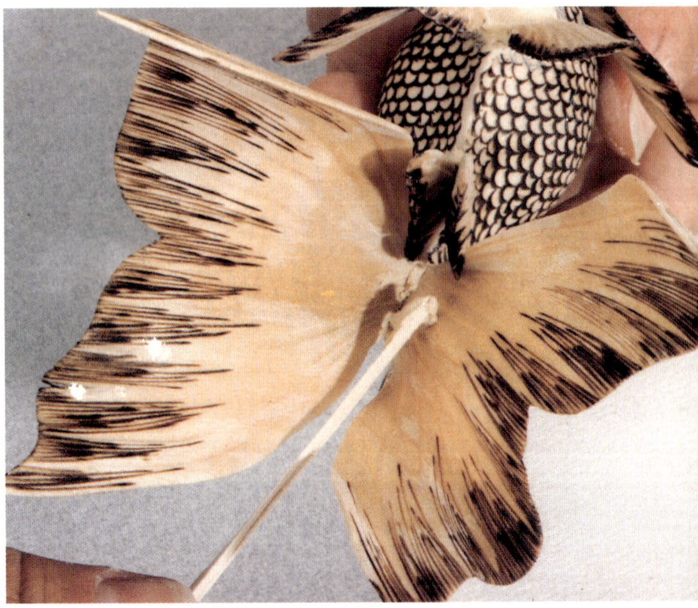

Apply putty between the conjunction of the two caudal fins.

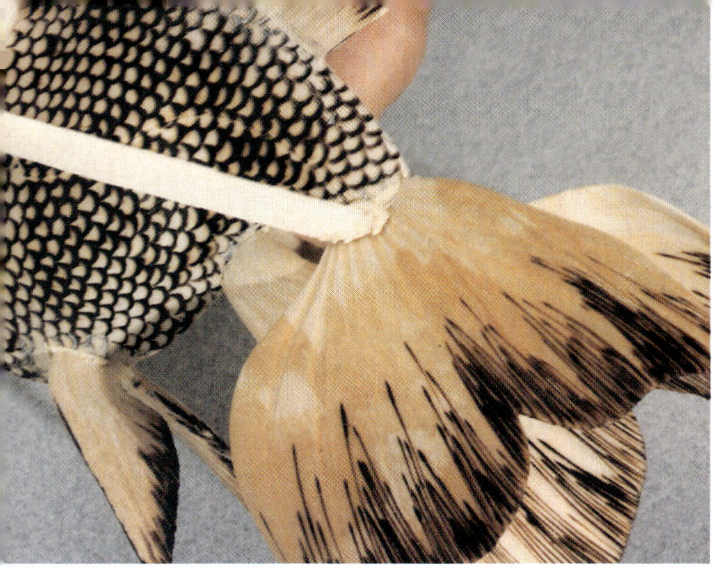

Fill in around the outside edges.

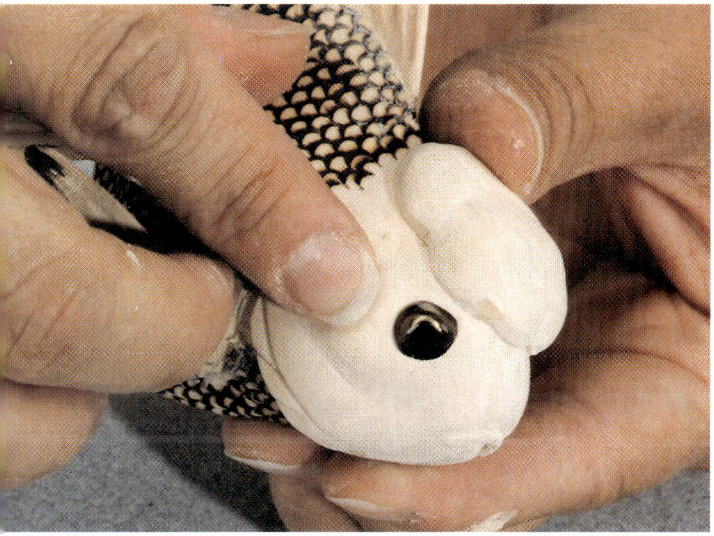

Test the fit of the eye by dropping it in the socket.

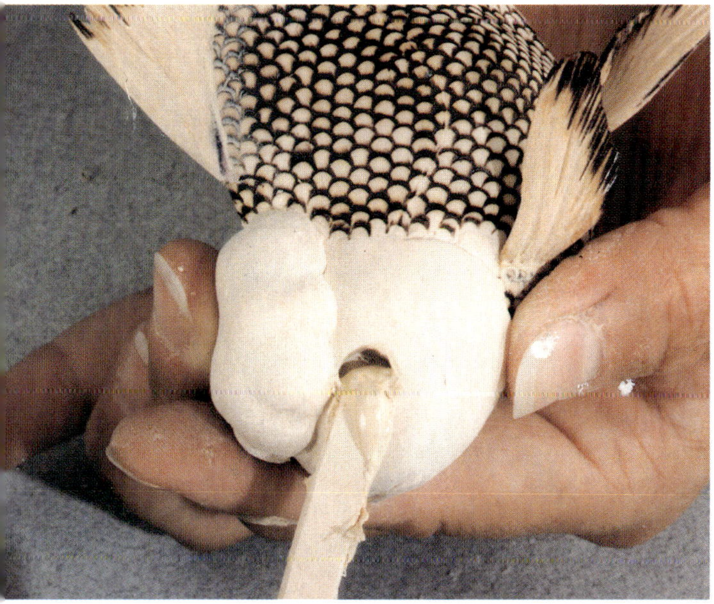

Fill the socket with the mixture.

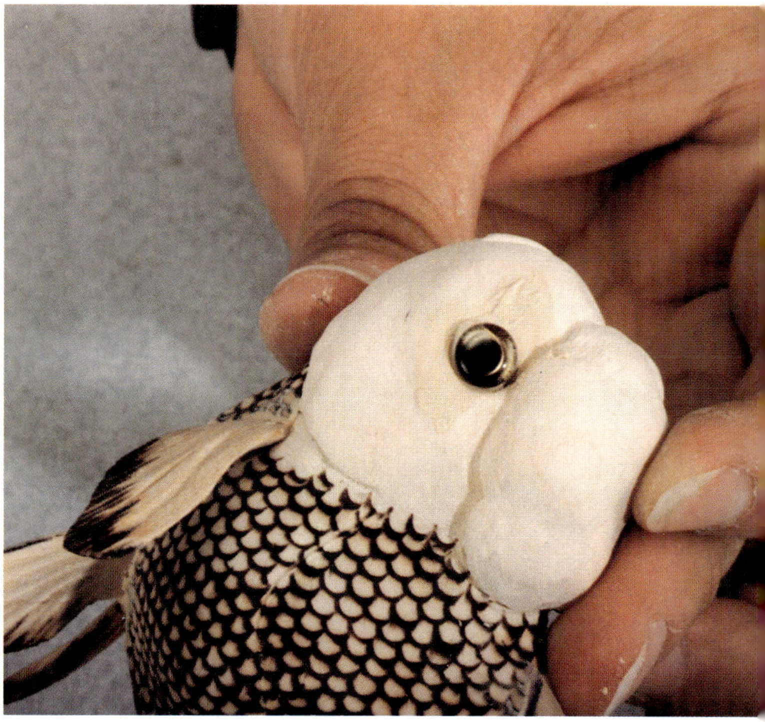

Set the eye in...

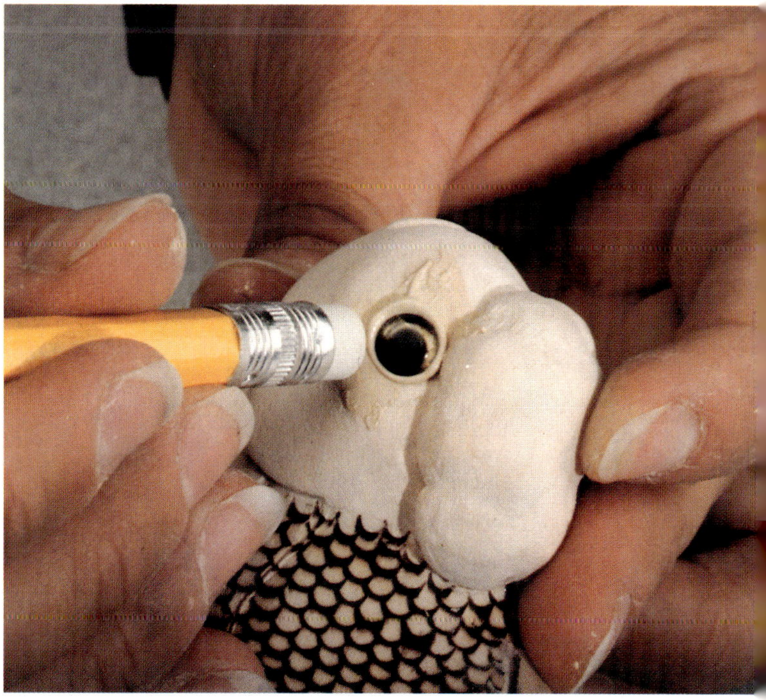

and tap it in place with a pencil eraser. Insert the other eye before adjusting.

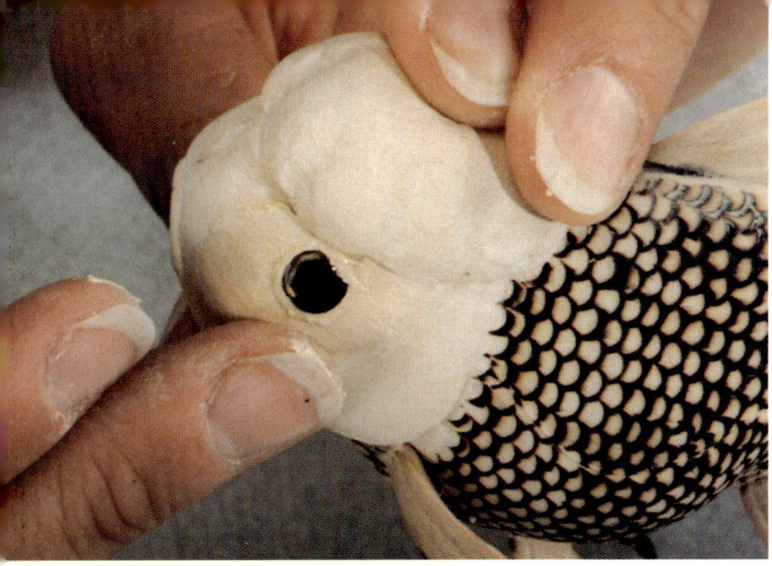

With a moistened finger wipe away the mixture to smooth it off.

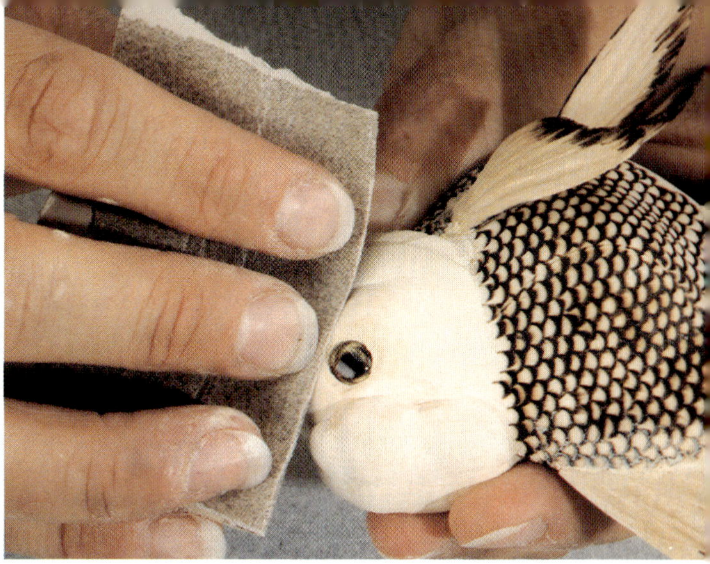

Lightly sand, being careful not to hit the eye.

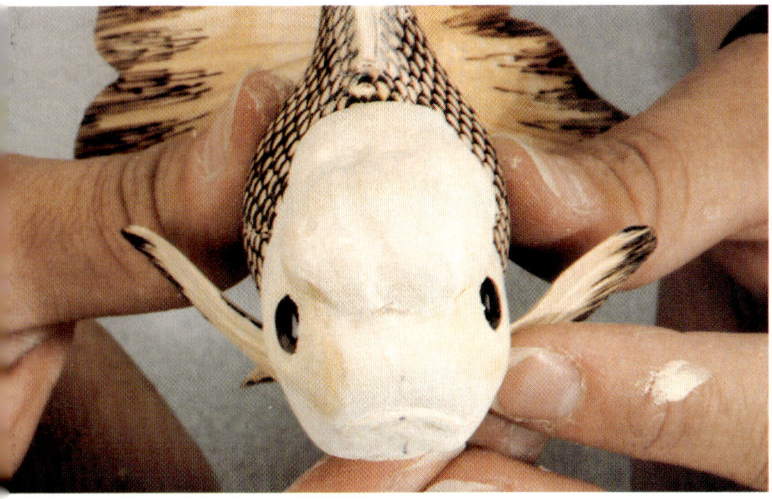

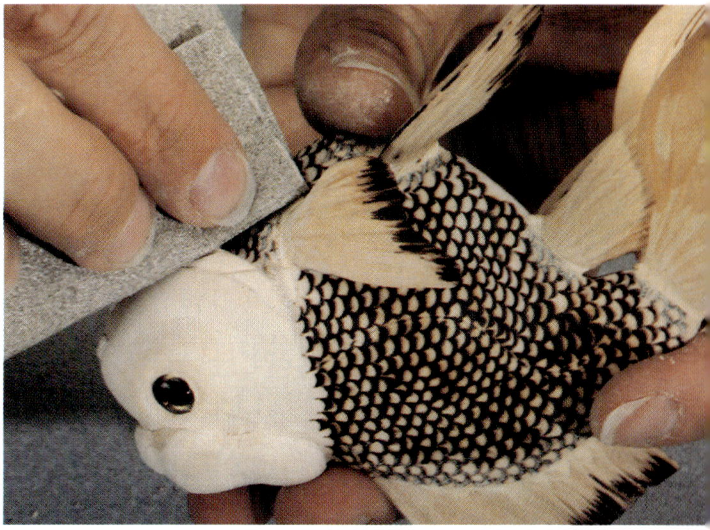

Continue sanding around the fin joints.

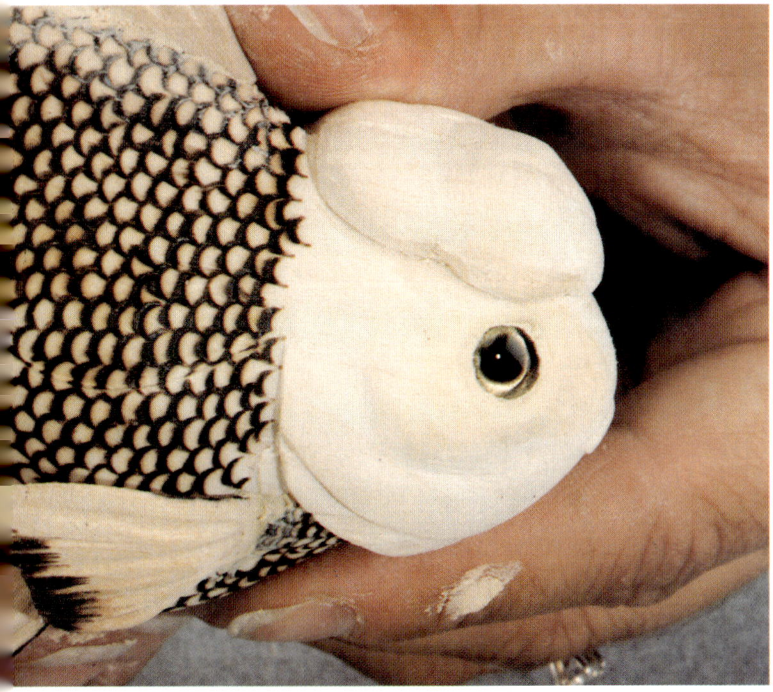

The eyes in place.

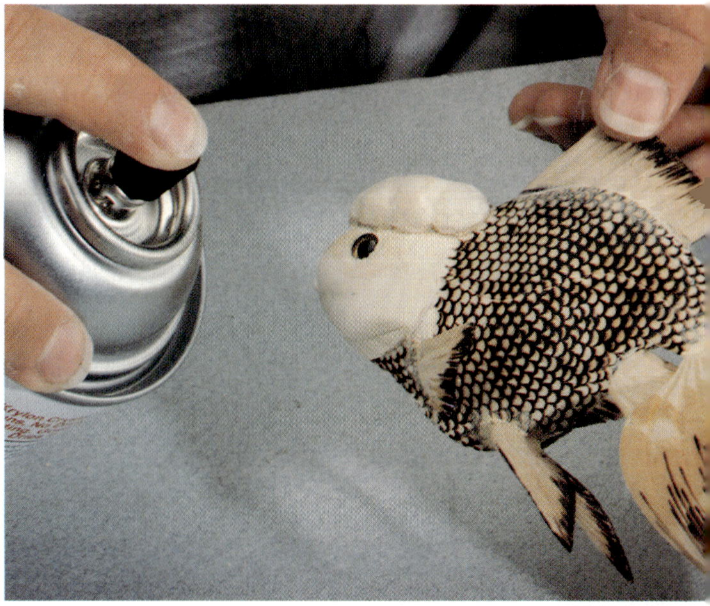

Apply a coat of Krylon Clear Coat.

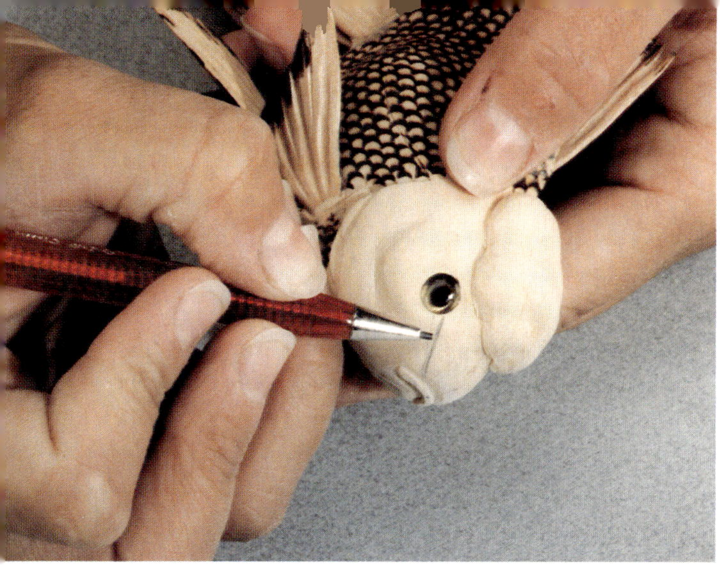

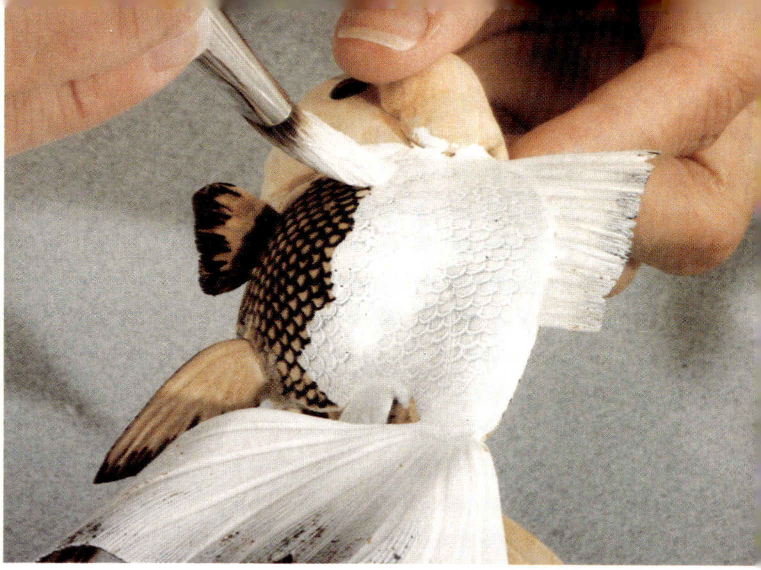

Before painting go over the fish and look for things that may have been forgotten. Here I need to add the nostrils. Draw a line from about a third of the way up the eyeball to a point about a third of the way up the side of the mouth.

When everything is completely dry, apply a coat of gesso in preparation for painting. I use a liquid acrylic gesso diluted approximately 50%. I apply two or three coats, though the super-glued tail may take extra. Work it into the scales.

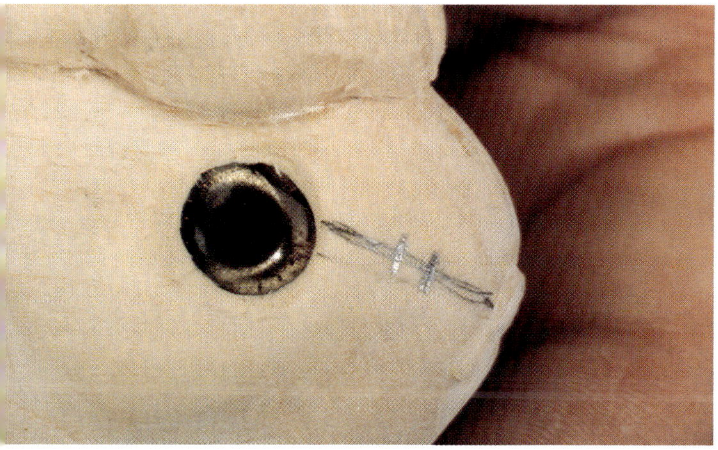

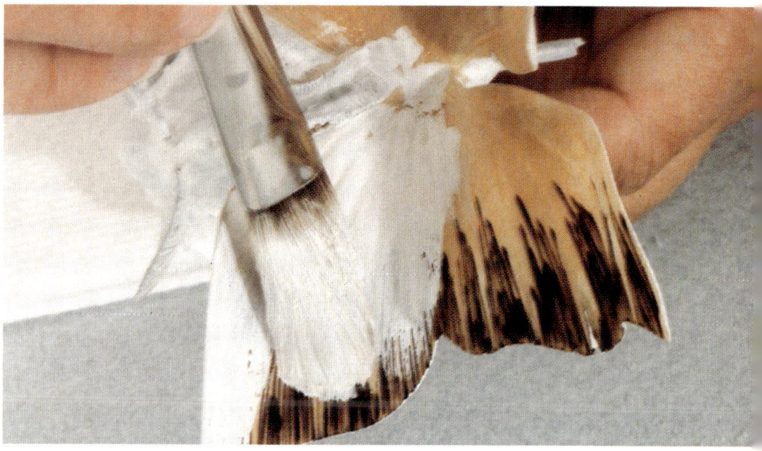

There are two nostrils on each side, marked with these hash marks.

You may need to work at getting the gesso into the burnings.

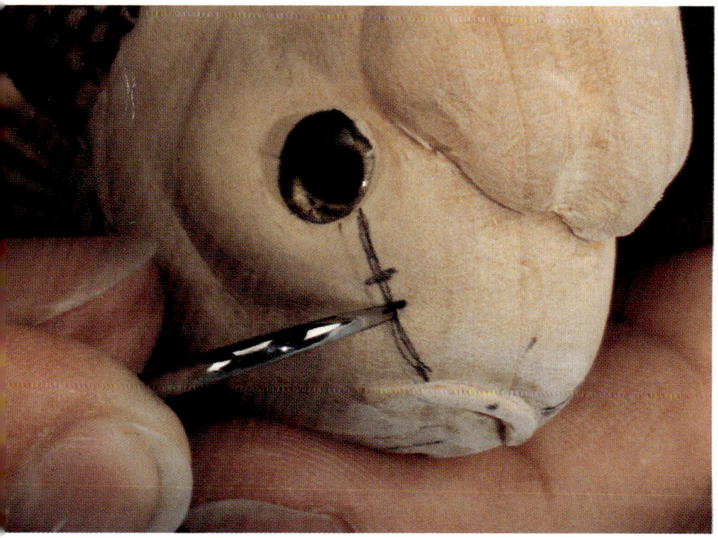

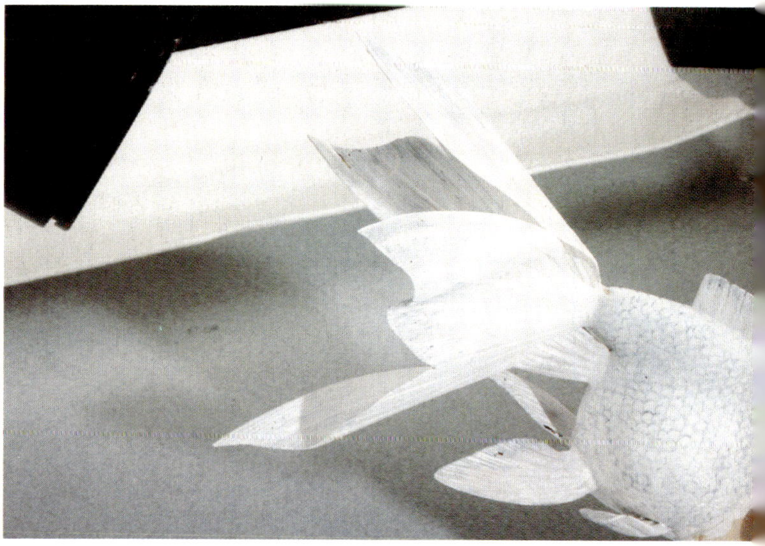

With a dental pick or similar instrument, make holes for the nostrils.

The gesso needs to be completely dry between coats. To accelerate the process I sometimes use a hairdryer. Don't use too much heat.

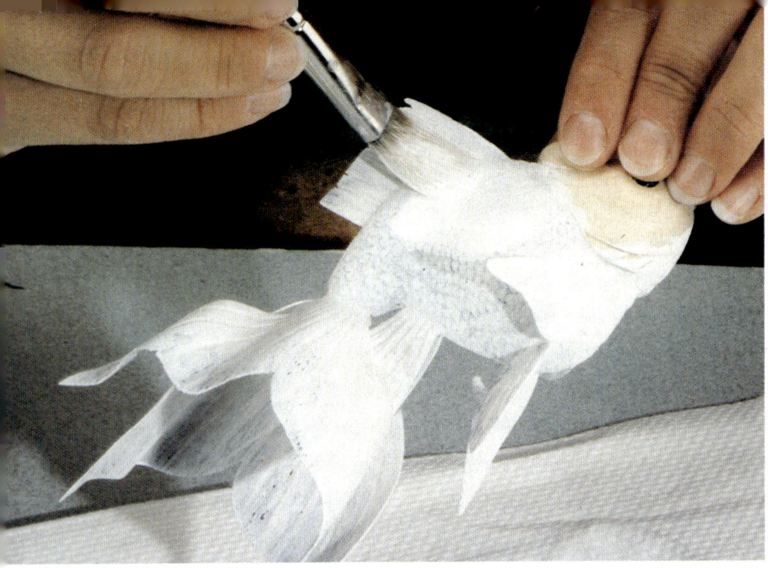

Apply a second coat to the body.

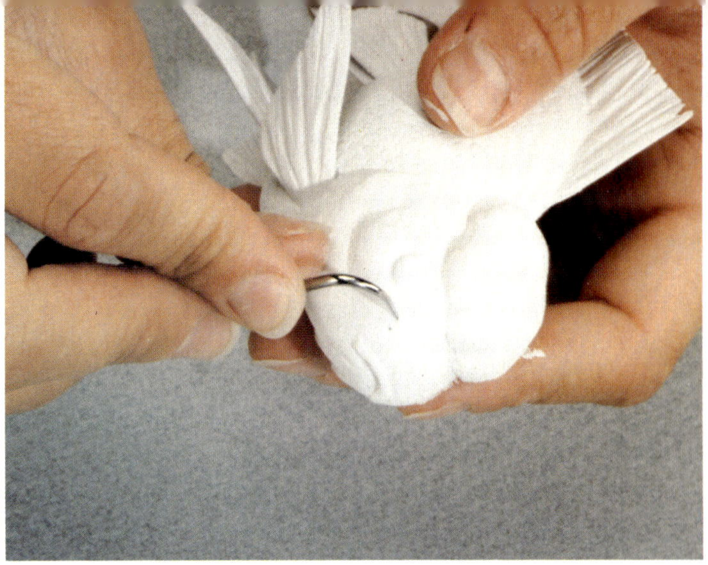

When the gesso is dry, clean out the nostrils with the dental pick.

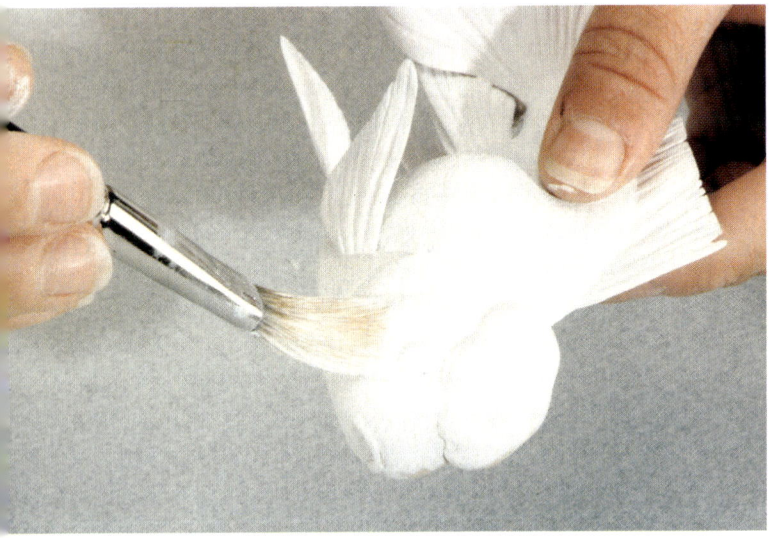

When the body is finished paint the head, going over the eyes with the gesso.

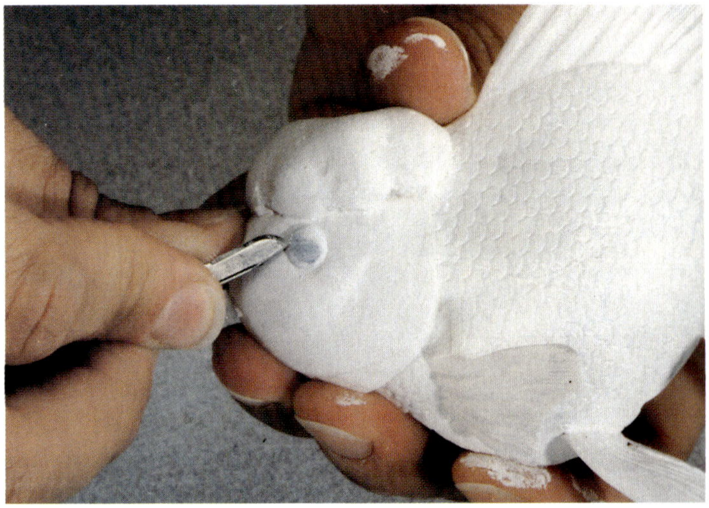

Clean the eyes with the knife. Start by running the point around the edge of the eye.

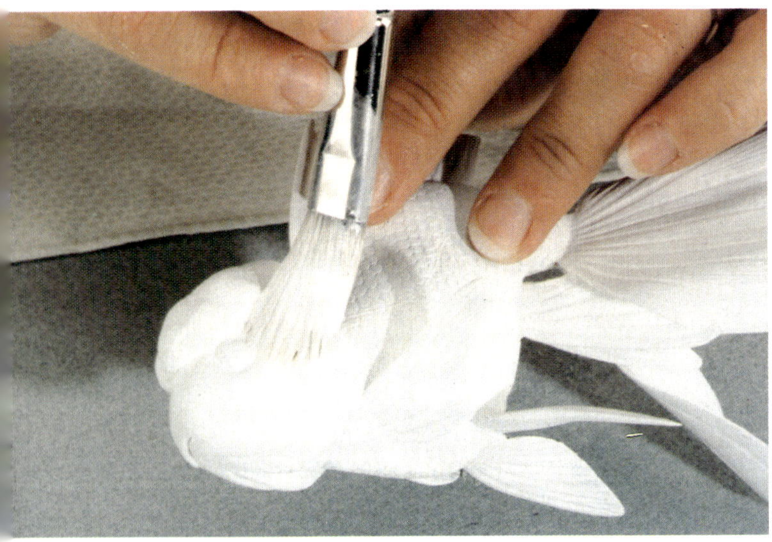

On the face, where there are no scales, be certain not to leave any brush marks that will mar the surface.

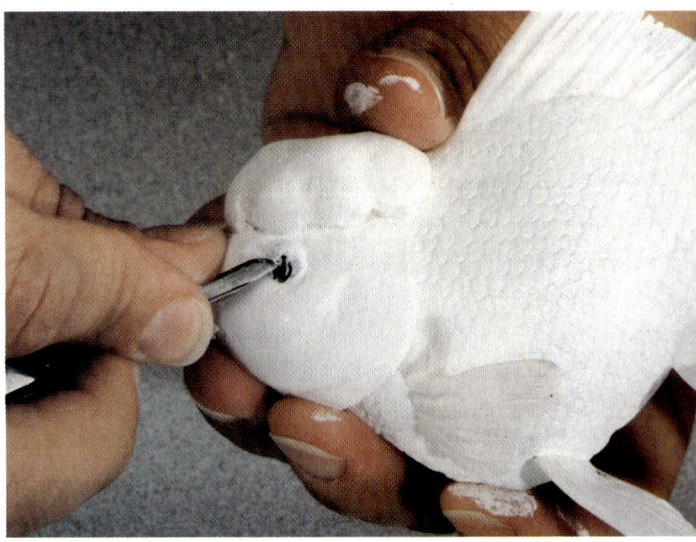

Scrape from the outside toward the middle. I like using a surgical scalpel for this. It has never scratched an eye.

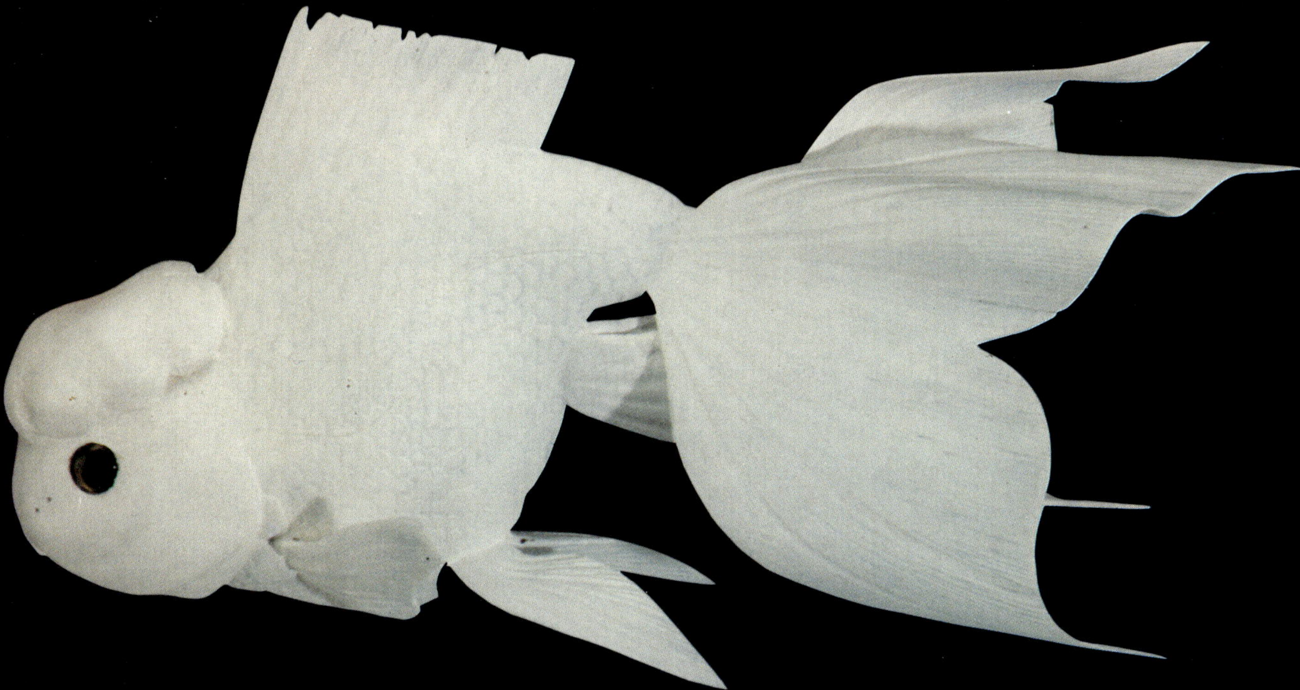

Ready for painting.

Carving the Base

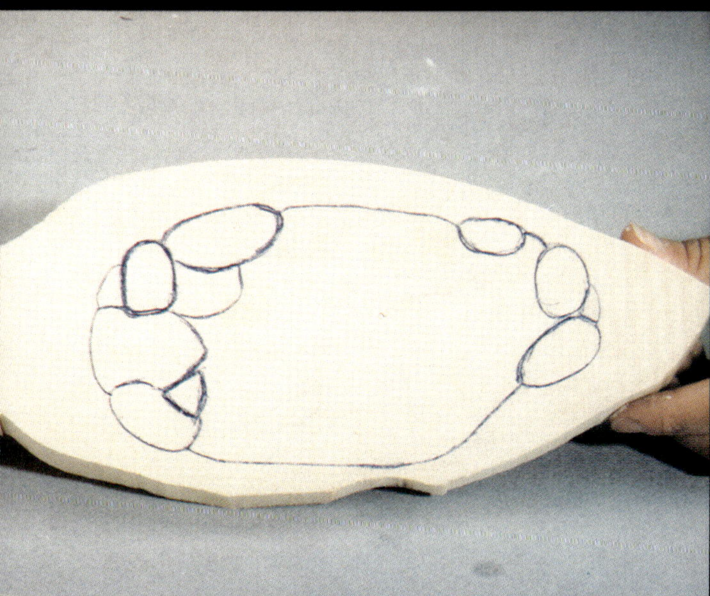

I make many of my bases from scrap wood. As you can see this was the salvage from a bass carving.

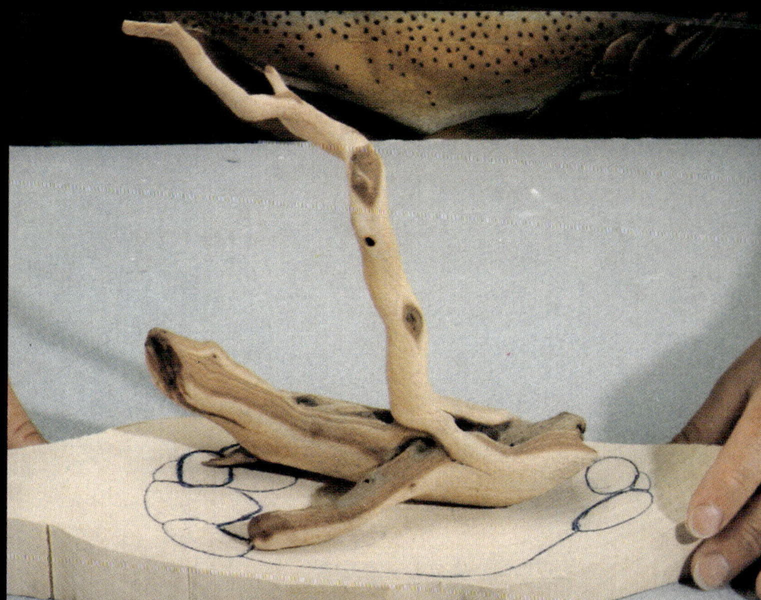

Since this is a domesticated fish, the setting should be aquarium-like. This will have a few rocks and a piece of manzanita root. It is sold in branches with the bark sand-blasted off.

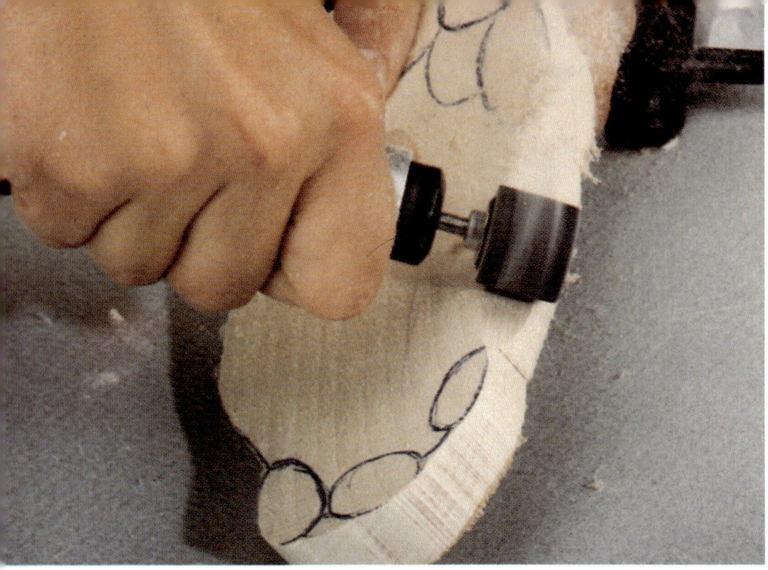

Saw the pattern out, then, with a sanding drum, take off the sharp edges of the central section.

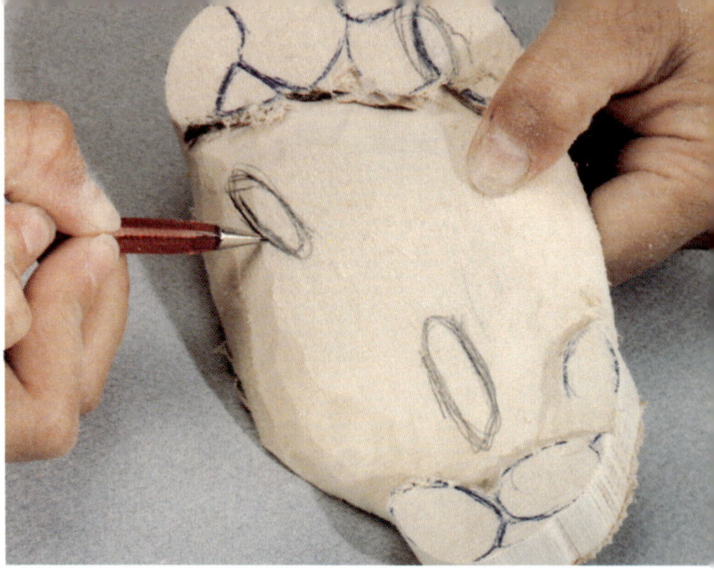

These circles are where the branch rests. The rest of the center area will be covered in gravel.

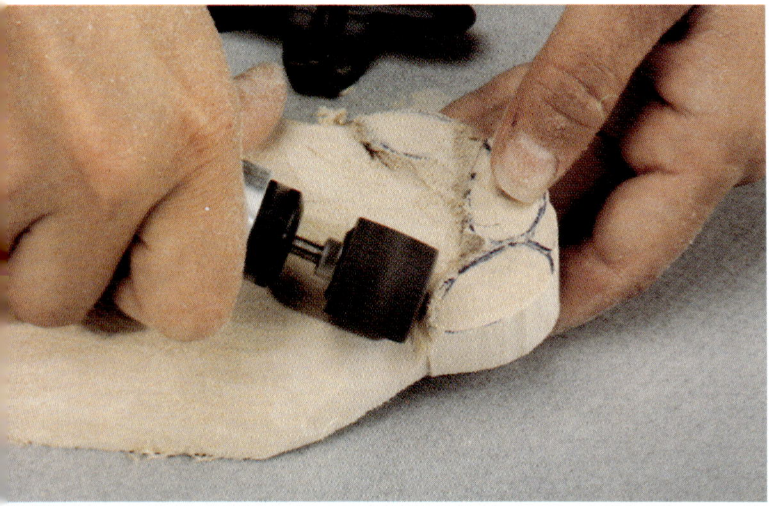

Go along the border with the rocks, bringing them out.

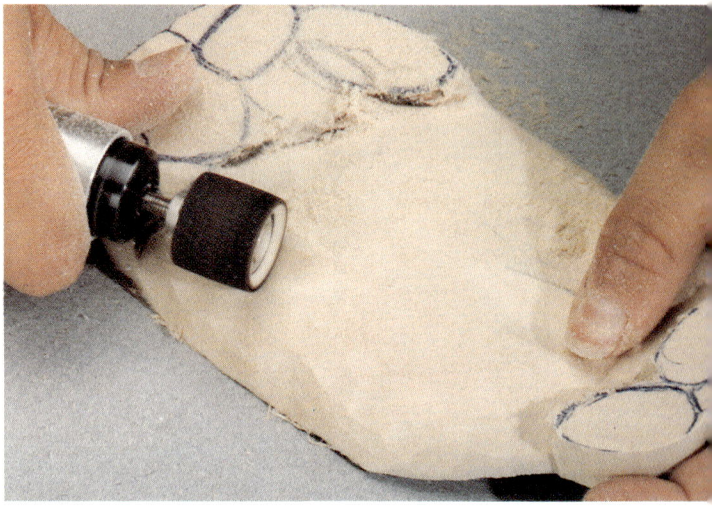

Cut a grove in the resting spots.

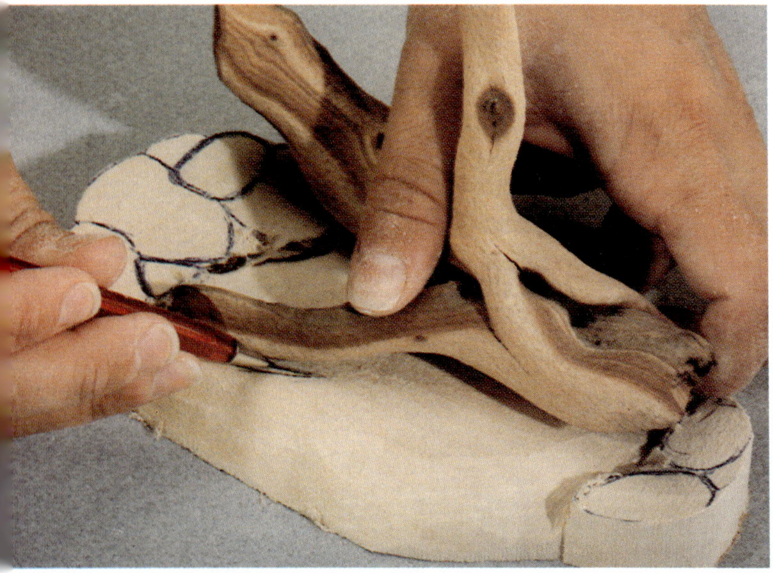

Decide where the branch will rest and mark the areas where it touches the base.

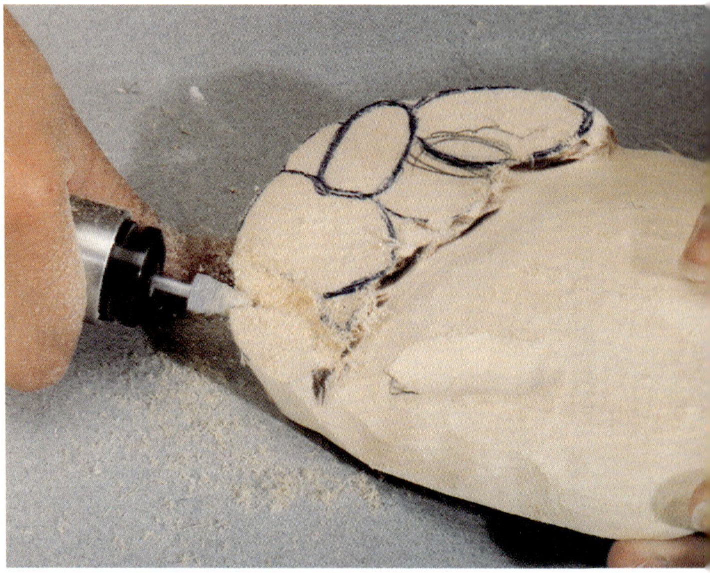

Switch to a carbide cone to establish the spaces between the rocks and begin to give them shape.

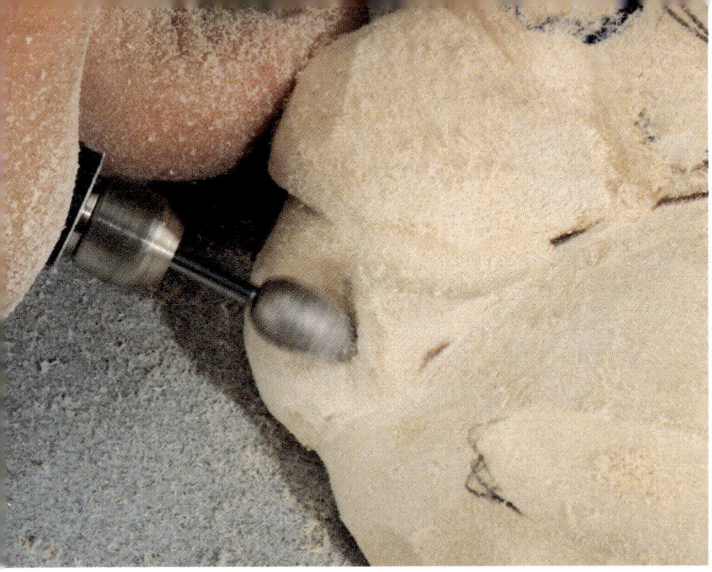

A ruby cone will do some of the finishing work on the rocks.

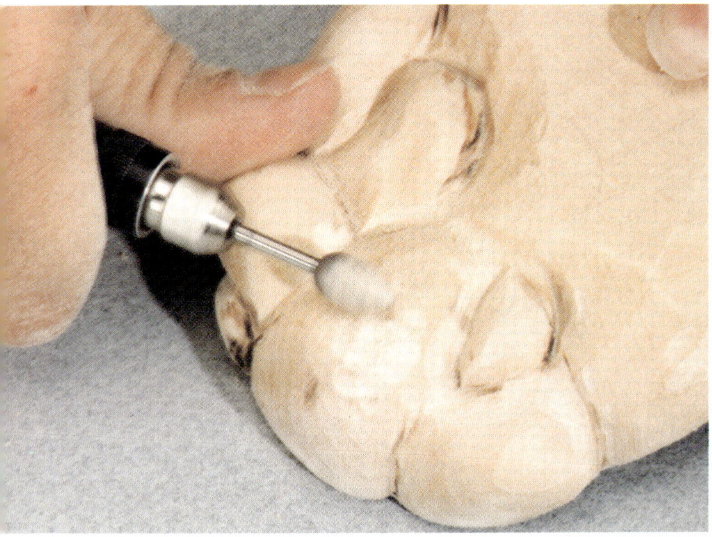

It can also be used to texture the stones. Here I simply touch the side of the bit to the stone in a series of little taps.

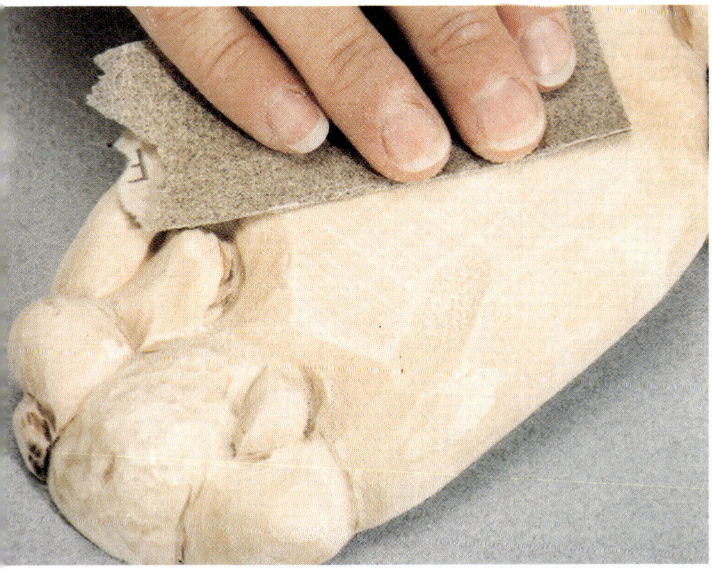

Sand the base with medium grit paper.

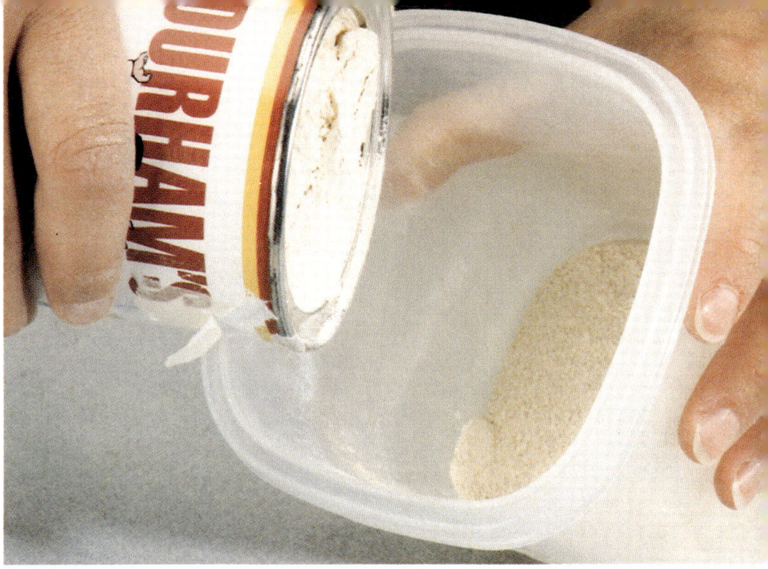

To make gravel I pour Durham's Water Putty™ into a container.

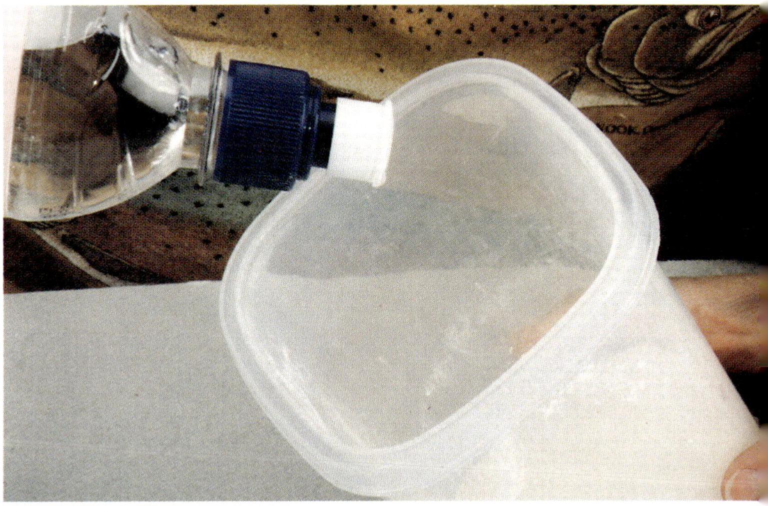

Add water.

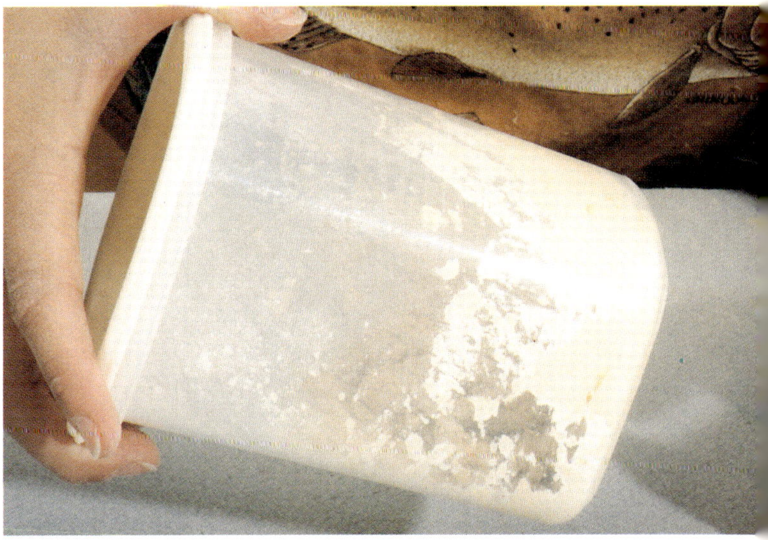

Seal the container and start shaking. If you end up with a glob, add more powder; if it is too dry, add more water. If you use a vigorous shaking technique...

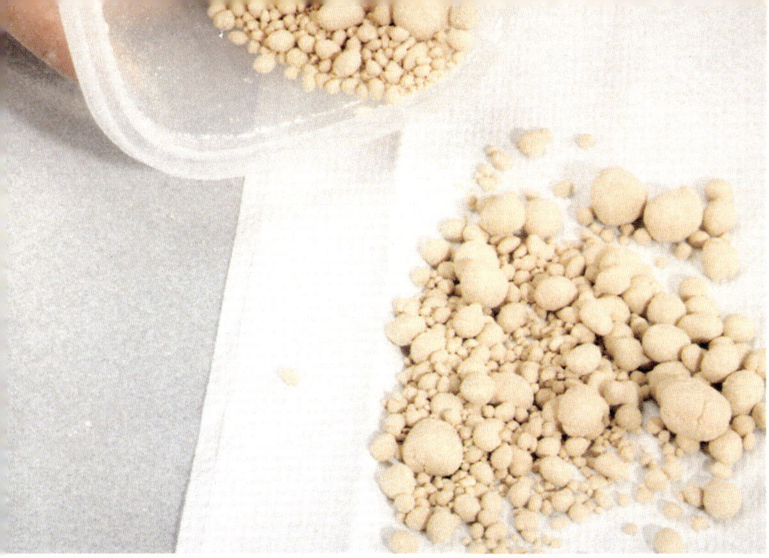

you should end up with a variety of different sized "gravel" pieces. I spread this out on a cookie sheet and let it dry overnight.

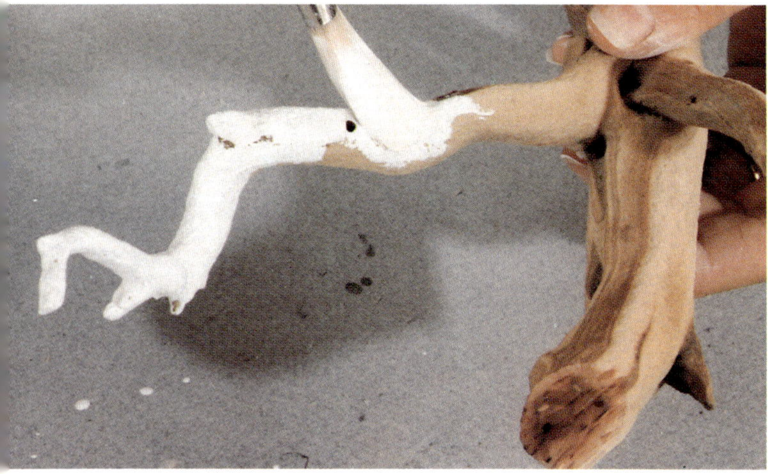

Gesso the branch.

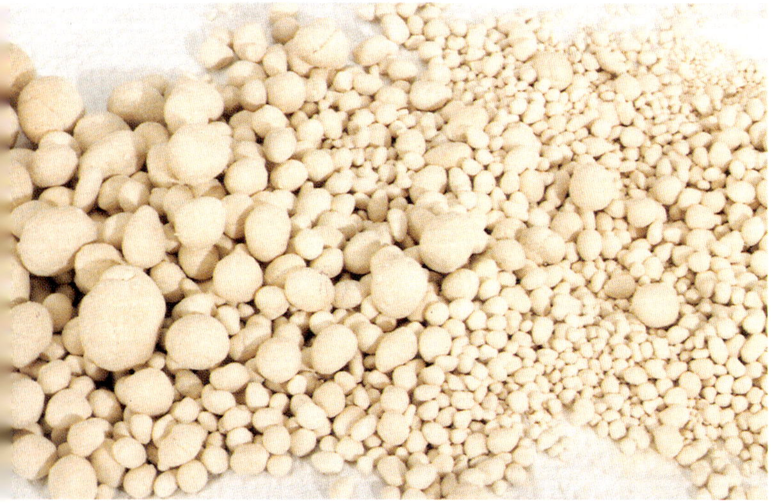

When the water putty dries it has produced a variety of pebble sizes. I skim off the larger sizes and keep them for future carvings. Here I want the small pebbles that look like aquarium gravel.

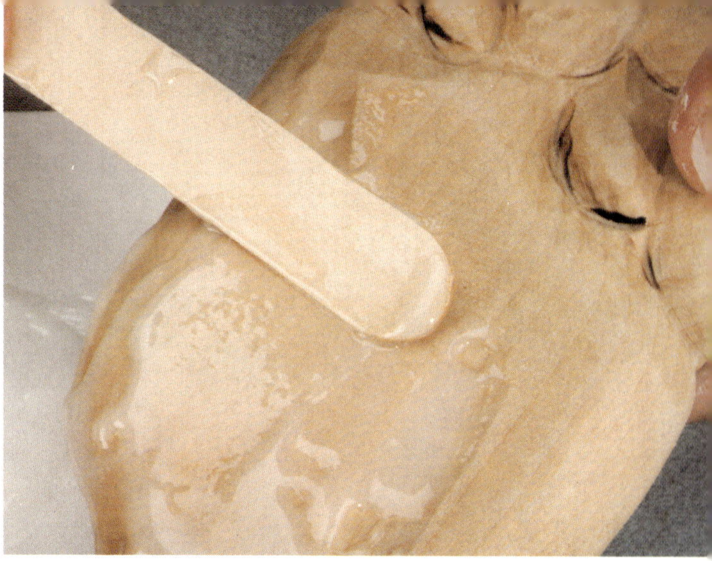

On the base, cover the area between the rocks with a coating of 2-part epoxy.

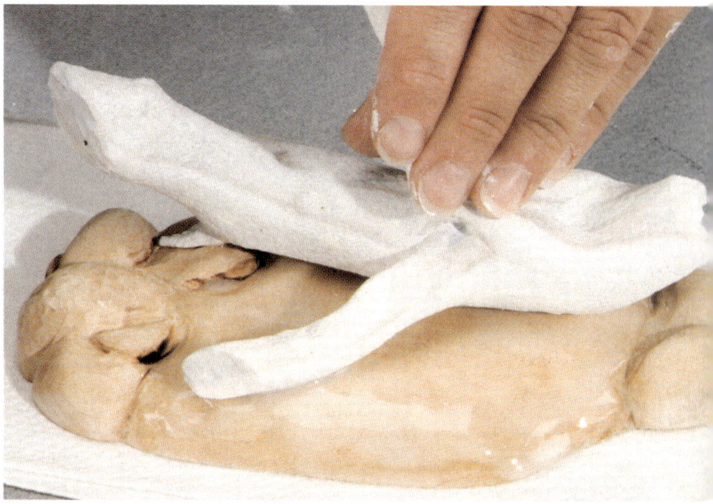

Glue the branch in place. I may peg it from the bottom in the final steps.

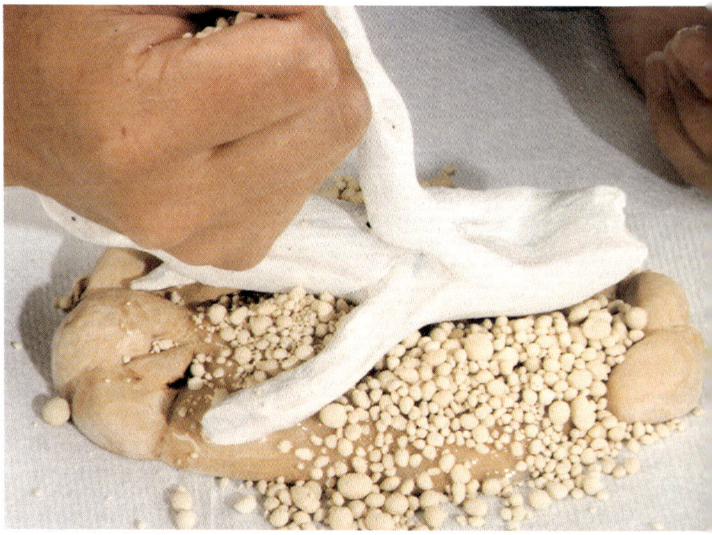

Pour the pebbles on the base. Where there is glue, they should stick.

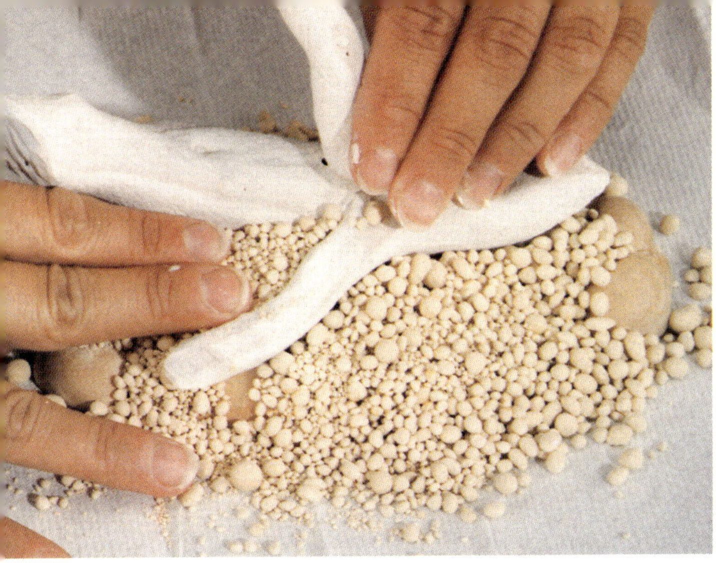

Press them into the glue.

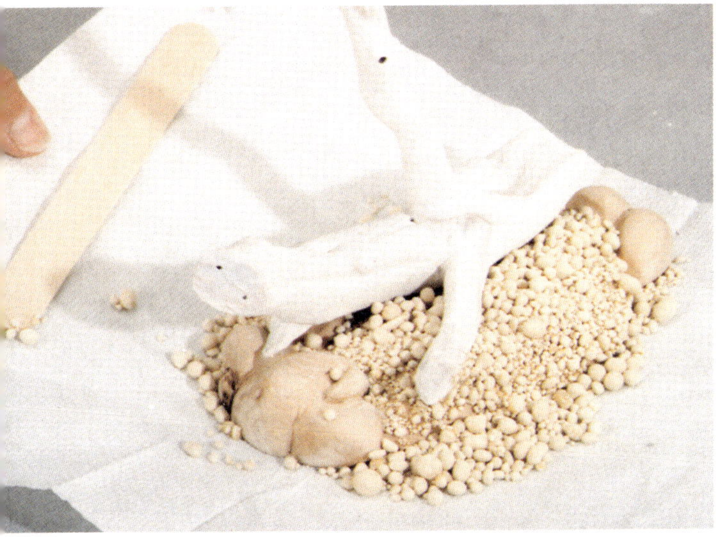

Set it aside until the glue has thoroughly dried.

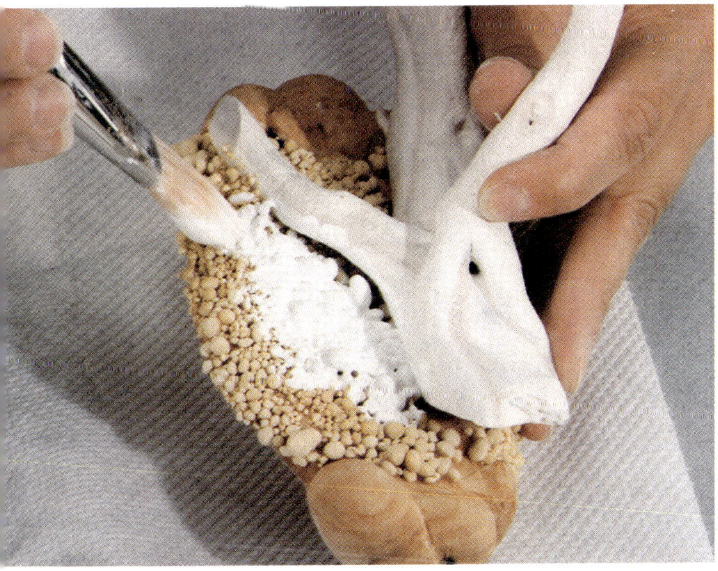

Gesso the base. To get into the pebbles, you will need to use a stippling stroke.

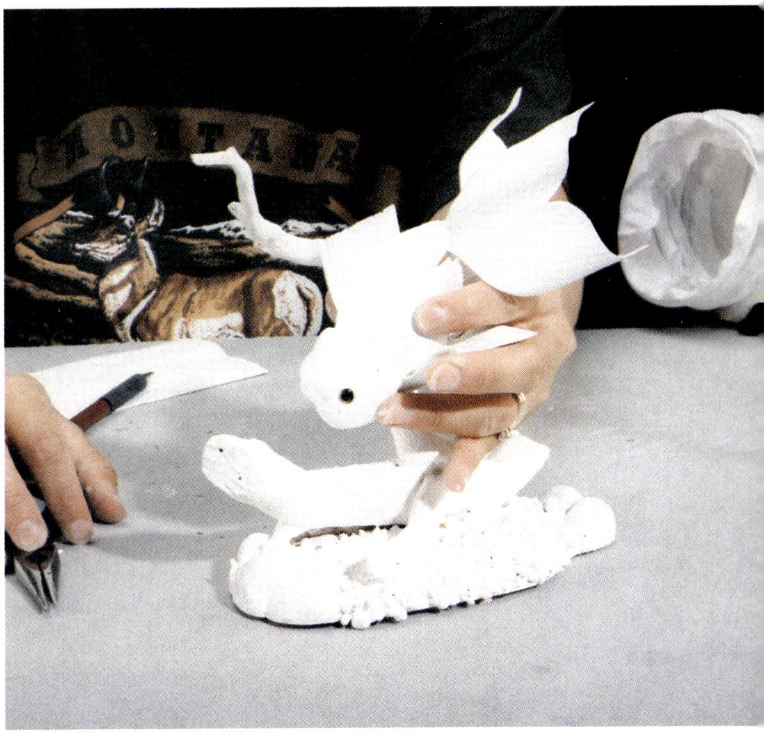

I want the gold fish to be heading at a downward angle. They feed by sucking in gravel and spitting it out.

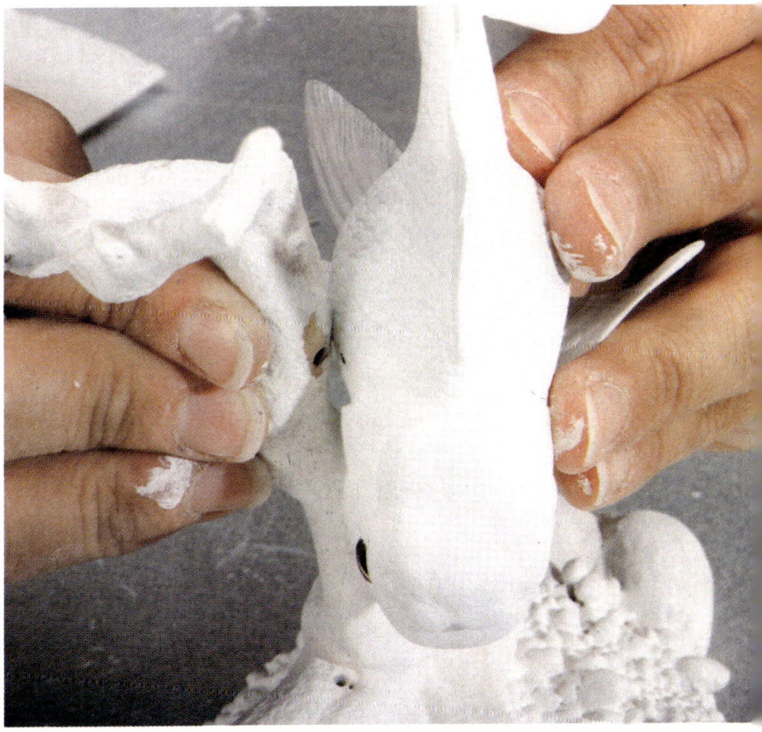

When I am satisfied with the position, I mark the spot where the hole must go into the branch and the fish.

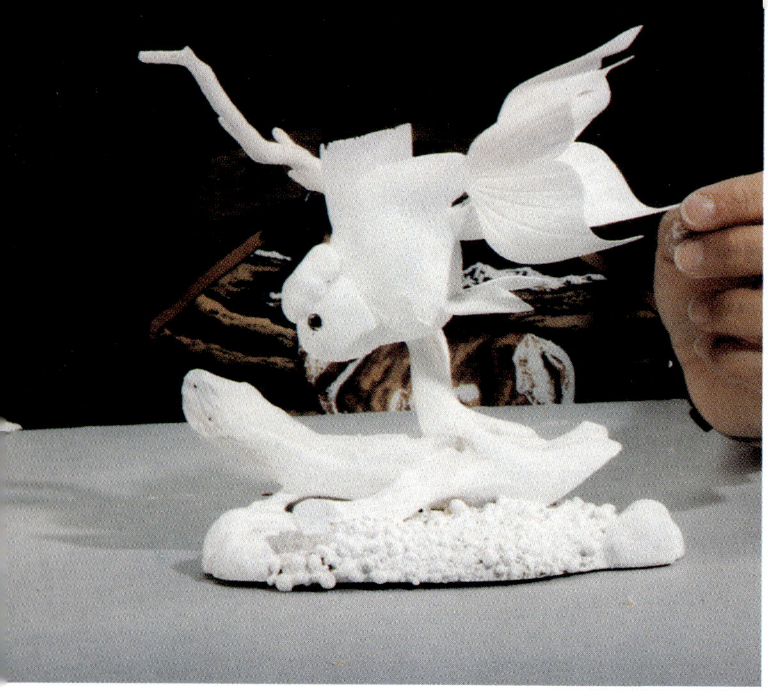

A couple fine tuning adjustments and it is ready for mounting.

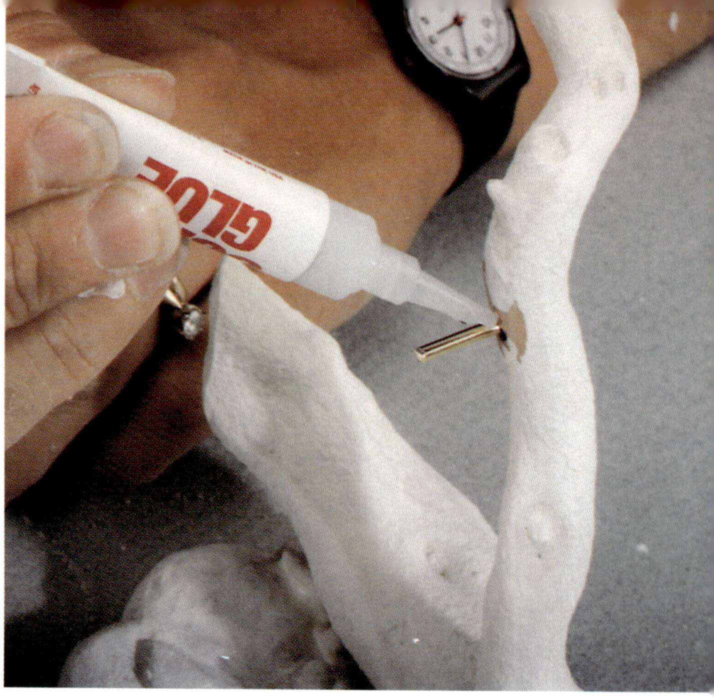

Because I had to bend the pin to get the position I wanted, I need to glue it in place now, before I forget what I have done.

Painting the Red Crane Crest

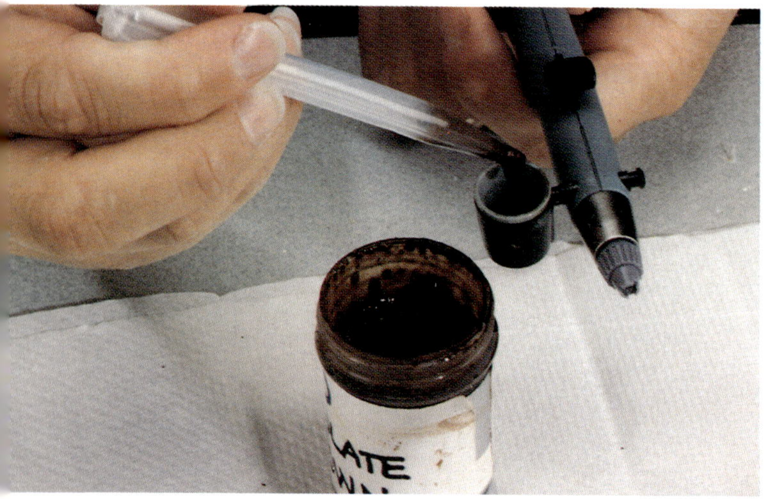

The base for the goldfish carving is what would be found in an aquarium, so there is no need for a natural look. I begin with an airbrush for the pebbles. The airbrush paint I use is Polytranspar from Wasco. This is an opaque chocolate brown. The airbrush is an Aztec, and is easy to use and clean. Mix the paints well before using. The pigments tend to settle in the bottom. I use a pipette to fill the paint cup and add enough water to bring the paint to the consistency of milk.

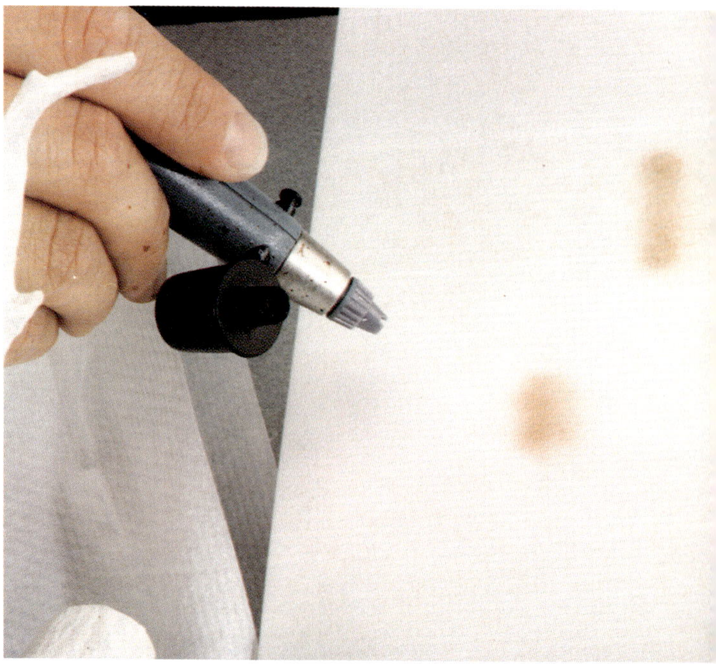

Always test the airbrush on scrap paper before working on the carving.

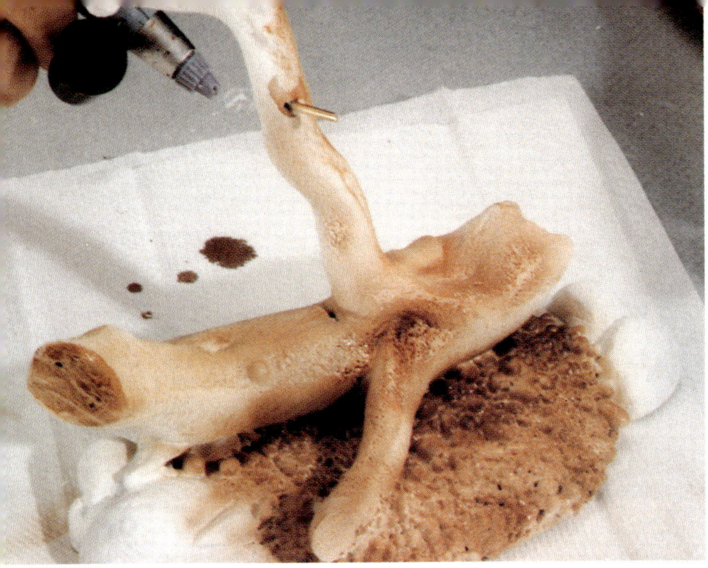

Paint the base to a mottled brown, except for the larger rocks. Continue up the branch. Don't worry about overspray at this point.

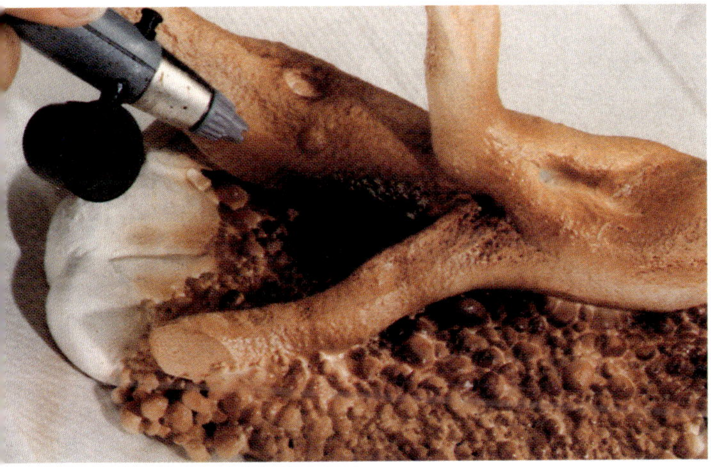

Get the pebbles darker in the areas under the tree to create a little shadow.

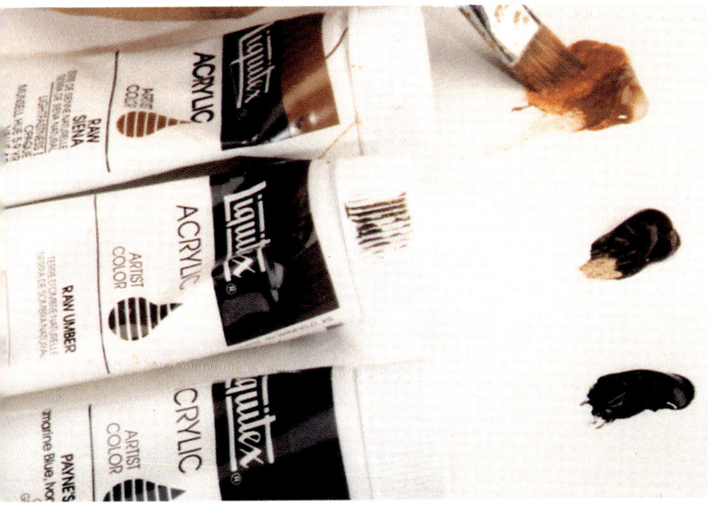

The larger rocks are brush painted with a combination of raw sienna, raw umber, and Payne's gray acrylics, straight from the tube.

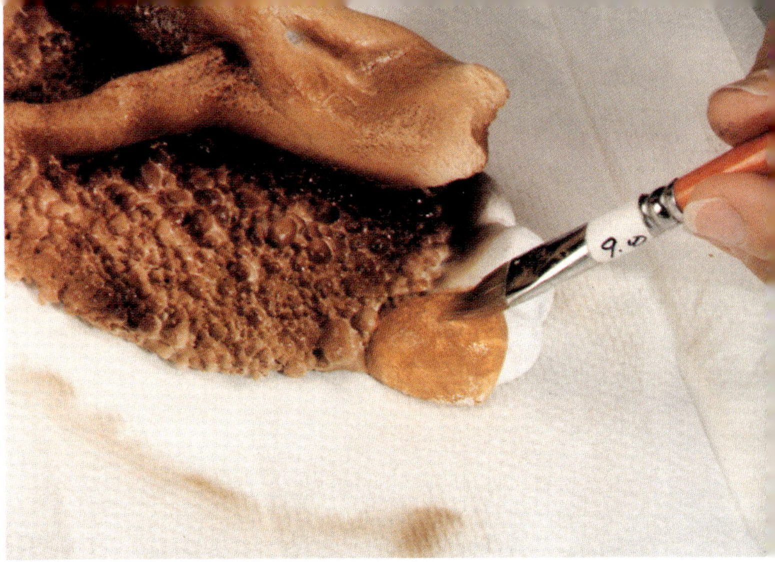

I don't have a particular order. I paint some light with raw sienna...

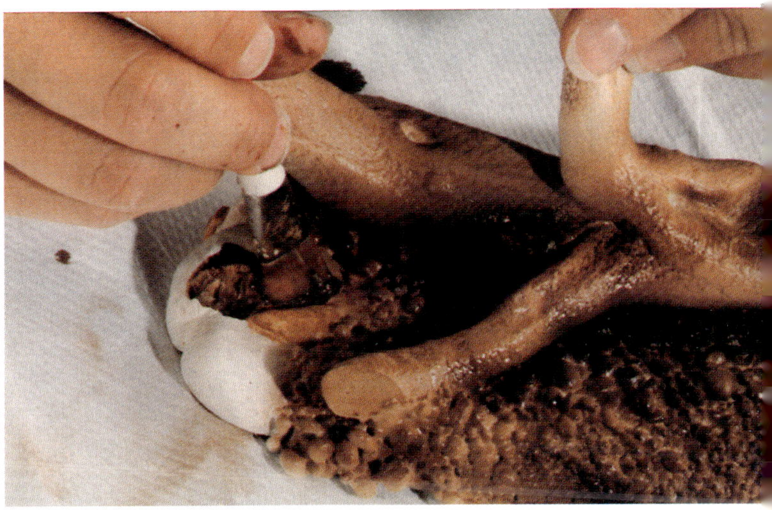

and some a darker shade with raw umber.

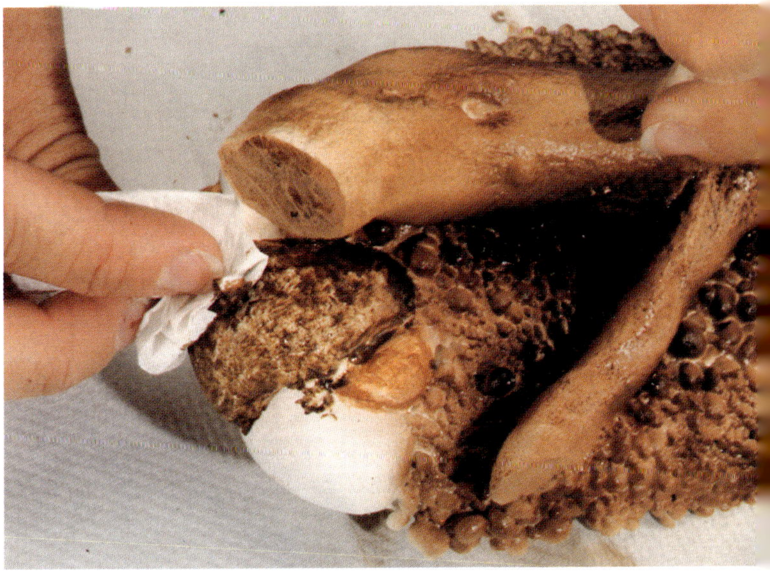

On these I am going to take off a little paint while they are still wet by dabbing them with paper towel.

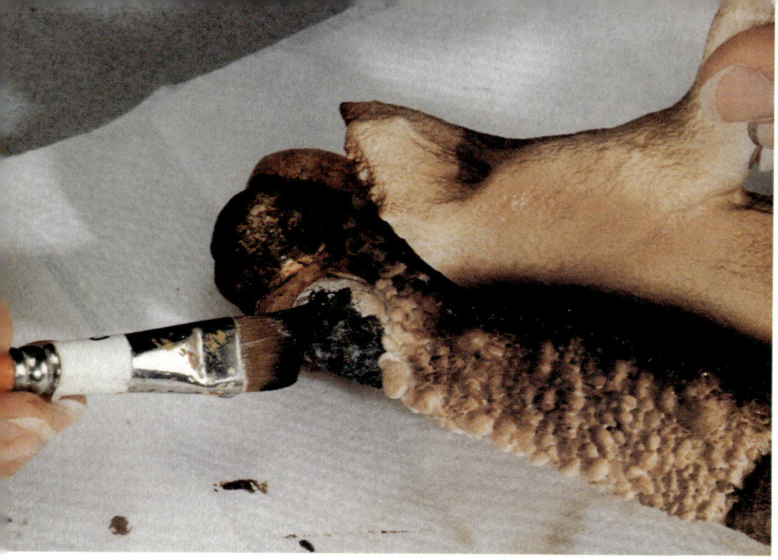

Payne's gray creates a nice contrast in the larger rocks.

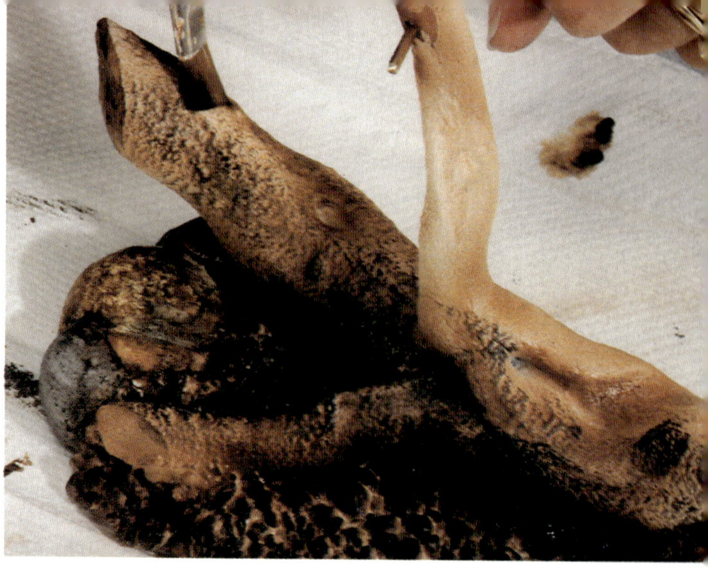

Use the same drybrush technique to go lightly over the wood, too, making it darker at the bottom.

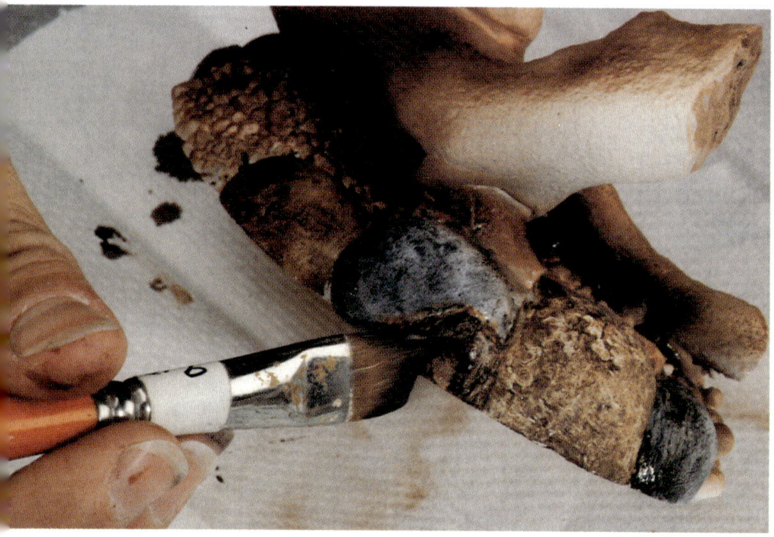

You can blend the colors slightly while they are still wet, dabbing flecks of one color onto another for a rock-like effect.

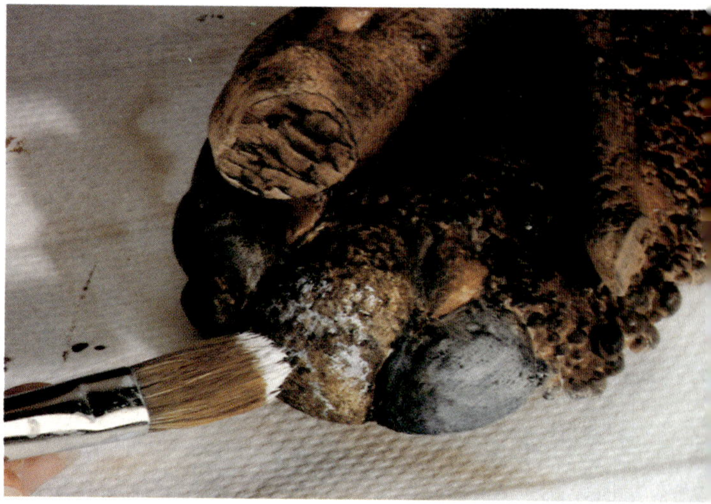

Load the tip of a smaller brush with titanium white and stipple some of the rocks...

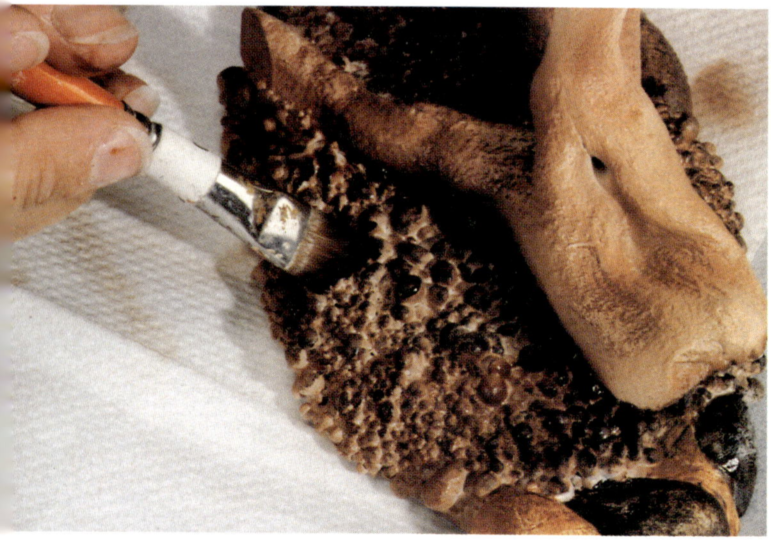

With a relatively dry brush go over the top of the stones with Payne's gray to give them some highlight.

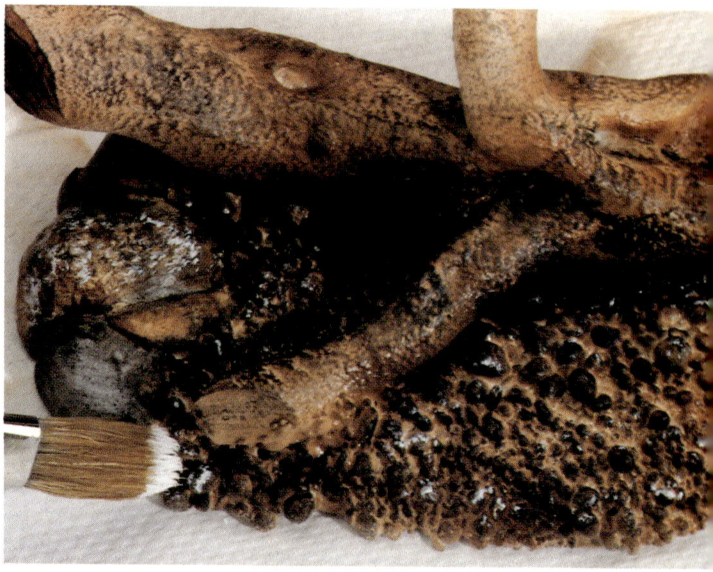

and some of the gravel.

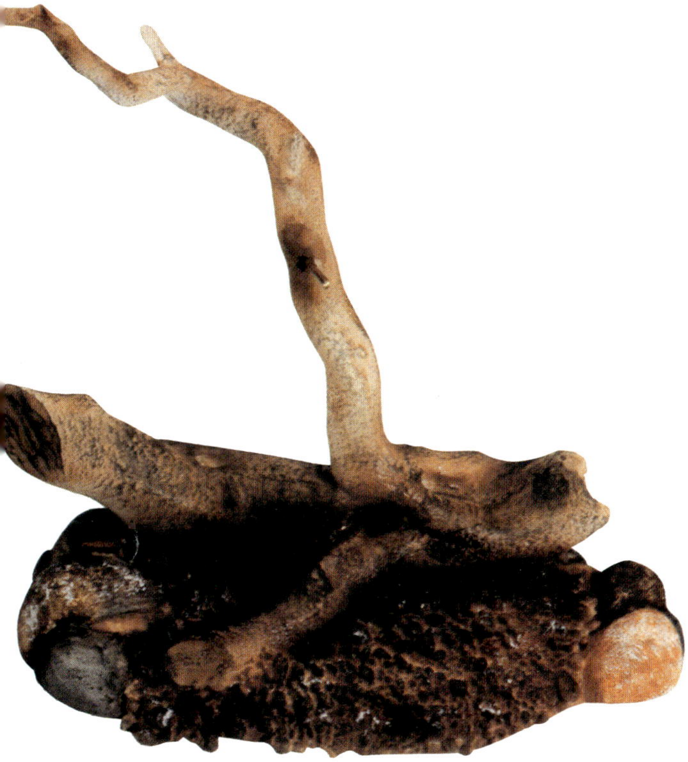

The base is painted.

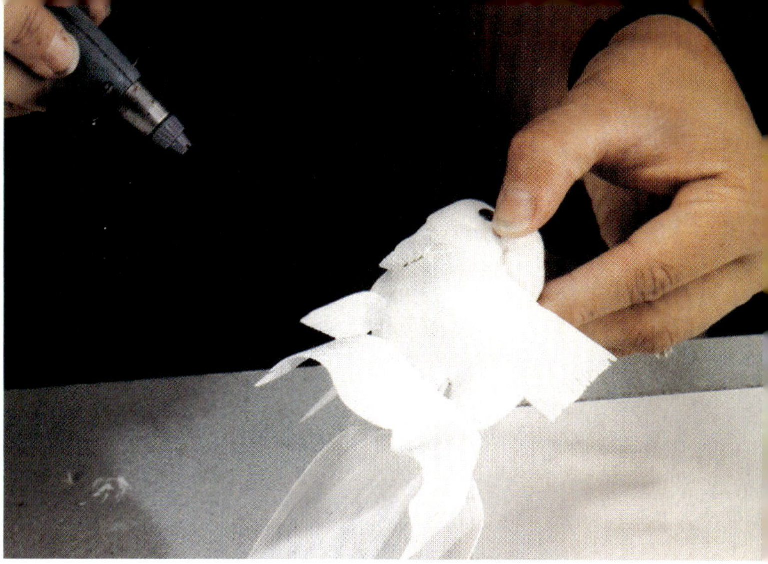

Holding the fish by the crest, paint the body with the white paint.

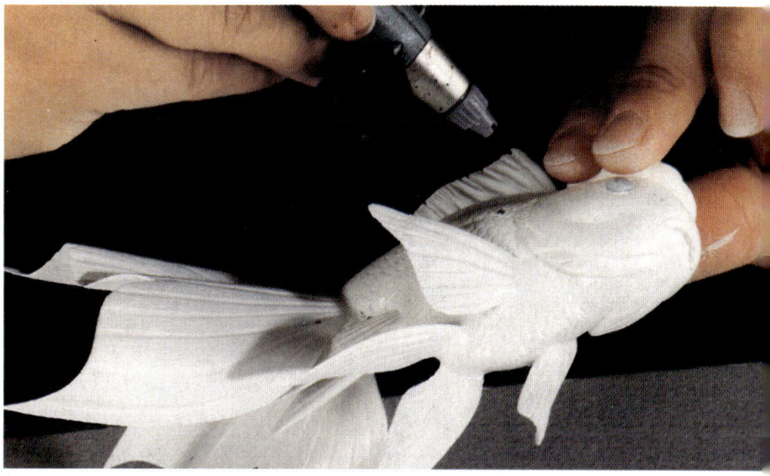

When dry we apply a coat of white "Pearl Essence" paint, a light refracting paint that creates a pearl-like gleam.

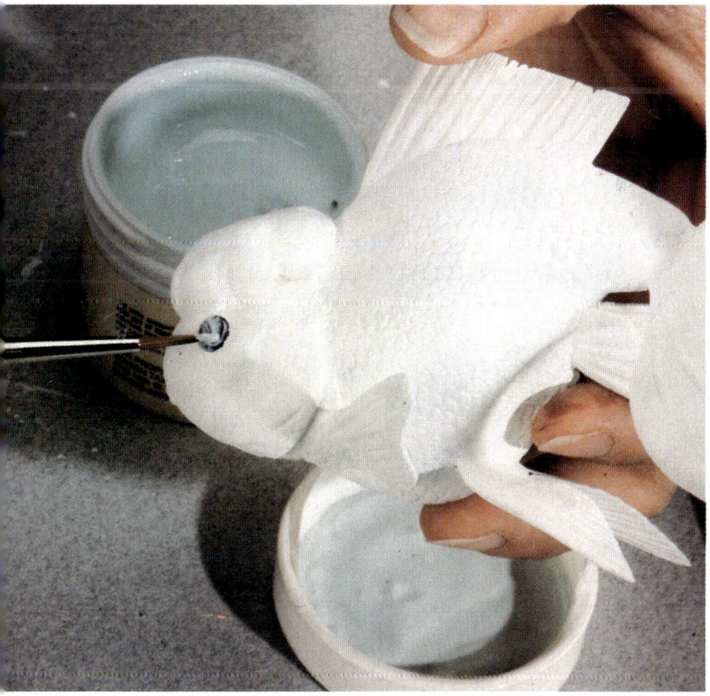

The first color for the Crane Crest is Superhide White. This is the primary color of the gold fish. Be sure your airbrush is thoroughly clean before using this color in it. First I coat the eyes with Eye-Protect™, a product that makes the removal of paint much easier. It dries clear.

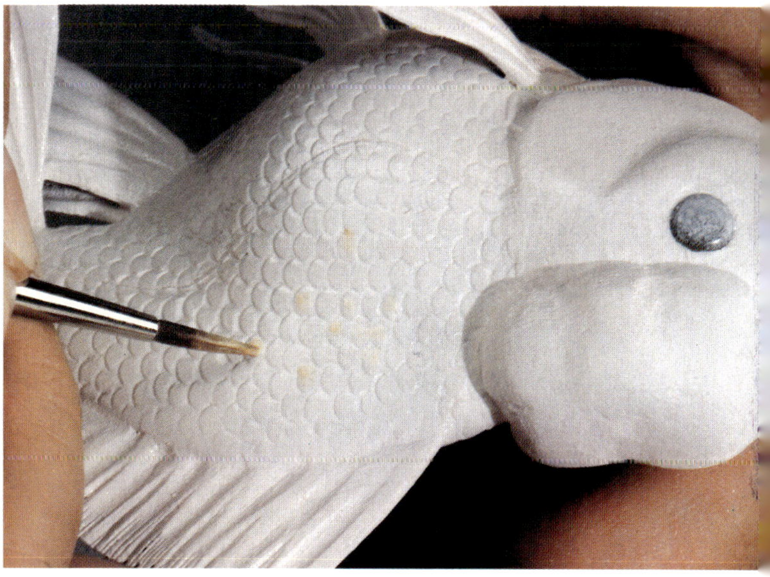

With a wash of light gold acrylics, randomly touch the tips of some scales. This creates a little shine.

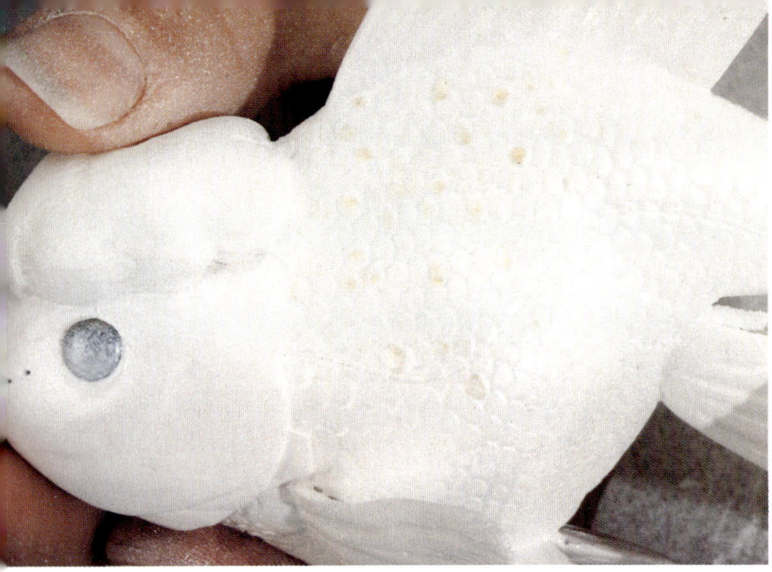

The result.

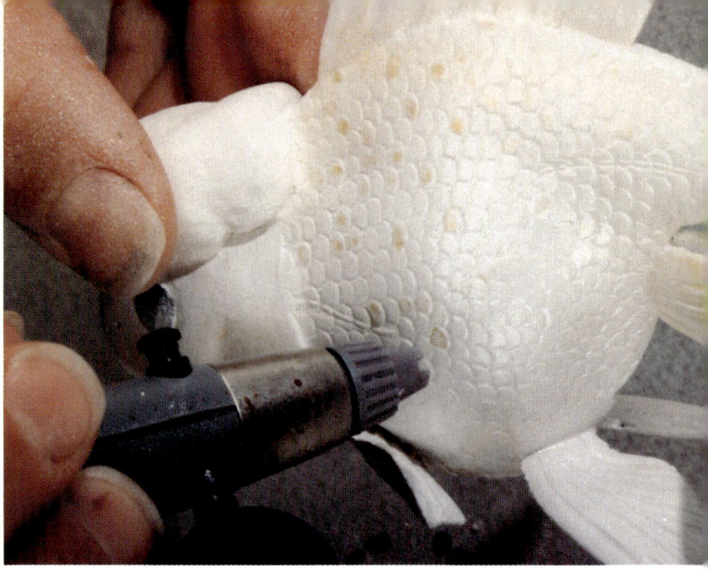

the butt of the ventral fin....

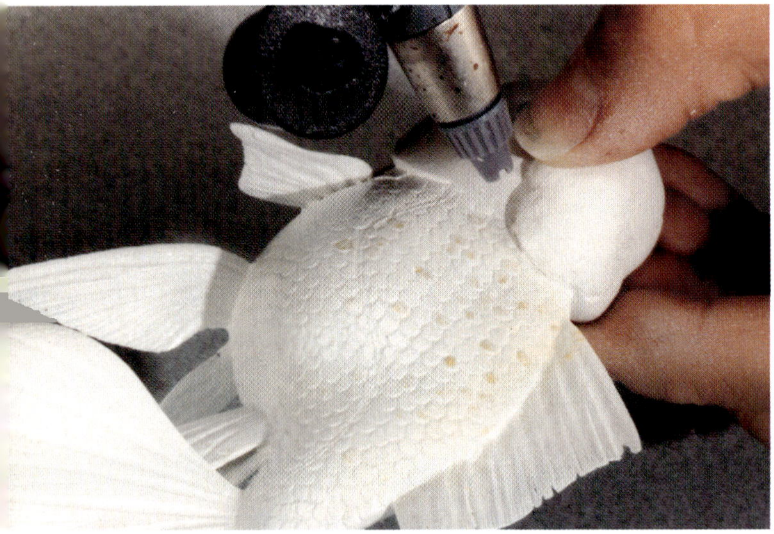

The highlights are airbrushed with a pearl finish sparkling gold paint. The sparkle paints need to be mixed very well. I add two or three drops of yellow ocher to strengthen the color. This is going on the back...

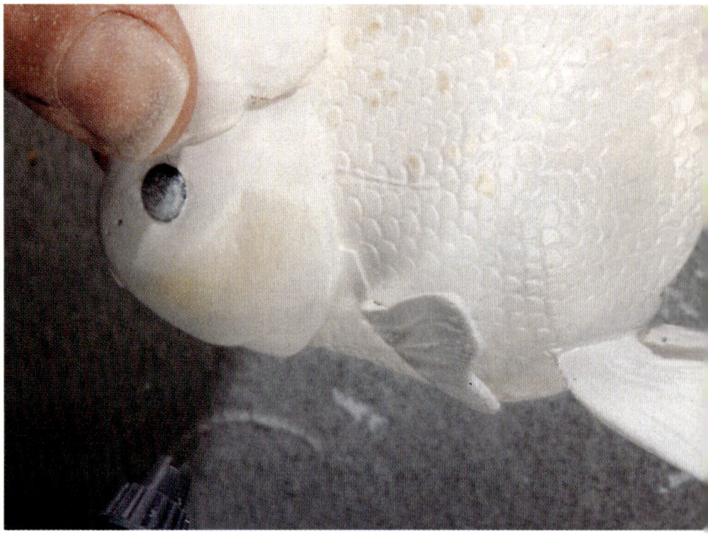

the gill plate...

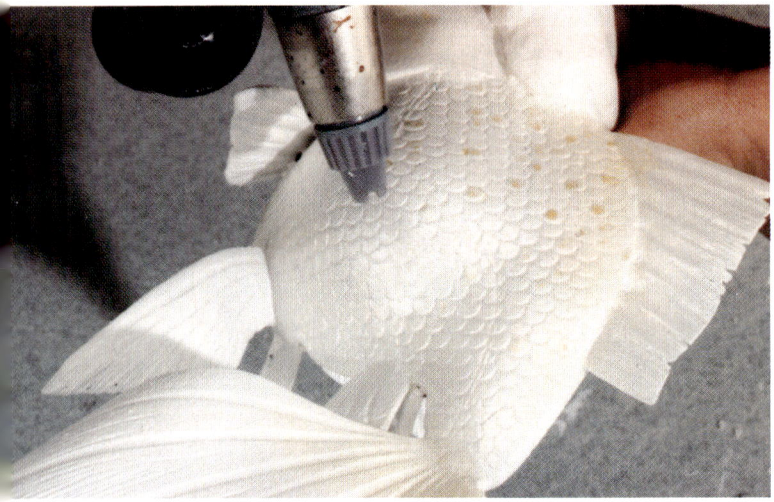

the caudal peduncle and the caudal fin...

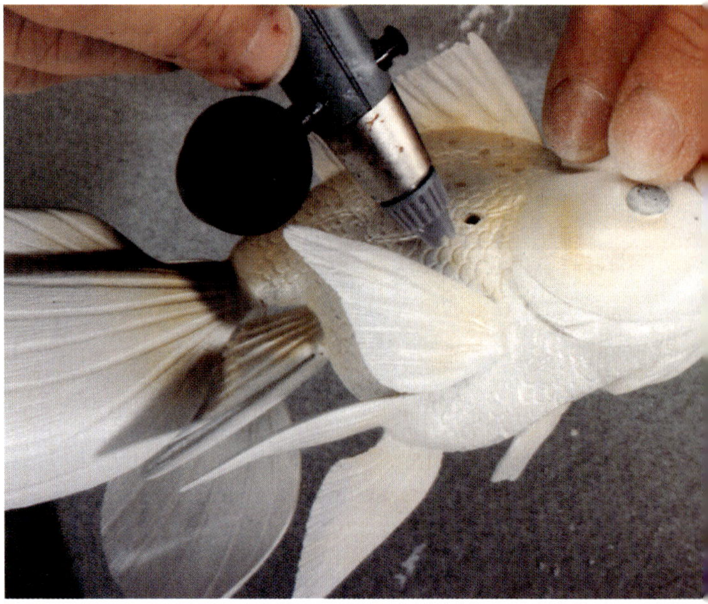

the pectoral fin butt...

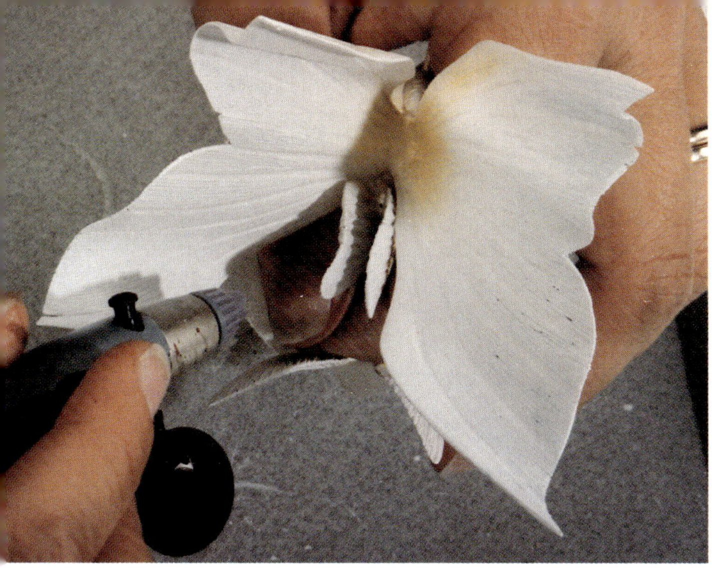

and inside the tail.

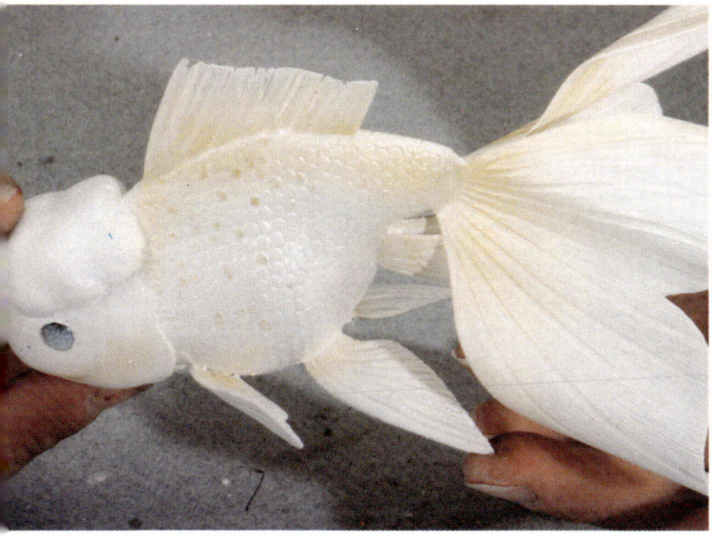

The gold highlights applied.

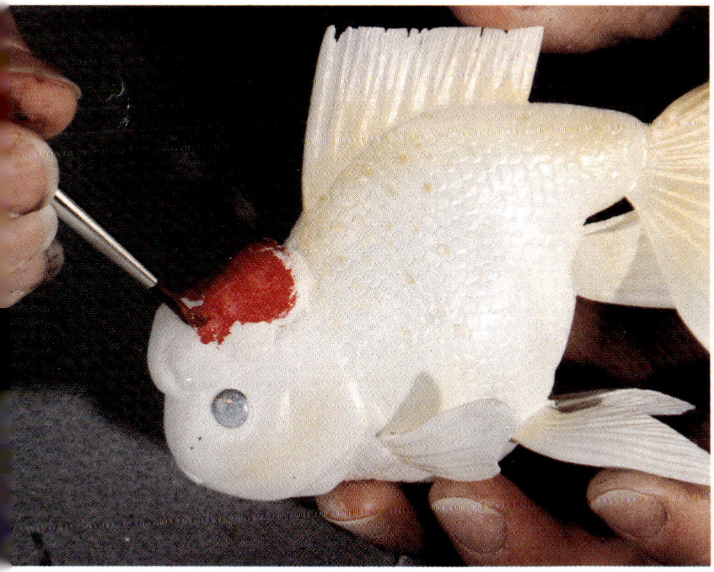

I will paint the crest with a brush. I begin with a coverage of bright, gill red.

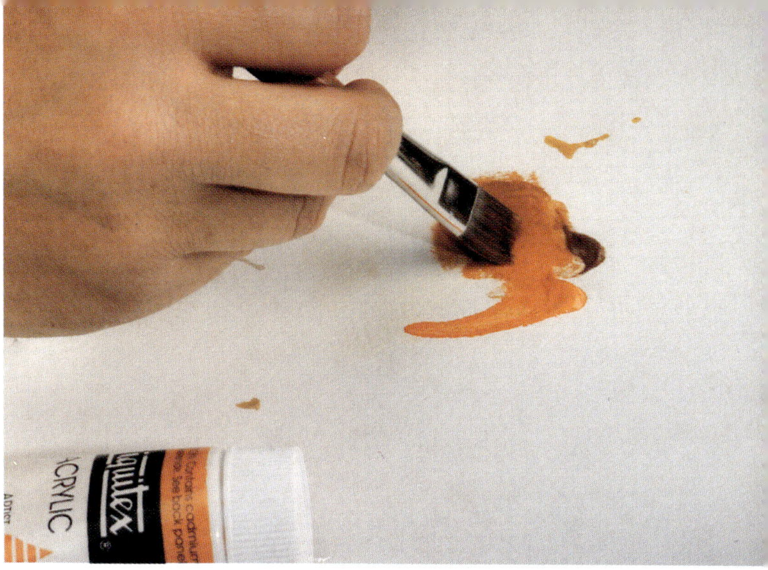

When the paint is dry I add a wash of a mixture of cadmium orange and raw sienna.

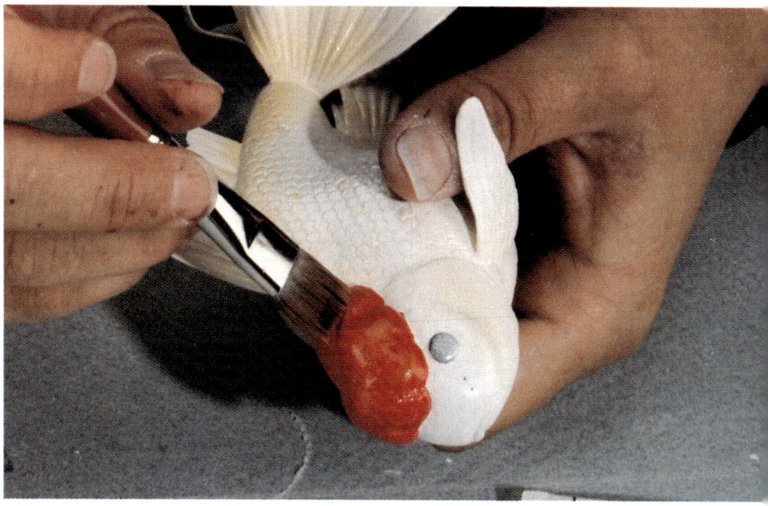

Brush lightly, hitting the high spots. This tones down the bright gill red.

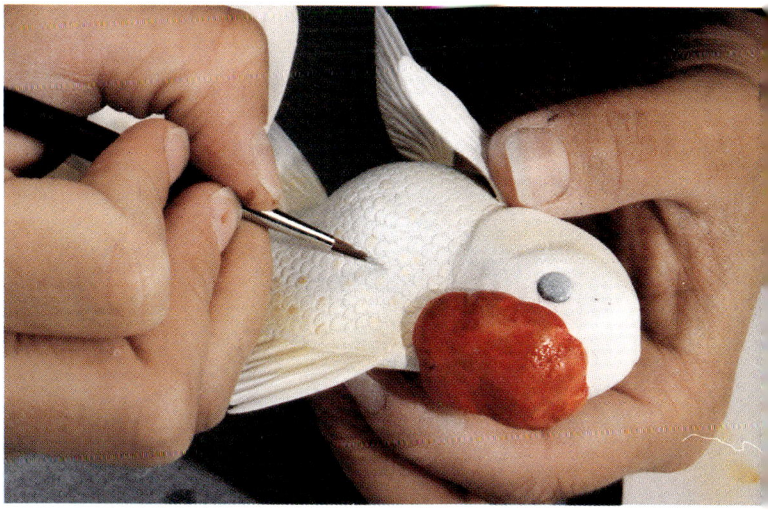

Next I paint a few randomly picked scales with iridescent white acrylic paint from the tube. This will not be seen until it catches the light.

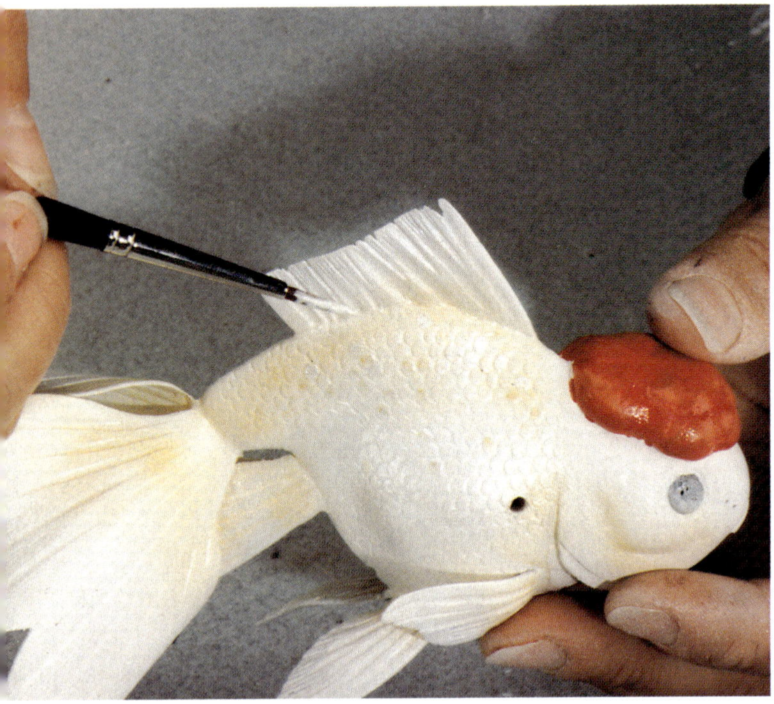

You can see the result most clearly in the areas that were airbrushed in light gold.

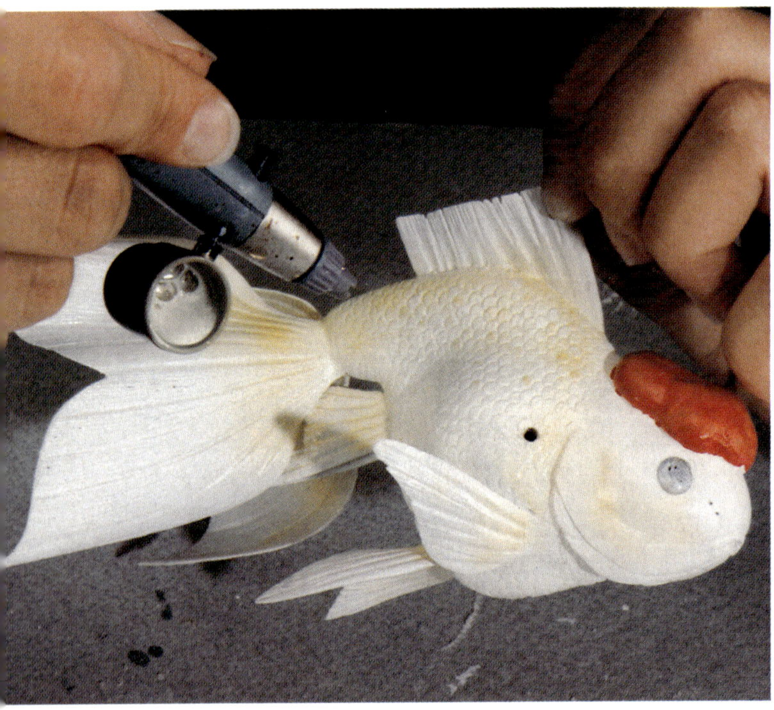

I spray the white areas of the fish with a shimmering gold, a paint that reflects light in only one direction, giving the carving a very natural look. This also softens the gold areas.

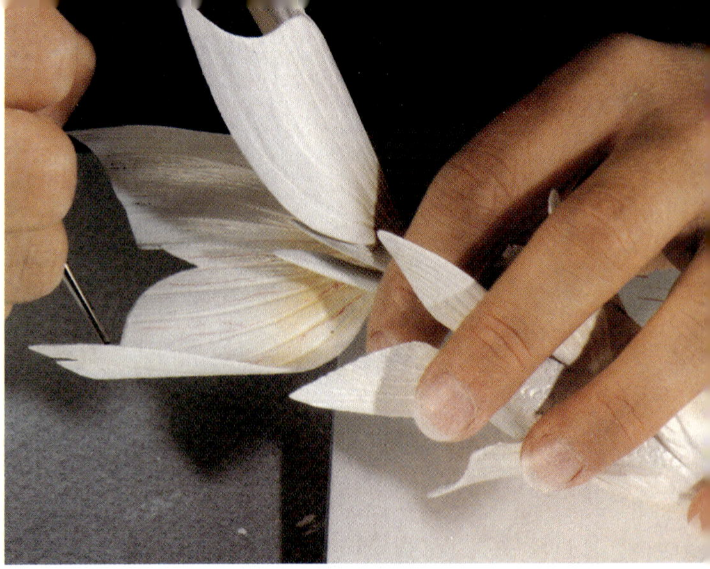

In the caudal fin I paint some very fine broken red lines in some of the veins.These should fade out before they reach the trailing edge. Paint the inside...

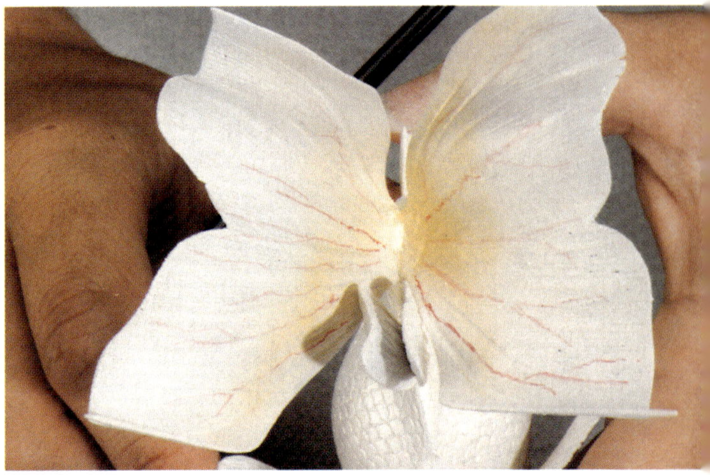

for this result...

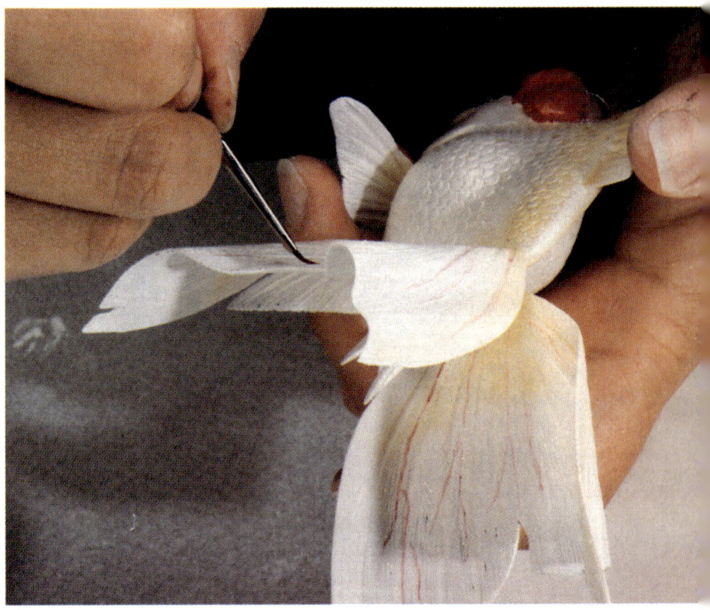

and the outside...

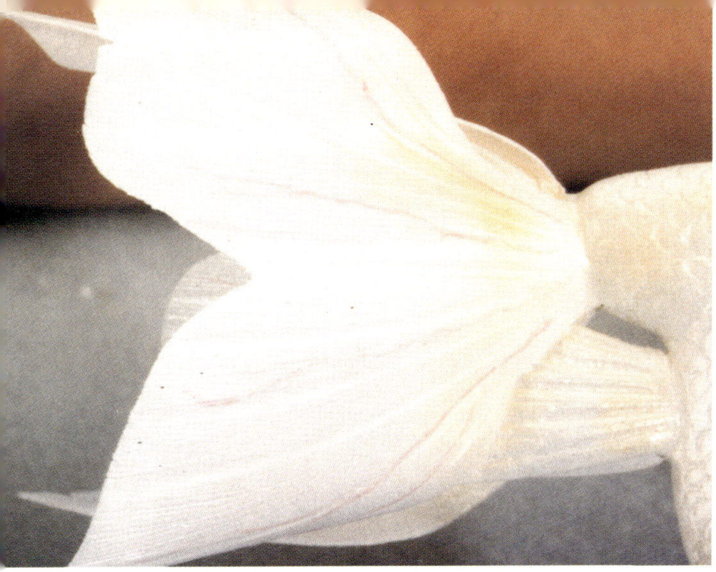

for this.

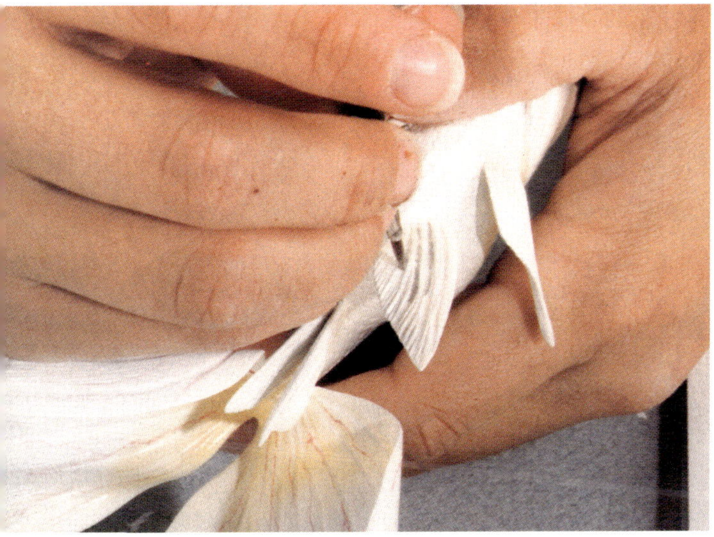

The final painting step uses a wash of Payne's gray to give the illusion of transparency to the fins. This is done by light painting the area between the rays. Start at a place that will not be noticeable to check your color.

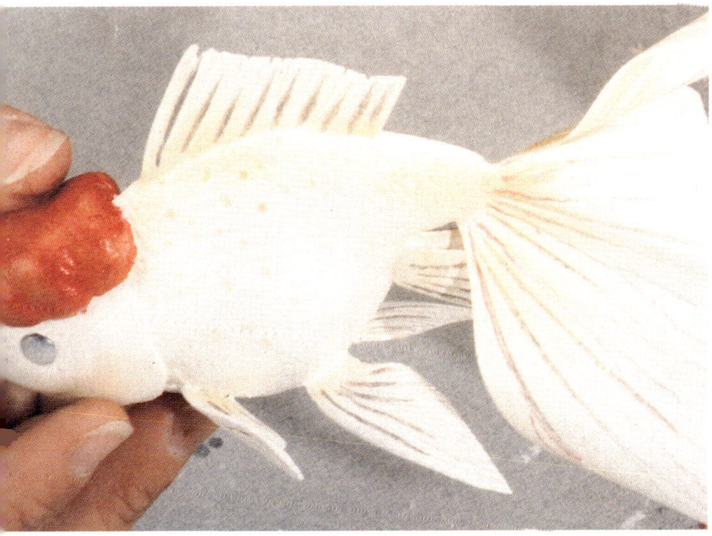

The result.

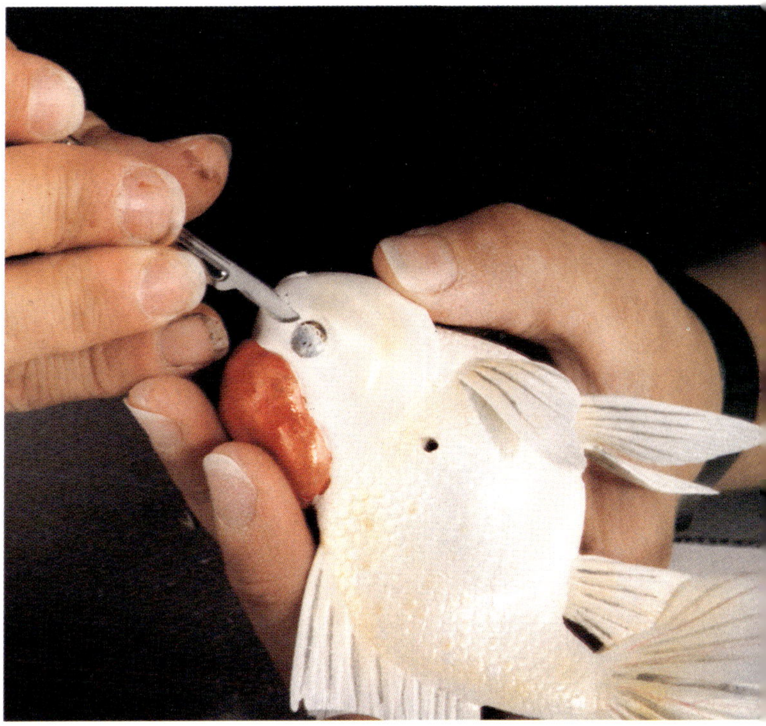

Carefully clean the eyes.

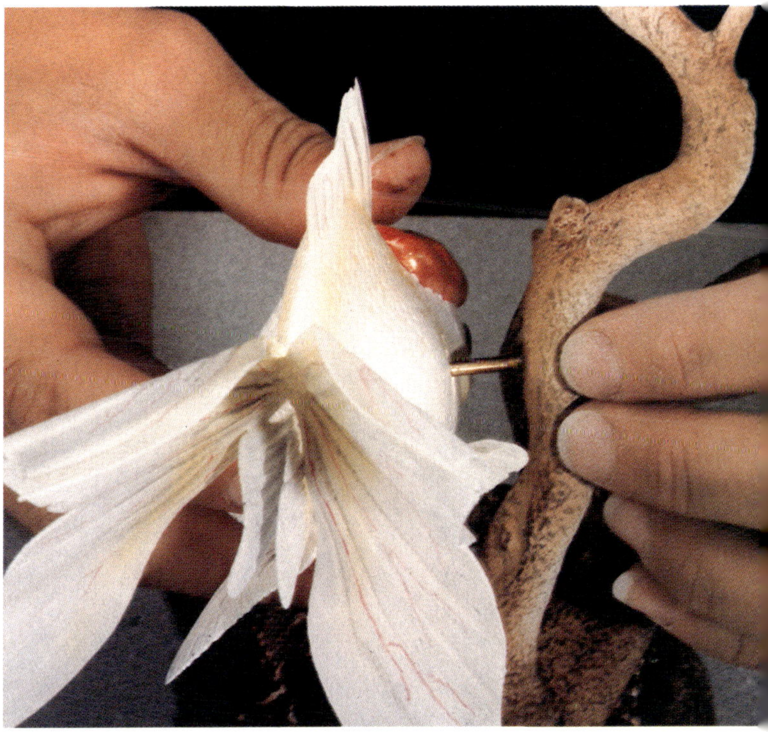

Glue it onto the habitat...

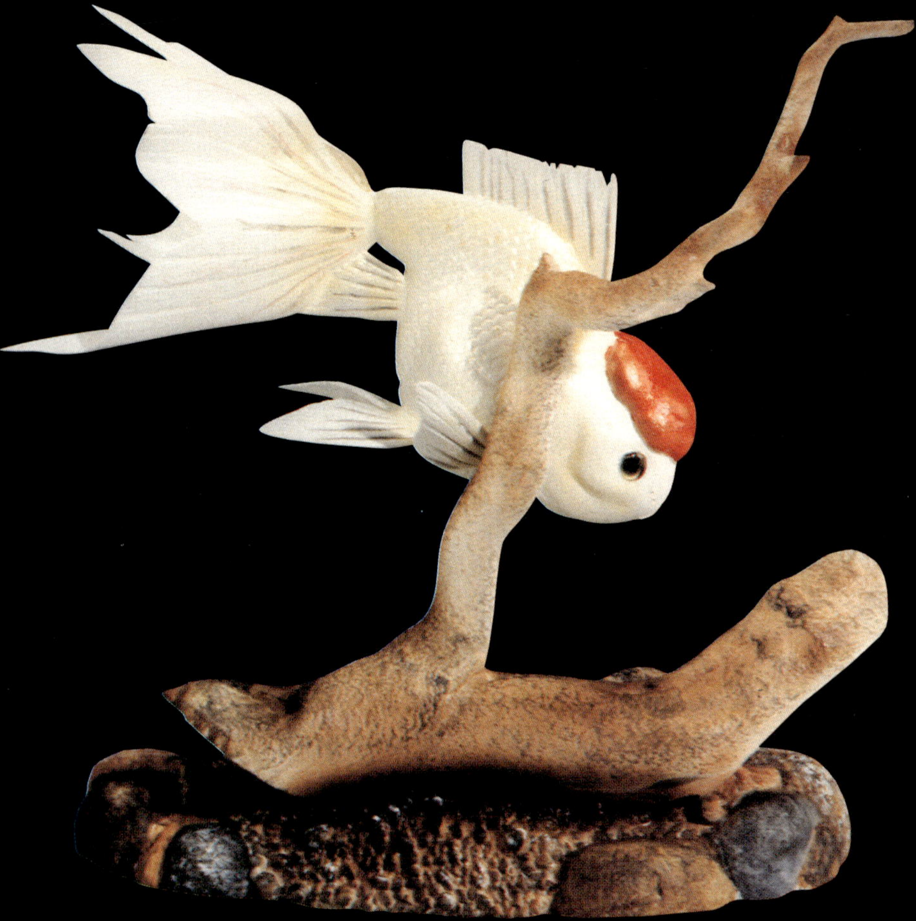

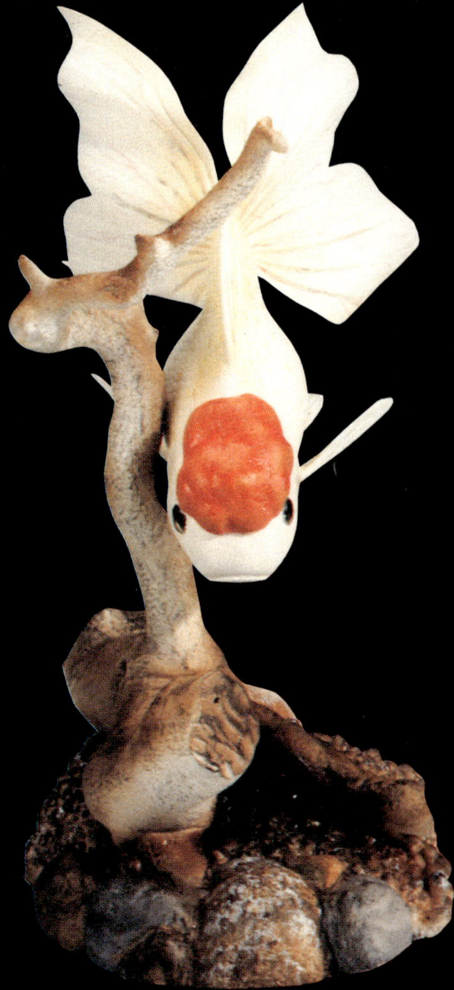

and it is done!

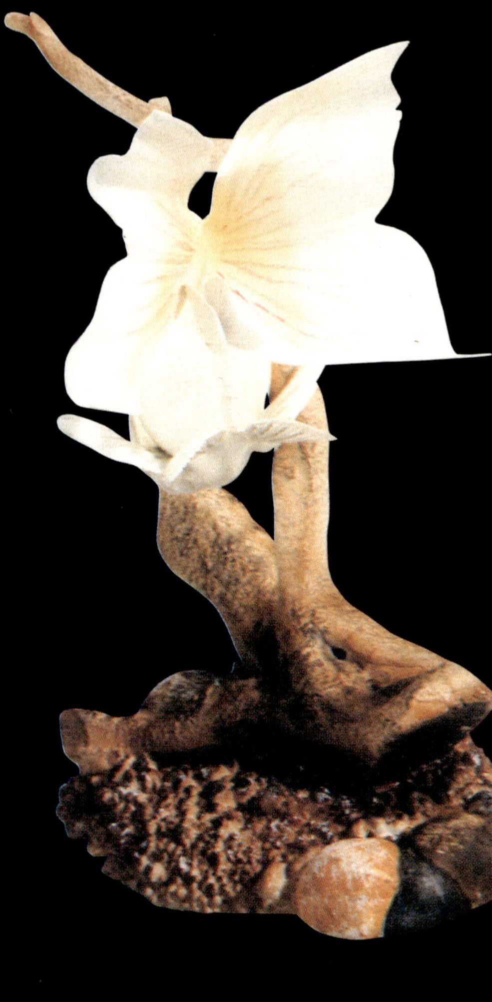

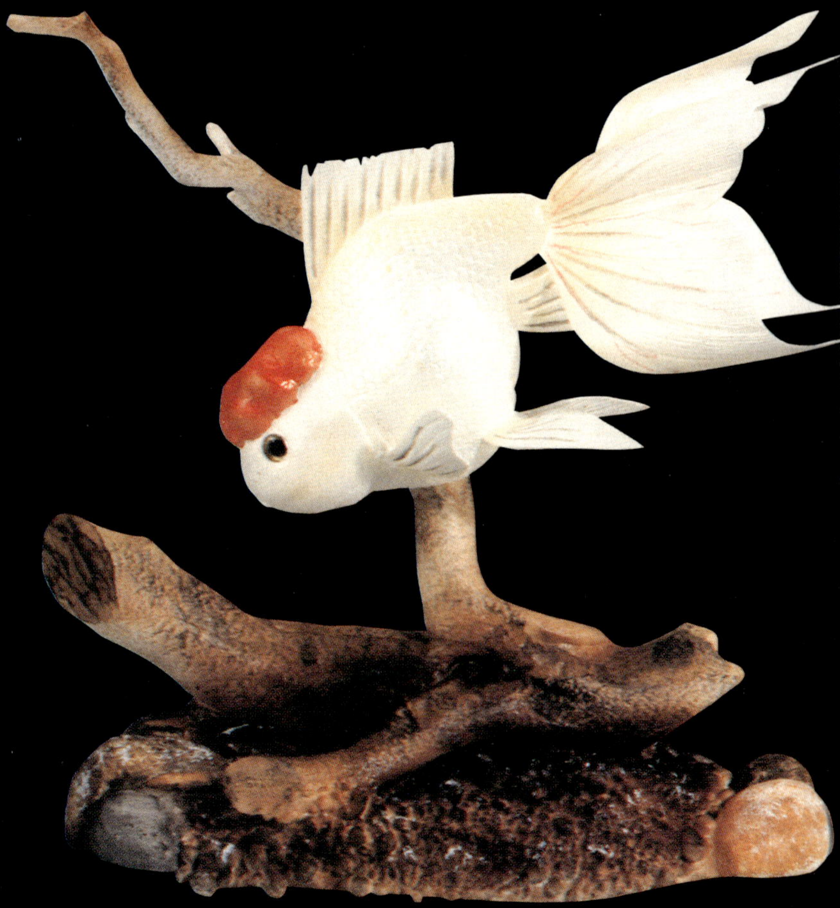

Fresh Water Angelfish

Pterophyllum scalare

CHARACTERISTICS

Coloration

* The natural coloration is brownish silver with several dark vertical bands that cross the body and enter the dorsal and anal fins. There are, however, many color variations.
* Four major dark bands
* Some secondary bands on the head
* Reddish spots on the back
* A red spot in the eye.
* The extended rays of the pelvic fins are bluish-white

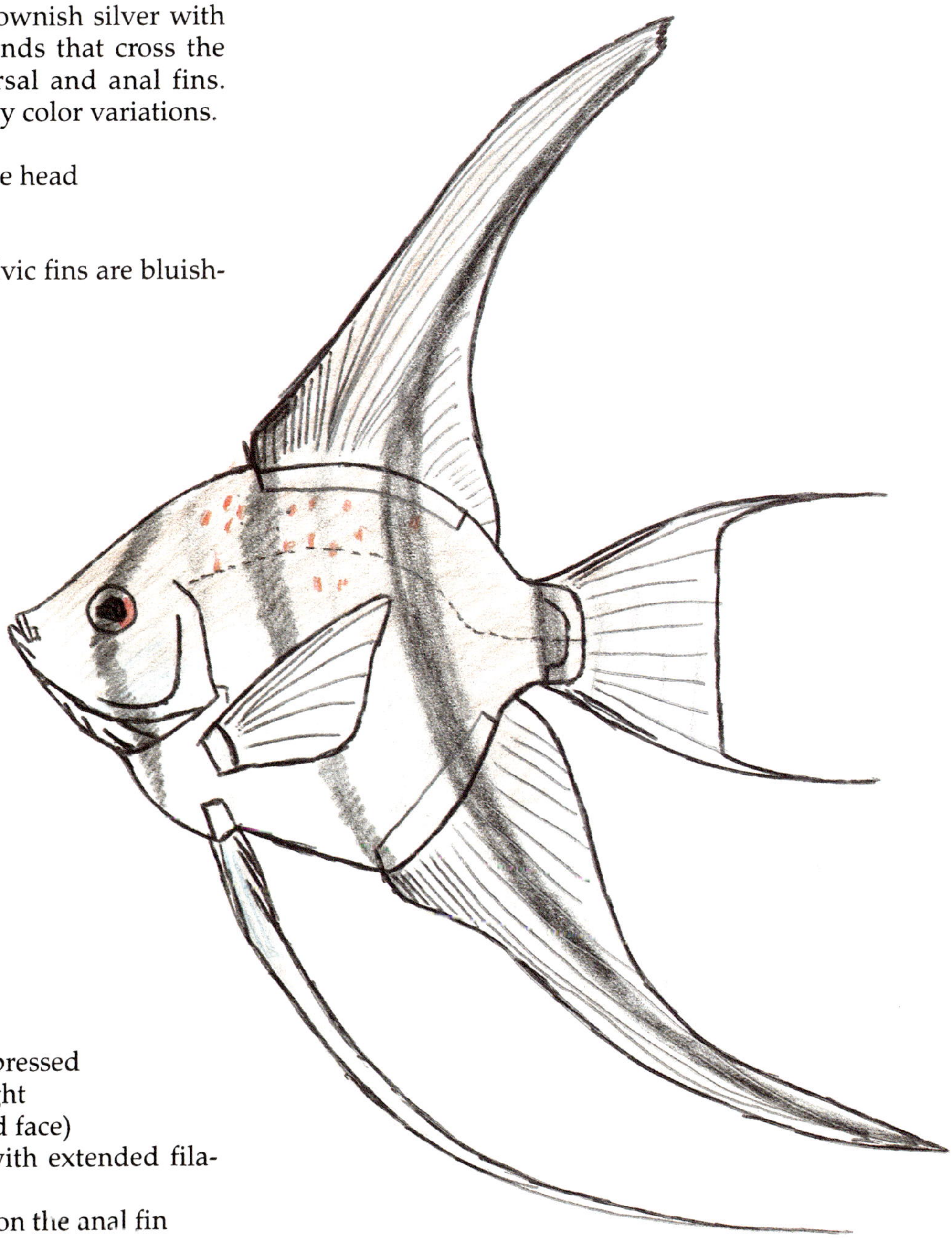

Physical Characteristics

* Disc-like body, laterally compressed
* Body 1/3 longer than its height
* Notch in the forehead (dished face)
* Long dorsal and anal fins with extended filaments
* 11 spines on the dorsal fin, 5 on the anal fin
* Thread-like pelvic fins
* The rays at the top and the bottom of the tail (caudal fin) are extended
* The tail rays split only once, dorsal and anal fin rays only occasionally split, and pectoral fin rays rarely split
* Juvenile fins end more bluntly

Fresh Water Angelfish

Pterophyllum scalare

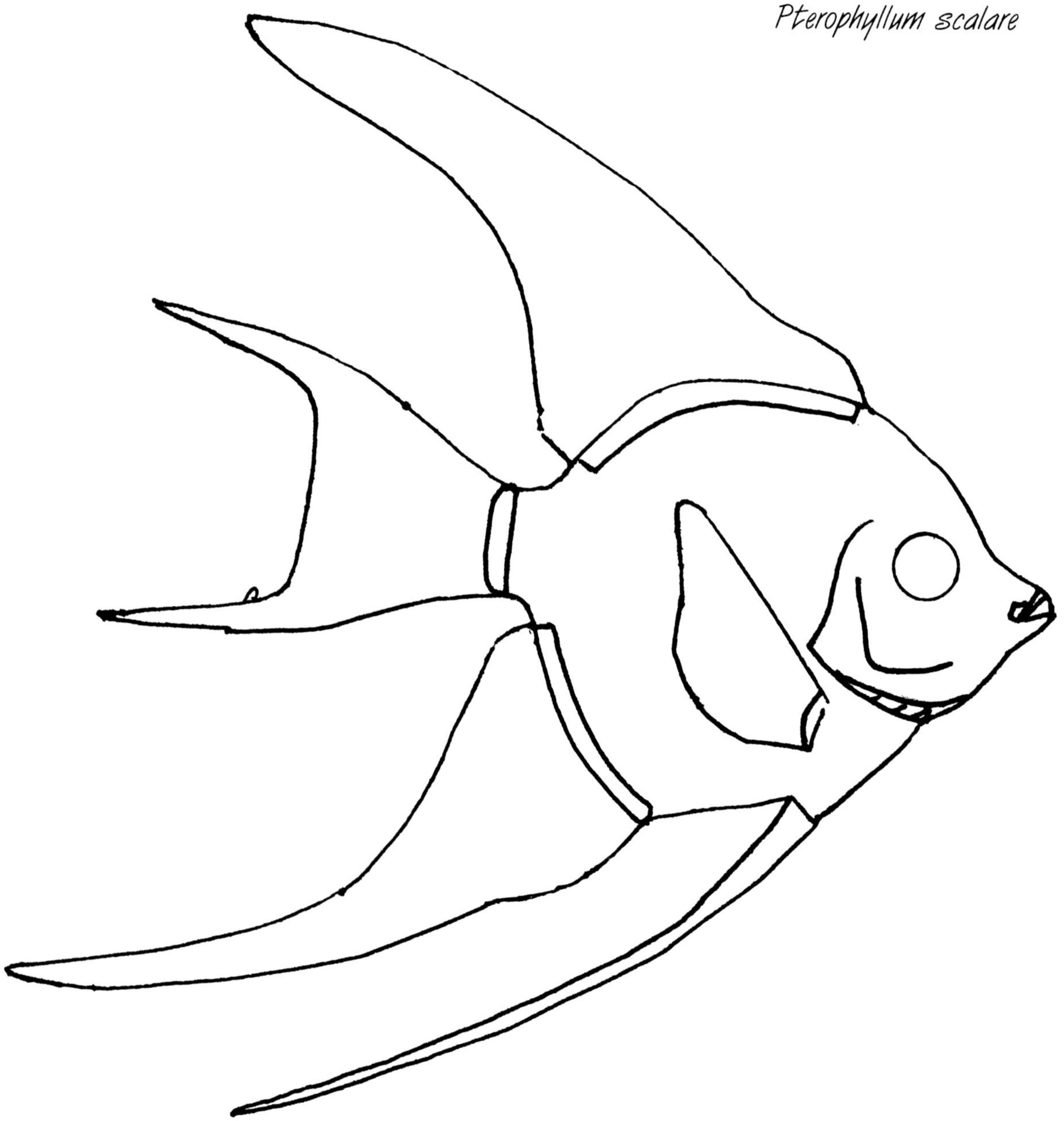

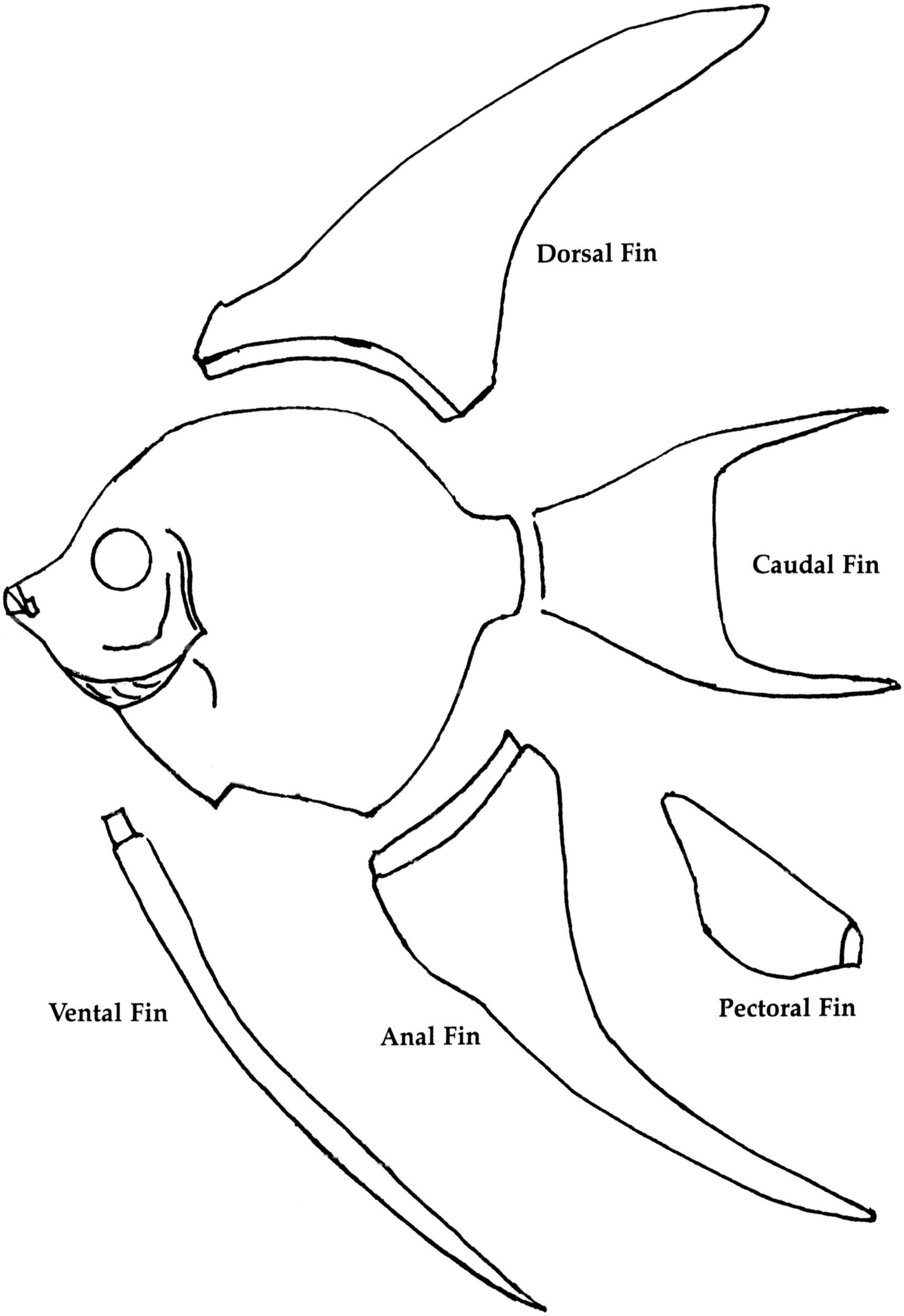
Dorsal Fin
Caudal Fin
Ventral Fin
Anal Fin
Pectoral Fin

Carving the Fresh Water Angelfish

This "peace-loving" community fish is native to South America. It is found in the Amazon, Negro, and Orinoco river systems. Its habitat is in the rivers' reed beds. It is on the leaves of the aquatic plants that the Angelfish lay their eggs. Although they are very difficult to tell apart, both the males and females stand guard over the eggs until they hatch.

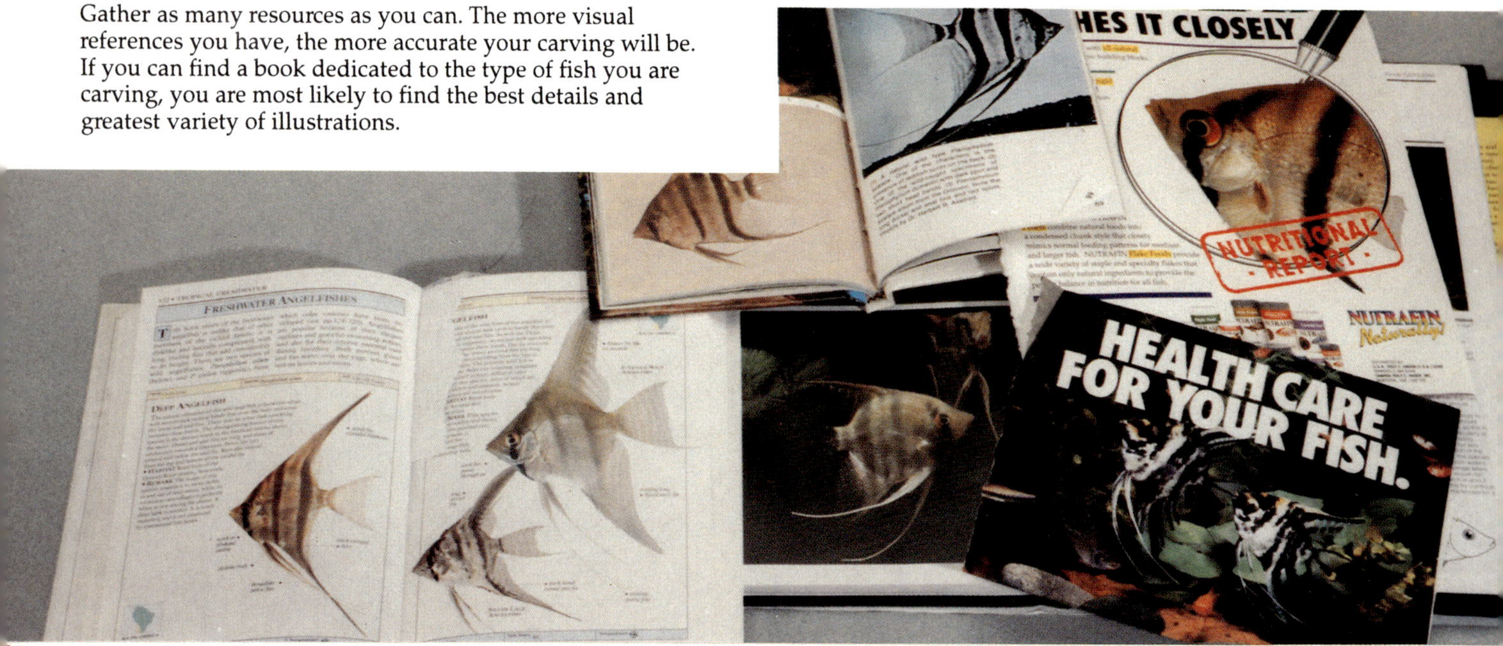

Gather as many resources as you can. The more visual references you have, the more accurate your carving will be. If you can find a book dedicated to the type of fish you are carving, you are most likely to find the best details and greatest variety of illustrations.

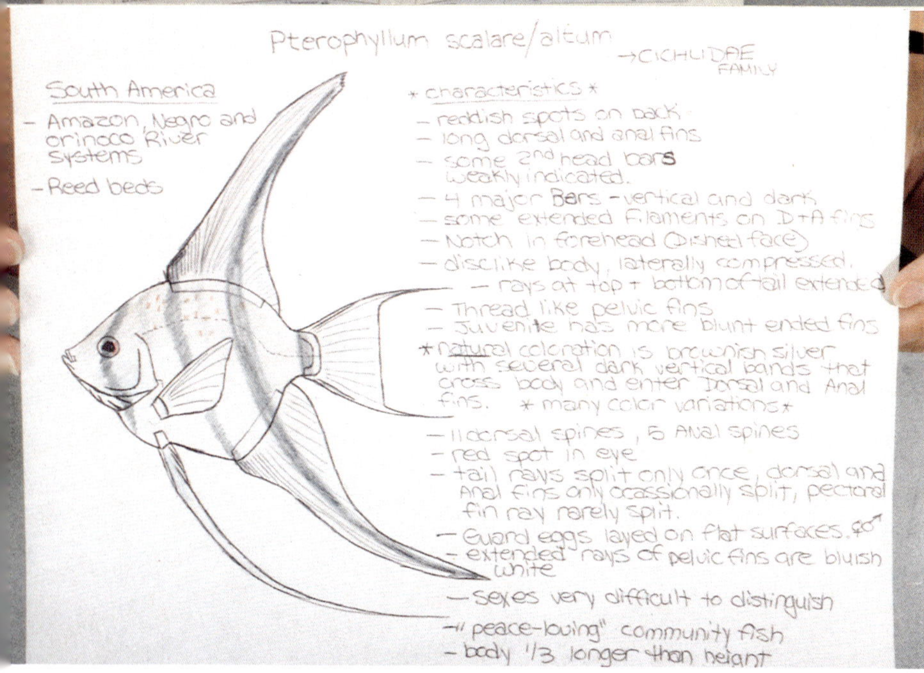

When preparing for a carving I try to develop a data sheet with as much information as I can glean, and a color pencil drawing of the fish.

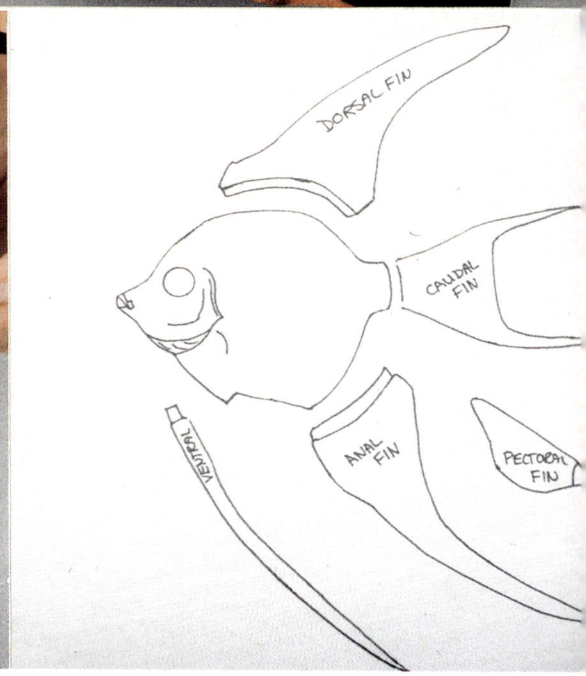

From the research I develop a basic pattern.

Opposite page:
I also keep an aquarium with examples of the fish I am carving. Photographs through the glass are nice referen

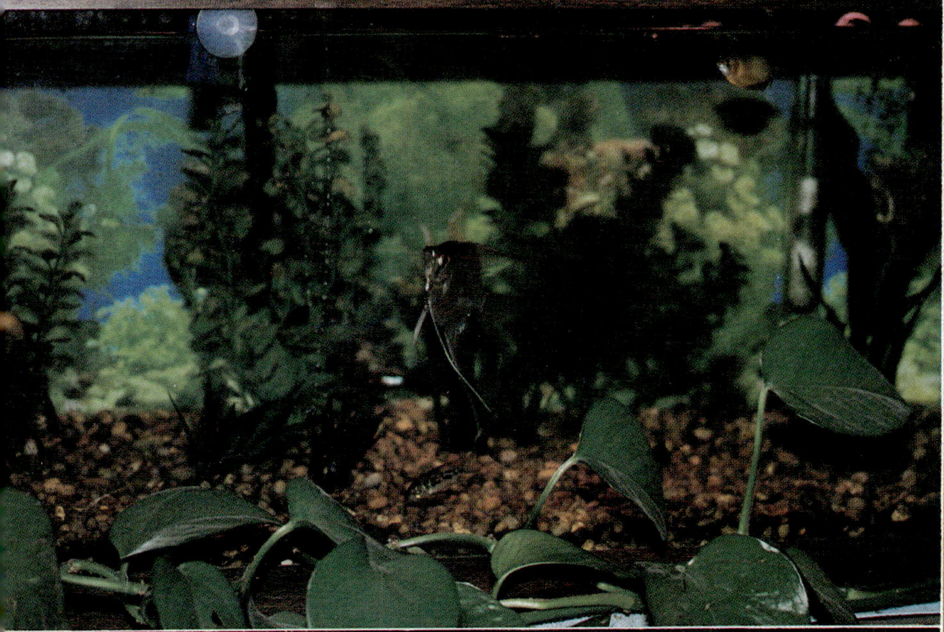

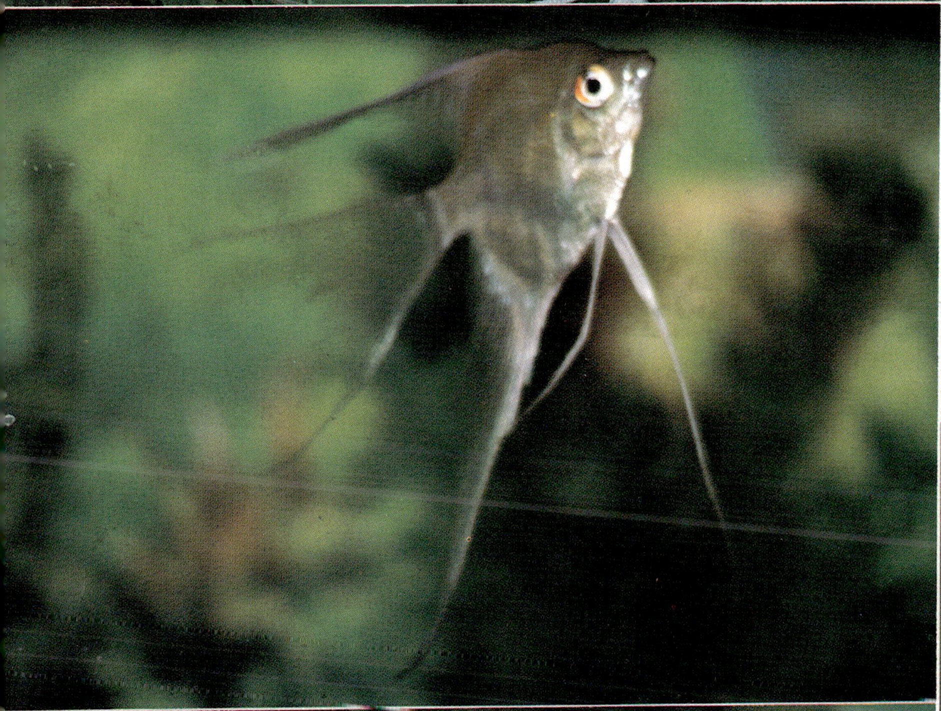

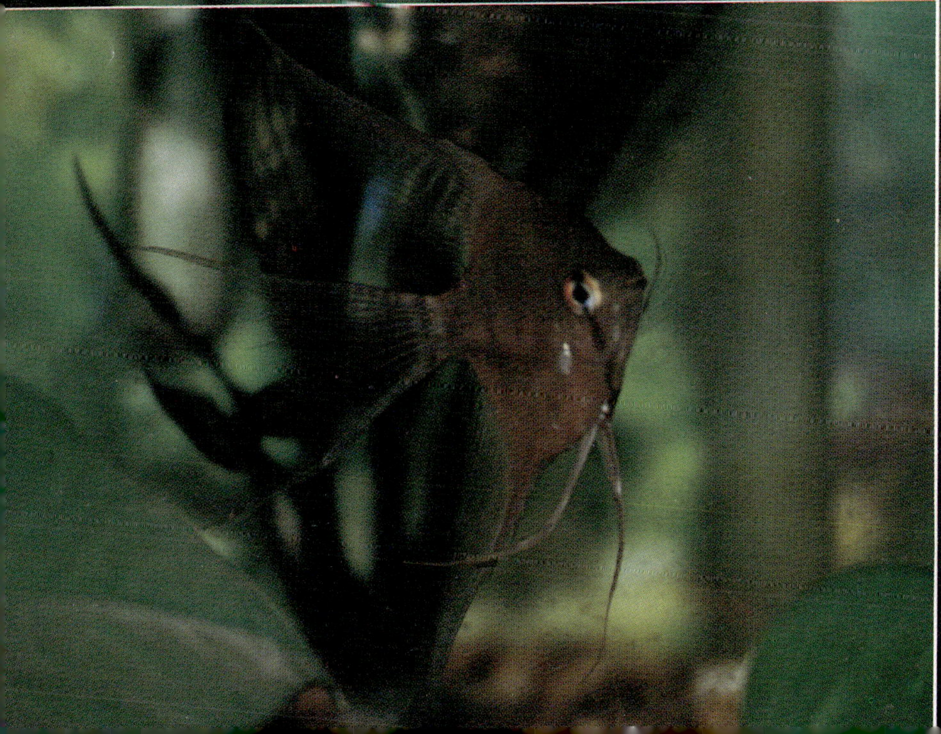

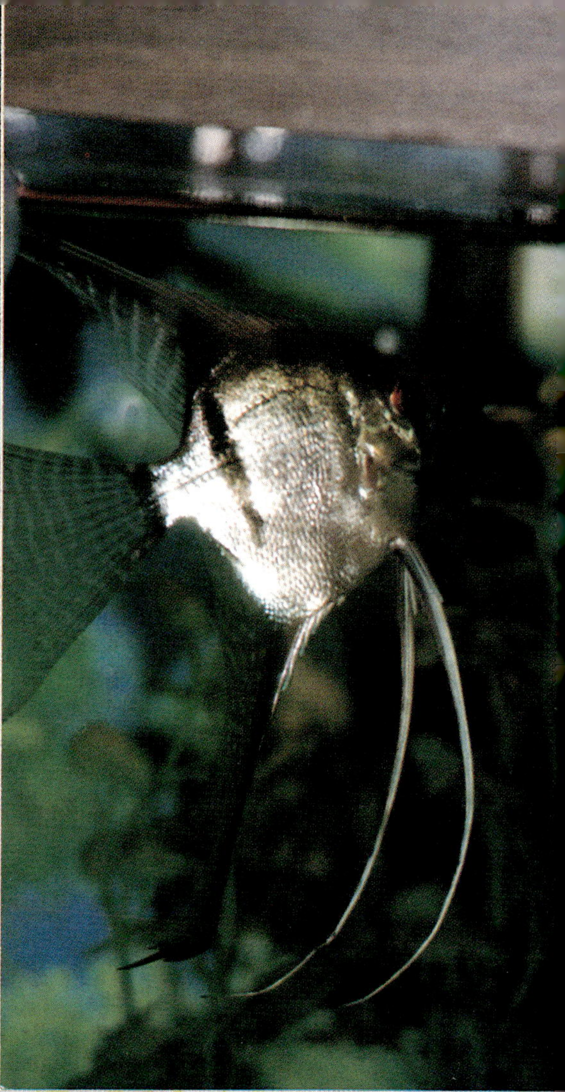

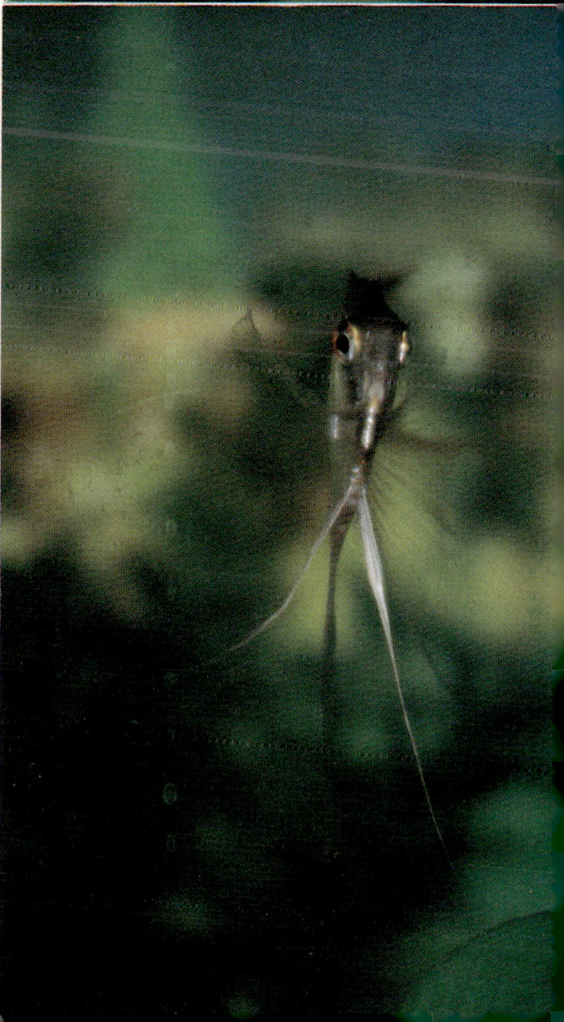

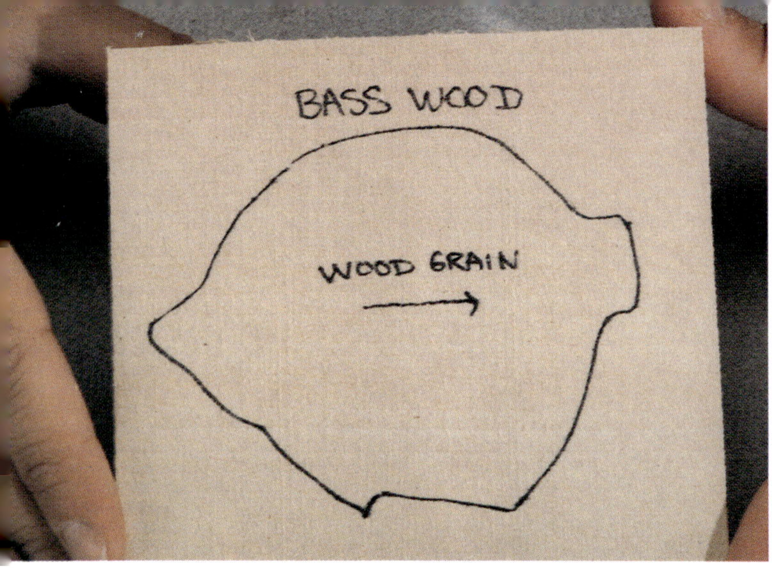

The body pattern is laid on a piece of bass wood 4" x 4" x 1". Draw in the body side view, which will be cut first.

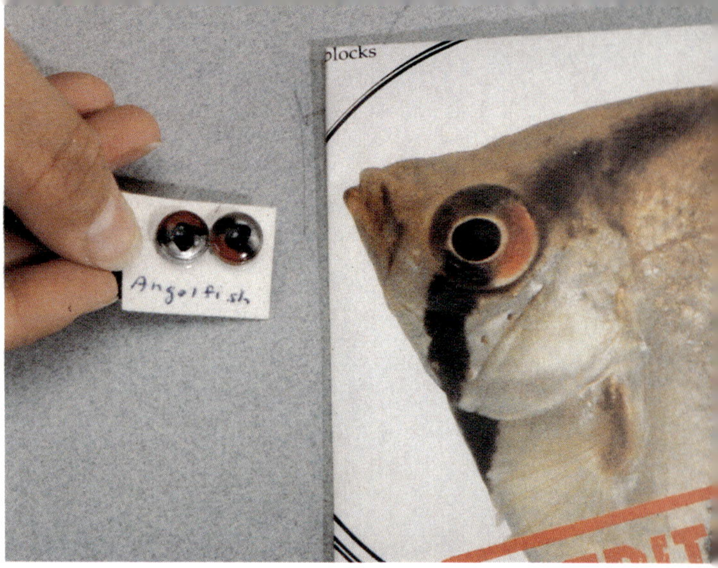

Order your eyes early. I sent Tohickon this picture, told them the size, and they custom-made the eyes. Custom-made eyes sell for about $4-5.

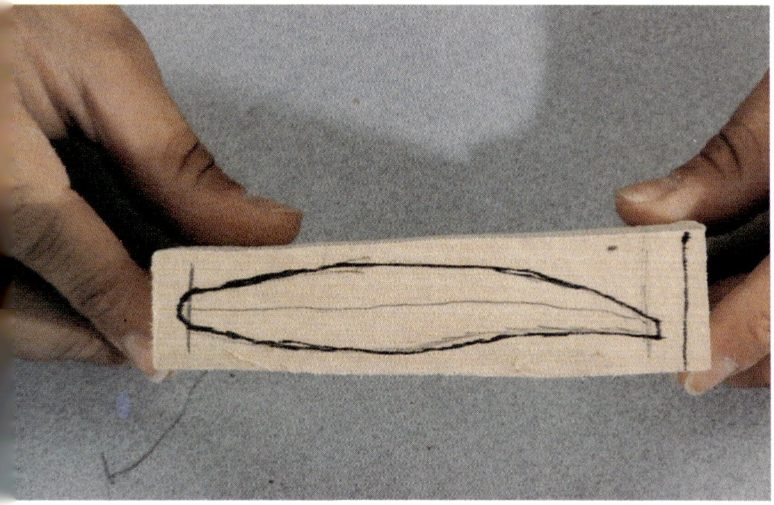

I also sketch the plane view to get an idea of how it will be situated in the wood.

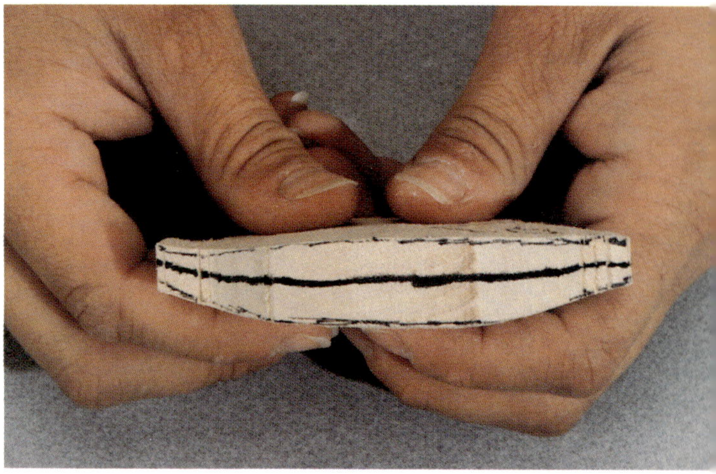

Cut the plane view on the bandsaw...

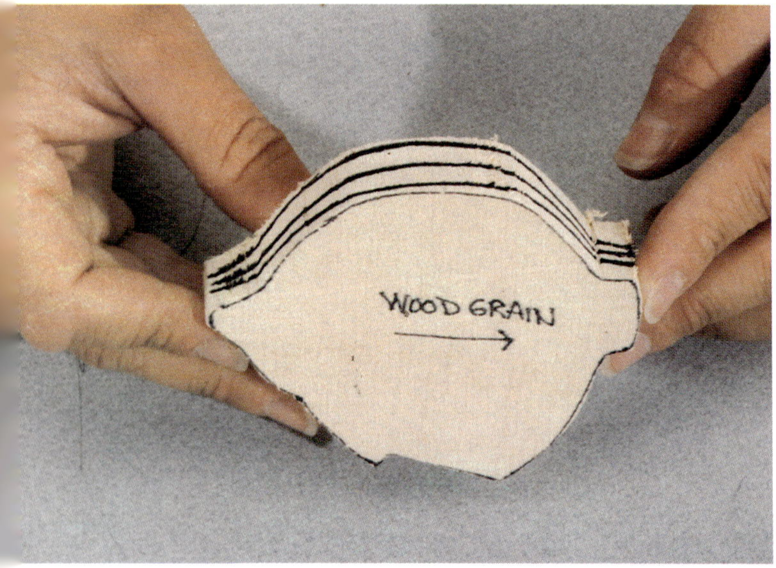

Cut the side view and redraw the plane view.

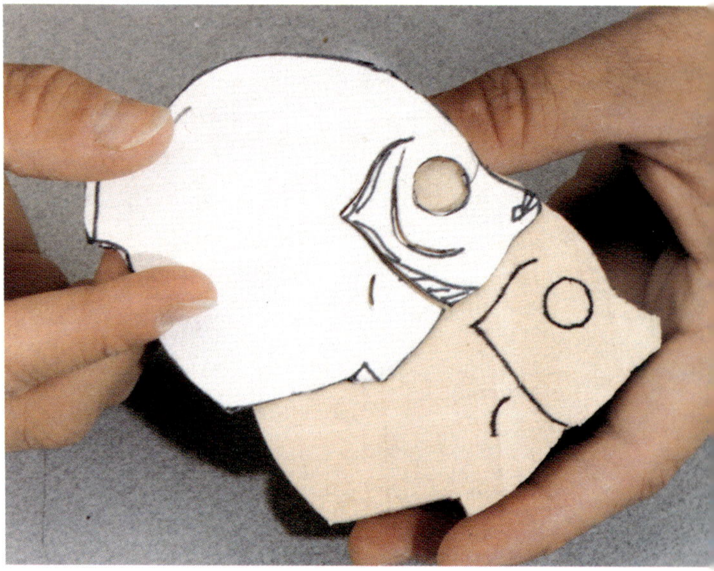

then use the pattern to draw in the details. Also draw a center line all around the edge.

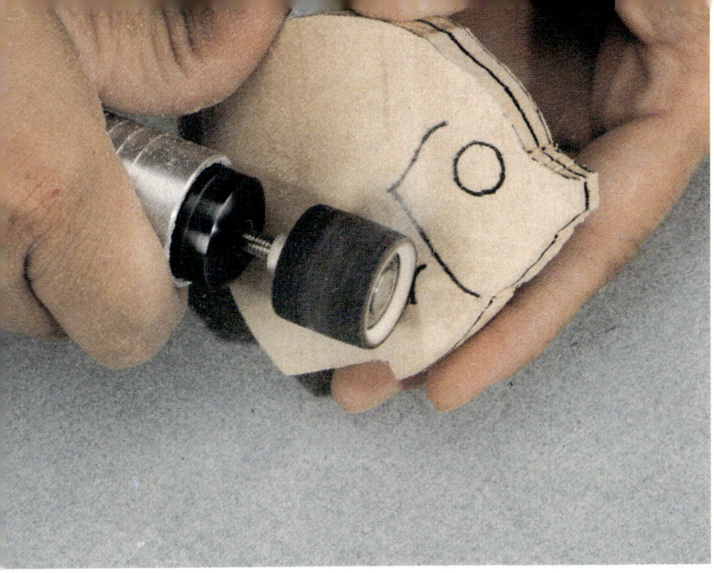

Use the sanding drum to relieve the body behind the pectoral fin joint.

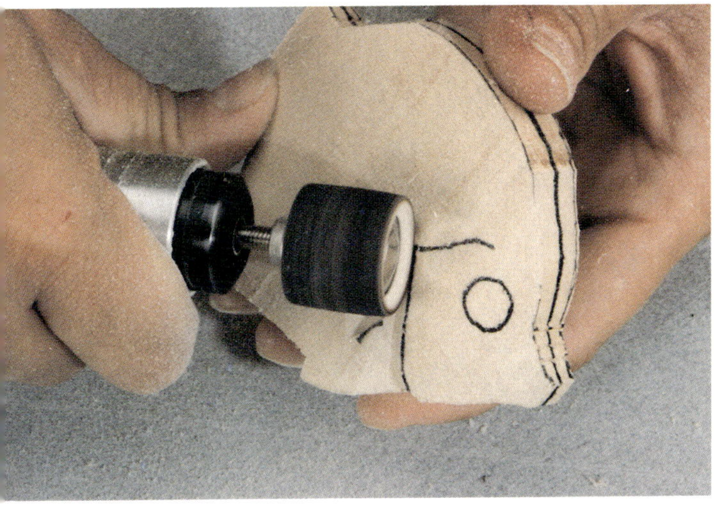

Do the same behind the gill plate, bottom and top.

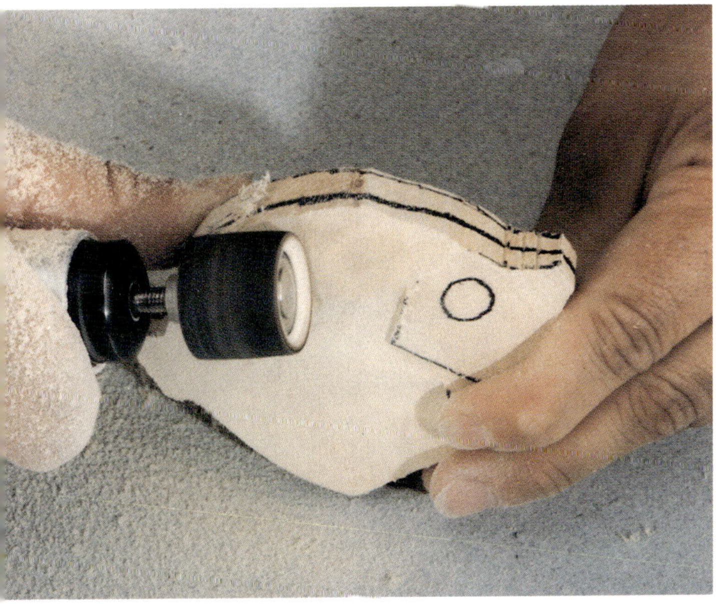

Continue using the drum to round the body at the edges.

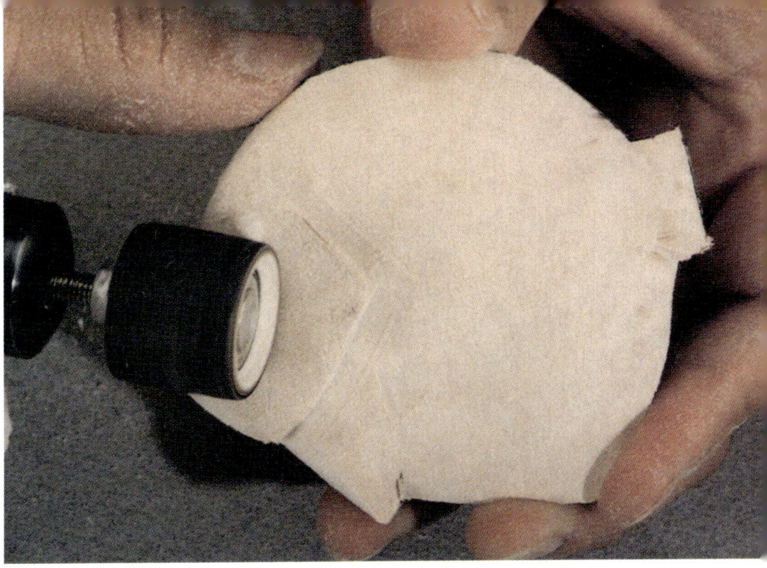

The result from the side...

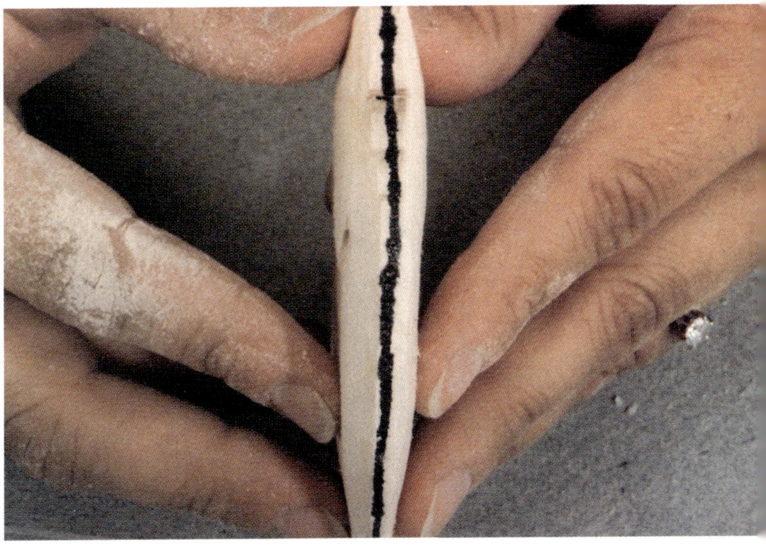

and the top. As you can see this is a very thin fish.

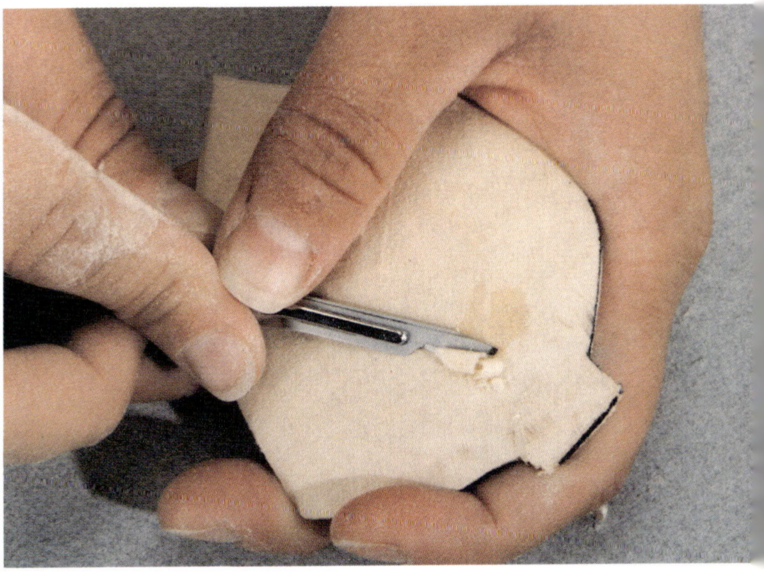

With the general shape established, smooth the surface with the knife.

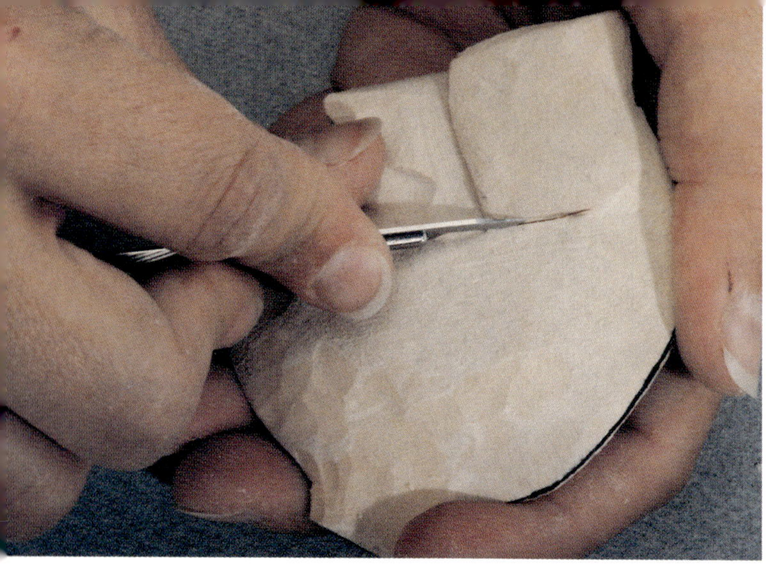

Cut stops along the trailing edge of the gill plate, top...

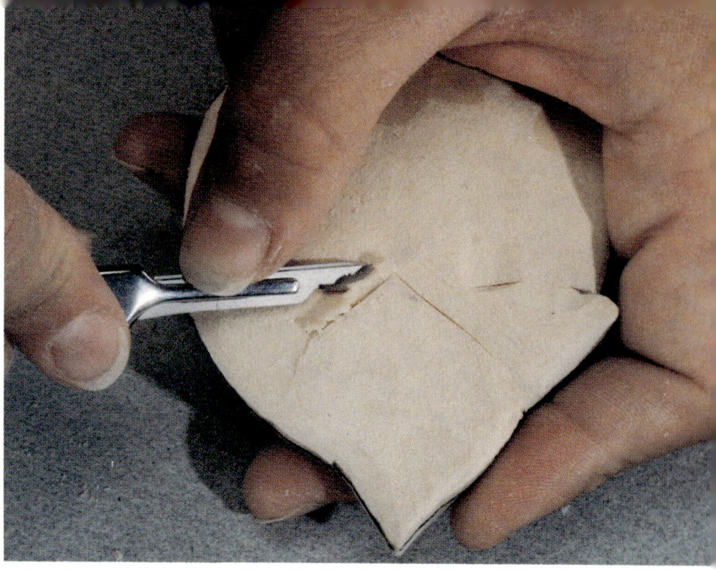

Trim back to the stops from the body at the gill...

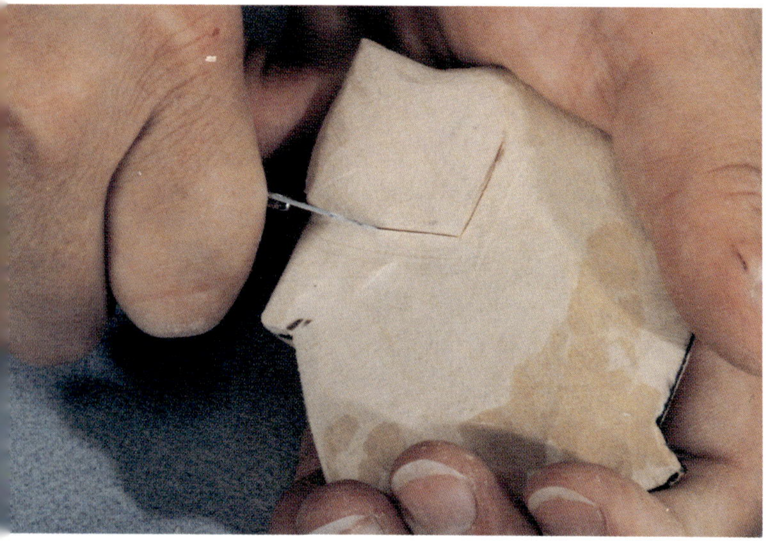

and bottom.

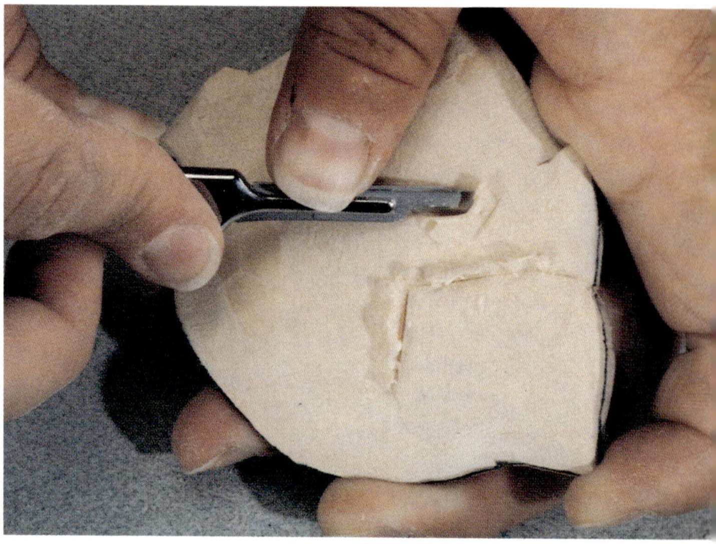

and the fin butt.

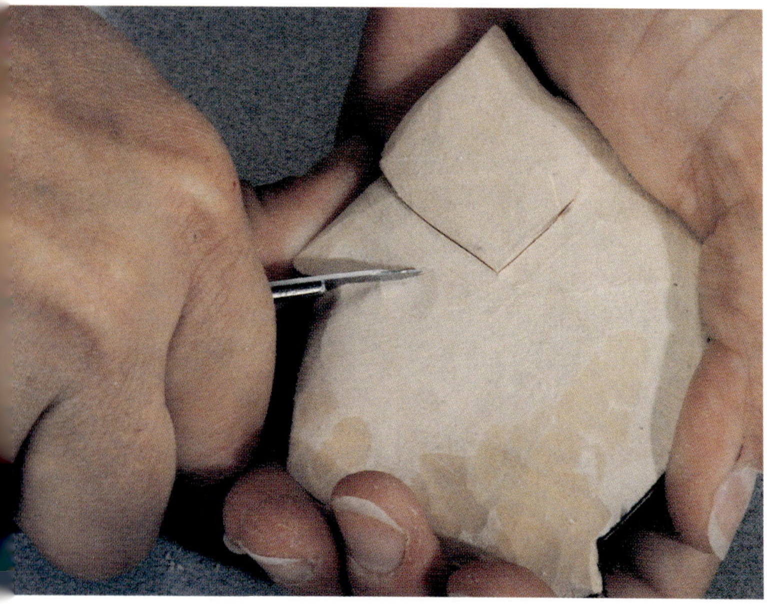

Also cut a stop at the edge of the pectoral fin butt.

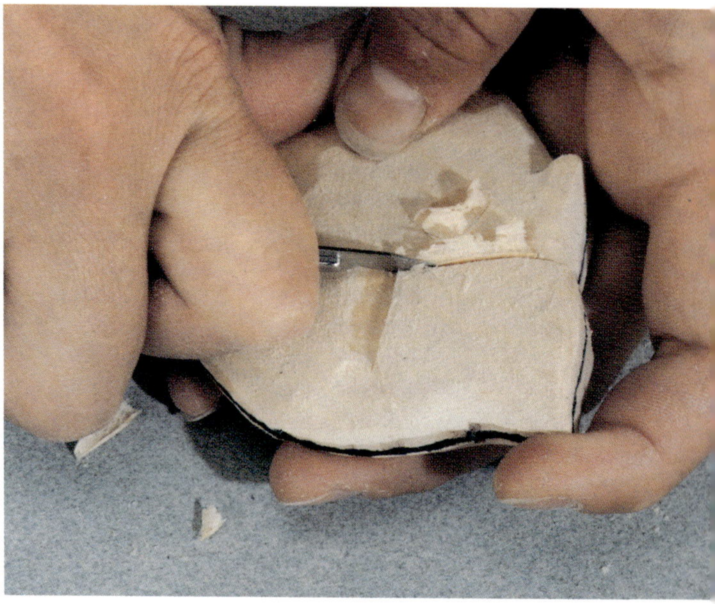

Trim off the shaving.

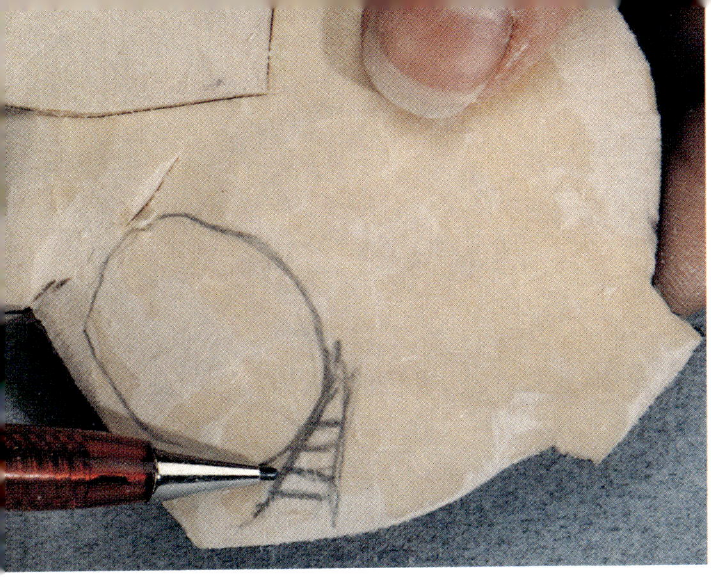

The oval, drawn here, is the area of the gut, and bulges out. The triangular area behind it is the visceral groove, and is concave.

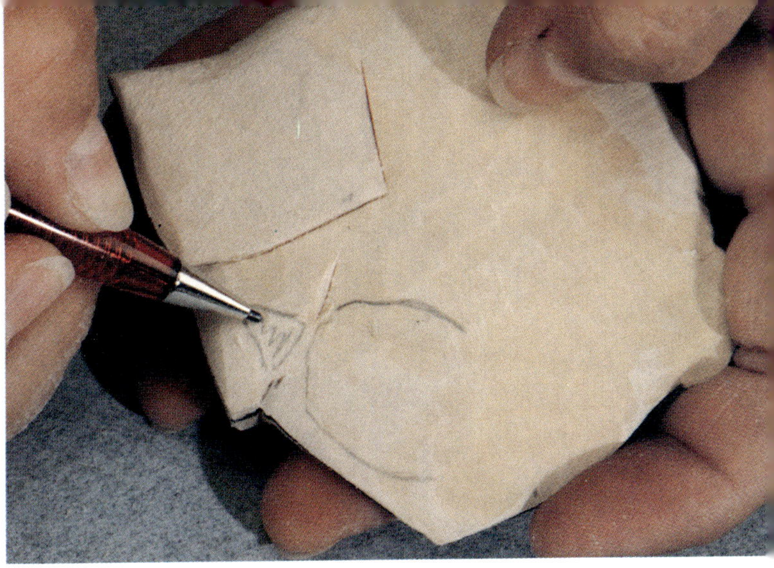

I will define the muscle of the pectoral fin by taking wood out between the pectoral an ventral fin.

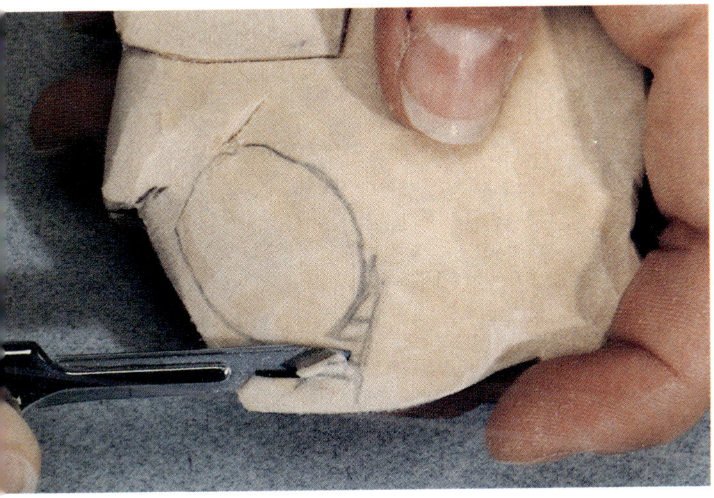

With a scooping cut, shave a small amount of wood from the groove.

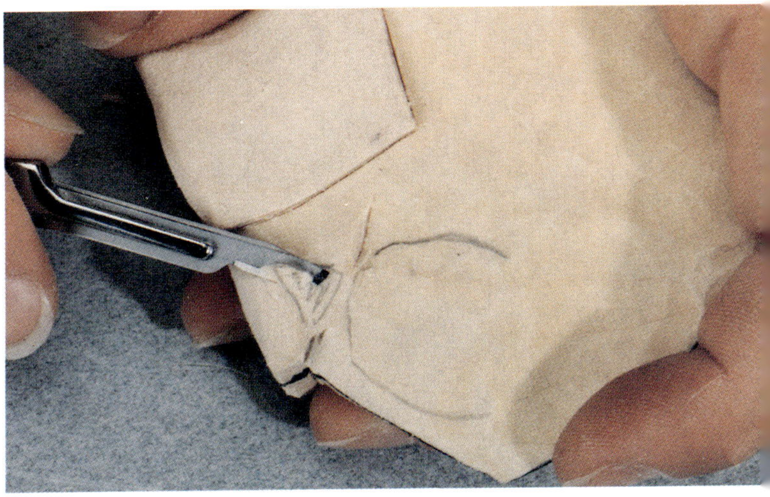

Use a scooping cut to slightly dish out this area.

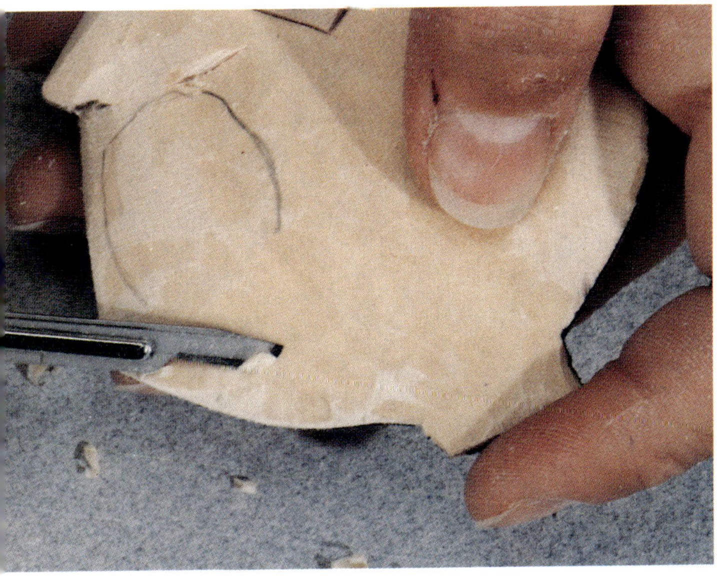

Blend the groove toward the back of the fish.

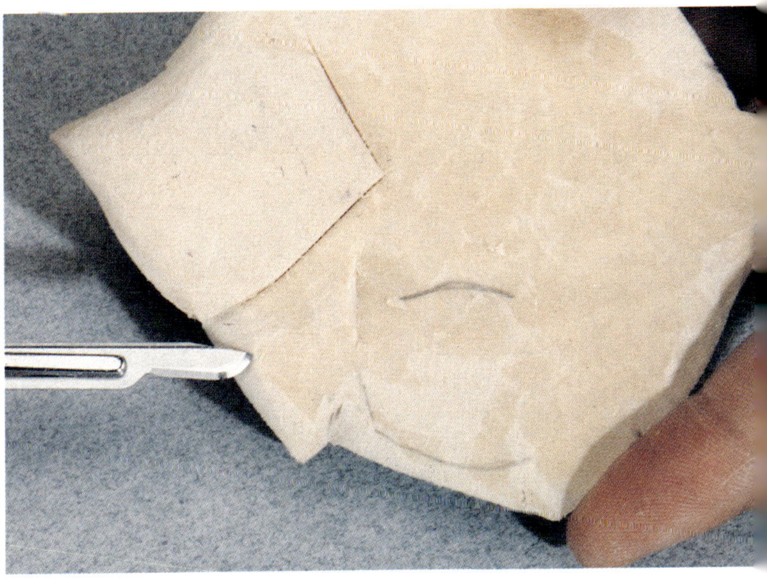

The result.

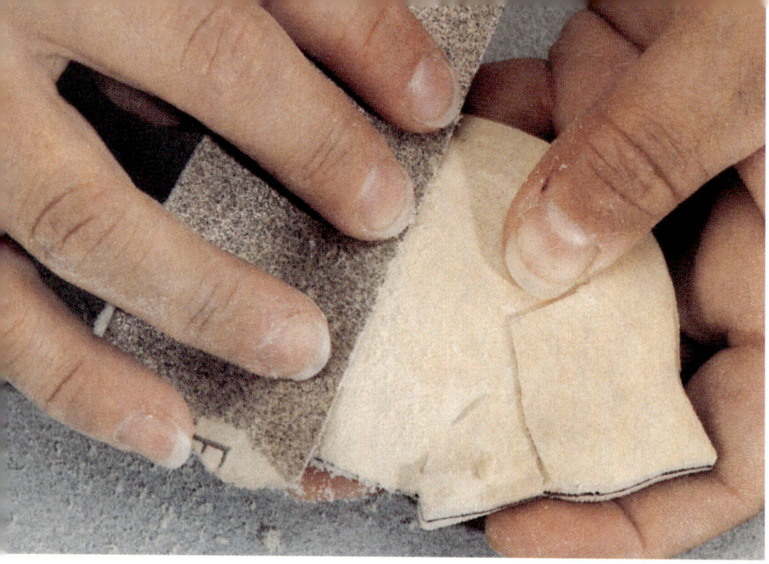

Sand the body, beginning with medium grit paper...

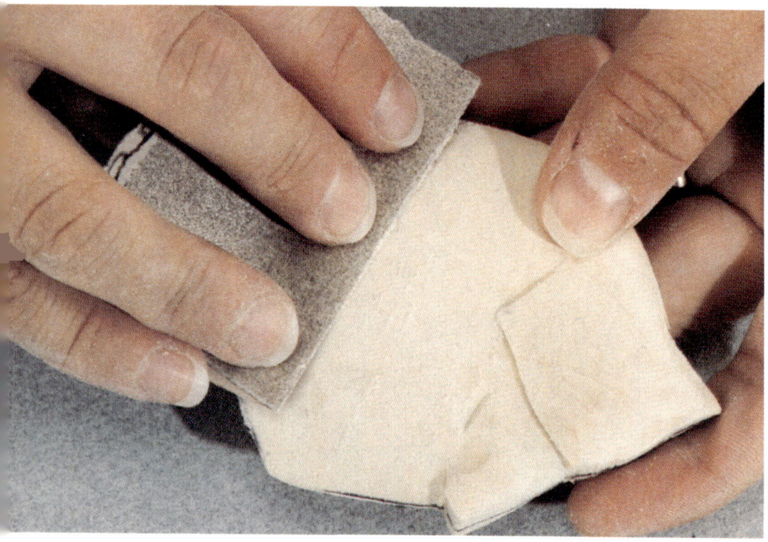

and finishing with a fine grit.

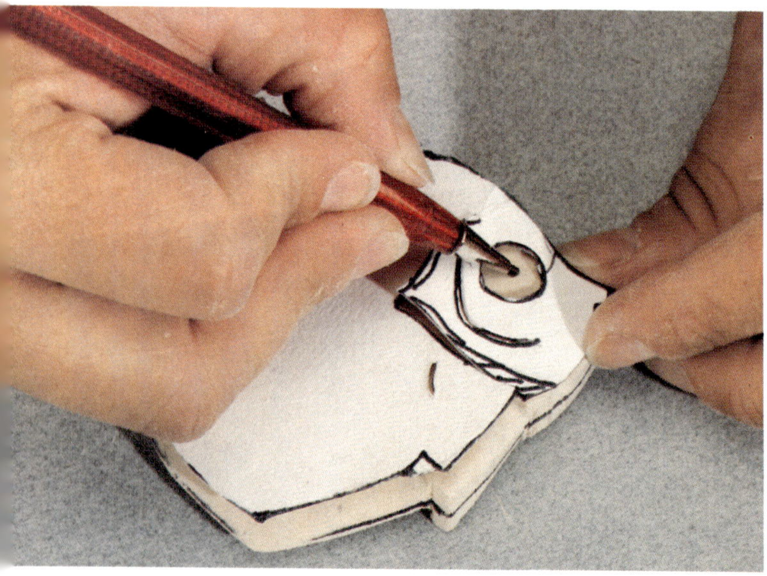

When you are finished sanding lay the pattern on the fish and mark the center of the eye.

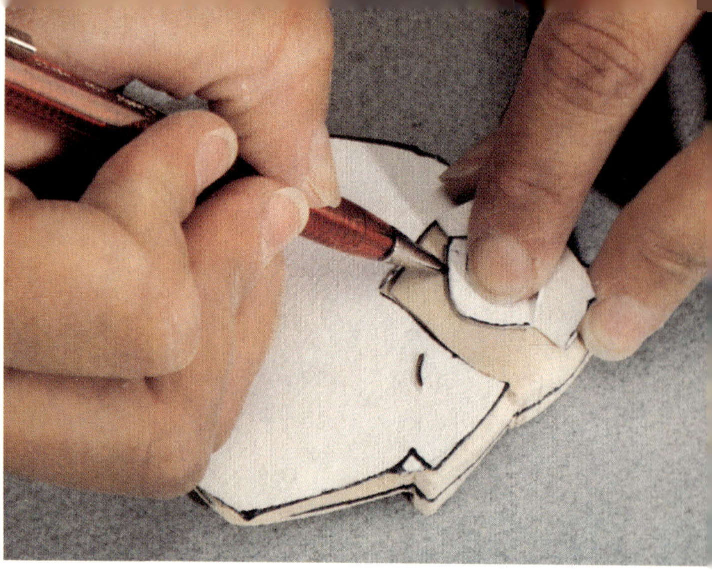

Fold back the pattern to draw the preopercle.

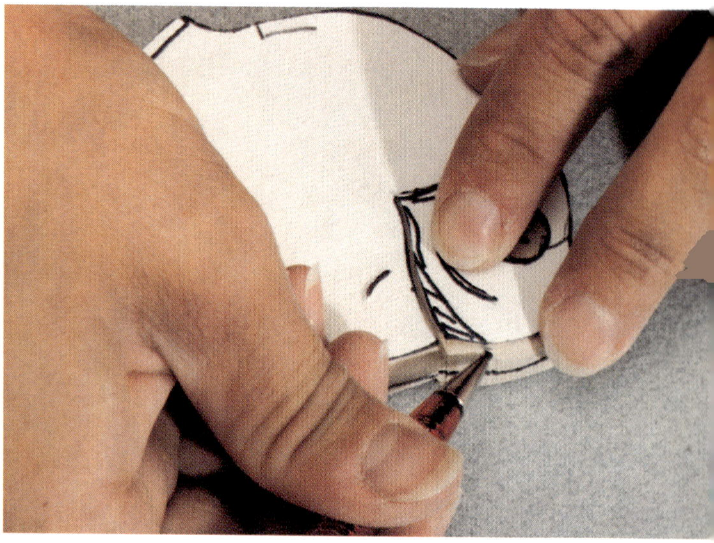

At the bottom of the gill mark where the branchiostegal rays begin.

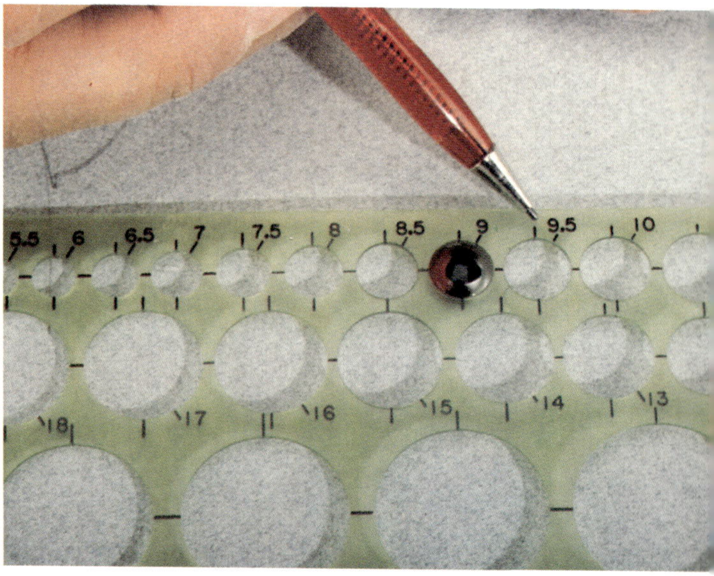

Size the eye. It is a 9mm eye, so I will use a 9.5mm template.

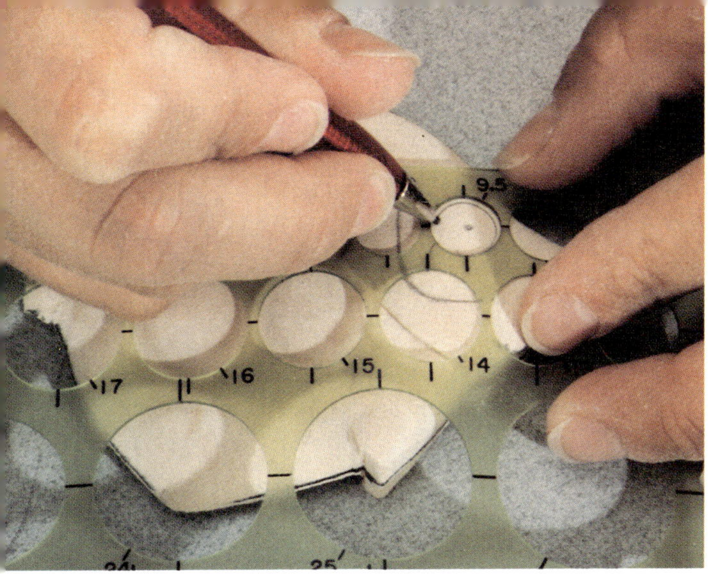

Center the dot in the template and draw the hole.

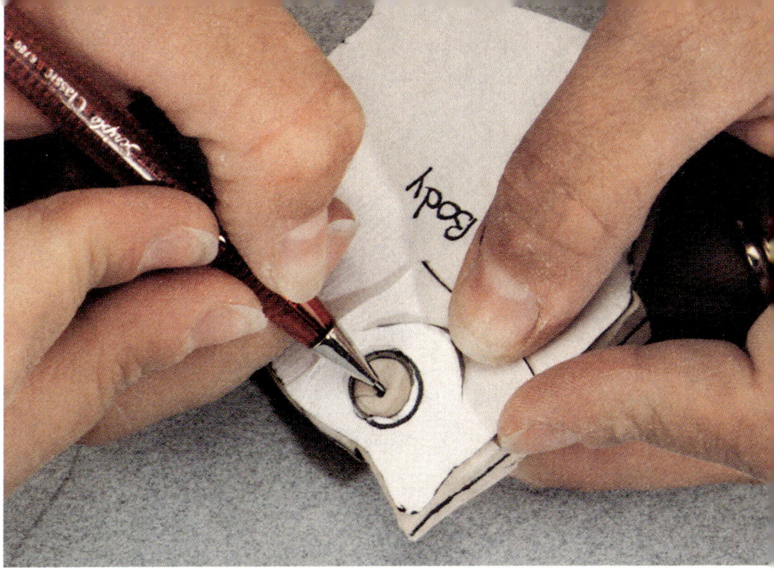

Then place the pattern on the other side and mark the center of the eye on the line you drew. Use the same template to draw the circumference of the eye. This is not a fool-proof method, and may require some adjustments.

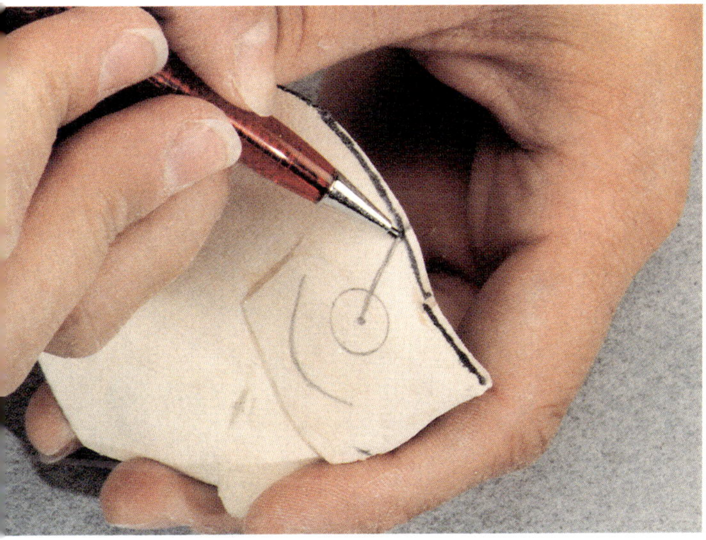

To locate the eye on the other side of the head carry a line up from the drawn eye...

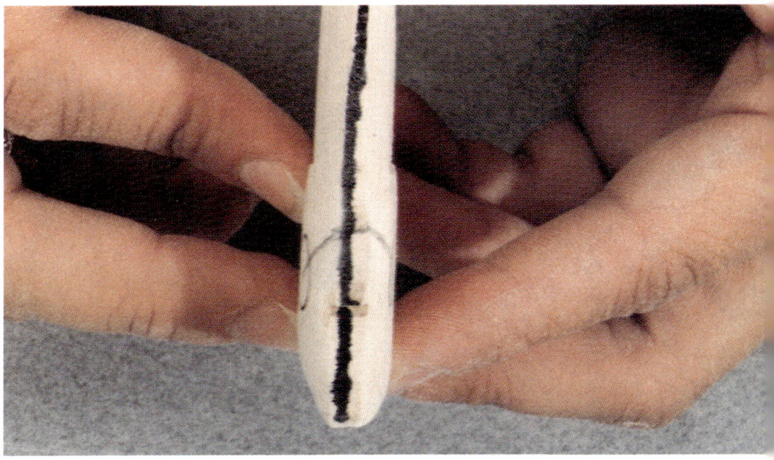

By looking from the top and front you can judge the placement of the eyes.

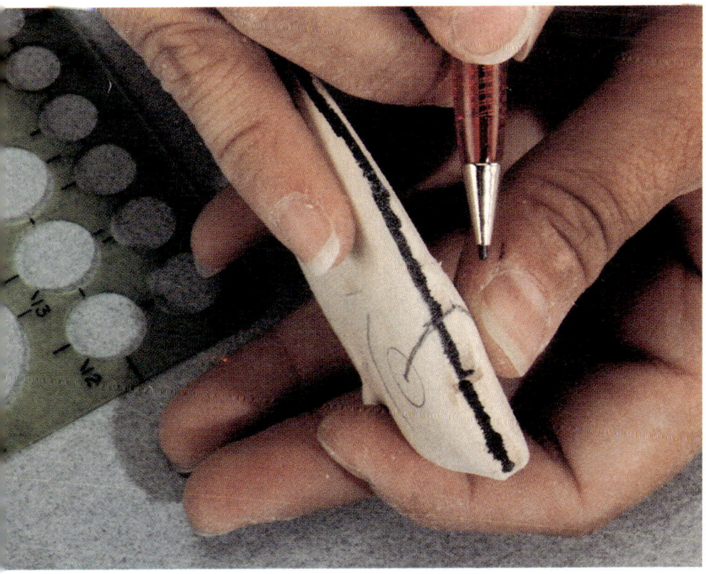

and over the other side.

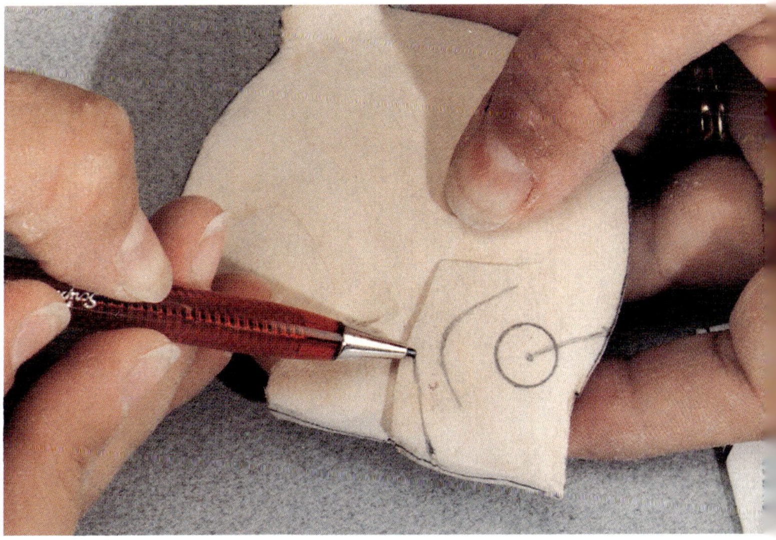

From the mark you made for the branchiostegal rays, draw the line to the gill.

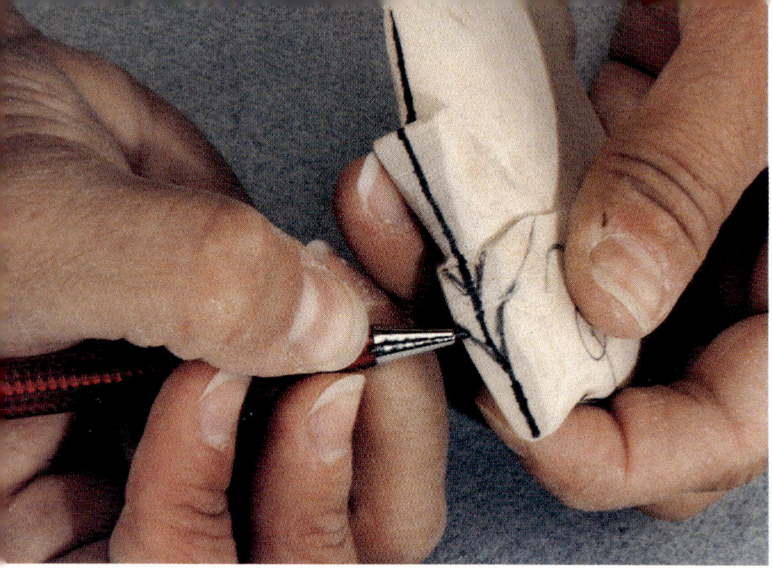

Continue the line under the lower mandible and join it with the other side. I've also drawn the shape of the trailing edge of the gill plate as it comes underneath.

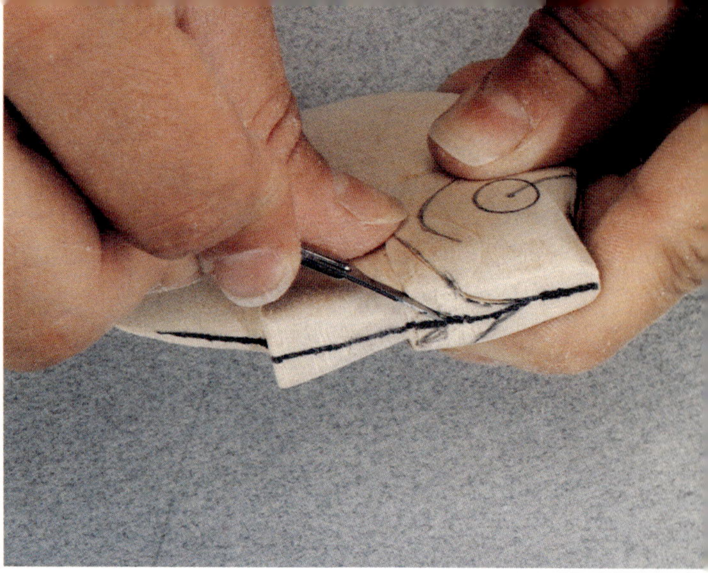

and the lower edge of the gill plate.

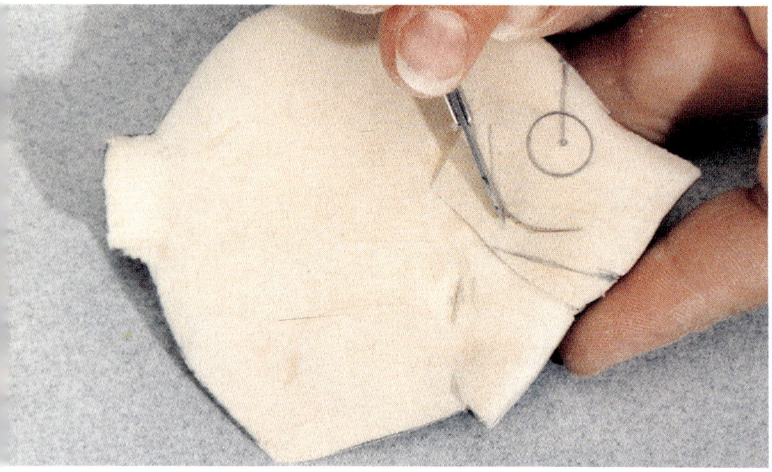

Cut stops on the preopercle.

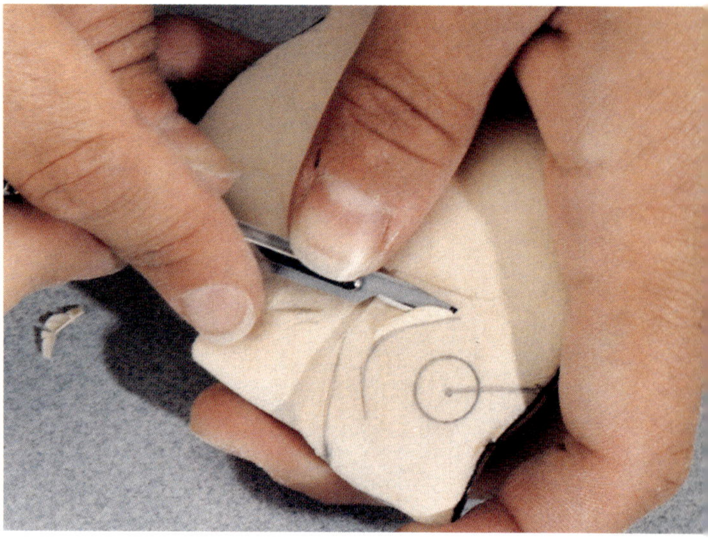

Cut back to each of these stops from behind.

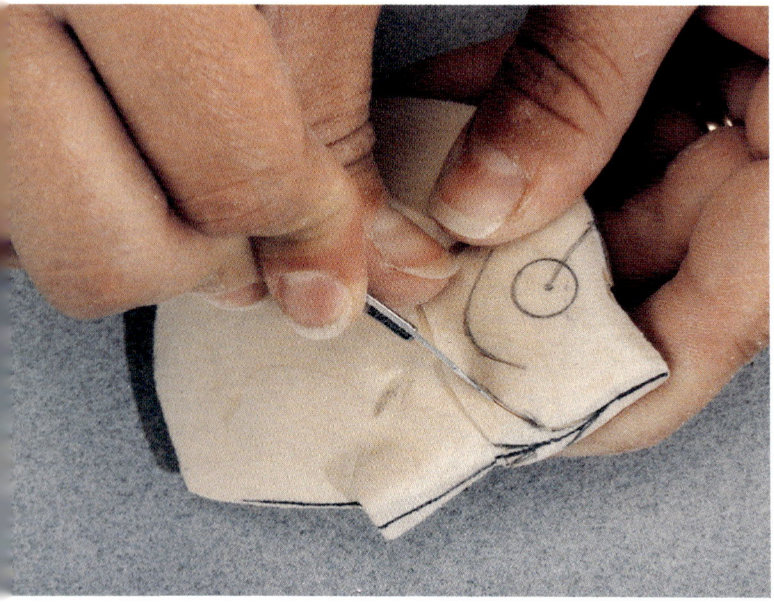

the forward edge of the branchiostegal rays...

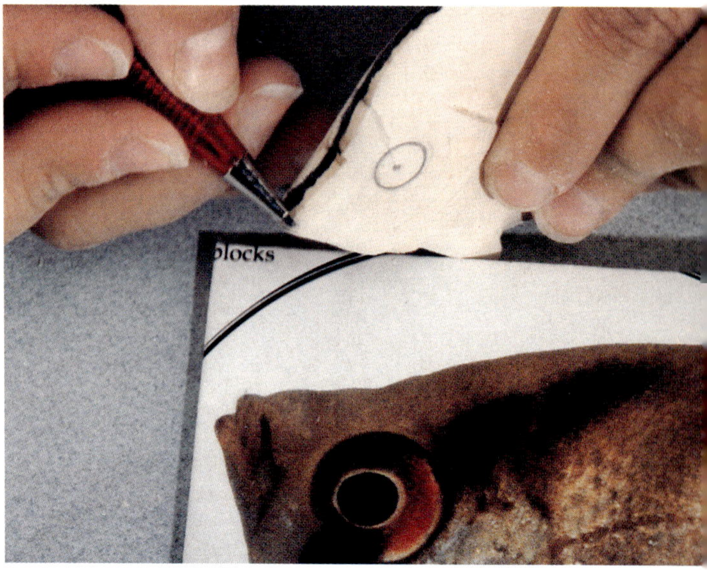

With reference materials at hand, draw the top of the upper lip.

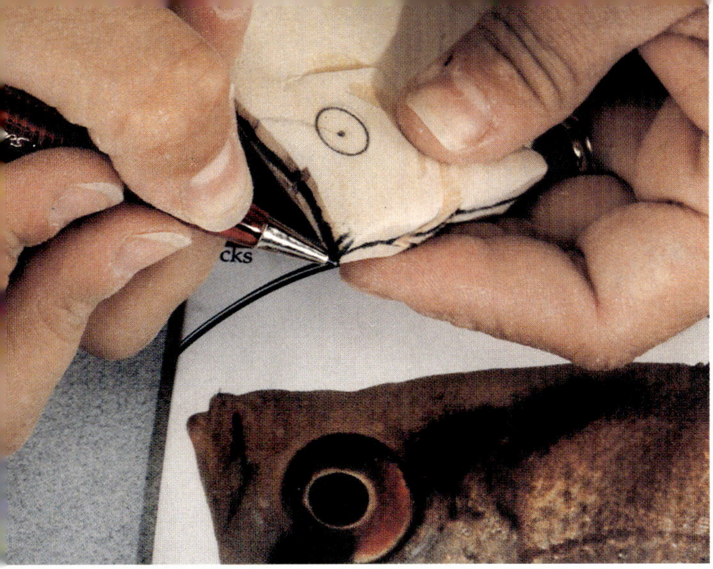

A line on the ridge is the lower edge of the mandible.

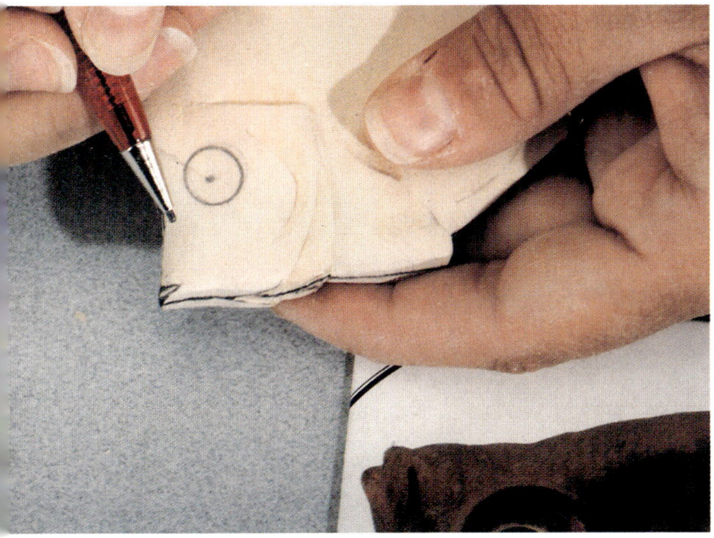

Carry the lines around the side where they come together.

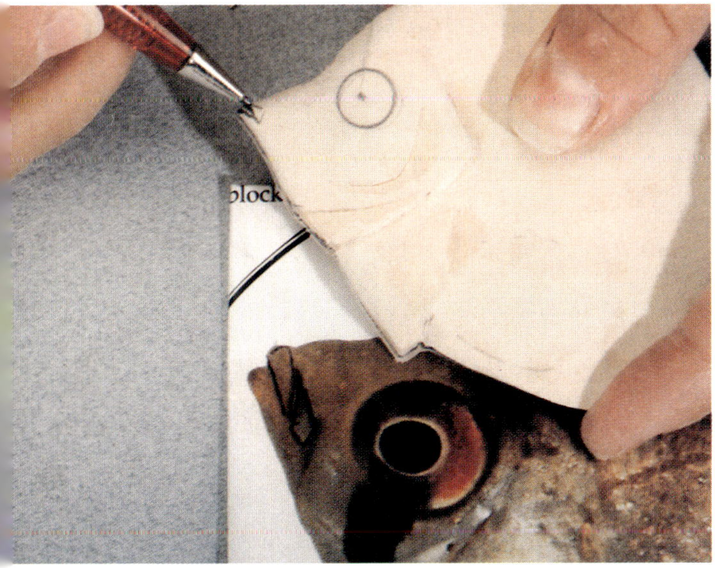

There is a triangular maxillary at the back corner of the upper lip.

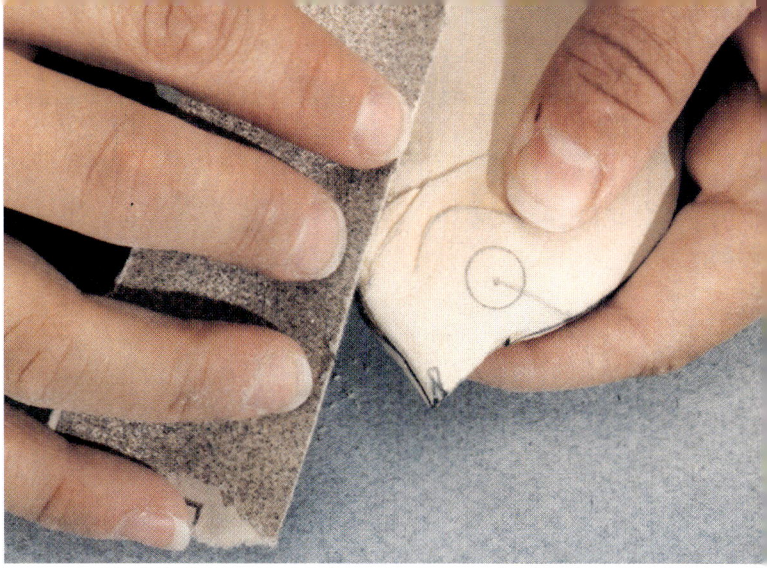

Smooth the areas behind the stop cuts to blend with the surround surfaces.

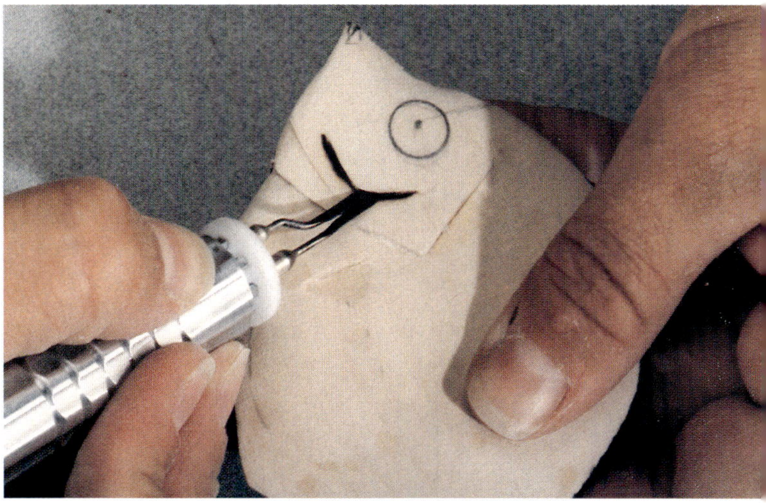

With the burner score the line of the preopercle.

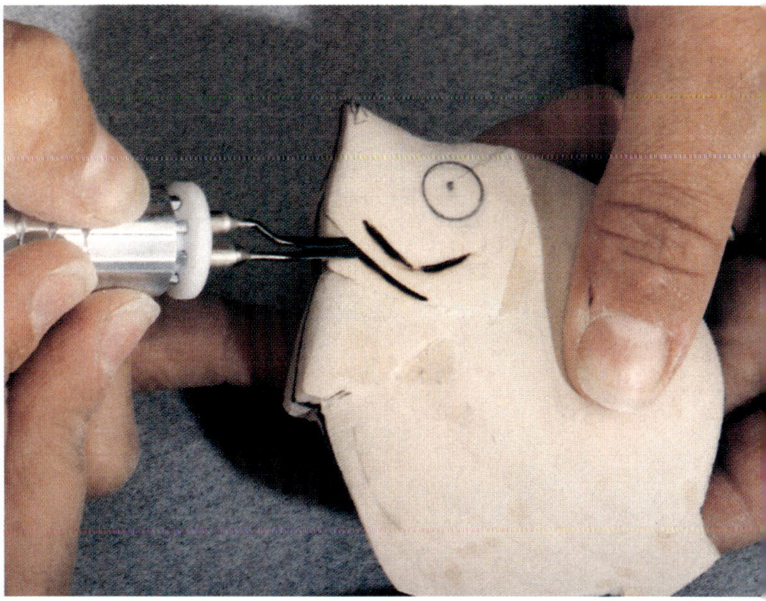

the leading edge of the branchiostegal ray area...

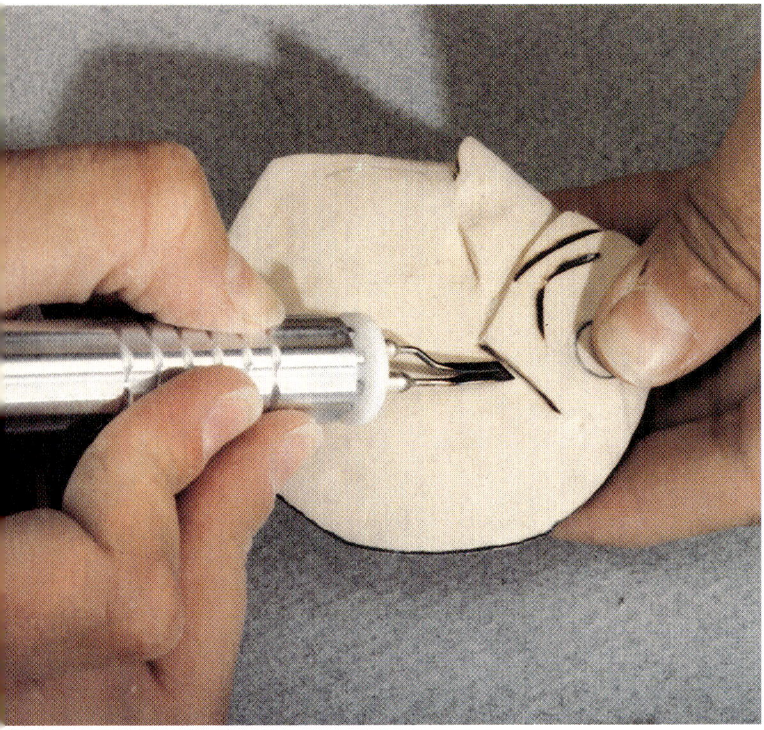

and behind the gill. This undercuts the area, lifting it slightly.

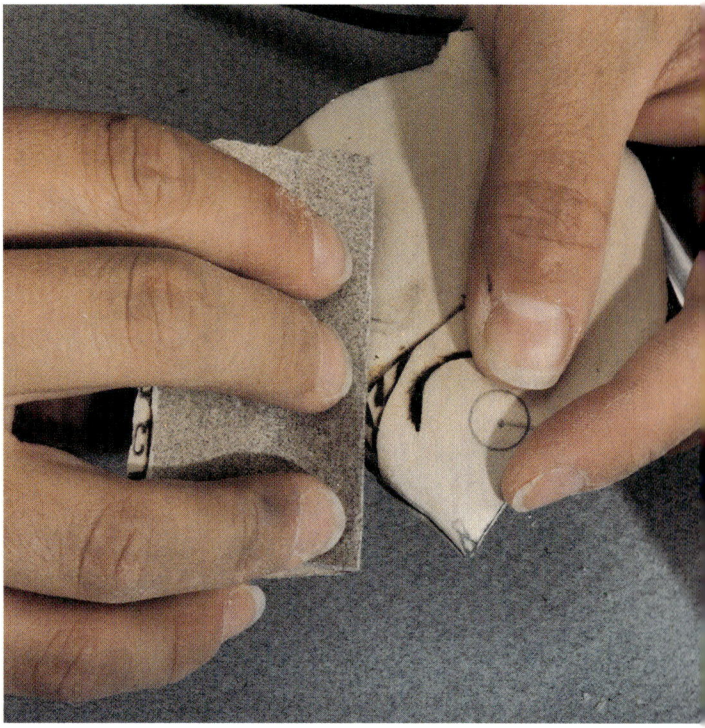

Slightly sand the burned areas.

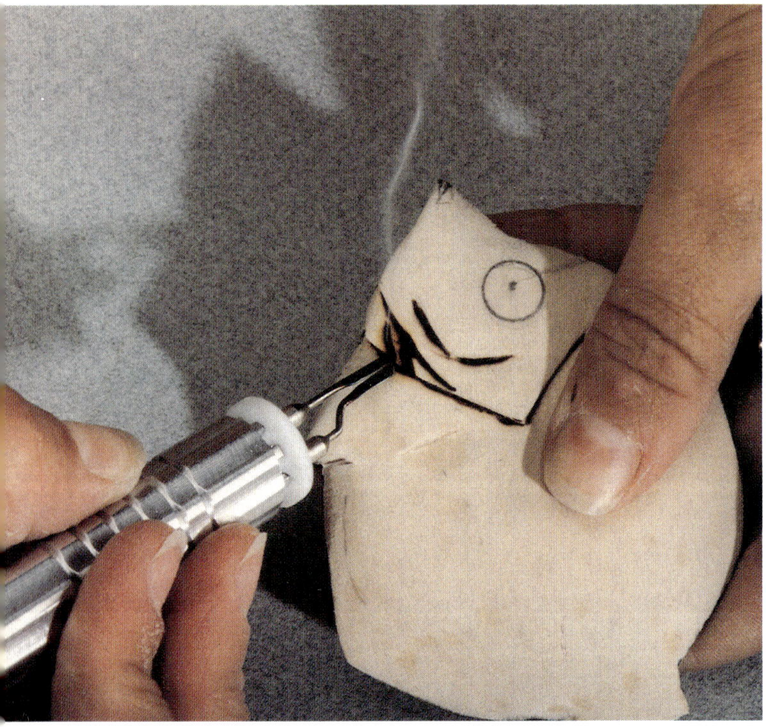

Burn in the rays. I use four on each side, though in competitions you would want to count the actual rays and be as accurate as possible.

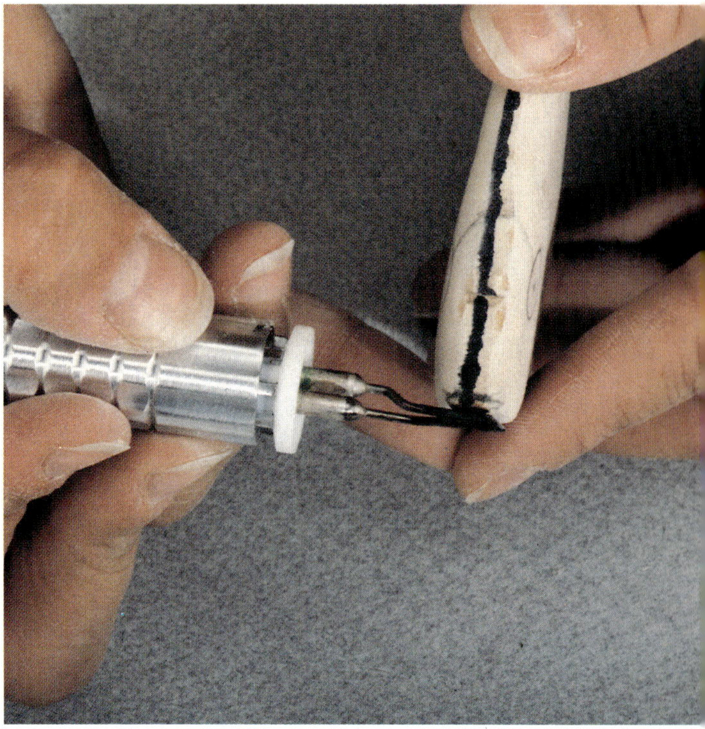

Burn in the lower line of the mandible...

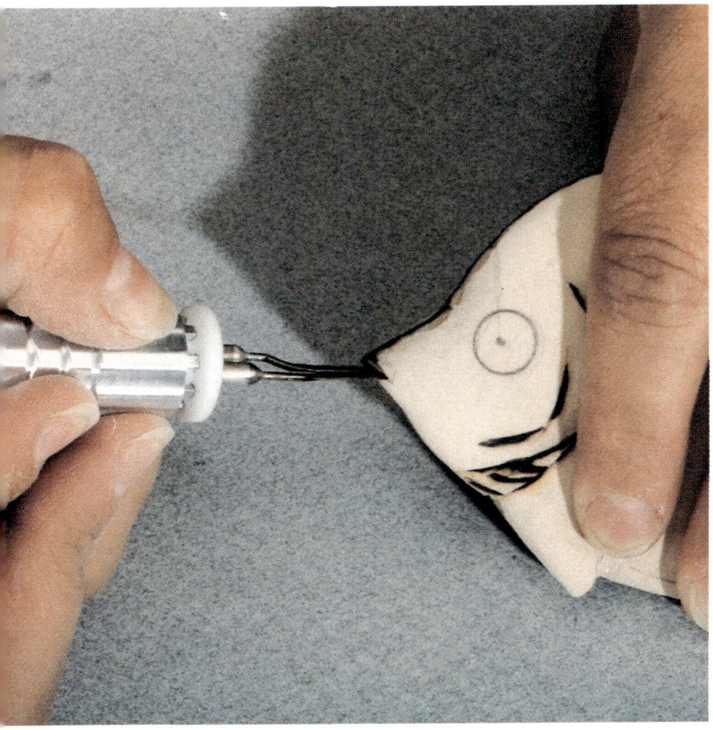

carrying the line around to the side.

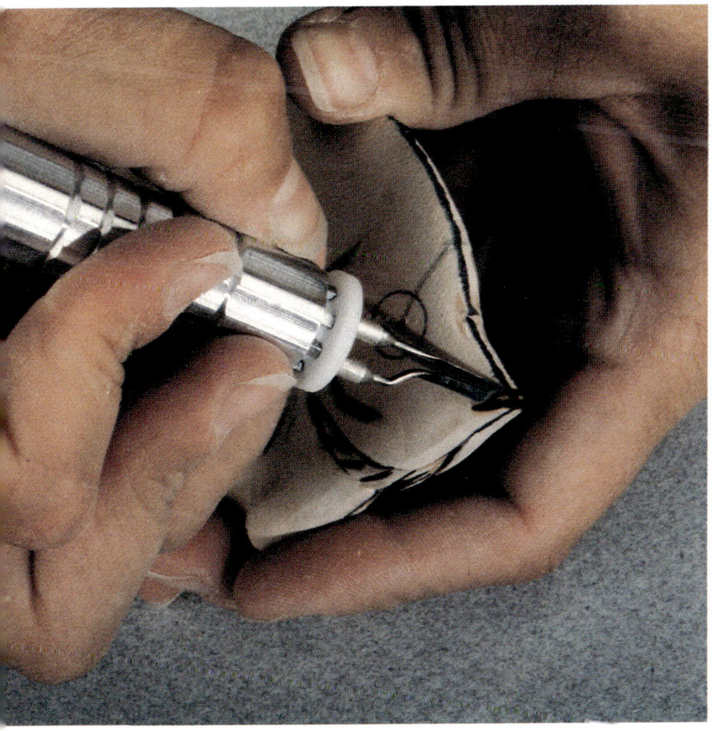

Burn the top line of the lip. These burns actually create stop cuts that I will carve back to.

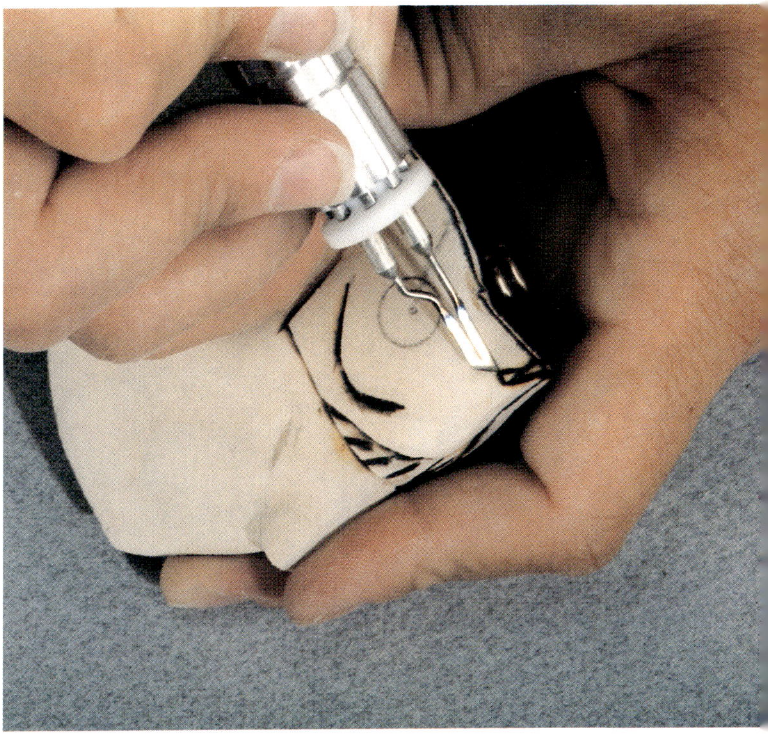

Burn in the maxillary.

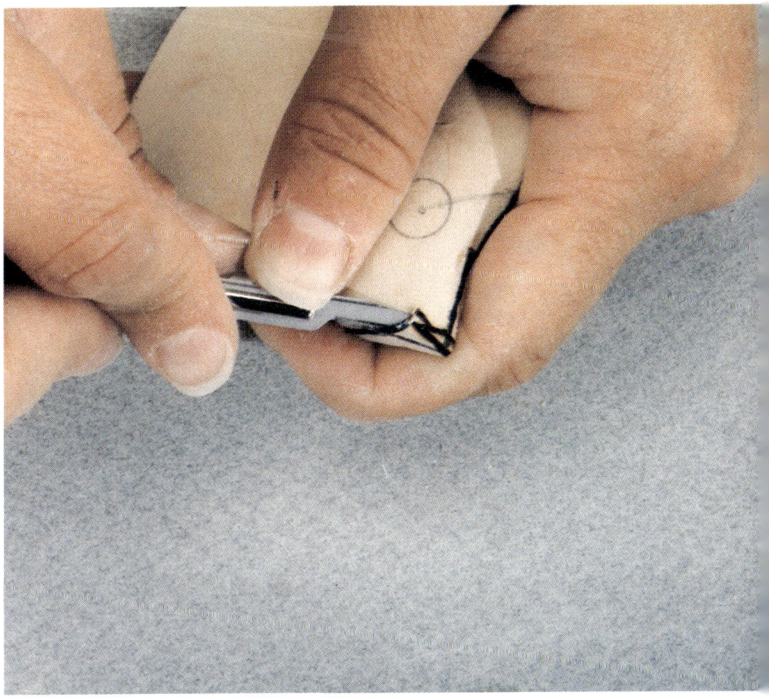

With a knife, carefully cut back to the stop created by the burning tool.

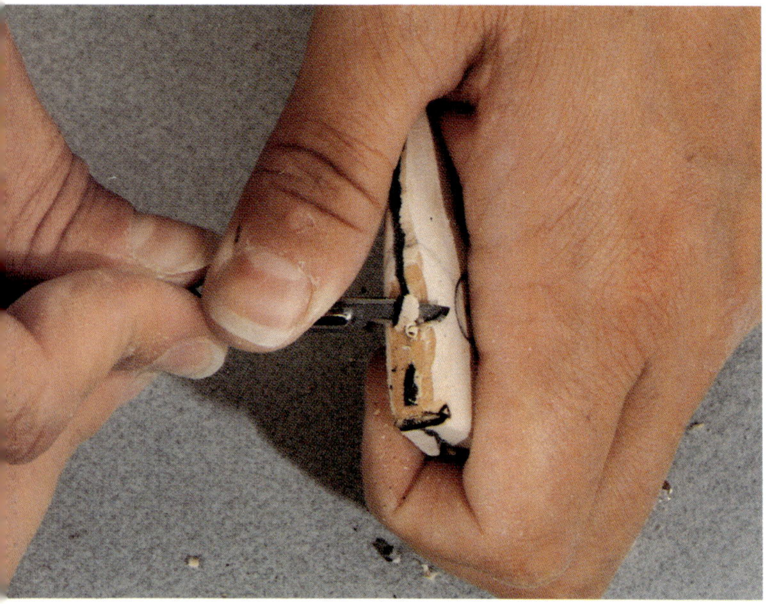

Now I can dish out the top of the head...

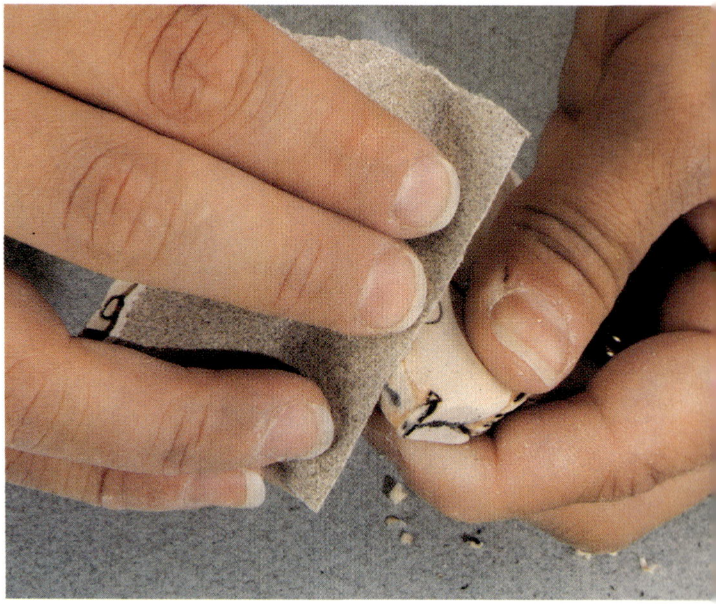

and lightly sand it.

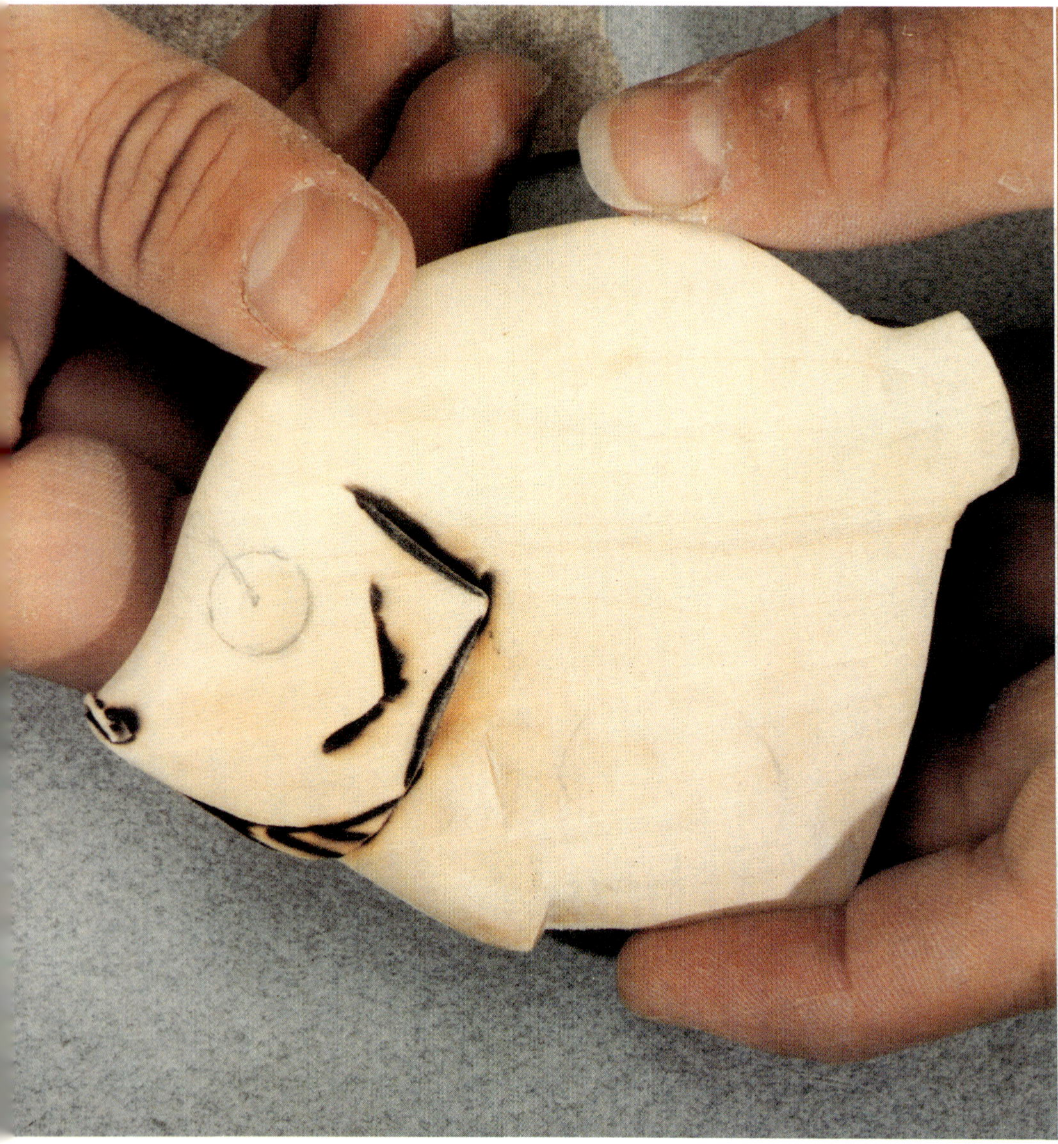

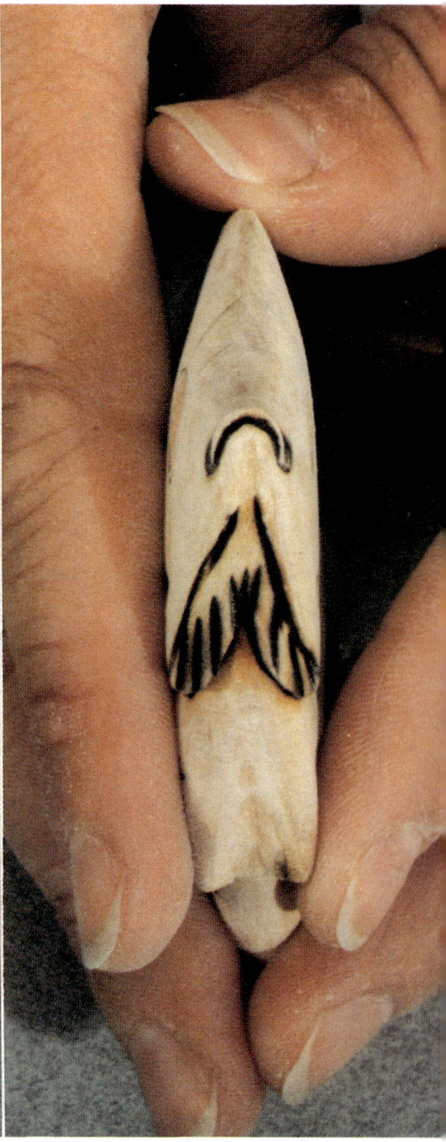

Progress.

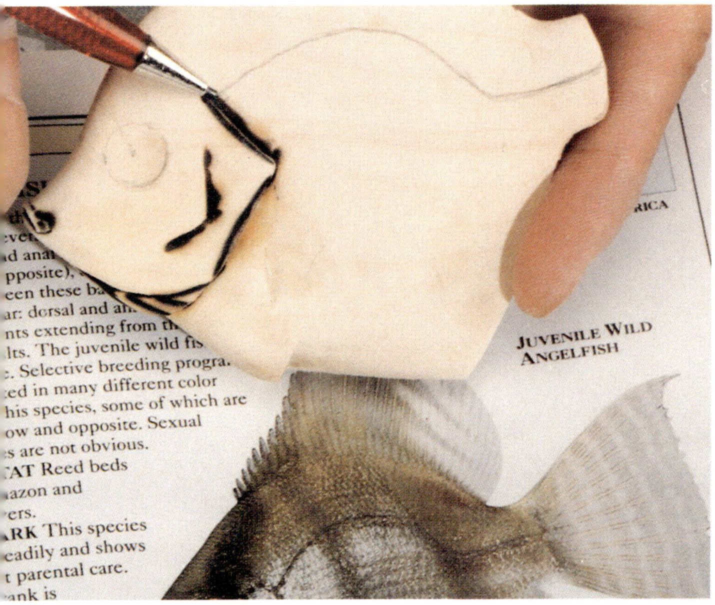

Refer to your drawings and draw the lateral line, starting in the middle of the caudal peduncle.

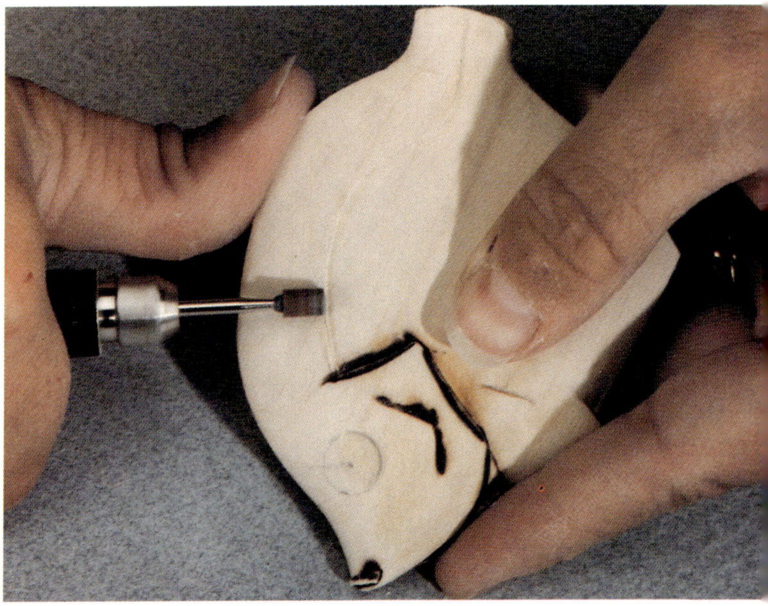

In the same way follow the top edge of the line...

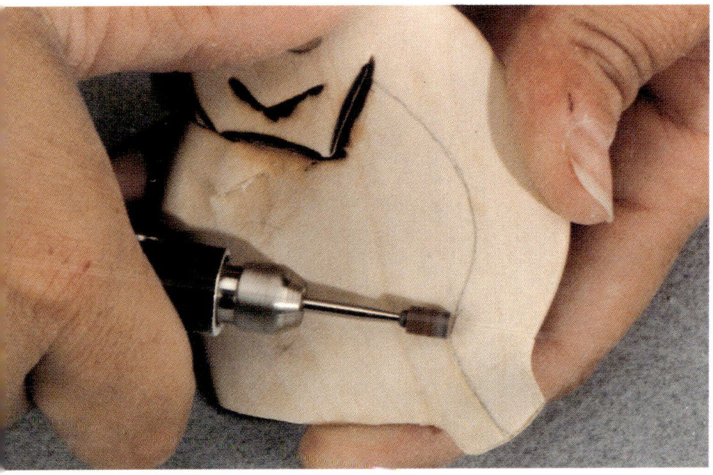

With a small cylinder grinding bit, follow the lower edge of the lateral line, reducing the body to bring the line out slightly.

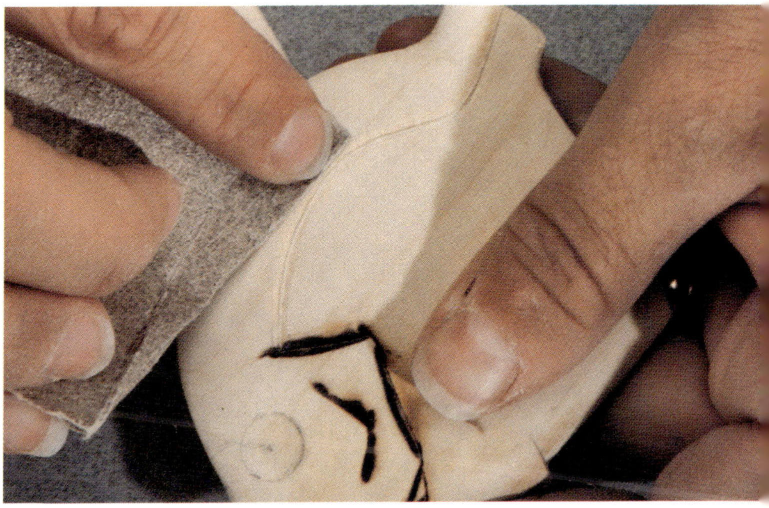

and sand to blend.

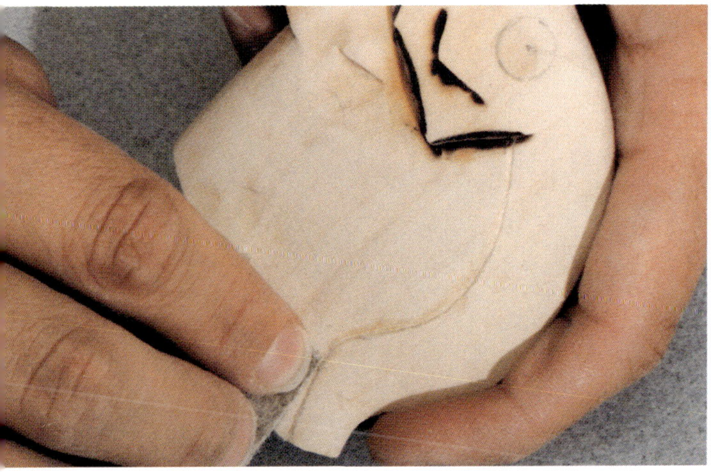

Lightly sand to blend the area with the body.

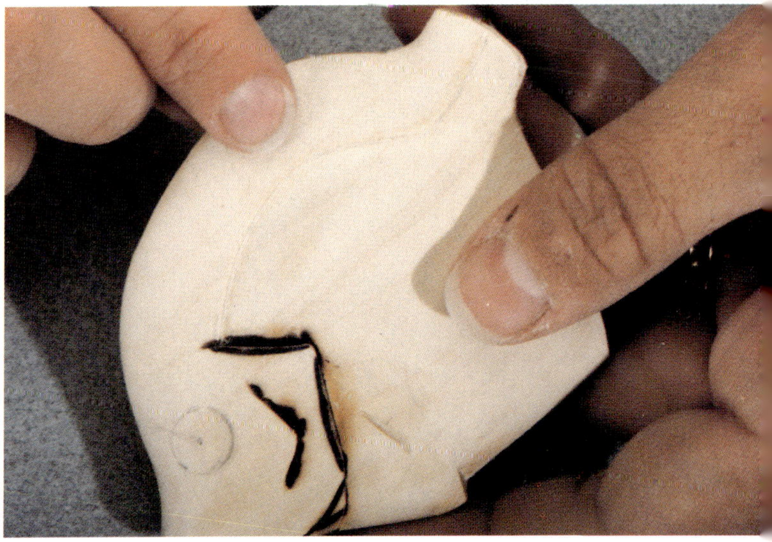

The result is a thin, raised lateral line.

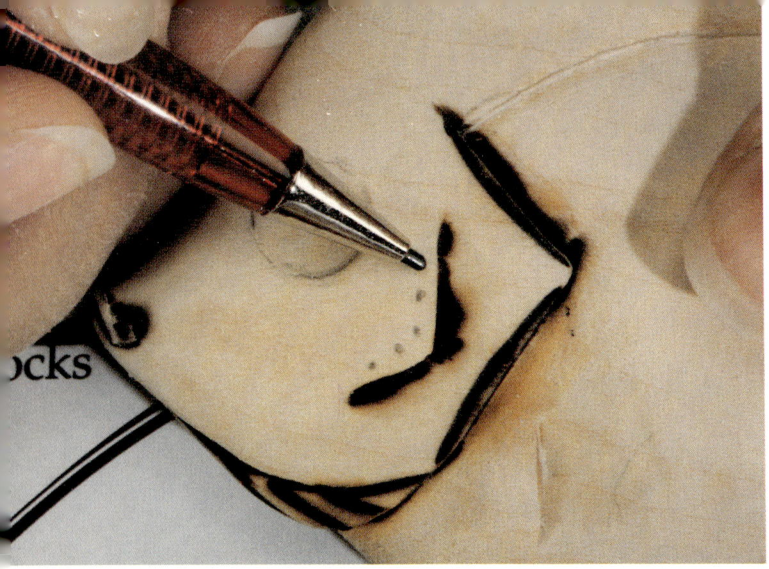

There is a series of holes in front of the preopercle, which I draw by hand.

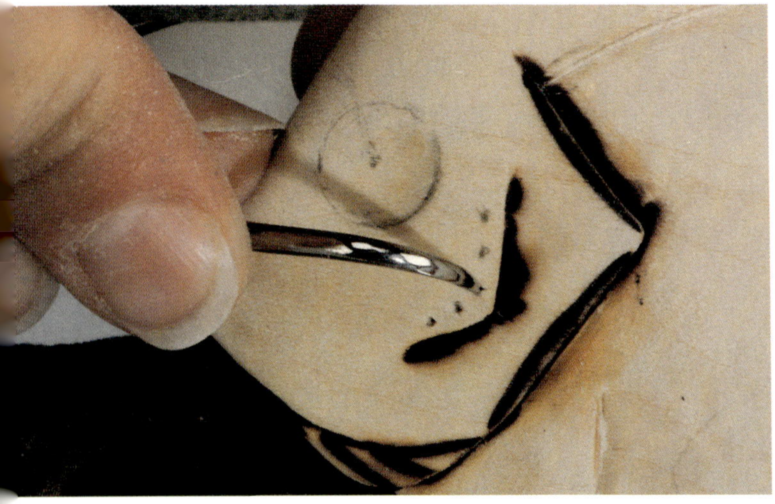

I punch them in with a dental pick.

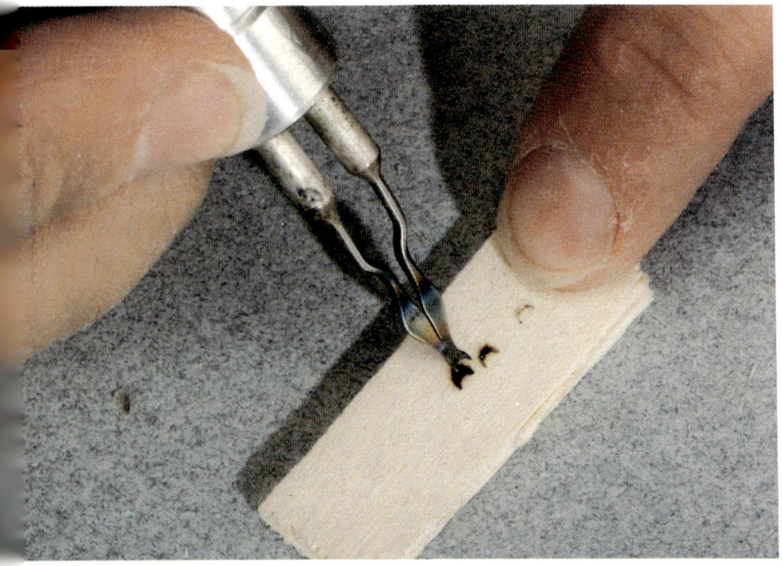

I use a small scaling tip for this fish. Always test the tip and the level of heat before actually burning the fish.

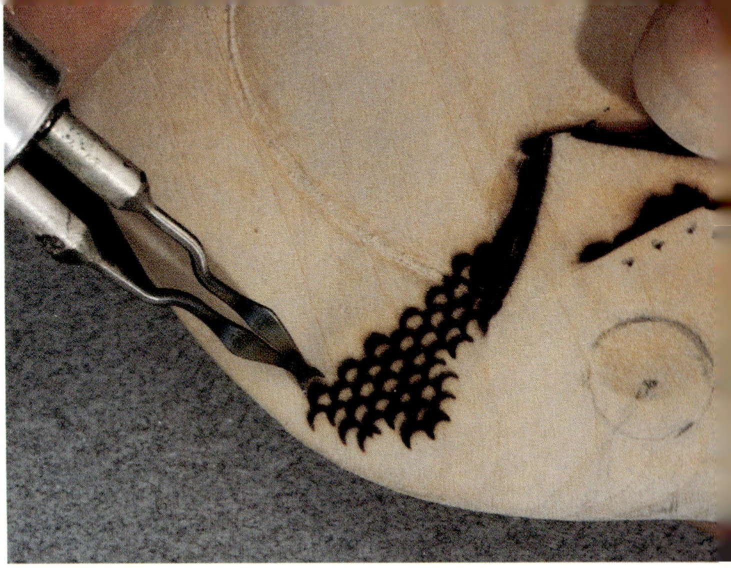

Begin the scales at the head and work back. Leave the edges of the body unburned for now. They require a smaller scale.

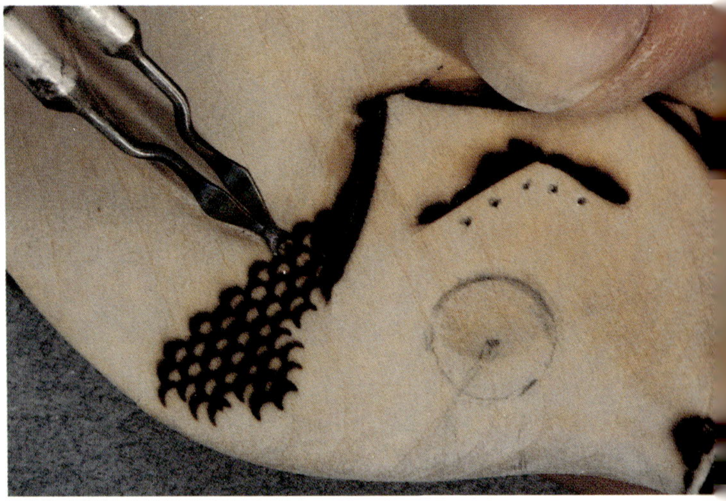

Burn through the lateral line. This breaks it up, just as it is in nature.

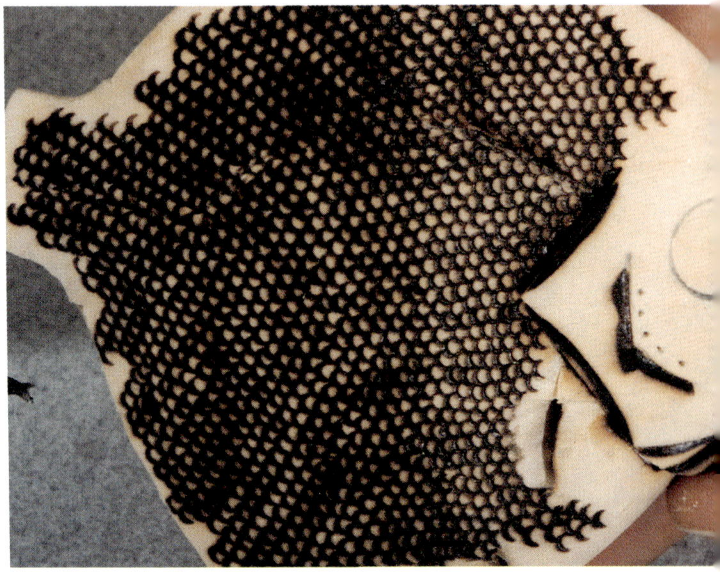

The larger scales complete.

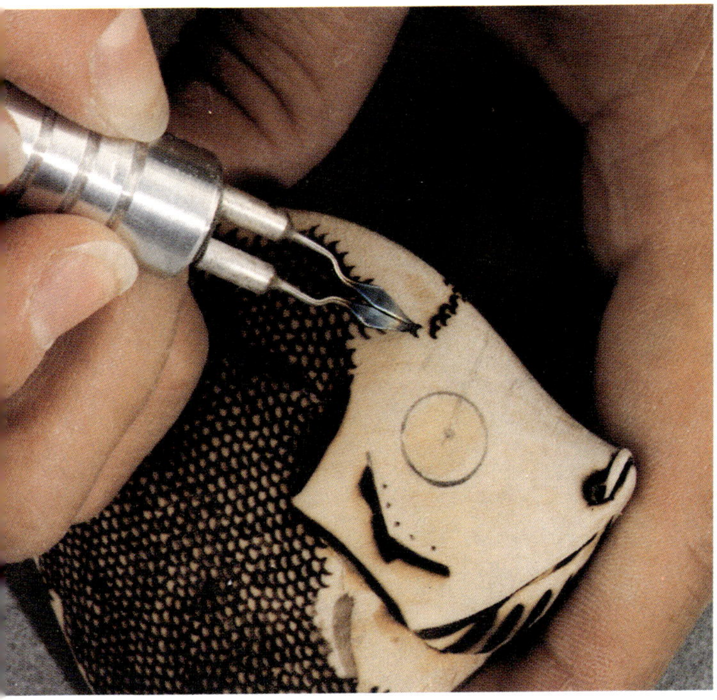

A smaller scaling tip is used to fill the gaps around the edges of the body. The face is not scaled so start here behind the head.

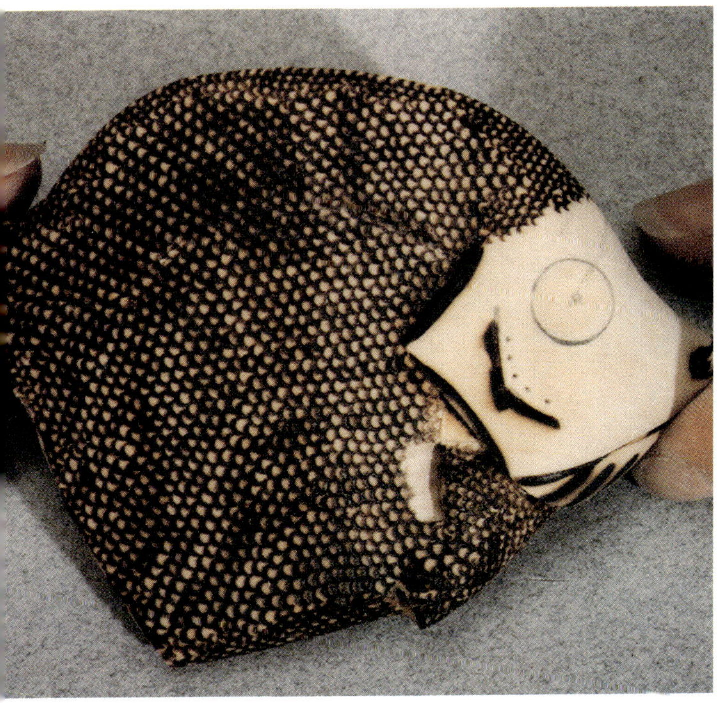

The scales are complete.

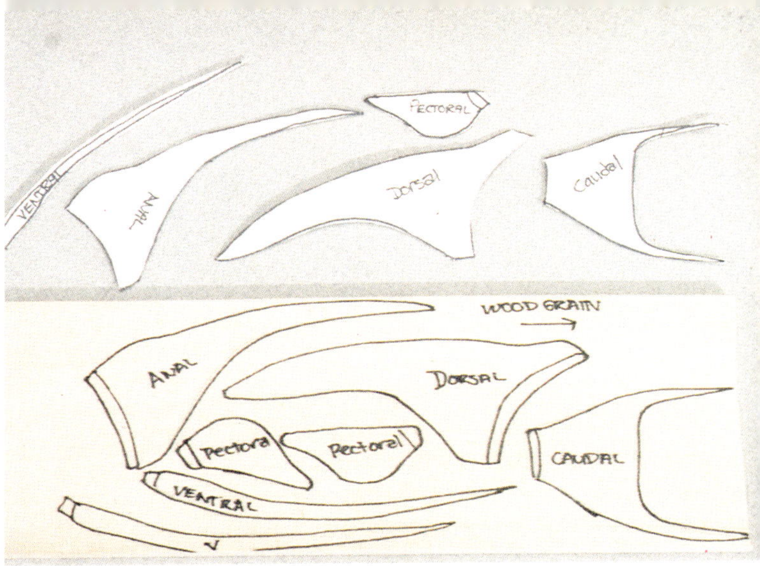

The fins are cut from a 1/4" thick piece of basswood.

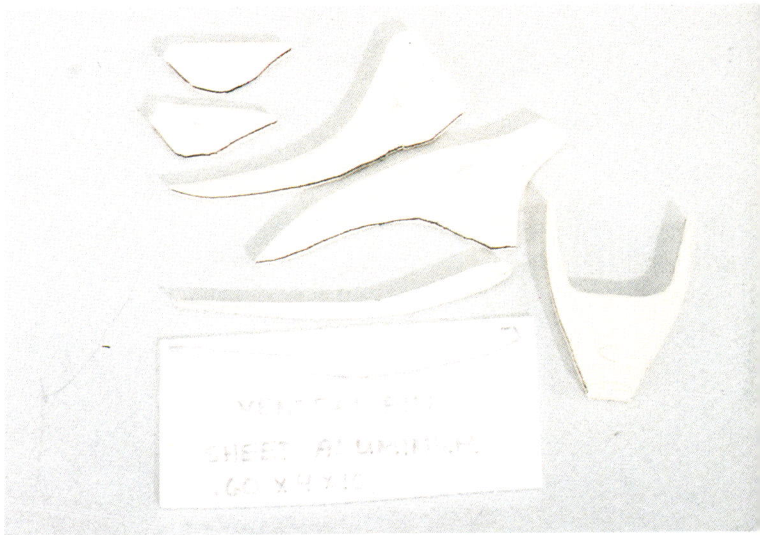

Cut the fins. One ventral fin will be from aluminum. I use this if a fin is going to support the fish in the habitat or if it is particularly exposed to damage. You can also get more movement from a metal fin.

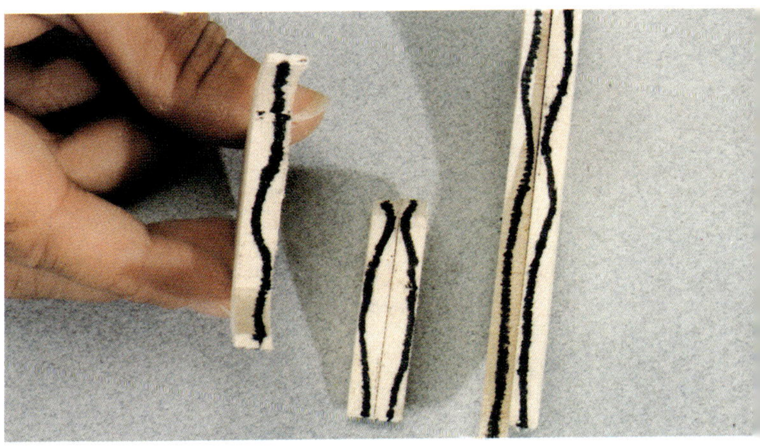

Draw the center lines with the kind of wave you hope to achieve. On the left is the trailing edge of the caudal fin. In the center are the pectoral fins. The anal and the dorsal fins are on the right.

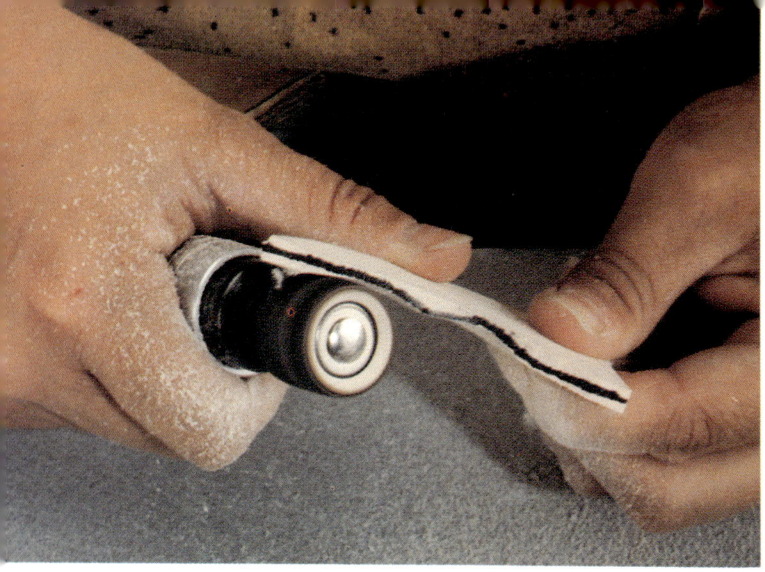

Use the sanding drum to shape the surfaces of the fins.

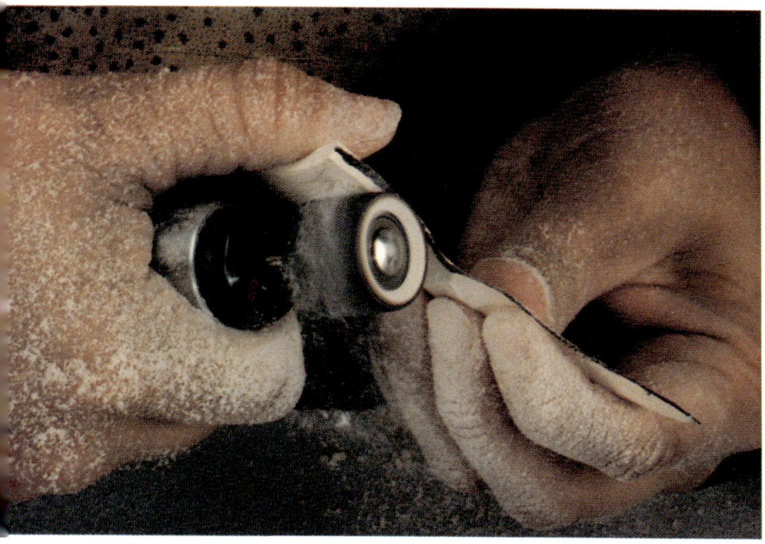

Reduce from both sides, leaving the center line intact.

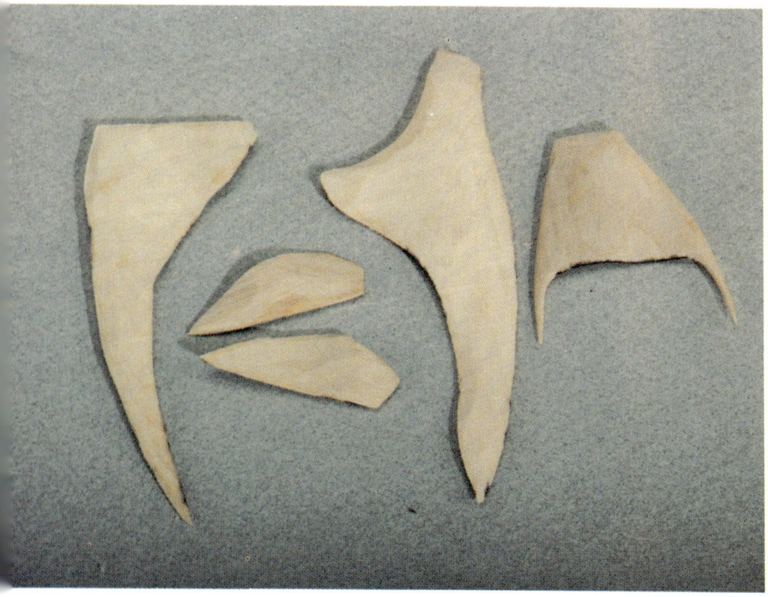

This grinding will take them to this stage.

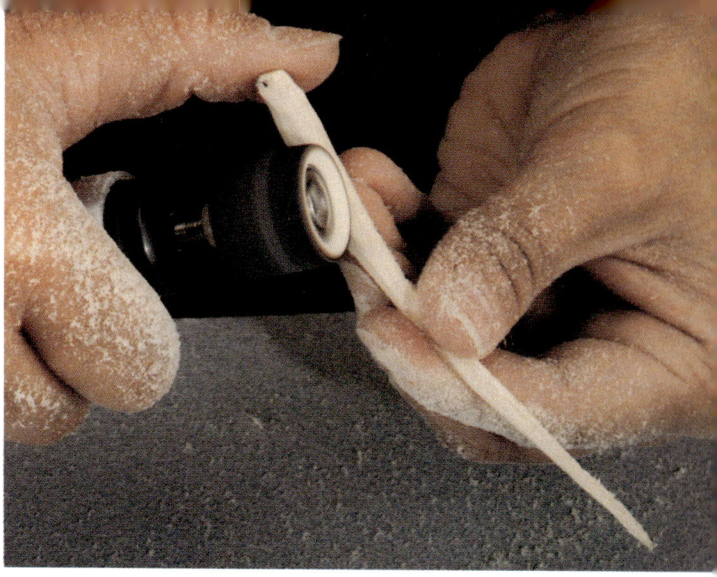

The ventral fin is very fragile. Until you are practiced (and even after) you may need to try two or three times.

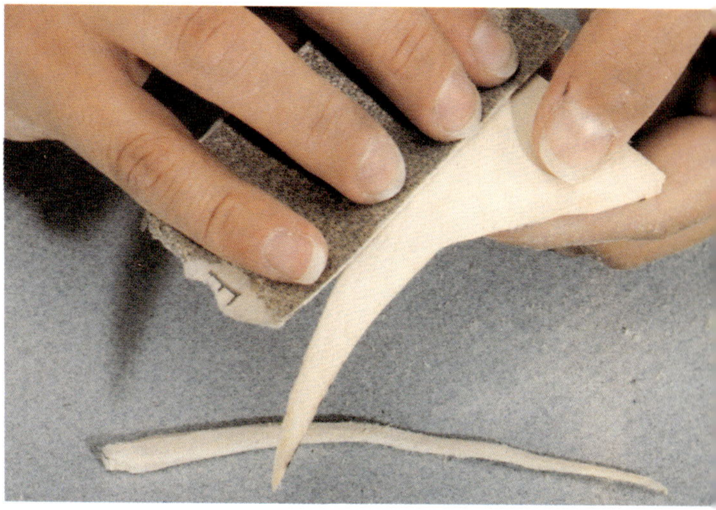

Sand the fins, first with medium grit paper. You can get additional thinness just by the amount of sanding you do.

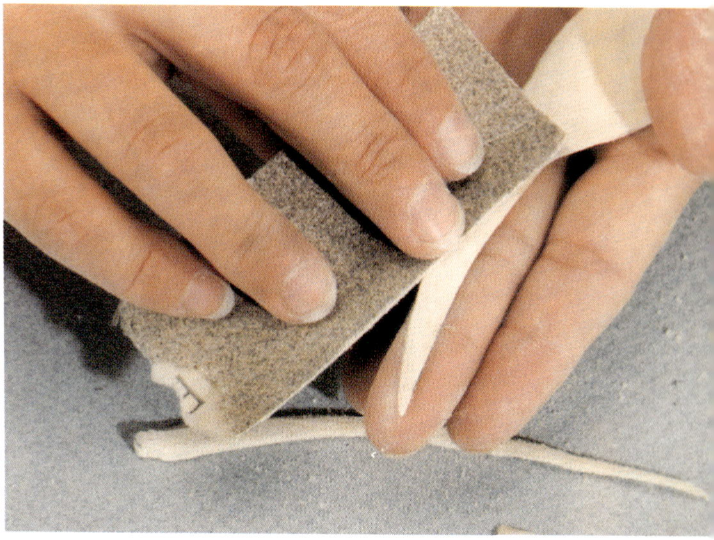

When sanding the tips I always support the work with my finger.

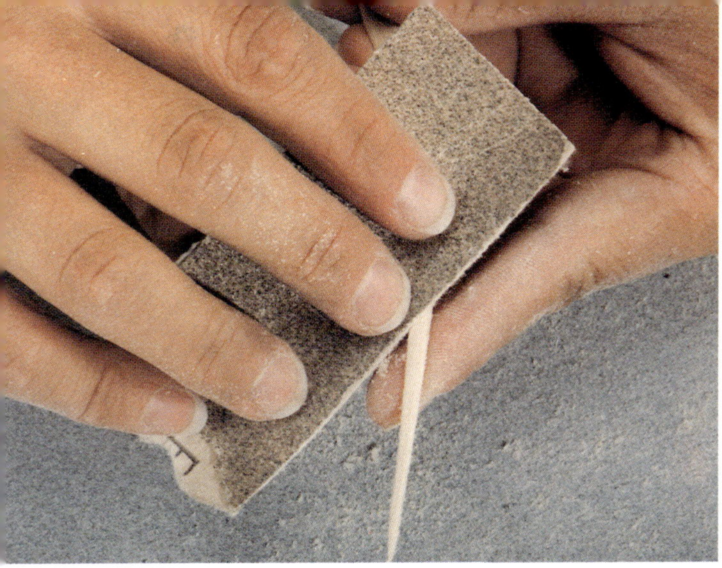

The ventral fin needs to be completely supported while sanding.

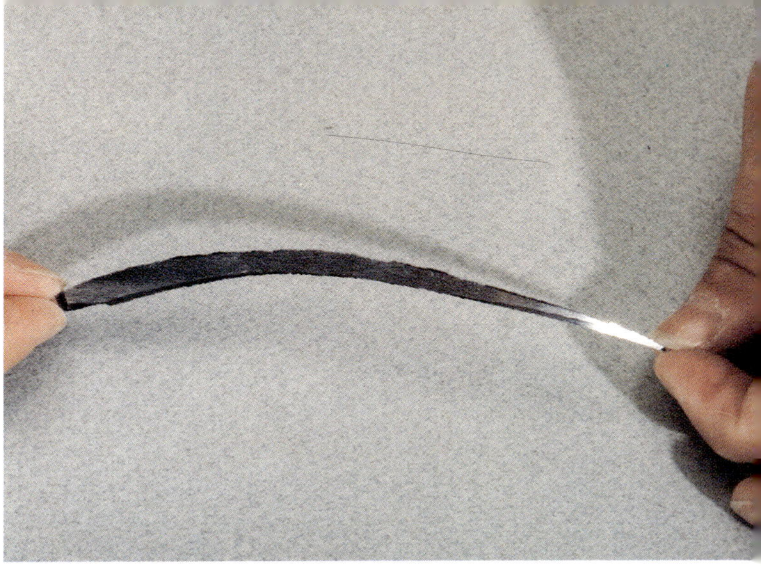

Cut the aluminum fin on a bandsaw. **FOR SAFETY: be sure to wear protective eyewear when cutting metal!**

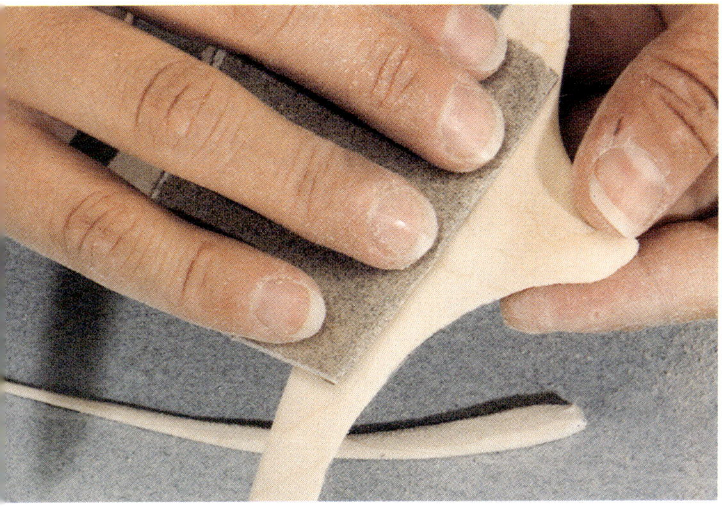

Continue with fine grit paper.

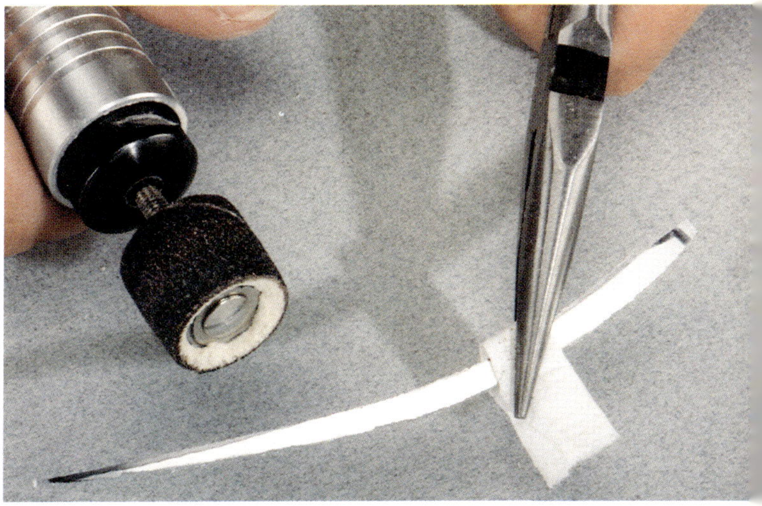

The metal gets very hot during sanding so you need to hold it with pliers. The paper keeps you from marking up the work with the tool. I use an old sanding drum for the shaping. When I'm finished, the drum will be ruined.

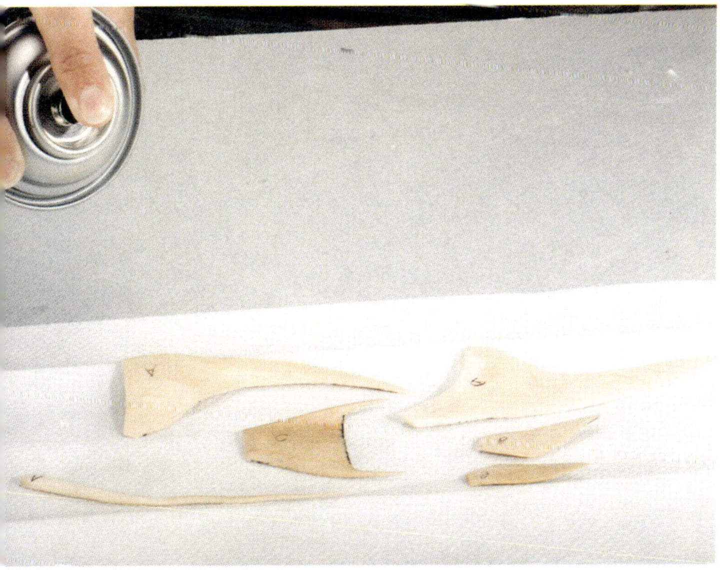

When the are completely sanded, lightly seal them with a Krylon Clear Coat acrylic.

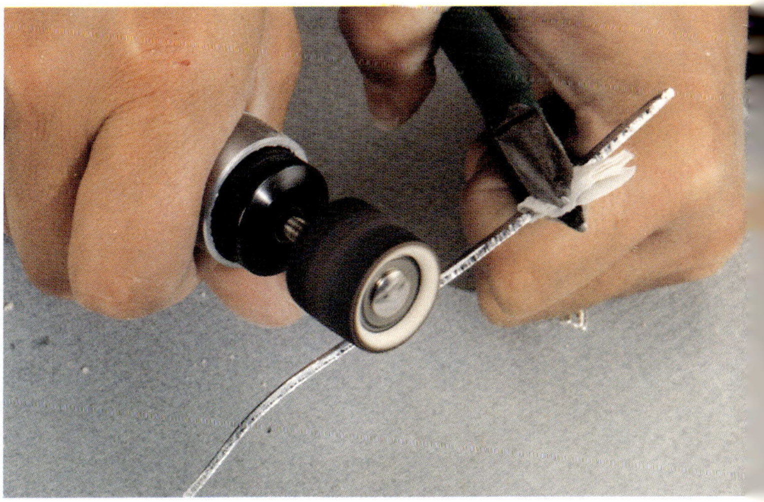

Thin and round the edges. Again **FOR SAFETY: be sure to wear protective eyewear when sanding metal!**

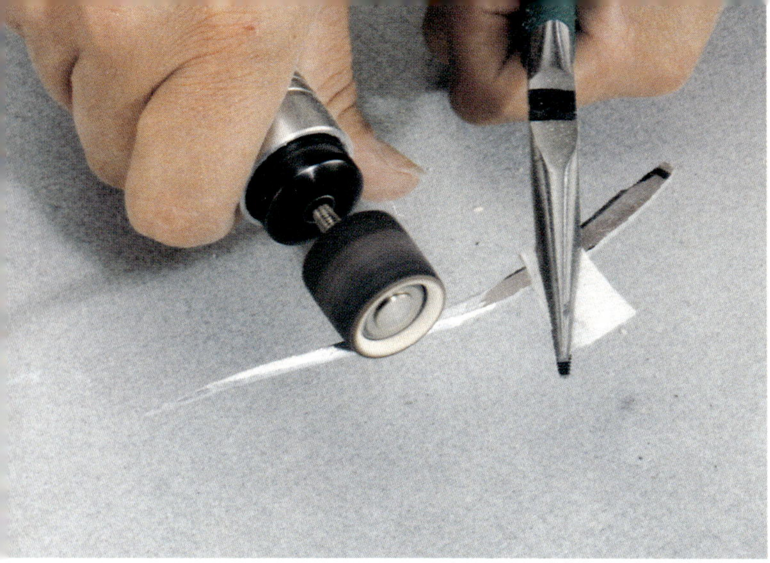

Rough up the entire surface. This will allow the paint to stick to it.

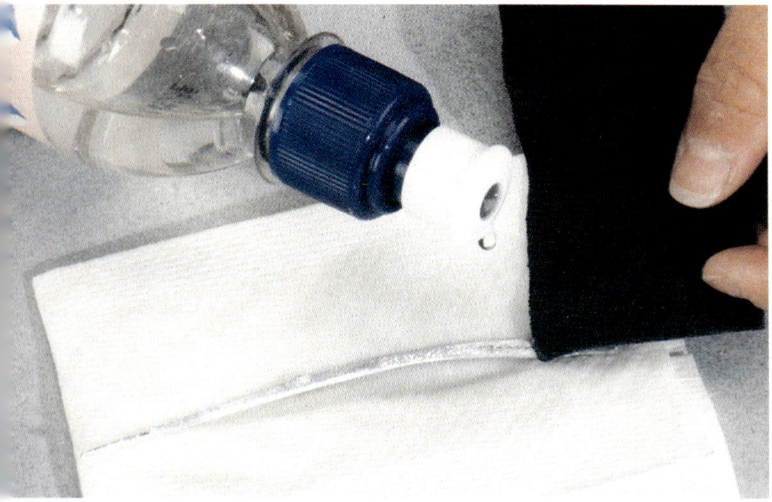

When the grinding is done, go over it with medium grit emery cloth. Moisten the surface before sanding...

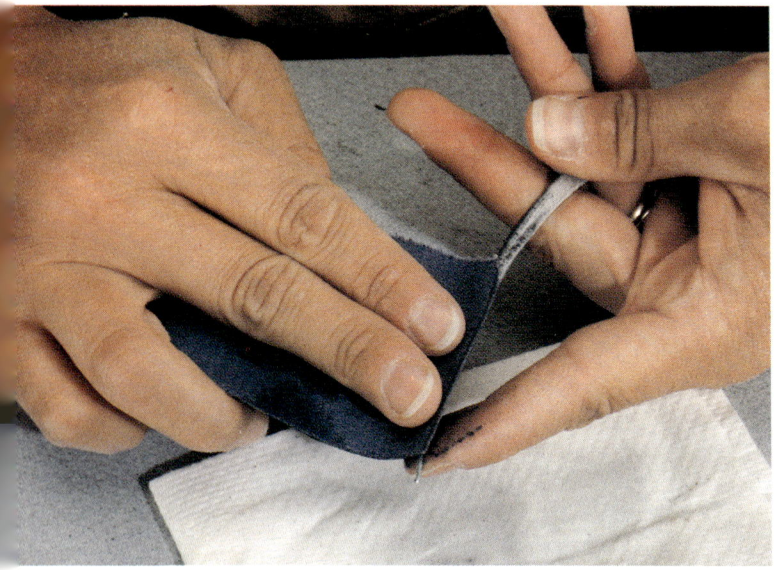

and sand to take off any burrs.

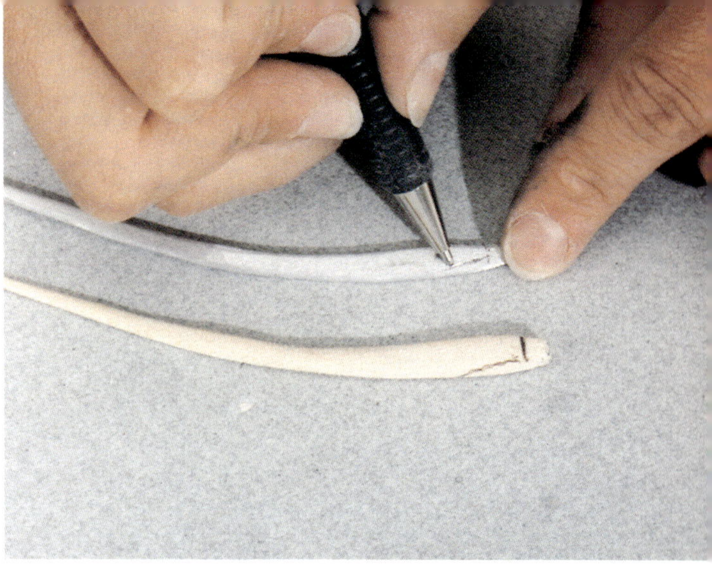

The ventral fins have rays, one on the leading edge and three on the trailing edge. Draw them in, first on the leading edge...

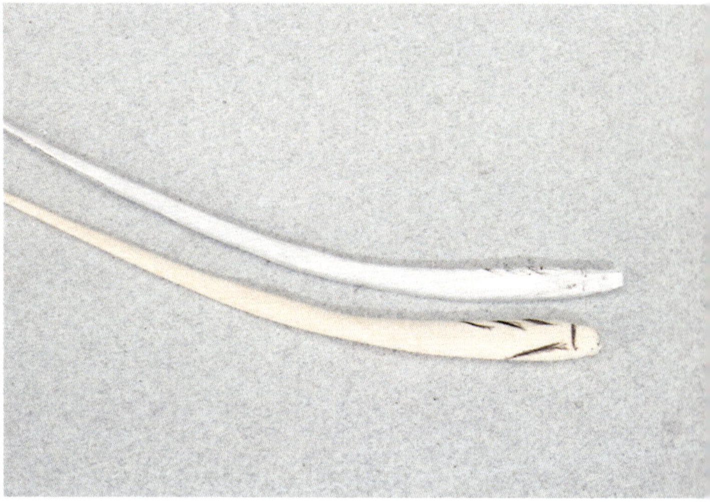

then on the trailing edge. These lines are where I will cut into the wood.

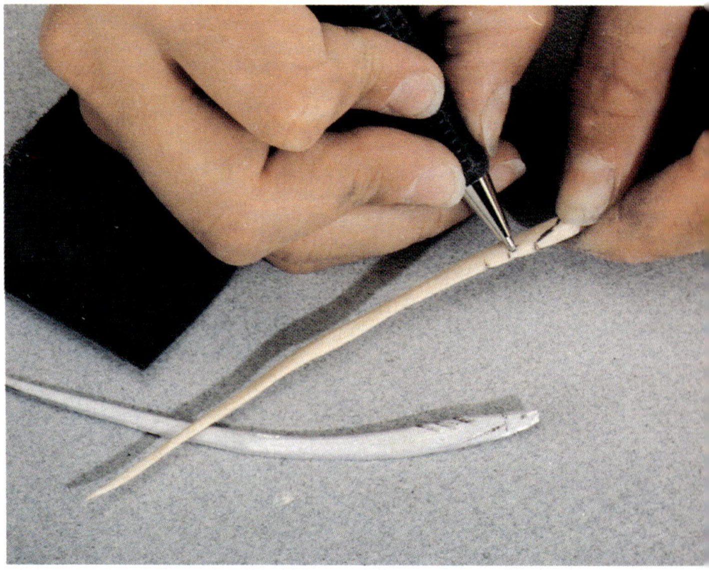

Carry the lines around to the other side.

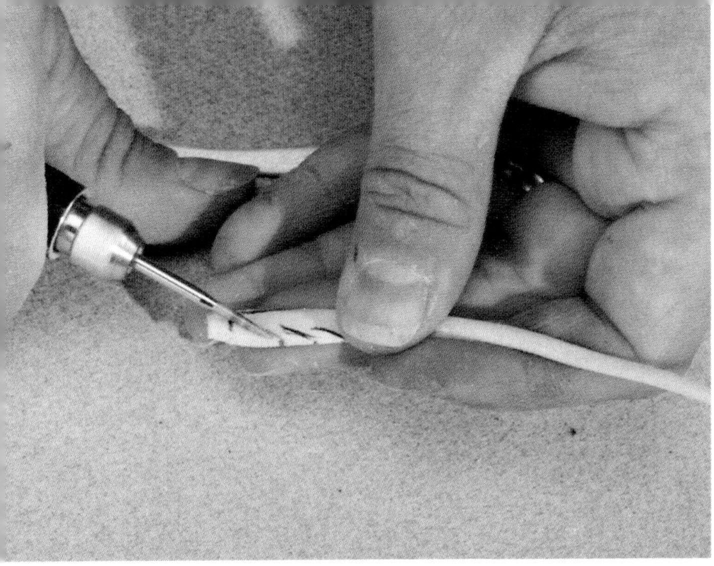

A diamond point bit will cut both the wood and the metal. Lay it on the line to create a groove.

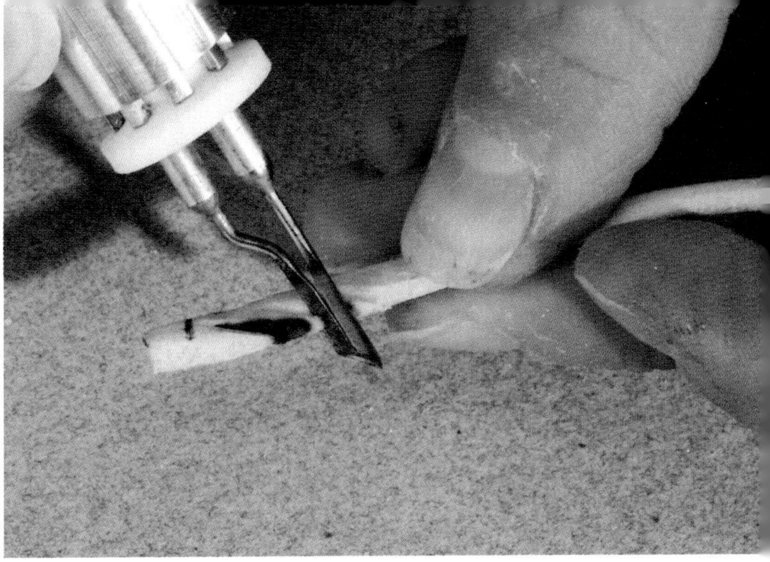

Clean it up with the burning tool, burning into the notch...

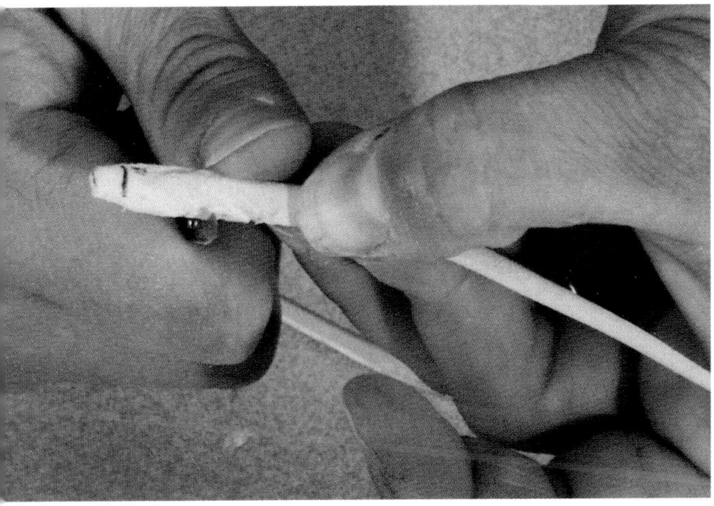

Make a stop cut on the edge at the groove...

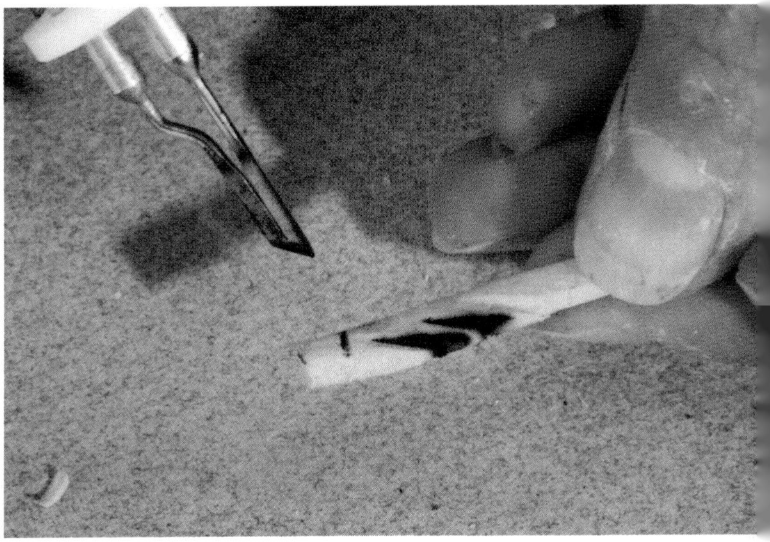

and dragging back along the groove.

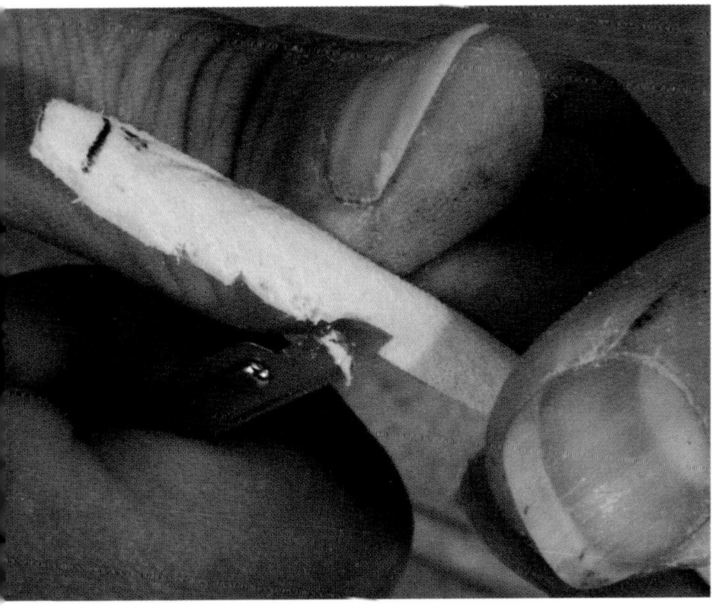

and cut back to it along the edge of the fin.

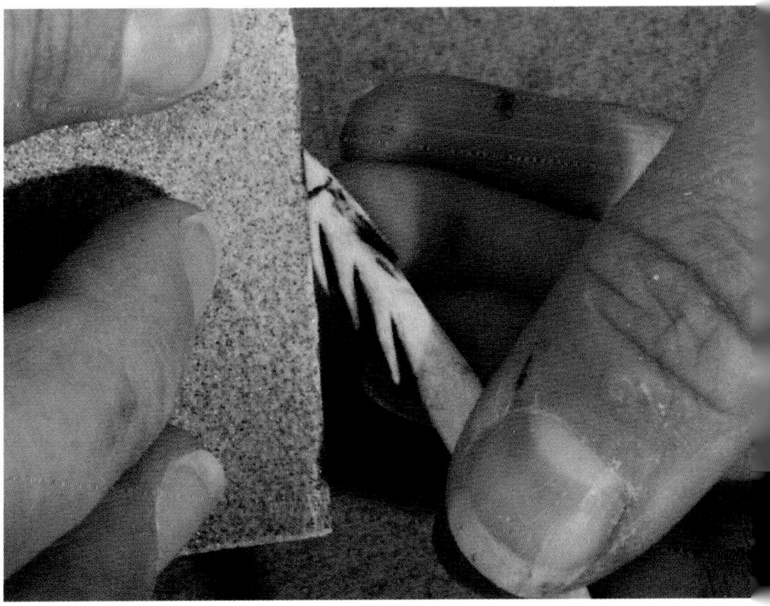

Lightly sand in the groves.

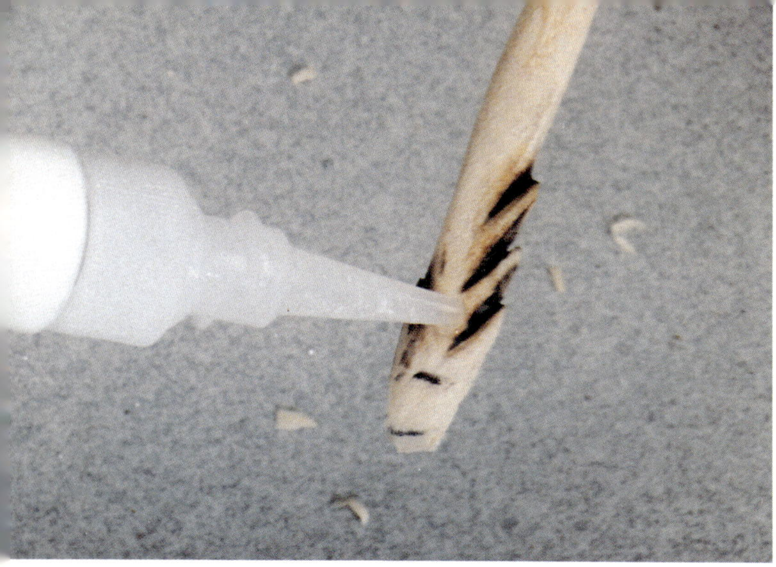

Super glue the entire fin to give it added strength.

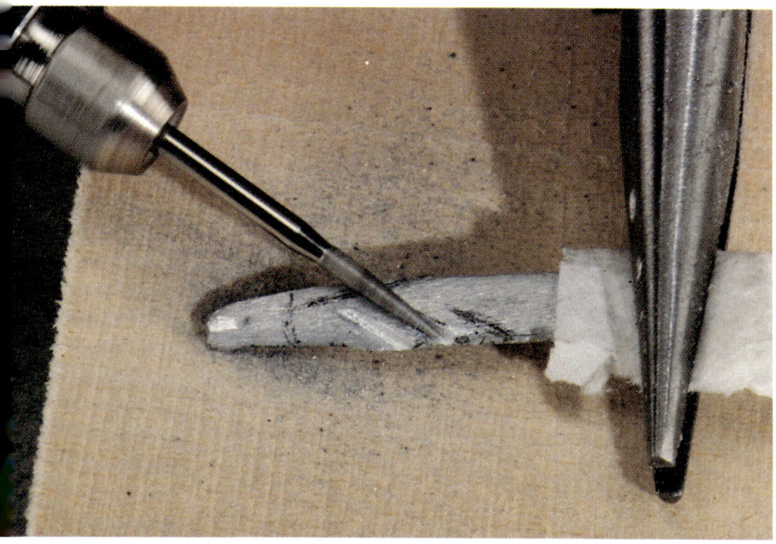

Use the same grinding technique with the metal. Because you can't burn the aluminum, you will never be able to get the same detail.

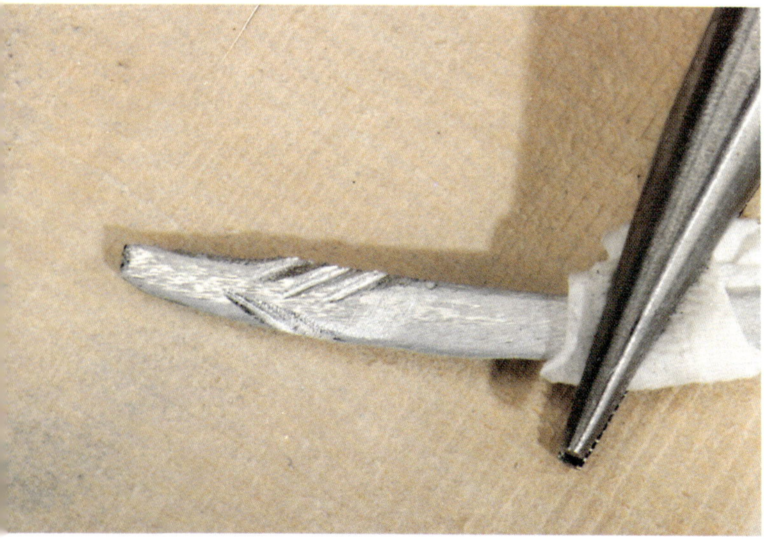

The result.

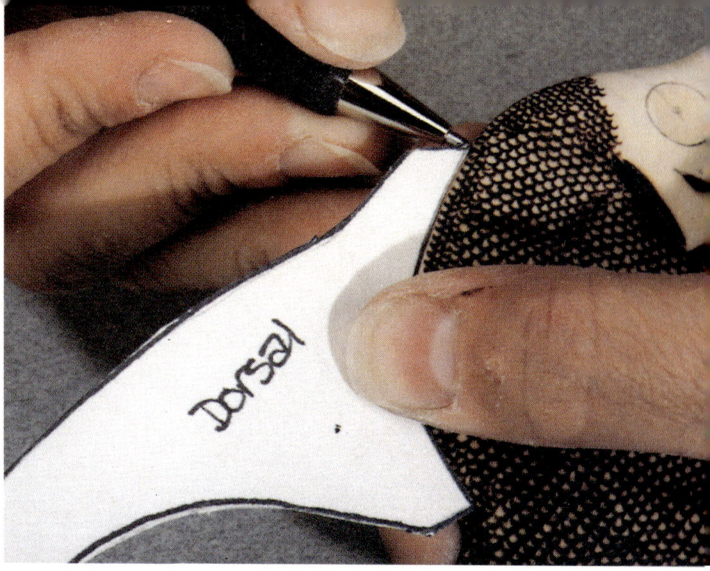

Hold the pattern to the top of the body, and mark the beginning and end of the dorsal fin.

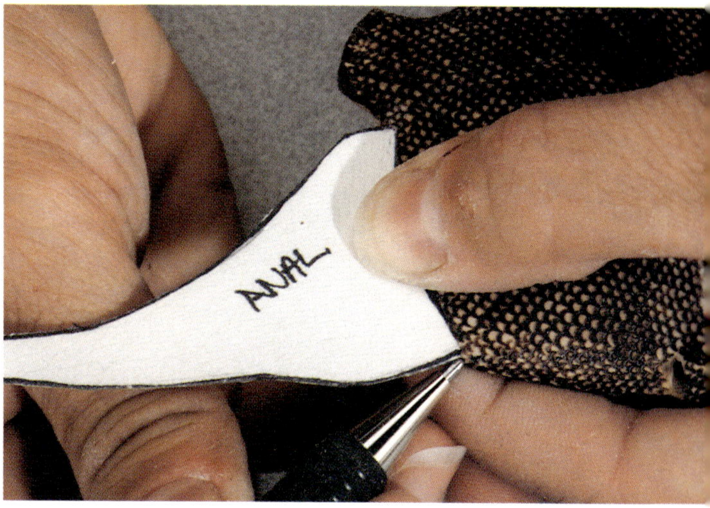

Do the same at the anal fin.

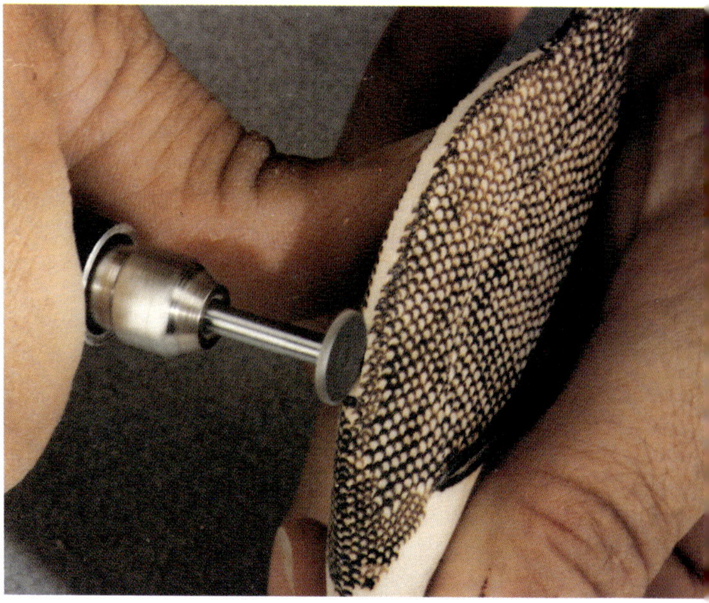

With a steel cutter, start at the line...

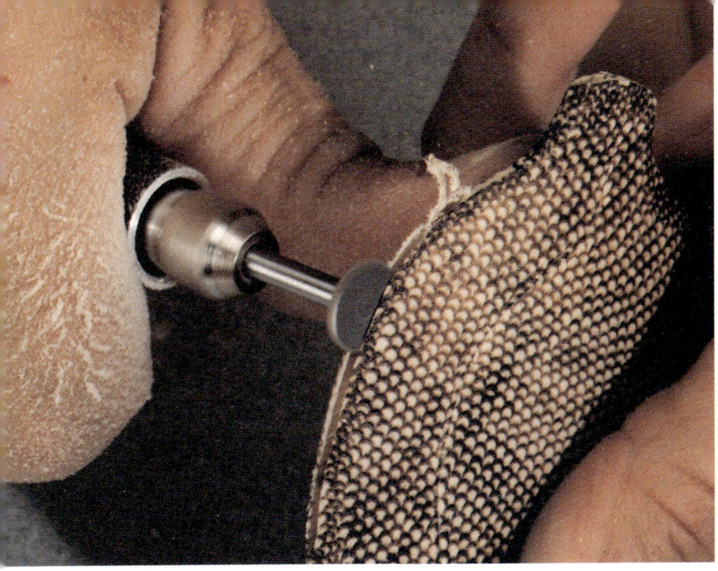

and cut a groove for the dorsal fin.

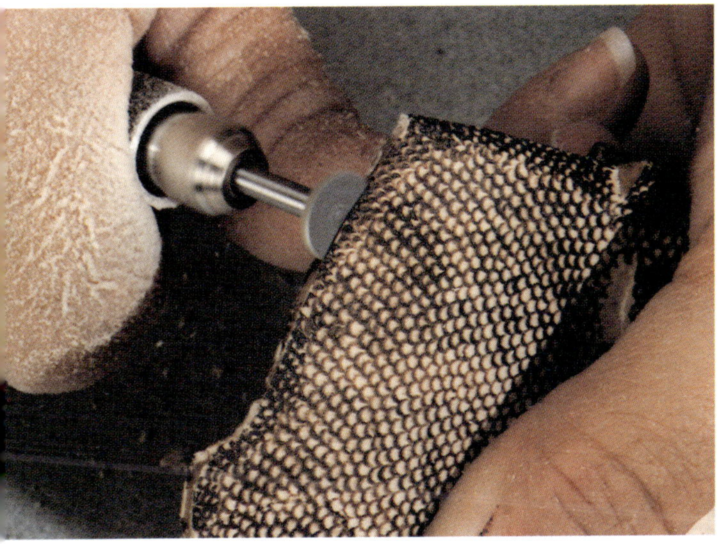

Do the same for the anal fin. The cutter's radius is the same as the depth of the tab on the fin.

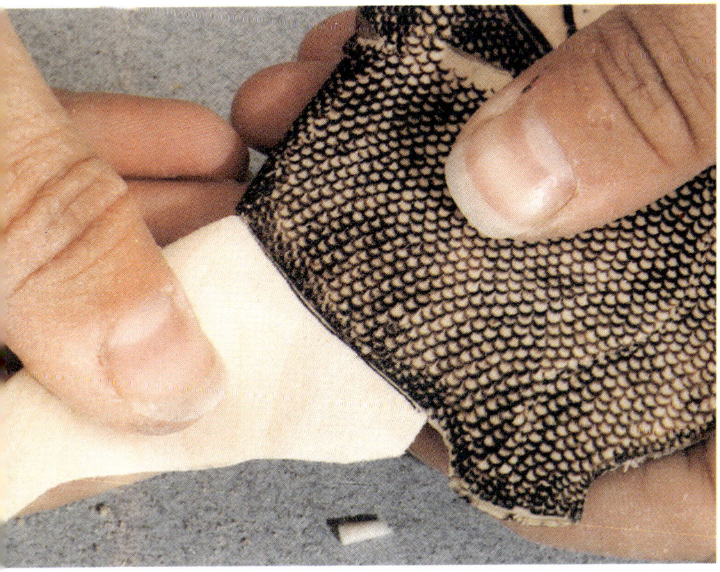

Check the fit.

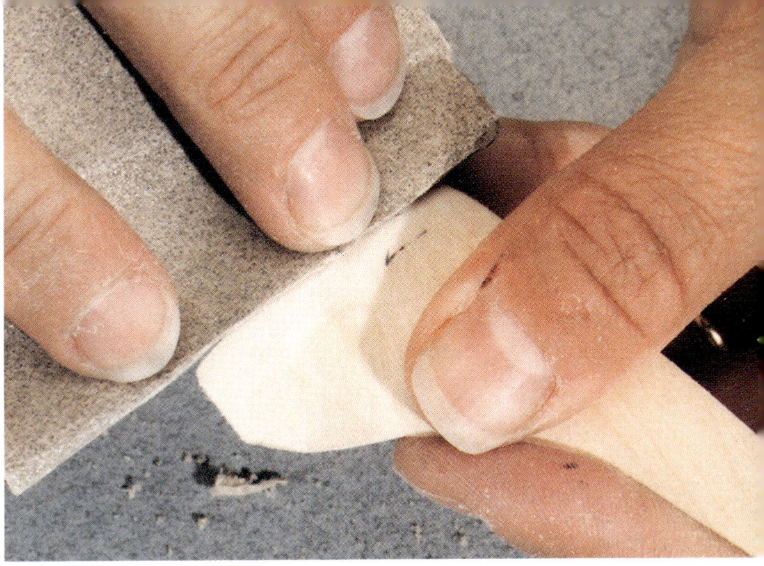

Making any necessary adjustments. Sand paper may be enough for some minor fixes...

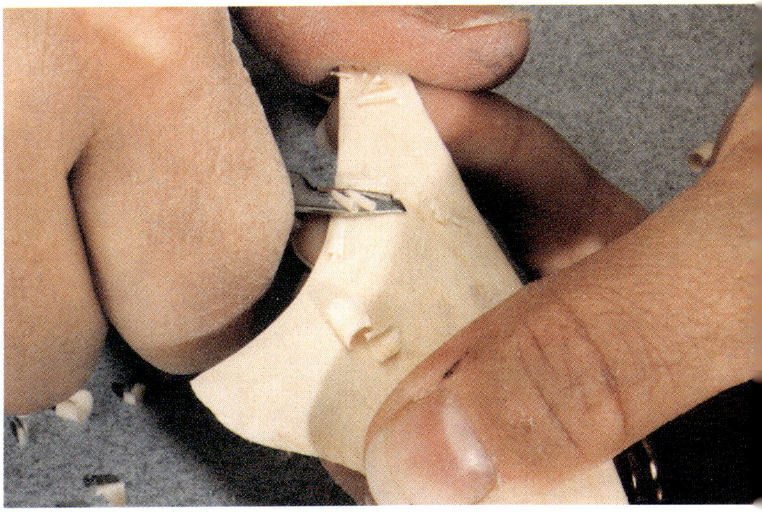

or you may need to use the knife.

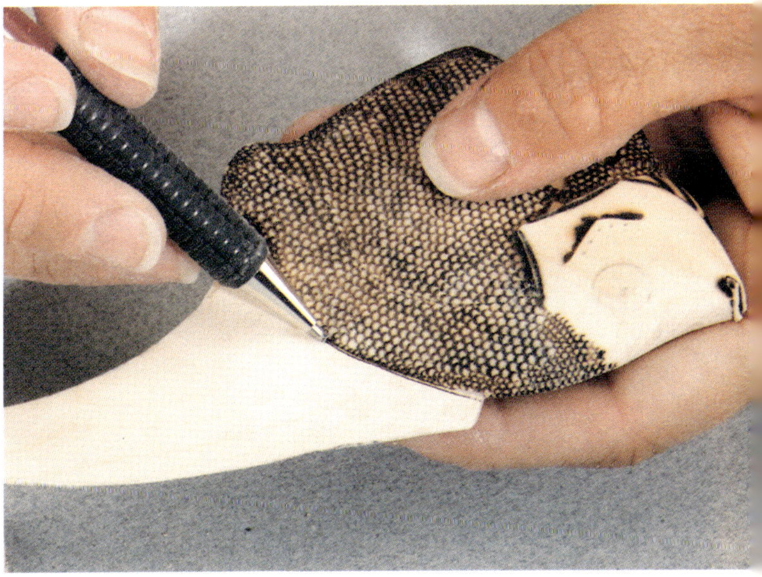

Mark the line of the body on the fin to check the depth of the tab.

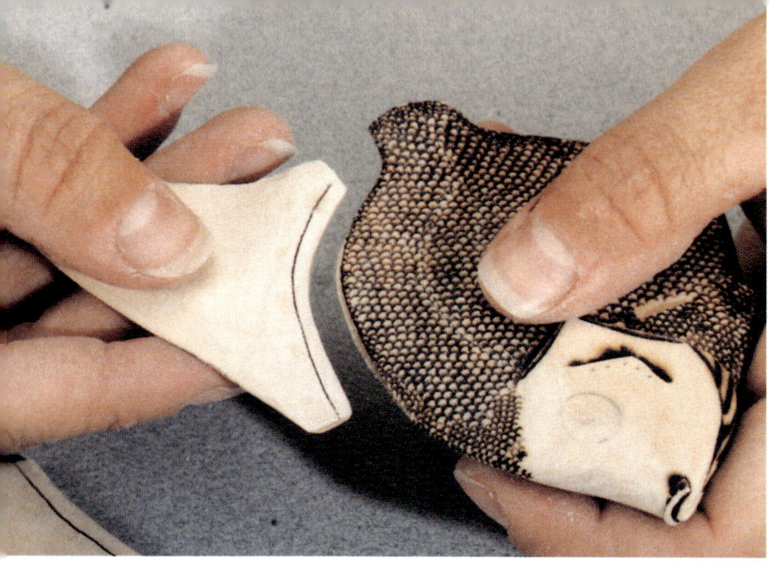

The tab is uniform, and with the line, I will be able to tell that it is inserted all the way when I glue it up.

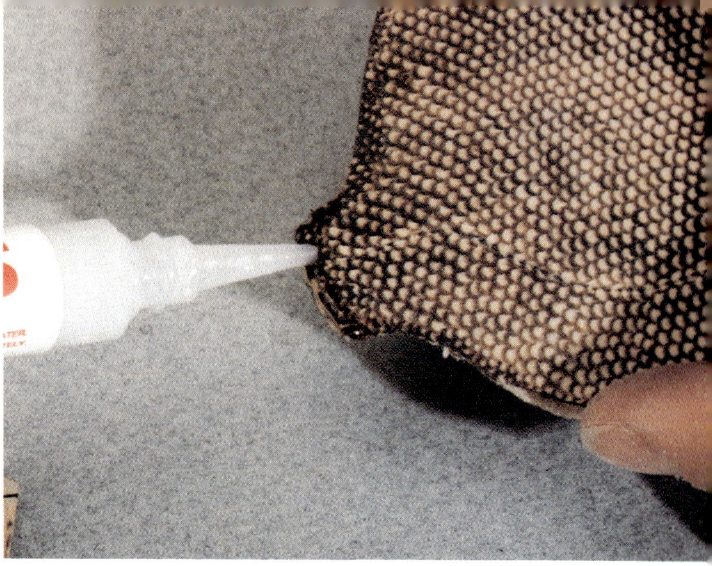

Reenforce the edge of the peduncle with super glue. In this case I had developed a small crack which the glue filled.

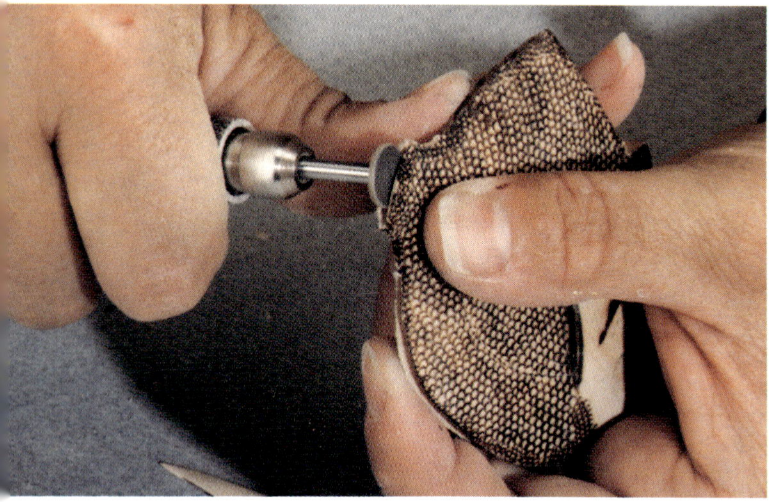

Use the same bit to cut the socket for the caudal fin.

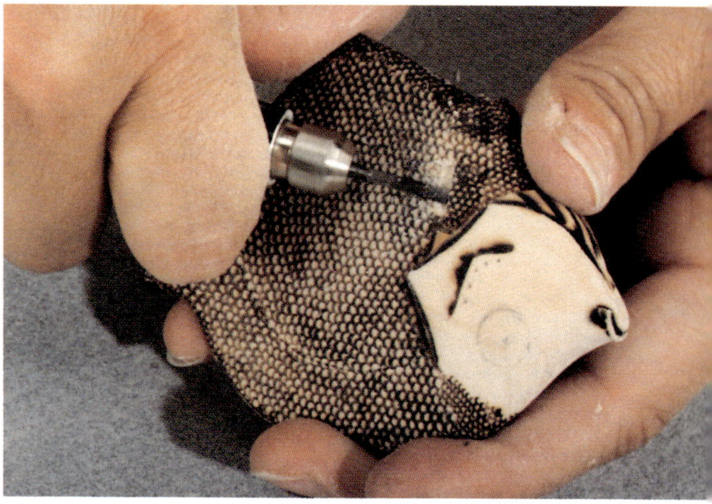

Change to the long shank carbide burr to cut the sockets for the pectoral fins. This goes deeply into the wood. Begin the cut gently until you get to the desired depth.

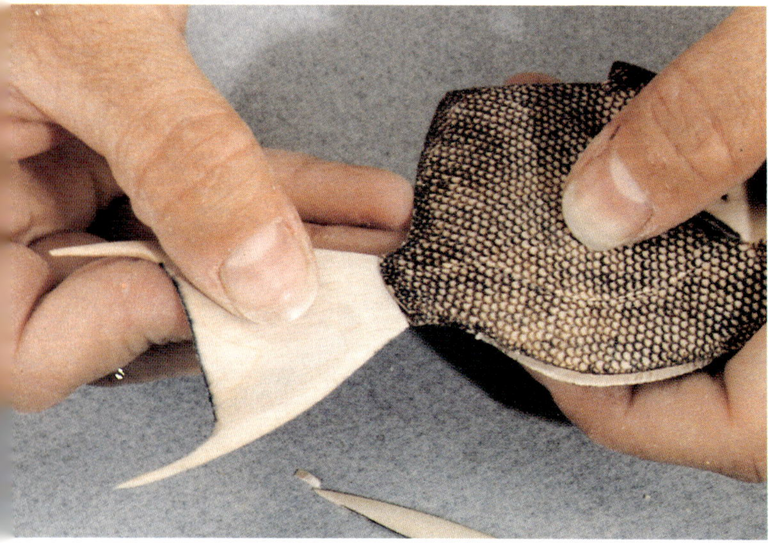

Check the fit of the caudal fin and adjust. With the socket the peduncle walls are very thin so use extra caution when checking.

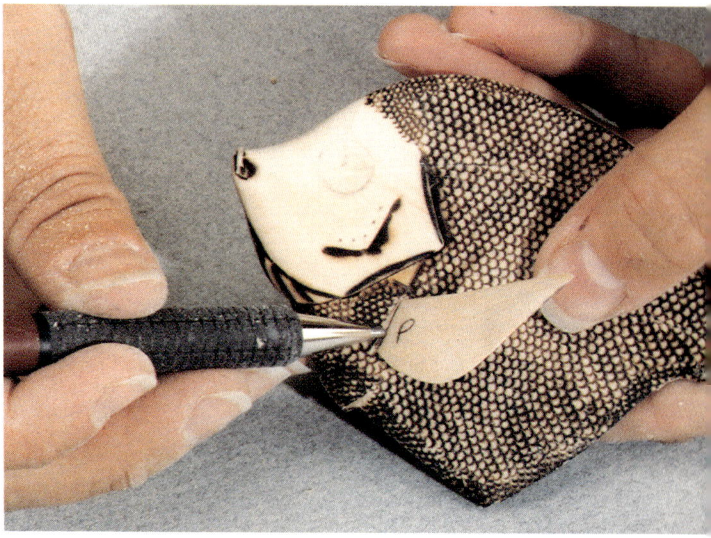

Fit the pectoral fin and mark it.

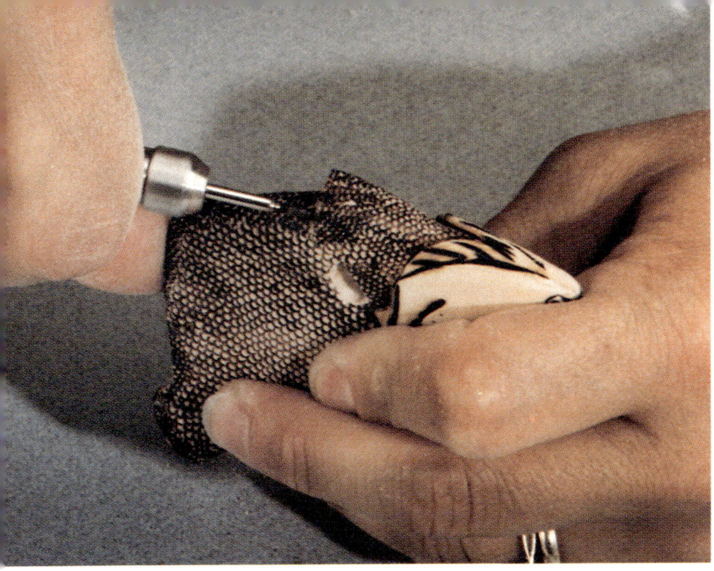

Switch to a finer diamond bit for the ventral fin sockets. The hole is much smaller and more delicate. When you reach the correct depth carefully enlarge the hole.

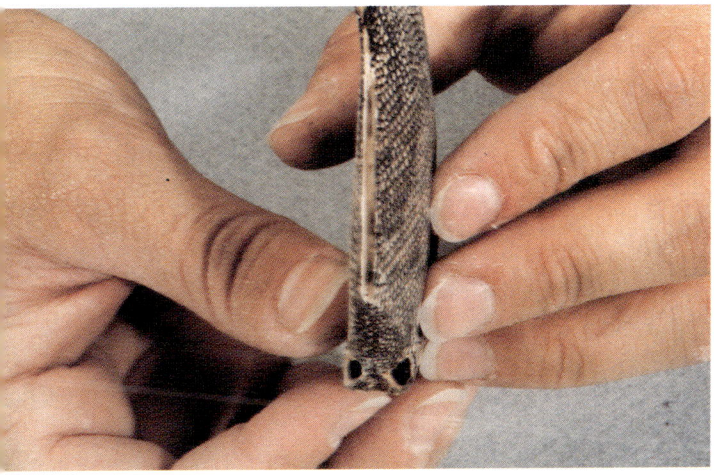

The result.

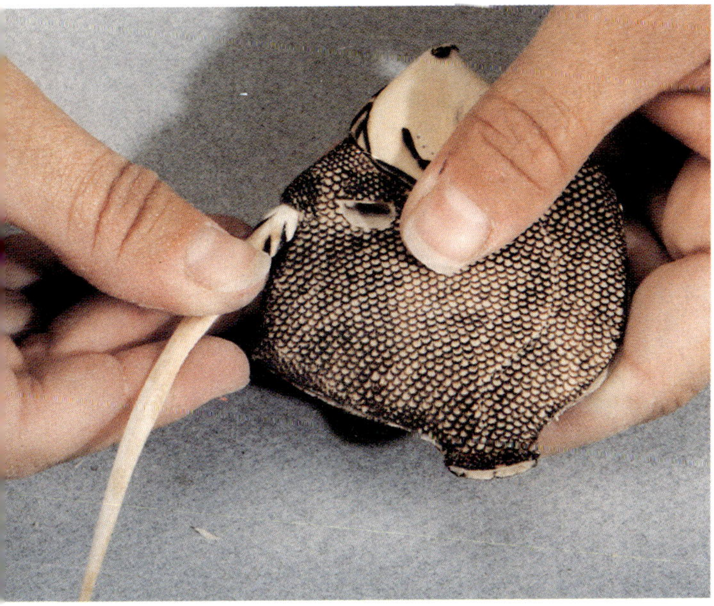

Test the fit and adjust.

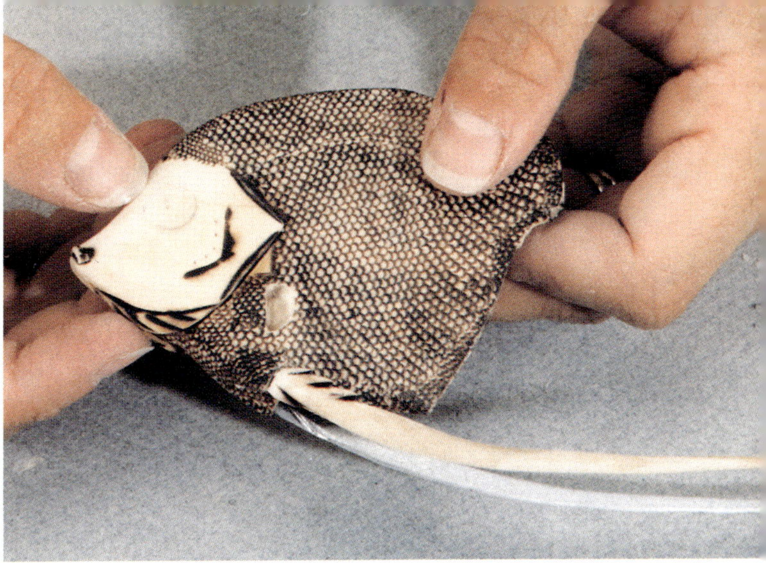

The result.

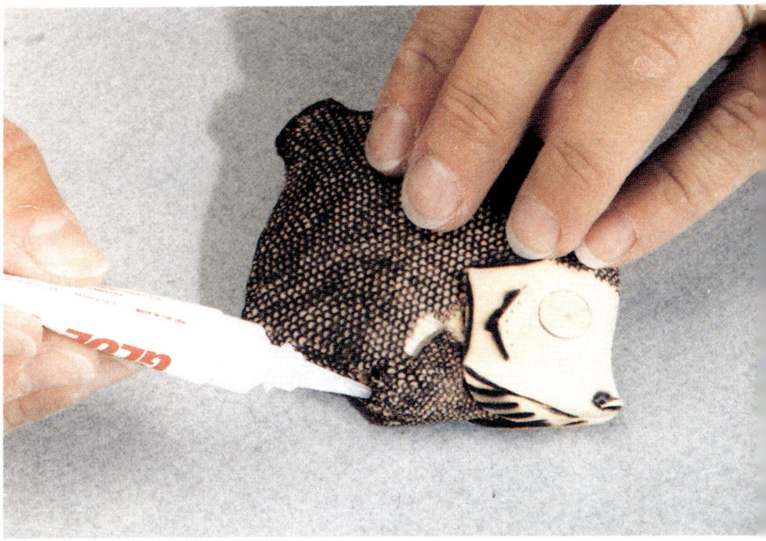

Reenforce the holes with super glue.

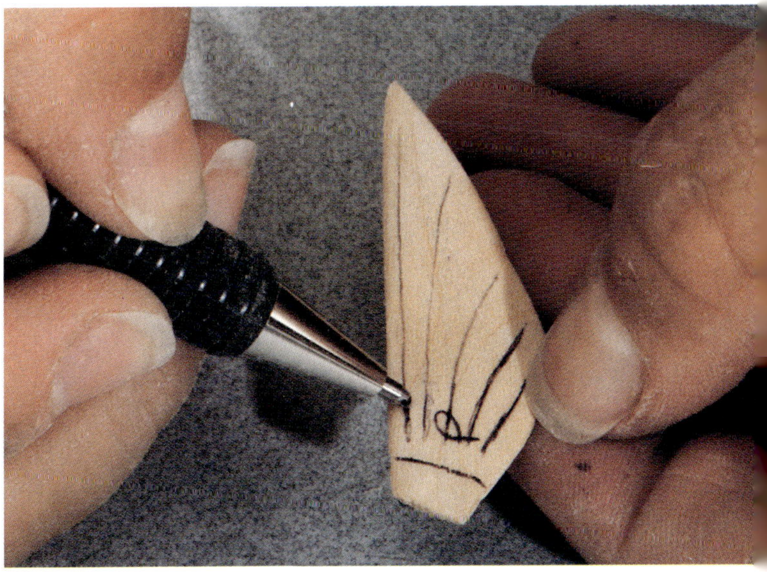

The pectoral fin will have five rays in this carving, though they have a few more in real life.

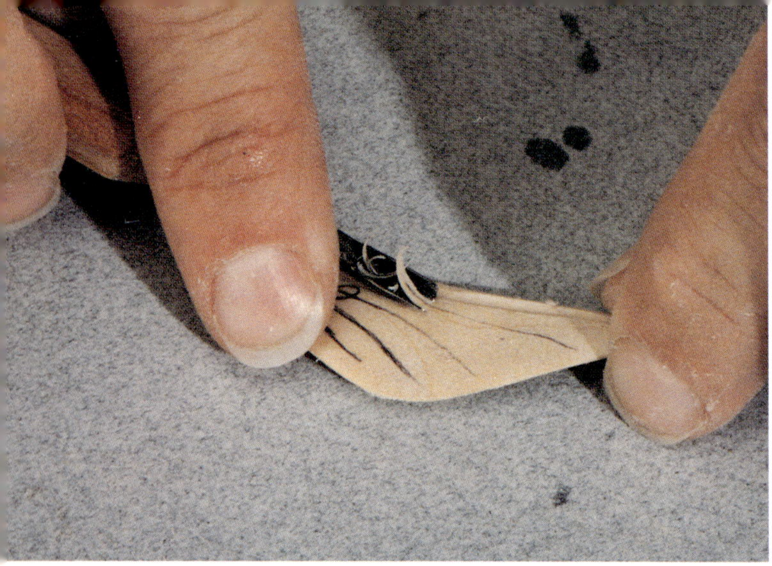

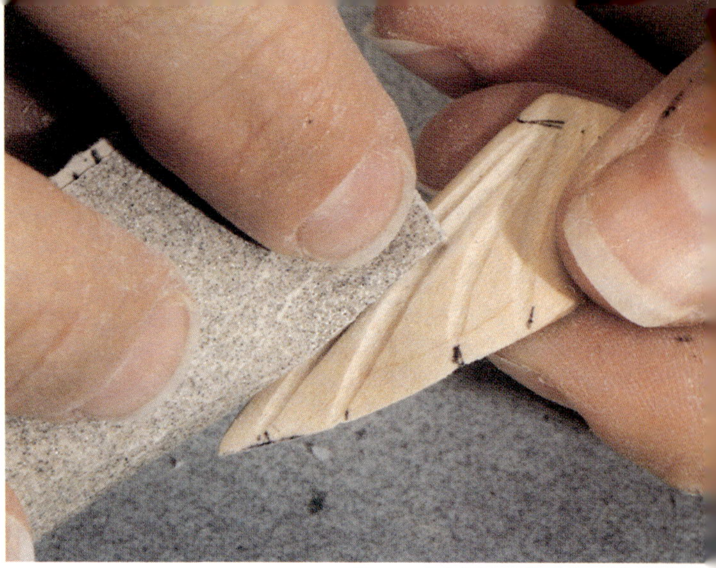

Carve the lines with a small u-shaped micro-gouge.

Sand the grooves to remove the sharp edge.

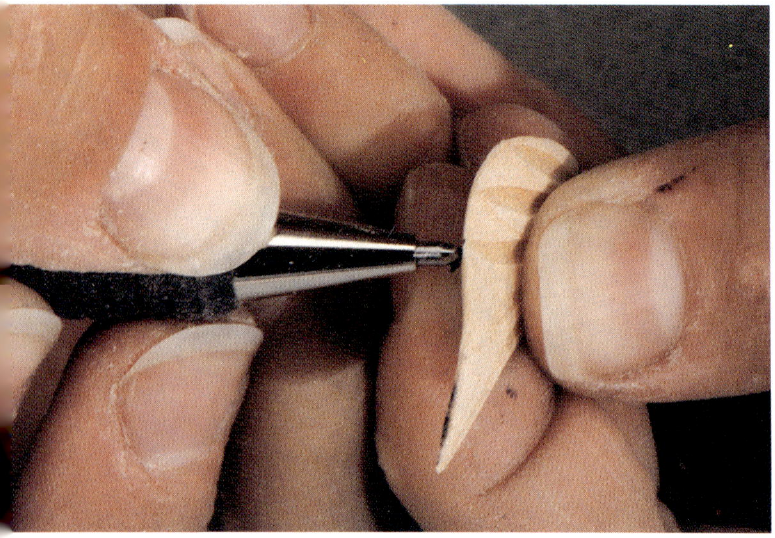

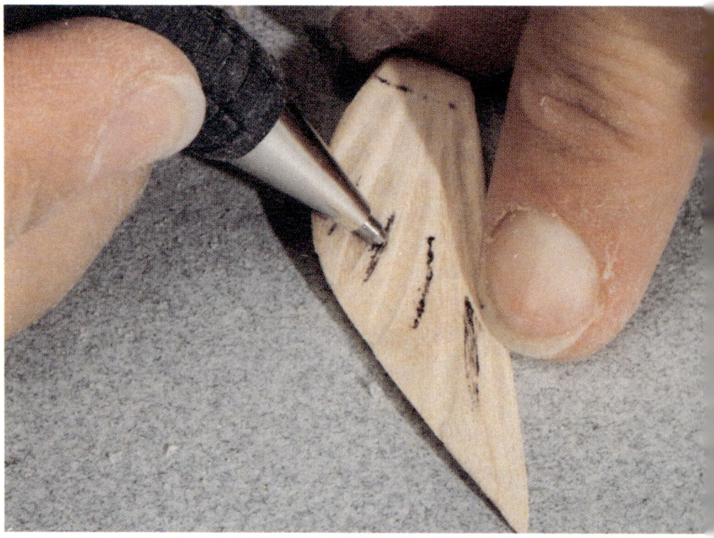

Look at the edge and on the other side mark where the grooves end.

With the micro v-gouge, I will bisect each of the rays at about these points.

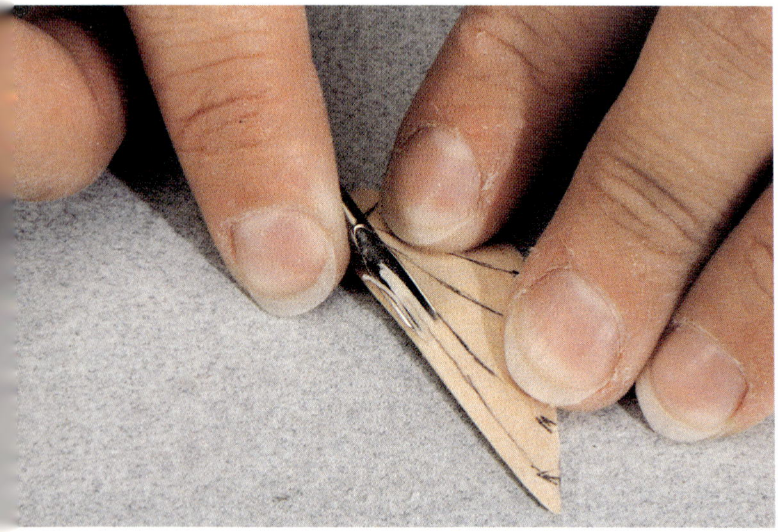

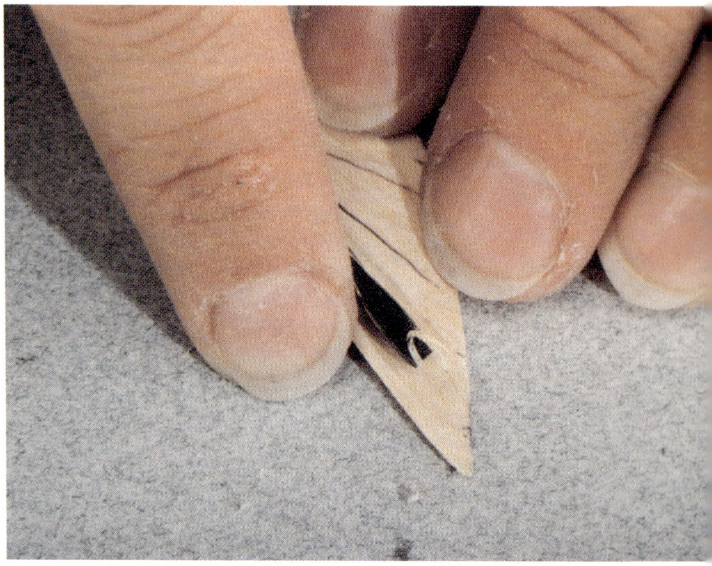

Draw the rays to match the other side, and carve in the same way.

Go almost to the end of the fin.

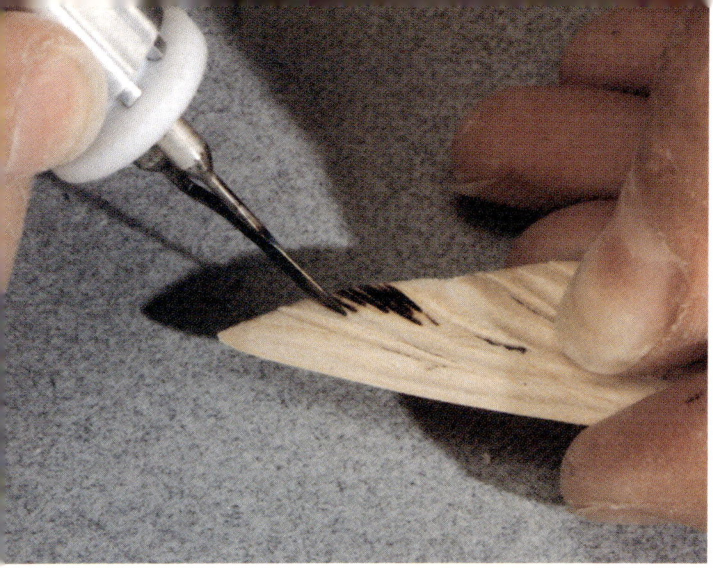

In the last third of the fin use the burner to split each ray even more.

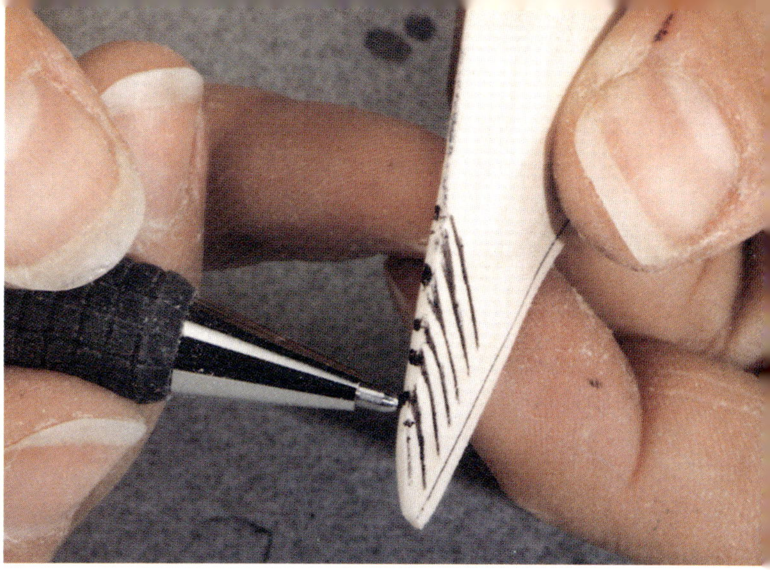

Mark the top edge and carry the spines down the other side.

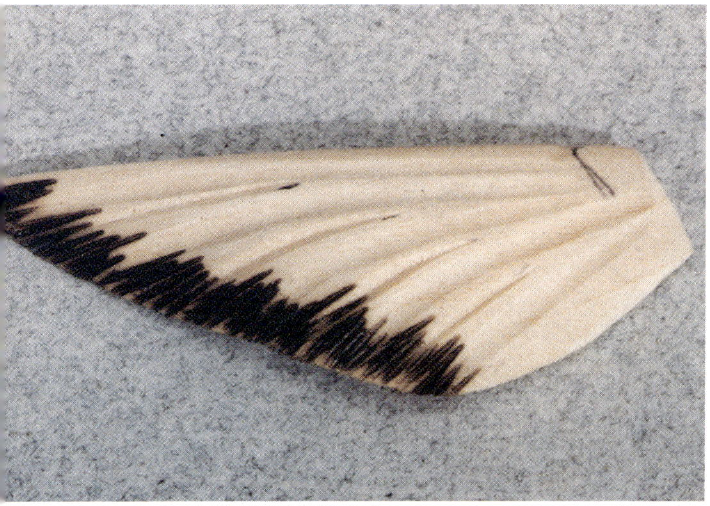

The result.

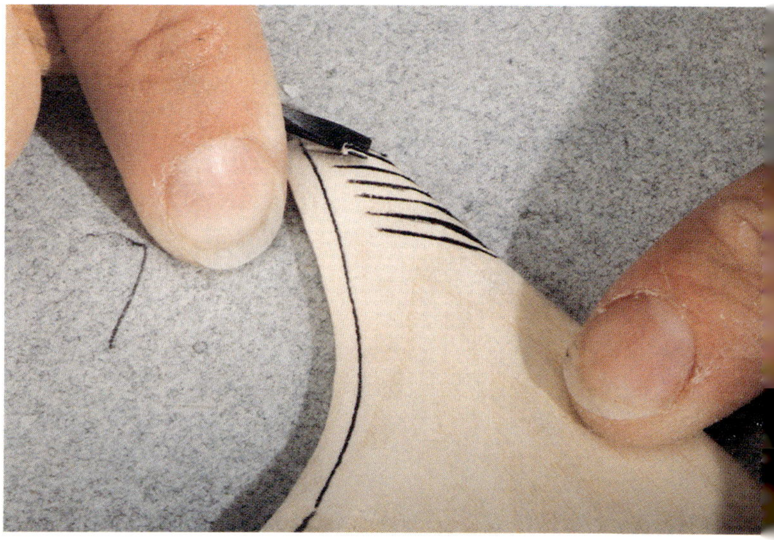

With the micro v-gouge, run up the lines of the spines. Do both sides of the fin.

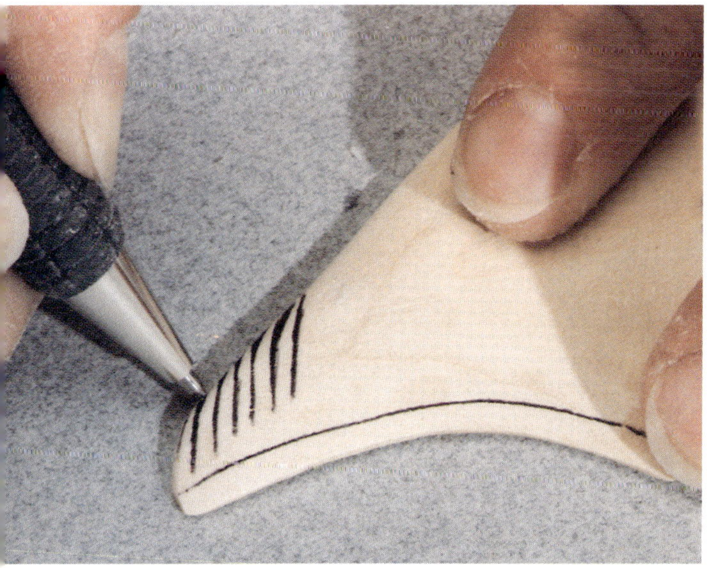

The leading edge of the dorsal fin is has spines. I use about six spines, though in reality there are more.

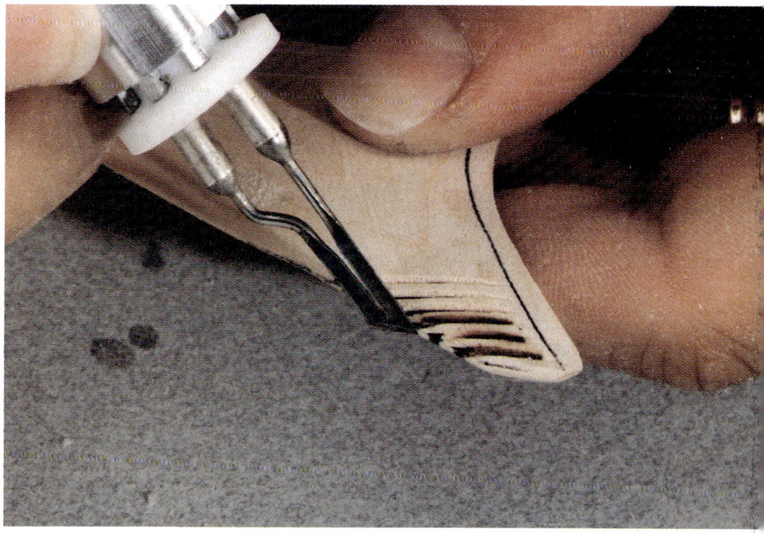

Burn it in a little, going deeper at the tips so the spiny rays looked raised.

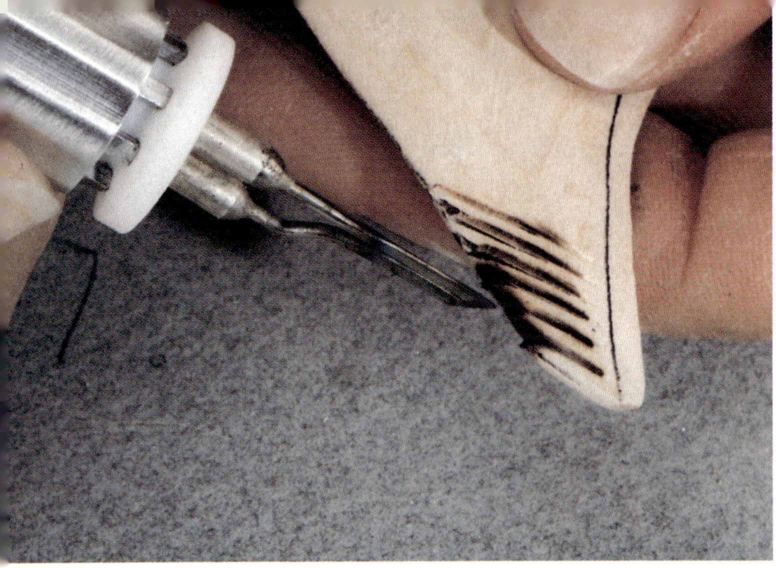

The burner helps bring out the points of the spines.

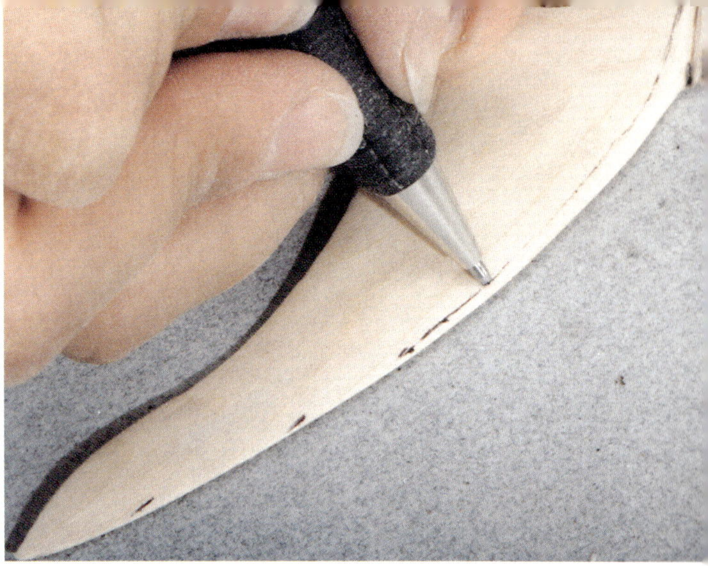

The rays in the dorsal fin don't split except at the tip.

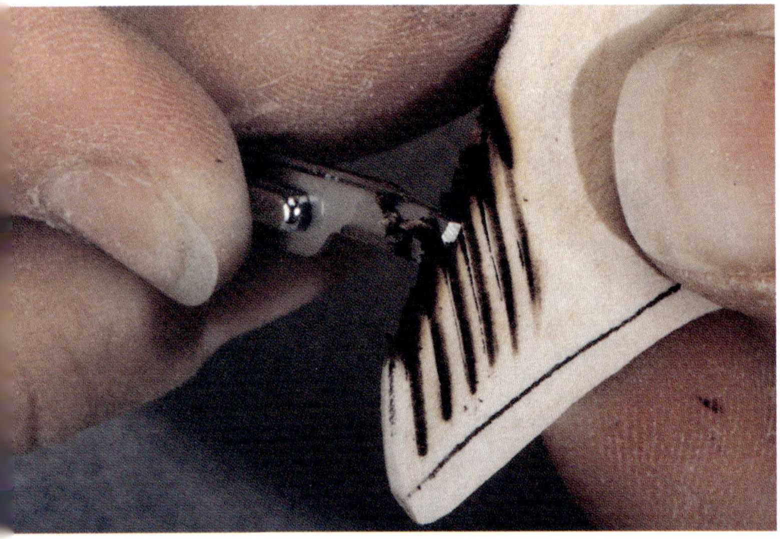

Trim the front edge of each spine a little more to curve it.

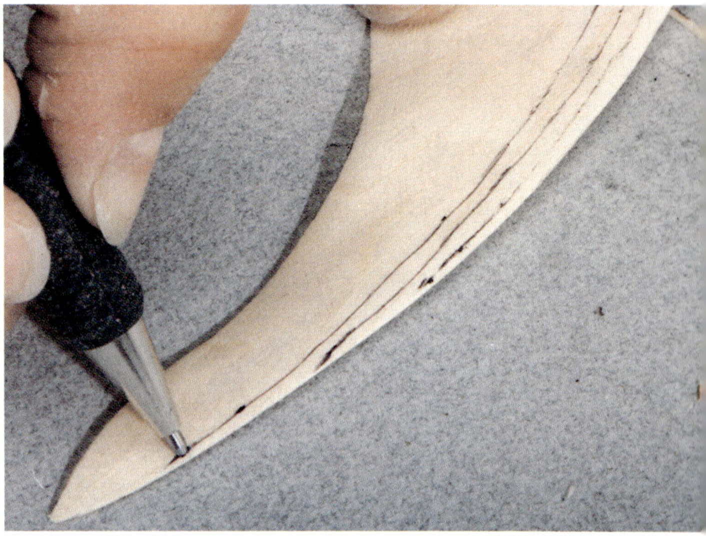

They do end as they meet the edge, as you can see with these three leading rays.

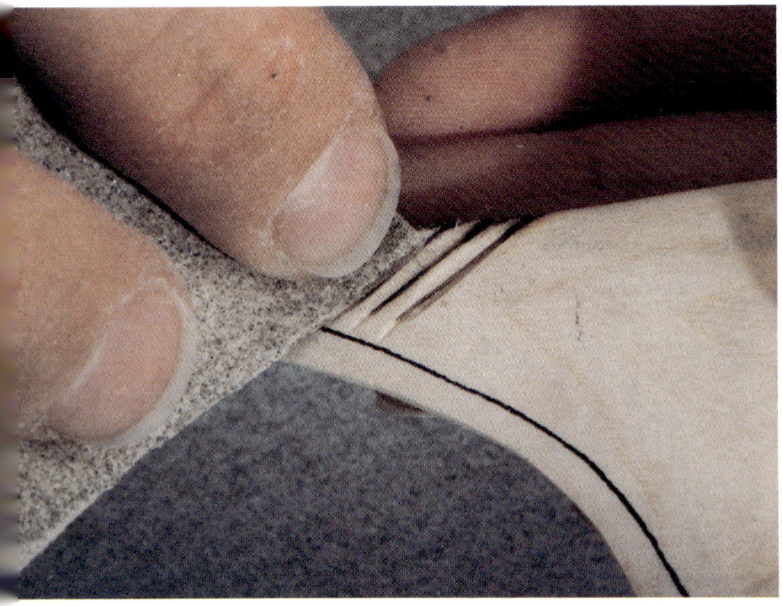

Lightly sand each spine to round it slightly.

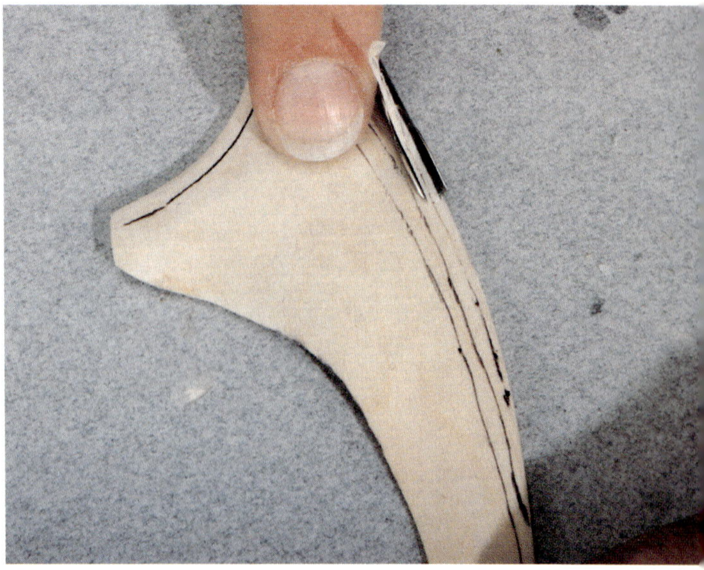

Cut the lines with the micro u-gouge.

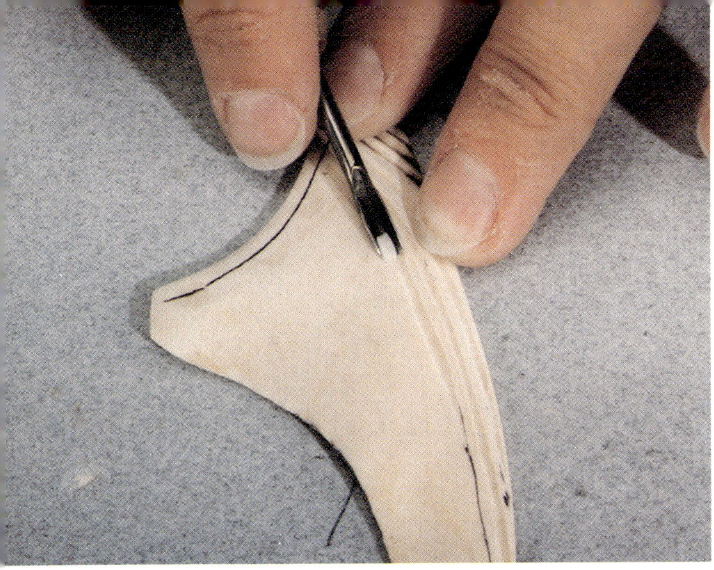

As you move in, switch to a wider micro-gouge for the base of the grooves..

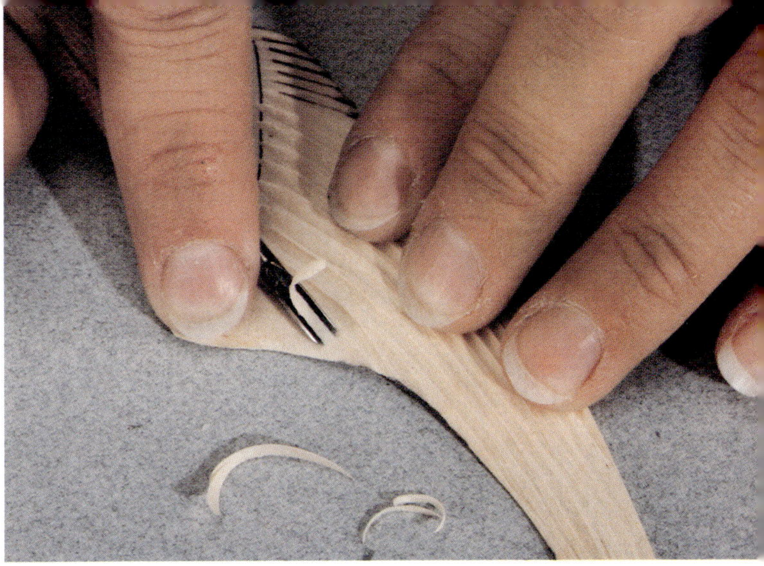

As you move toward the trailing edge, the rays end as they run off the fin.

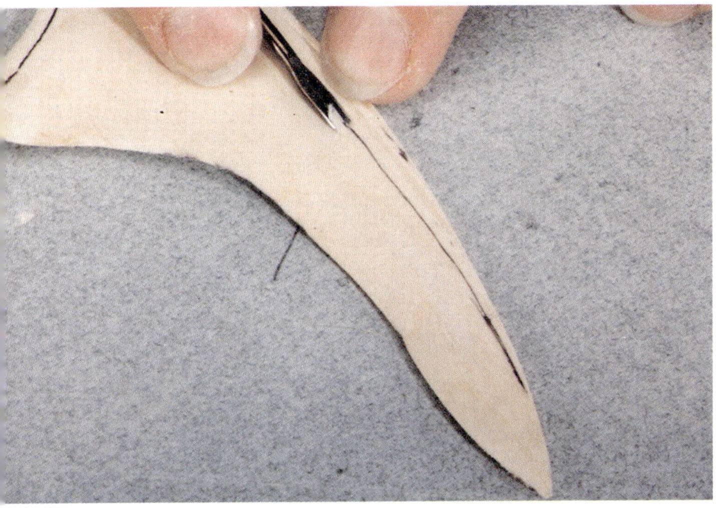

and about halfway up, go back to the narrower tool.

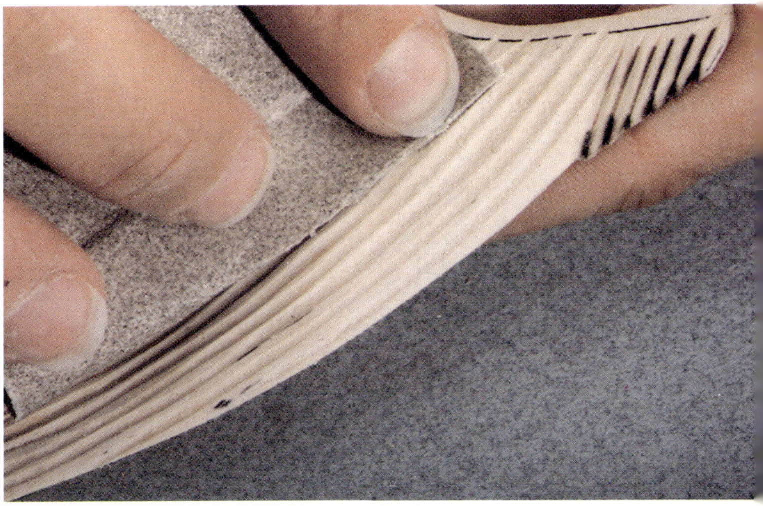

Sand lightly to round off the edges.

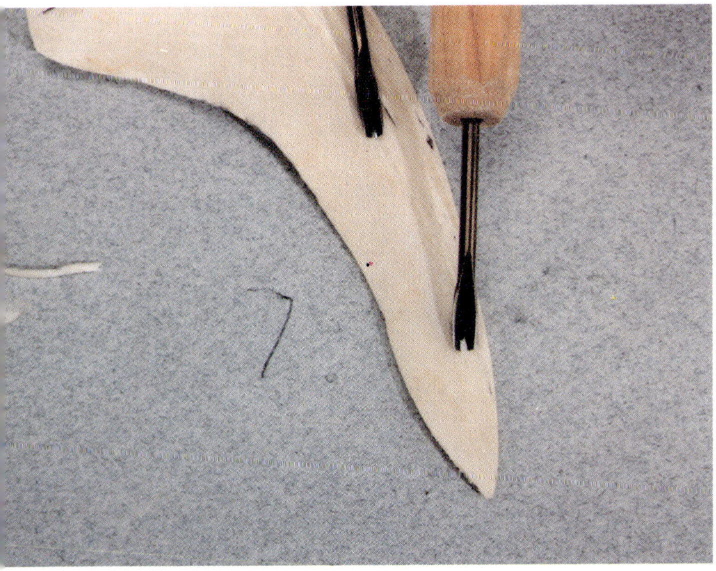

For the last part of the groove, where the rays get crammed at the tip of the fin, switch to the micro v-tool.

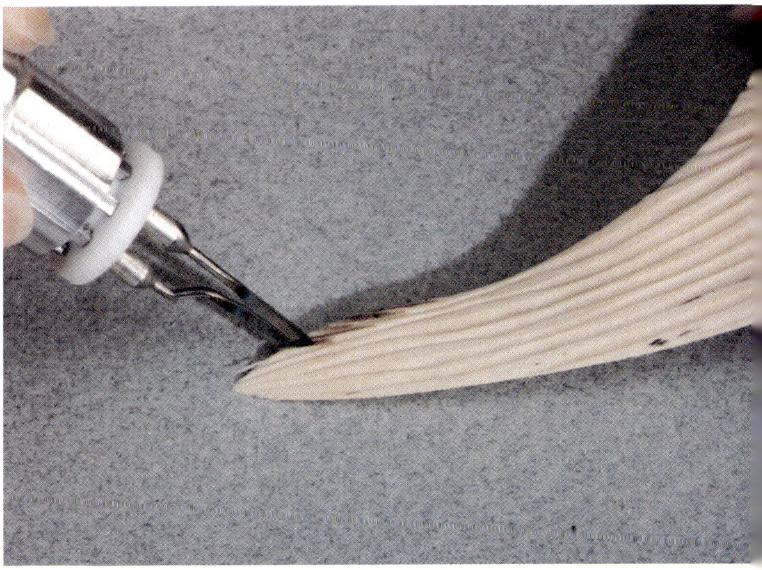

Use the burner to add a few more detailing marks at the tip of the fin...

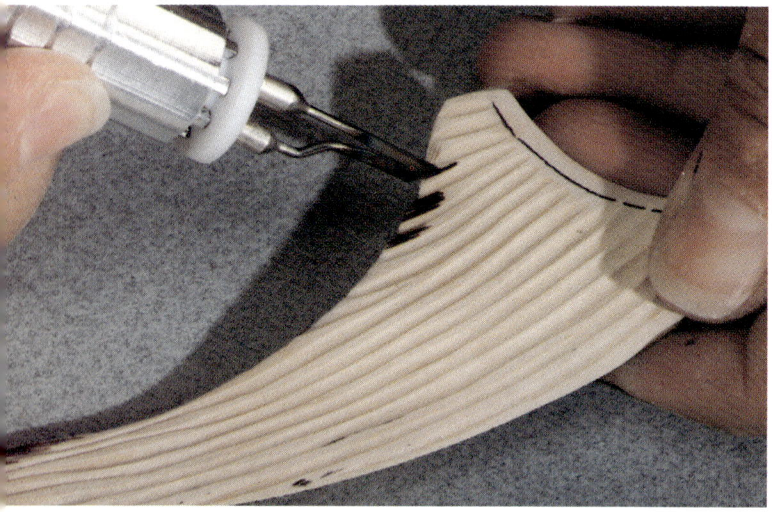

and at the trailing edge.

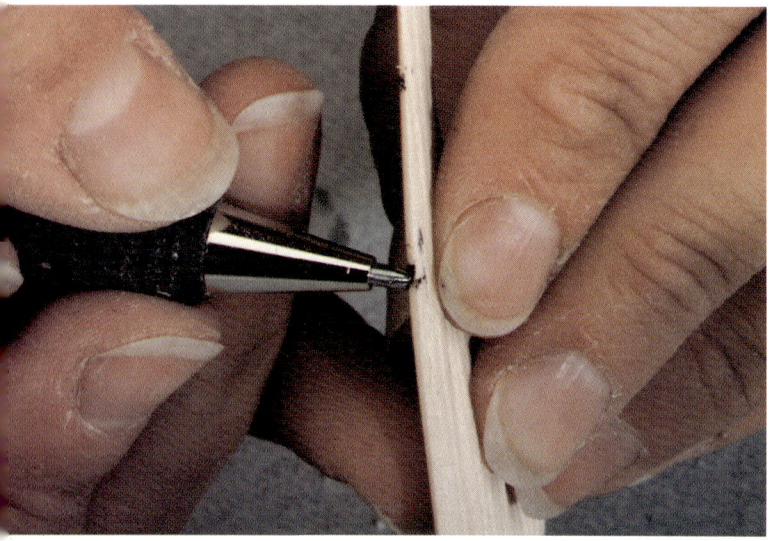

On the opposite side I match where the rays end on the leading edge, but do not worry about matching the others.

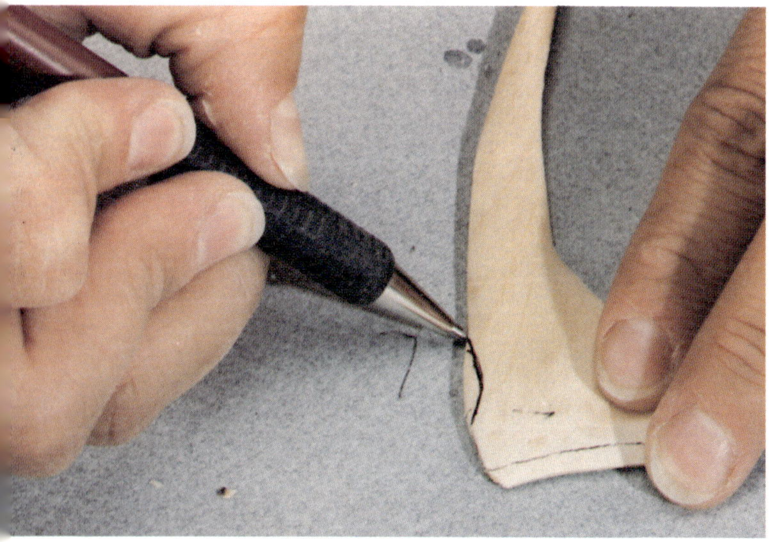

Moving to the anal fin, I want to shape the leading edge. This will give me room for the fin spines.

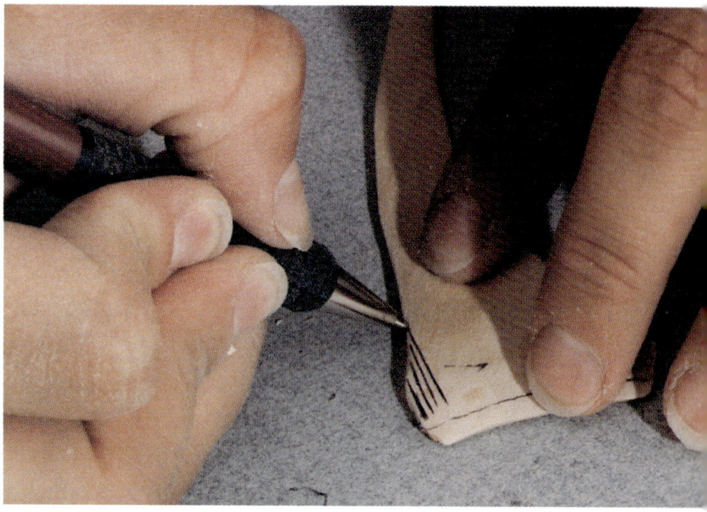

Add four spines to the leading edge as you did on the dorsal fin.

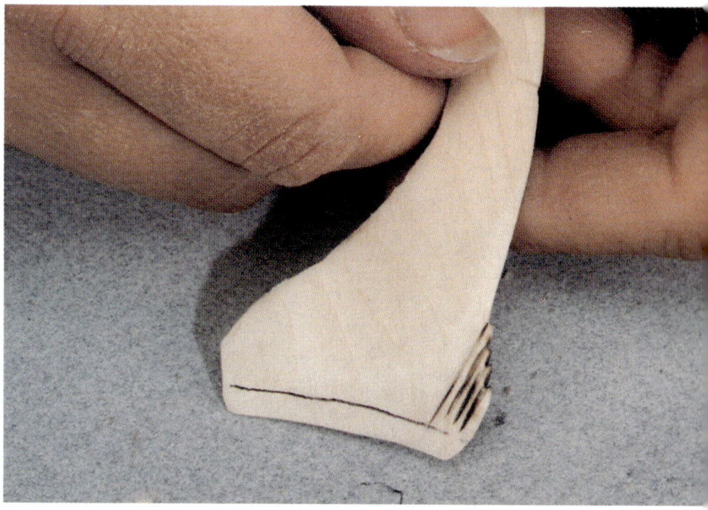

The result.

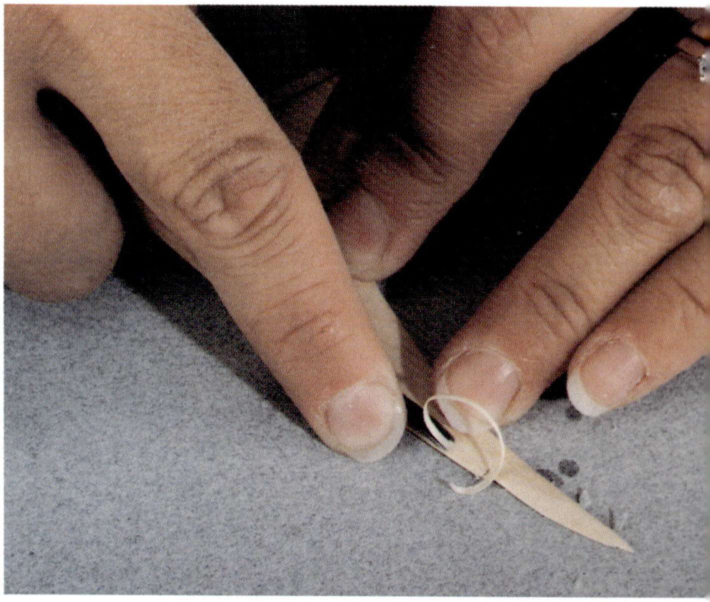

Add the rays as you did on the dorsal fin.

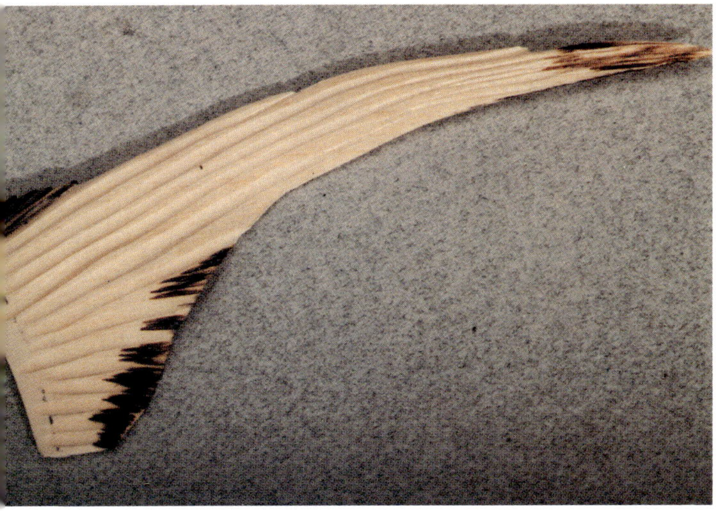

Burning details at the tip and at the base on the leading and trailing edges finishes the anal fin.

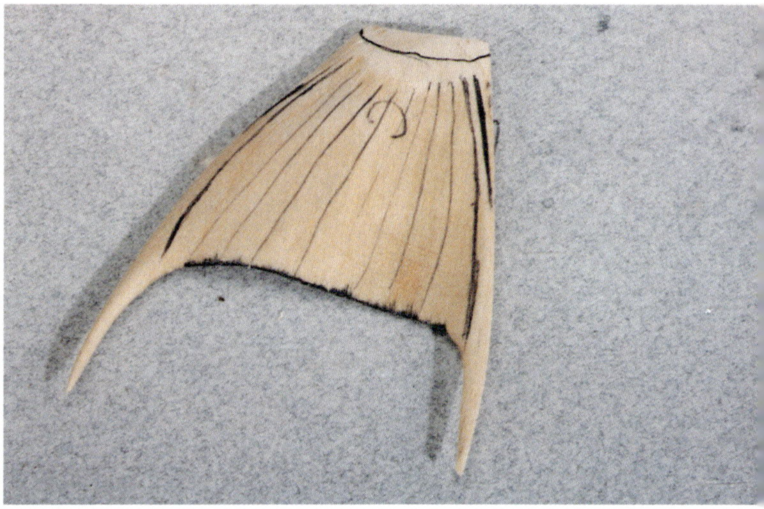

Draw the others, working toward the middle.

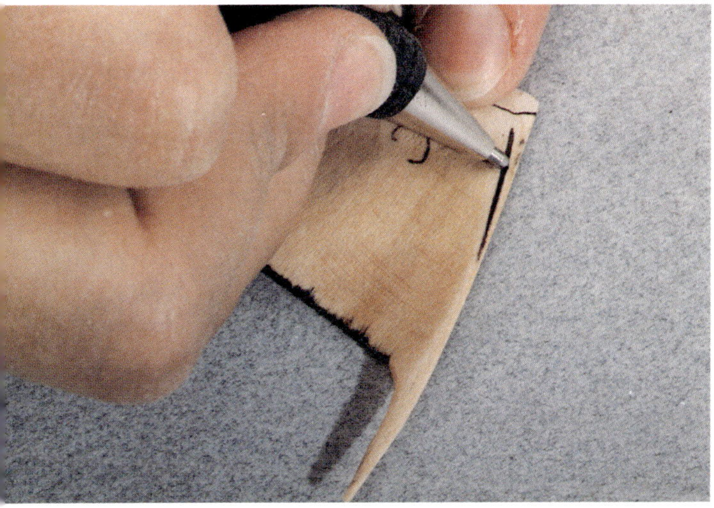

The caudal fin will have 10 rays, though the real one has somewhere around fourteen. On each edge the first ray runs off the side...

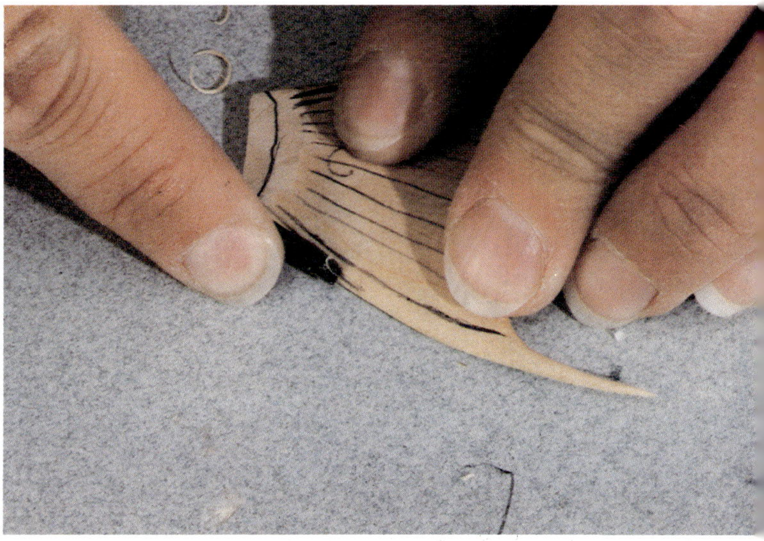

With the micro v-tool, run the first rays off the sides.

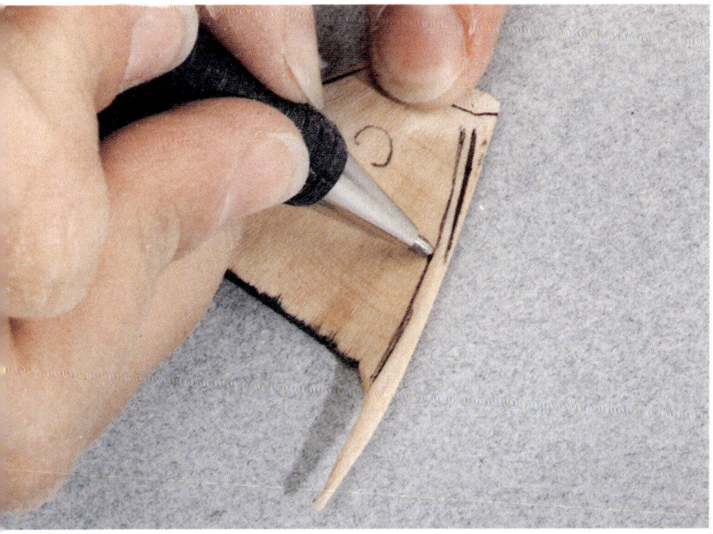

and the second ray includes the "trailer."

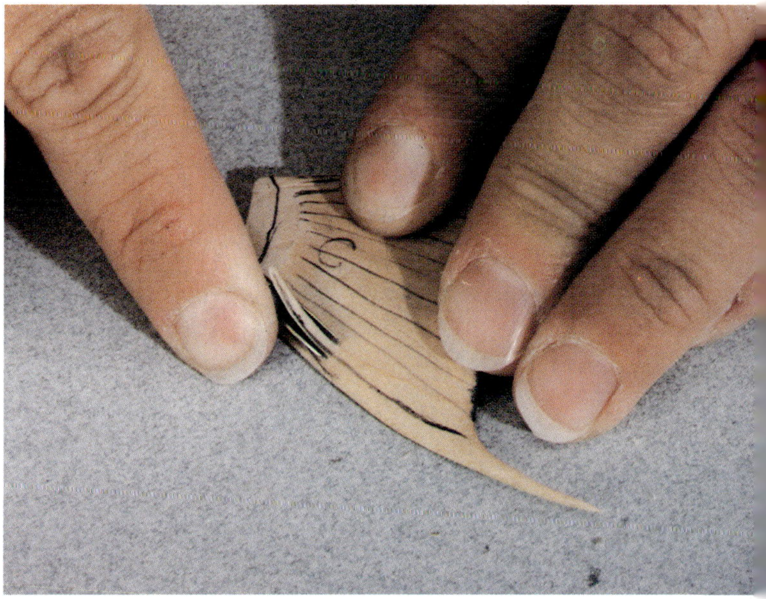

The other rays are carved using a micro u-gouge.

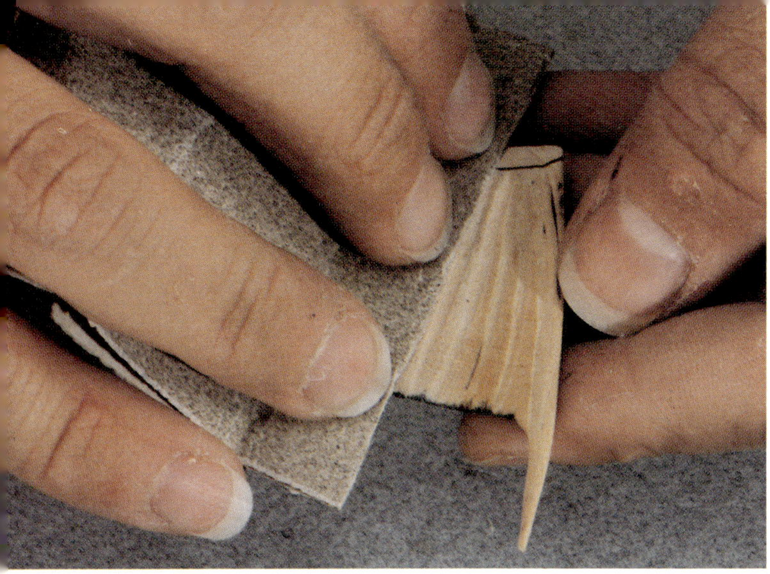

Sand them lightly rounding over the fin rays and making them look more delicate.

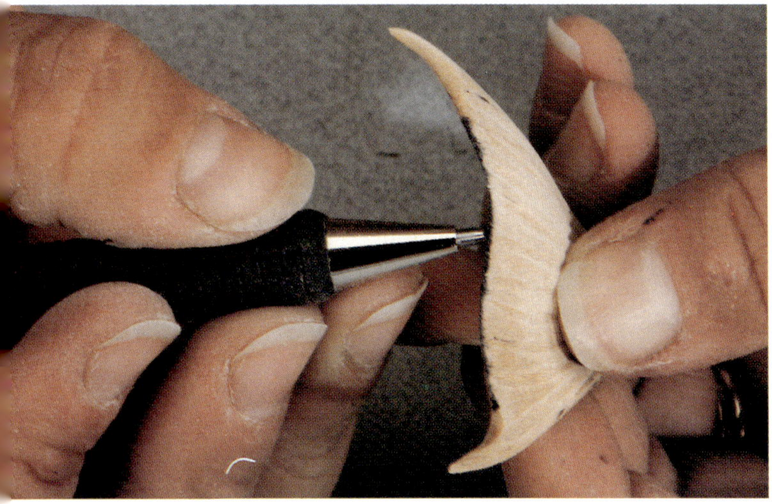

Mark the rays so you can match them on the other side.

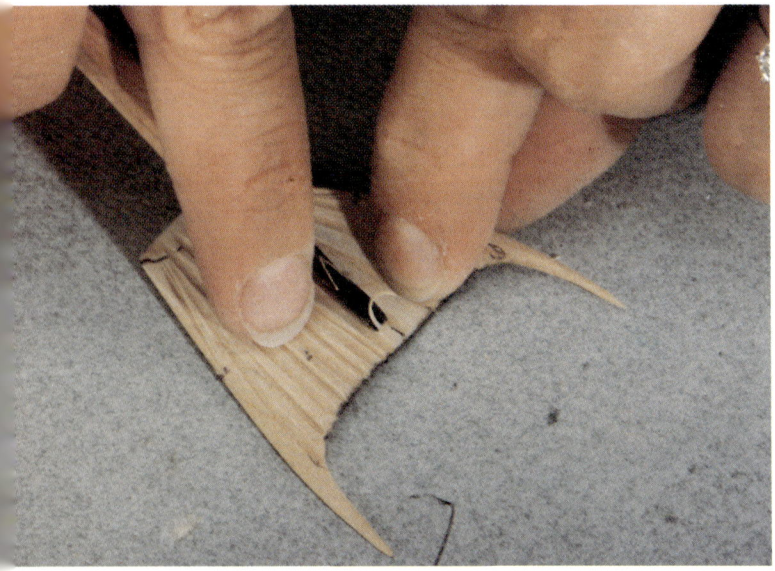

Starting about halfway up the caudal, use the v-tool to bisect the rays.

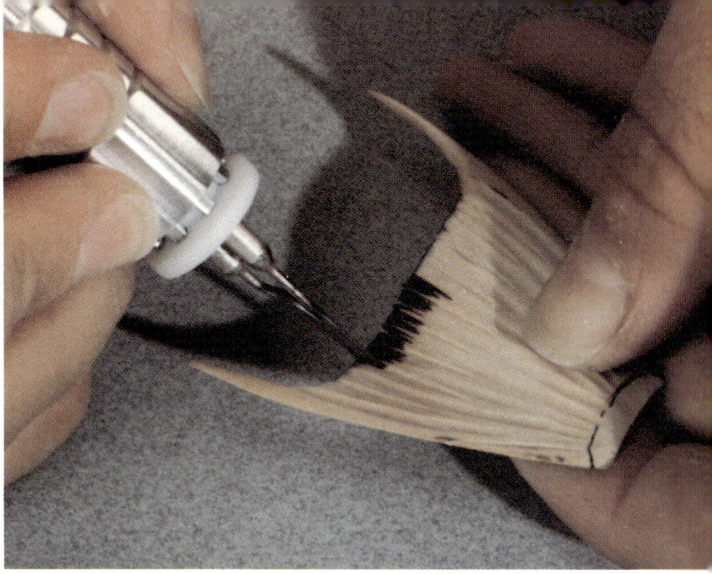

Further divide the last third with the burner.

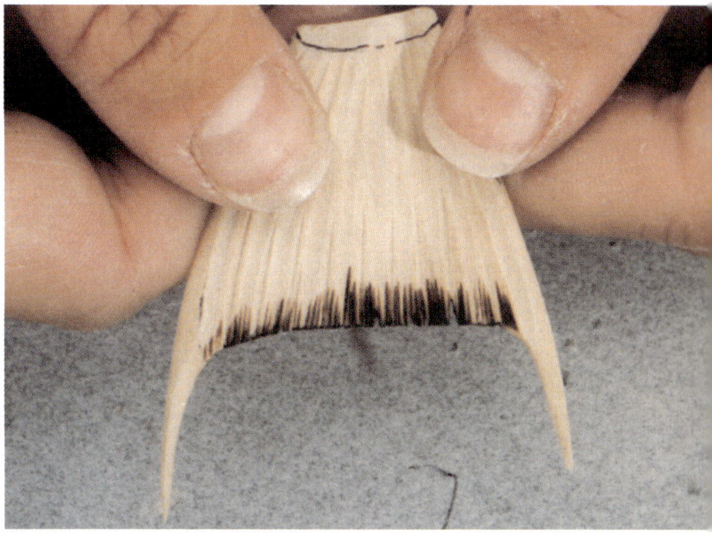

The result. Notice that I've created some imperfections in the trailing edge. This is common with these fish in nature.

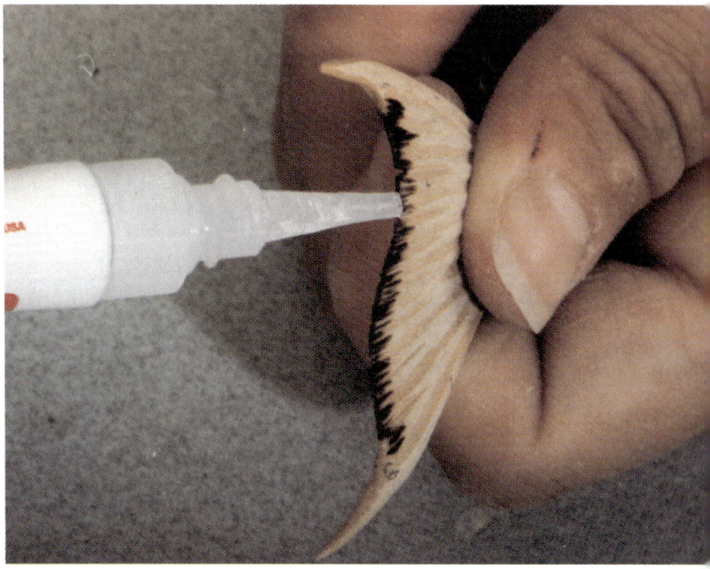

Super glue the tips and the edges of all the fins for strength.

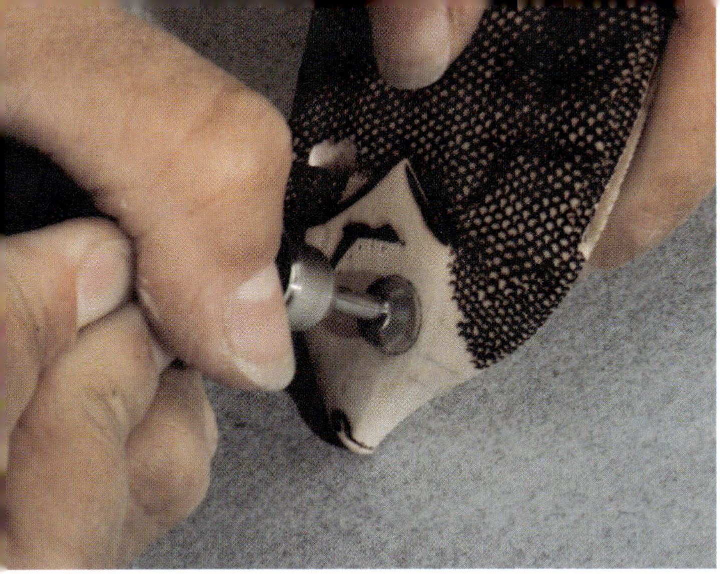

While the fins dry we can cut the eye socket. With this larger eye I can use a carbide countersinking bit. It has a point on the cutting surface that can be aligned at the center point.

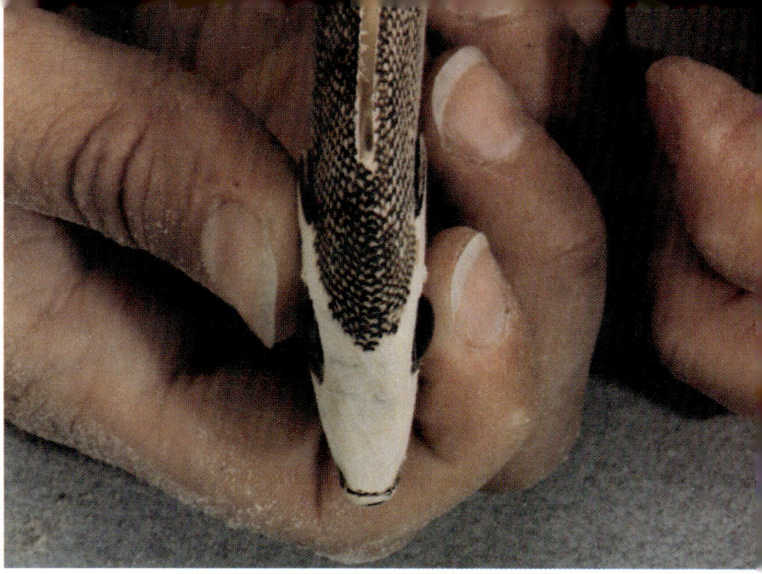

Check the alignment of the eyes from the top and the front. Again, you can make adjustments. The putty will hide any mistakes.

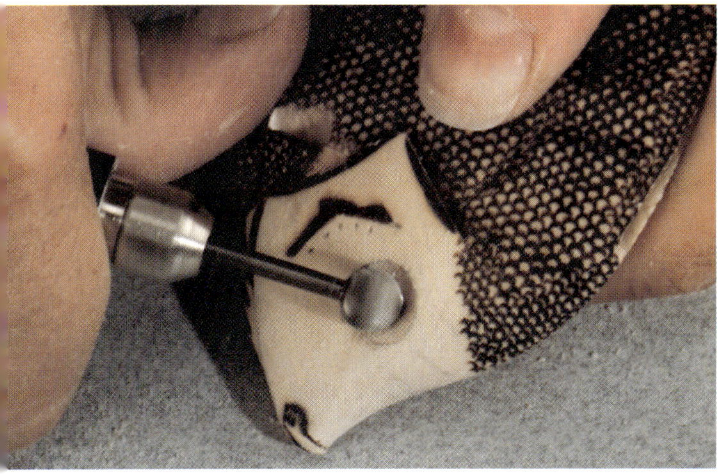

With the hole started I switch to a ball cutter to establish depth.

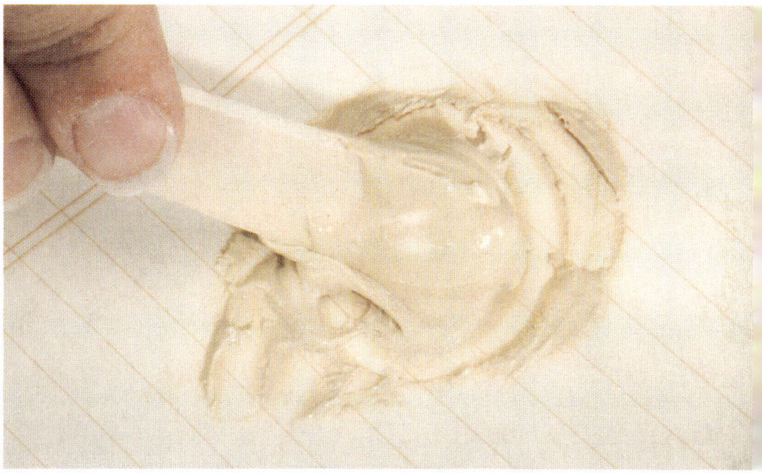

Mix the putty for the eyes.

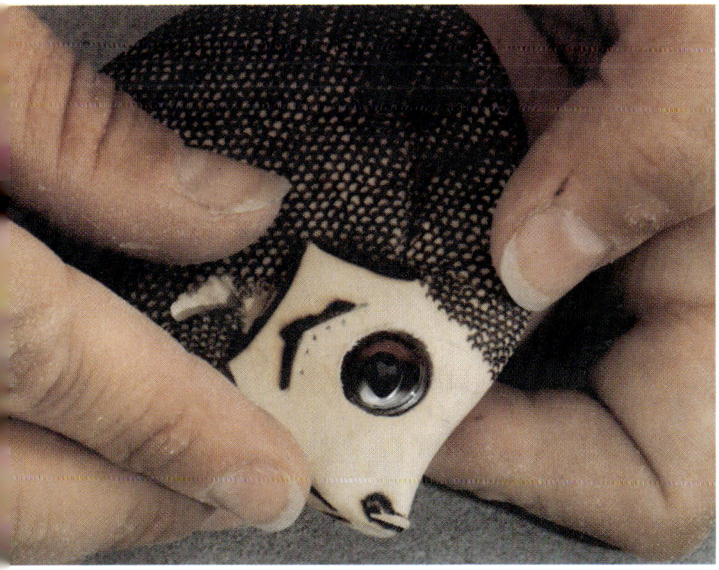

Test fit the eye, adjust the socket until it drops in.

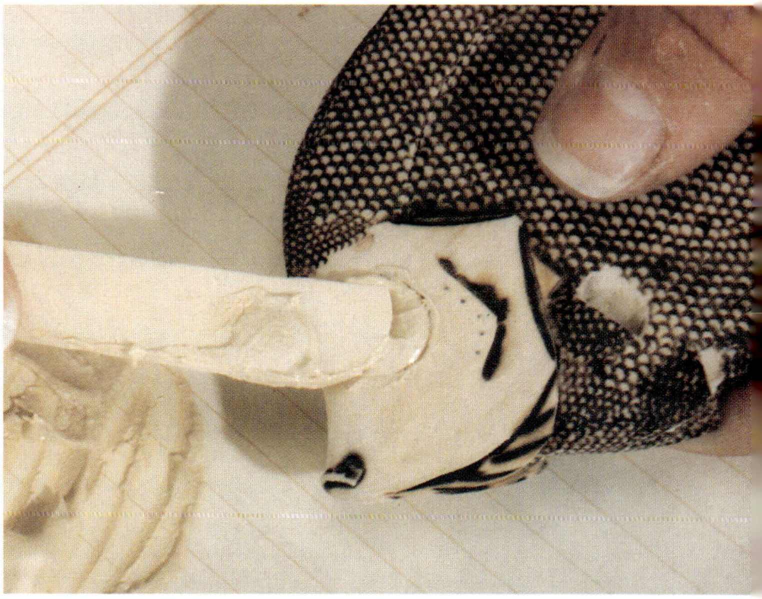

Fill the socket with putty...

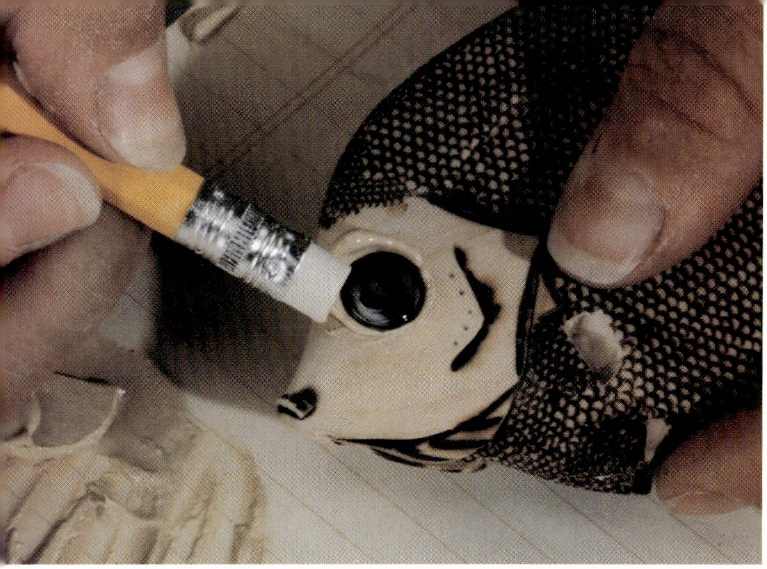

and put the eyes in place, silver side forward.

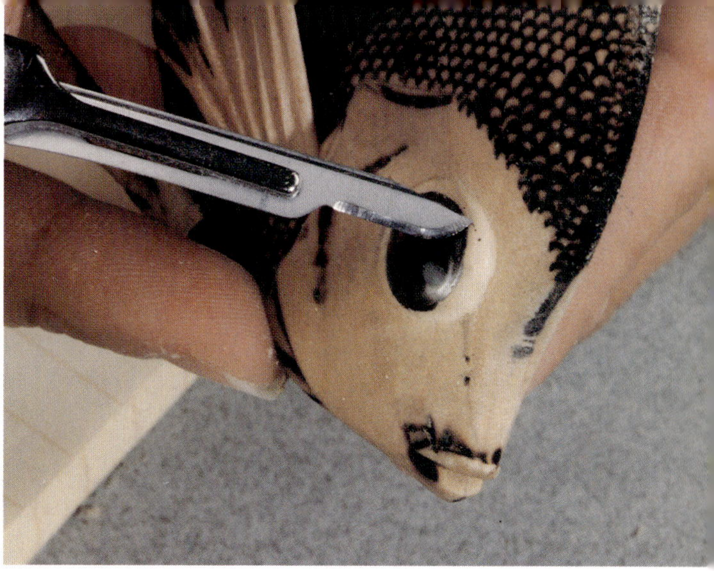

The result will be this fleshy edge to the eye.

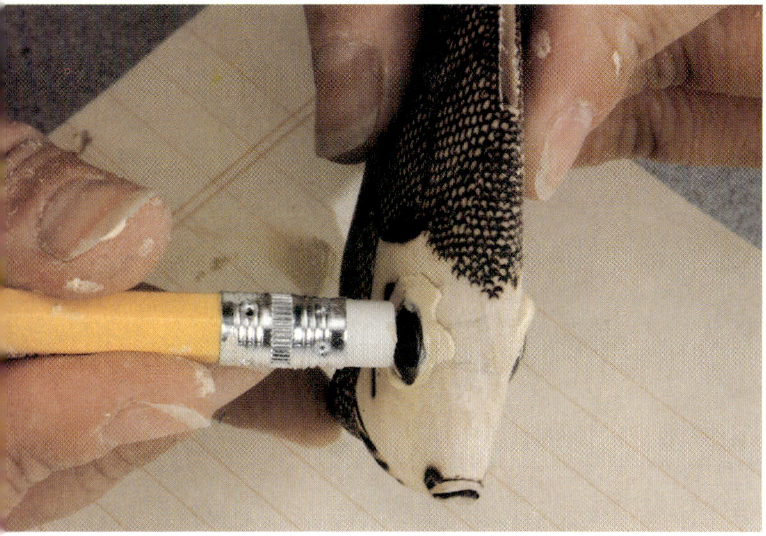

The bottom edge should be flush with the face and the top edge protruding. For adjustment, you can turn the eye a little with the eraser end of a pencil.

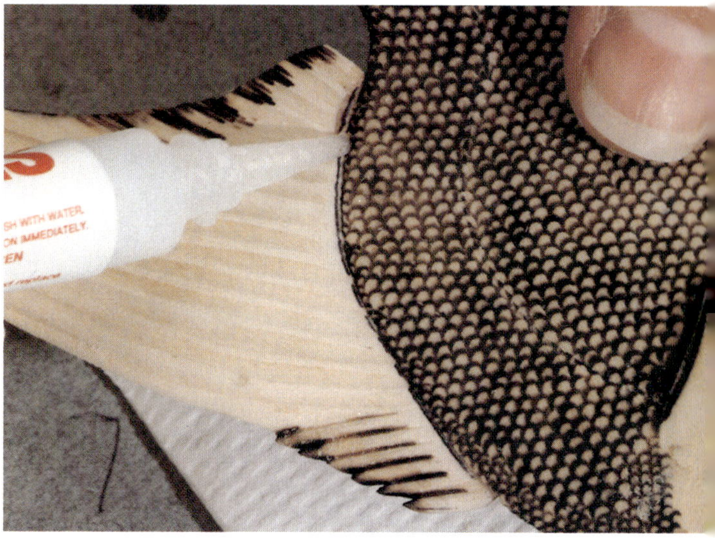

While that is setting we can attach the fins. The fit on this model is so close that they can be super glued into place. Put the fin in place and run a bead of super glue along the joint on each side. Capillary action will pull the glue into the joint for a strong bond.

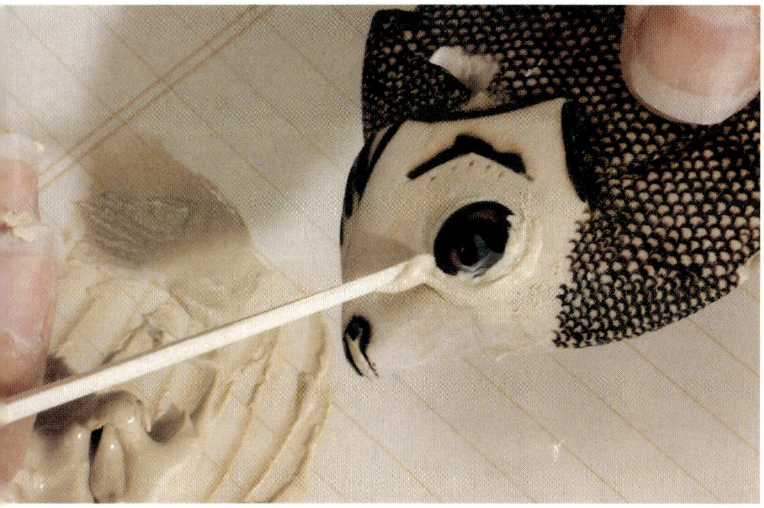

With extra putty fashion the sclerid capsule on the top of the eye.

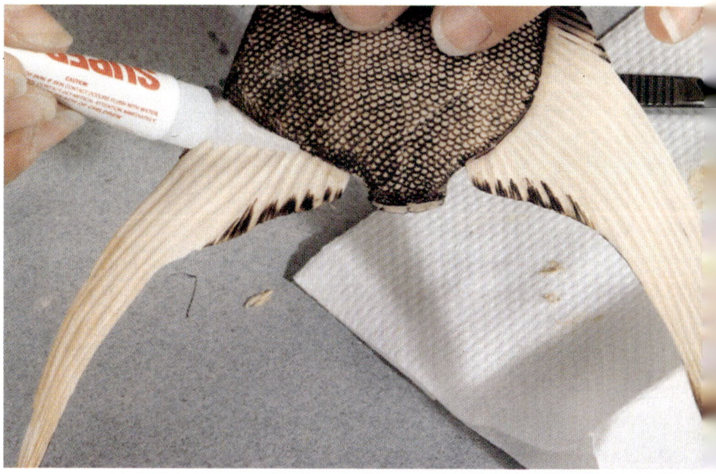

The anal fin is next and is done in the same way. If the fins didn't fit so well I would use the putty I used for the eyes.

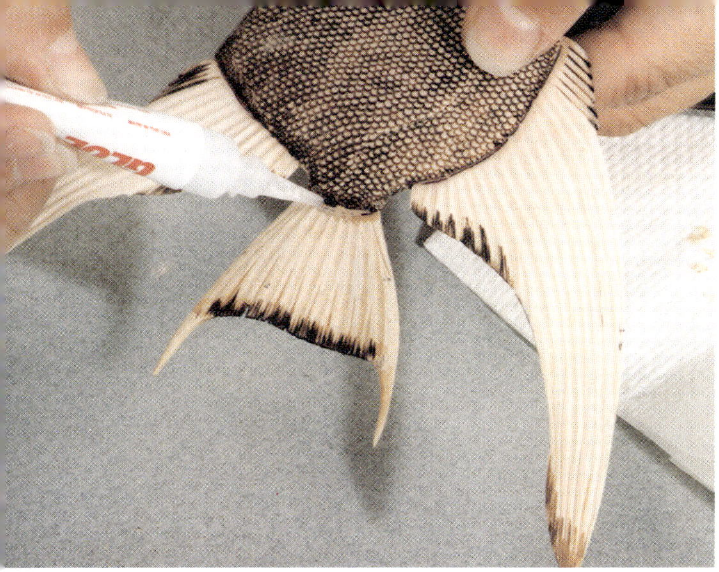

After the anal fin follow the caudal fin...

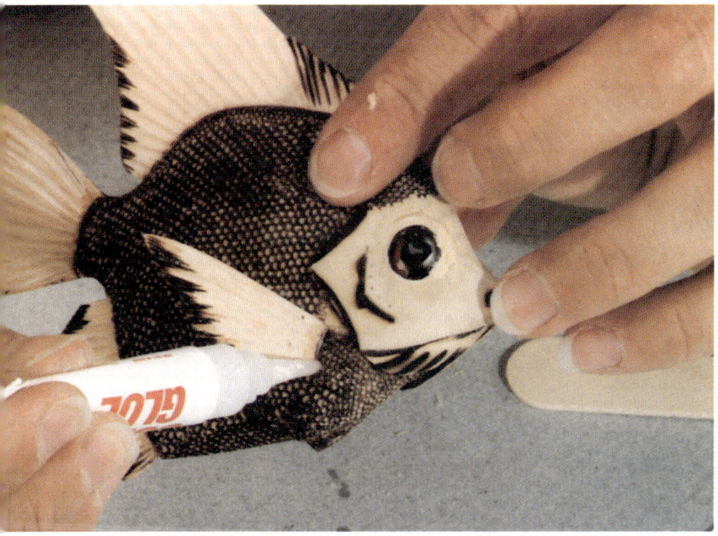

the pectoral fins...

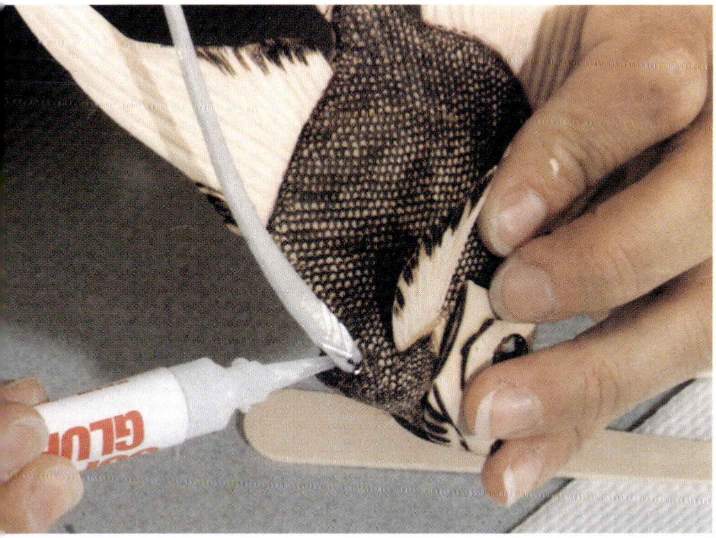

and finally the ventral fins. The metal ventral fin will be bent into position when it has set and we mount the fish in the habitat.

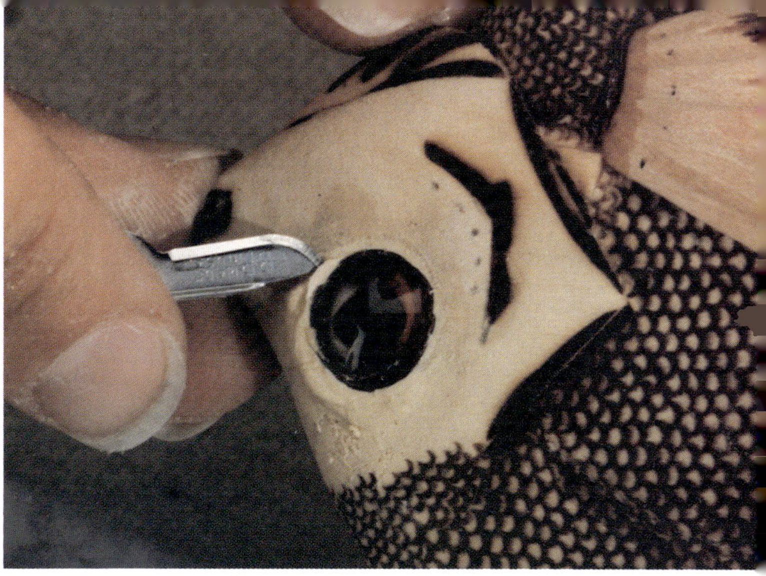

When the putty at the eye has set I can clean it up. I begin by running the knife around the edge of the eye and taking off that putty.

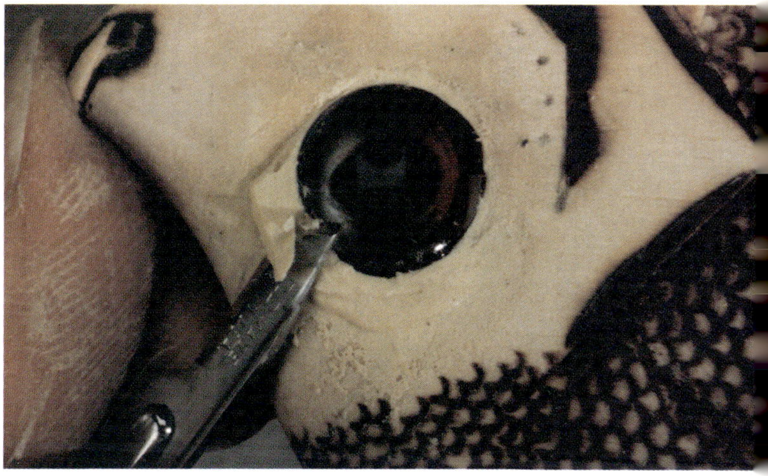

Carve away any extra putty in the sclerid capsule.

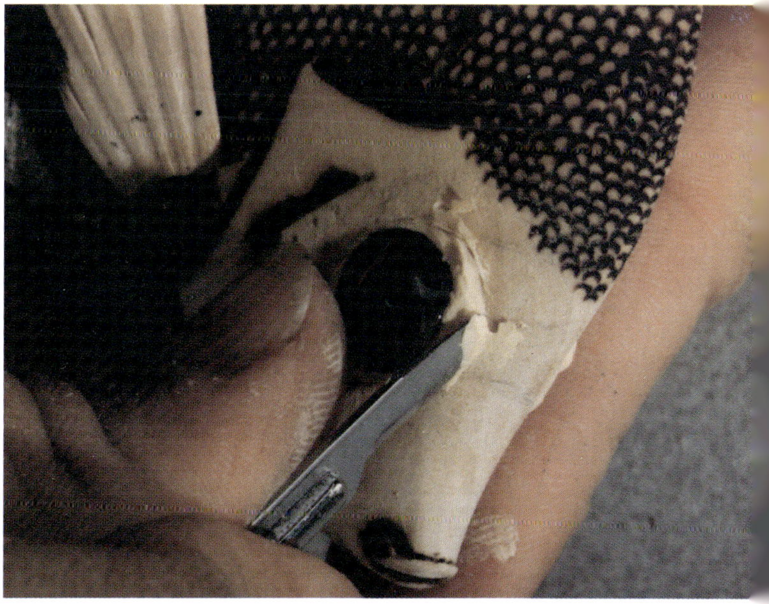

Round off the top edge.

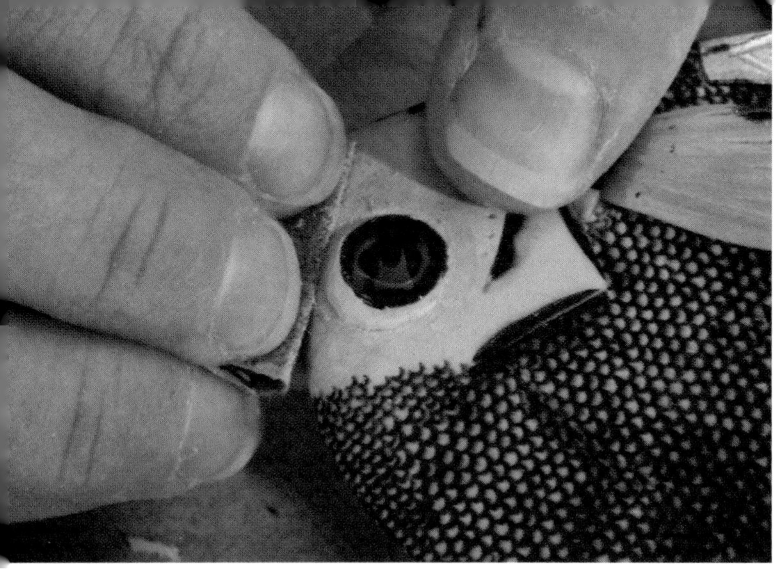

With a light touch, being careful not to scratch the eyeball, smooth and blend the sclerid capsule.

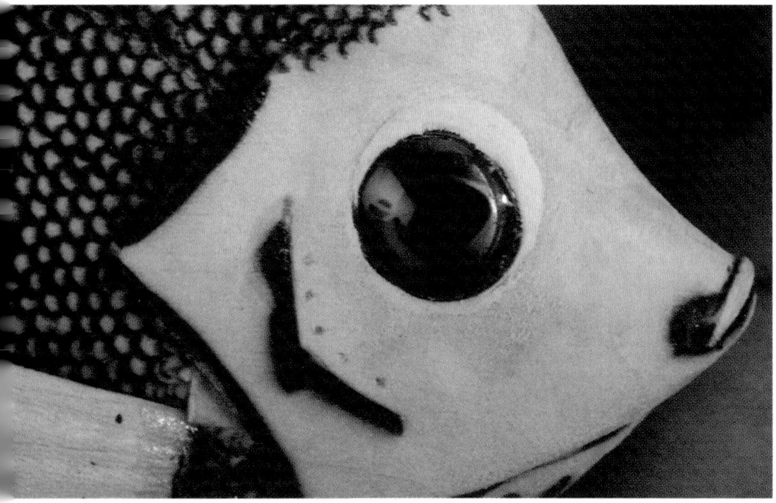

Progress. A little further clean-up is necessary.

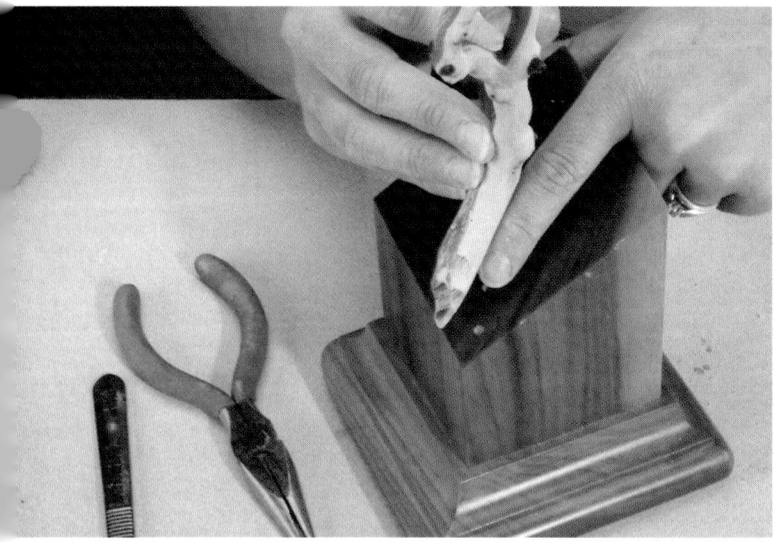

The angelfish and its mate will be mounted in a natural setting set on a finished wood base. I cut one surface of the branch to match the angle of the broken pedestal base.

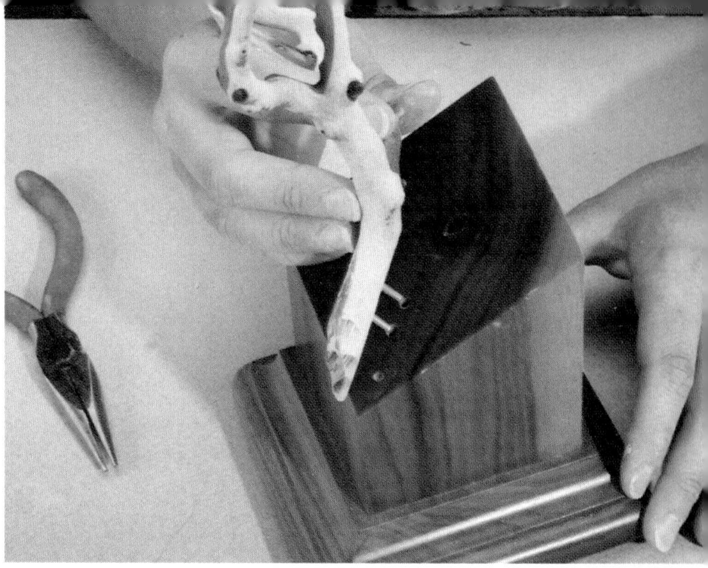

Matching holes are drilled in the base and the branch to join them. A larger hole in the base will hold foliage.

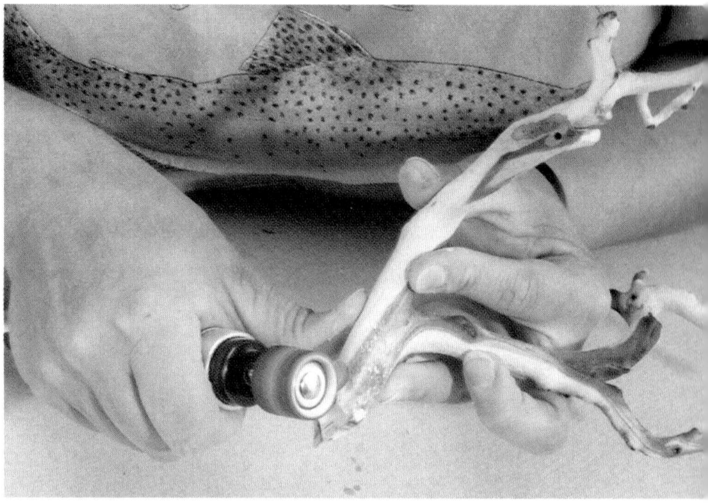

To make the branch more stylized I grind the end of main trunk...

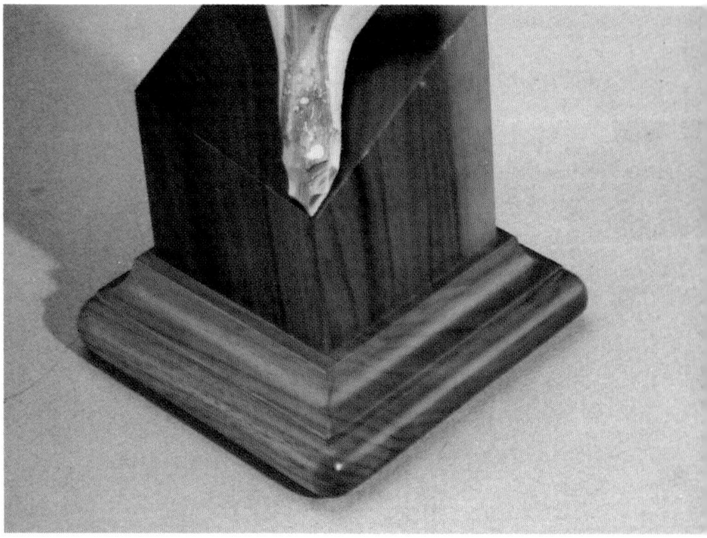

so it matches the corner of the base when it is mounted. The branch will be painted in the end.

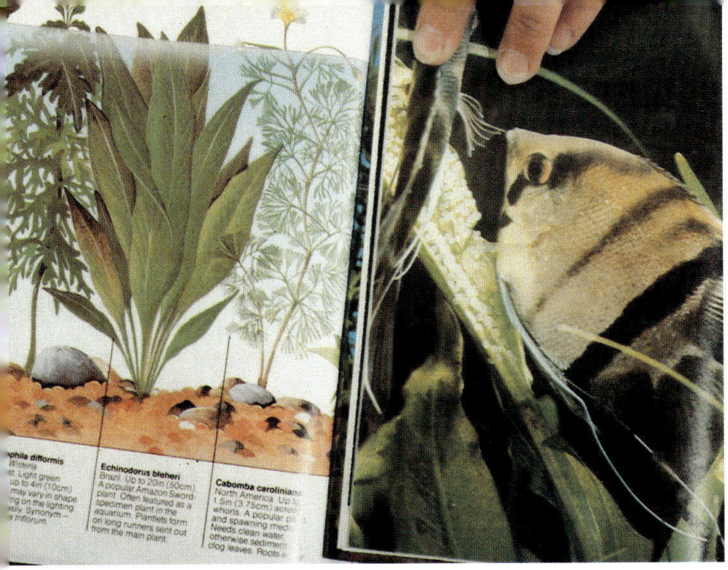

The scene I am after is something like the scene on the right, with the fish laying eggs on the plant. The plant is a Amazon Sword Plant, seen in the drawing to the left.

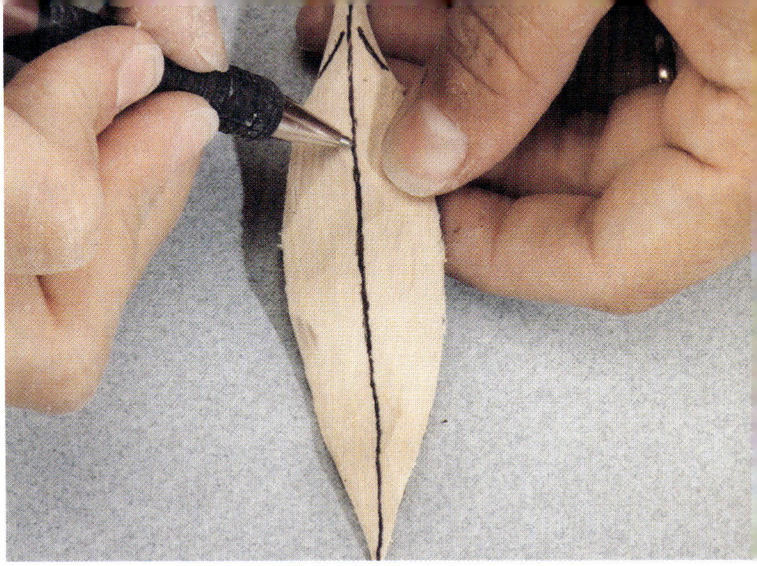

The leaves have a front and back. The center line in the front is a groove, drawn with a line.

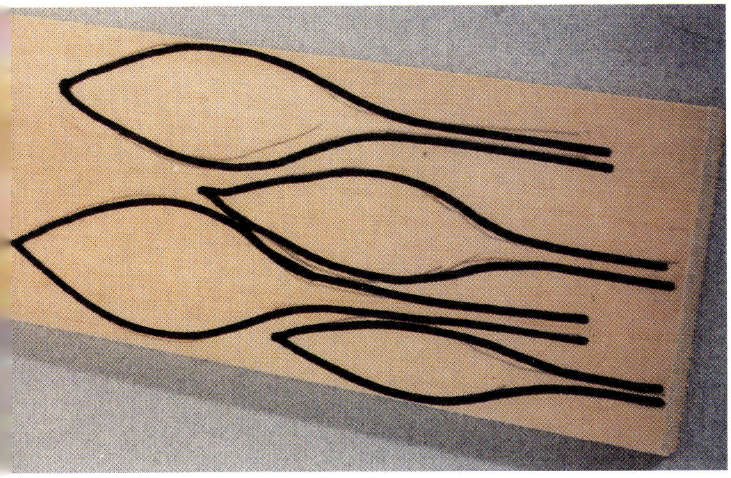

The four leaves of the plant are laid out on 1/4" bass wood.

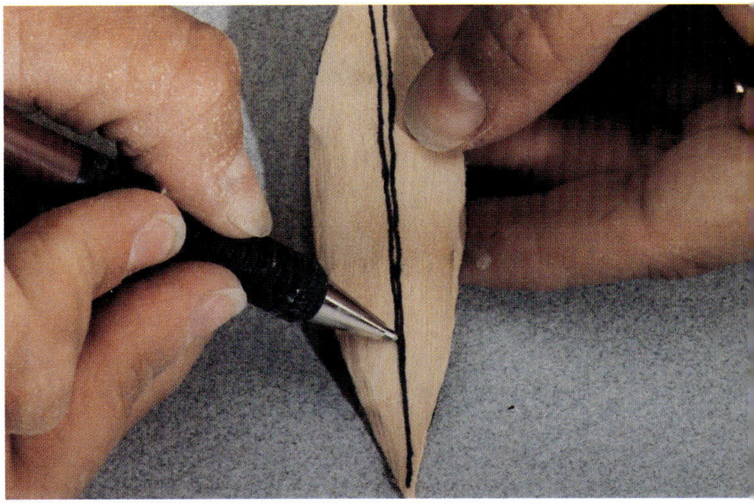

In the back the center line is raised, tapering to a point.

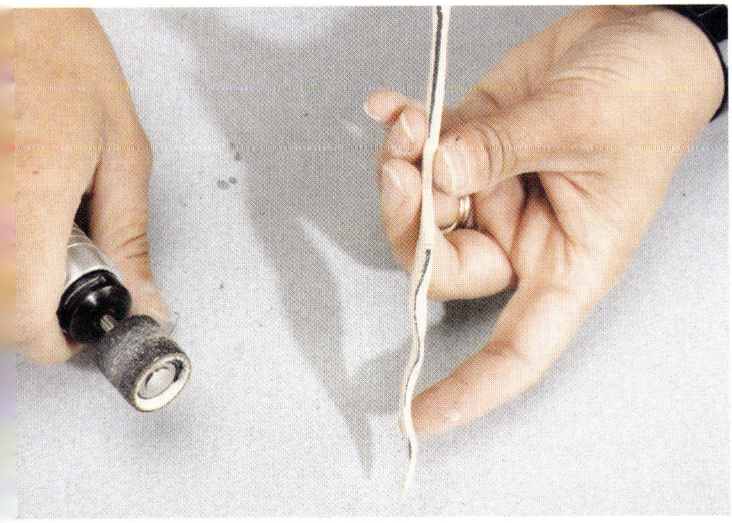

They are cut out and ground, just like I did with the fins, to get some undulation in the surface. The center line around the edge is drawn randomly and the grinding is done with the rotary drum.

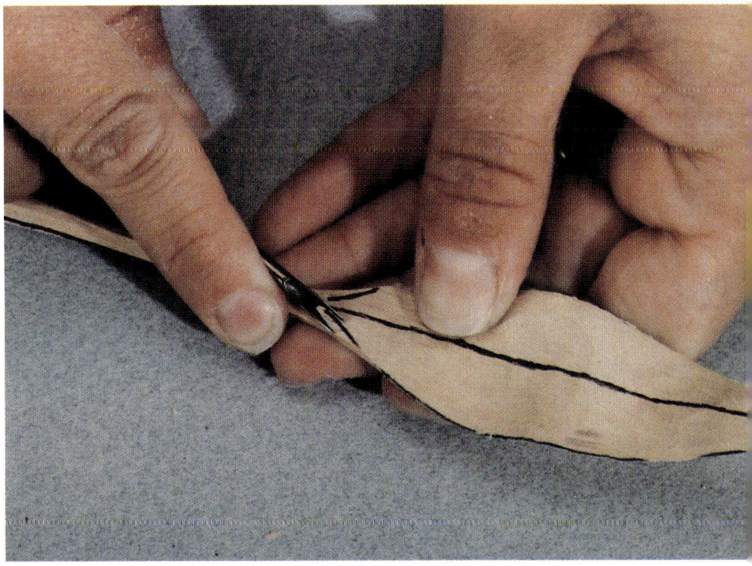

On the front I use a wide micro gouge where the edges of the leaf blend into the stem.

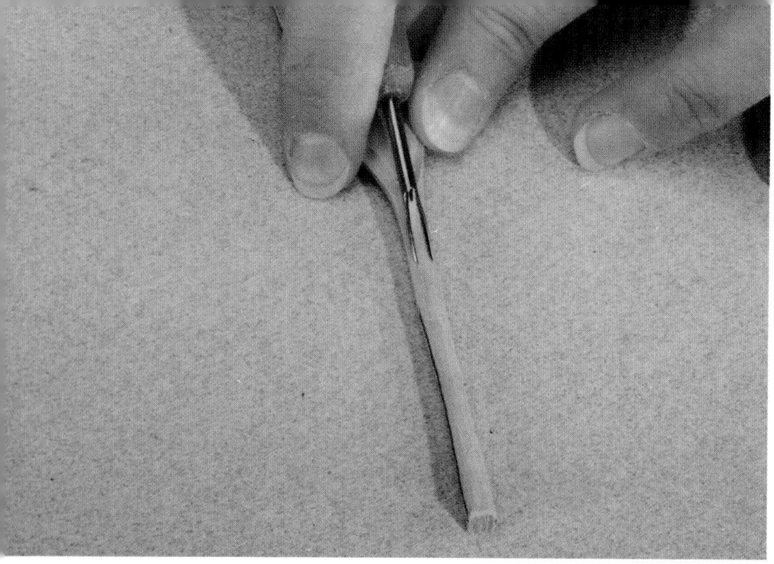

The front of the stem is concave so I run the gouge down its center.

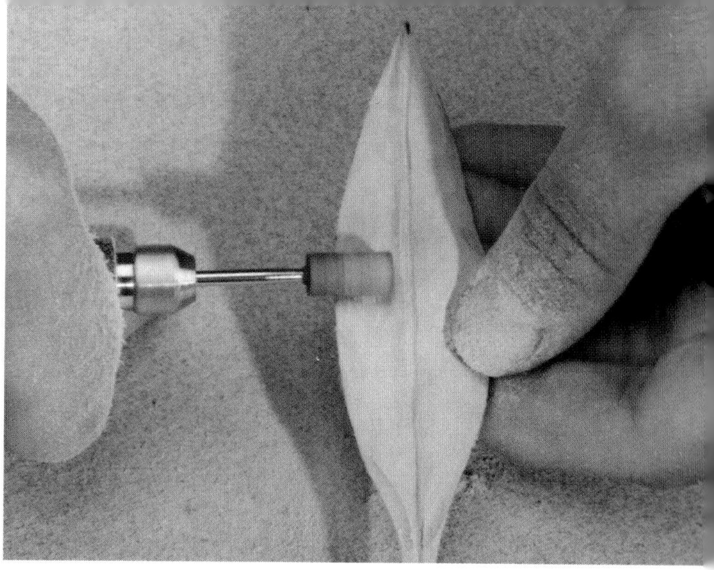

Blend the surface out to the edge.

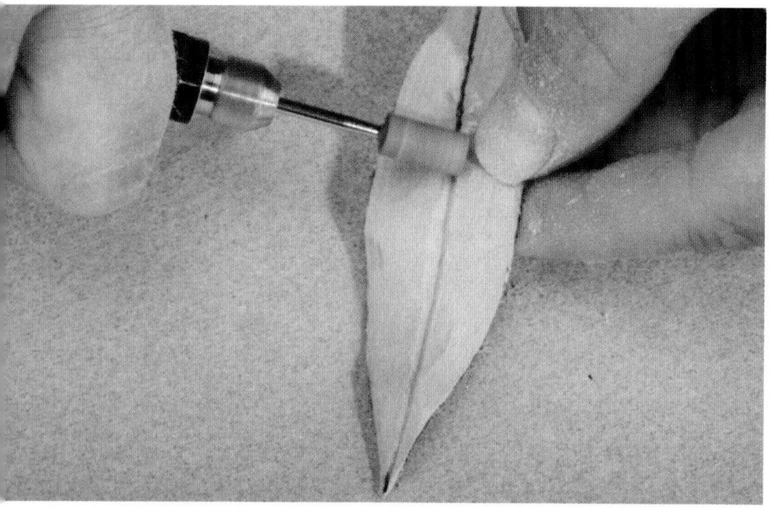

Run the edge of a grinder down the concave line of the leaf.

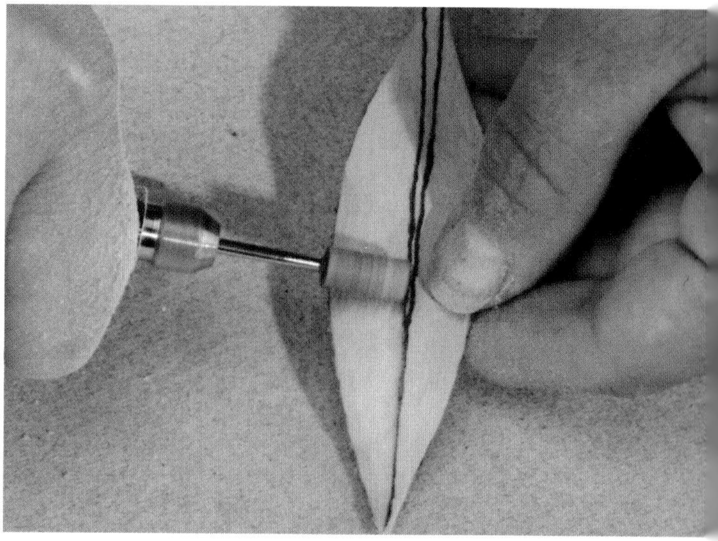

On the back of the leaf, hold the grinder nearly flat against the surface to cut along the sides of the center line. This will bring it out. Come up the other side.

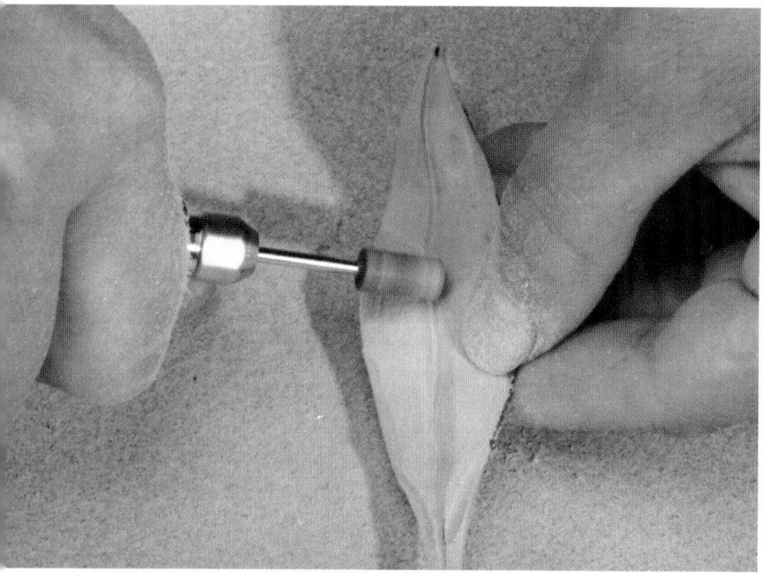

Flatten the angle of the cut and round over the leaf surface into the groove on each side.

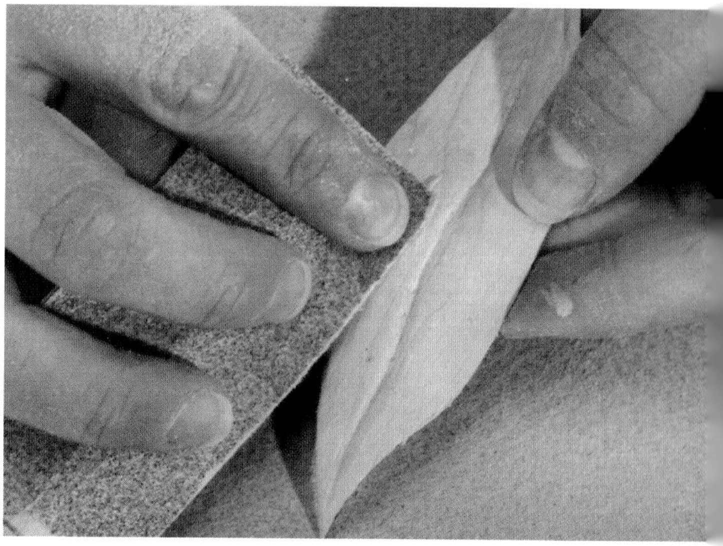

Lightly sand, front and back.

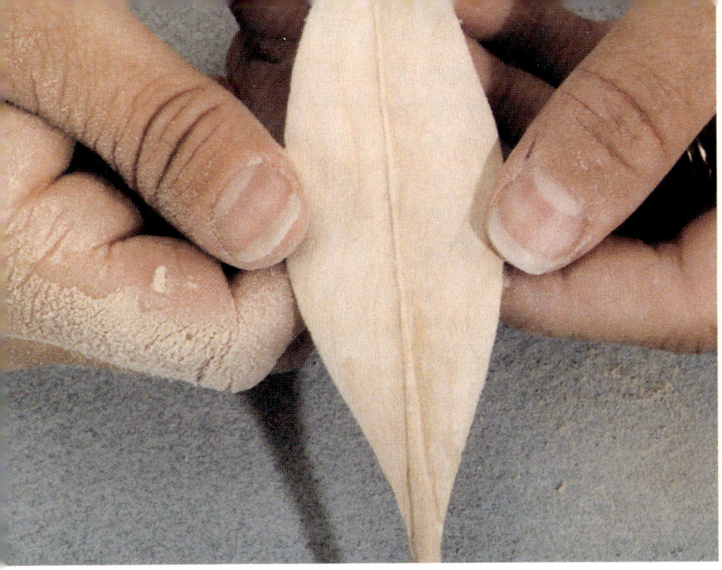

The result.

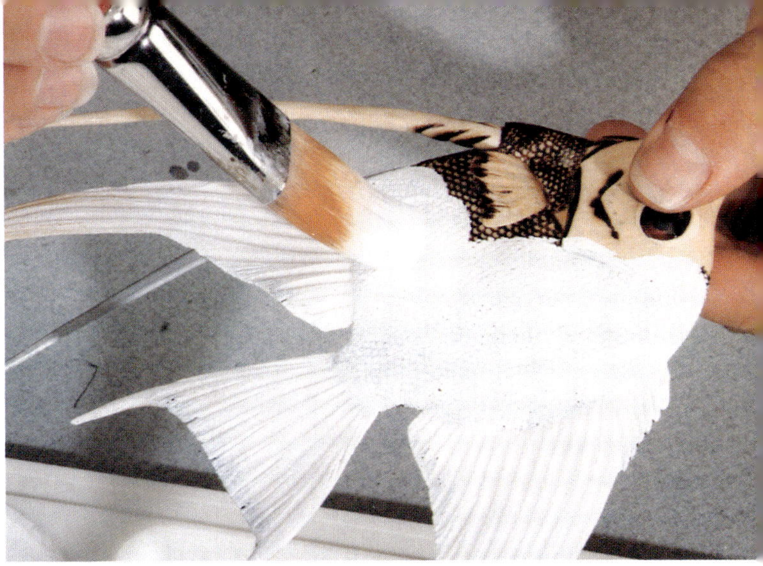

Let it dry completely before applying gesso. Work the gesso into the grooves and the scales.

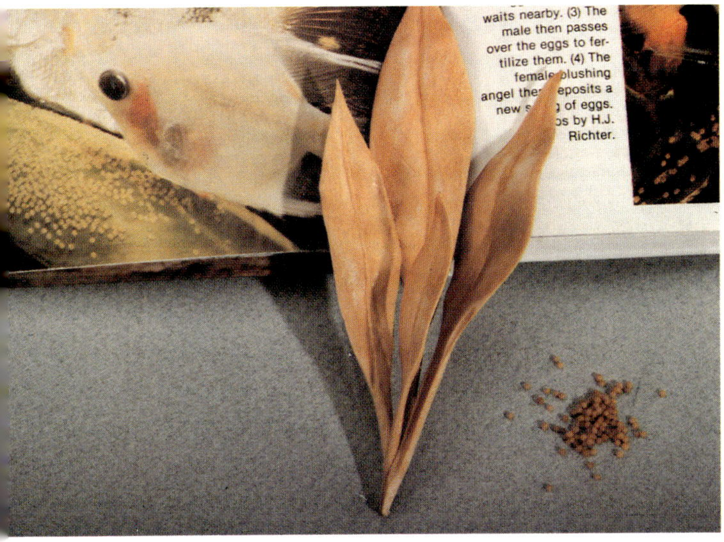

Four leaves are glued together at the base. The eggs are formed from Super Sculpey™ and will be glued on the plant. Super Sculpey™ is a modeling clay that is baked in the oven to become rock solid.

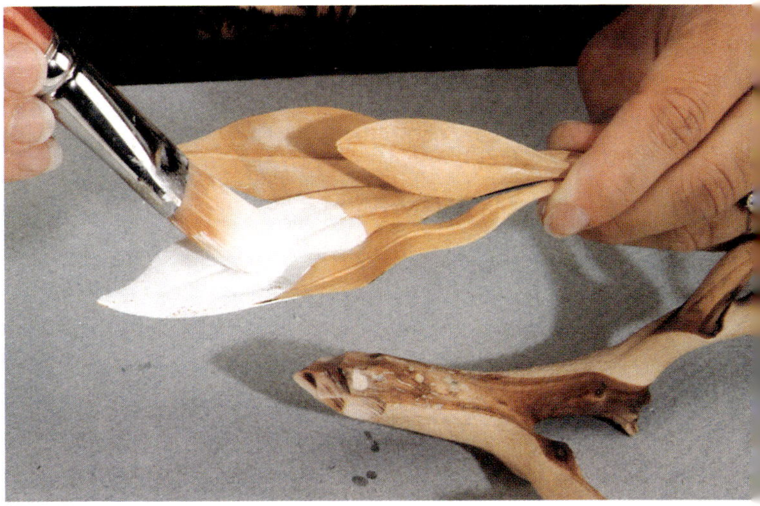

Gesso the sword plant and the branch.

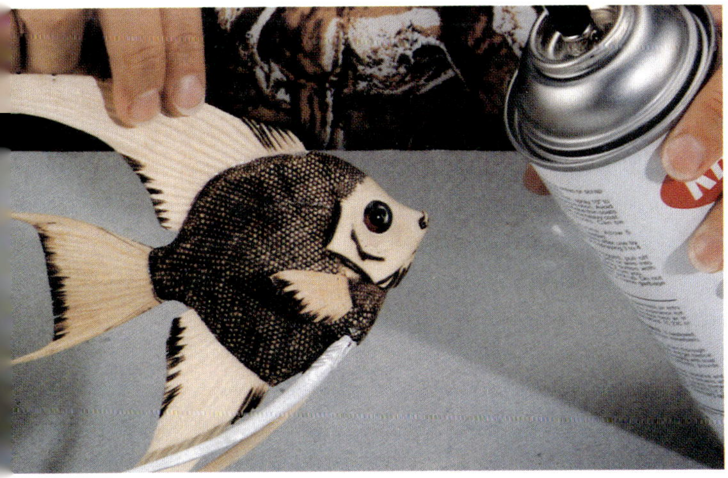

When the clean-up and carving are complete, add a coat of clear acrylic.

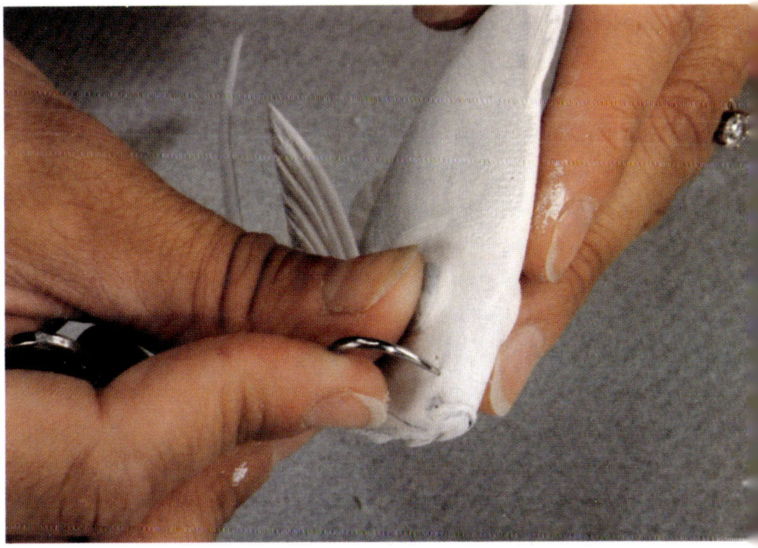

Again, I forgot the nostrils, but it is easy enough to do now. At the same time I can clean up any of the holes along the gill that were filled with gesso.

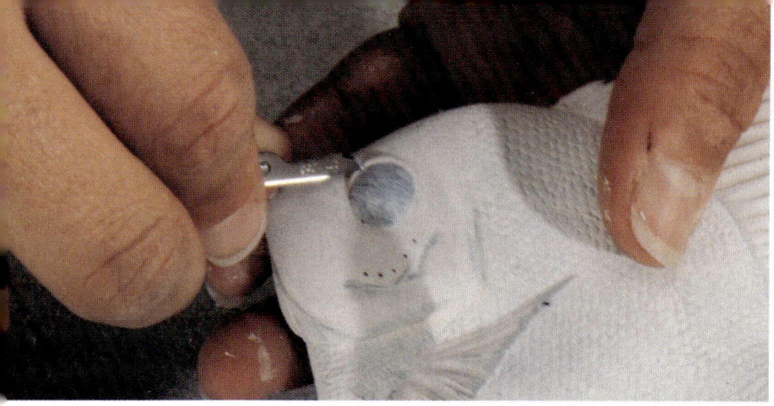

Begin cleaning the eye by cutting around the perimeter.

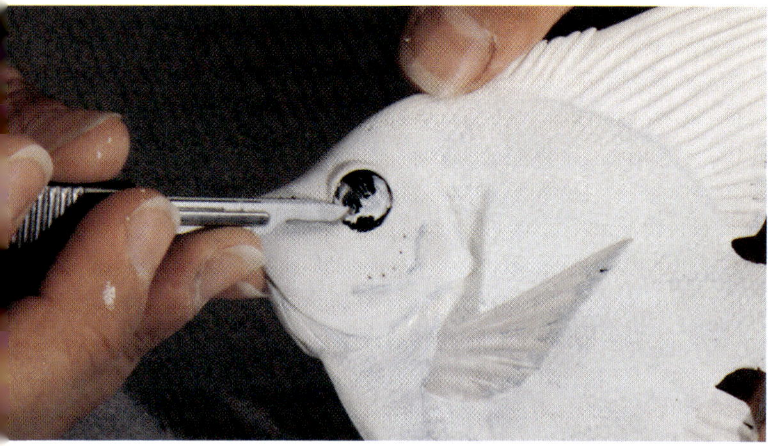

Then scrape the eye free of any gesso.

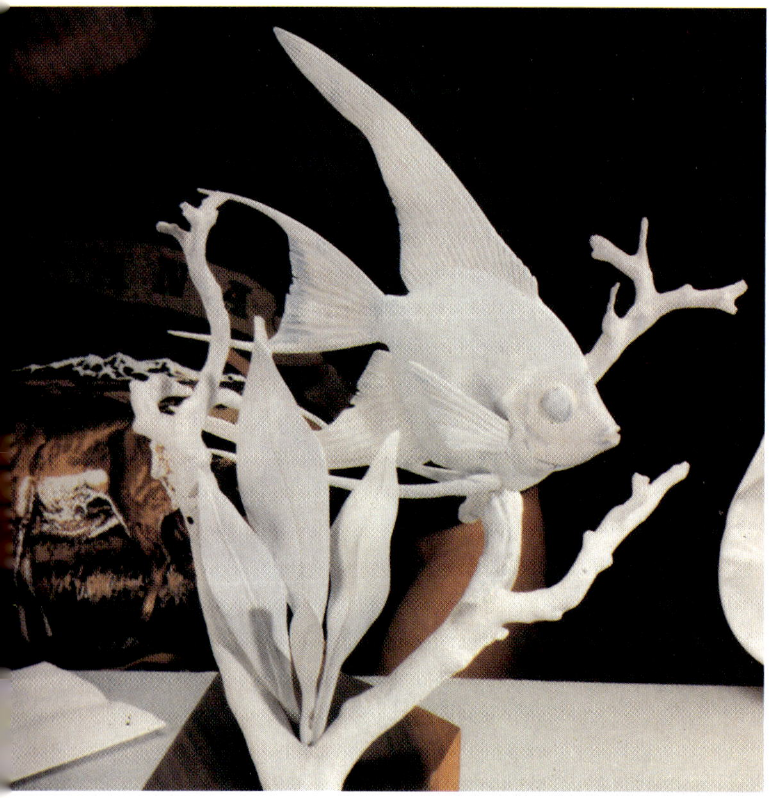

We need to determine the setting of the fish. This will be a two-fish construction. One angelfish is attached to a back branch by a tab in it's metal ventral fin.

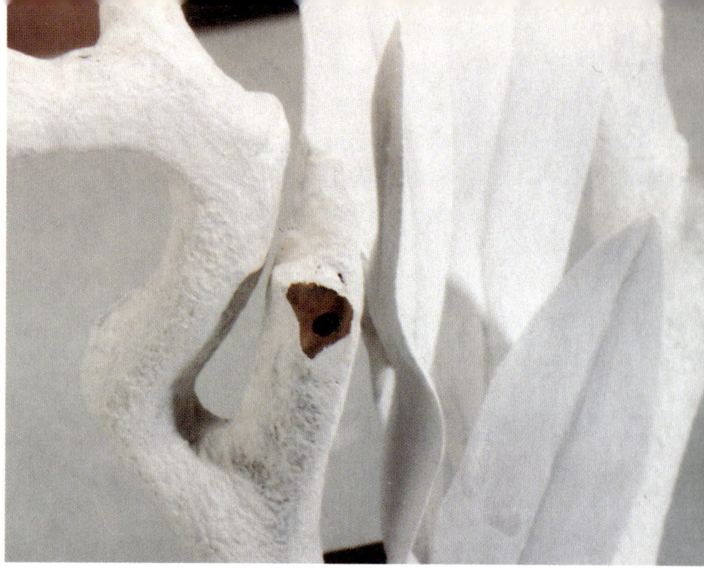

I want the fish we carved to be on the forward branch, lower than the other. I have drilled a hole in the branch for the pin, and flatten the area around it where the fish will touch.

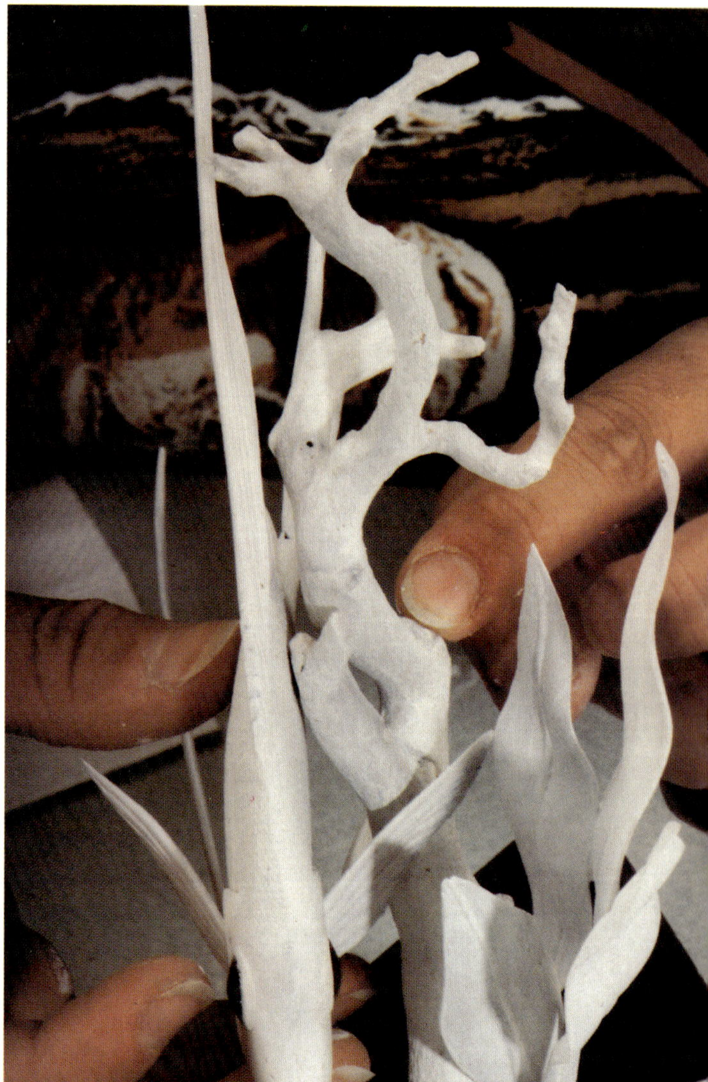

Adjust the placement of the fish. Here I want the left pectoral fin to be free. I mark the spot where it will attach.

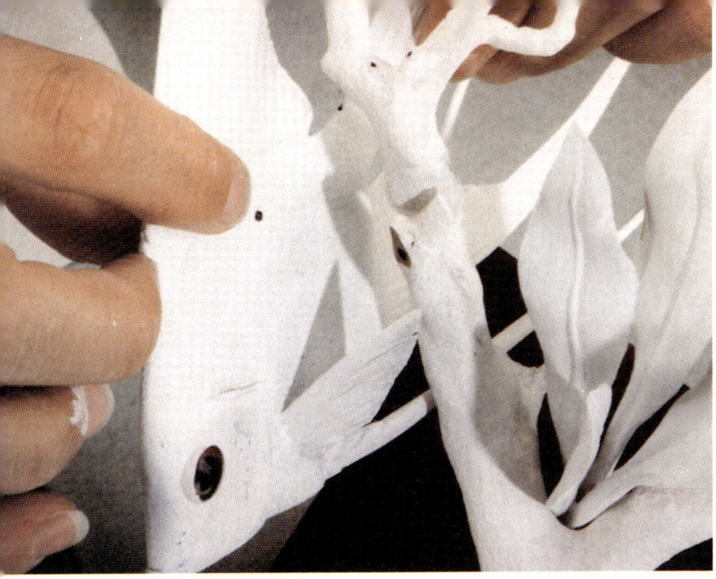

Unfortunately the spot where the peg enters the fish is going is very thin, so I will need to be careful how I drill and how long I make the pin.

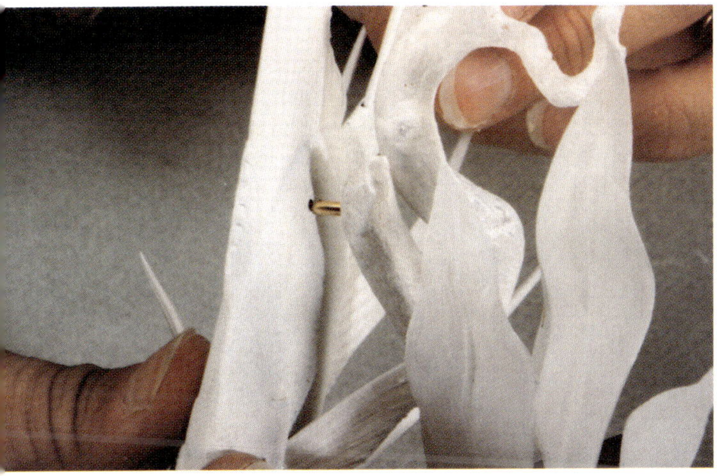

With the pin in place, check the angle for drilling.

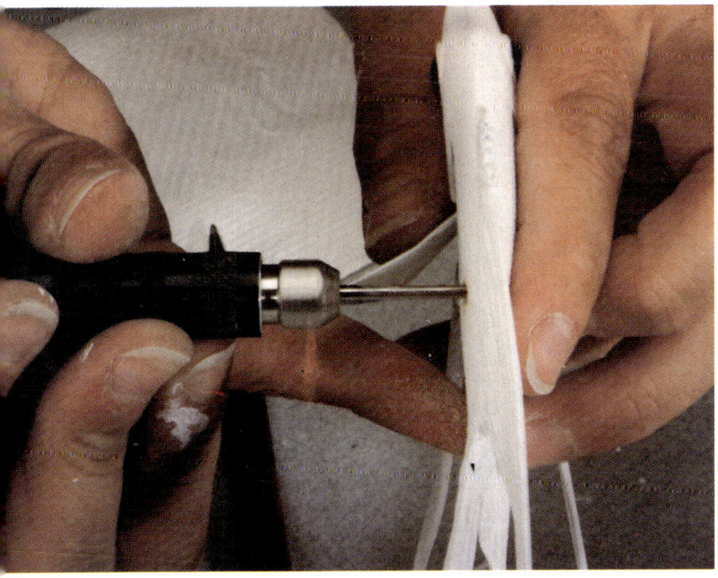

As I drill I keep one finger opposite the hole so I can feel if it starts to emerge. I also check the depth often.

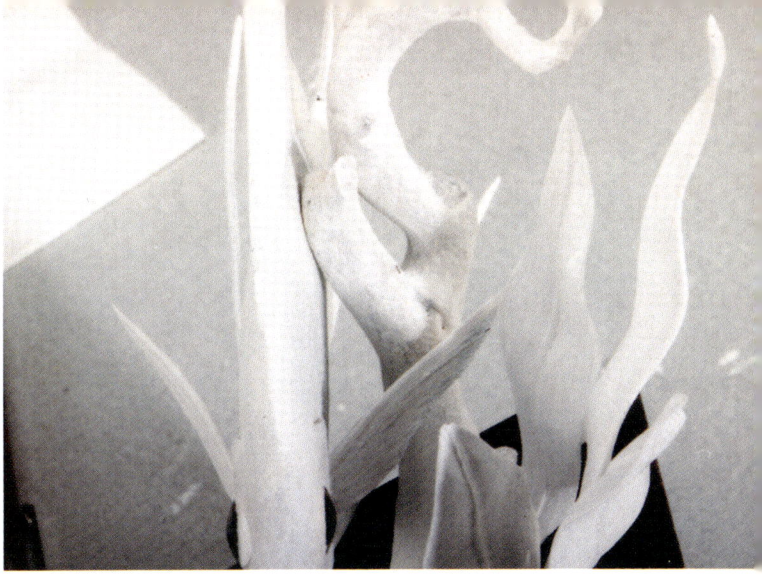

I got a good fit the first time.

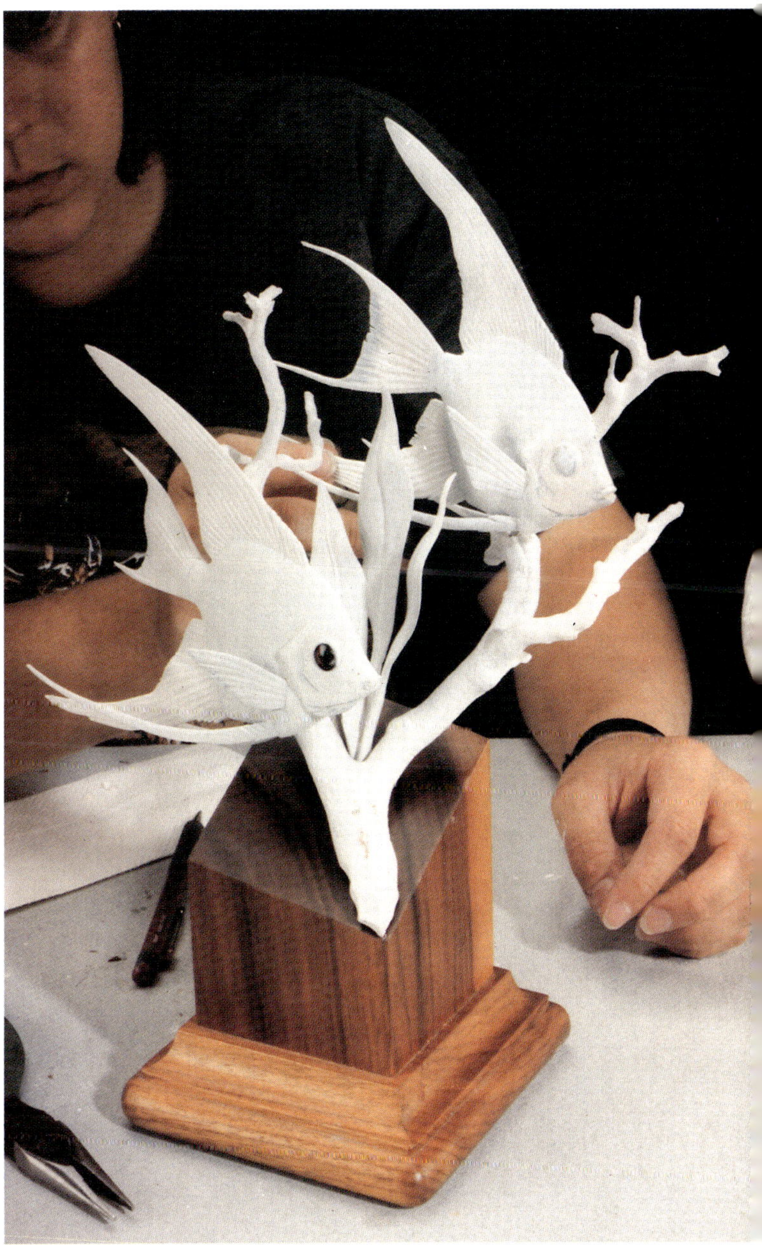

This is how the assembly will look when it is finished.

Painting the Fresh Water Angelfish

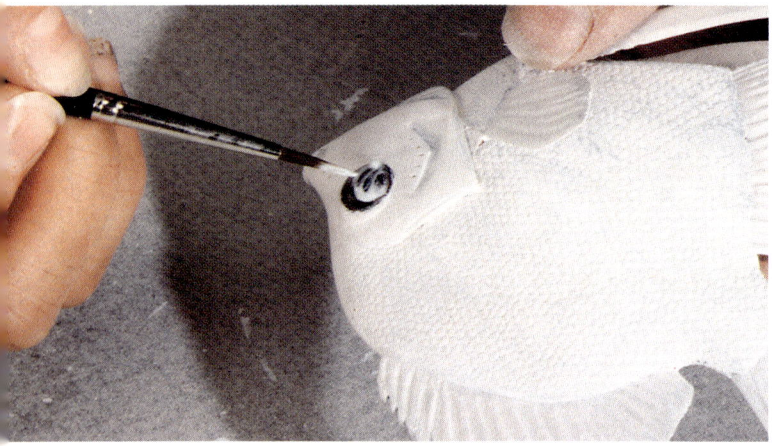

Eye-Protect is applied to the eyes to help in the clean-up.

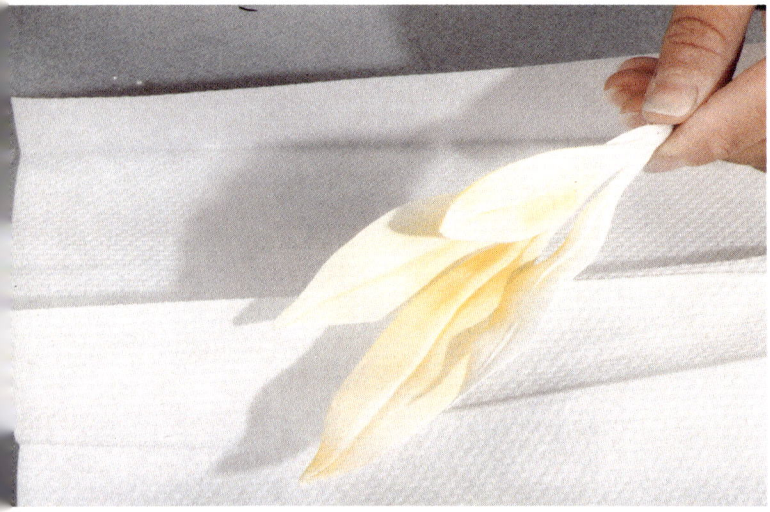

The sword plant has an undercoat of cadmium yellow.

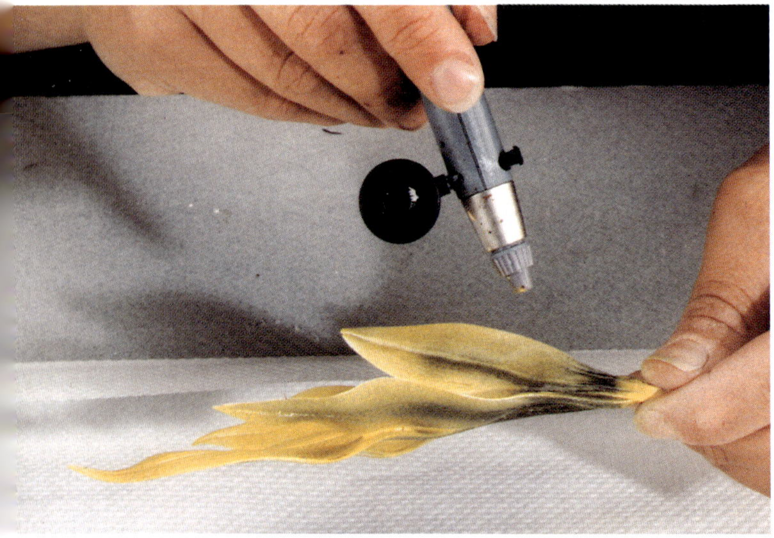

When the entire plant is undercoated, I go over it with Hooker's green. Apply it over the yellow, painting darker at the bases and up the centers of the leaves.

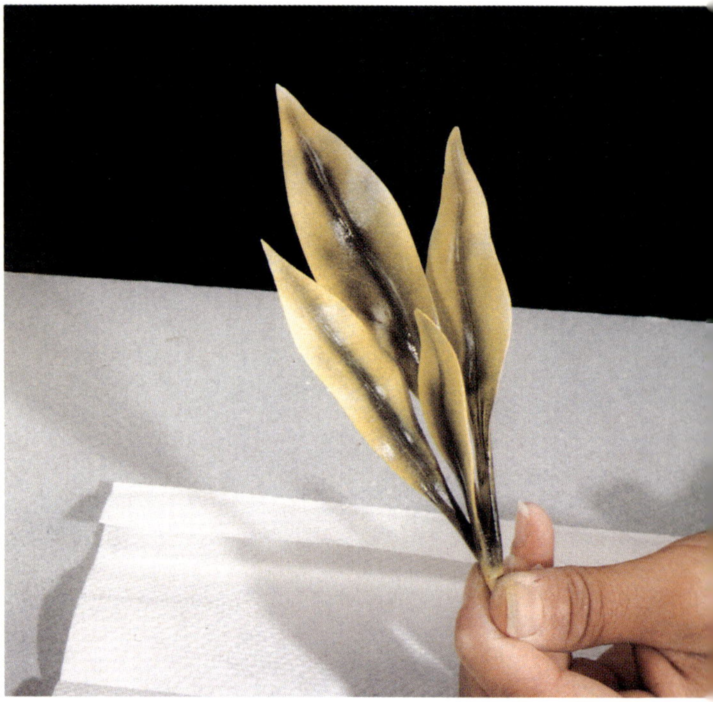

The result.

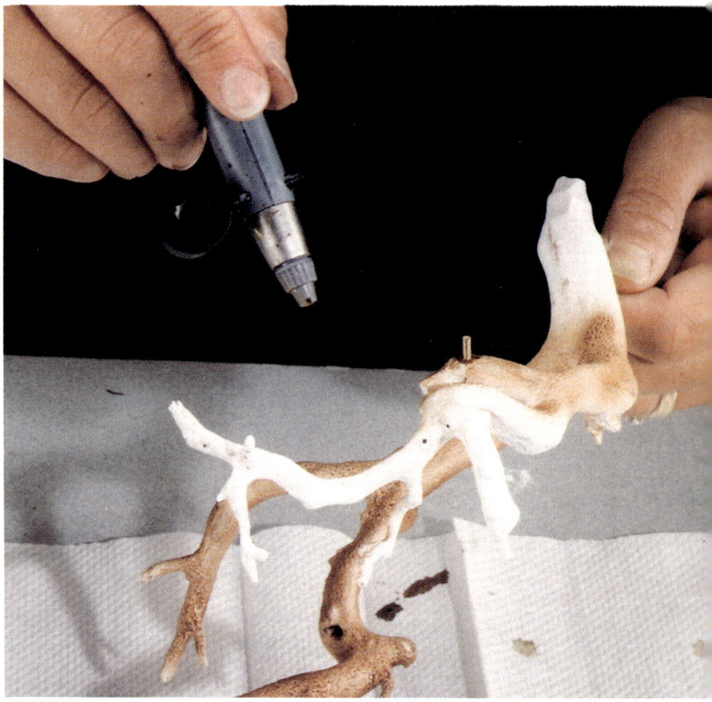

The branch is the muddy brown of bog wood. The undercoat is an airbrushing of chocolate brown.

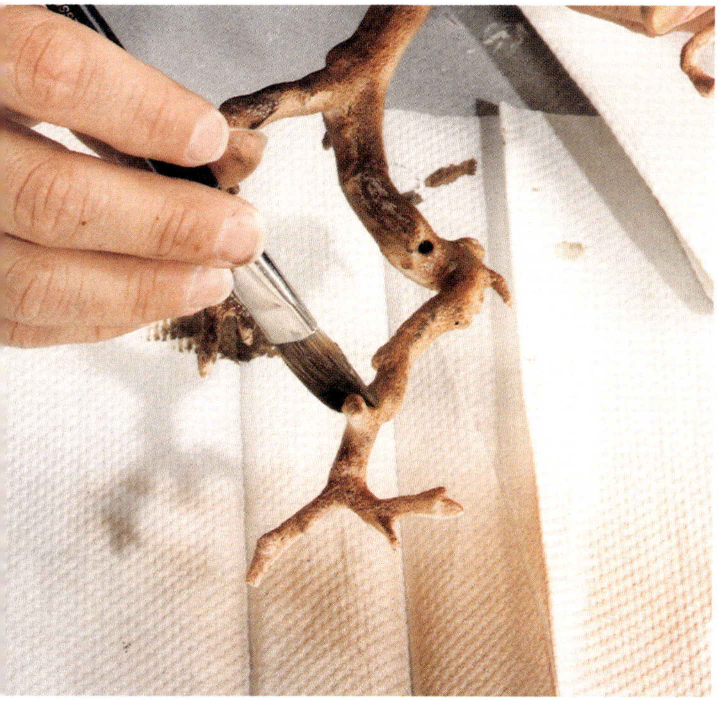

Dry brush over the chocolate brown with a raw umber, hitting the high areas of the branch.

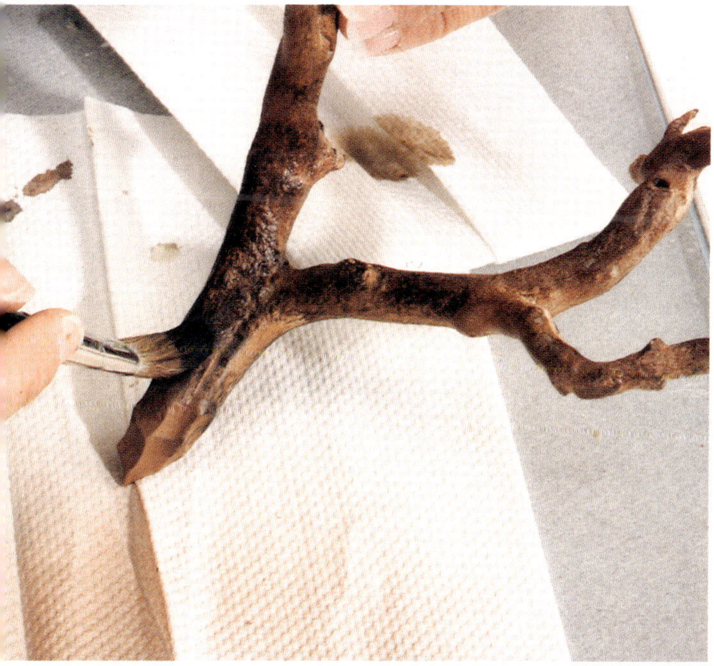

Go over this with a dry brushing of Payne's gray. I want it to look like it's starting to rot.

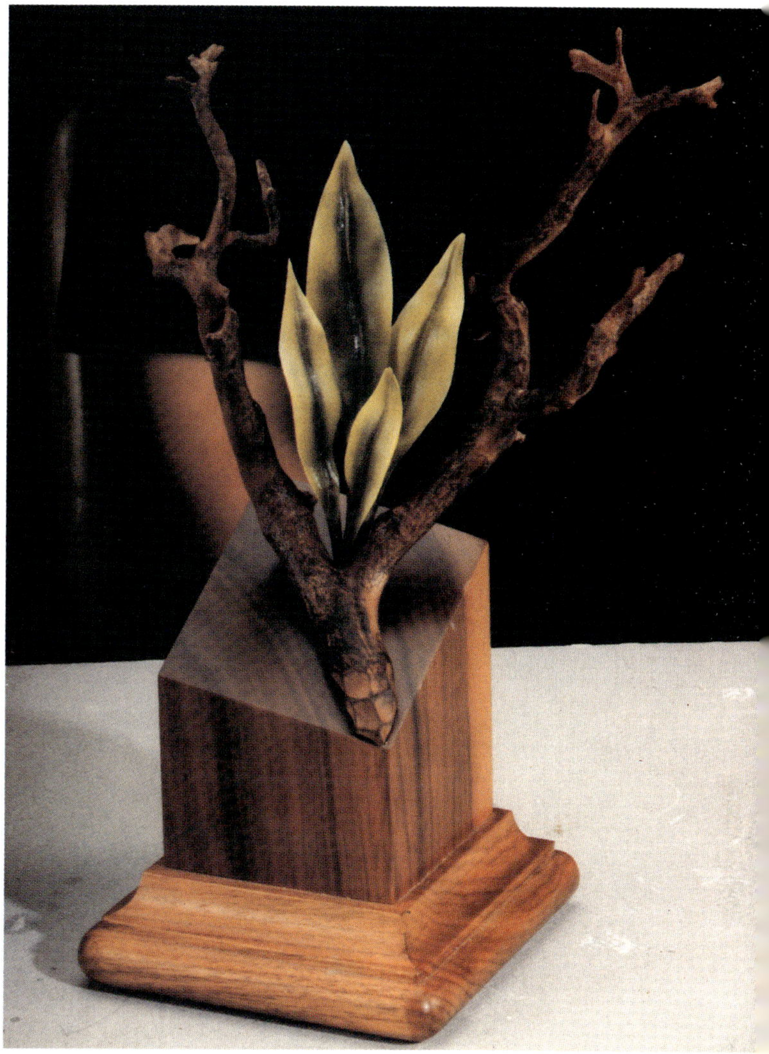

The result. Glue the branch in place with super glue.

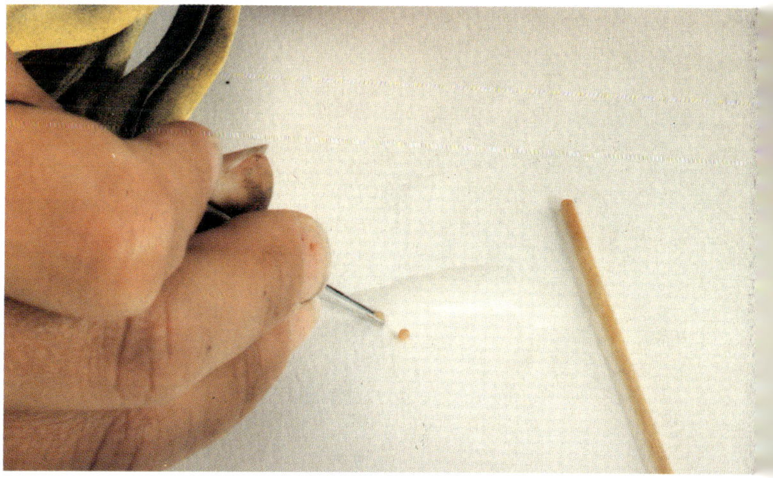

The eggs are put on the leaf one at a time. The female normally makes a pass, laying a row of eggs, and is followed by the male who fertilize them. This action is repeated several times, so the eggs appear as irregular rows on the plant. These rows may clump together where they meet. With small tweezers touch the egg to the epoxy...

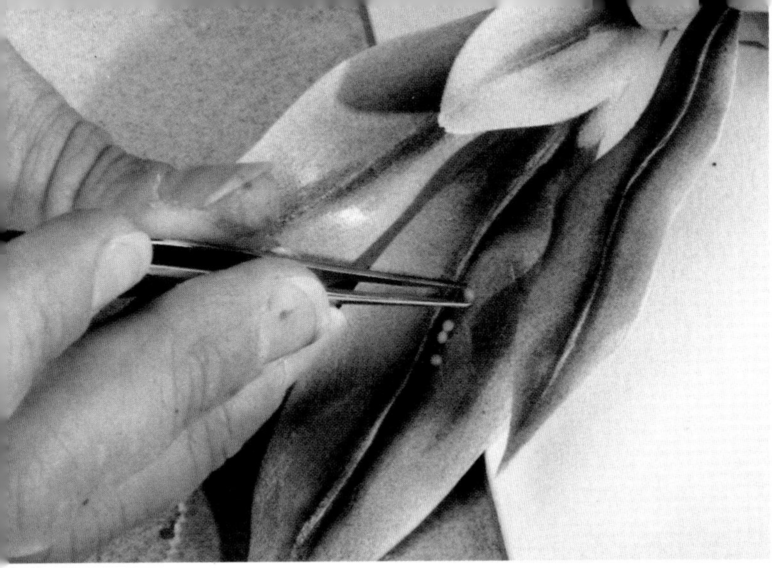

and lay it on the leaf.

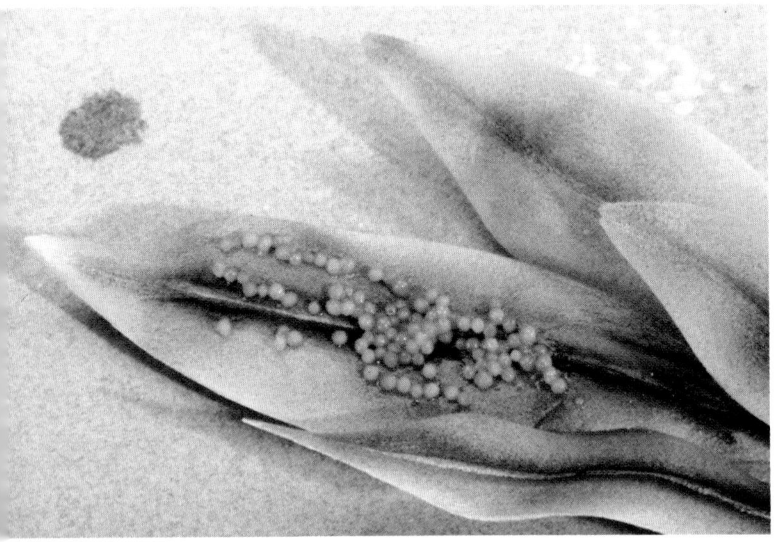

The result. Epoxy the leaf into the base.

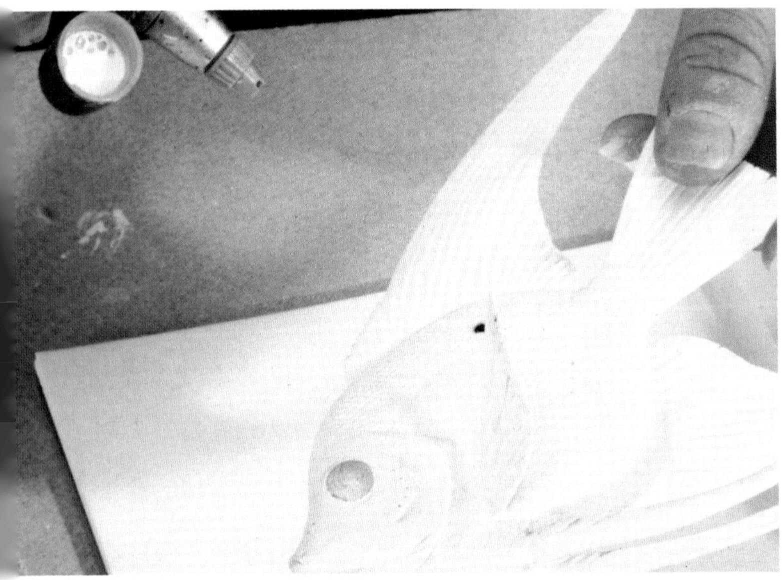

The wild angelfish has a silvery gold body with bold black stripes. Start the painting with "Super-hide" white.

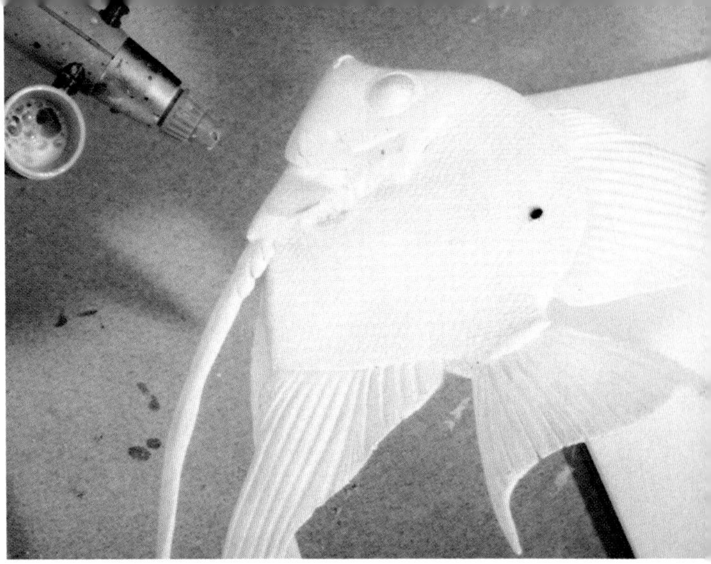

When the white is dry, apply satin white pearl to the belly and lower gill area. This gives the belly a pearly sheen.

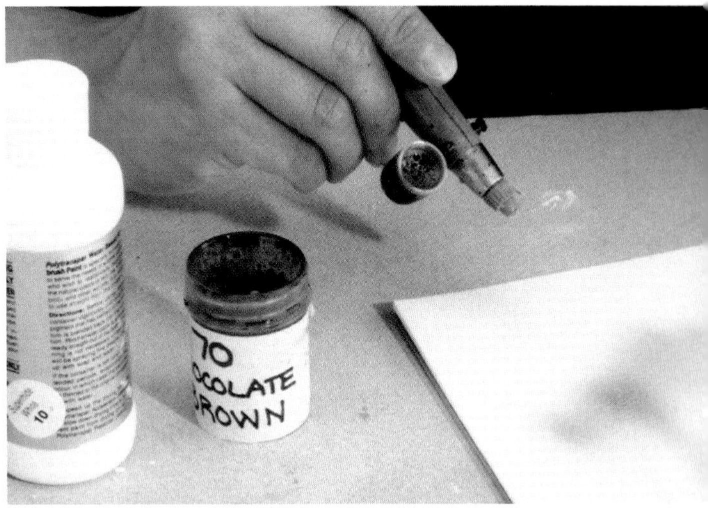

A mixture of chocolate brown and Super-hide white provides the color for the upper body and fins. Be sure to mix the color thoroughly and test them before using.

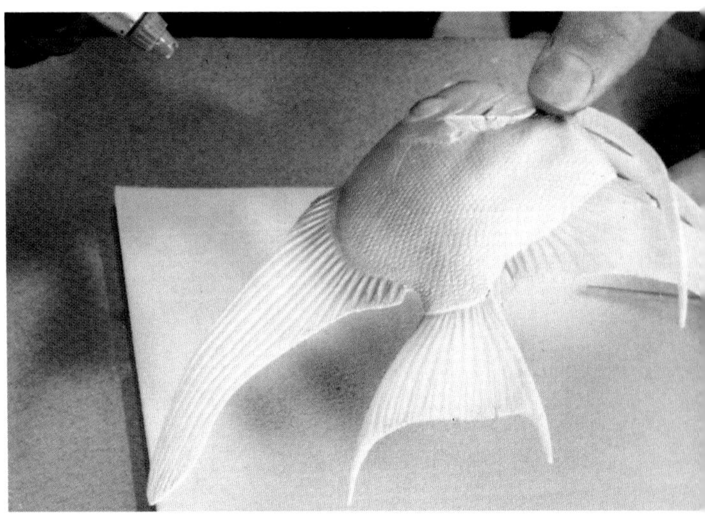

The body is darker along the back and fades out toward the belly.

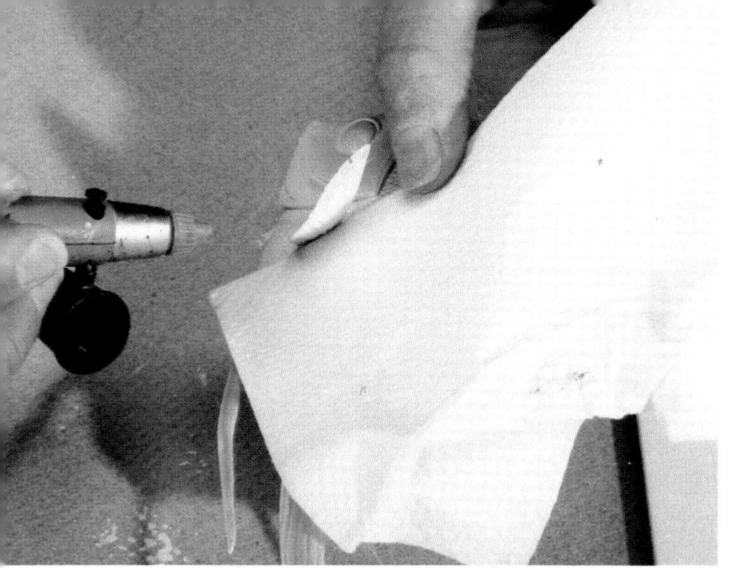

Mask the belly when painting behind the pectoral fins.

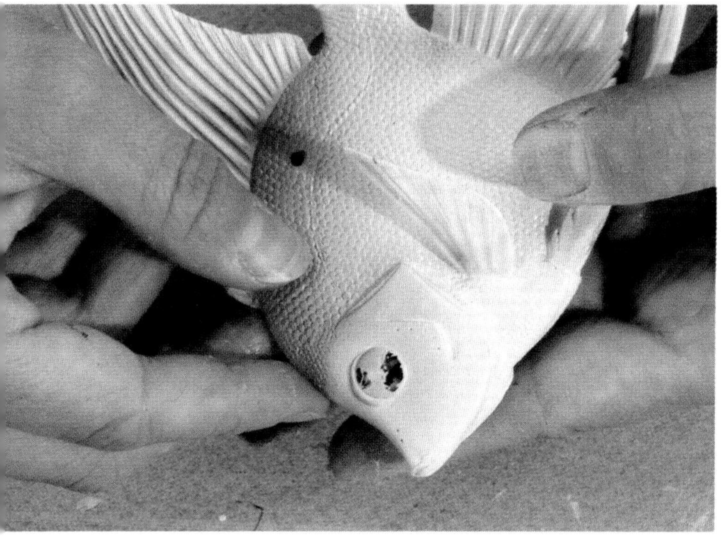

The stripes are done with black. I hate this stage. One slip and a lot of damage happens to an almost finished carving. Be careful and use your references. The dark stripe carries through the eye, so I need to scrap the eye a little so I can align it.

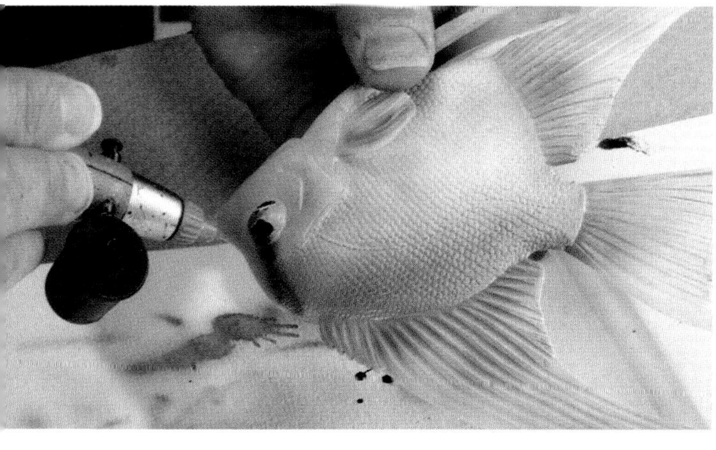

The first line goes from the eye toward the dorsal. Gradually build the line using good care. This is usually one of the darker lines.

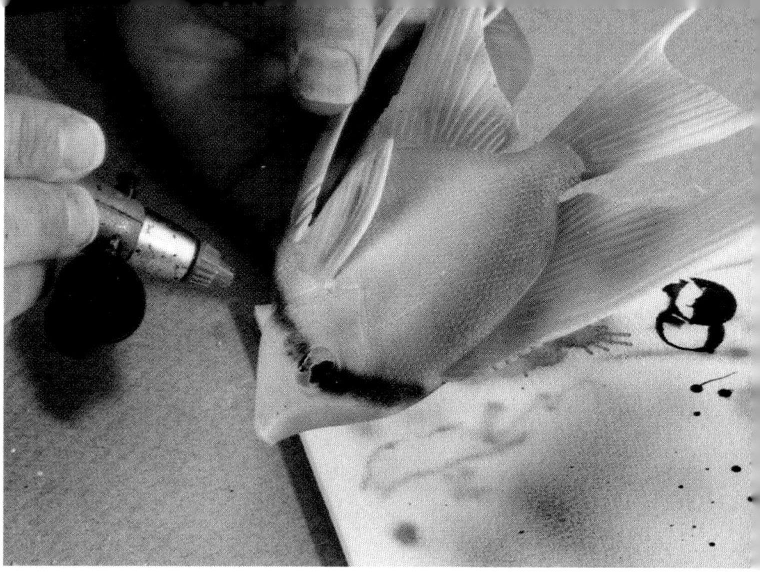

Continue the line down from the eye, toward the butt of the ventral fins.

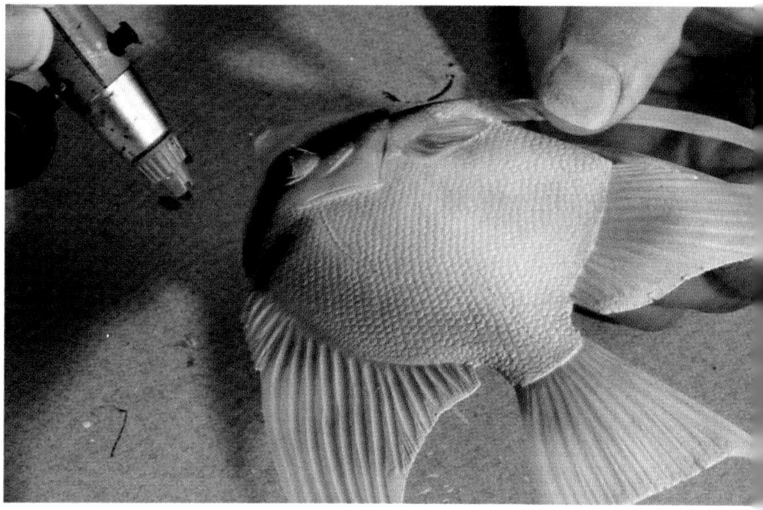

Next do a false stripe down from the back, ending at about 1".

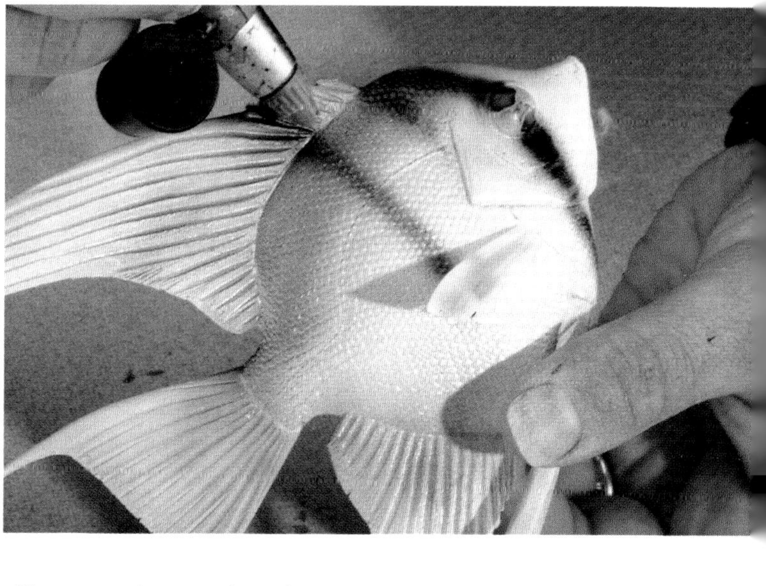

The next stripe runs from the start of the long spine in the dorsal and to behind the pectoral fin, where it will fade out.

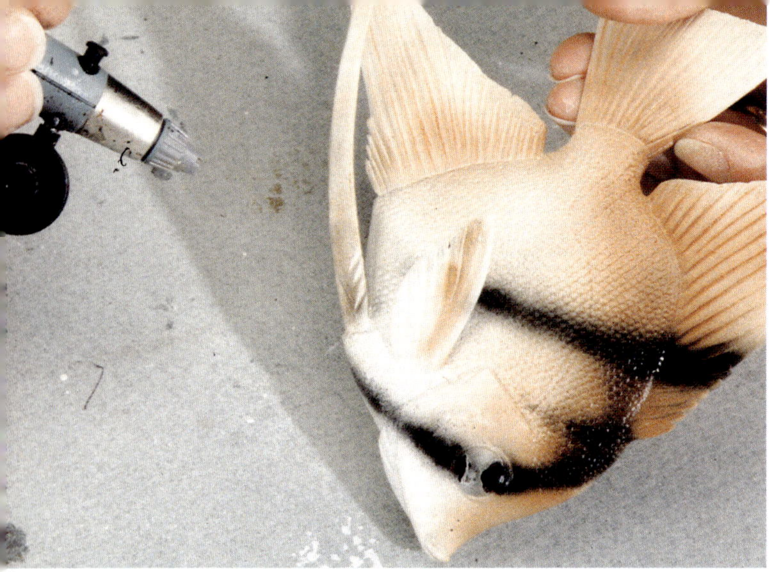

Slightly darken the base of the ventral fin.

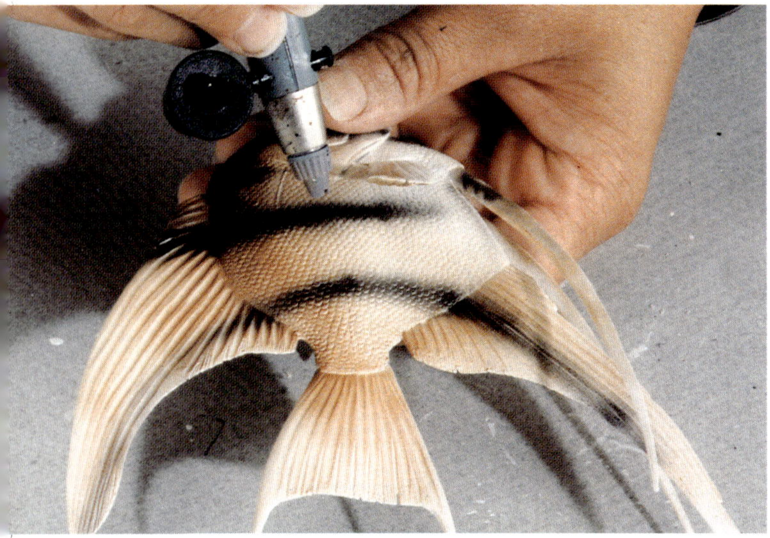

The longest stripe goes from the tip of the dorsal, across the body just before the caudal peduncle, and continues to the tip of the anal fin. I tilt the fish so it slopes away from the spray. This allows the overspray to fade toward the posterior of the fish, as it does in nature.

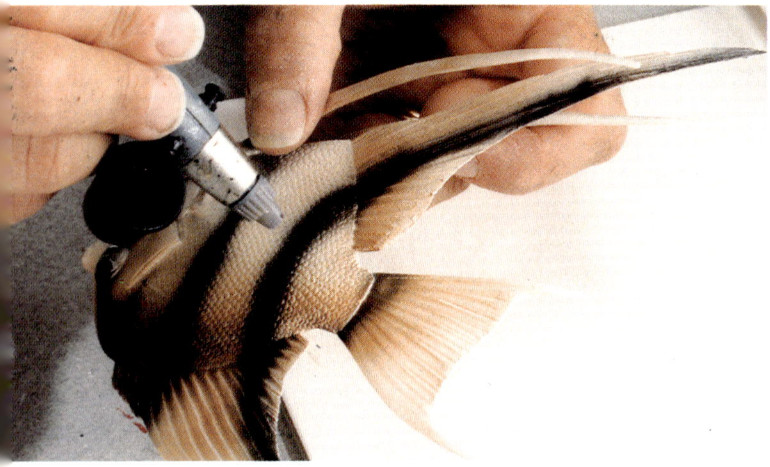

There are four stripes in the tail. The first is at the butt of the fin.

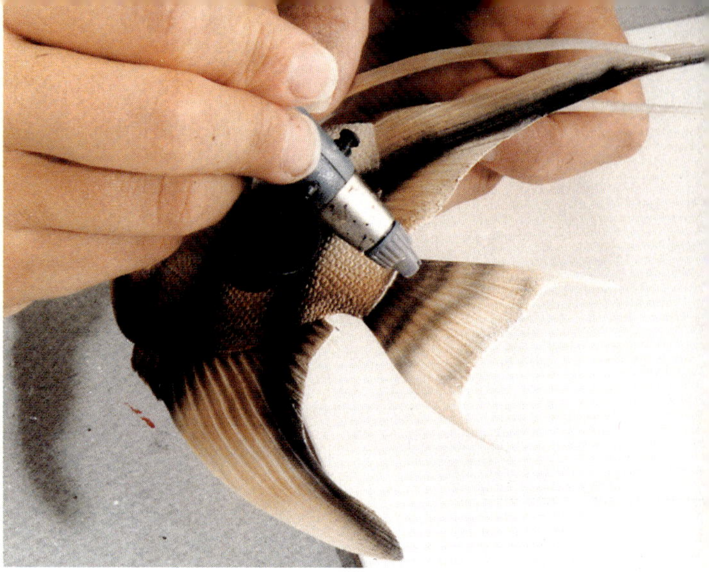

Two others are across the width of the tail, and the fourth is at the trailing edge.

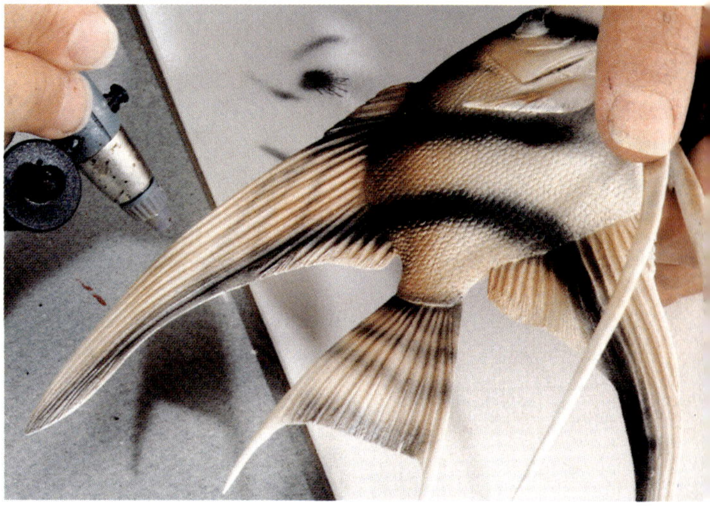

A few light misting stripes go across the rays of the dorsal...

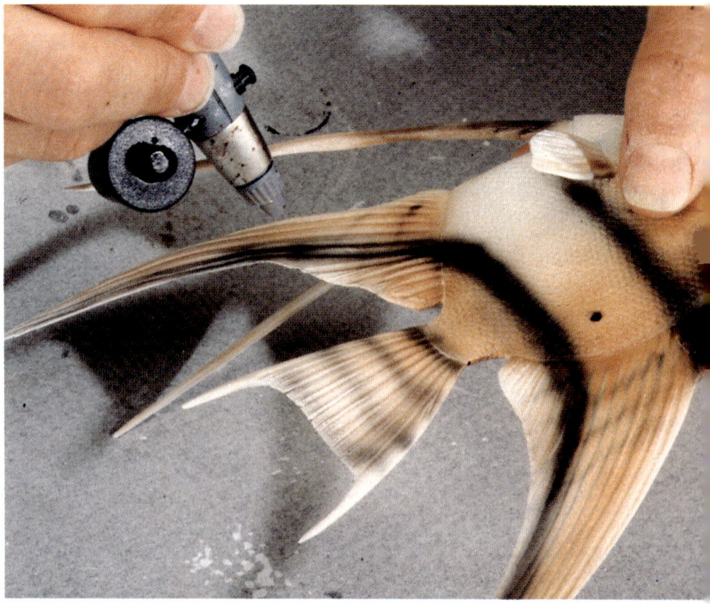

and, even more lightly, on the anal.

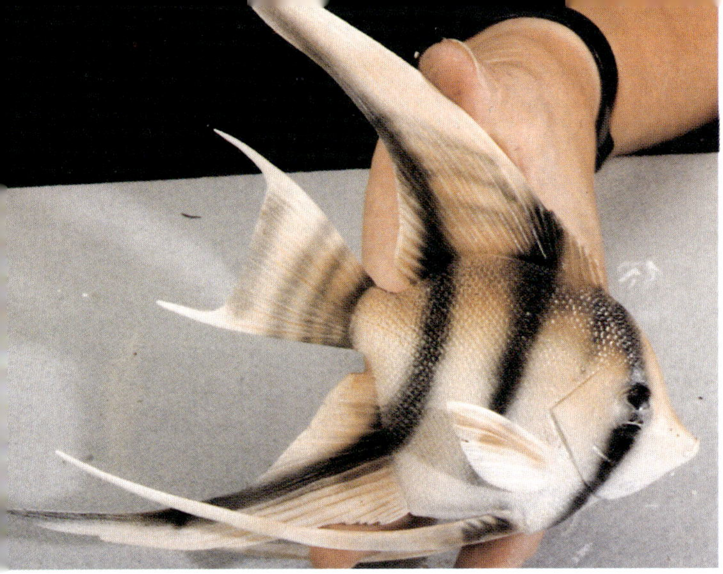

The black applied.

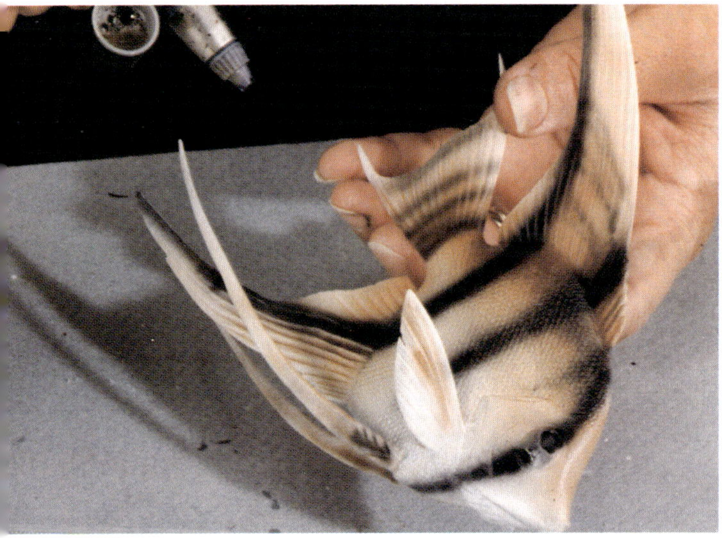

The whole fish is then covered with a bronze gold reflector paint. This adds sparkle but not much color.

You can see how this brings the finish to life.

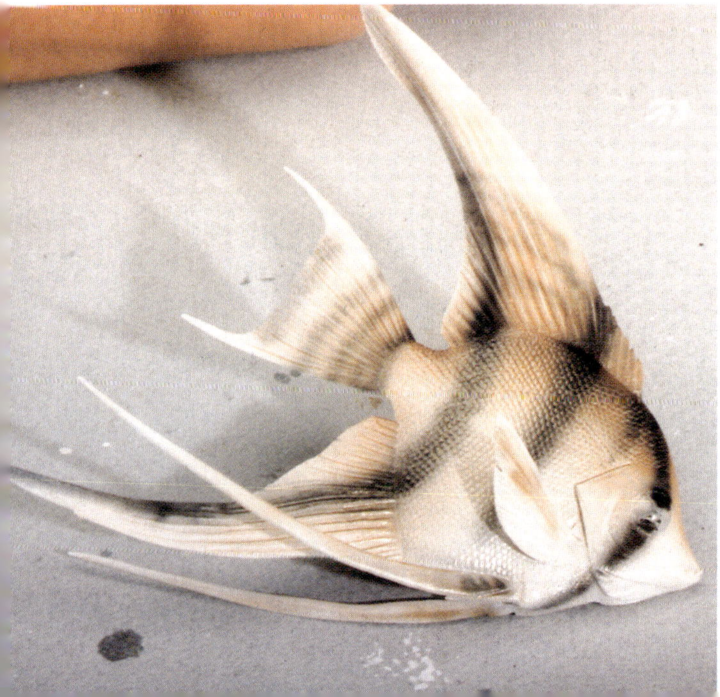

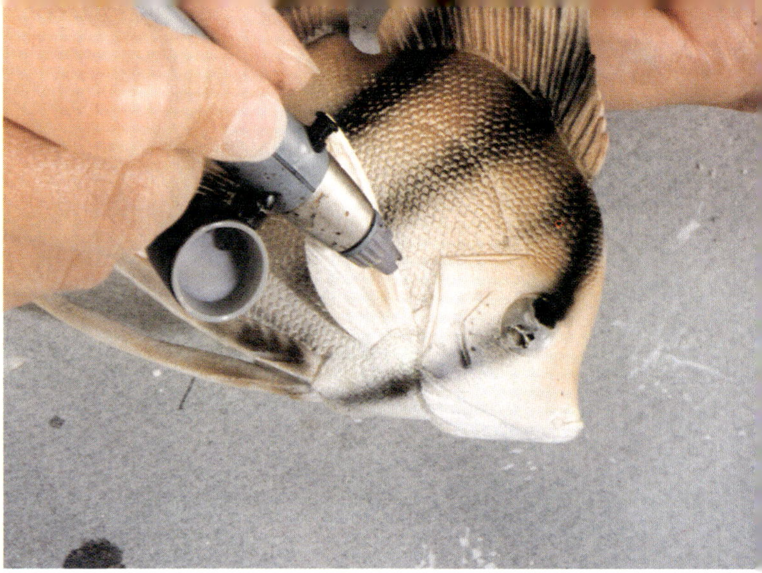

Finally I add some iridescent blue to the lower jaw...

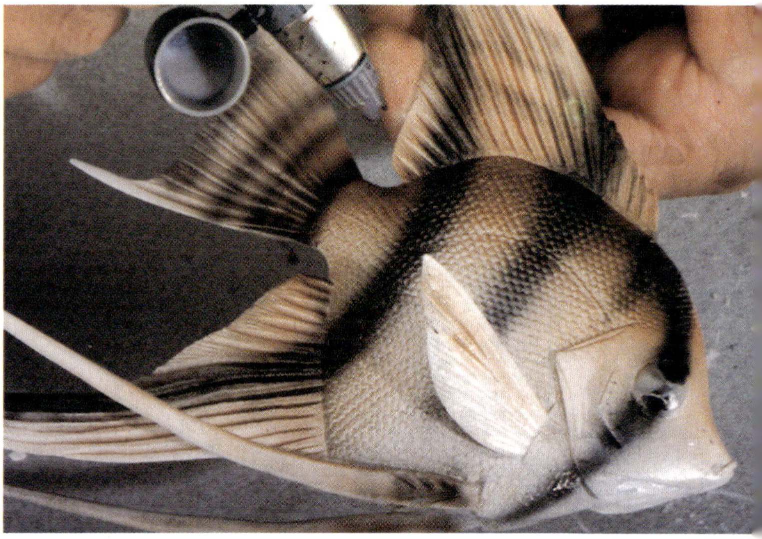

and the center of the body.

Paint random scales along the shoulder of the fish with red ocher.

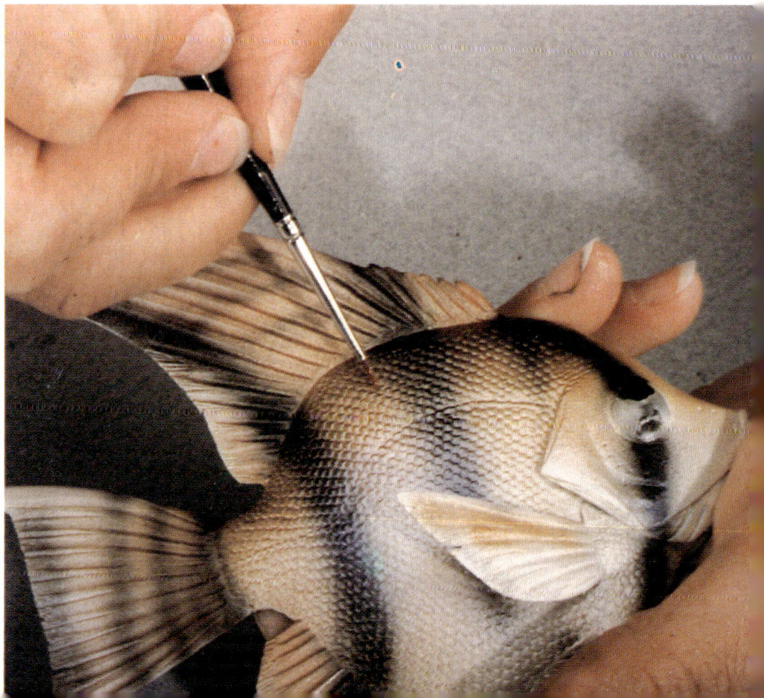

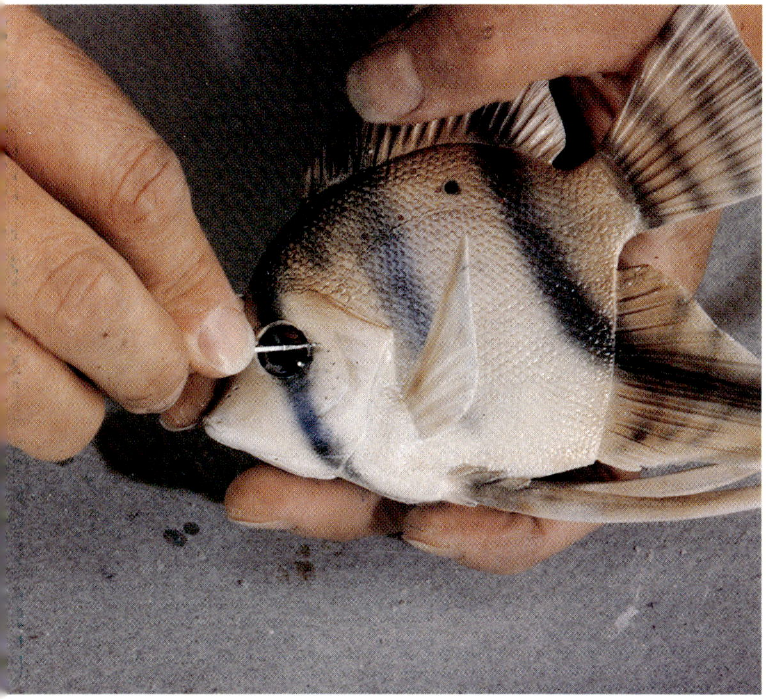

Clean the eyes.

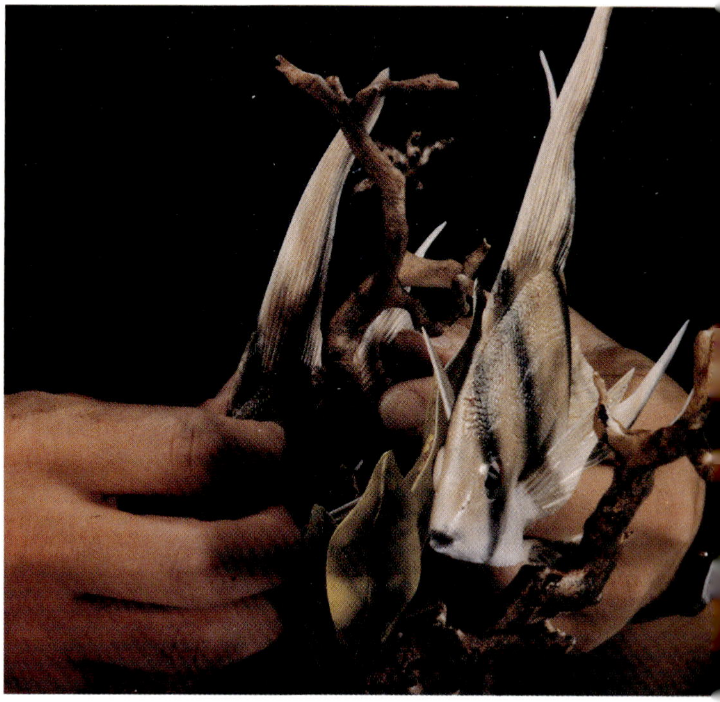

Check the position and glue the fish to the habitat.

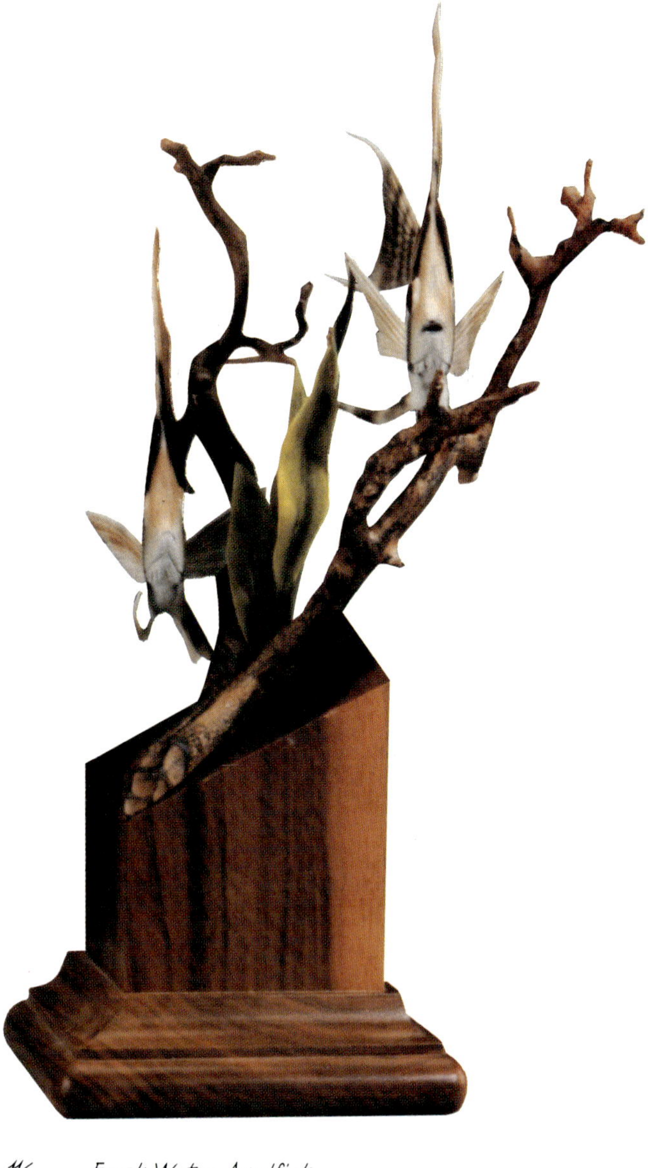

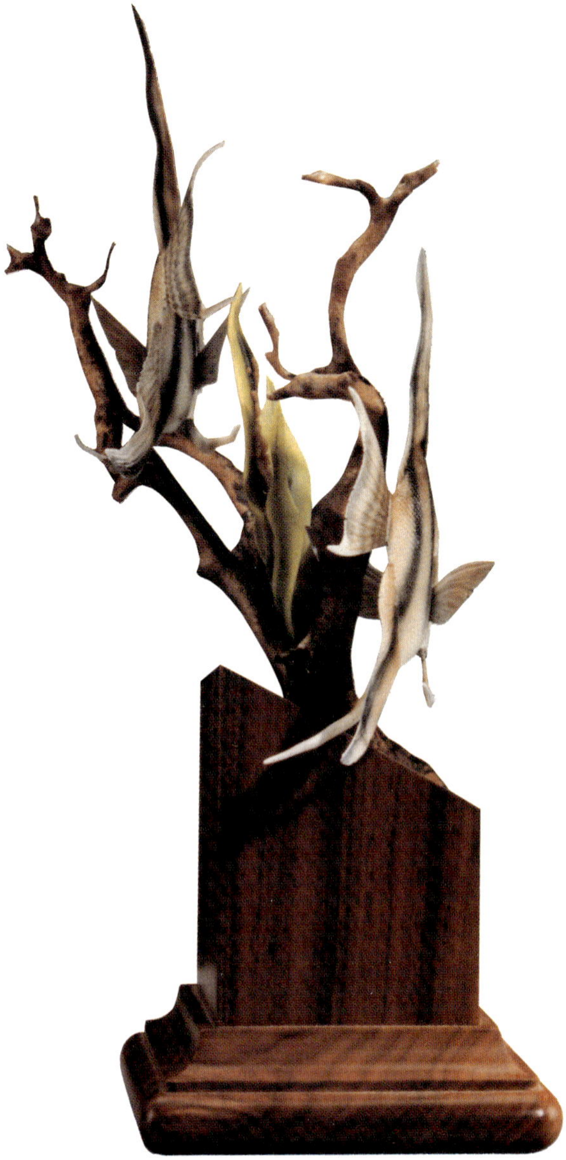

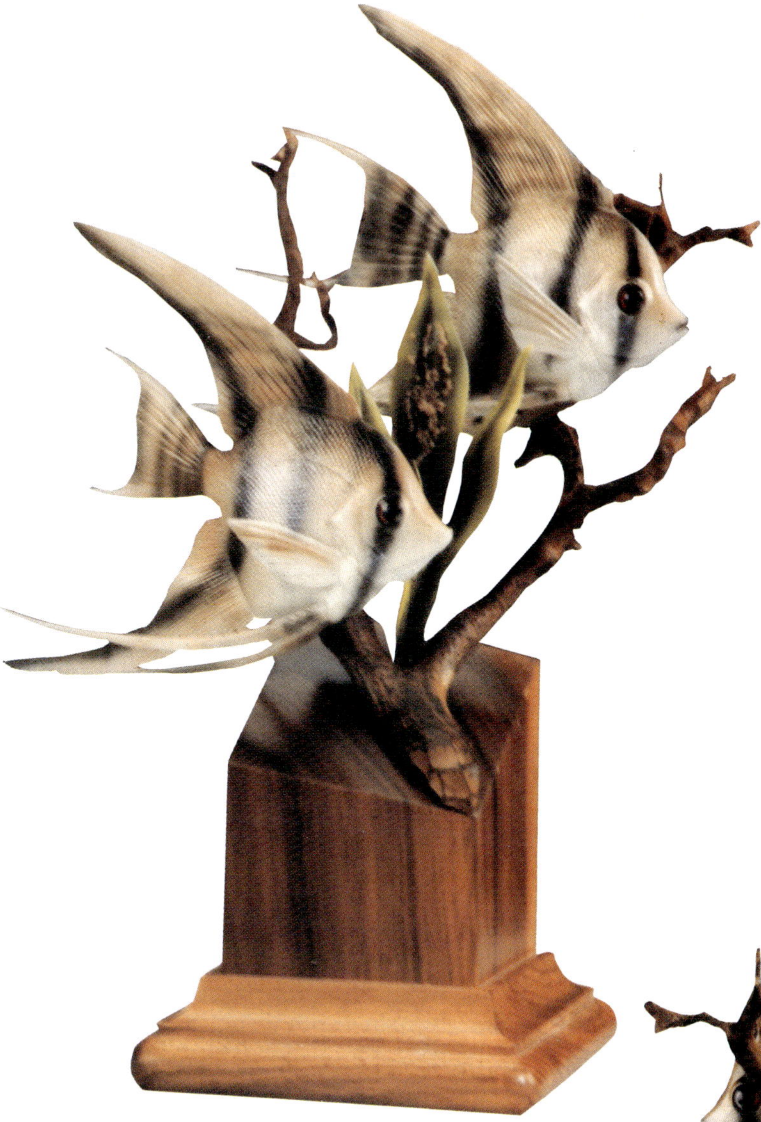

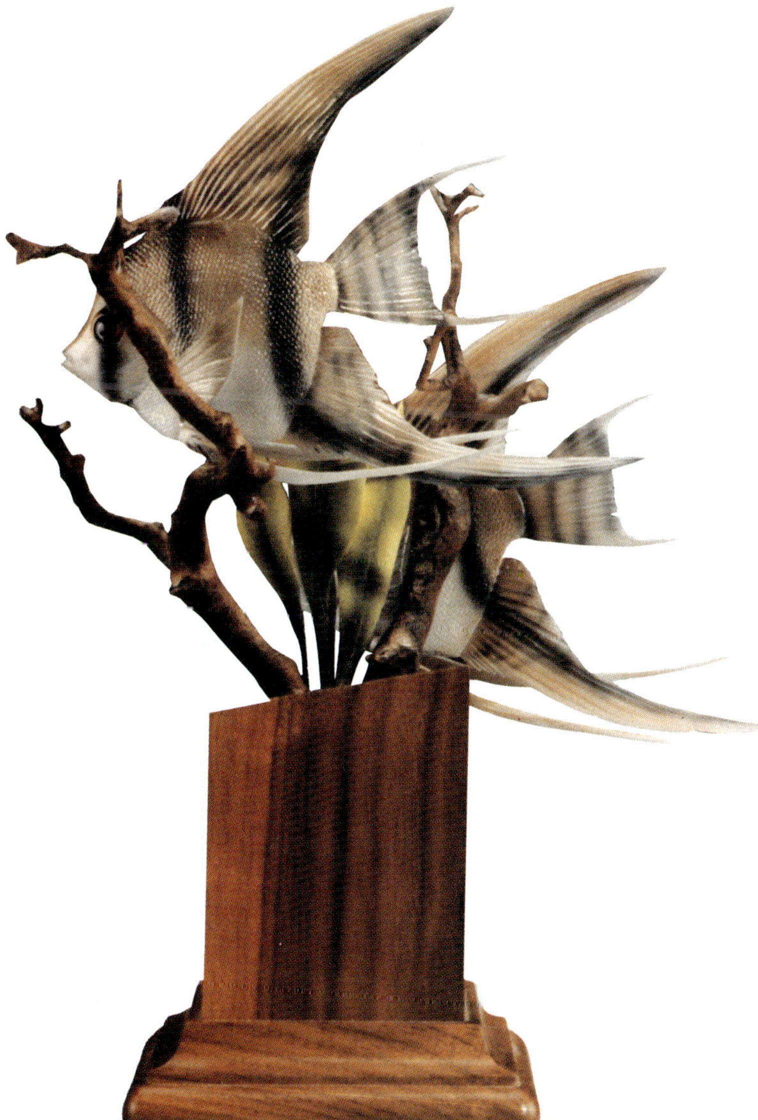

Long-Nosed Butterfly

Forcipiger flavissimus

CHARACTERISTICS

Coloration

* Markedly bright colors, this one being bright yellow/gold
* Velvety black triangle on the top of the head from the tip of the snout to the beginning of the pectoral fin
* The bottom of the head is blue/green
* Clear pectoral and caudal fins
* Dark eye-spot on the anal fin
* blue line on the trailing edge of the anal and dorsal fins.

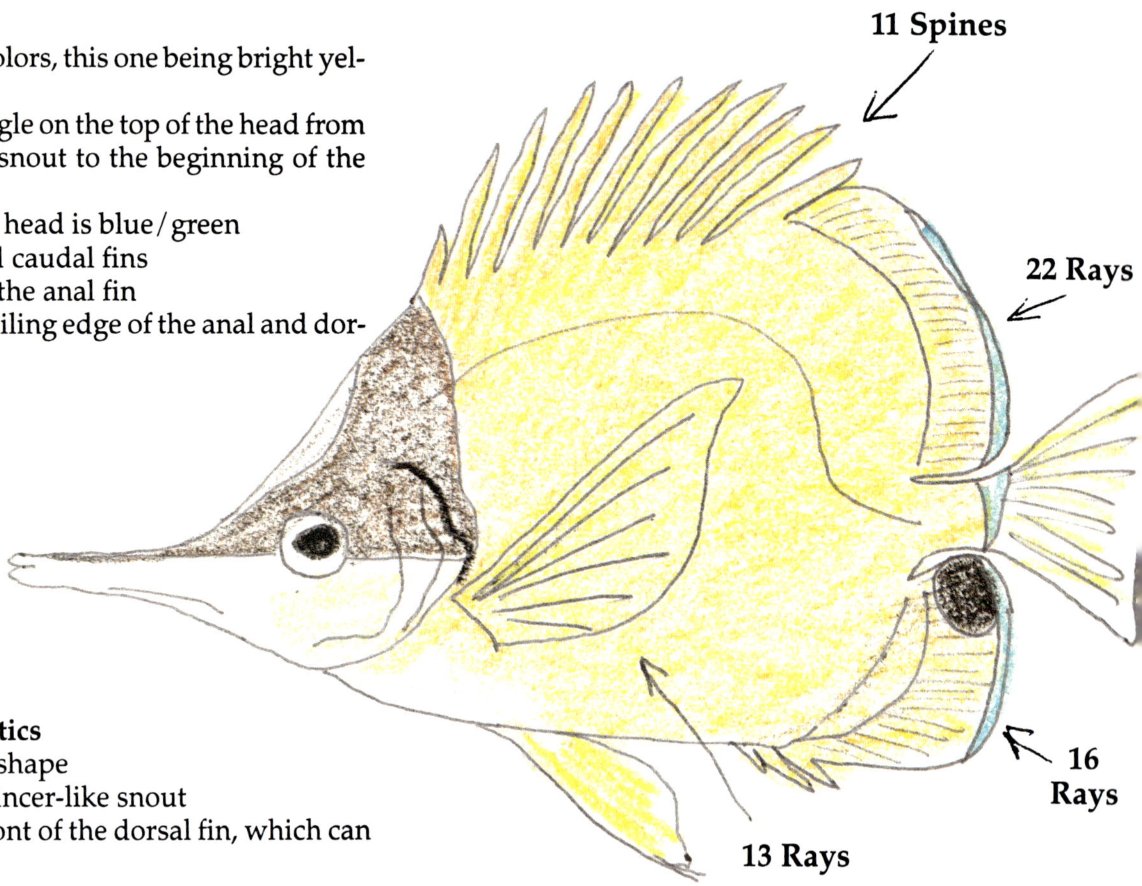

Physical Characteristics

* Chaetodon body shape
* Extremely long pincer-like snout
* 11 spines at the front of the dorsal fin, which can unfold.

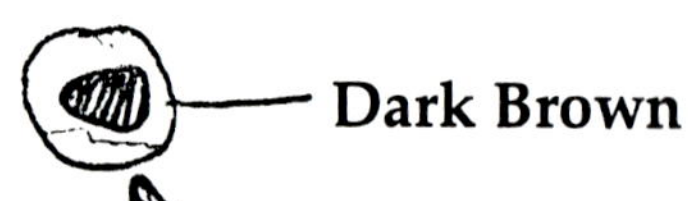

—Tropical Indo Pacific
—6"
—Digs for it's food out of narrowest crevices
—Territorial
—Lives in pairs

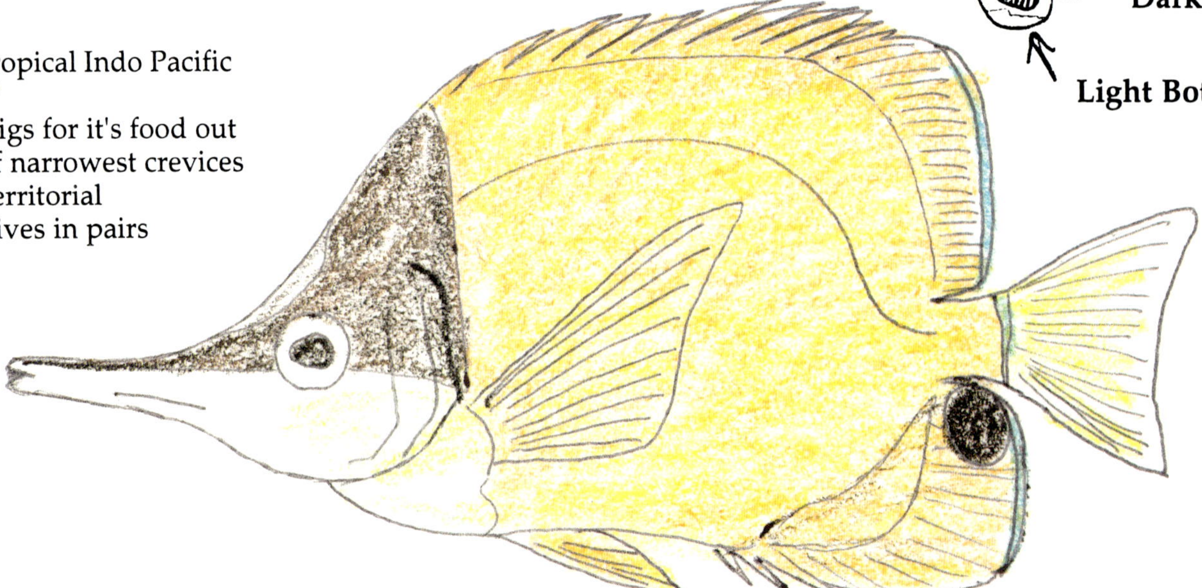

Long-Nosed Butterfly

Forcipiger flavissimus

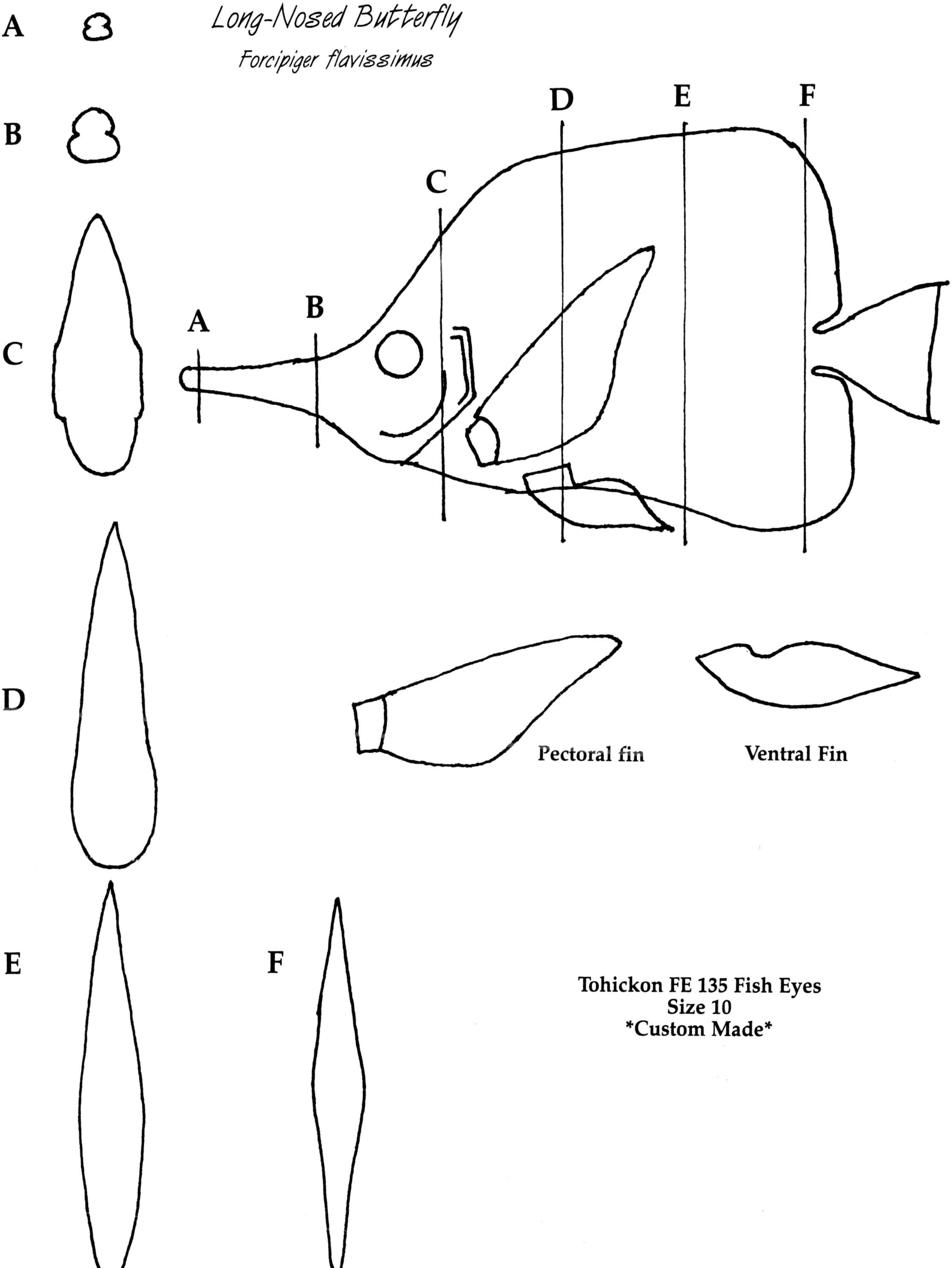

Tohickon FE 135 Fish Eyes
Size 10
Custom Made

Carving the Long-Nosed Butterfly

This salt water fish is a native of the tropical Indo-Pacific. They live in pairs and are highly territorial. They are normally six inches long and uses their snouts to dig for food in the narrowest crevices.

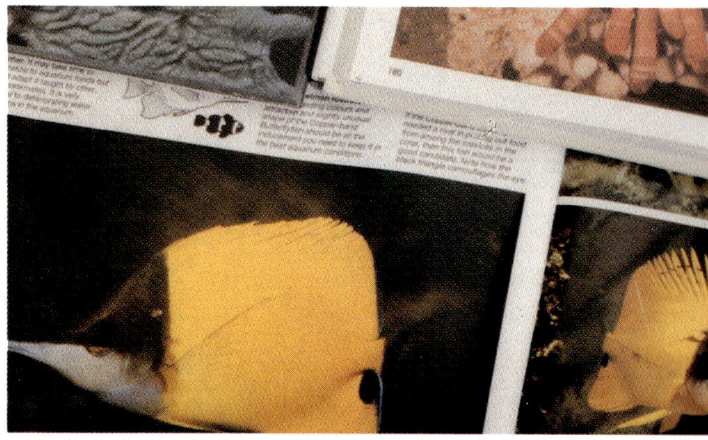

Gather together as many reference materials as you can find. These photos show the Long-Nosed Butterfly Fish, some sea urchins, and some coral, all of which will be part of this project.

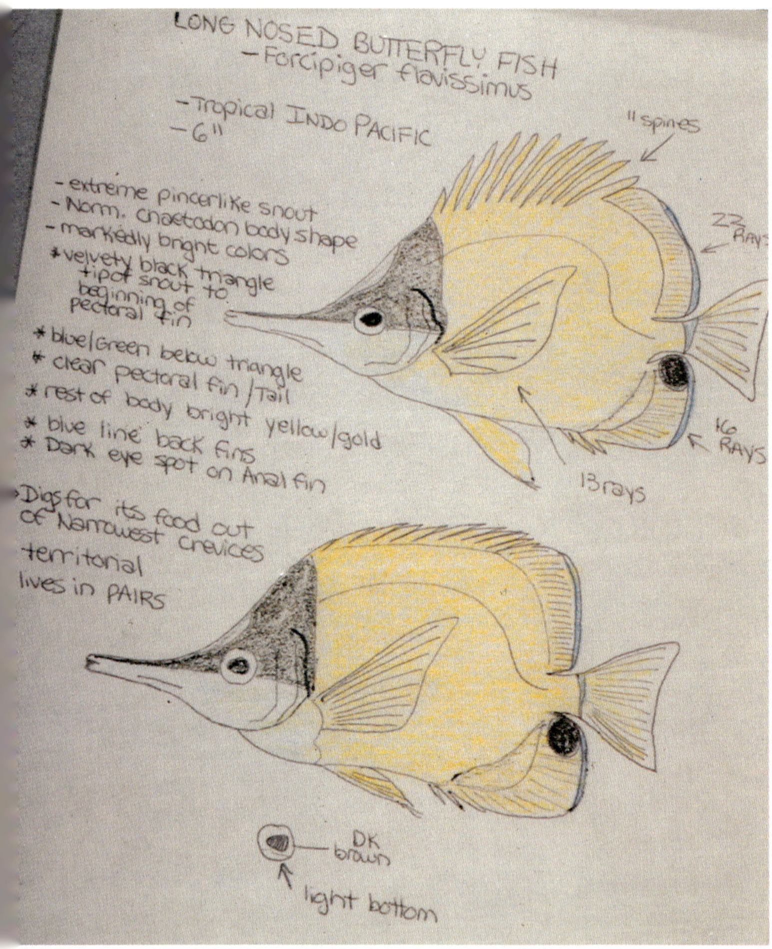

Again, I usually make up a fact sheet on a fish, including a colored drawing.

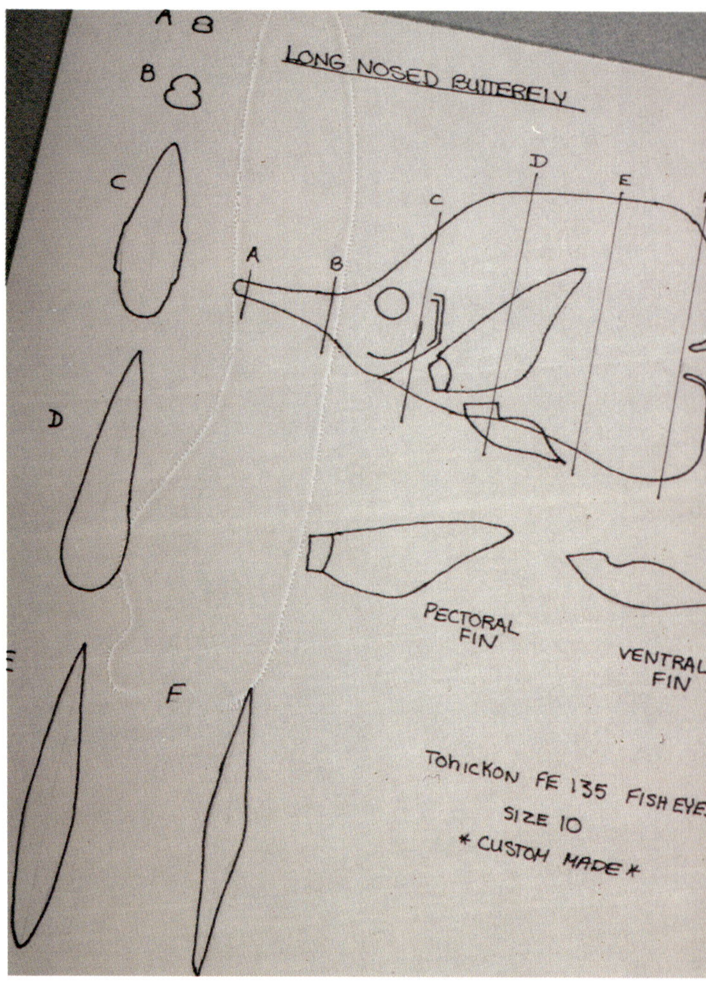

From there I make my patterns.

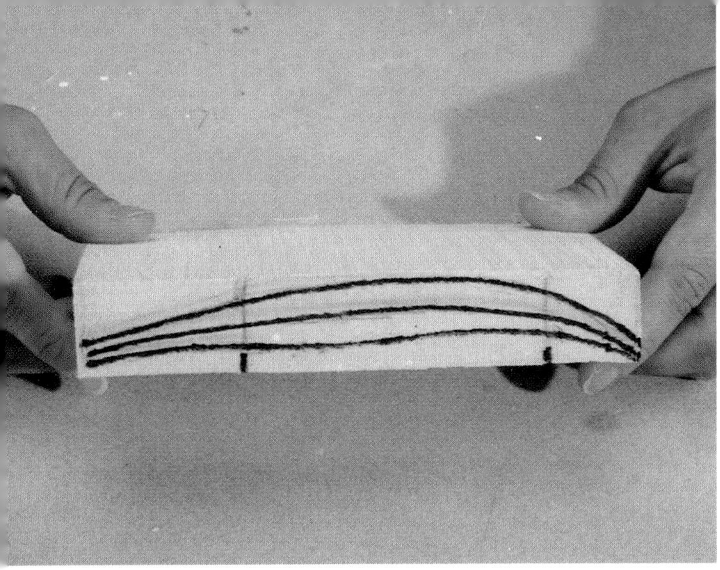

Because of the curve of this fish, I cut the top pattern first. This is bass wood, 6 1/4" x 3 3/4" x 1".

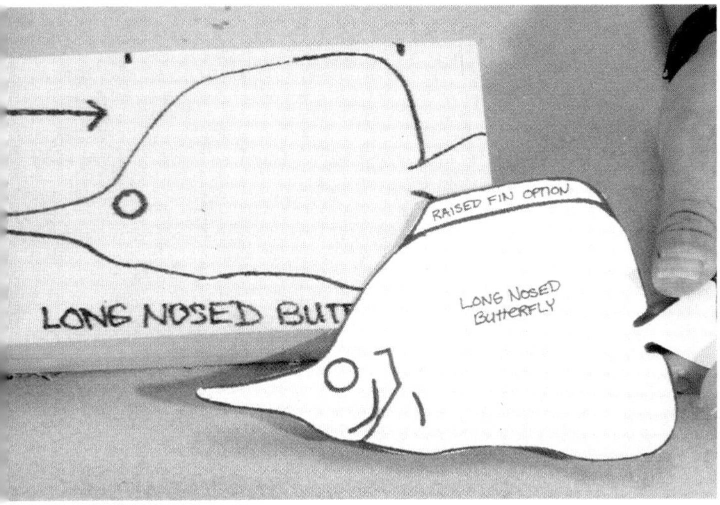

Then I lay the profile pattern on the concave side of the blank, and cut it.

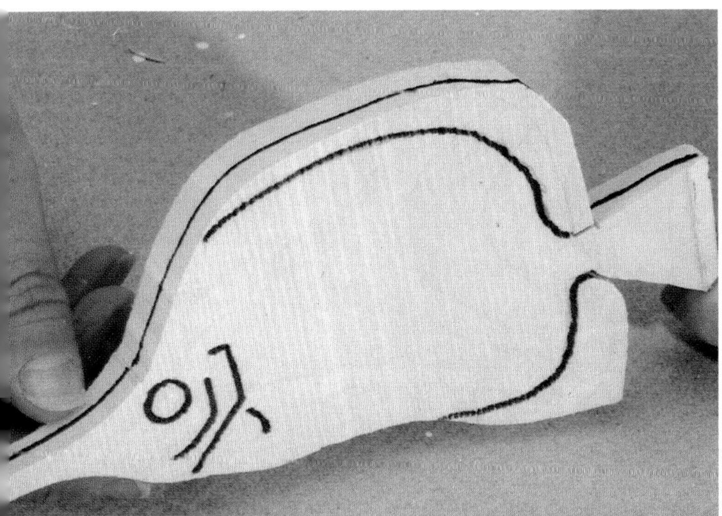

The result. I have added the facial features.

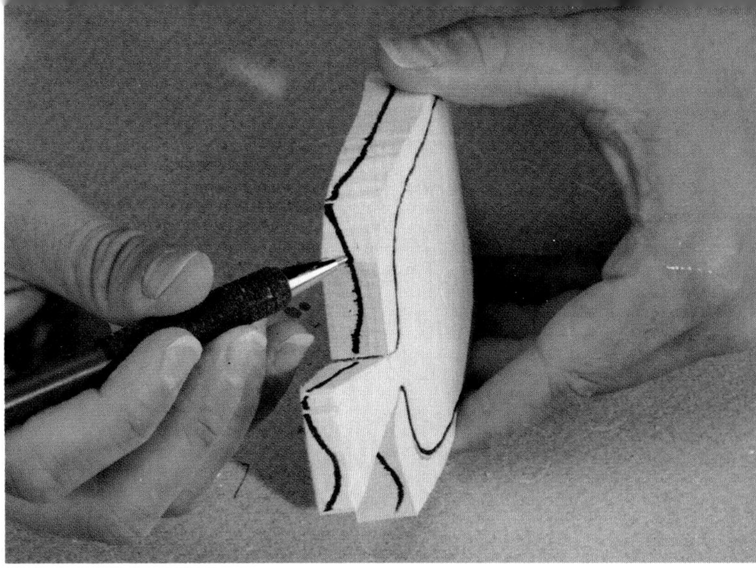

This blank has the dorsal, anal, and caudal fin as part of it. The pectoral and ventral fins will be applied. When drawing the center line, you need to put the undulation in them.

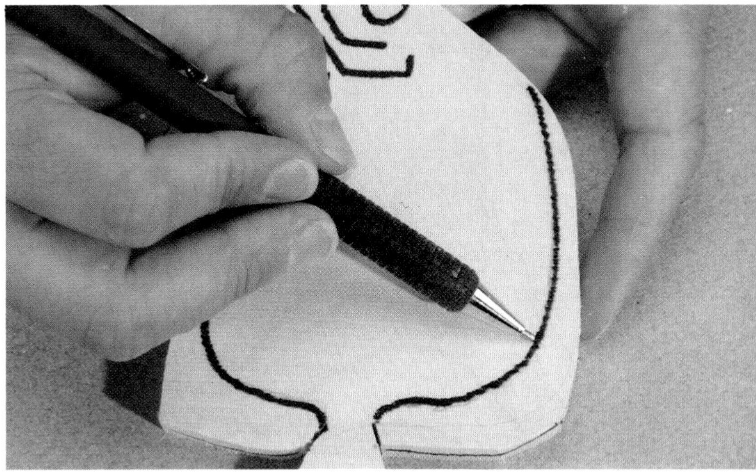

Add the line where the fin will meet the body. The pattern allows you to have the fin up or down. This fin is down, but we will be carving a pair, one with the fin up and one down. The same techniques will apply to both.

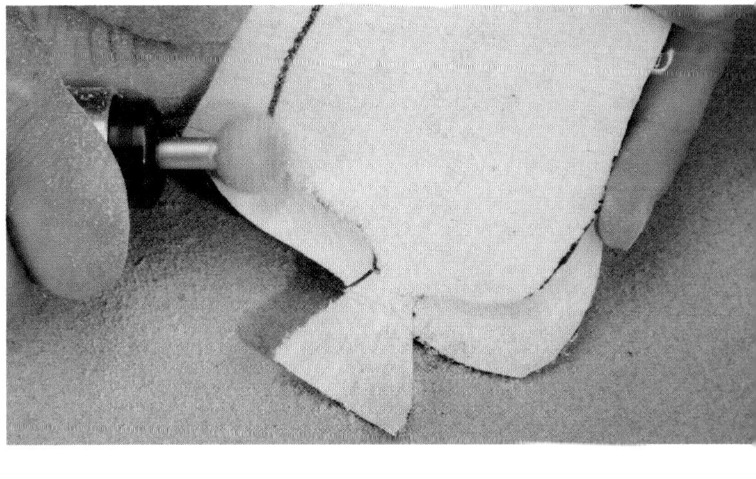

I get the contour of the fins with 1/2" carbide cutter by Kutzall. This is a very aggressive cutter and can easily injure the carver, so **BE CAREFUL!** Start at the caudal fin and follow the line of the body, shaping the dorsal and anal fins.

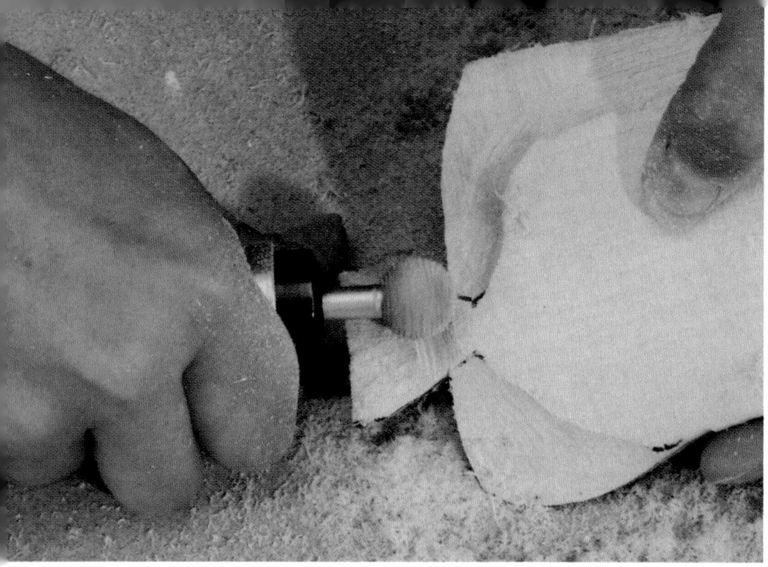

You can also use the bit to shape the caudal fin.

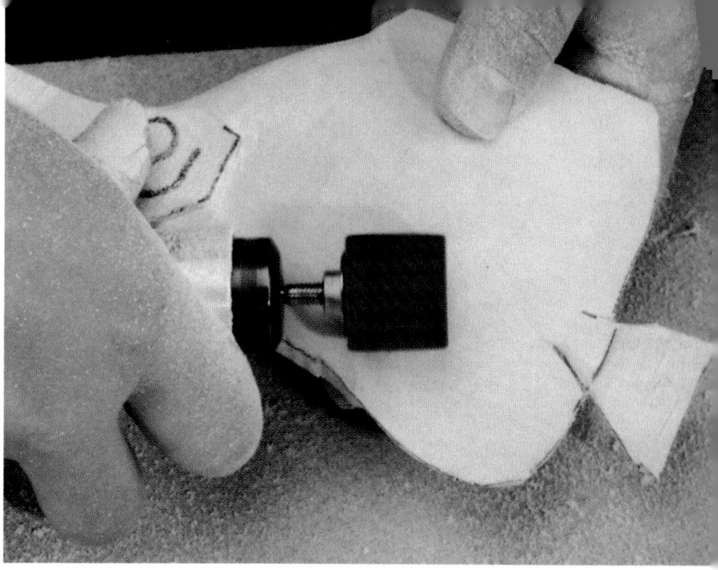

At the same time round the belly.

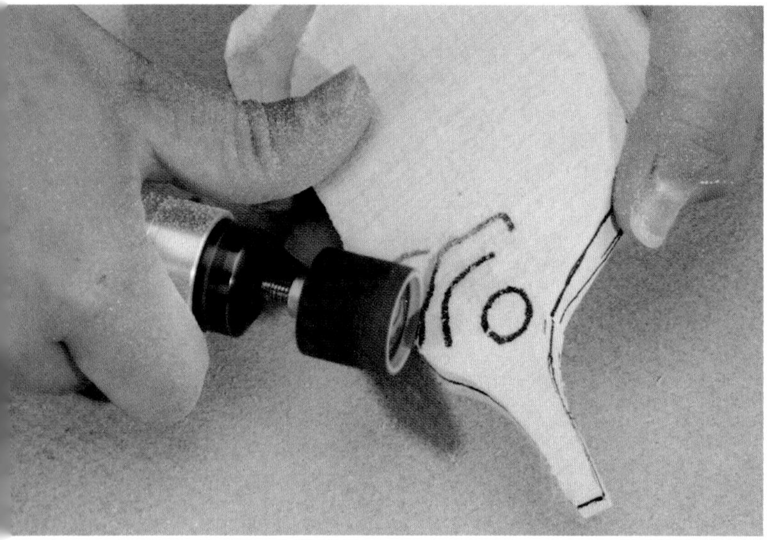

Change to the sanding drum to cut along the edge of the gill plate.

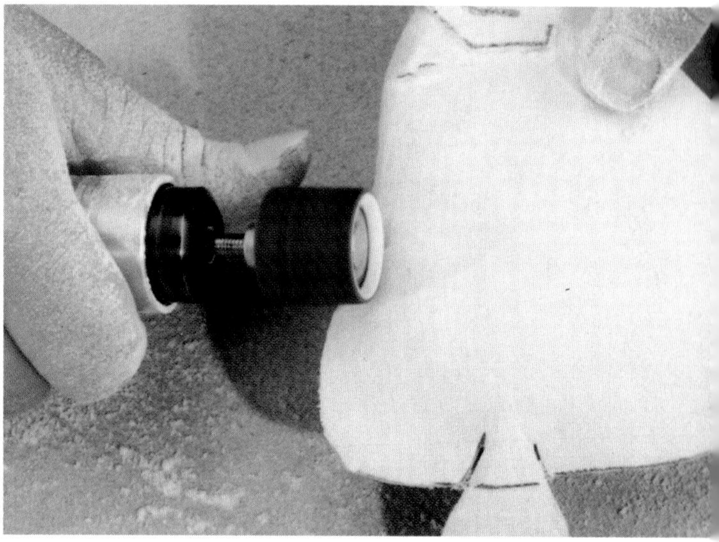

Create the visceral groove along the back edge of the belly.

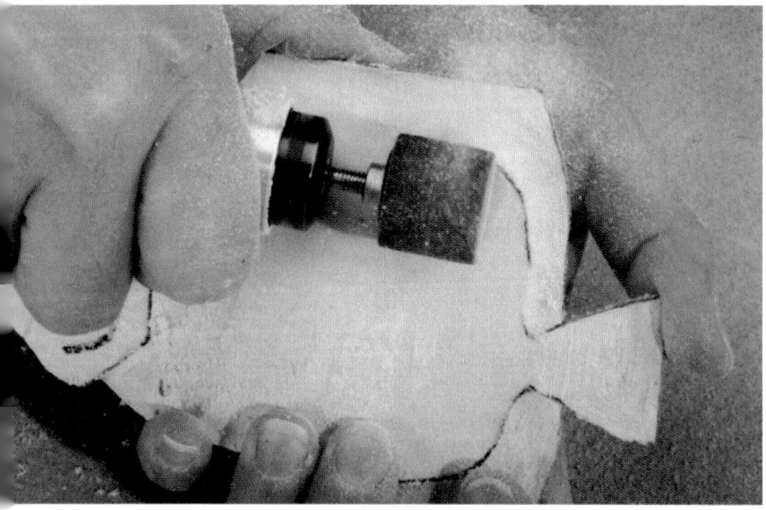

Continue with the sanding drum, and blend the body and the fin. This will also smooth some of the marks left by the Kutzall.

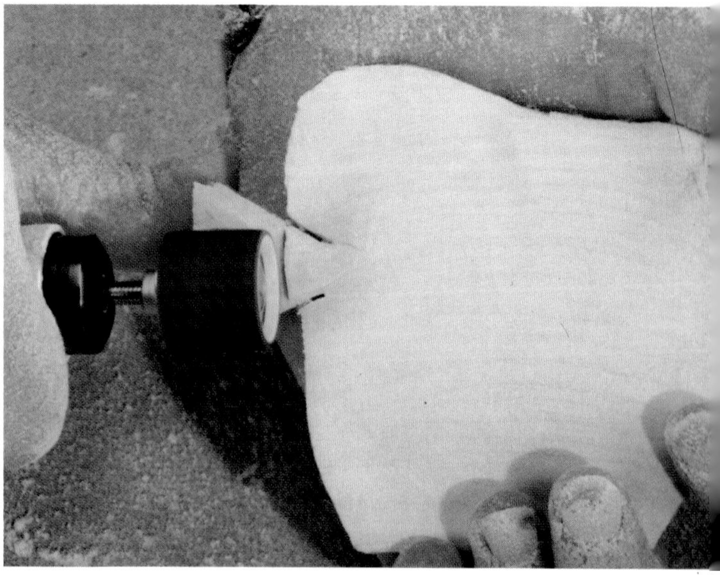

Run the edge of the grinder along the edge of the caudal peduncle.

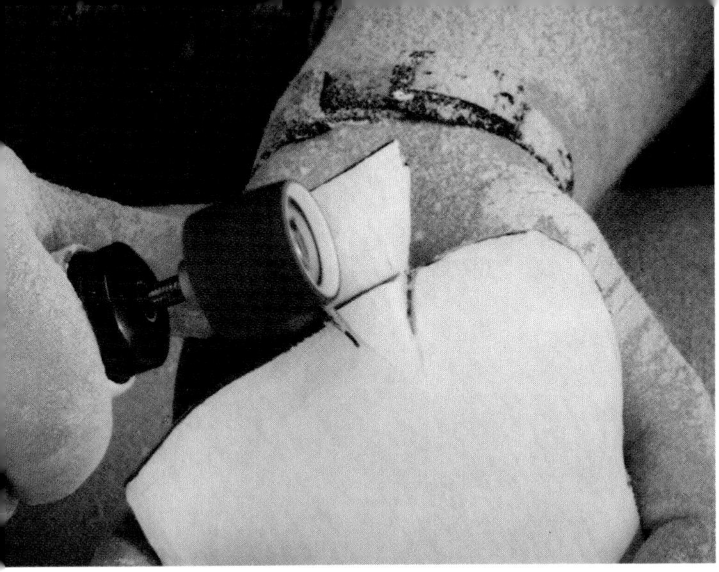

Taper the tail down from this line. The line will be blended later, but denotes where the scaling ends and the caudal fins begins to taper radically.

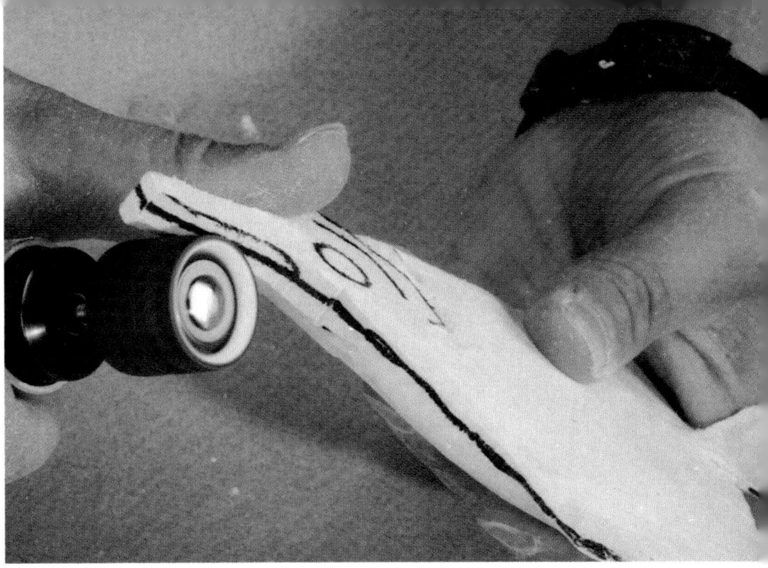

Round over the snout. This long maxillary looks like it is all mouth, but, in reality, only the tip has the mouth.

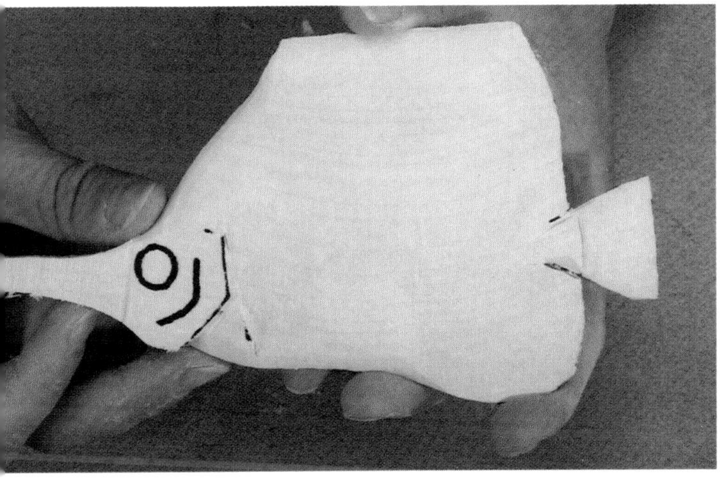

Progress, from the side...

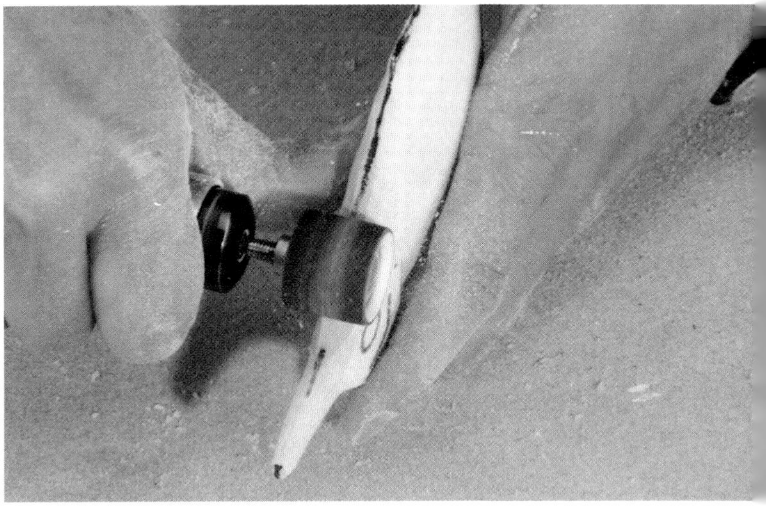

There is a flattened area between the eyes that can also be created with the grinder.

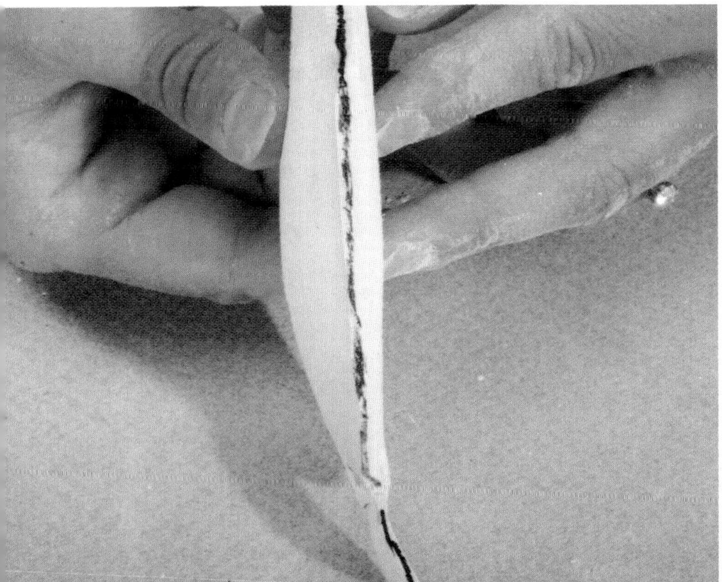

and the plane view.

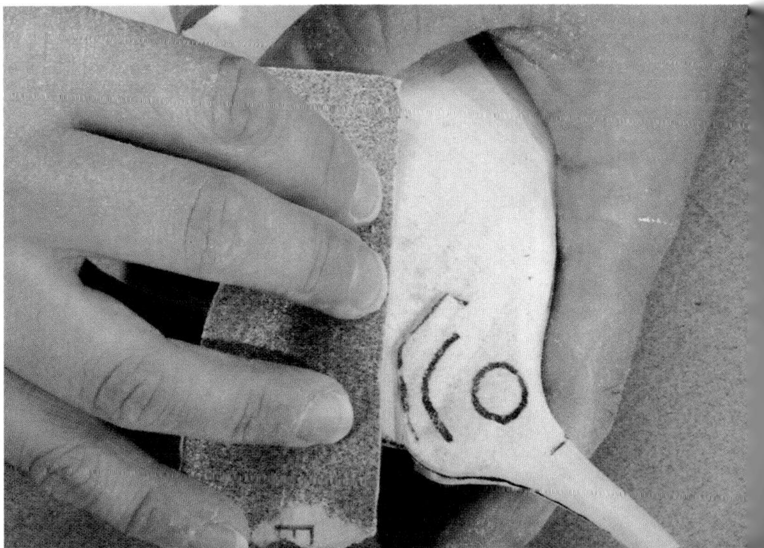

Sand the whole fish.

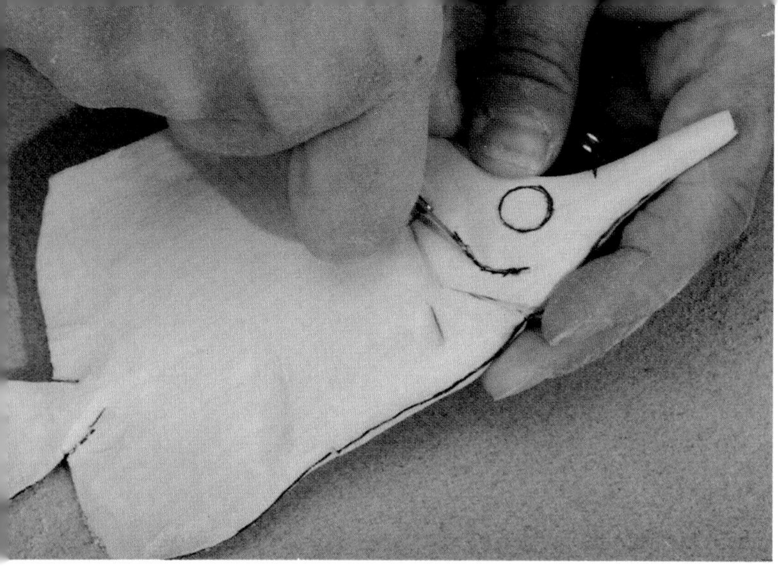

Cut a stop in the preopercle...

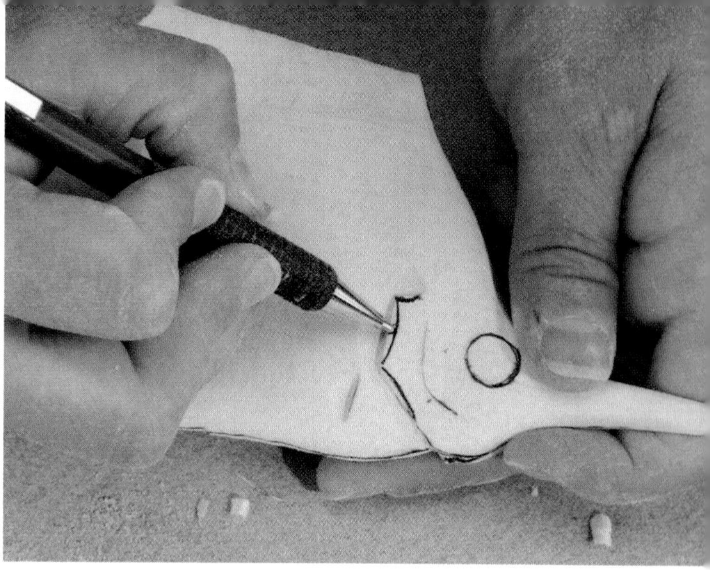

The structure of the gill gets thinner at the edge, one part ending on this line, and the rest trailing off. This line will be burned in later.

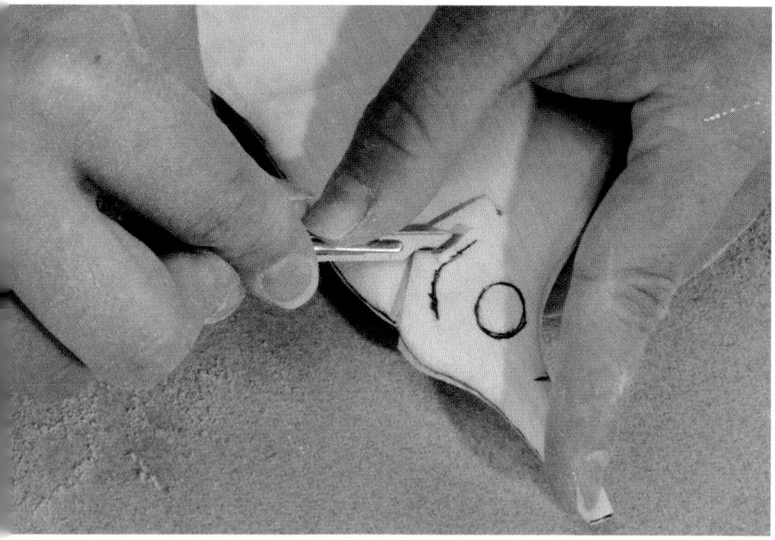

and cut back to it from the opercle.

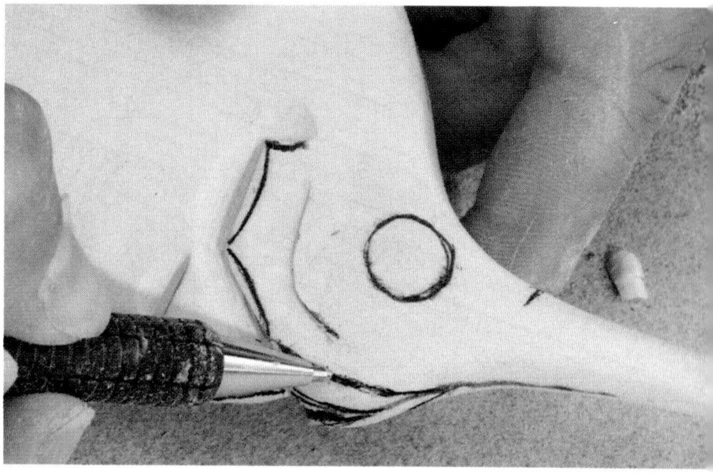

This lower line is where the branchiostegal rays begin.

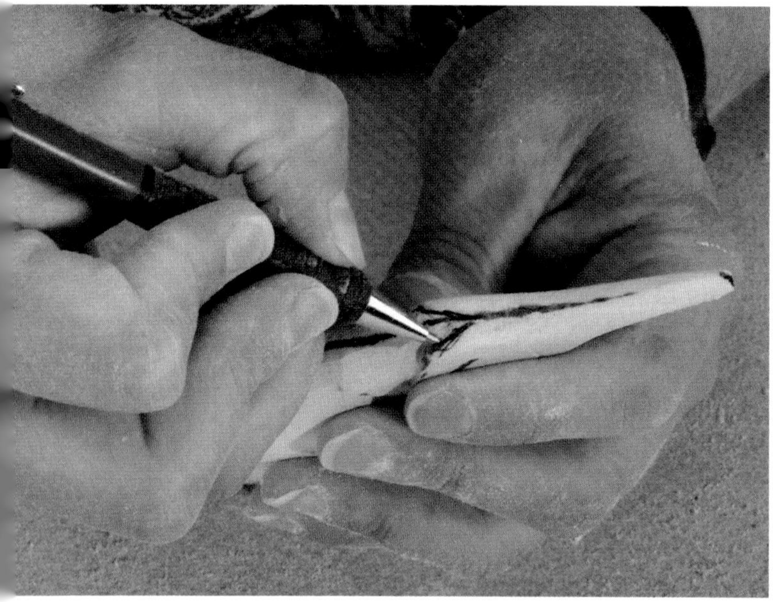

Mark the trailing edge of the gill plate beneath the head.

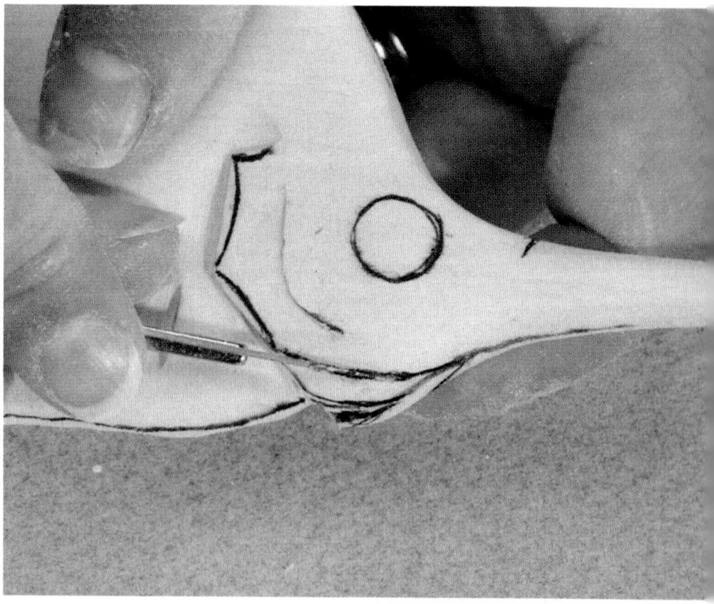

Cut a stop in this line...

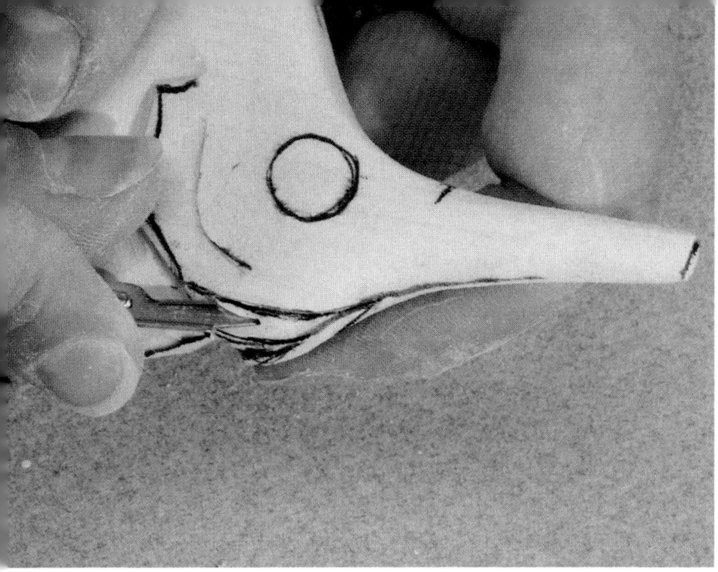

and trim back to it from below.

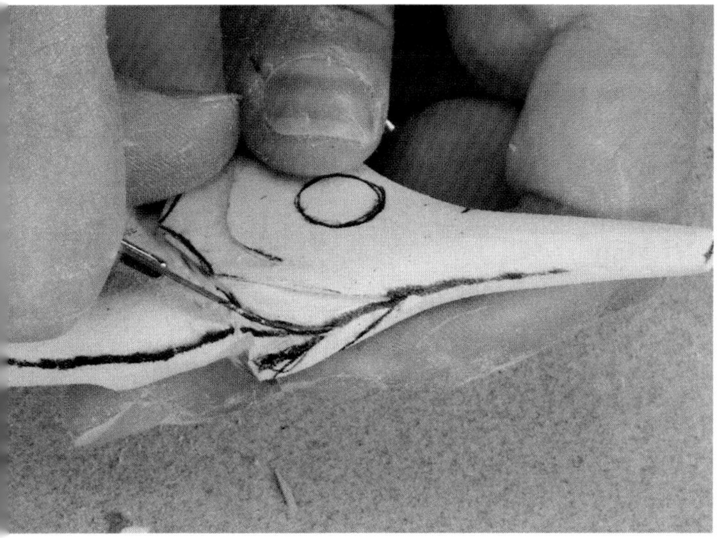

Cut a stop in the back edge of the gill...

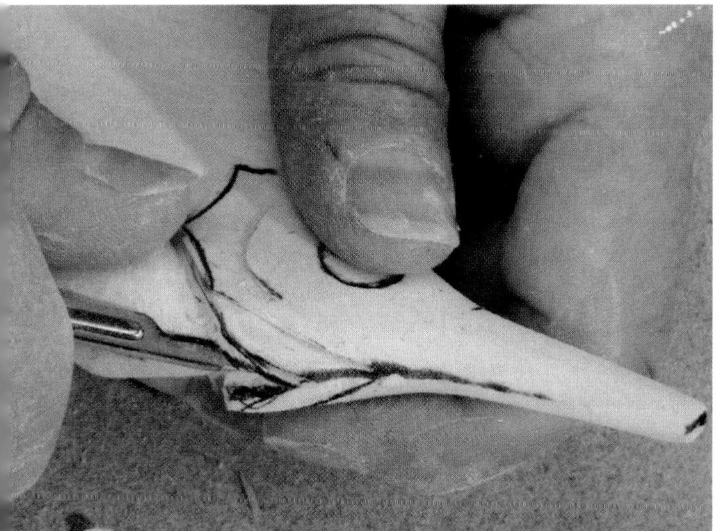

and cut back to it from behind, taking out the chunk of wood where the lines meet underneath.

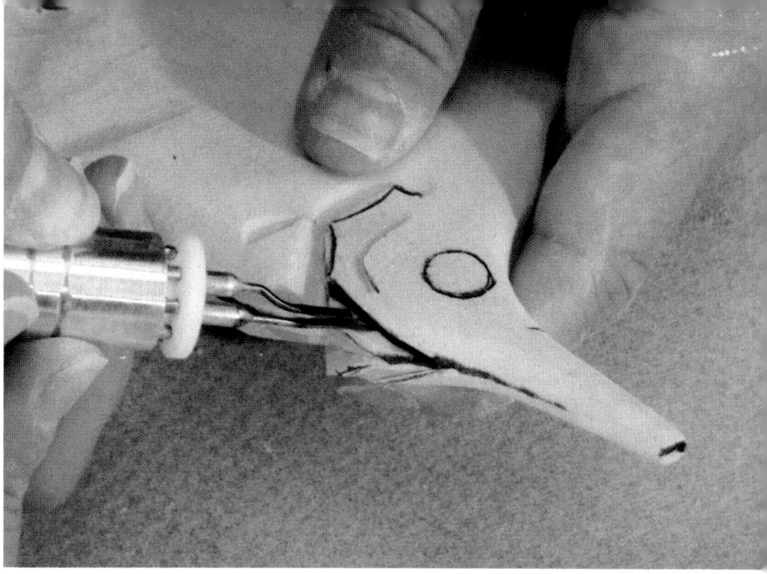

Burn these lines to clean them up.

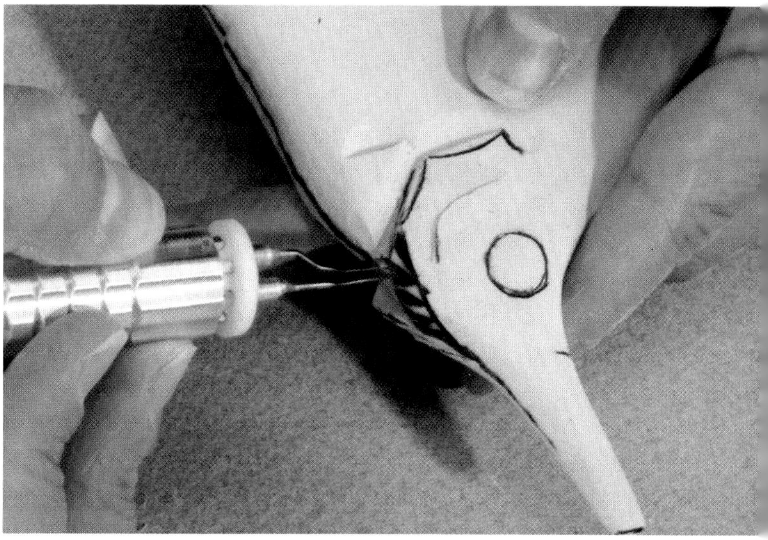

Continue with the branchiostegal rays.

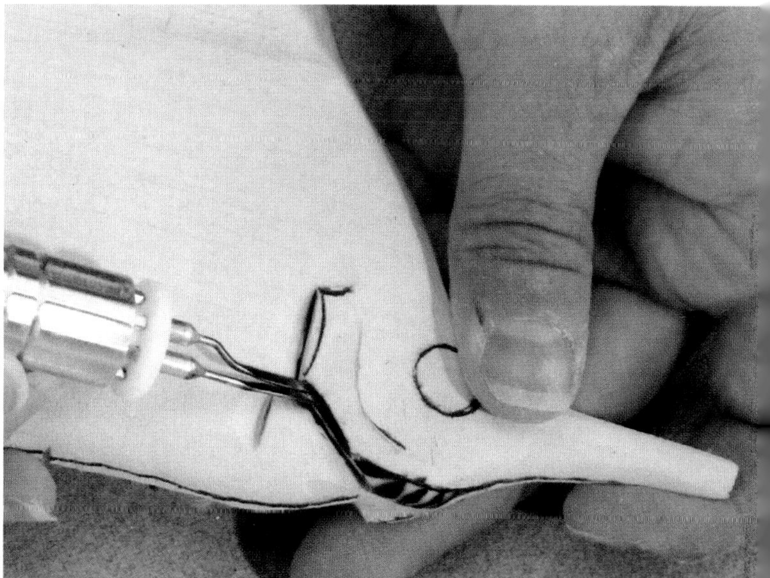

Burn in the depression at the back of the gill plate.

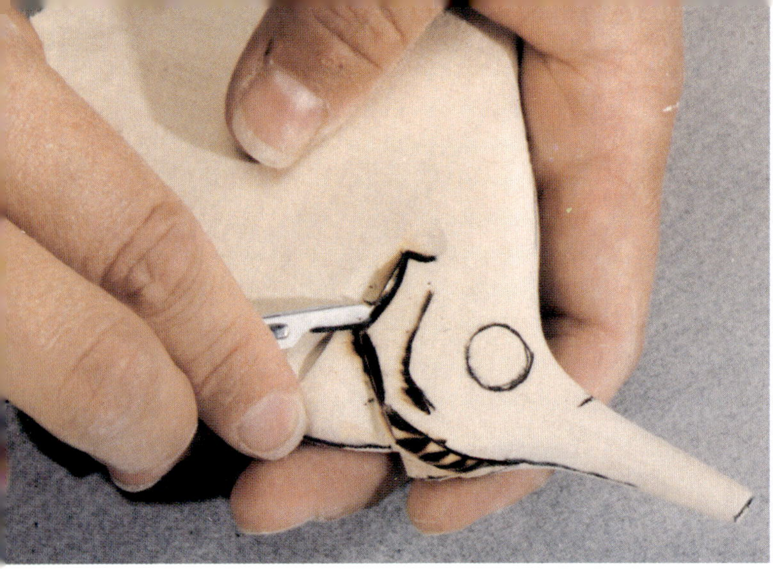

Clean up the burned area of the gill plate with a knife.

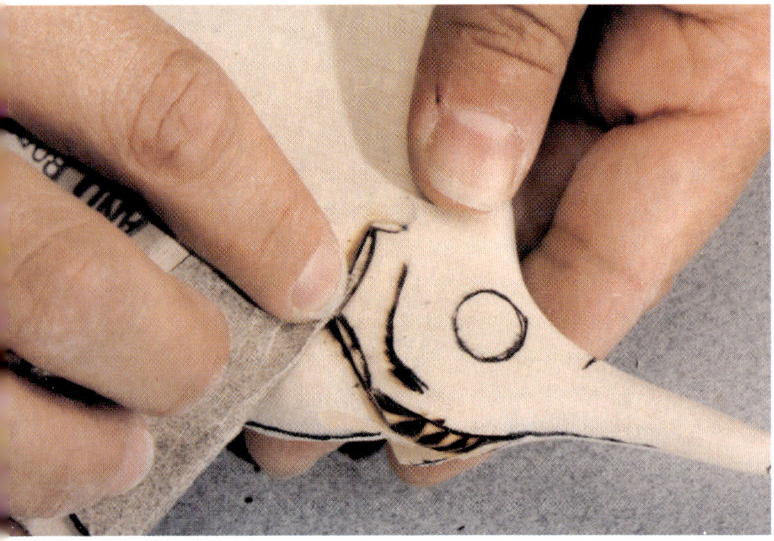

Lightly sand it with fine paper.

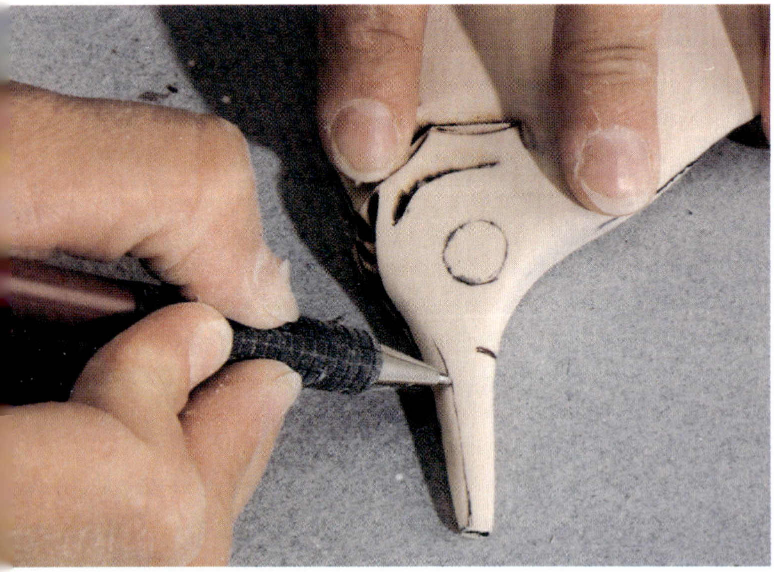

Draw in the line of the snout. The mark on the top is where there will be a slight ridge.

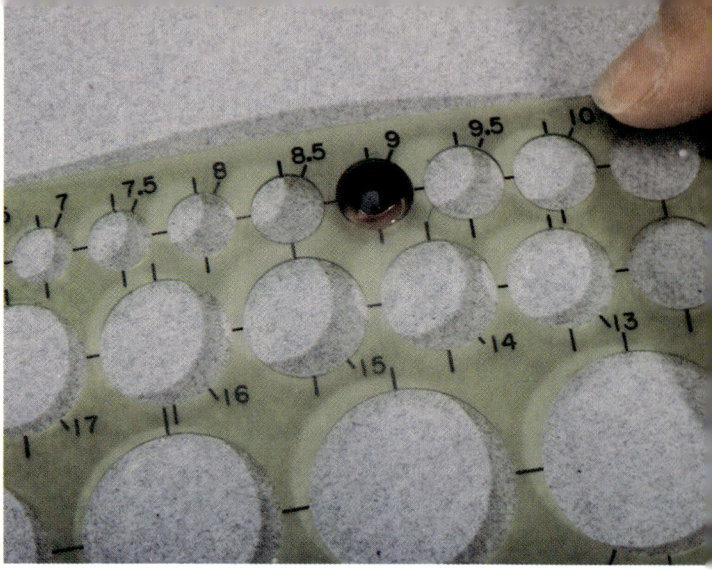

The eye measures 9mm so we need a socket that is 9.5mm.

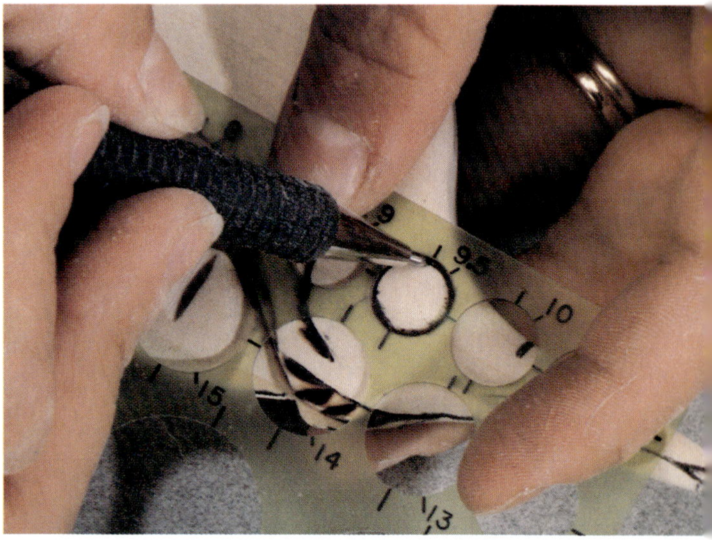

Draw the holes on each side, using the pattern for placement, and making sure the holes are aligned side-to-side.

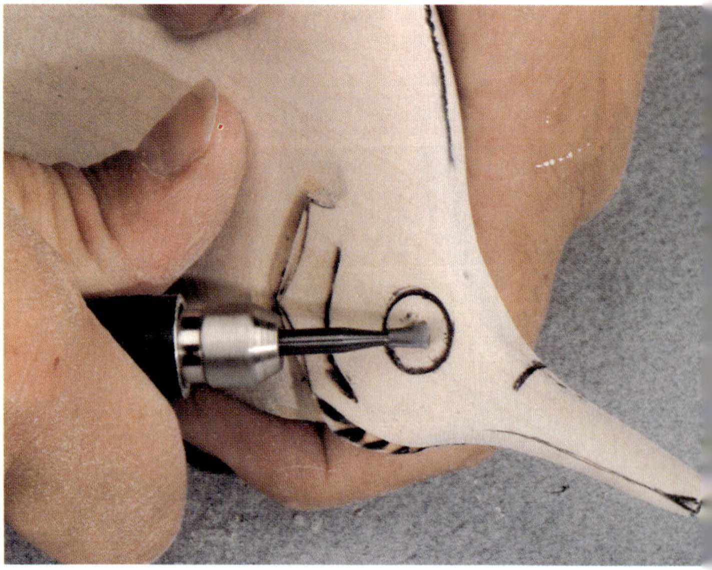

Make the start of a hole in the middle...

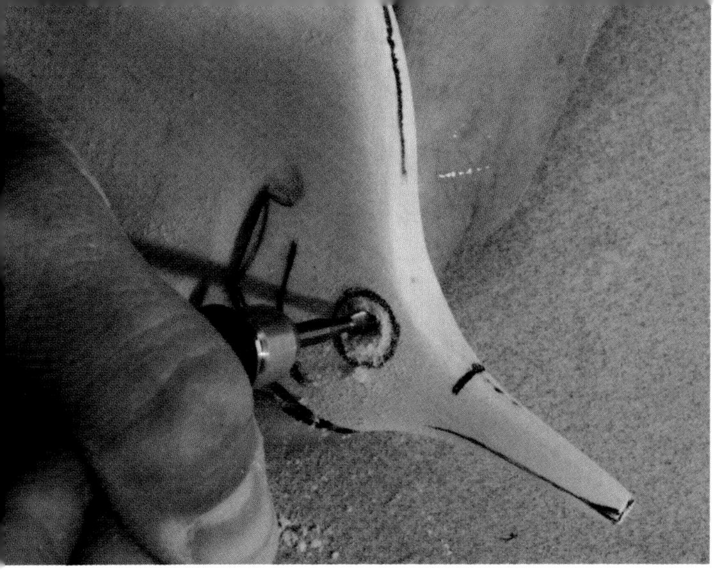

and widen it out to the perimeter. I am using a carbide burr that flares out at the end. This is probably my favorite tool for cutting eye sockets.

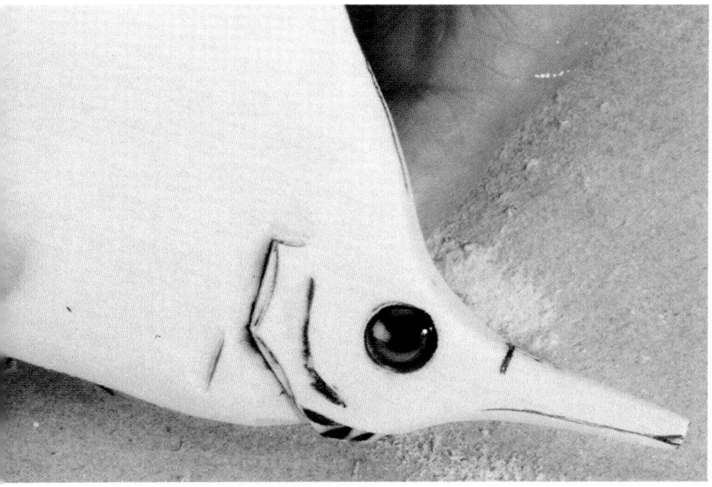

Adjust until the eye fits easily into the socket.

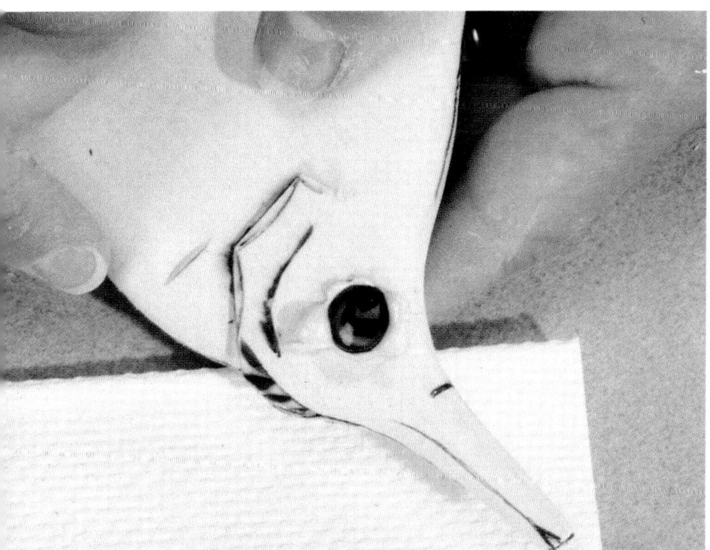

Fill the socket with the Tuf-Carve™ putty and insert the eye. The narrow end of the oval pupil goes forward in the eye.

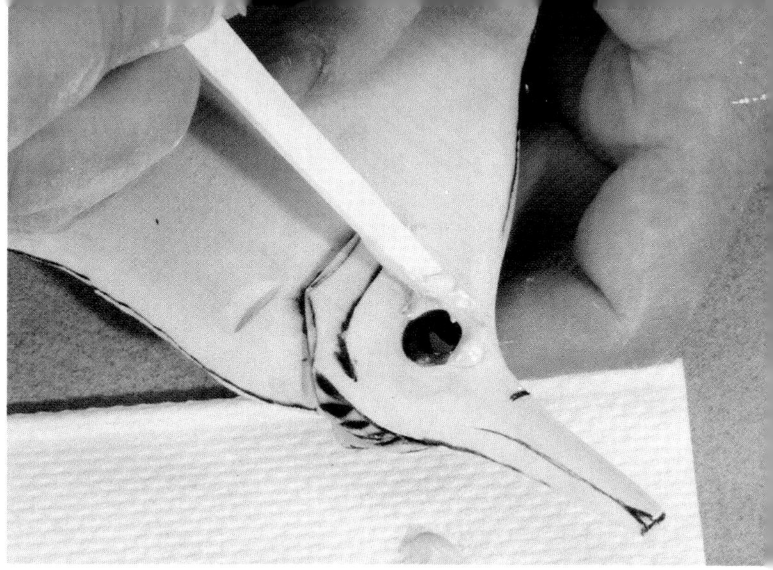

Clean up around the lower eye, but add some extra above for the scleric capsule.

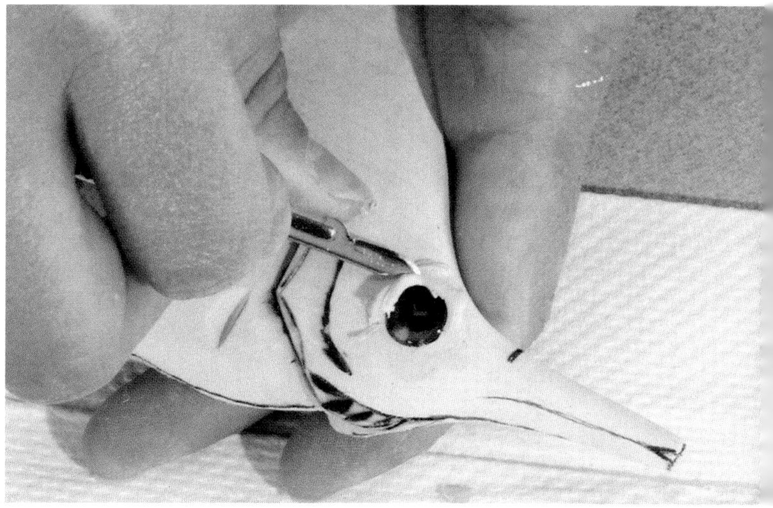

When the putty has set, clean the glass eye. Tohickon eyes have a groove around the perimeter that you can follow with the knife.

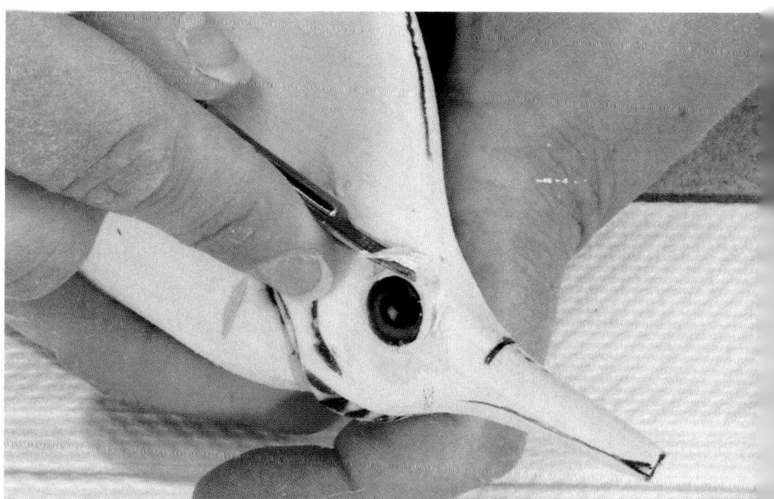

Cut along the edge of the capsule, cutting off the extra and leaving the ridge of the capsule itself.

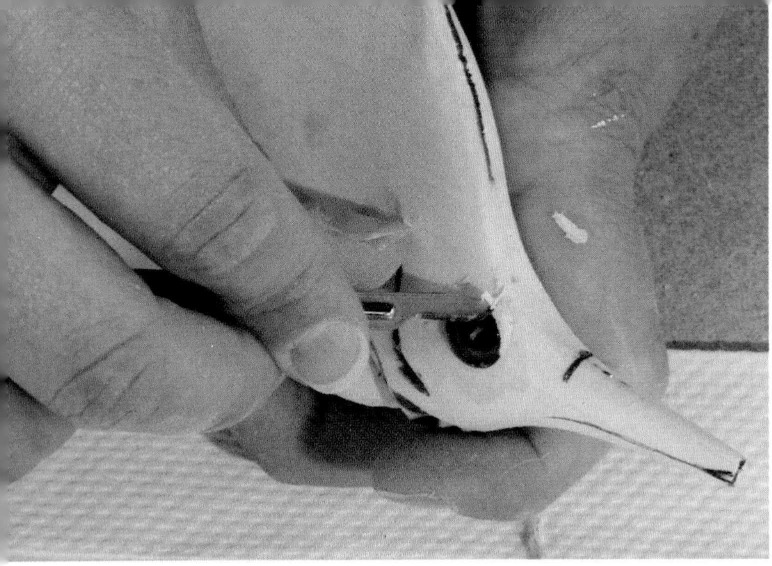

Clean up the edge of the capsule.

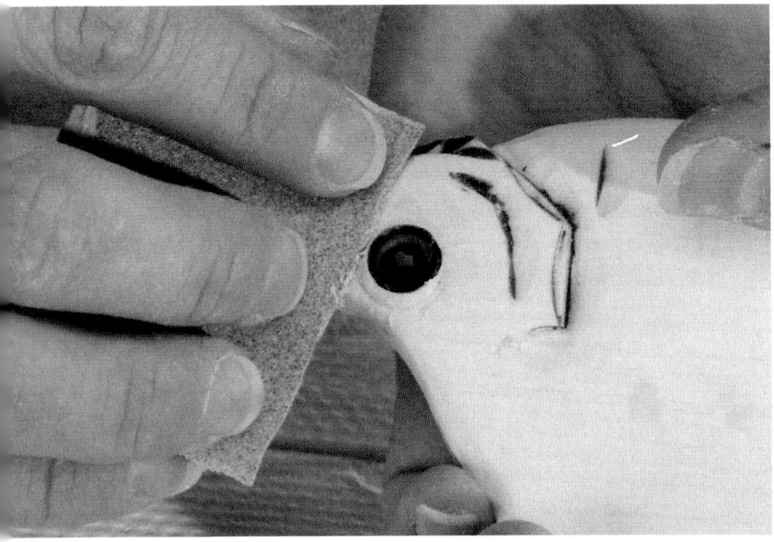

Carefully sand around the edges. It is easier to sand the Tuf-Carve™ while it is still a little wet.

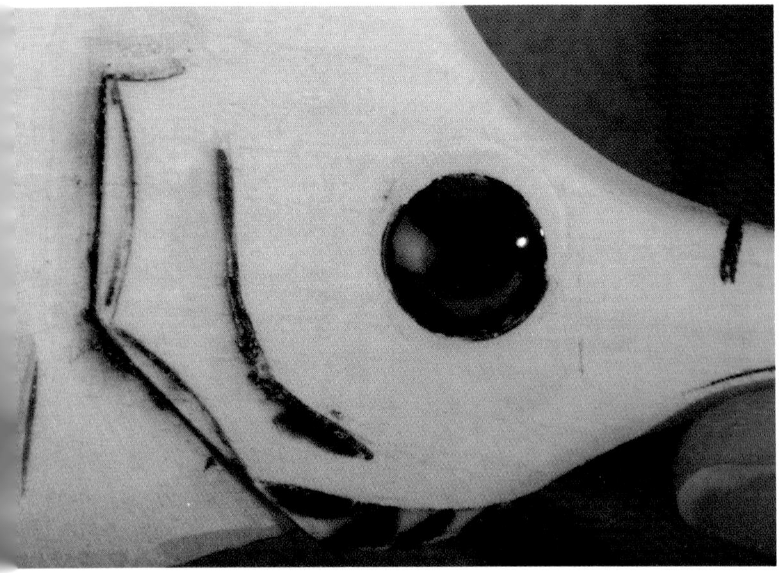

The result

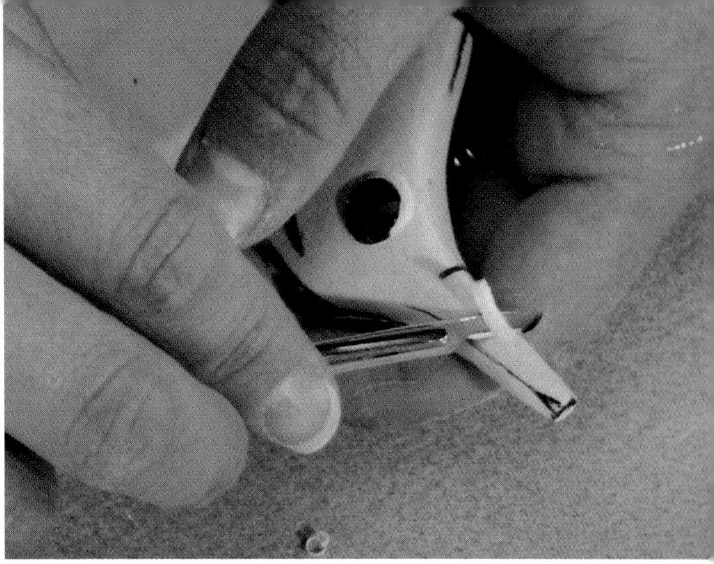

Working from the ridge to the end, narrow the snout even more.

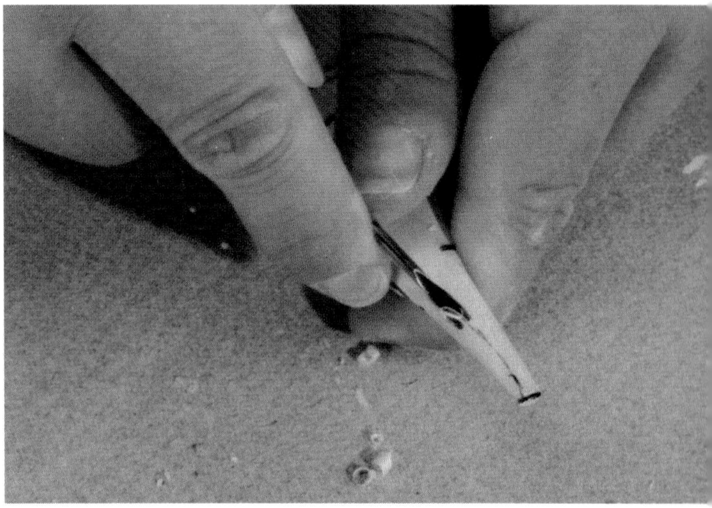

With a micro v-tool follow the snout line on both sides.

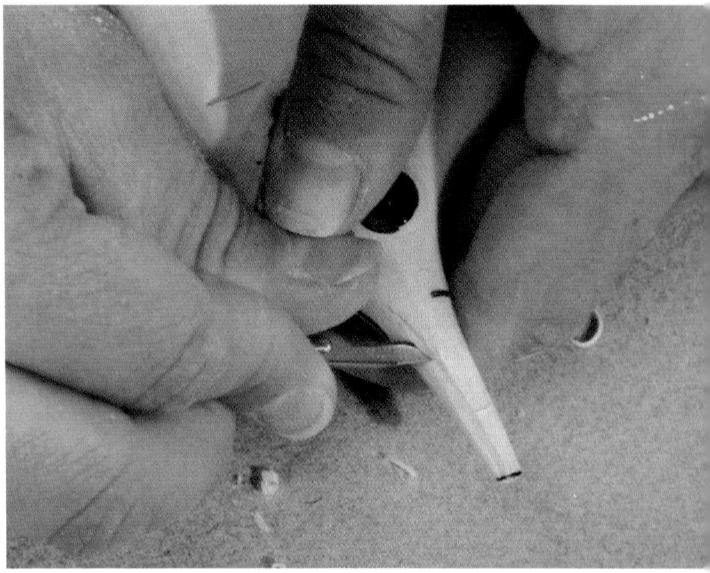

Clean up the edges on both sides of the line with the knife, blending it with the snout.

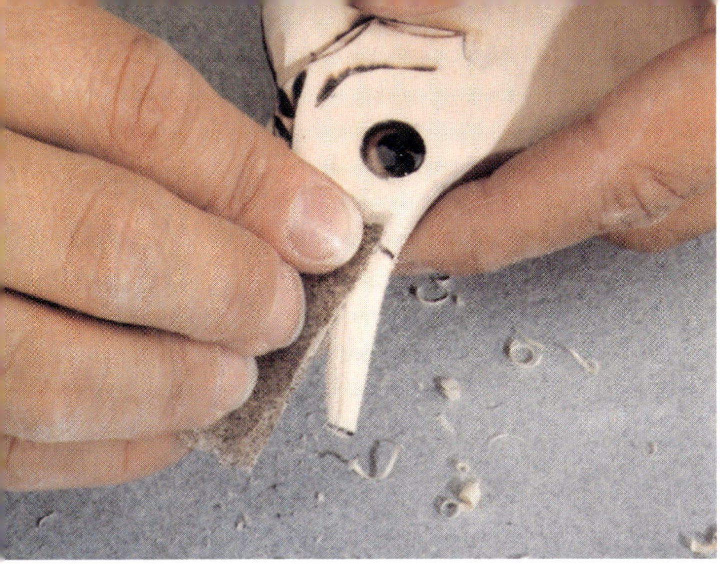

Lightly sand the area, first with medium paper, then fine.

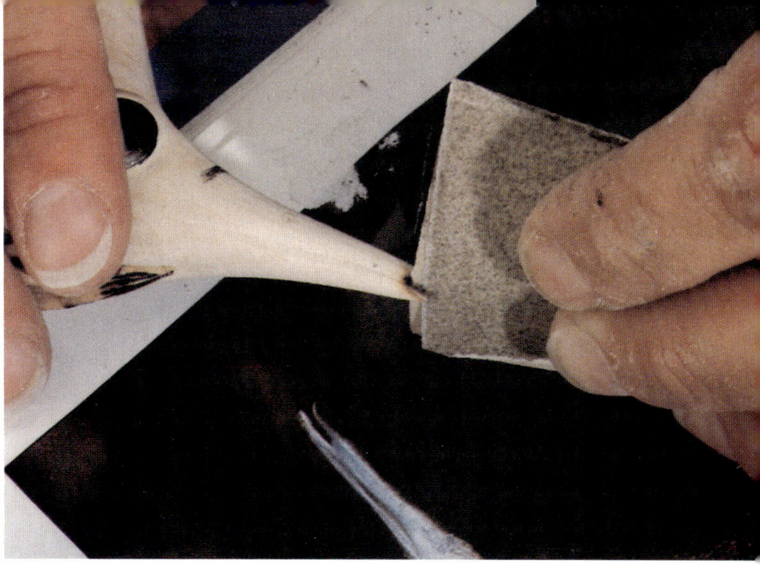

and lightly sand the burnt area. The sanding can take the mouth deeper.

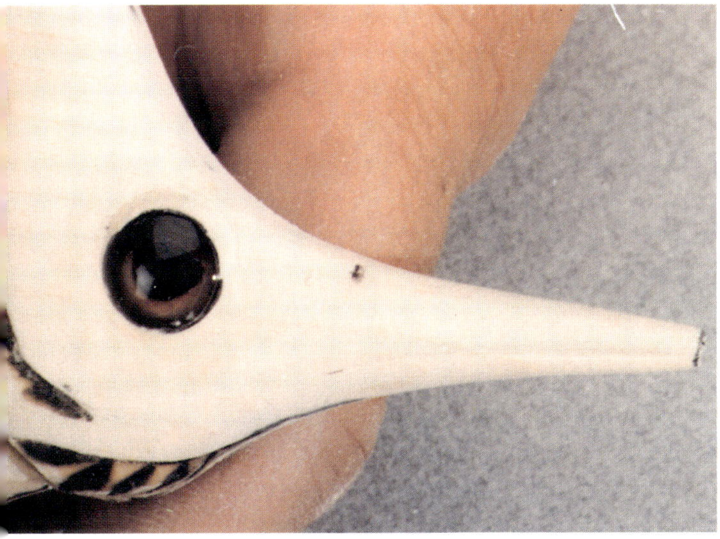

Complete.

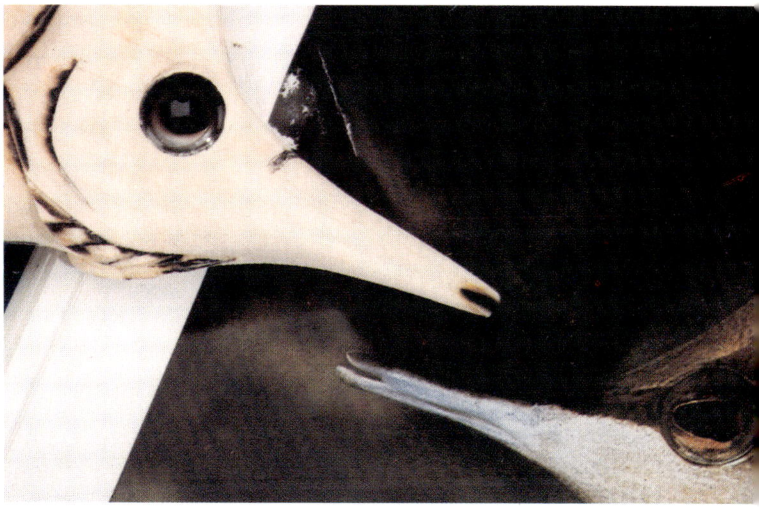

The result.

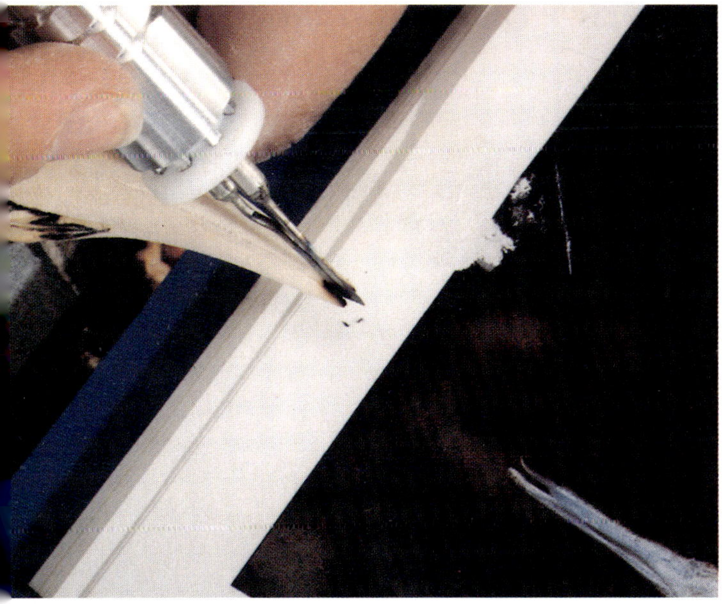

The mouth is at the end of the snout. I burn it in...

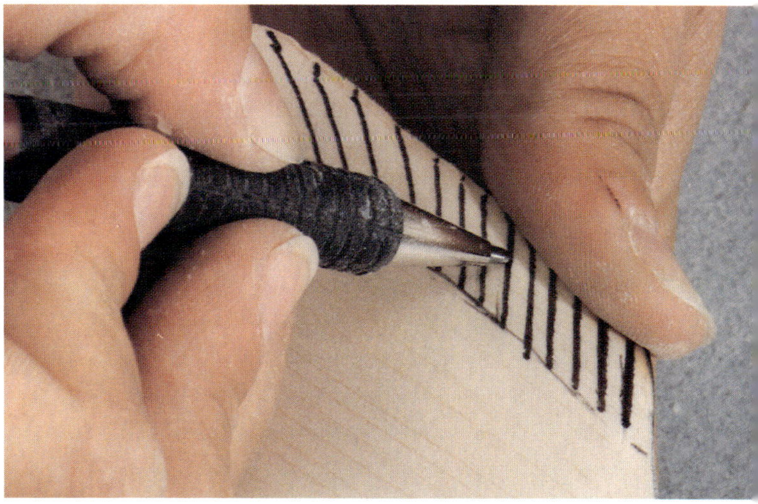

Redraw the line between the fins and the body and starting with the dorsal, draw the fin spines. There are ten strong spines at the top that will be carved separately. The rays that trail these are less distinct. In nature there are 22 rays in this fish.

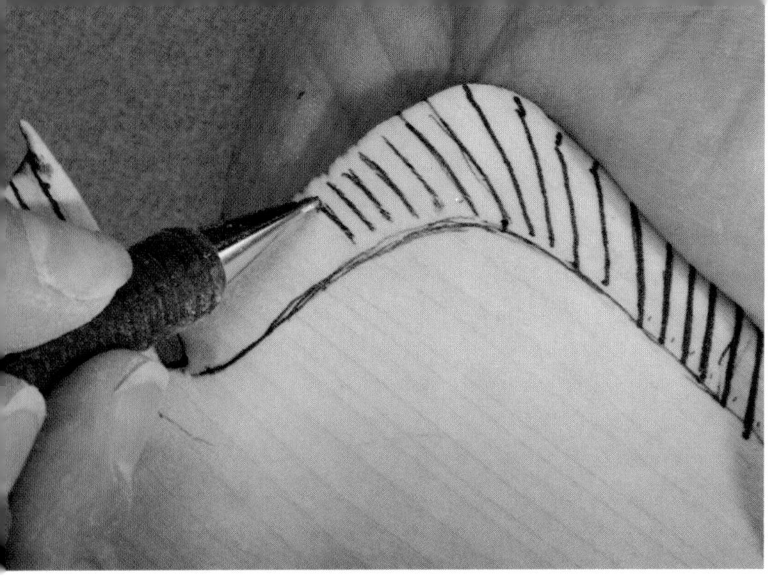

Draw a few of these trailing rays as guides.

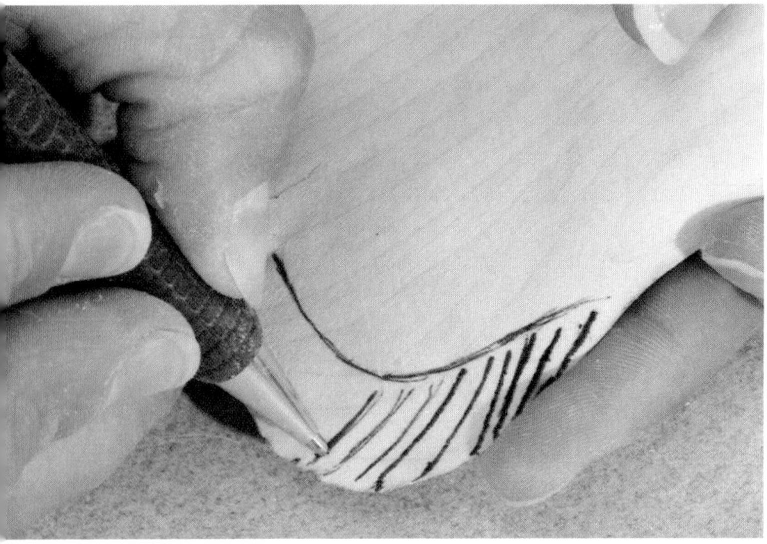

Draw three major spines on the anal fin and continue with the guidelines for the rays. There are sixteen rays following the spines.

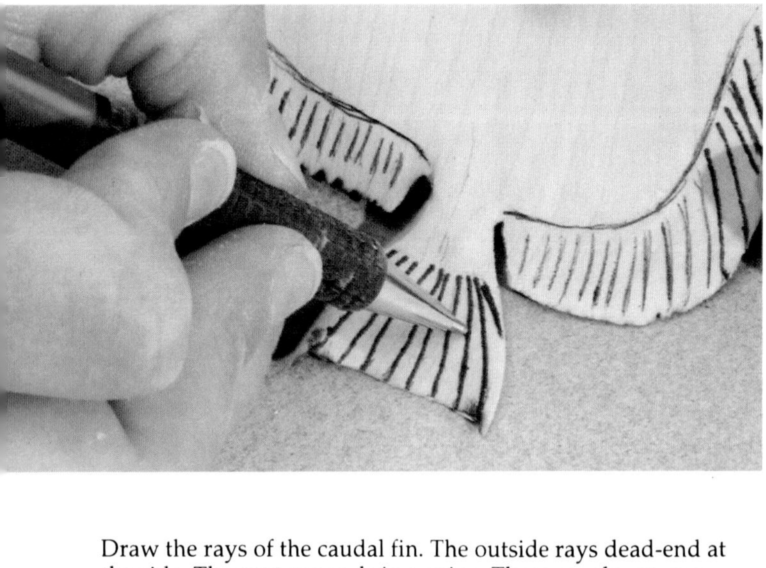

Draw the rays of the caudal fin. The outside rays dead-end at the side. The next ray ends in a spine. There are eleven rays in total.

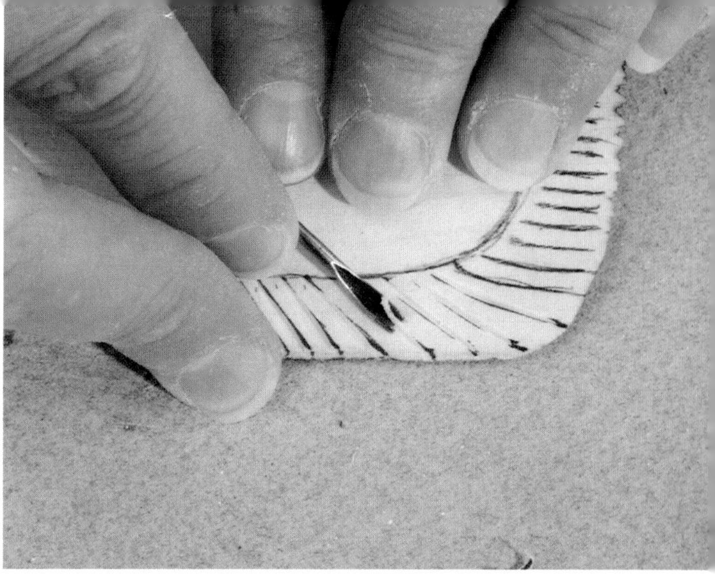

Start with the dorsal fin and cut the spine lines. Do the same on the three anal fin spines.

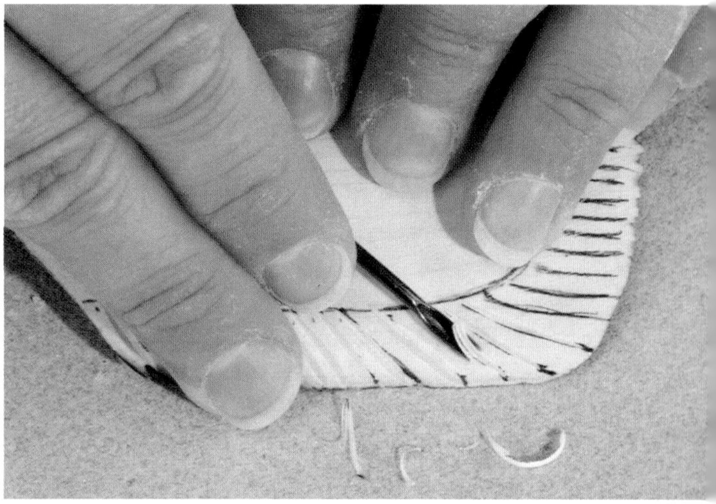

Switch to a small u-gouge, and go over the spine lines again to round the rough edges, then continue on all the ray lines on all the fins. The back of the dorsal fin is thin, so be careful. The breaks that are created on the trailing edge of the fin are desirable.

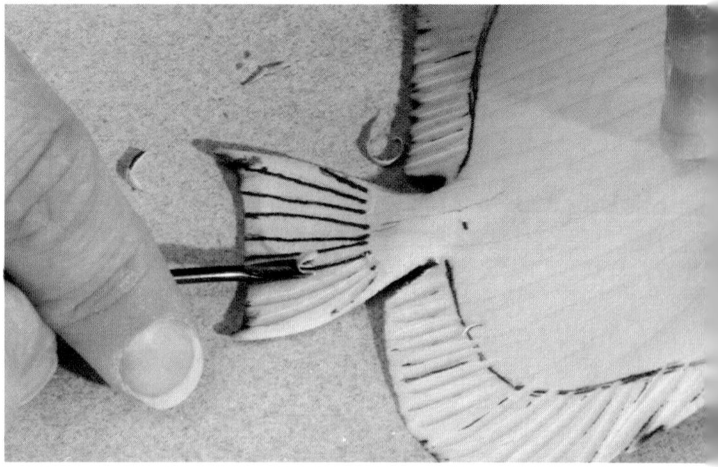

Sometimes the curve of the fish will require you to cut in the opposite direction.

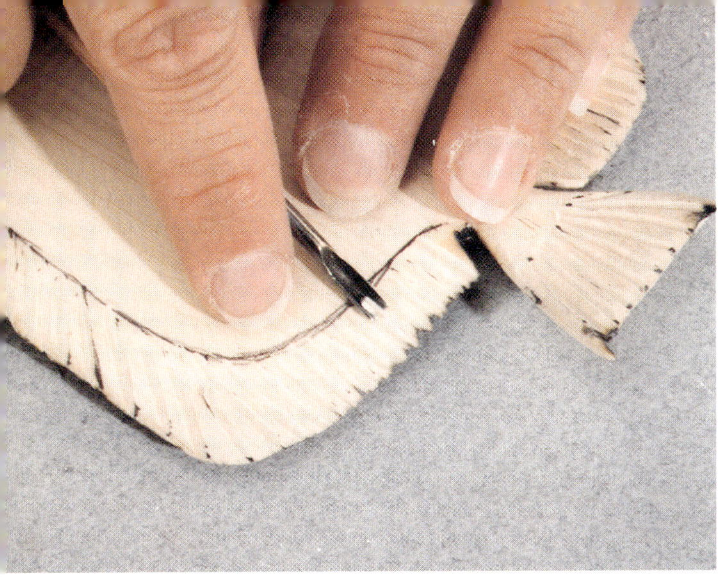

I switch to a slightly wider gouge to go over the first third of the rays as they leave the body.

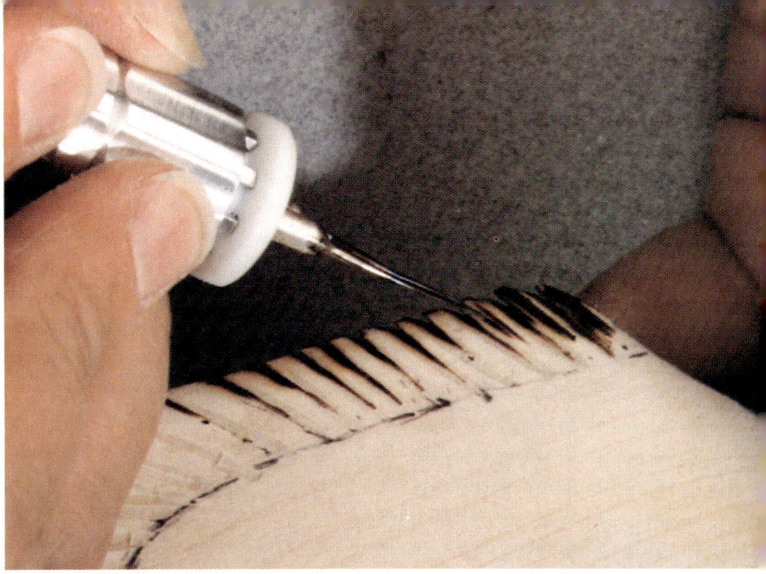

The spines of the dorsal have a little texturing which I do with the burner.

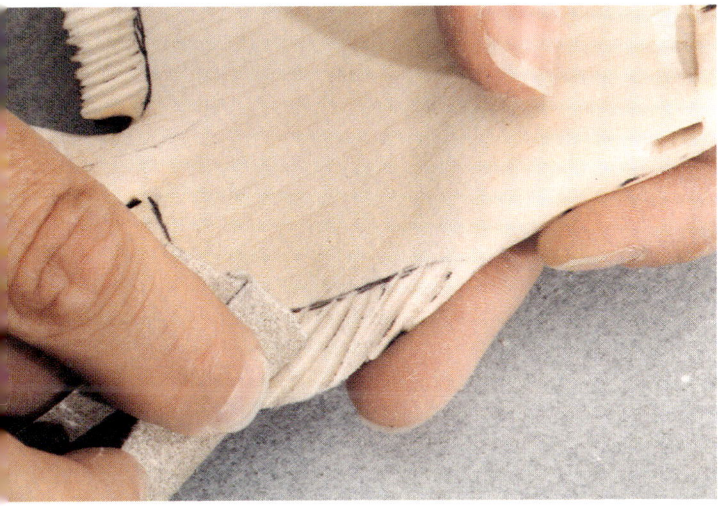

Sand all the edges.

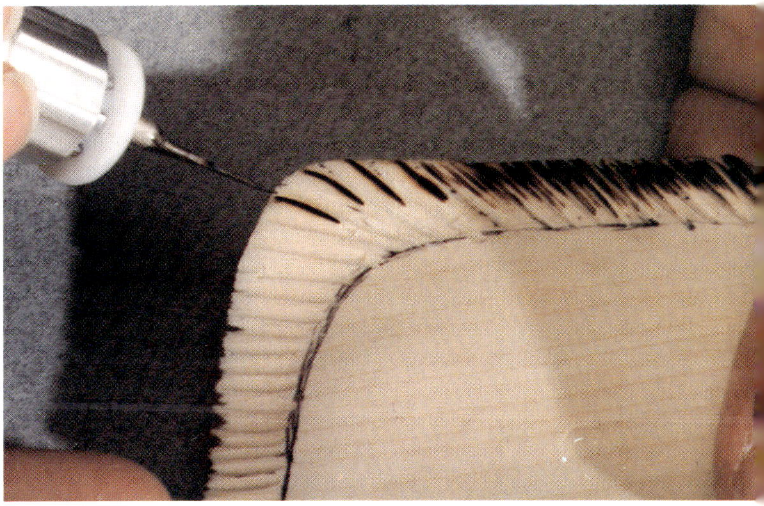

Bisect the ends of the rays of all the fins...

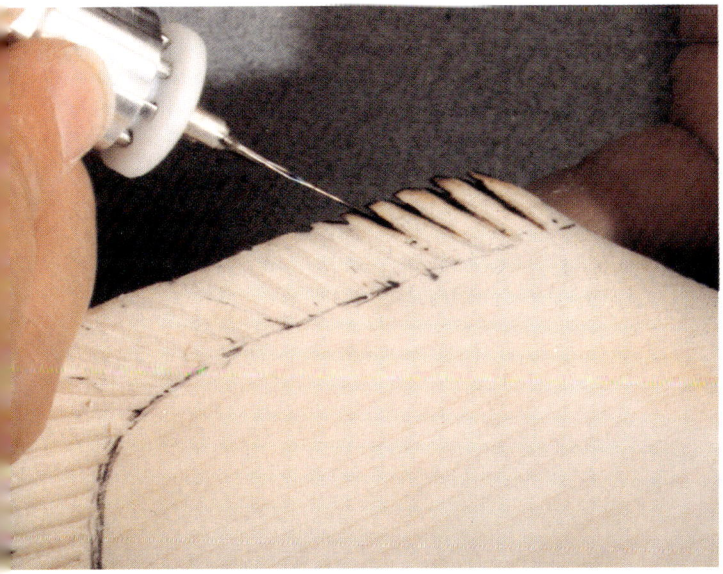

Burn the trailing edges of the spines, using the burner to separate their tips.

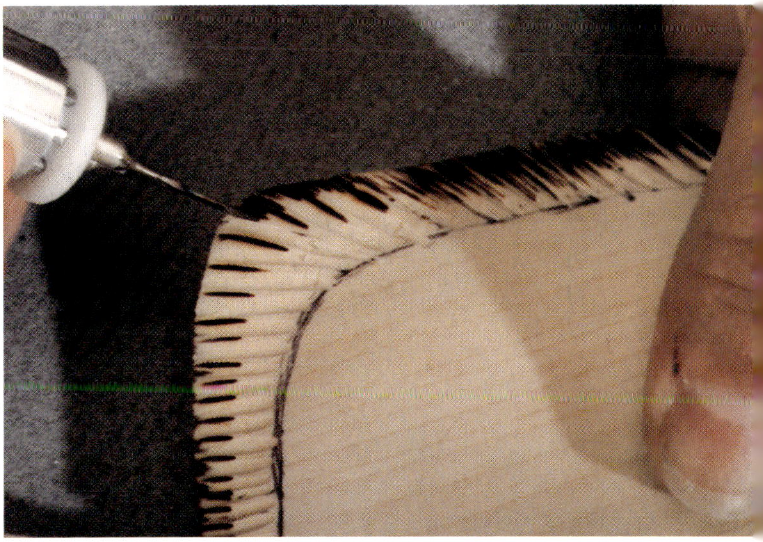

Then go back and divide the very ends again with more burn lines. Occasionally the burning tool will go right through, making a ragged edge, but that is all right.

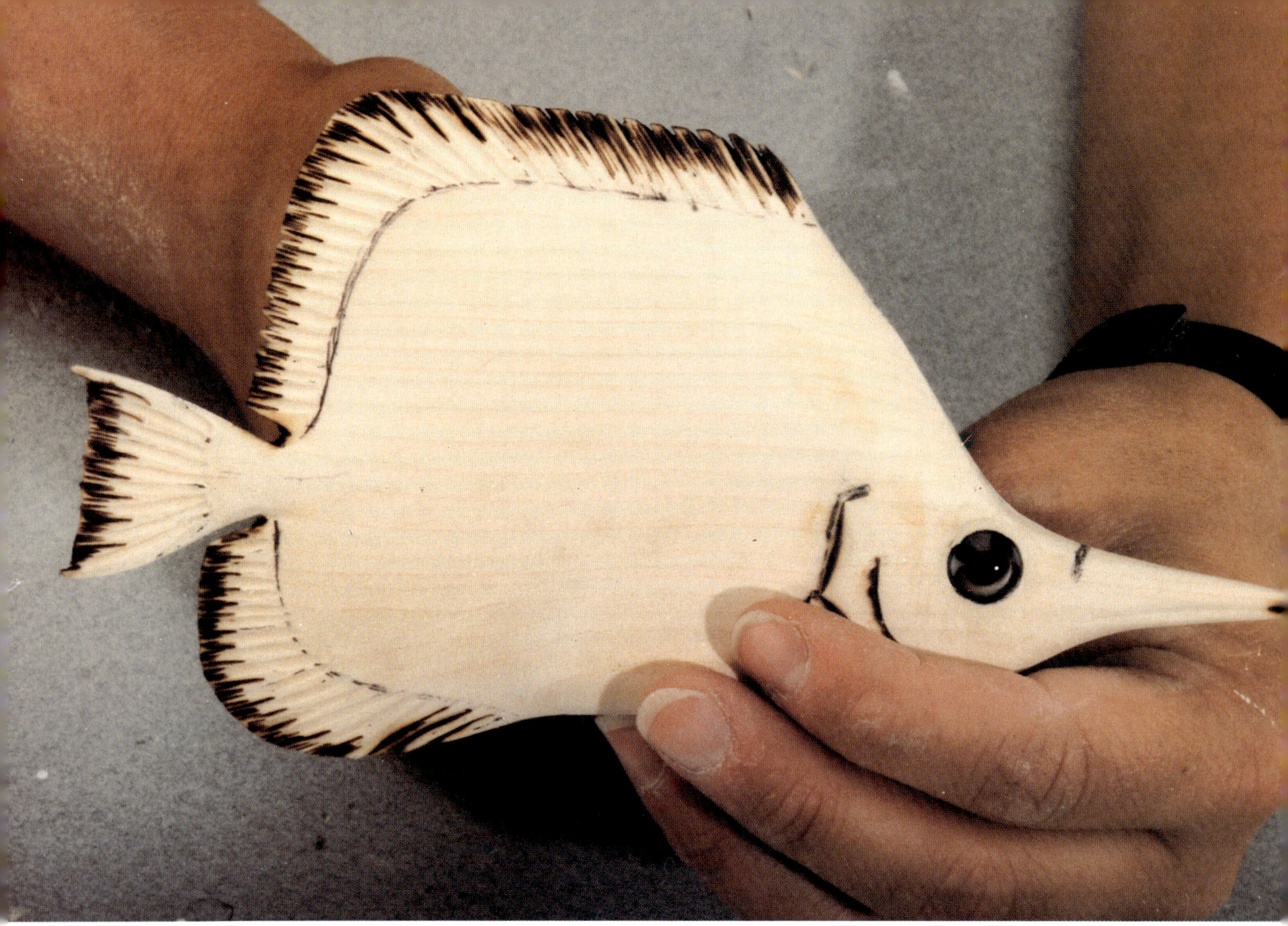

The fins complete.

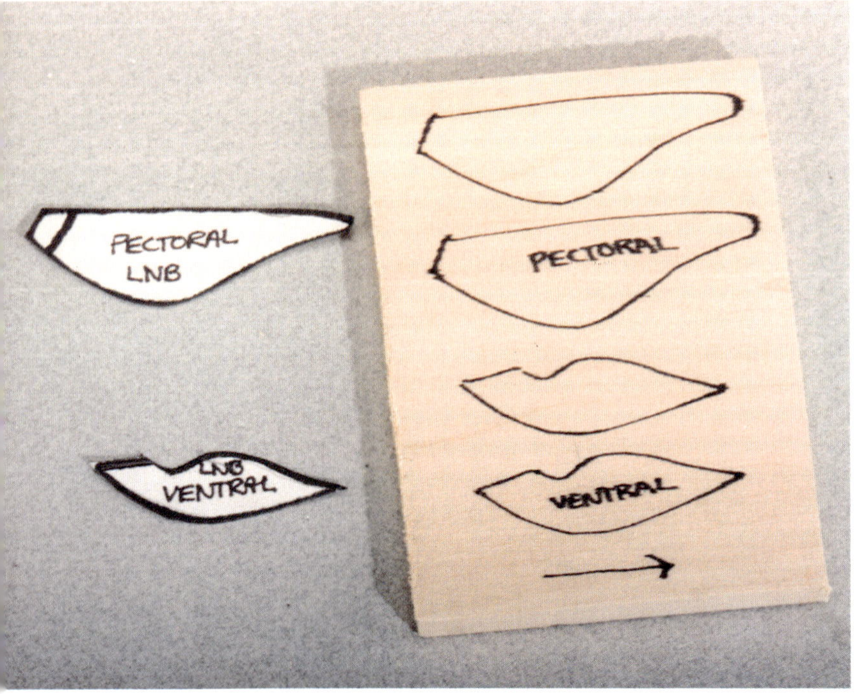

Cut the remaining fins from 3/8" bass wood.

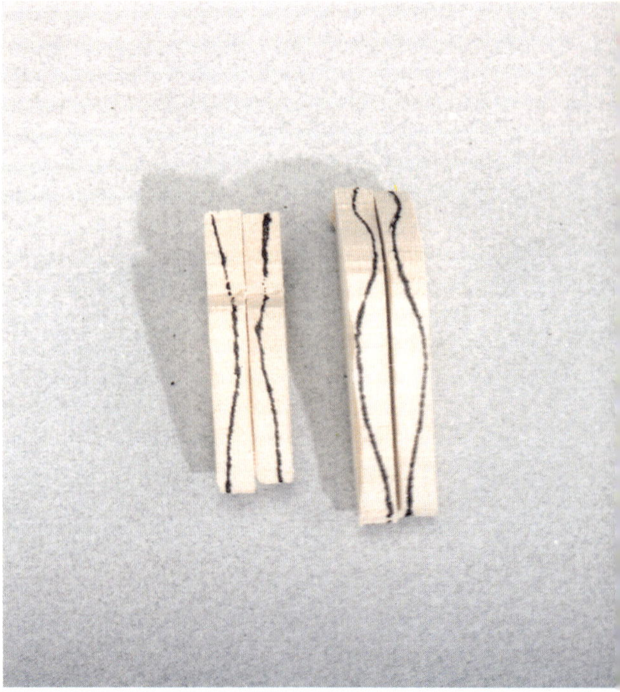

Draw the center lines to establish the curves...

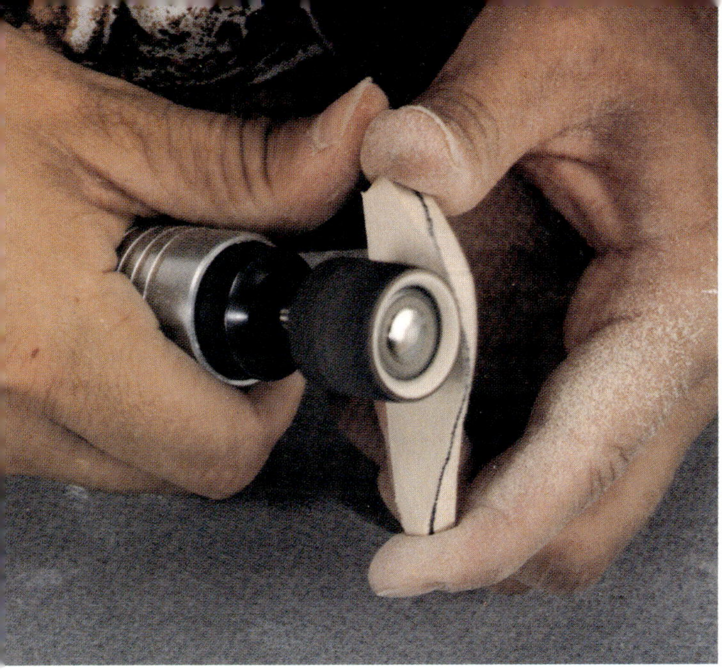

As with the other fins, they are ground to shape...

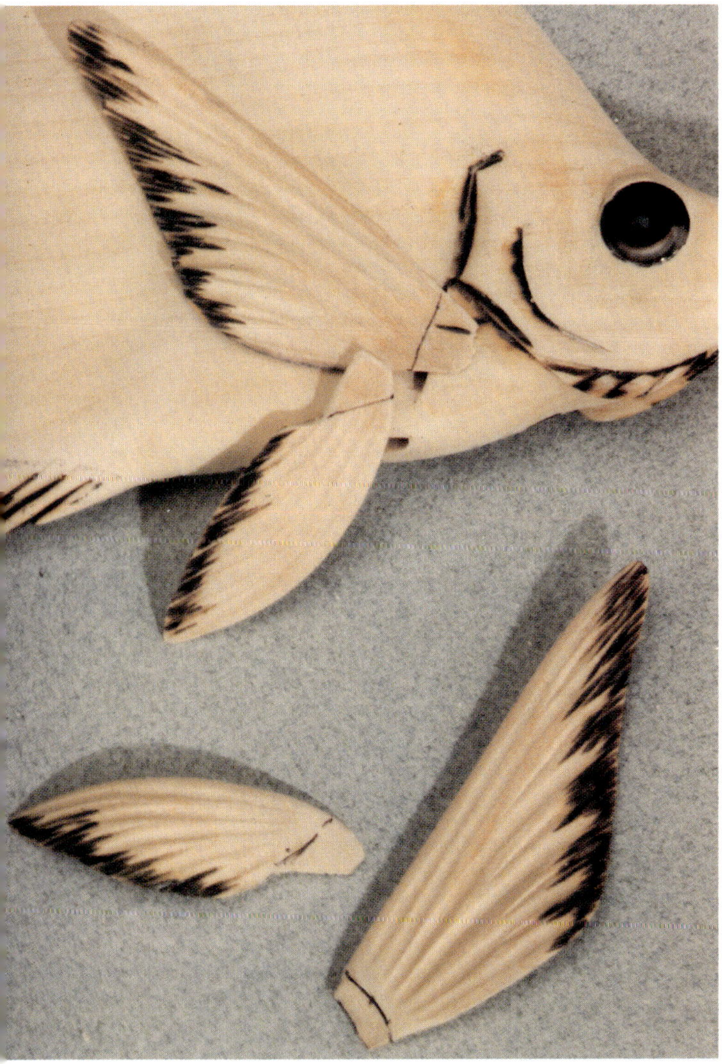

then carved and burned to arrive at this finished state. Remember to run a bead of super glue down the edge for strength. Refer to the other projects if you need more detailed instructions.

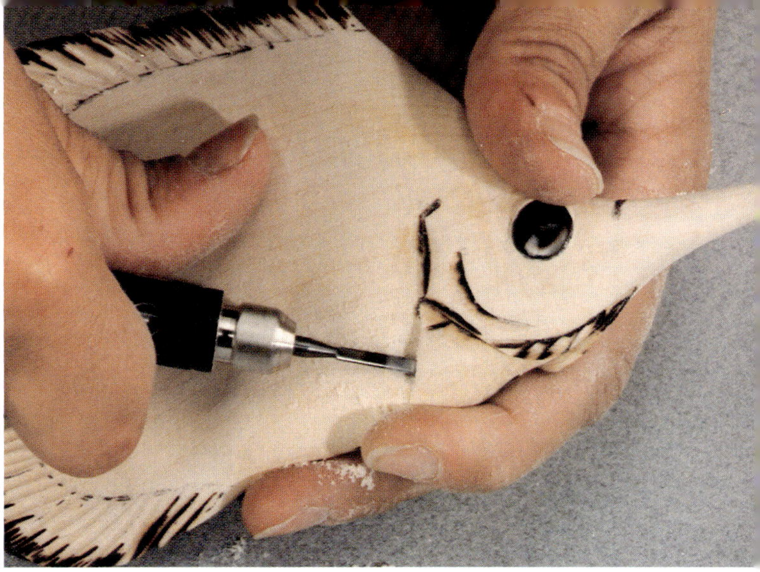

Cut the socket for the pectoral fin..

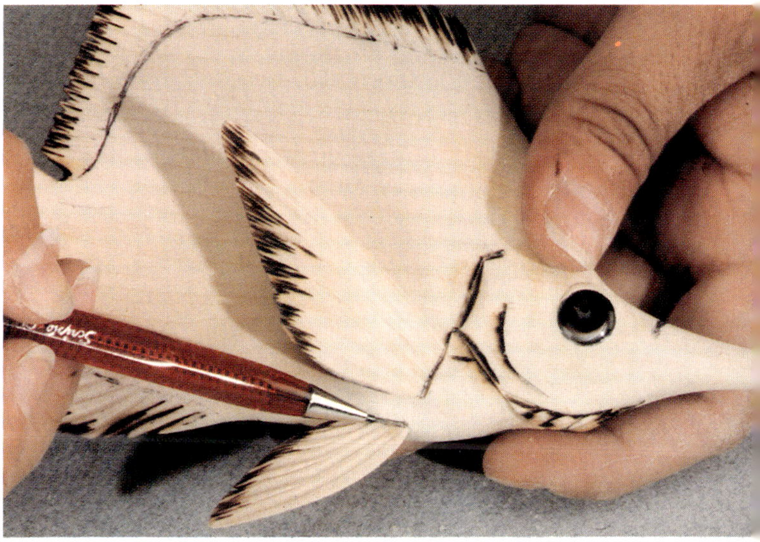

and the ventral fin.

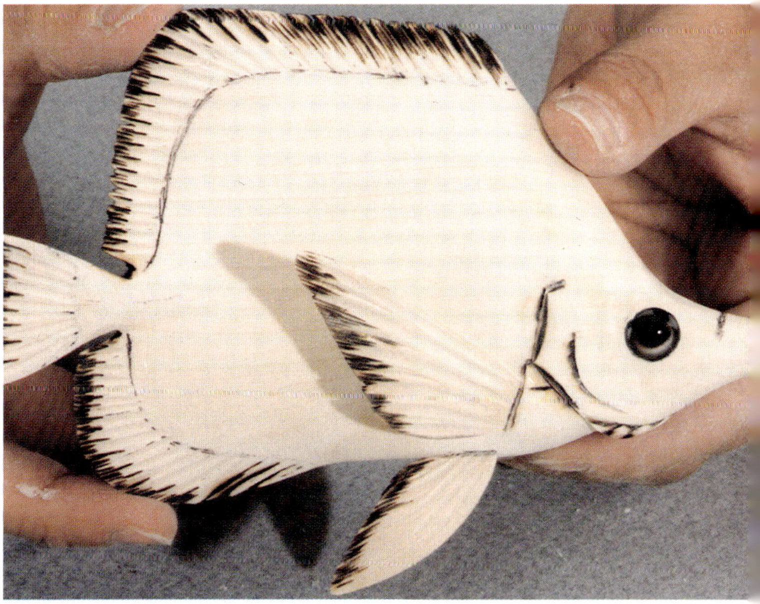

Check the fits and make adjustments. Everything fits.

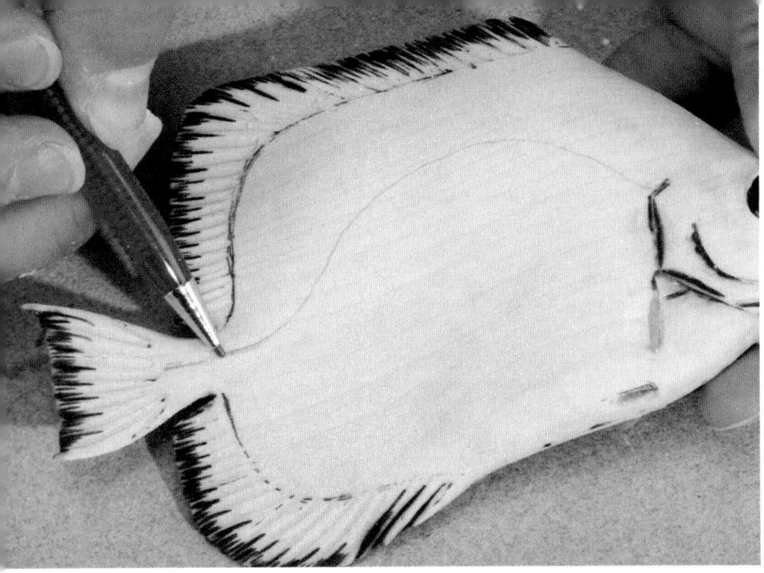

The lateral line starts at the top of the gill and takes a high arching route to the center of the tail.

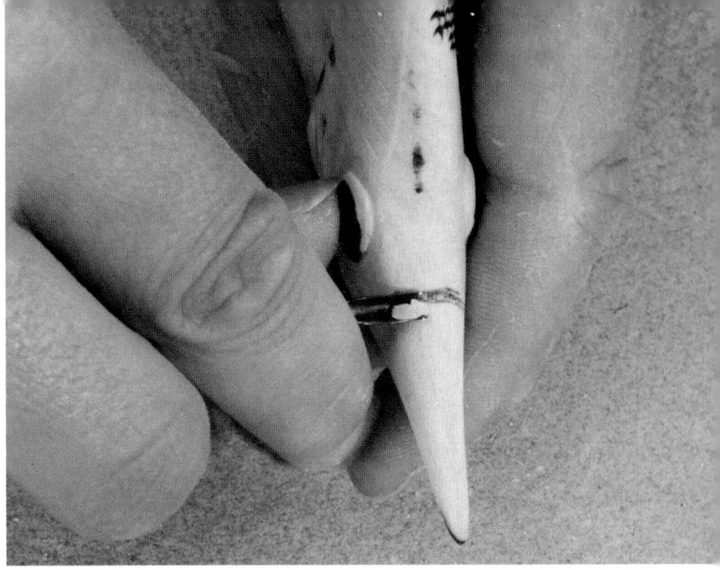

The ridge on top of the snout is created by relieving both sides of it with a micro-gouge.

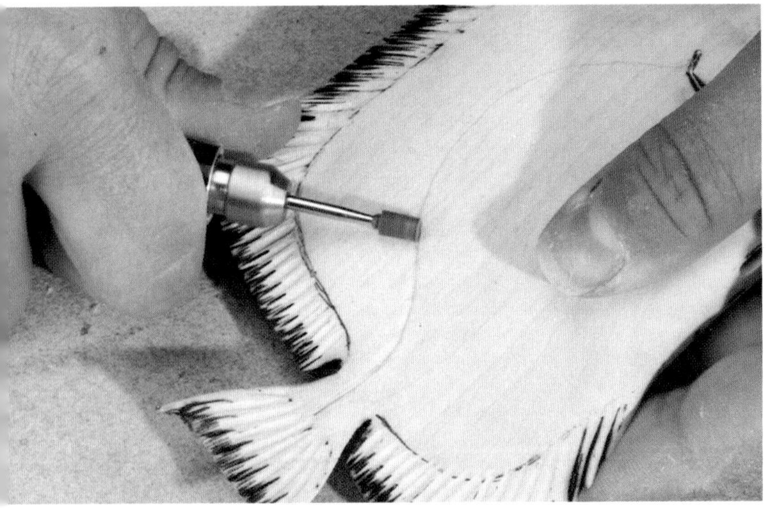

As before we create the lateral line by relieving the wood on each side of it with the grinder.

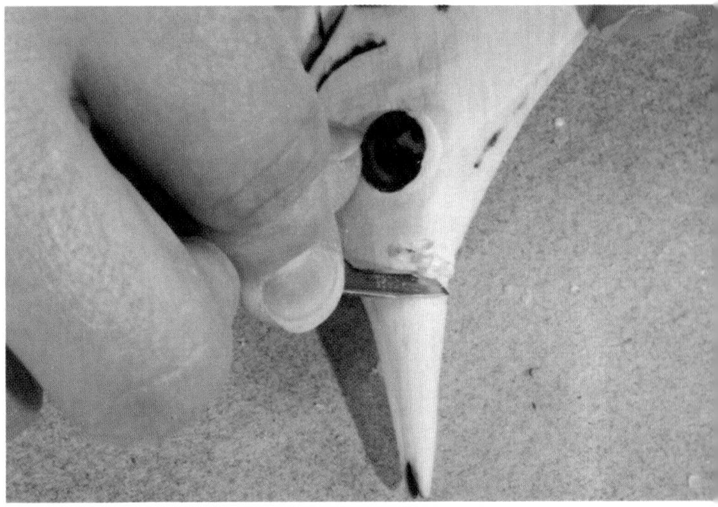

Blend the snout and head back to the channels with a knife and sand it smooth.

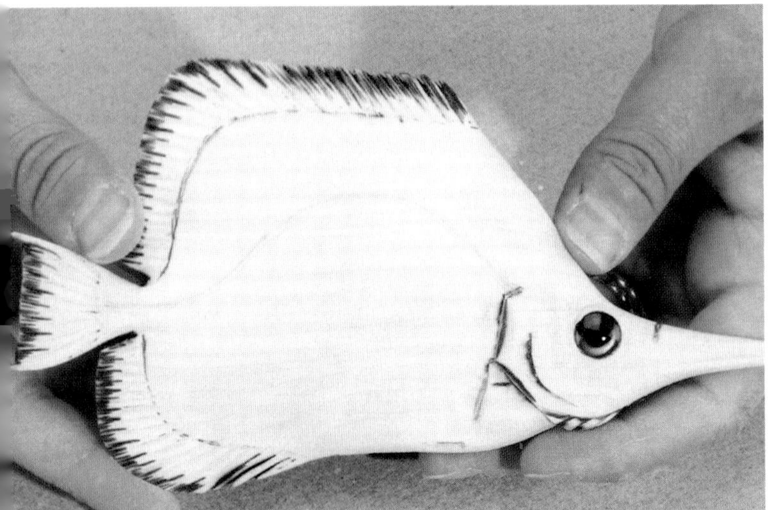

Blend the groove the grinder created back into the body by sanding, for this result.

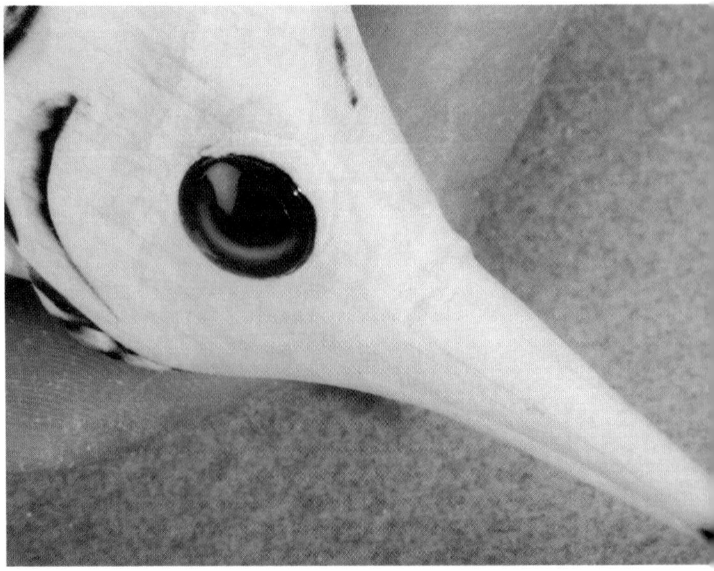

The result.

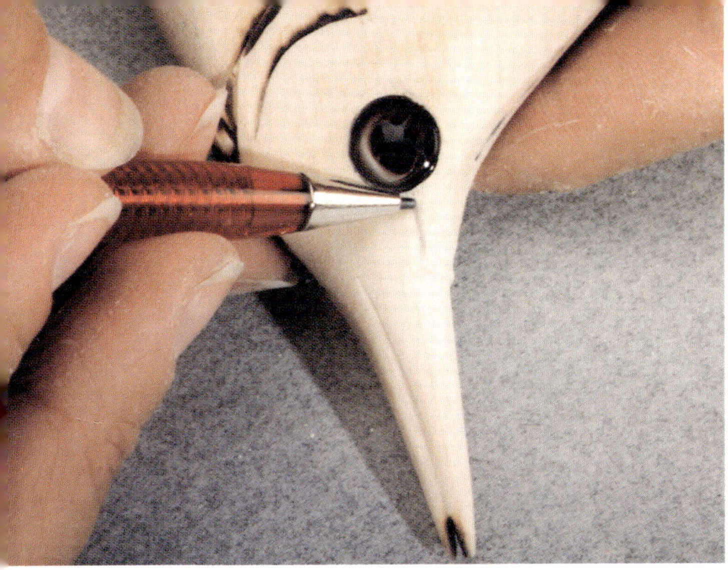

The nostrils are formed with a dental pick. They are placed on a line directly forward of the upper third of the eye, running to the ridge of the snout.

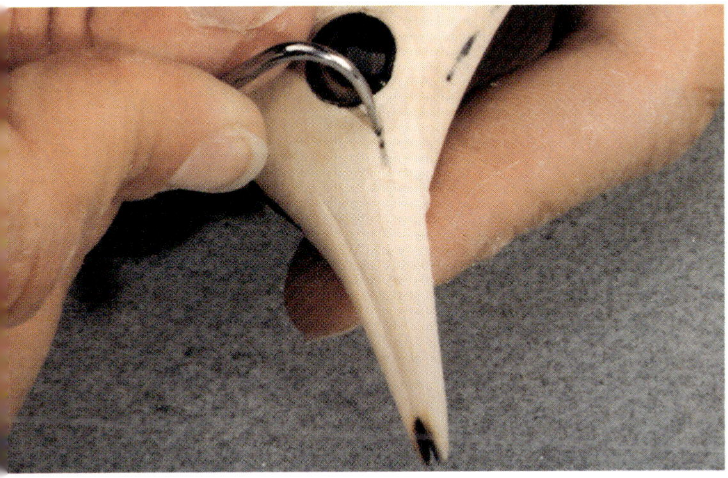

Make two little holes in the middle of this line.

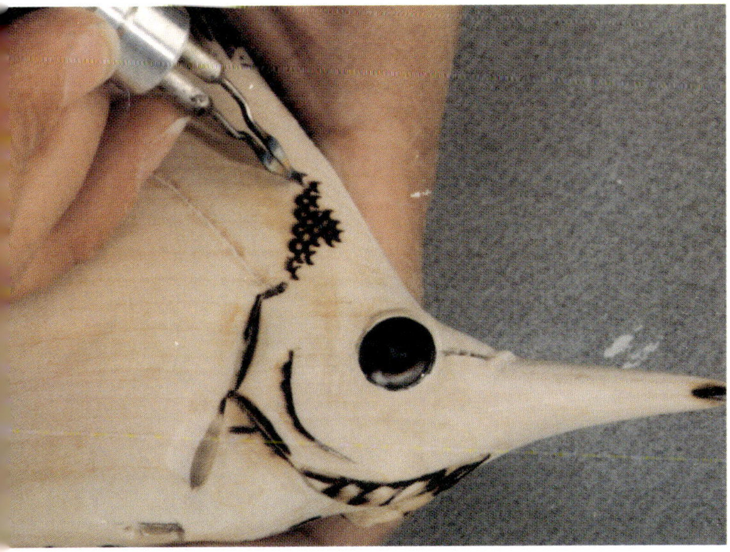

The scales are of two sizes. Begin with the larger size and do the main body, leaving the outside border and the face for the smaller size.

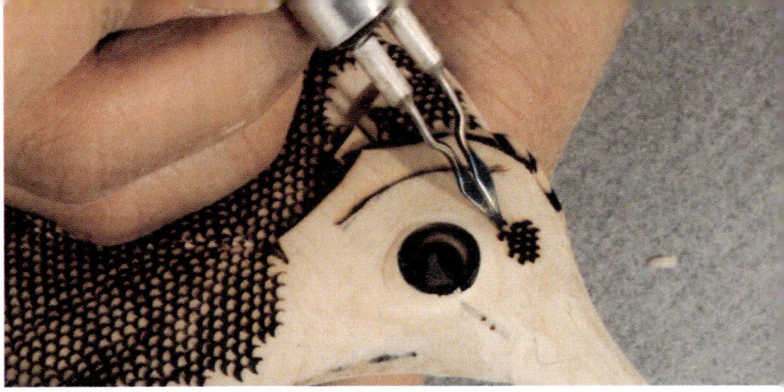

The scales of the face start at the back edge of the snout and cover the gill plate.

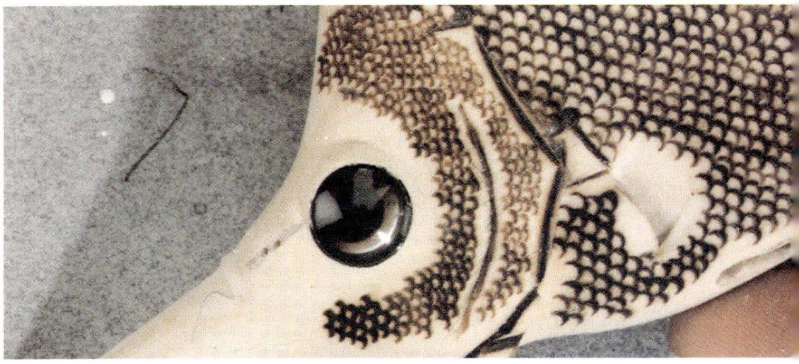

The small scales on the head complete.

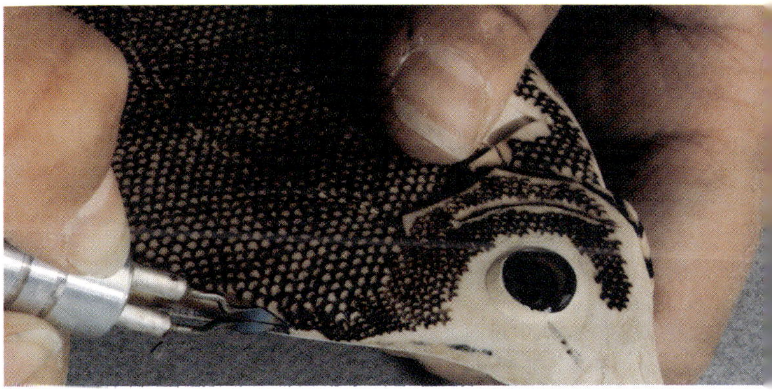

Fill in the border areas around the edge of the body with the finer scales.

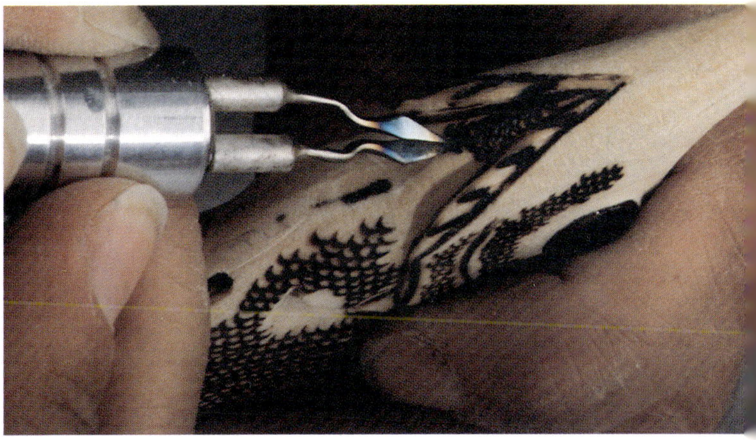

Begin the underside where the gill plates meet.

Ready for the fins.

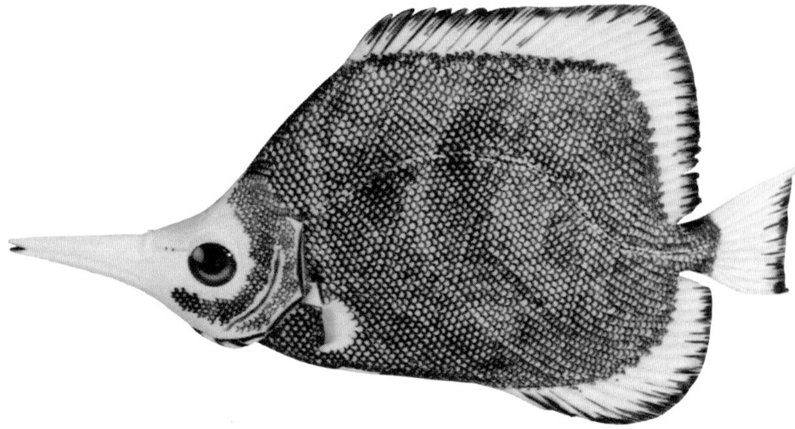

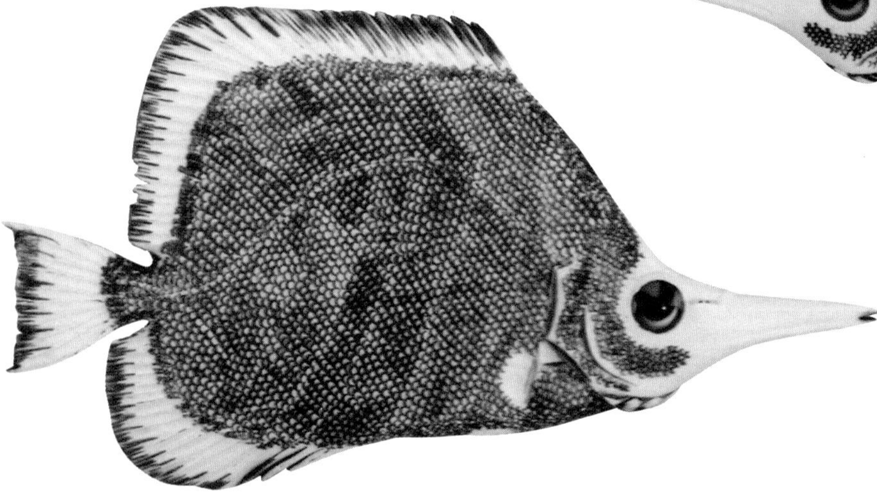

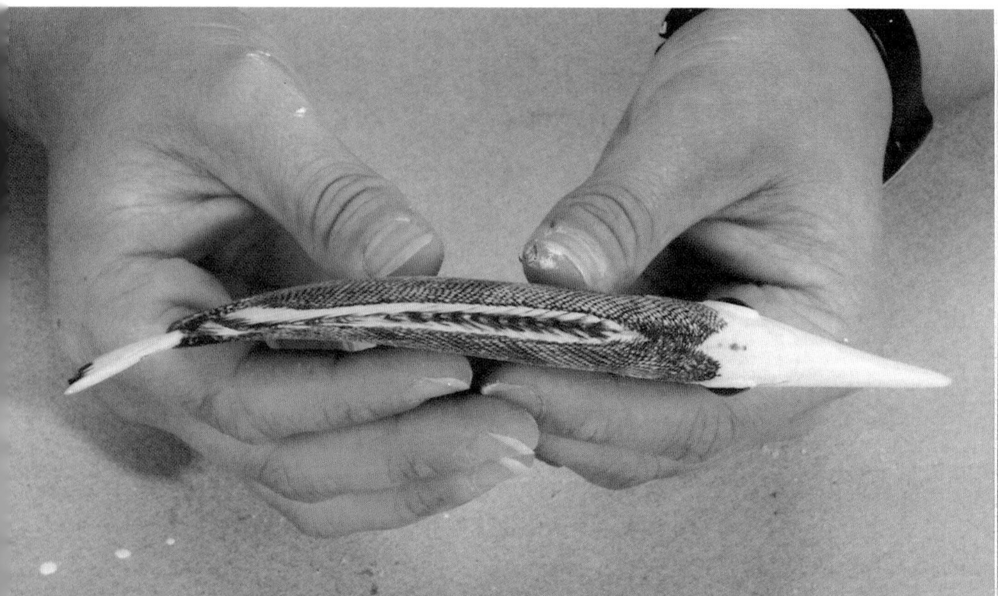

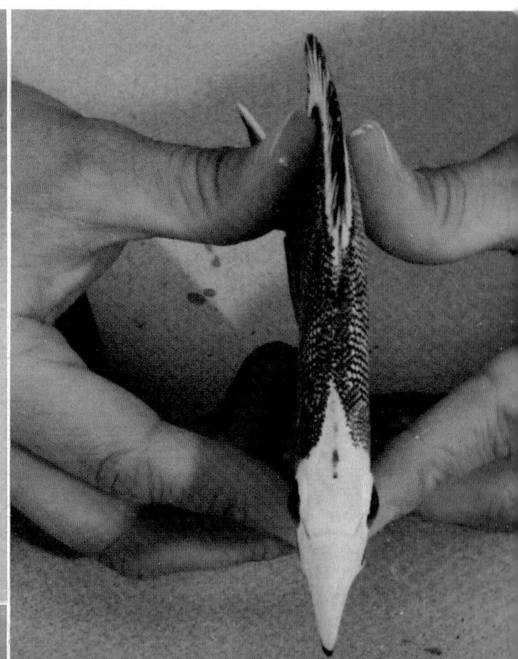

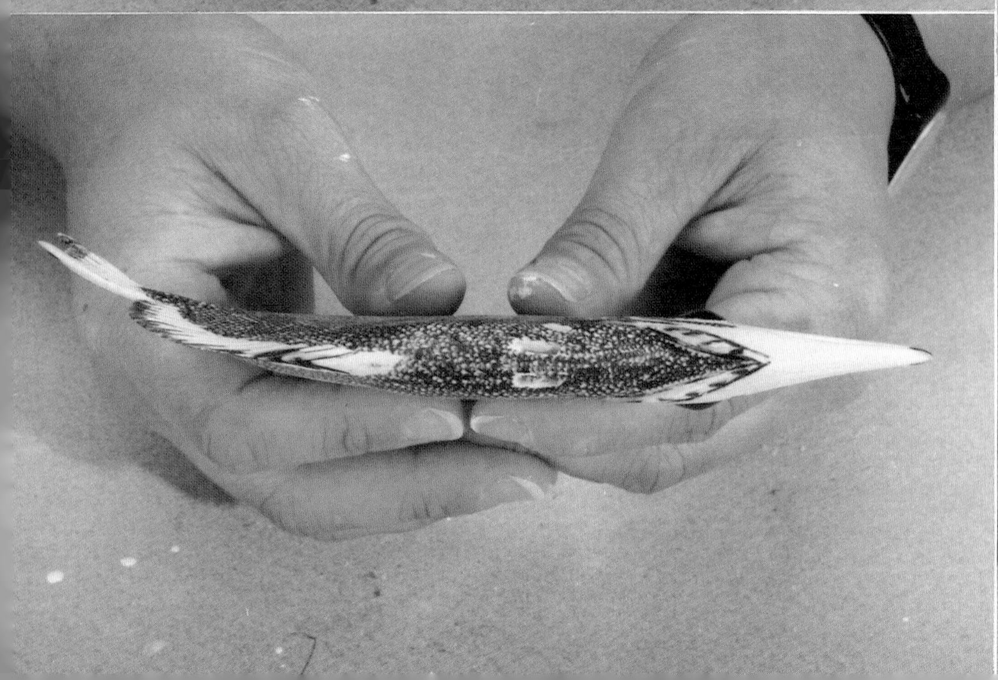

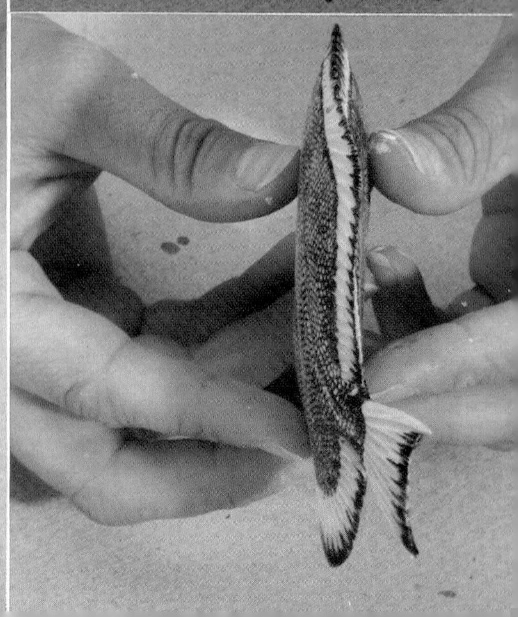

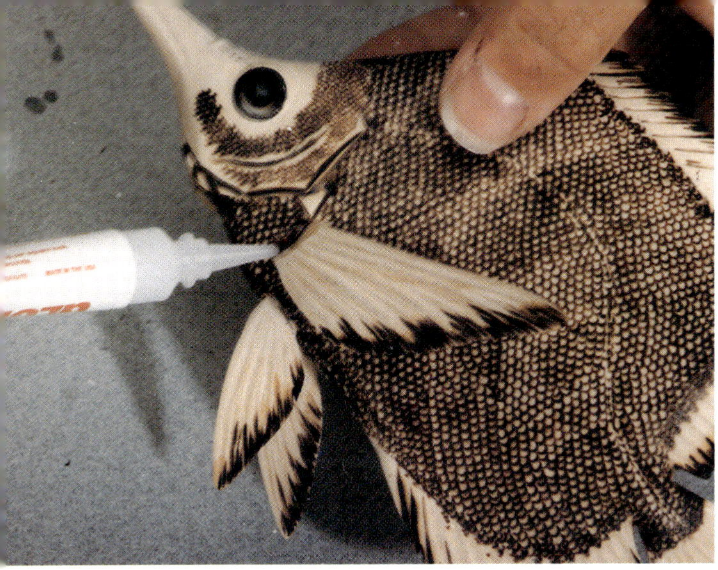

If the fit is tight enough I can use super glue to hold them in place. If not I would use Tuf-Carve™. With super glue, a bead of glue along the joint will be carried into the socket by capillary action.

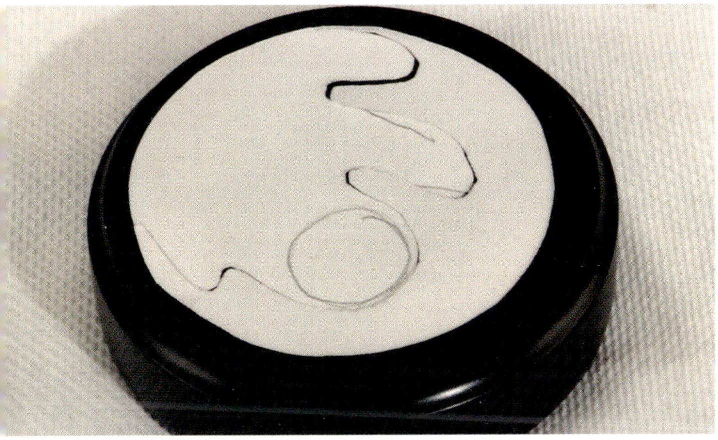

The carved ground will sit on a black lacquer base. Make a cut out pattern for the coral. The smaller round circle will be a sea urchin.

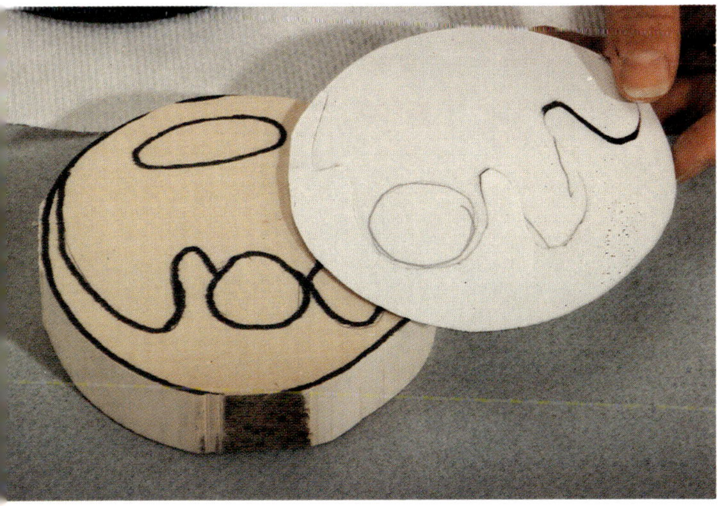

Lay the pattern on a piece of bass wood scrap. The thickness can vary, but the thicker it is the more the coral can be piled.

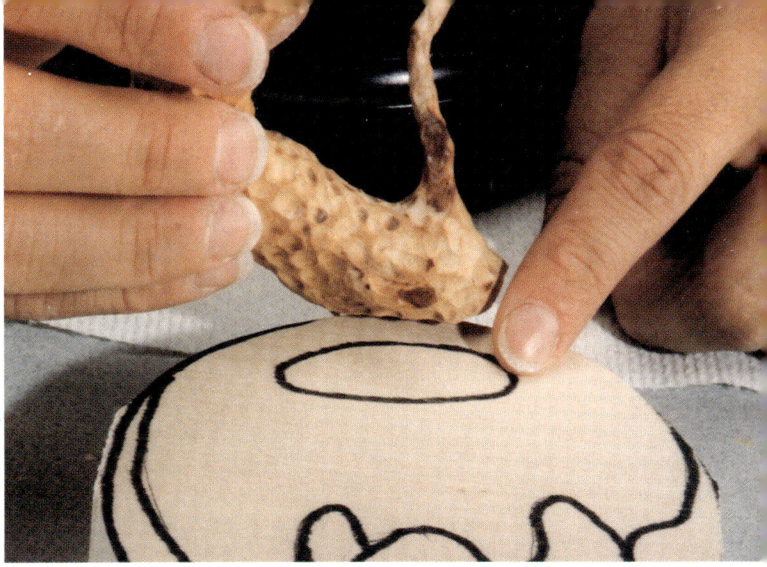

The oval marks the point where the branch will rest. I mark it now so I won't grind it away in error.

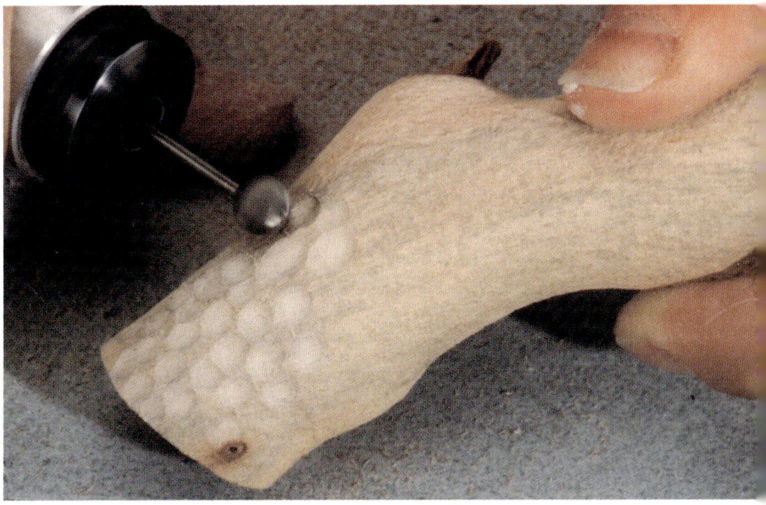

The branch is textured with a round cutter. Simply touch the cutter on the branch in a random way.

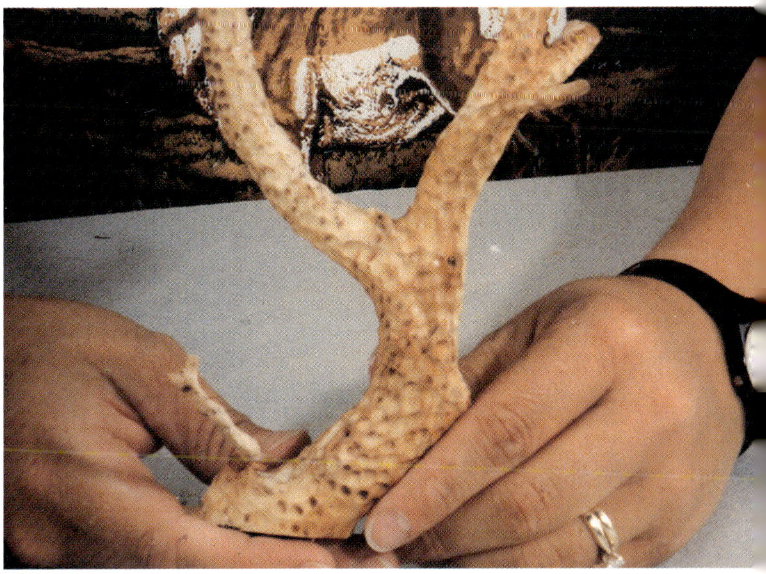

This creates the coral polyps.

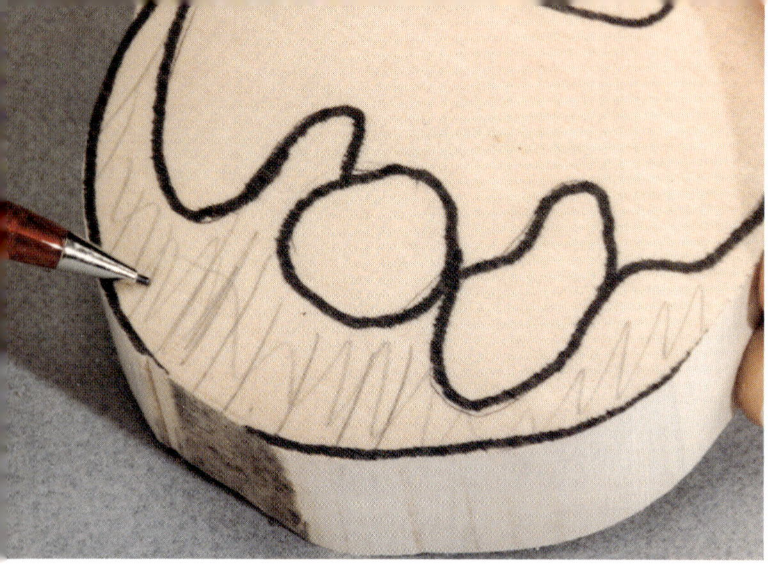

This front area will be lower, so I remove it with a Kutzall bit.

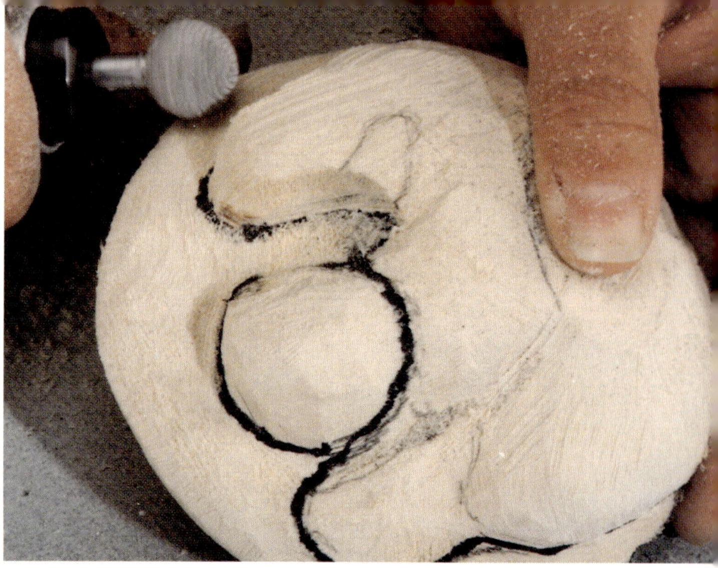

The final base will have a hemispheric sea urchin, some mounds of coral, and a flat space for attaching the coral branch.

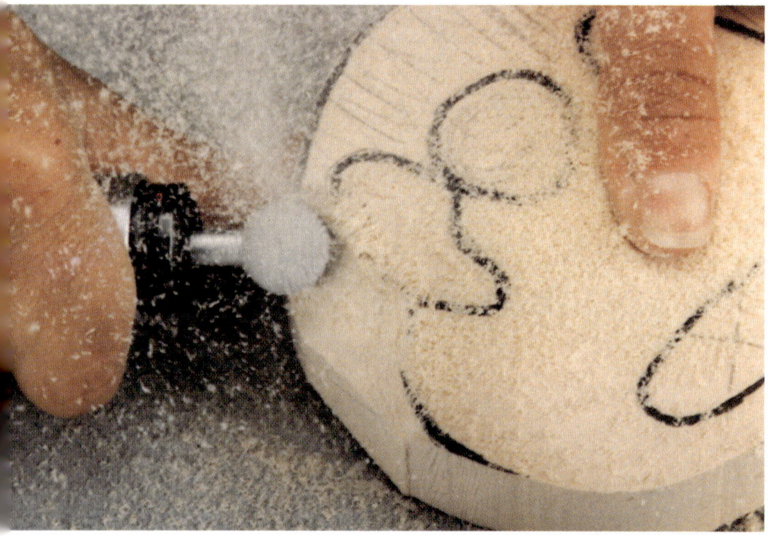

Remember this carbide cutter is aggressive and somewhat **DANGEROUS.** Keep a tight grip on the work.

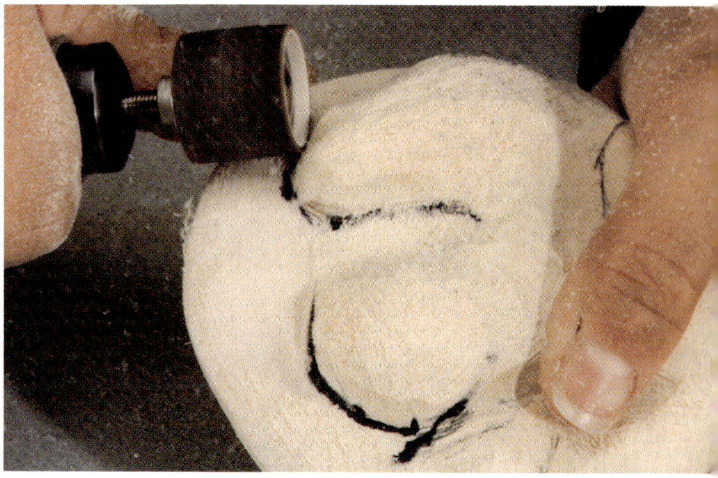

With a fine sanding drum, clean-up the Kutzall marks.

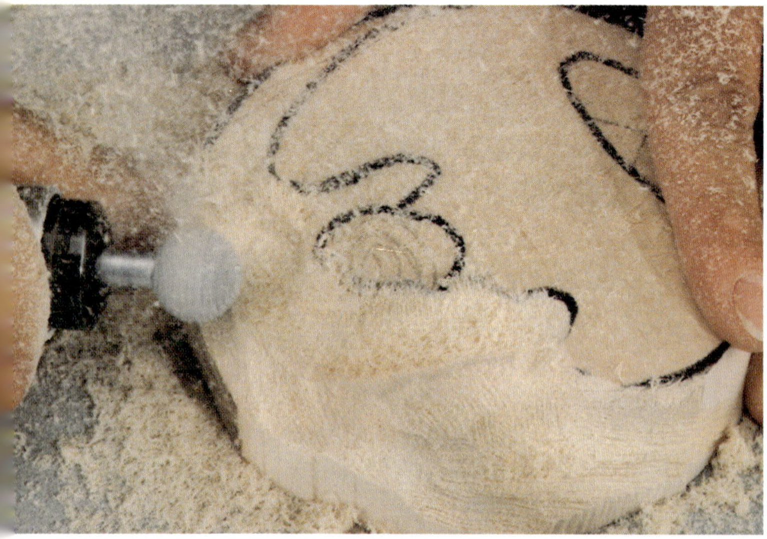

Work around the sea urchin space, leaving it untouched for now. Some of the coral may be reduced to various depths.

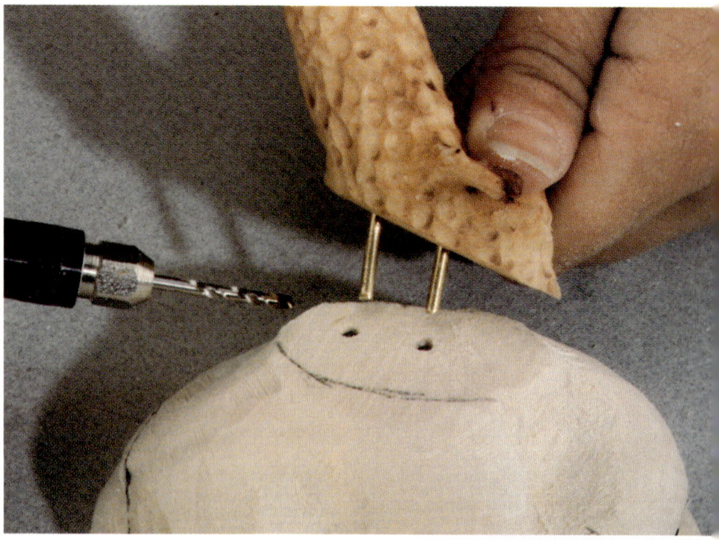

When the base is roughed out, drill the holes for the pegs that support the coral branch. Put the brass rods in the branch first, then mark the base and drill the holes.

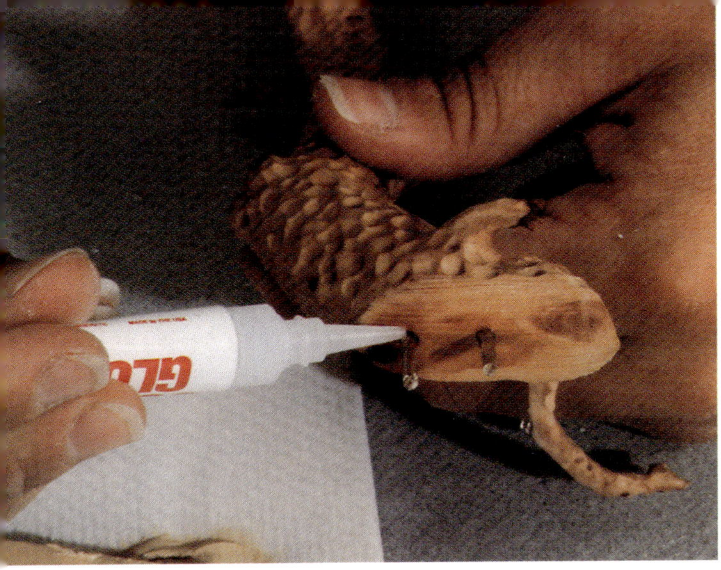

Check and adjust the fit, then glue the pegs to the branch.

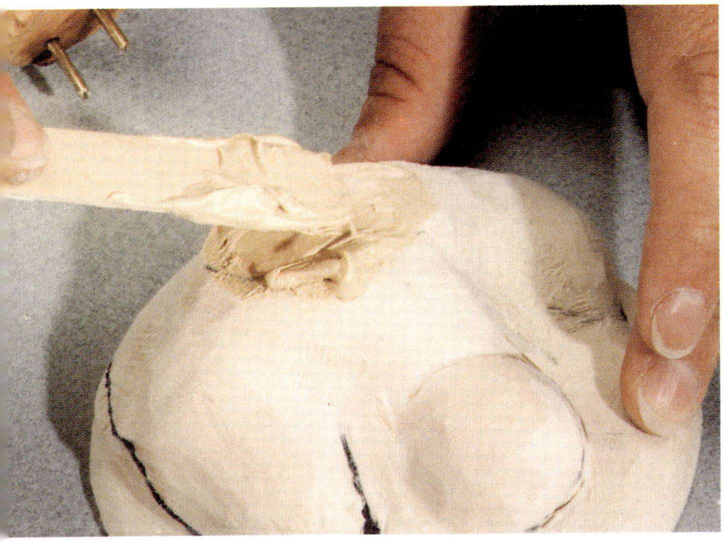

Smear Tuf-Carve™ on the base, pushing it into the holes.

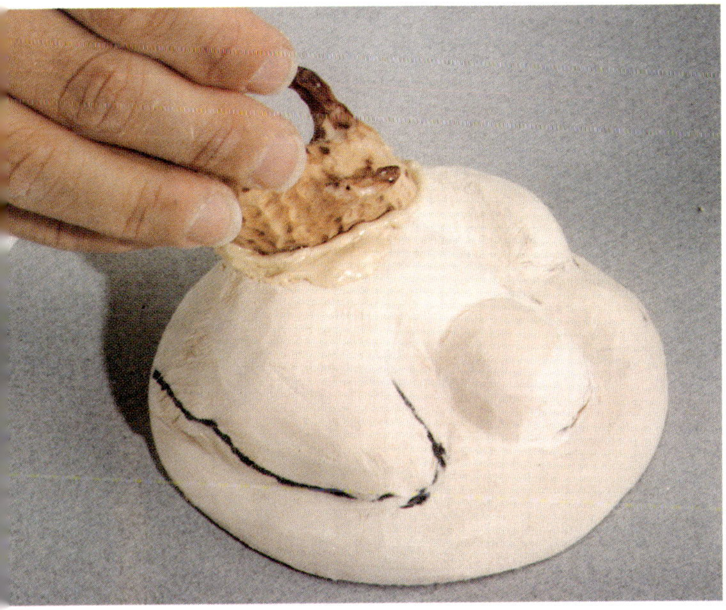

Push the branch into place...

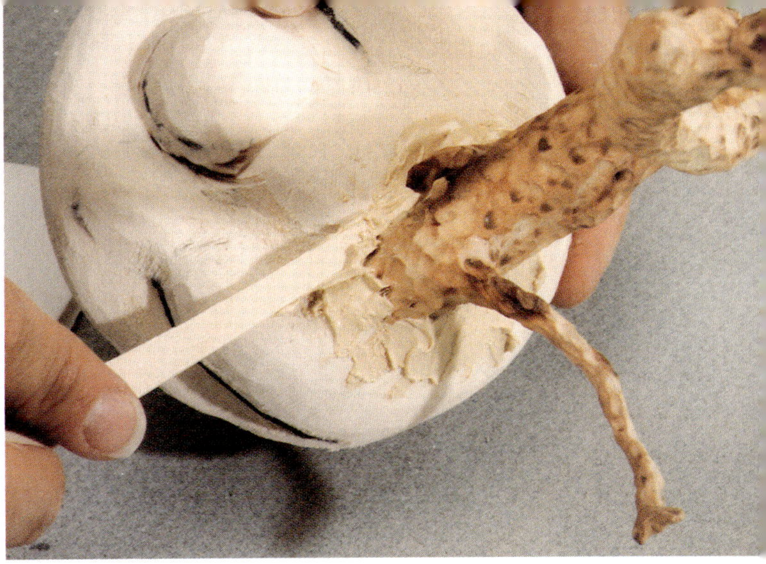

and smooth out the excess putty. Most of this will be carved away, so neatness is not important at this time.

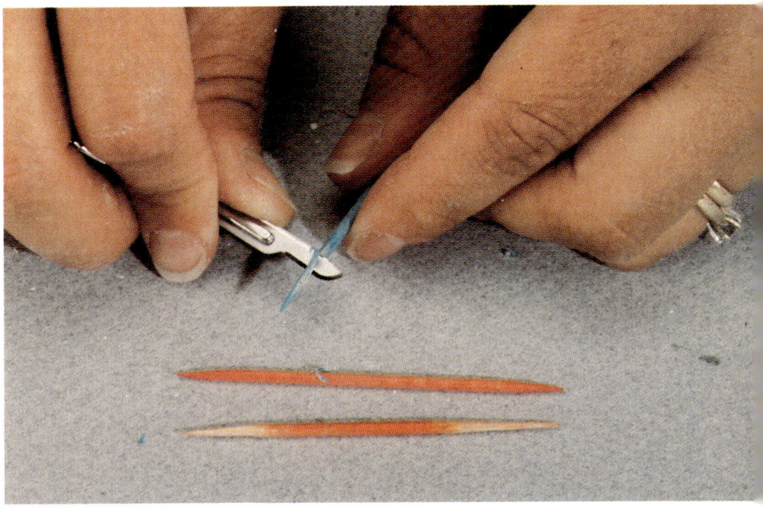

While it is setting I can work on the sea urchin. The rays are made from round tooth picks. To prepare them I shave the ends to a very sharp point.

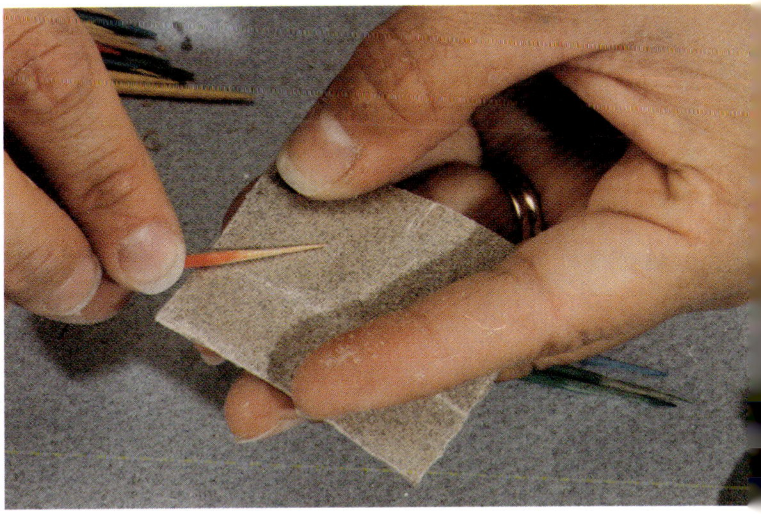

This is followed with a sanding of fine paper. They become quite sharp, so don't stab yourself.

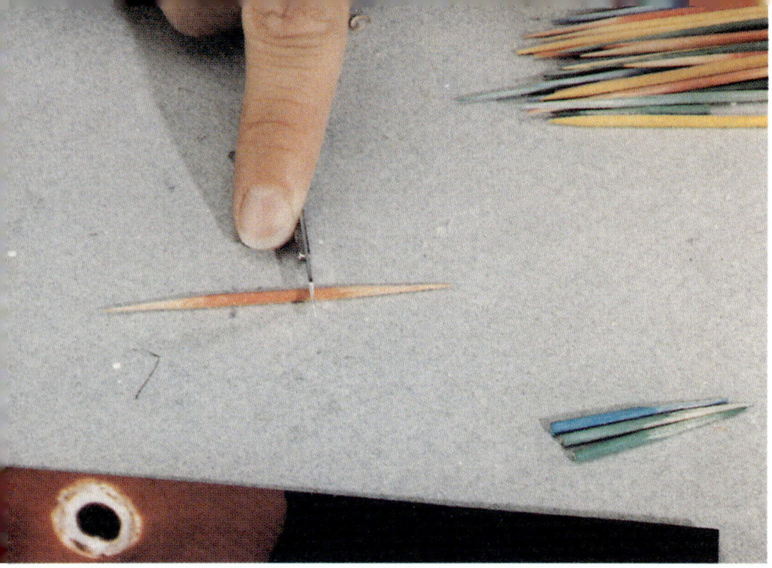

A sea urchin has short and long spines, so I cut the toothpicks into 1/3 and 2/3 length segments. If you simply score the toothpick with the knife it will break cleanly.

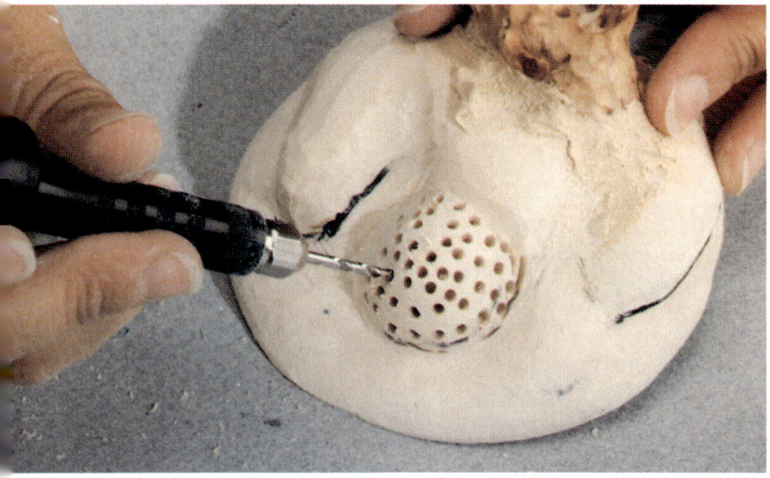

Drill holes for the spines. The holes are random in this one, though if you do some research you will find that urchins have different forms.

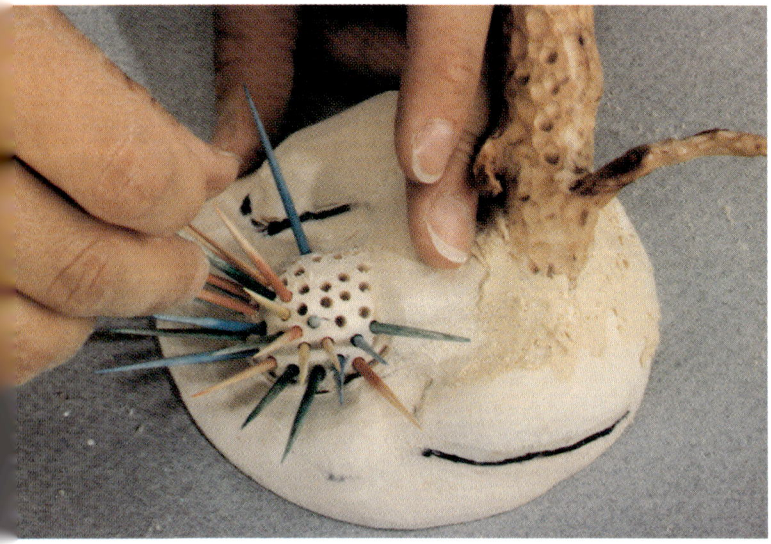

Test fit the spines.

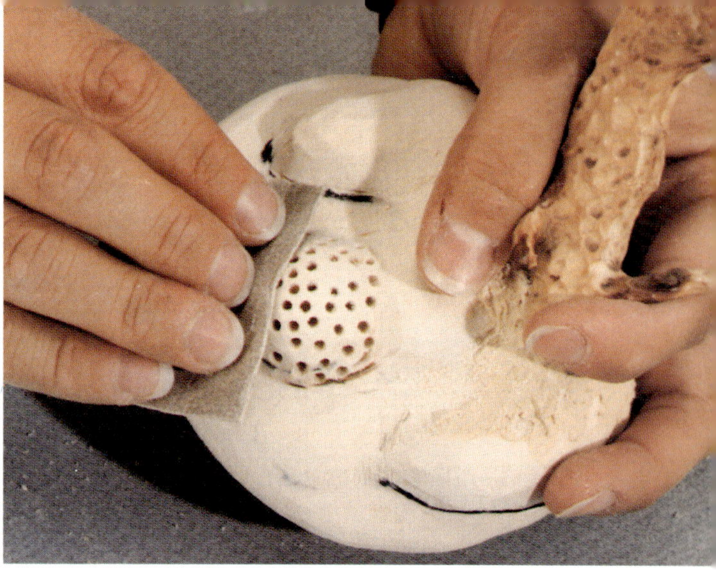

Lightly sand the sea urchin body to get rid of any excess.

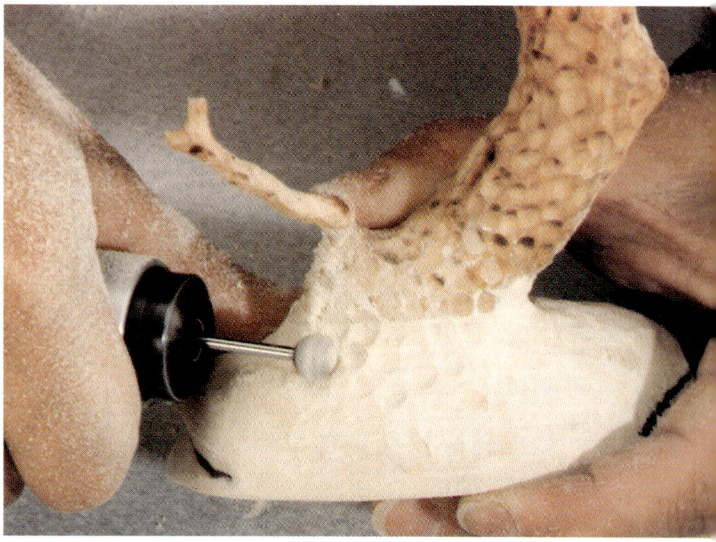

After cleaning away some of the adhesive putty, texture the coral in the base the same way you did on the branch. This is a ruby ball cutter, and I use it to make an invisible transition between the branch and the base from which it is growing. After painting the seam will disappear completely.

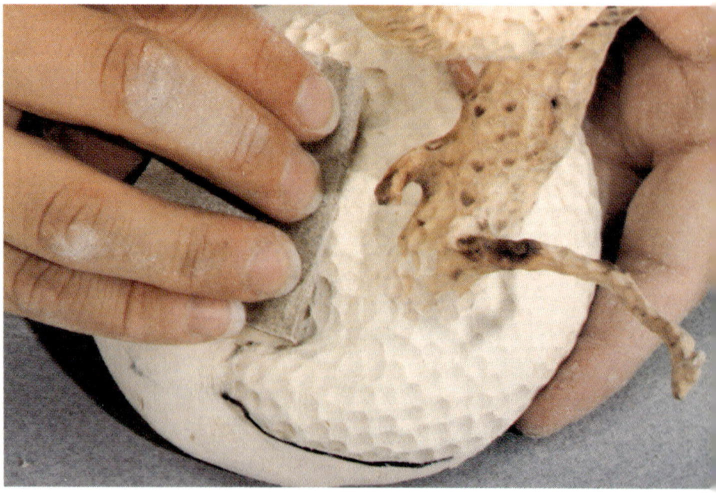

Go over the coral lightly with sand paper.

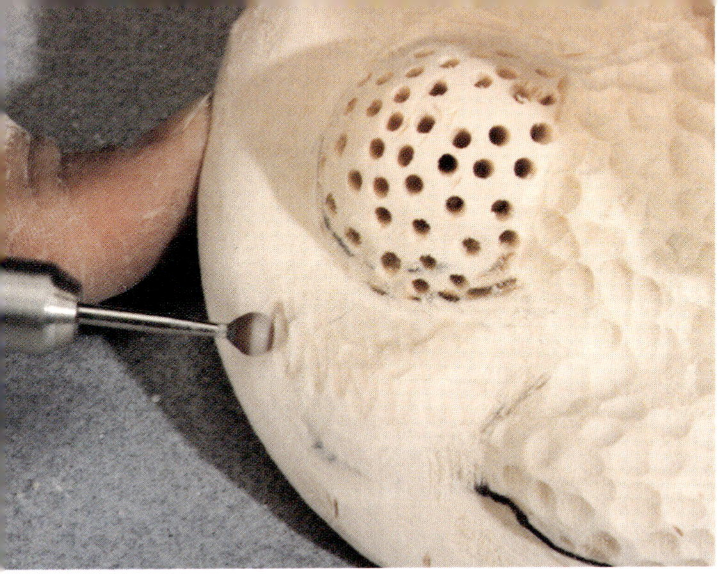

The ground coral is textured with a series of wavy lines. When two corals meet like this, they engage in mortal combat over the "turf." Over a number of years one will kill the other completely.

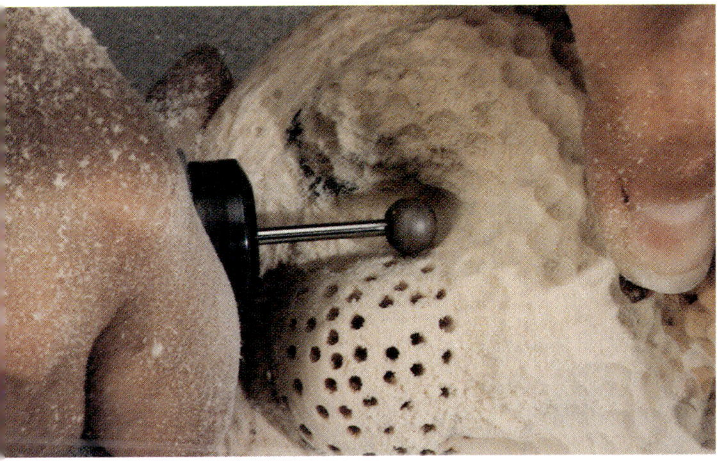

At the point of contact, I make the indentations deeper, reflecting the war going on. In the painting process these areas will be painted darker.

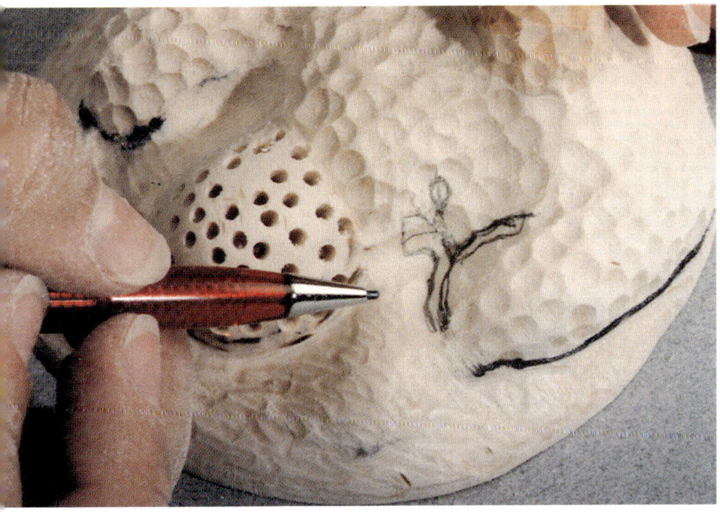

This conflict is further evidenced by the deep crevices between the corals. Draw them in...

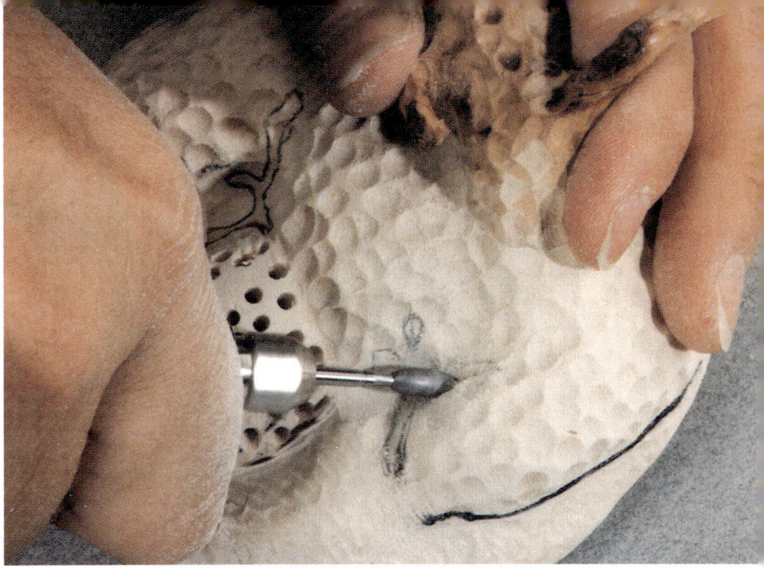

and carve them with a pear-shaped rotary bit.

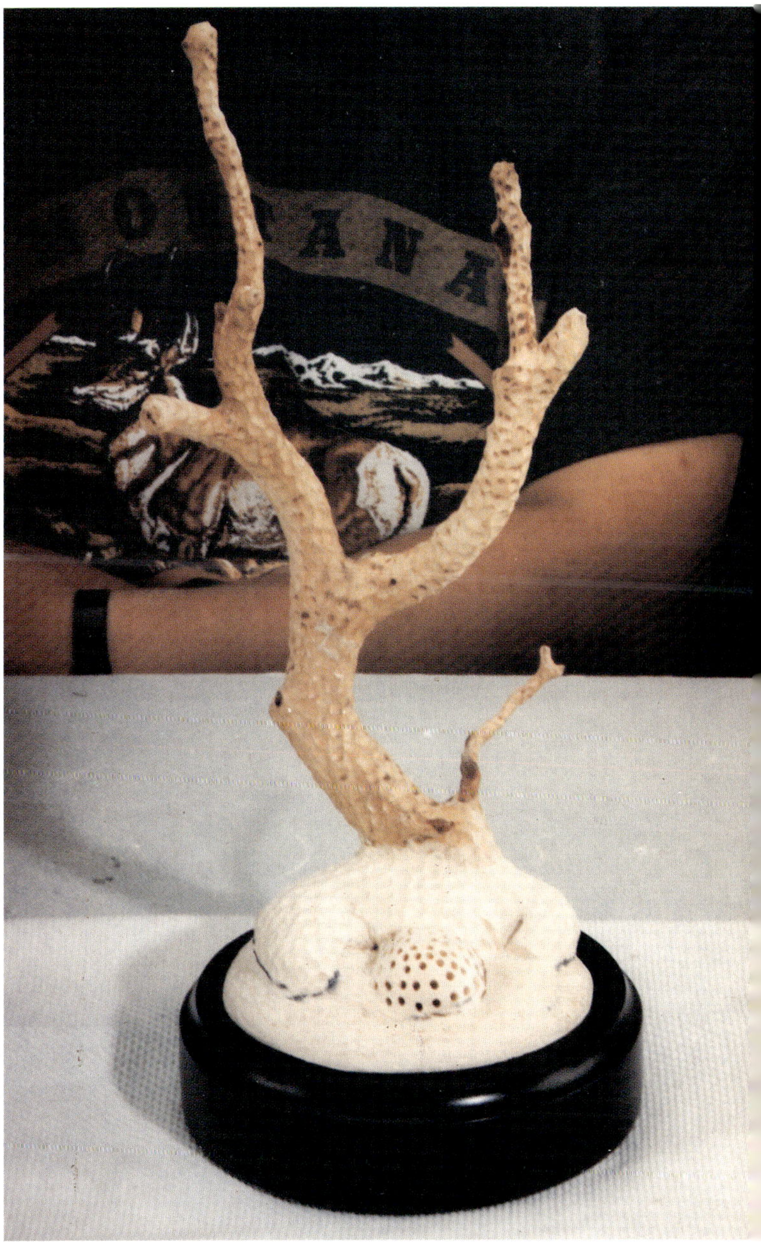

Ready to be sealed and gessoed.

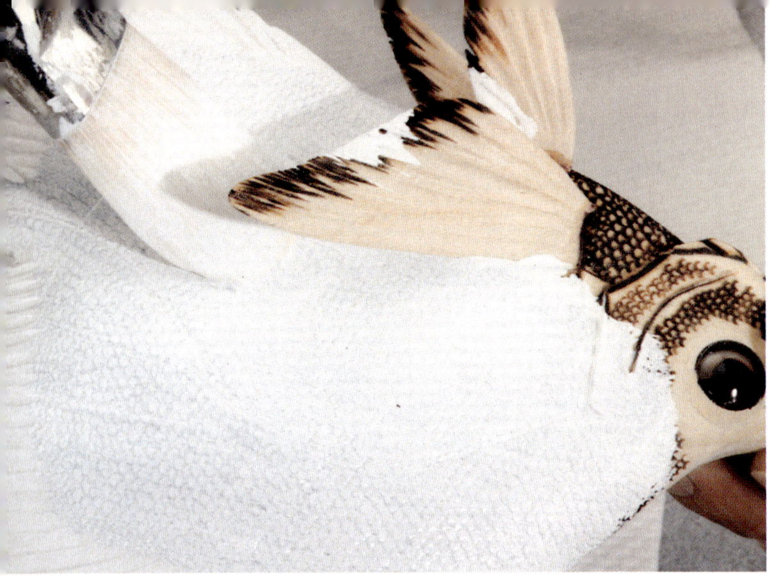

Gesso the Long-Nose, working it into the scales and avoiding brush and drip lines.

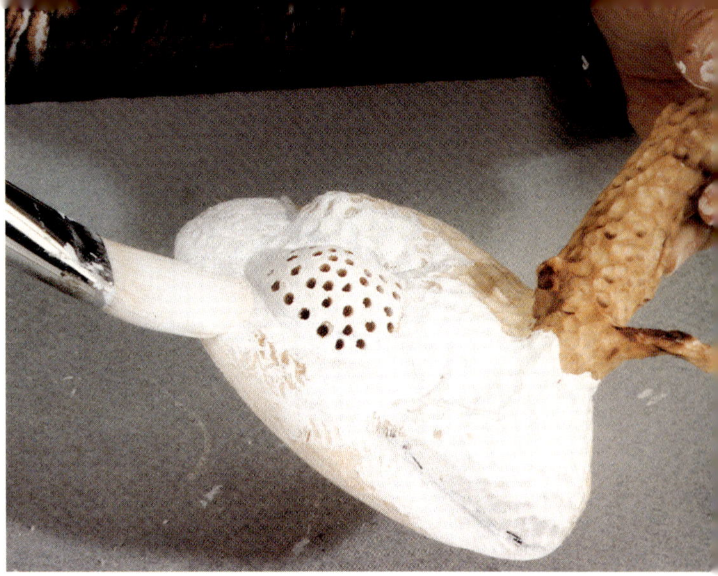

After a coat of clear acrylic sealer has been applied, gesso the habitat. The spines of the urchin will be painted separately. Any gesso that clogs the holes of the urchin needs to be cleaned with a toothpick before it dries.

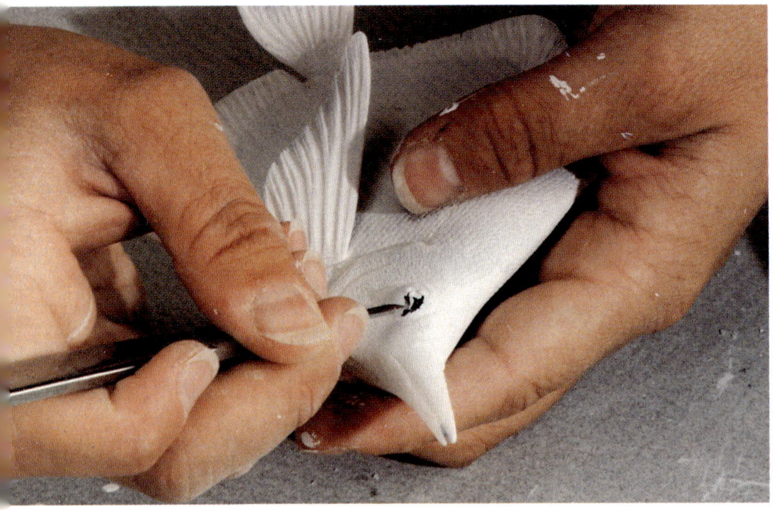

Clean the eyes by running the knife around the perimeter, then scraping them.

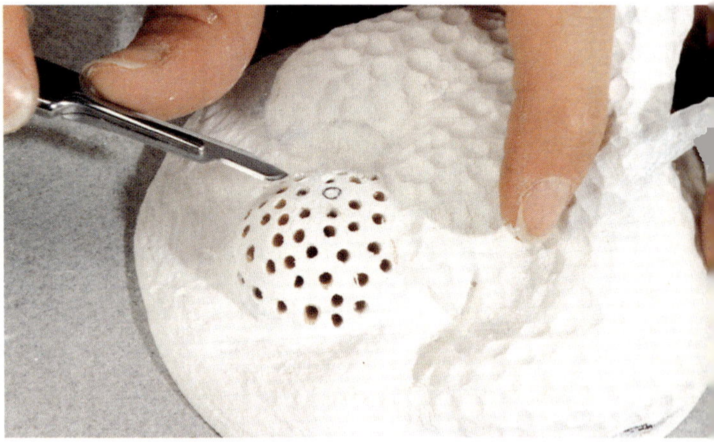

I forgot the anus of the urchin which is at the top. It is just a small shallow hole. Draw it in...

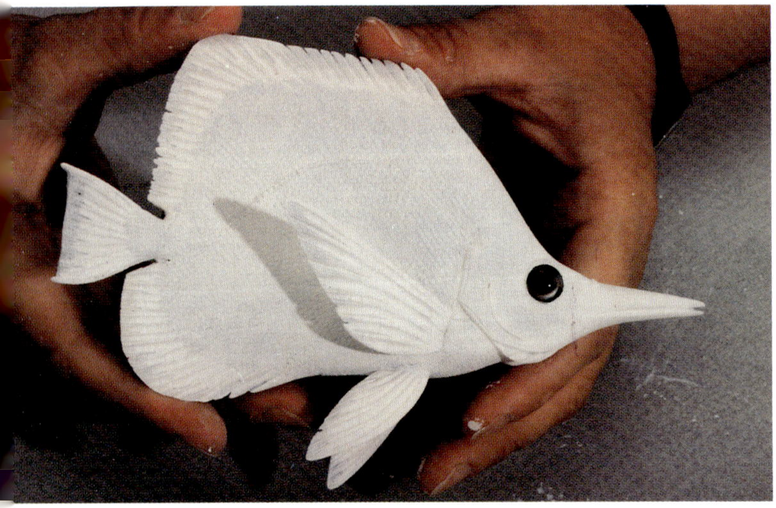

Almost ready for painting. Because of the small scales the burning was particularly dark. I may need to add one more coat of gesso.

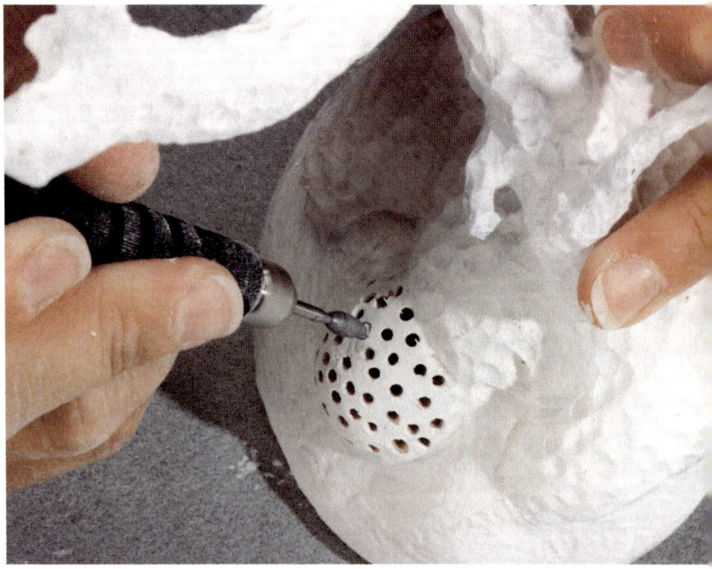

and create it with the rotary tool.

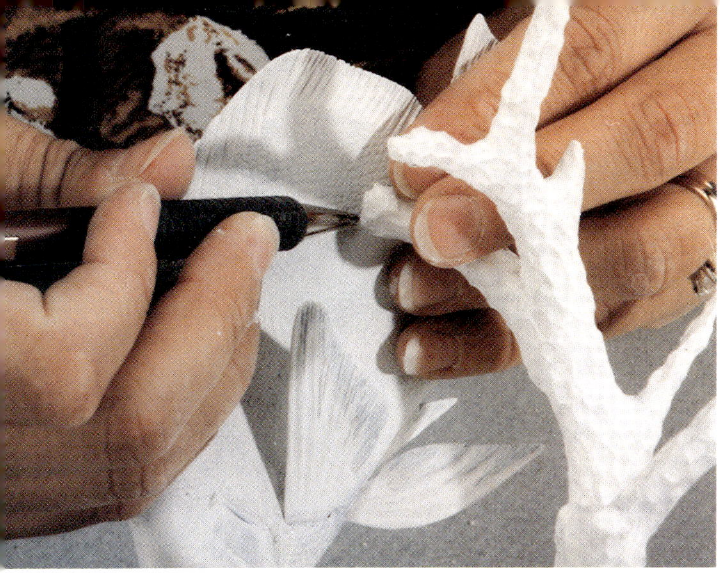

The design of the long-nose setting is designed to be a swirl. This involves two fish and the urchin. I am sure about the position of the lower left fish, so eyeballing it I make the spot for the pin.

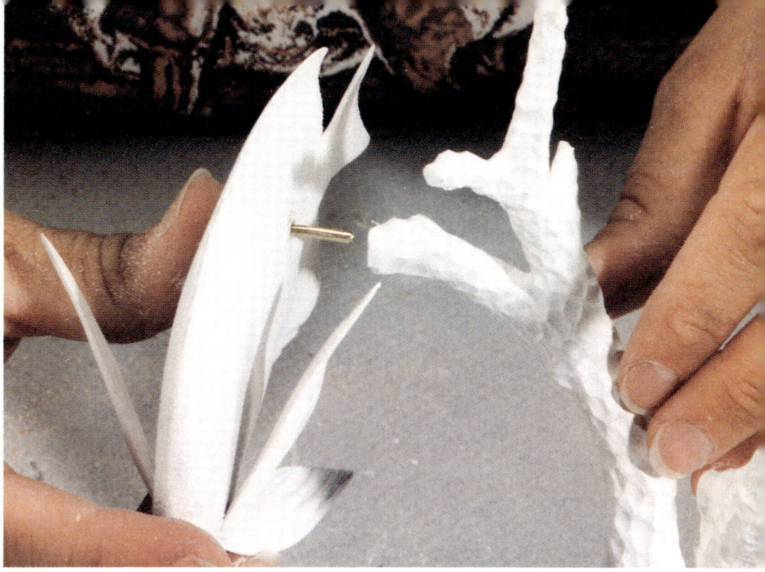

Insert the brass pin and mount the first fish.

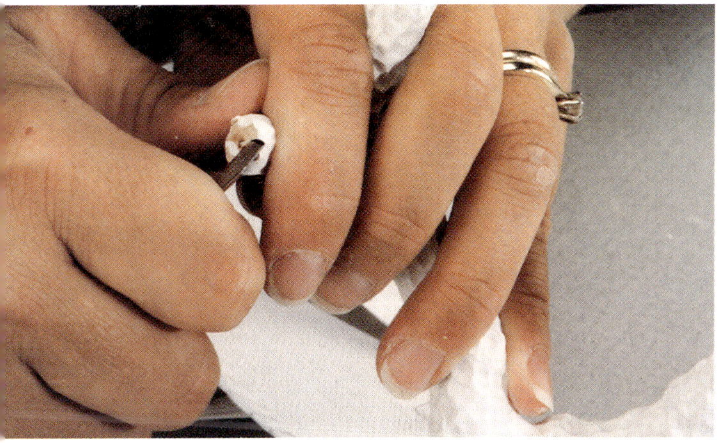

I didn't quite like the angle, so I can adjust it by trimming the coral where it will attach.

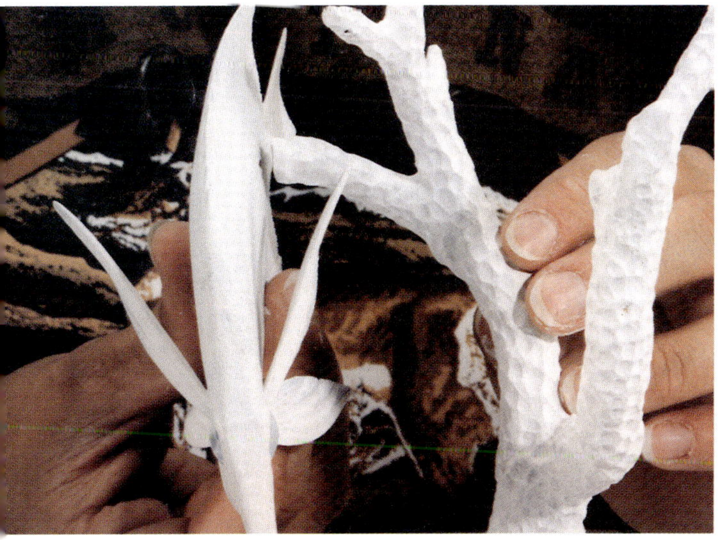

This allows the plane of the fish to be perpendicular instead of slanting inwardly at the bottom.

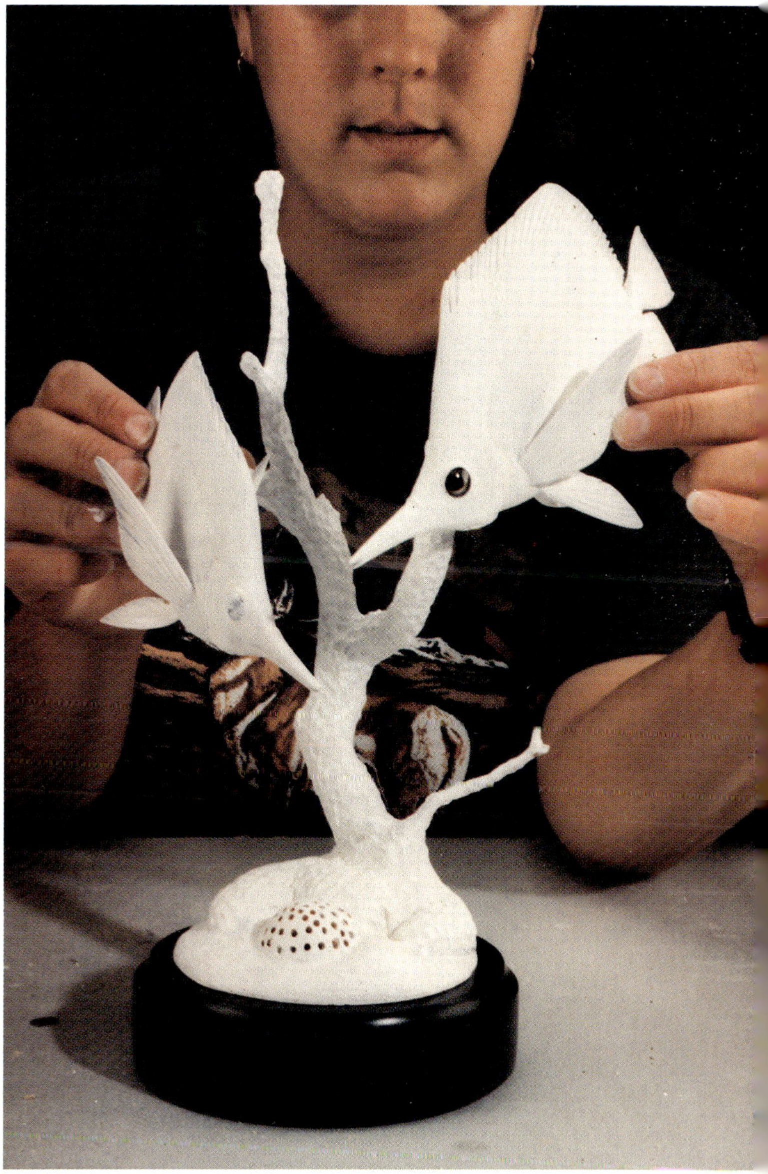

Follow the same procedures with the second fish. I want it higher, but also facing in and down to focus the viewer's attention to the center of the piece.

Painting the Long-Nosed Butterfly

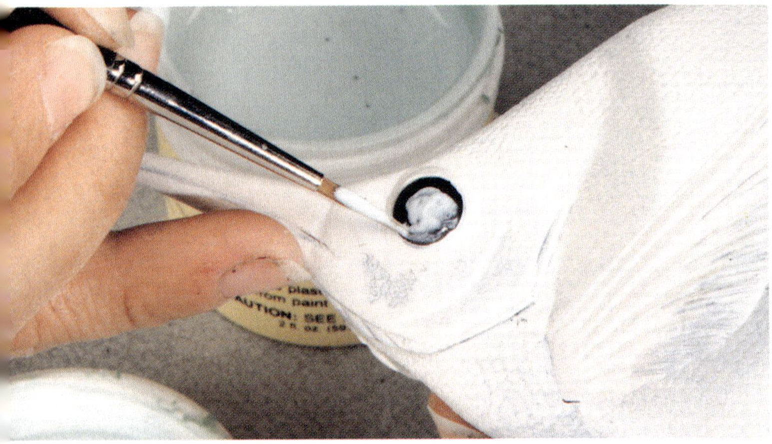

Cover the eye with Eye-Protect™ and set aside to dry while you paint the habitat.

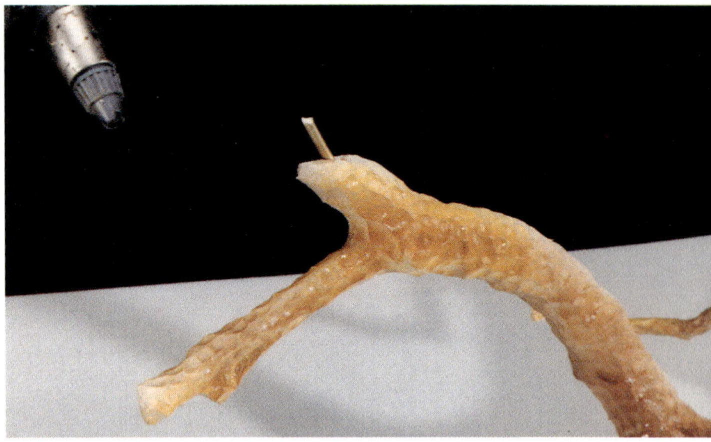

Add a little cadmium yellow to the tips. This will pick up the color of the fish.

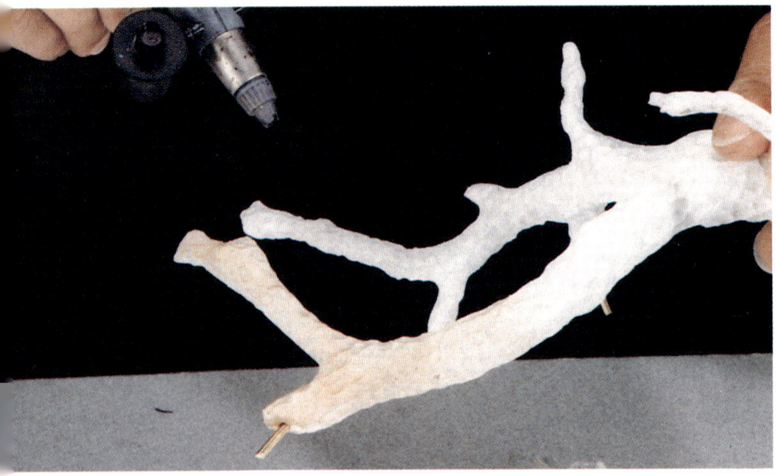

The coral will be light brown at the top and change to a greenish-brown at the bottom. the opposing coral will be yellow. Start with a light spray of chocolate brown at the top.

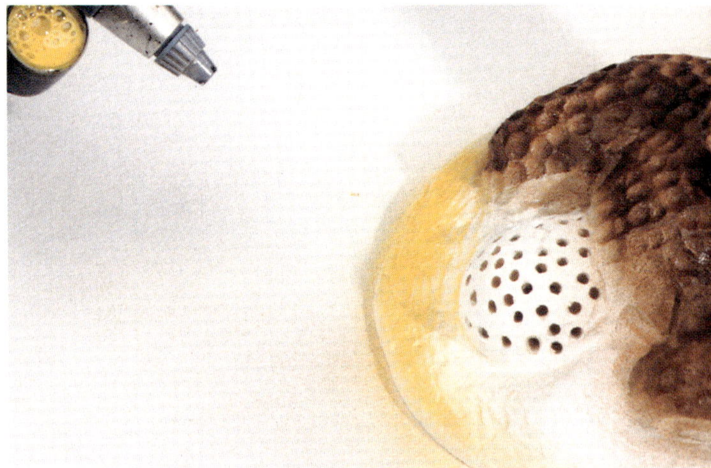

While the yellow is in the airbrush, I'm going to lay a light yellow base in the lower coral.

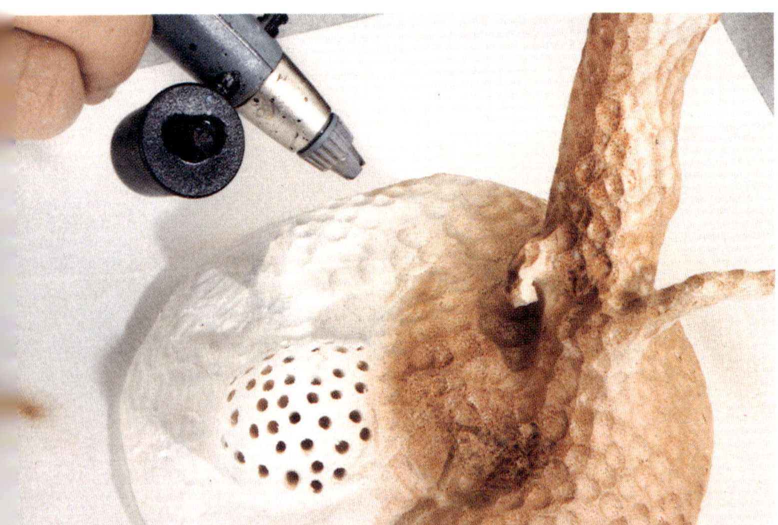

Continue down into the base.

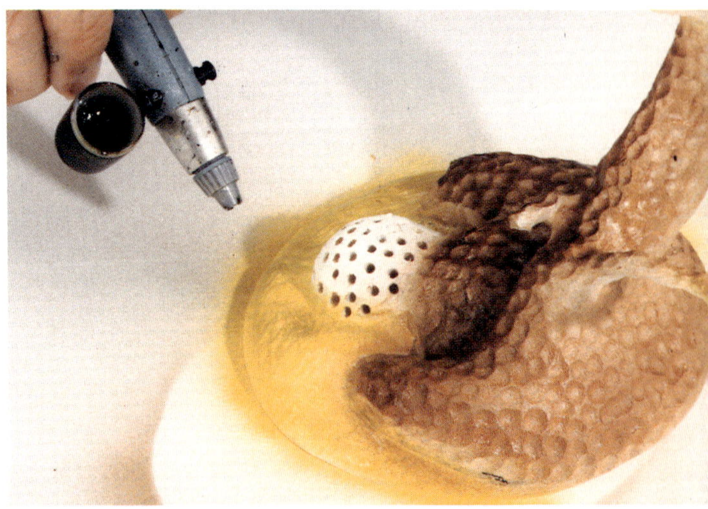

A "Dark Bass and Trout" green is applied over the two corals at the bottom of the habitat. This will tone down the yellow and give depth to the brown.

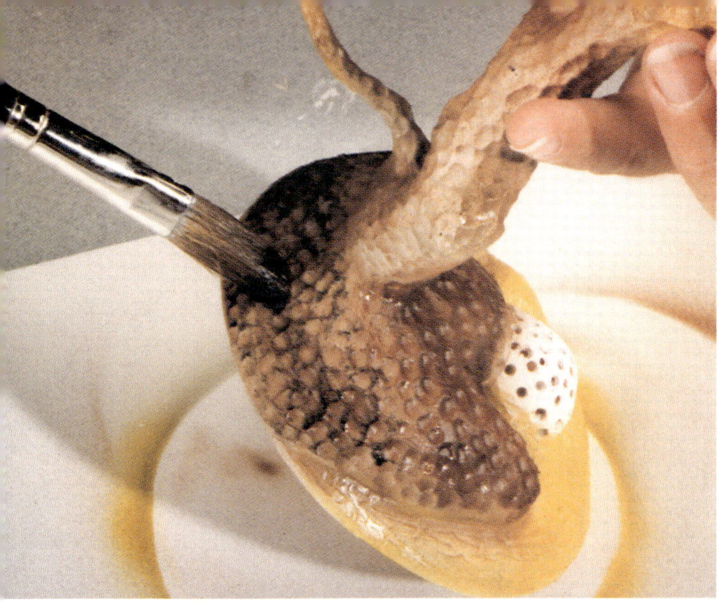

When the green is dry, dry brush over the brown coral with Payne's gray. Use less as you get to the top.

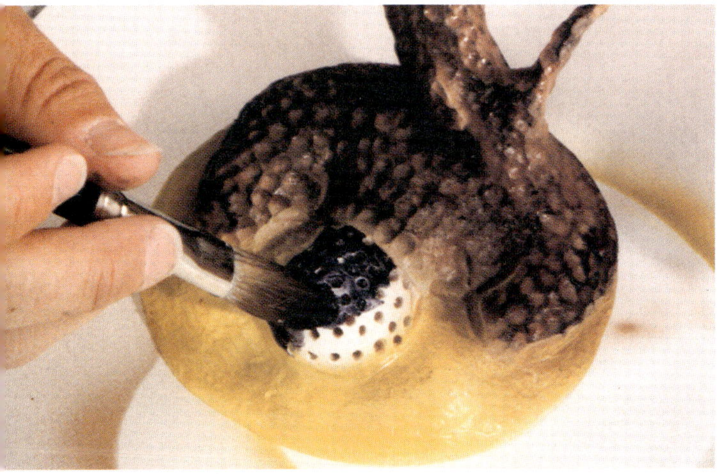

Add a little violet to the Payne's gray to get a deep purple gray, and paint the sea urchin.

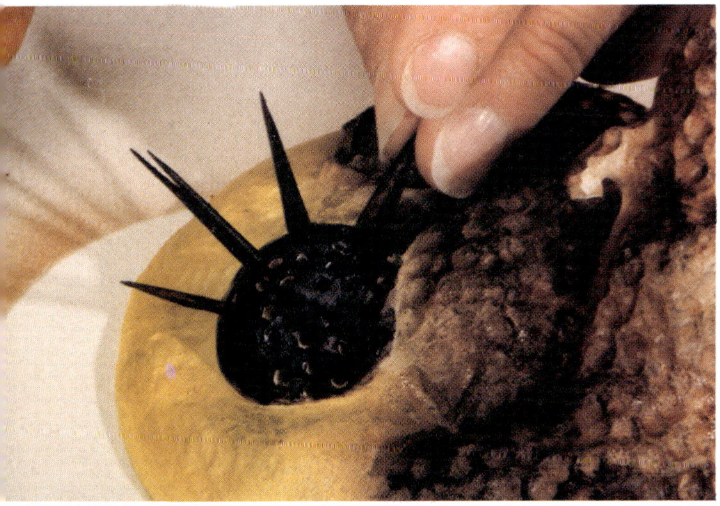

The urchin spines are painted the same color and, when dry, are placed into position. I put the short ones in first to avoid getting stabbed. Stagger their position.

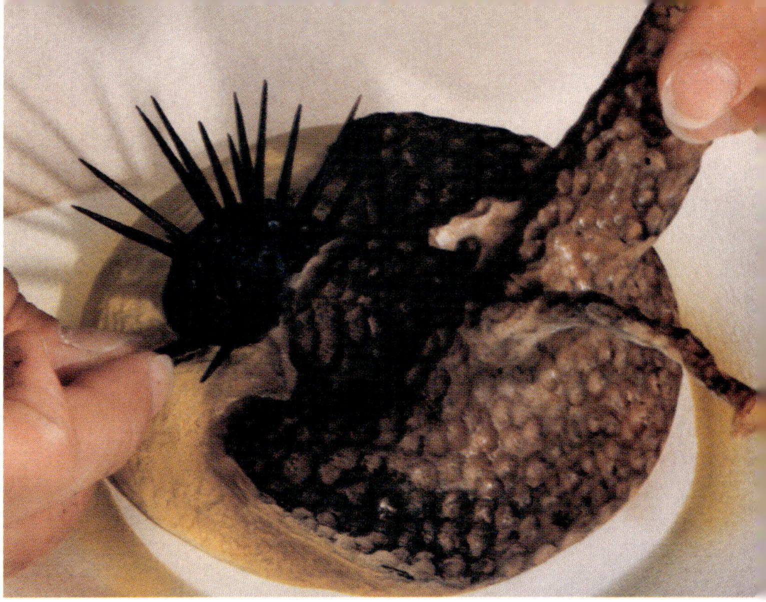

Fill the remaining holes with the long spines.

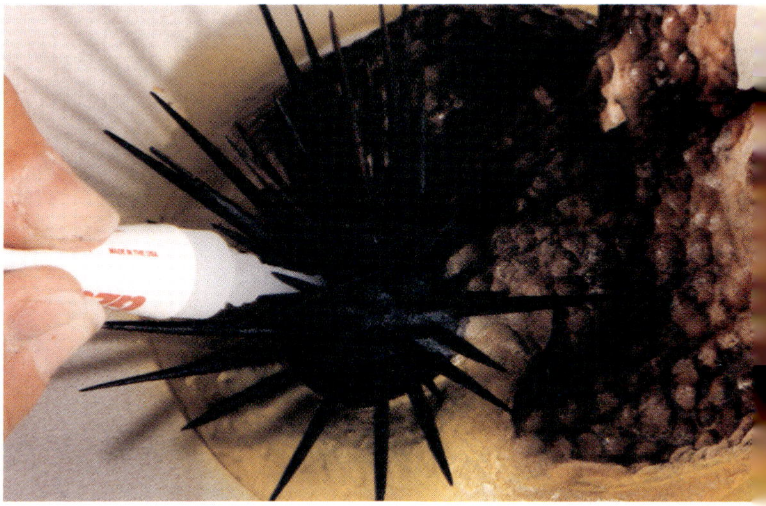

A touch of super glue at the base of the spine will be drawn into the socket by capillary action. While that dries move to the fish.

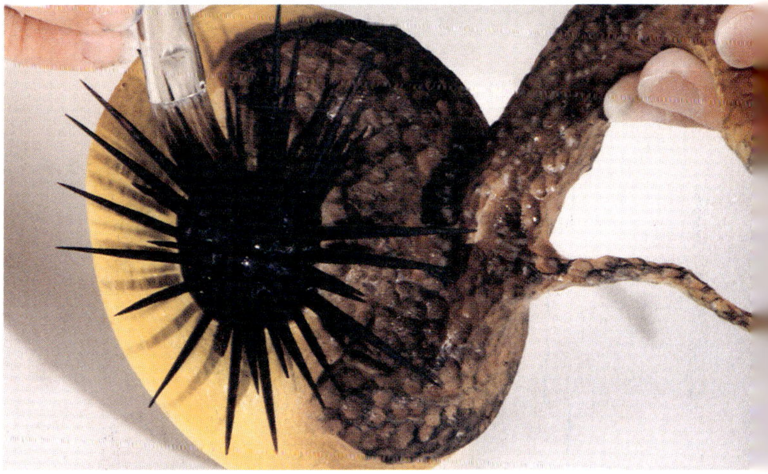

Apply some dark Payne's gray into the middle of the spines. The lower portion of the spines and the body will pick this color up.

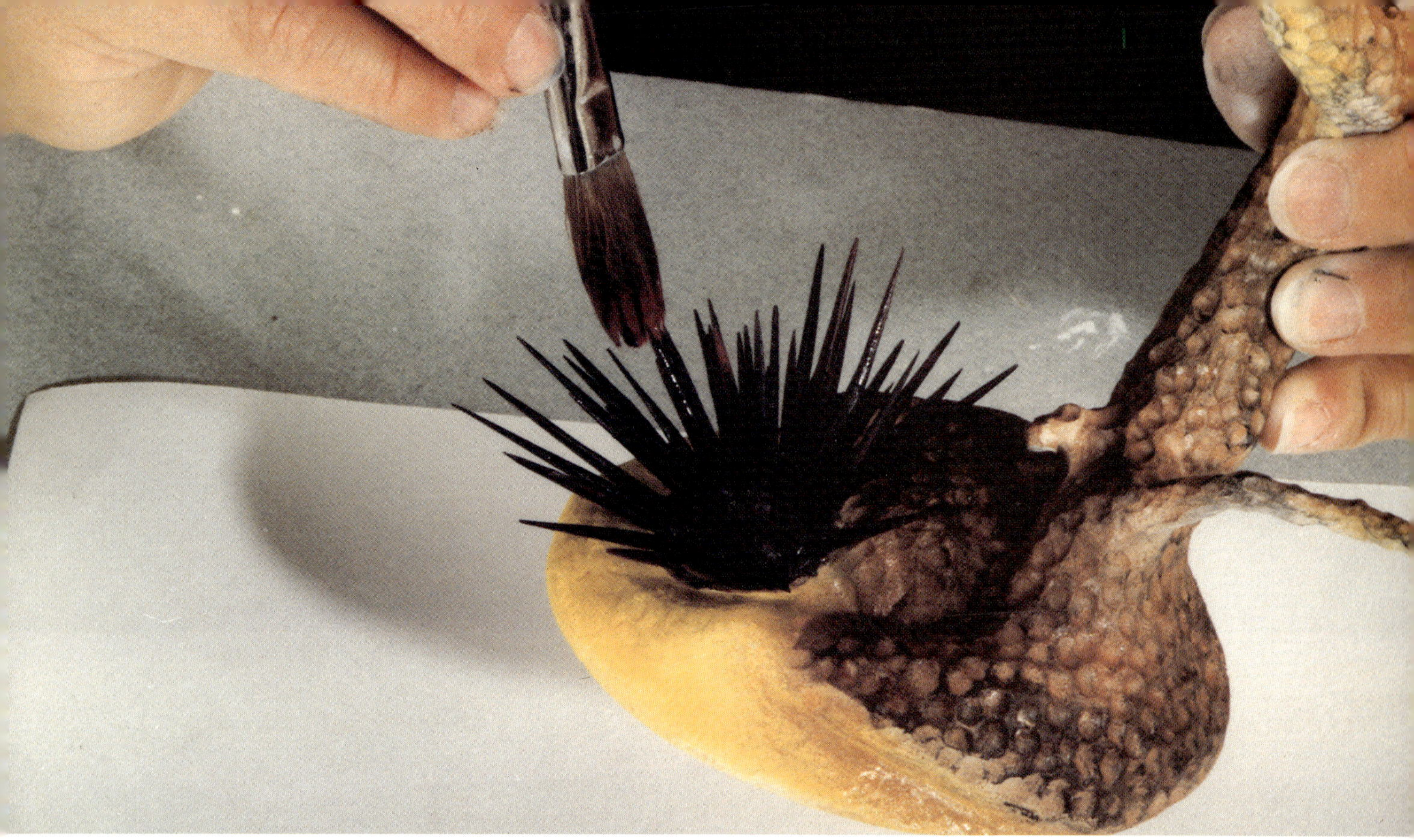

Paint the upper half of the spines with tube violet acrylic paint. This will take two coats to lighten them up.

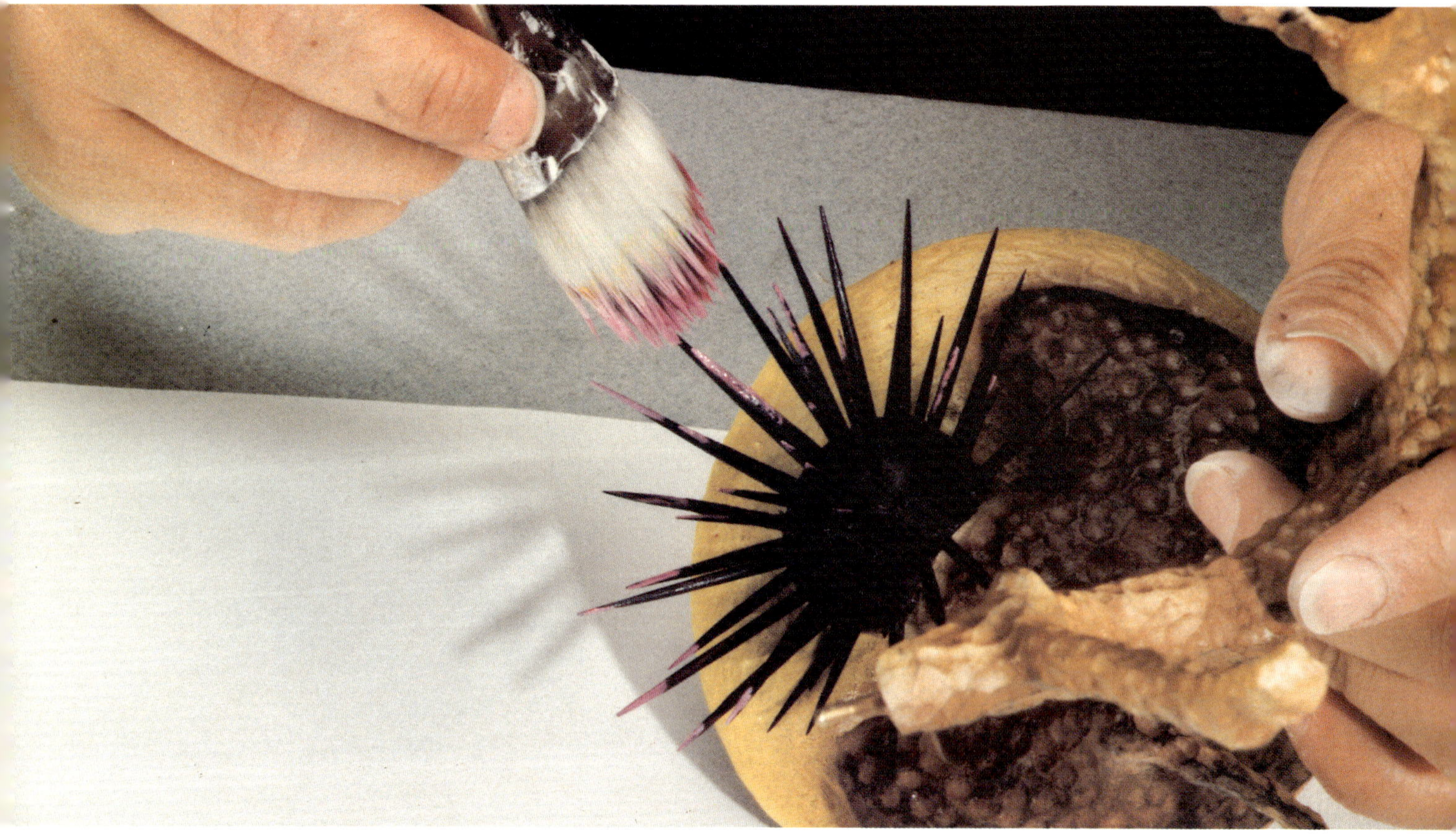

Mix some violet and white to get a hot pink. Lightly brush the tips of the urchin spines.

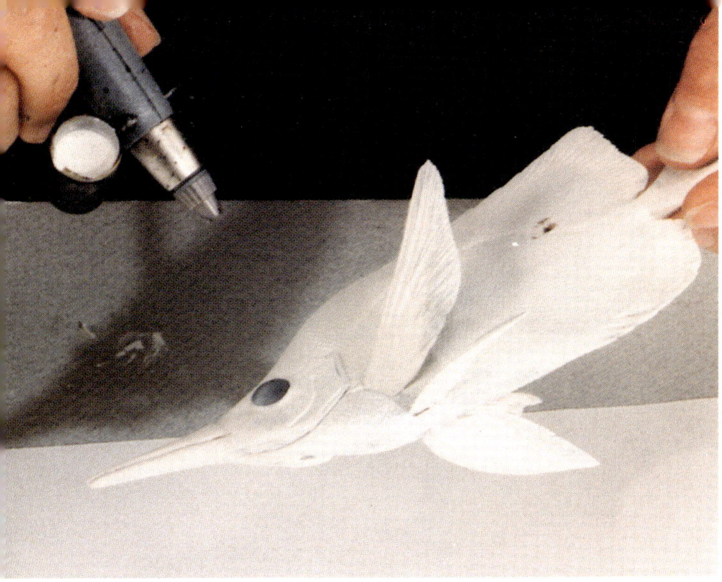

The first coat on the long nose is Superhide white.

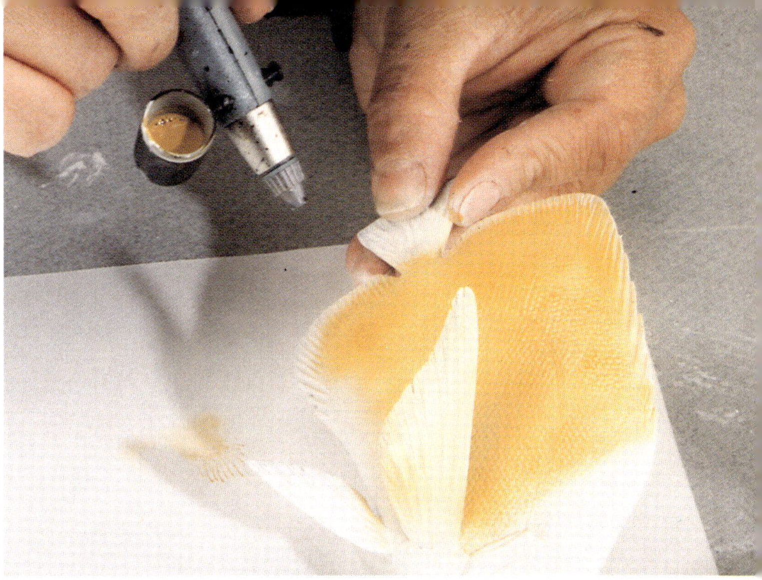

Blend lighter as you get to the bottom.

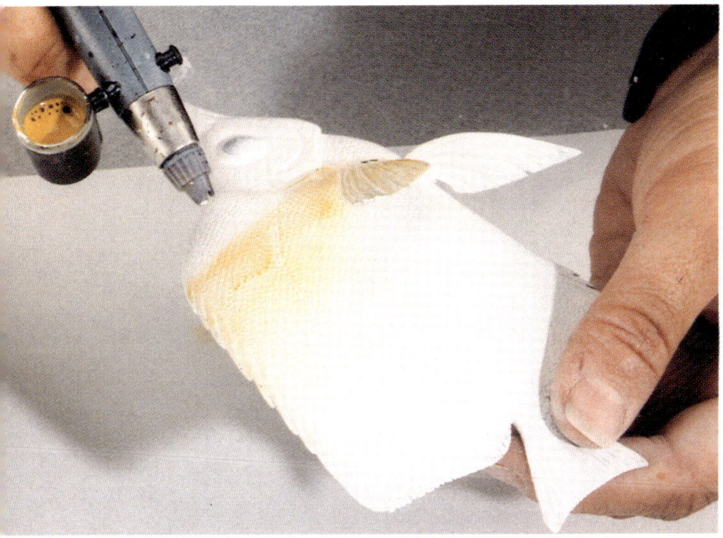

When the first coat dries, paint the body of the fish with yellow ocher. Paint back from a line connecting the pectoral fin and the leading edge of the dorsal fin.

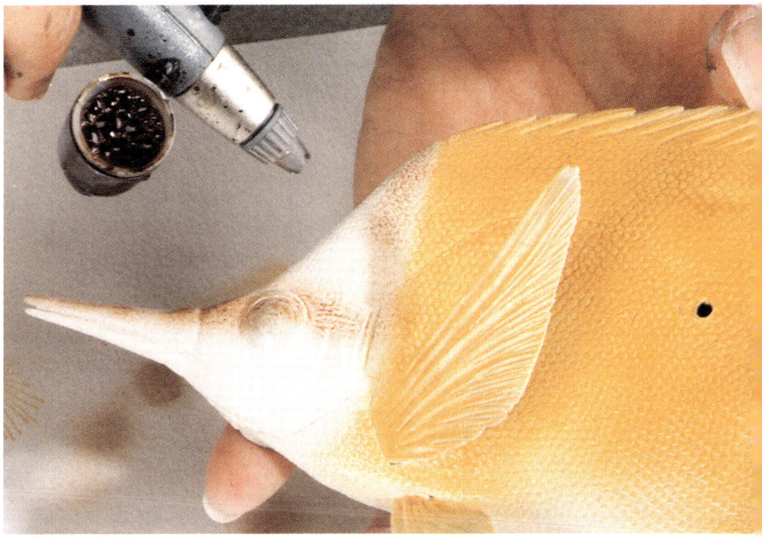

Chocolate brown is used on the head triangle and, as a light mist, on the caudal fin. The line goes through the top half of the eye.

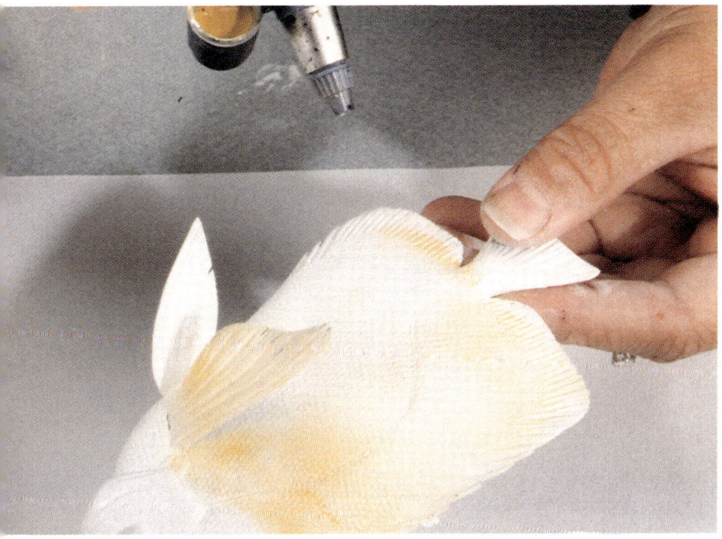

Paint the fins with a light coat.

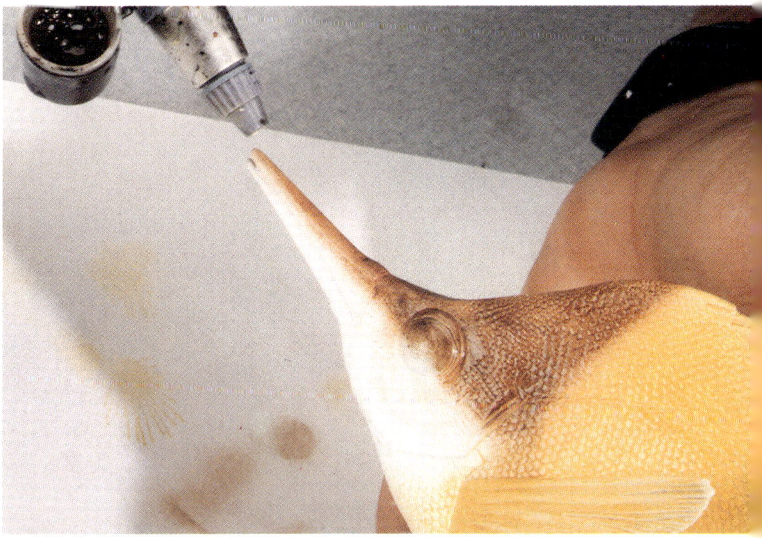

There is a slight misting of brown under the eye.

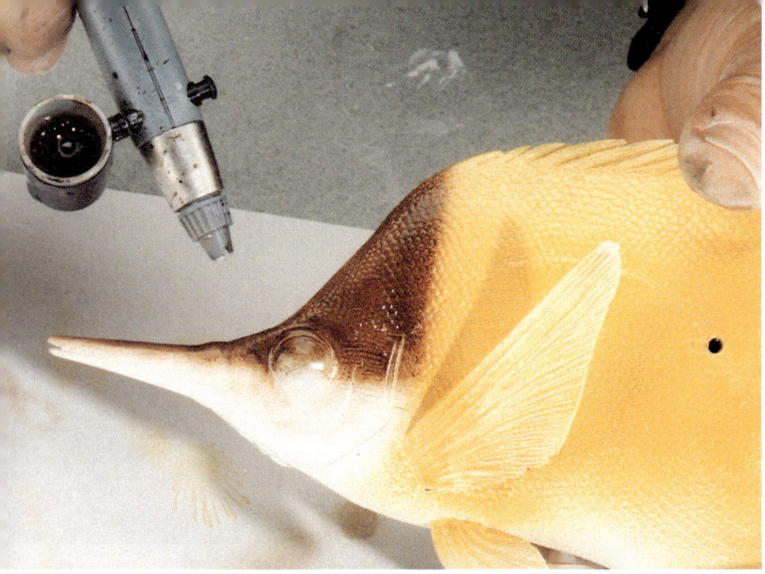

Continue to build the color by adding coats.

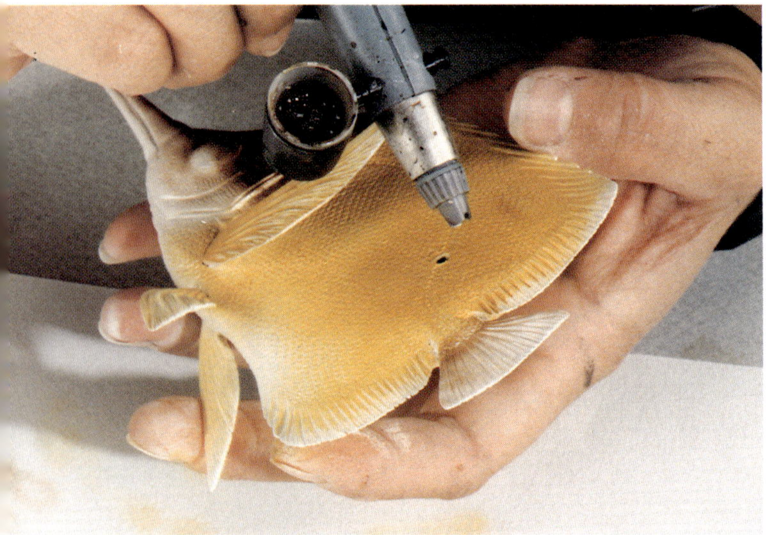

Lightly spray the caudal fin with the chocolate. It is actually translucent, but since this will be in a dark habitat it is picking up dark colors. This extends slightly onto the peduncle.

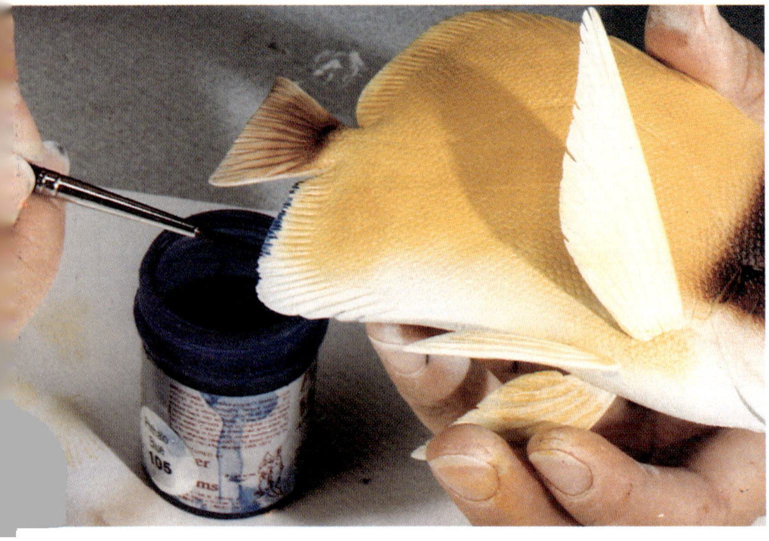

I brush thalo blue on the trailing edges of the anal fin...

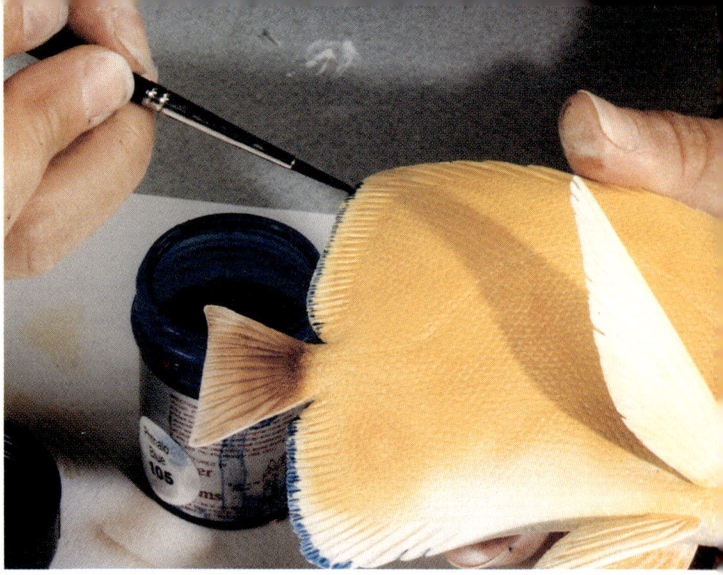

and the dorsal fin.

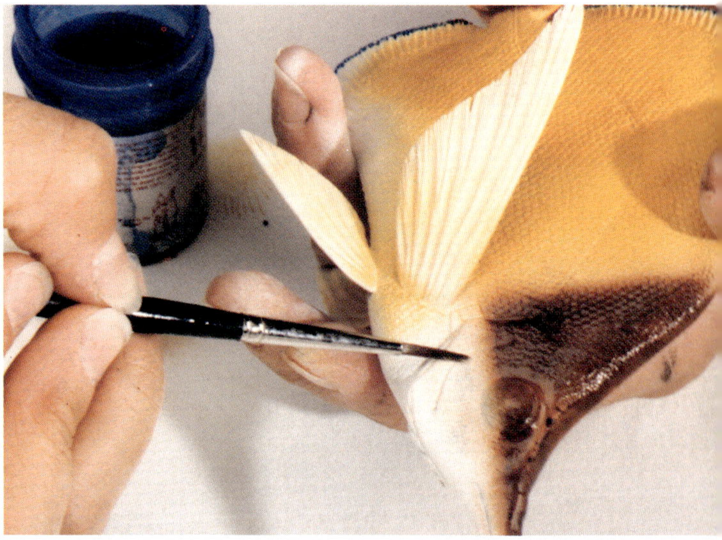

Stipple a little blue under the chin.

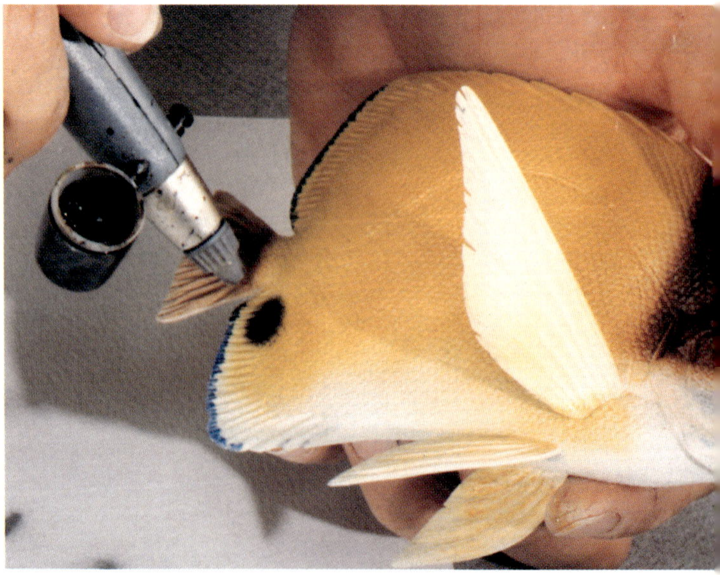

The spot at the top of the dorsal fin, just below the caudal peduncle is black.

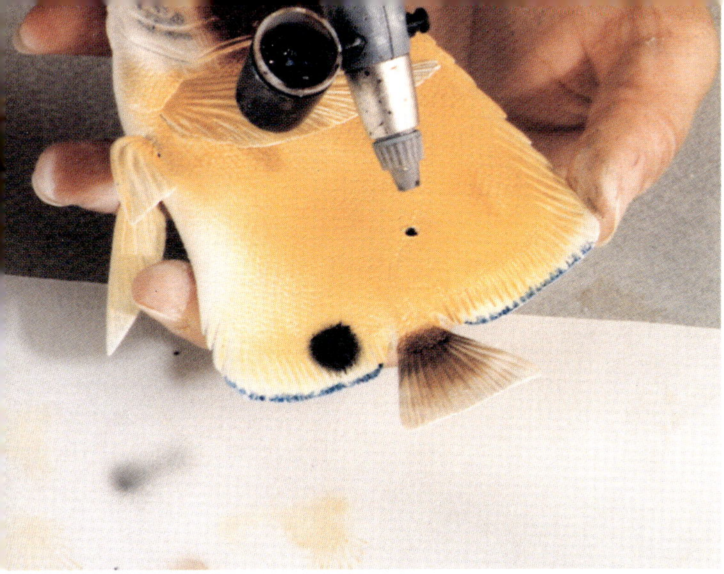

Mist the tail with black.

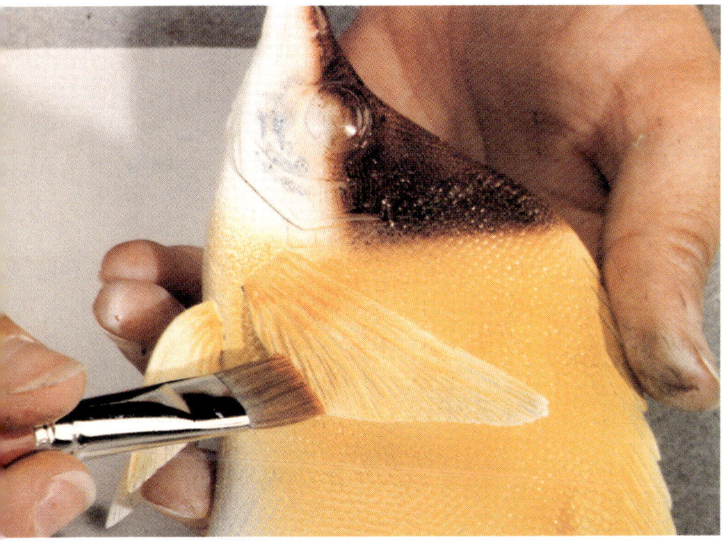

With cadmium orange dry brush all the fins, including the tail. You just want to pick up the raised areas.

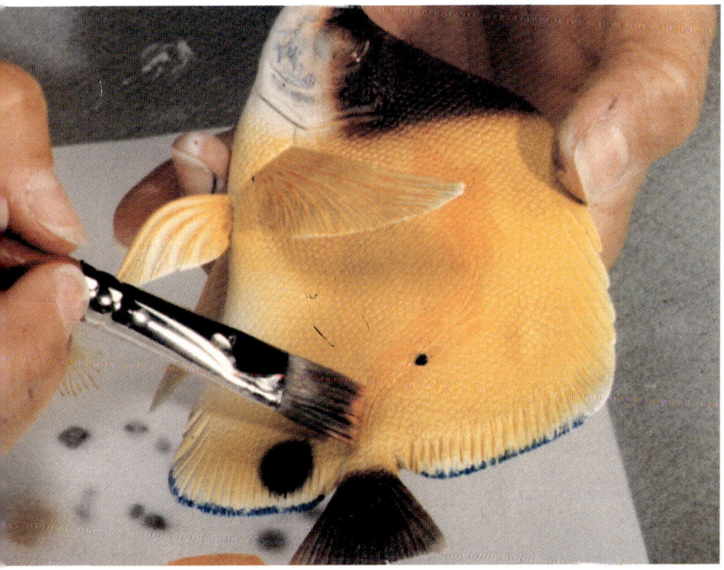

Follow the lateral line with a dry brush cadmium orange.

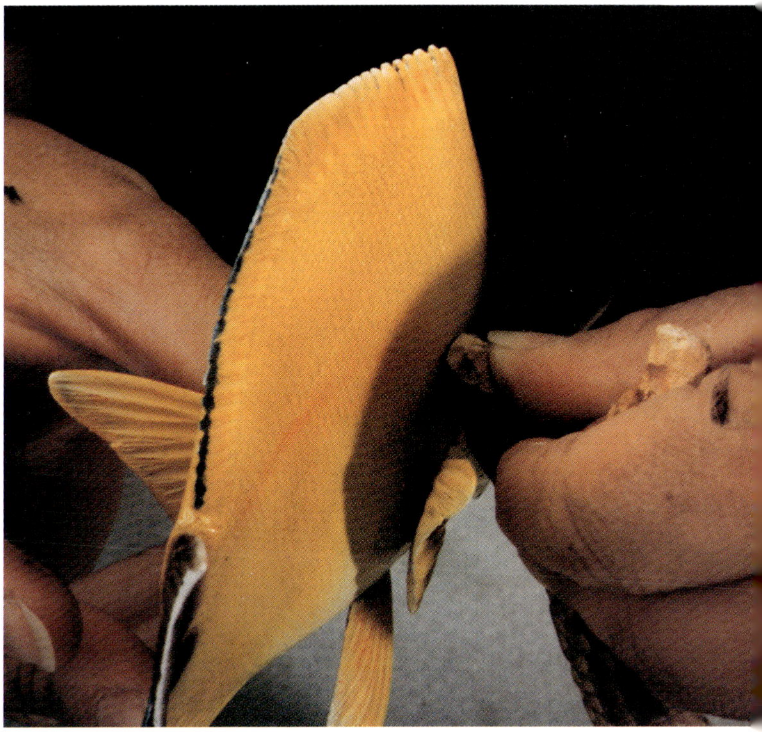

Mount the fish in the habitat.

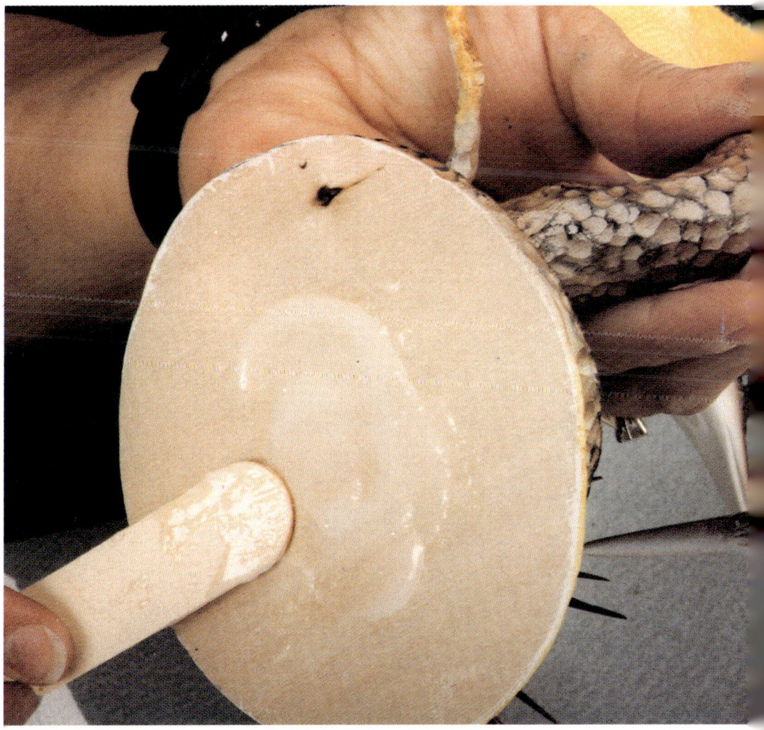

Epoxy the habitat to the base. This can be reenforced with a screw from beneath. Apply the glue only to the center.

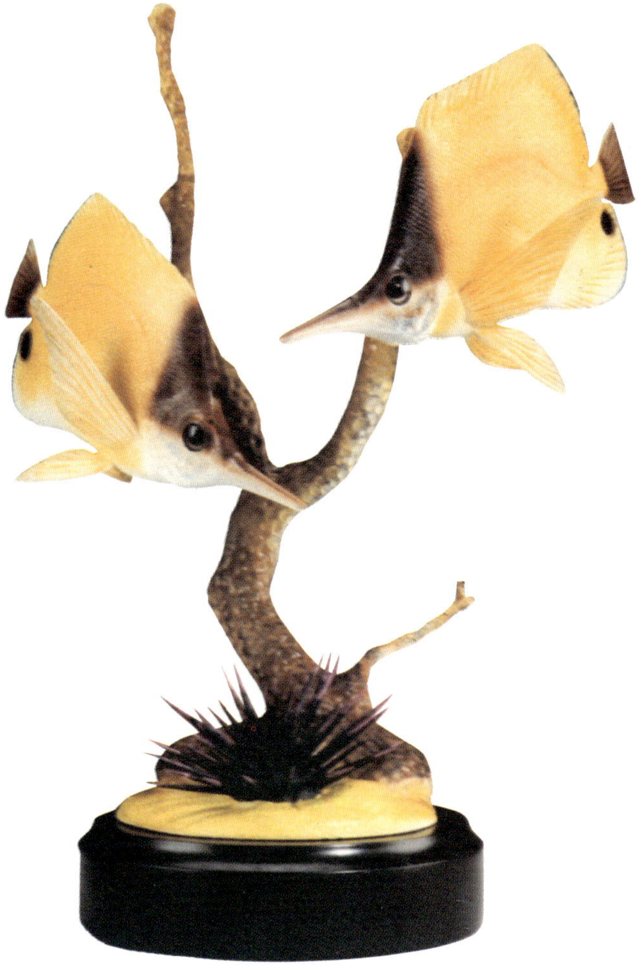

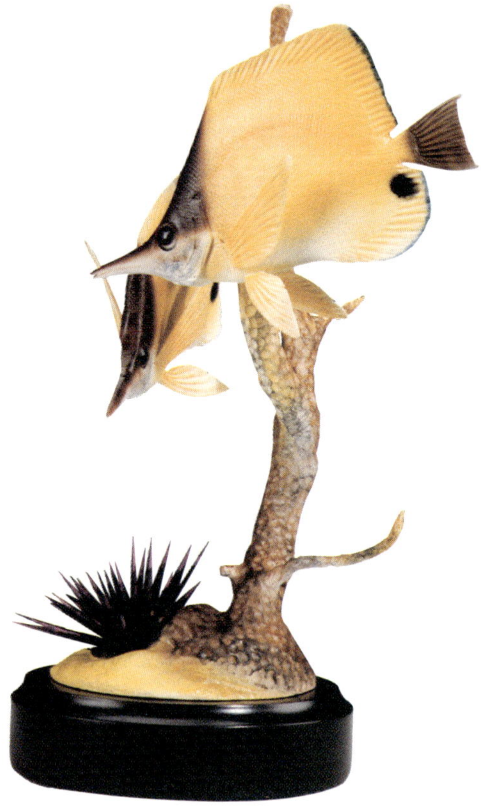

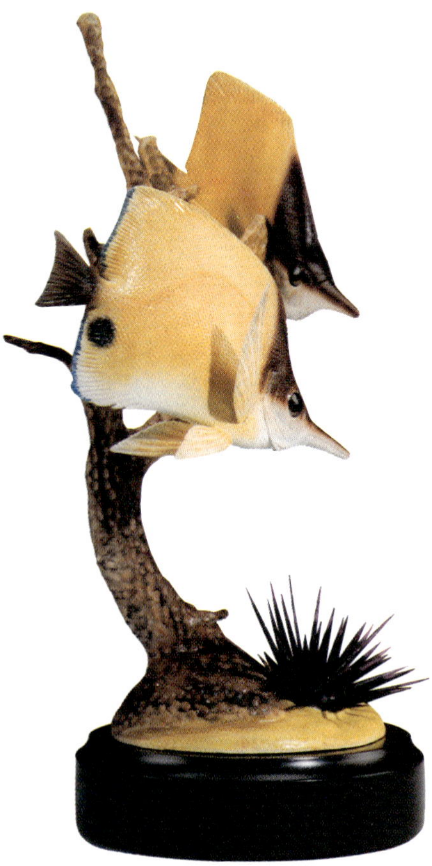

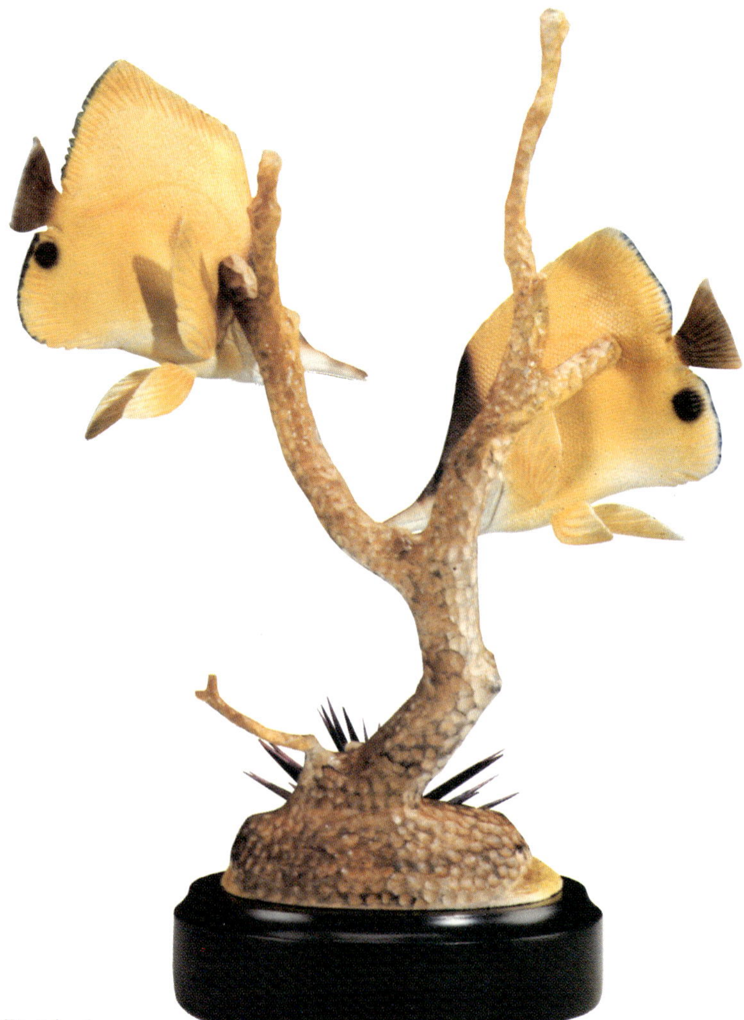

Finished.

The Gallery

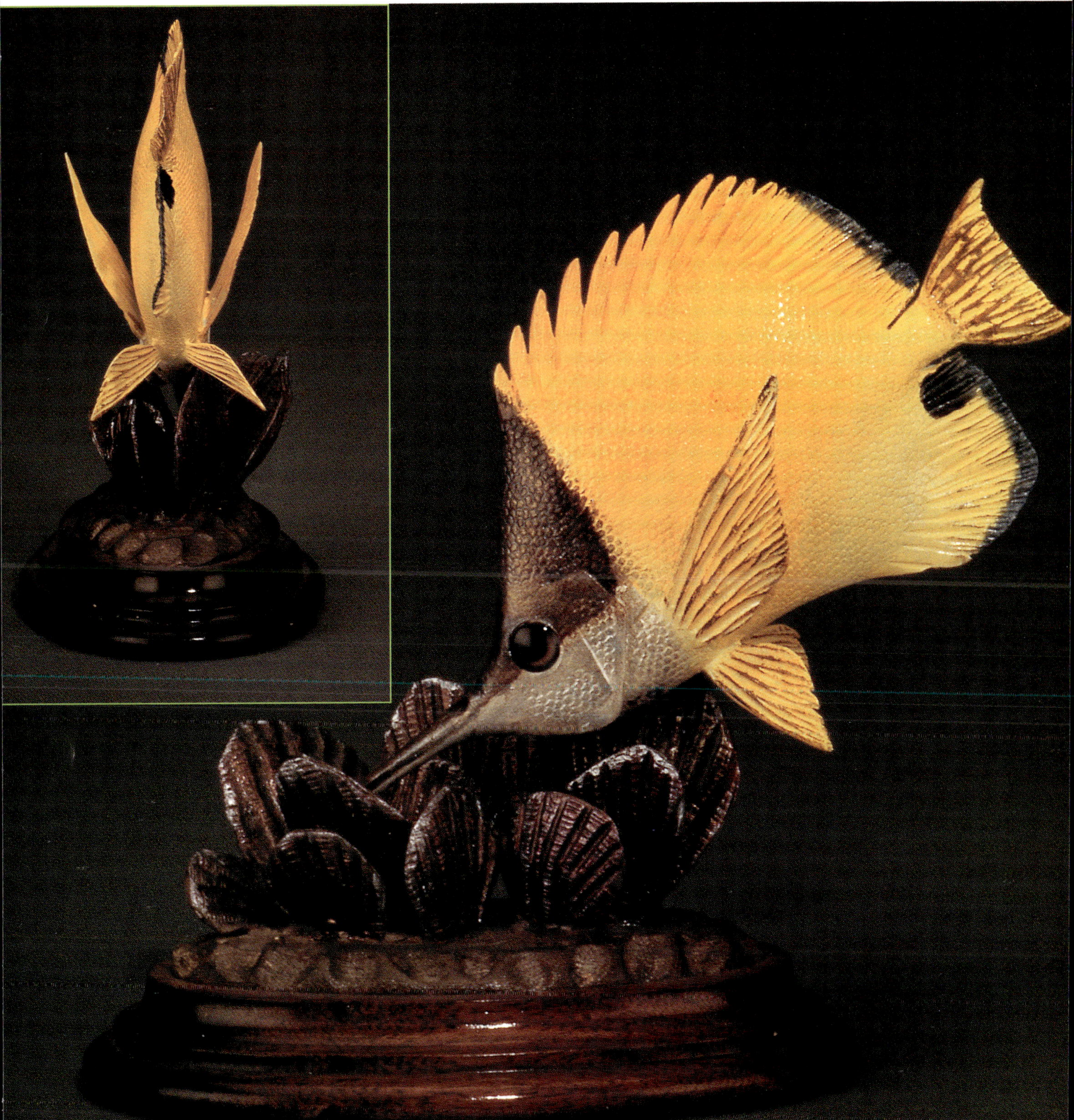

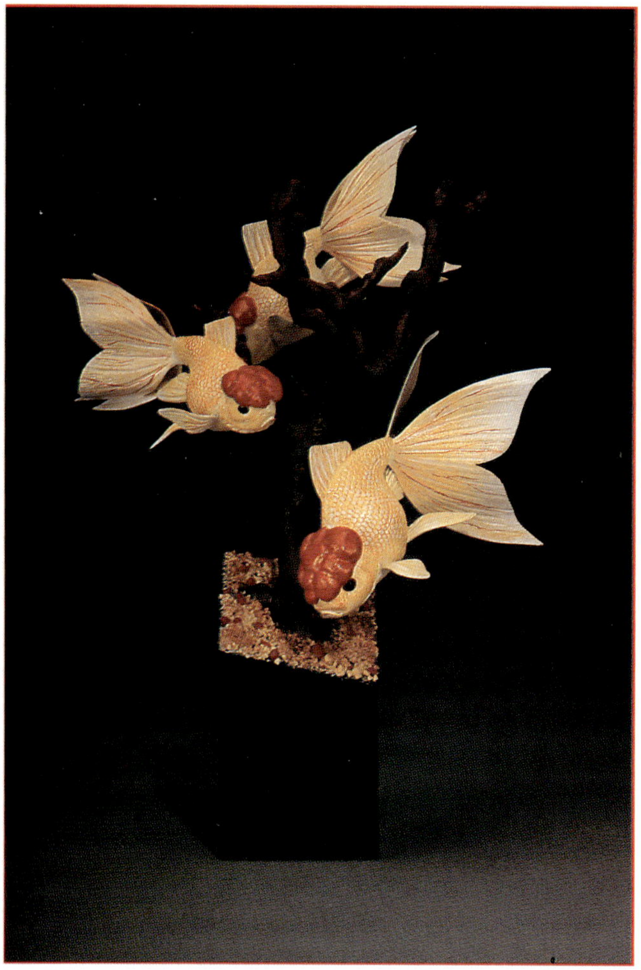

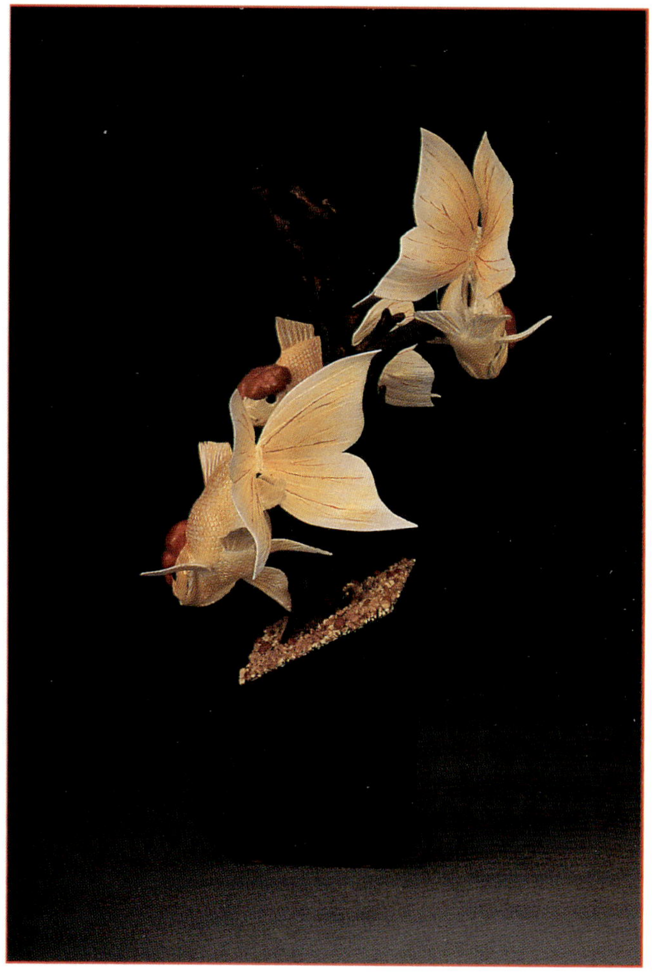

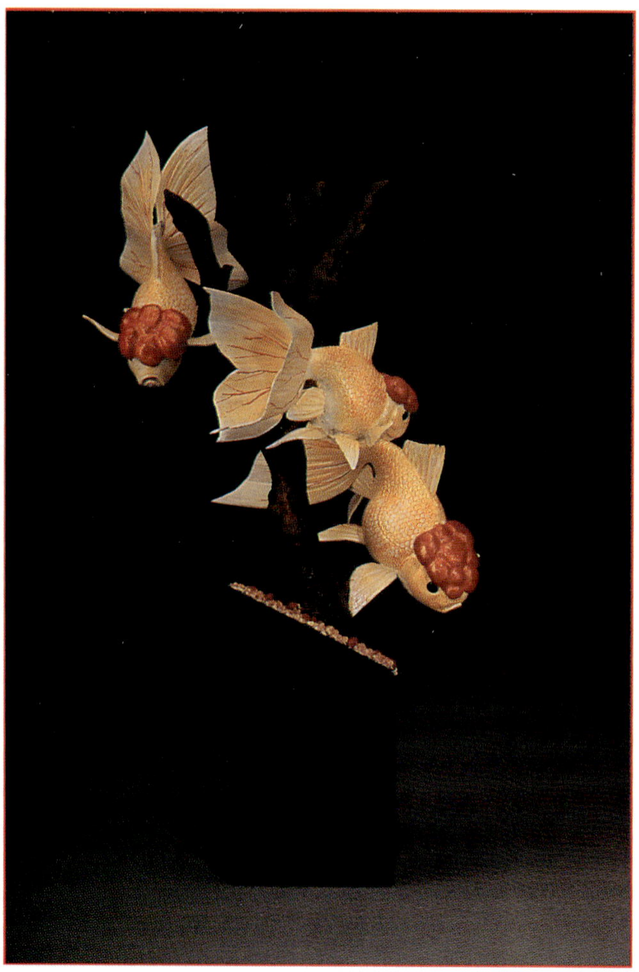

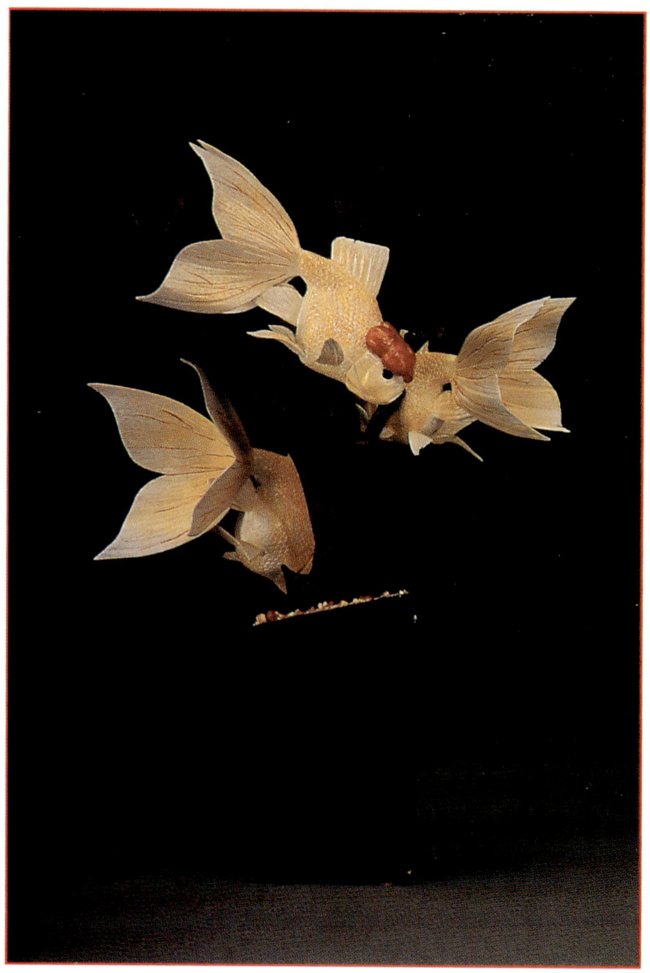

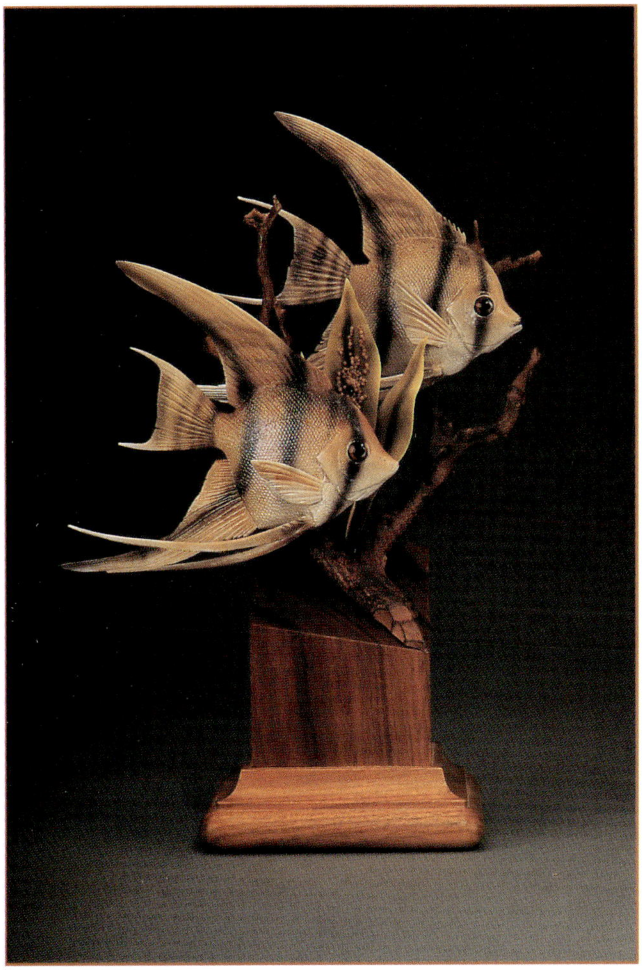
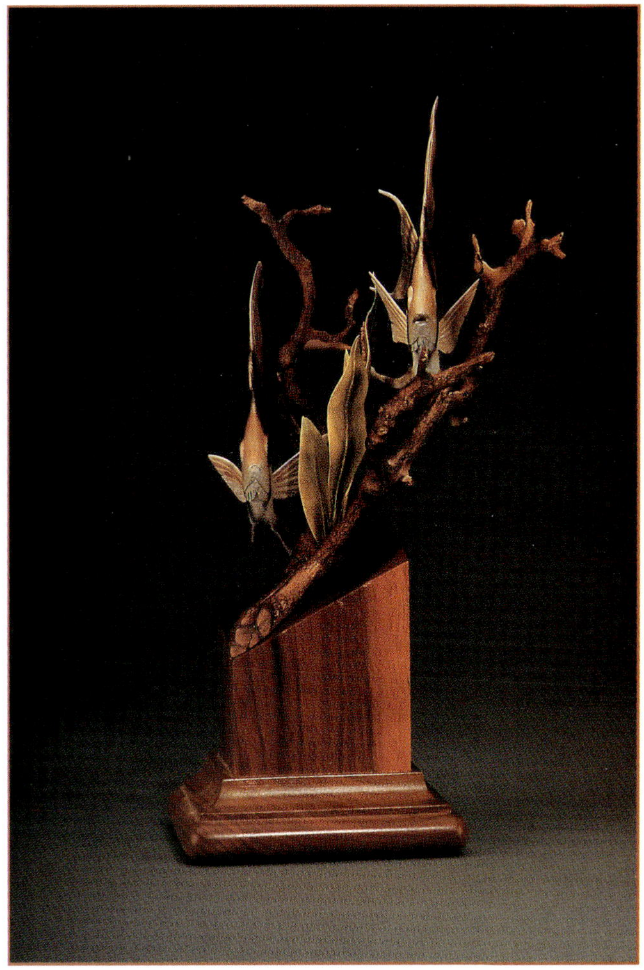
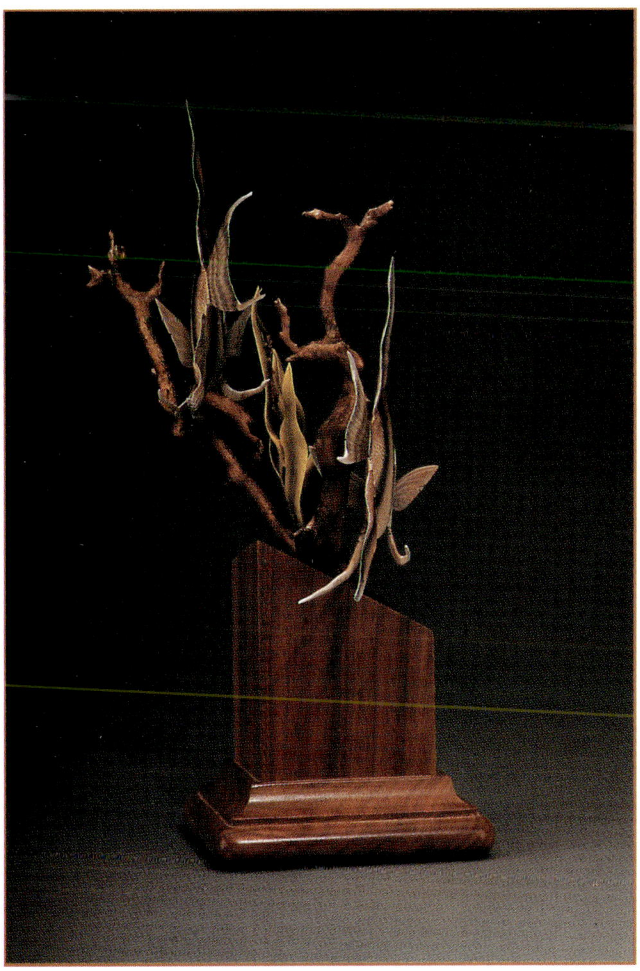
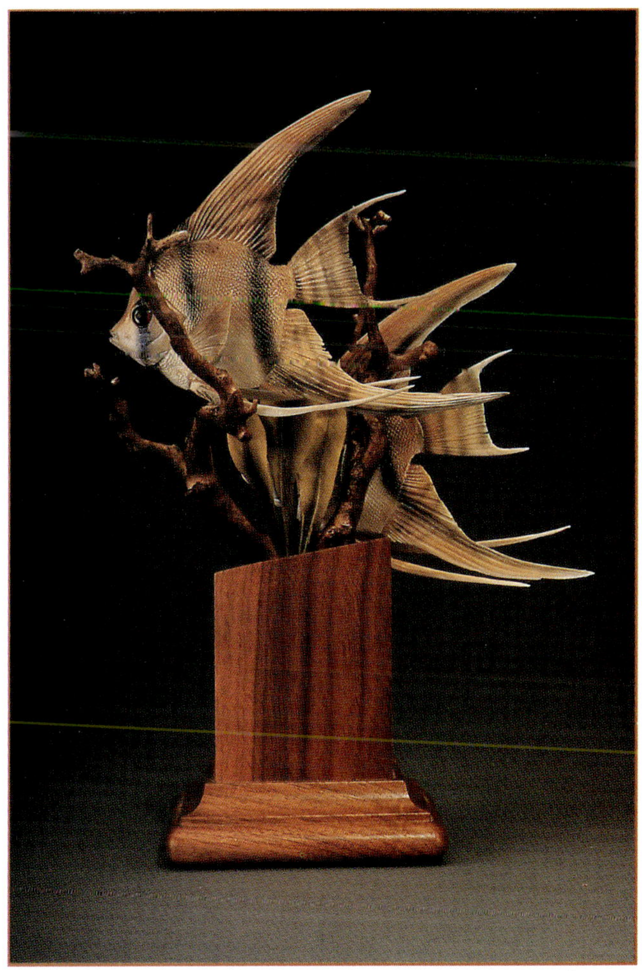

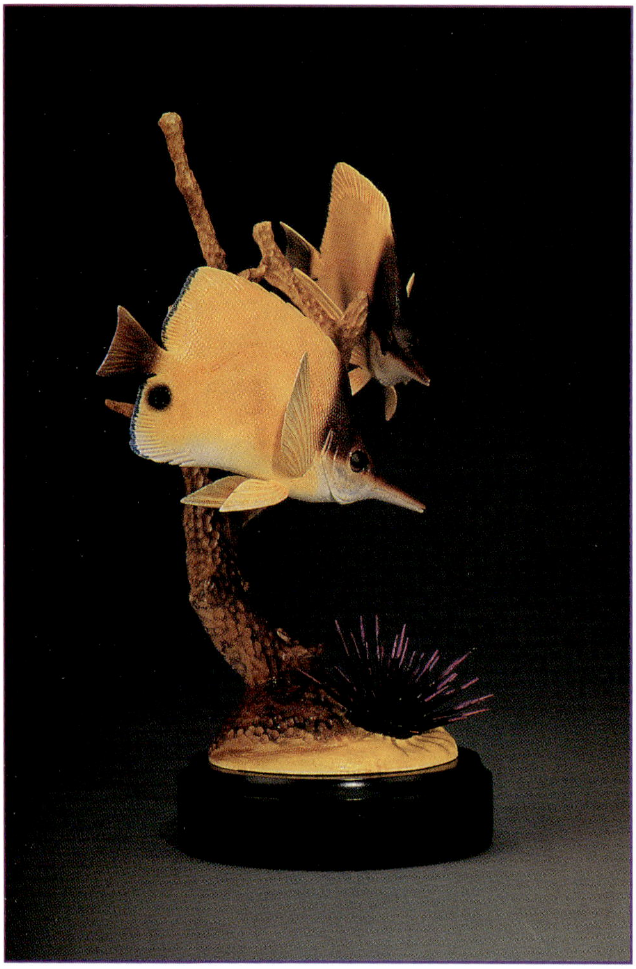

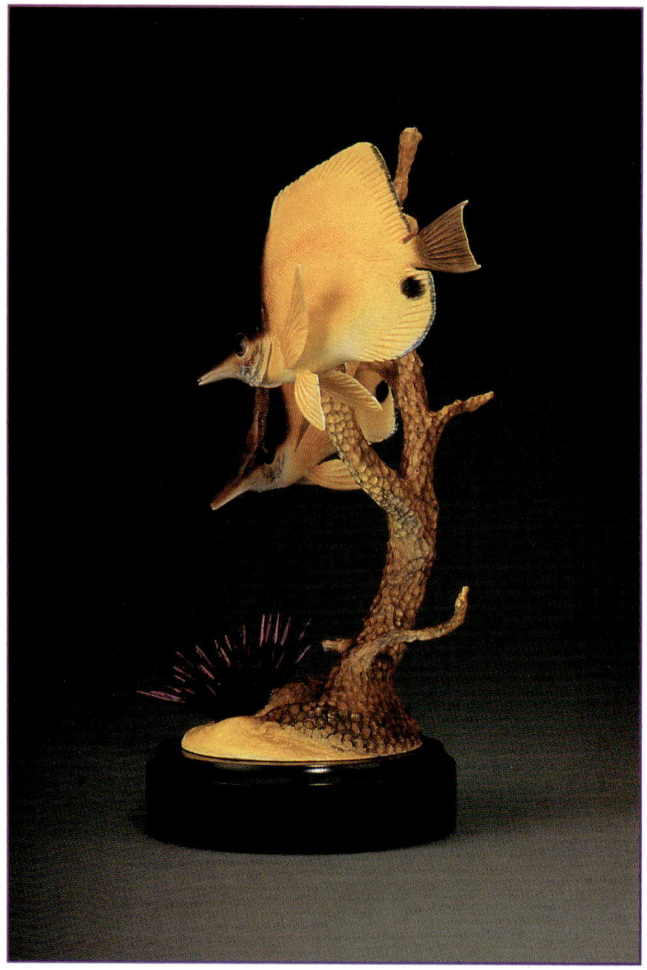

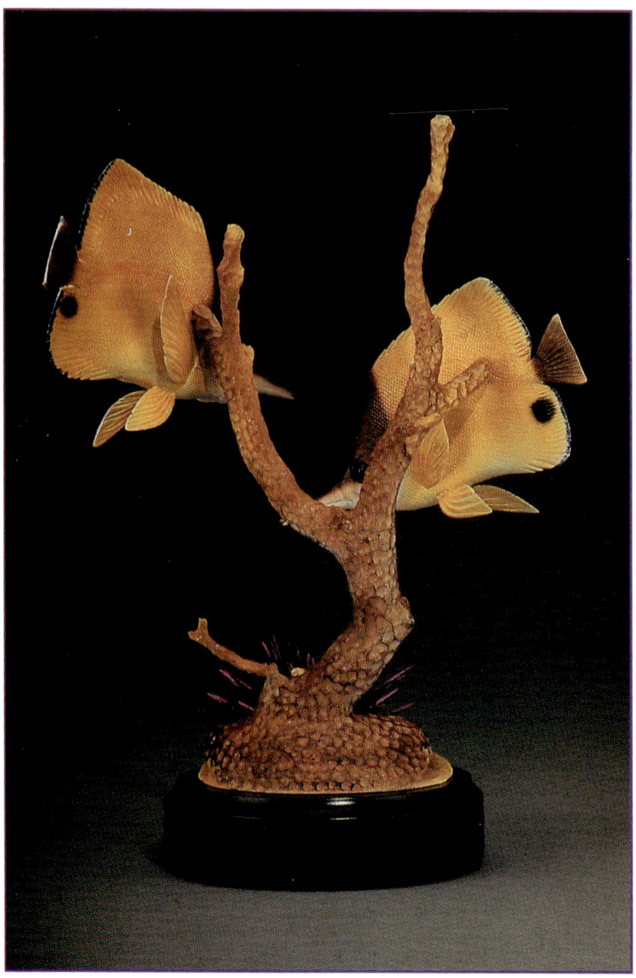

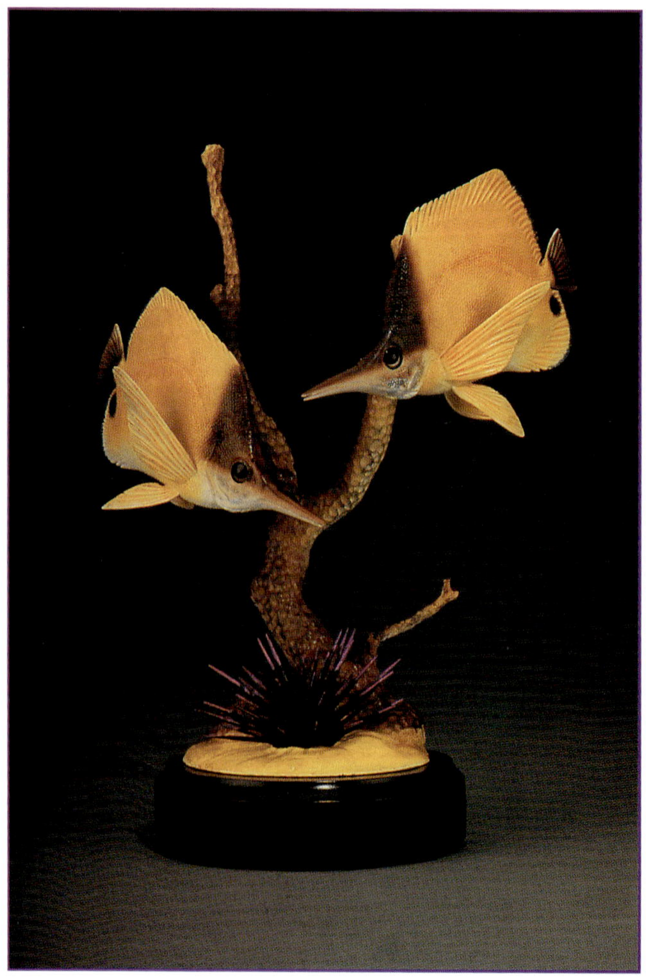

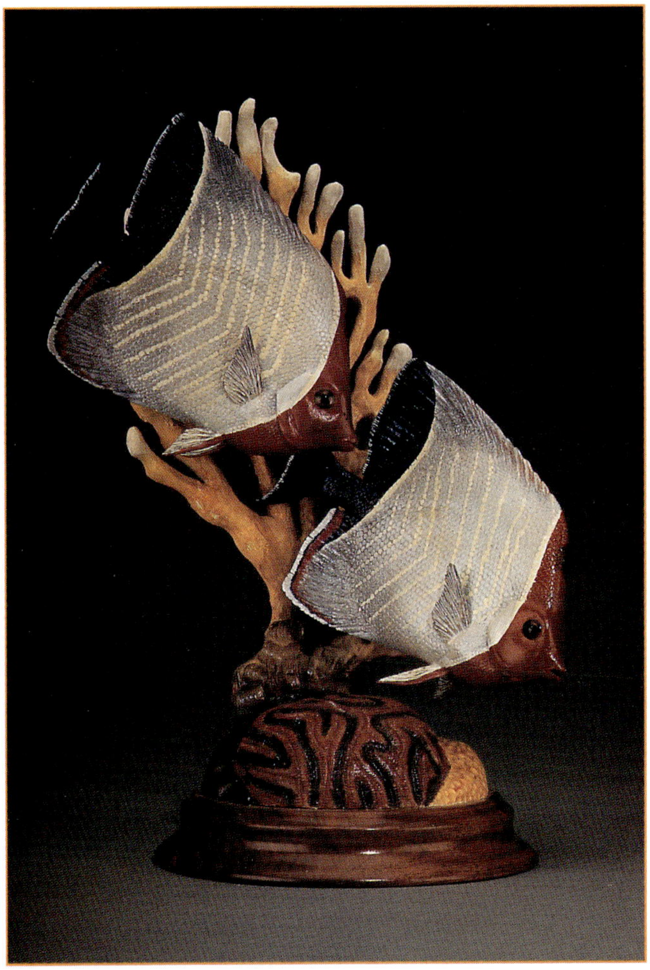

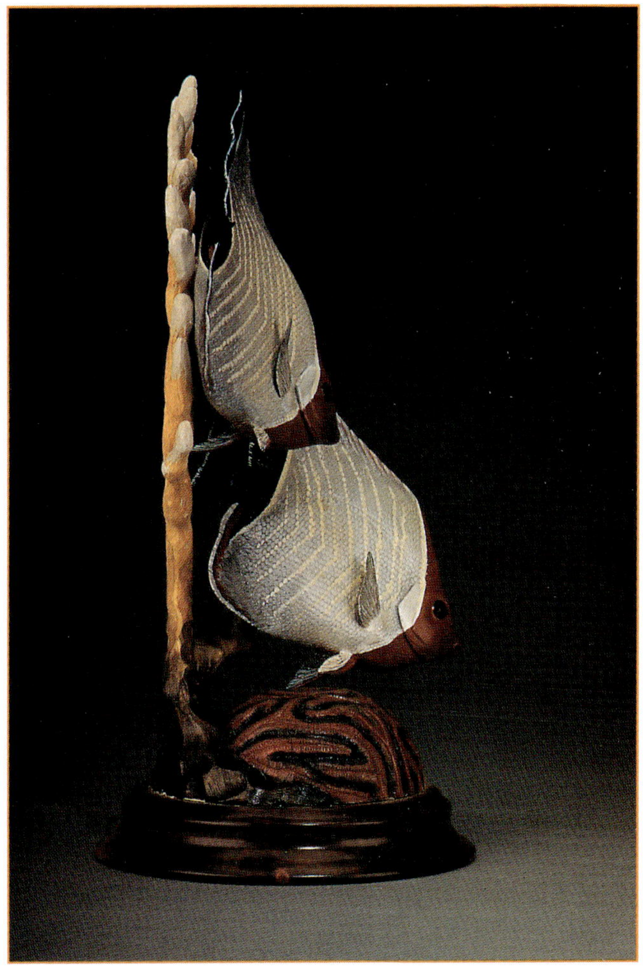

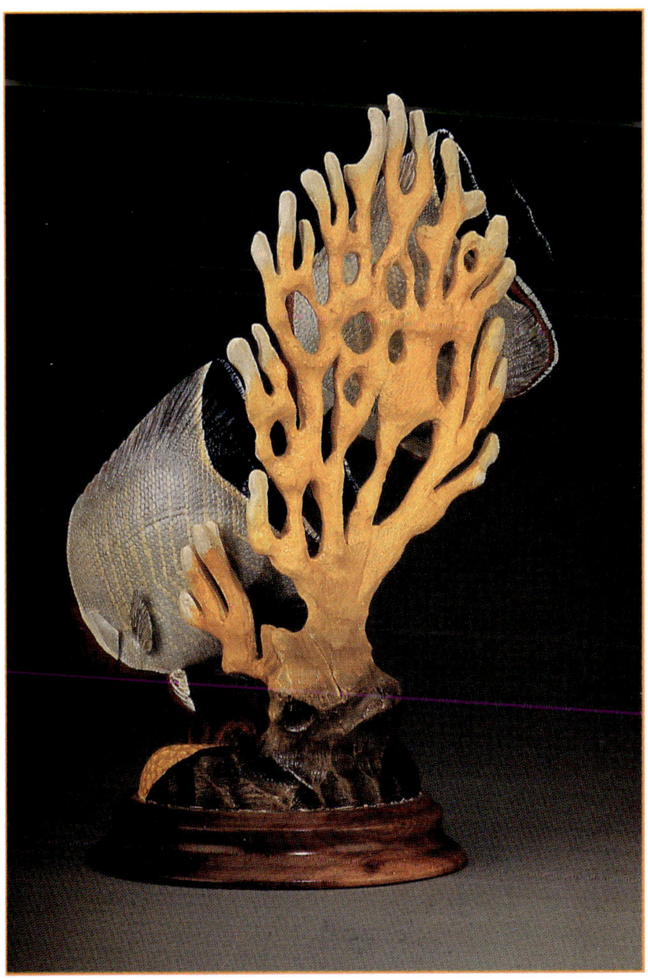

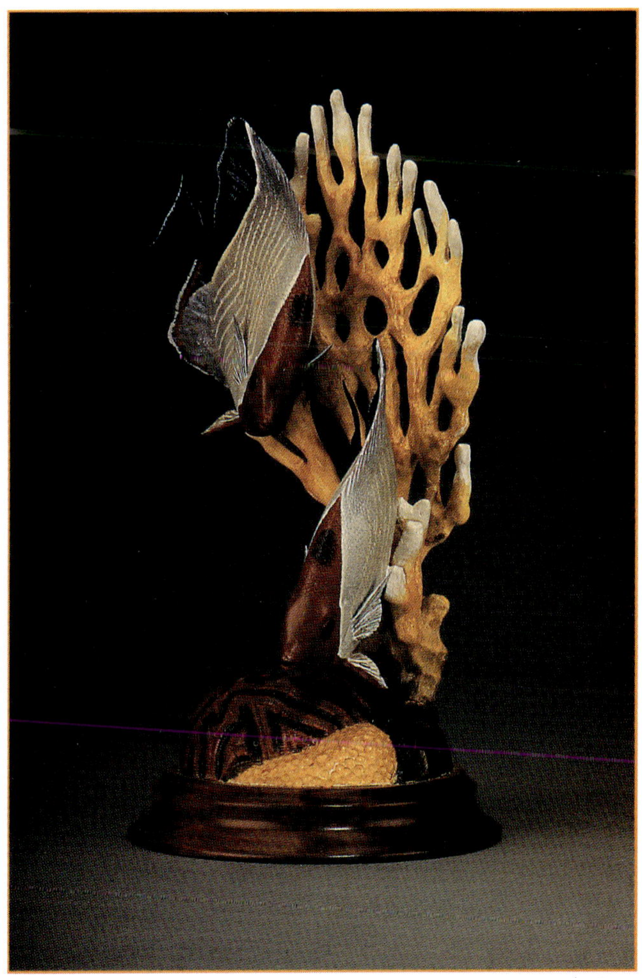

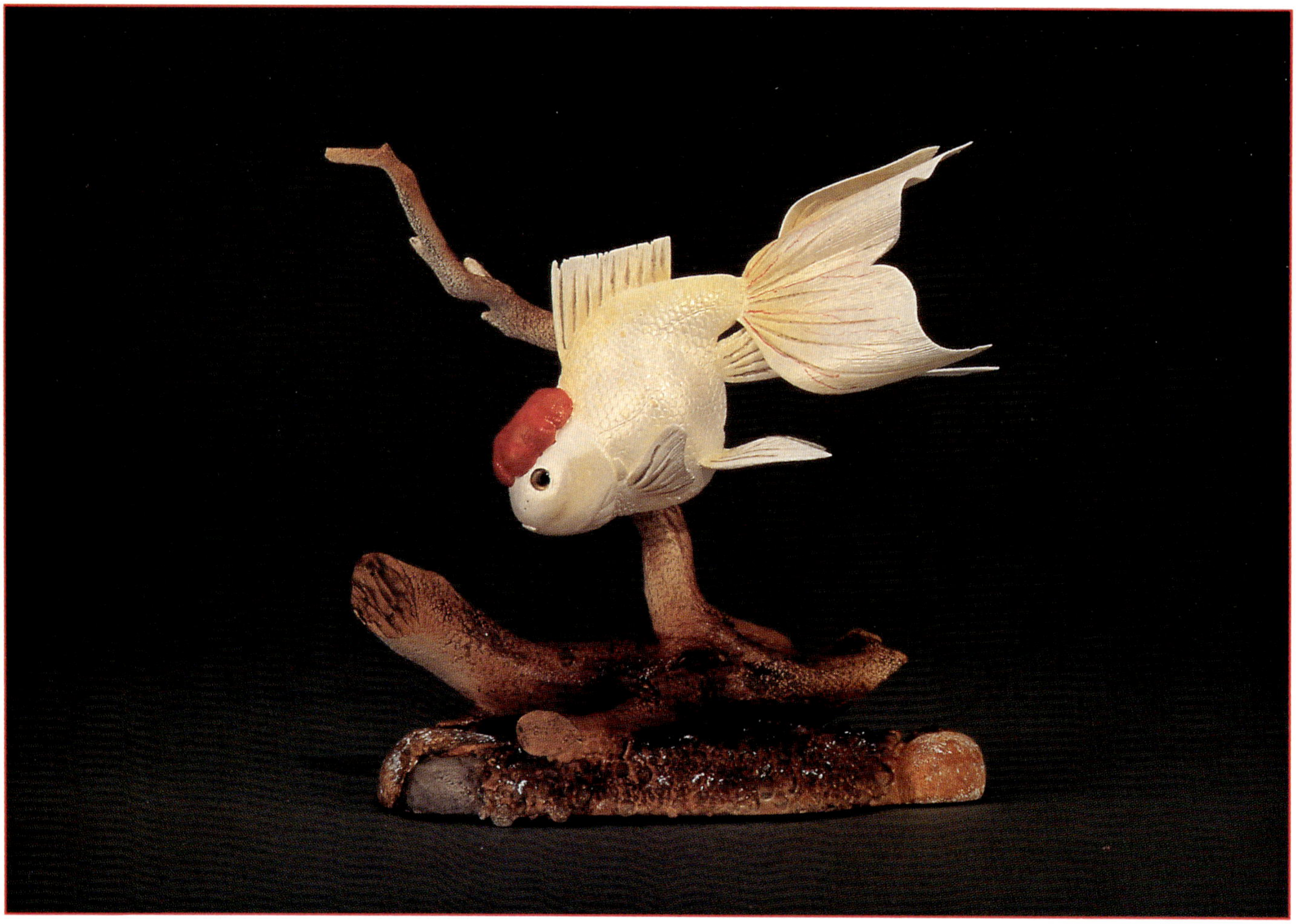

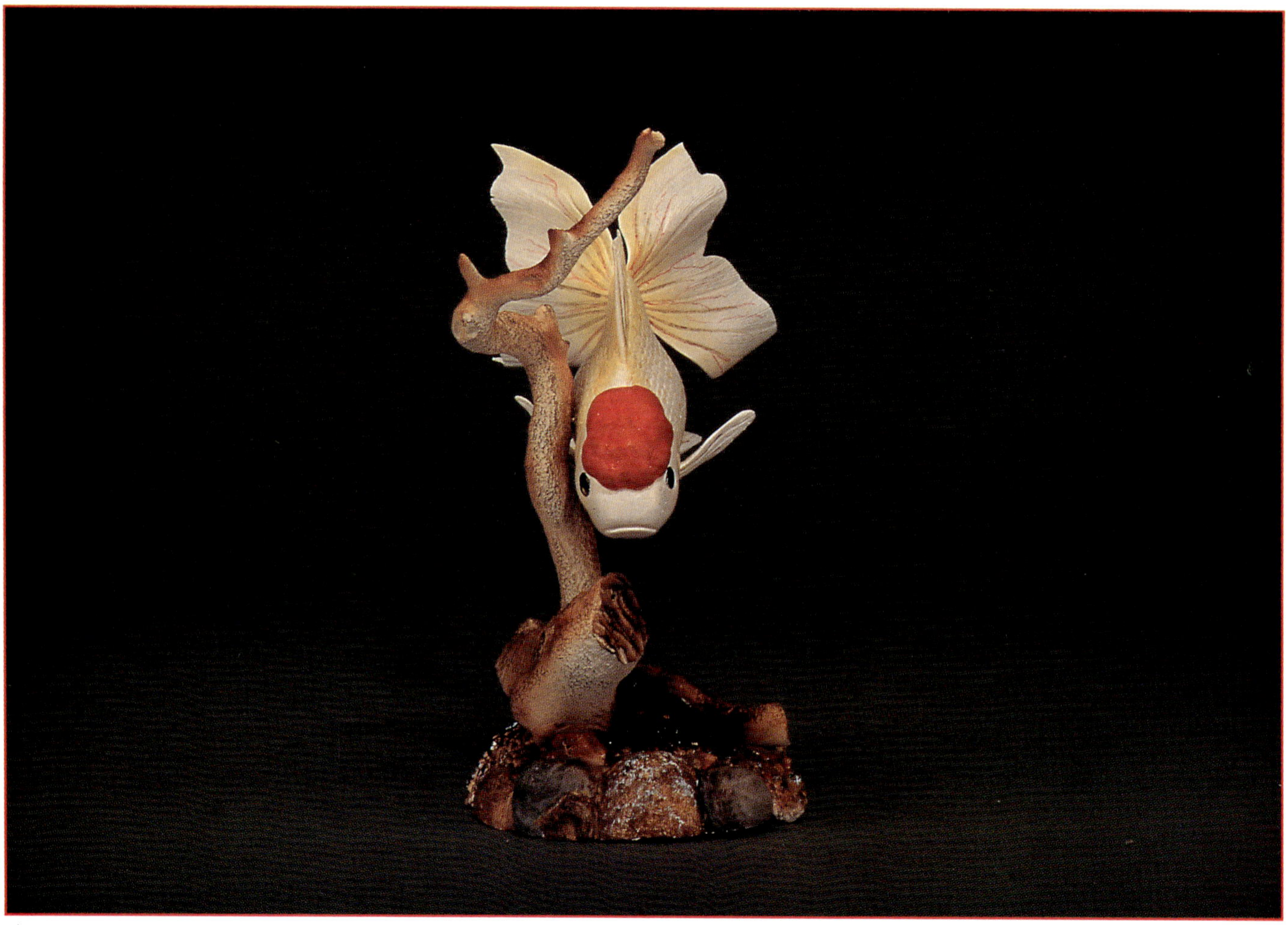

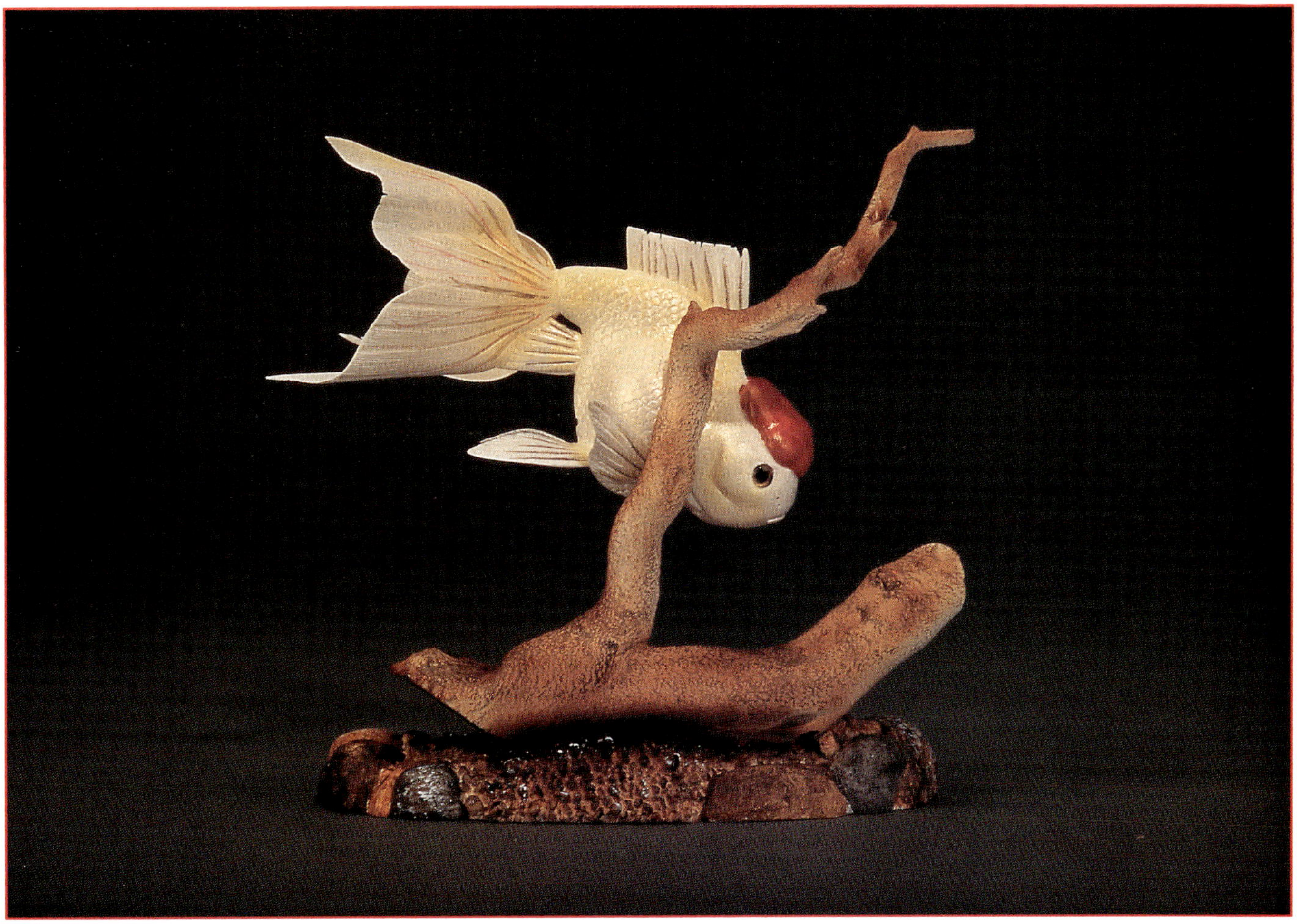

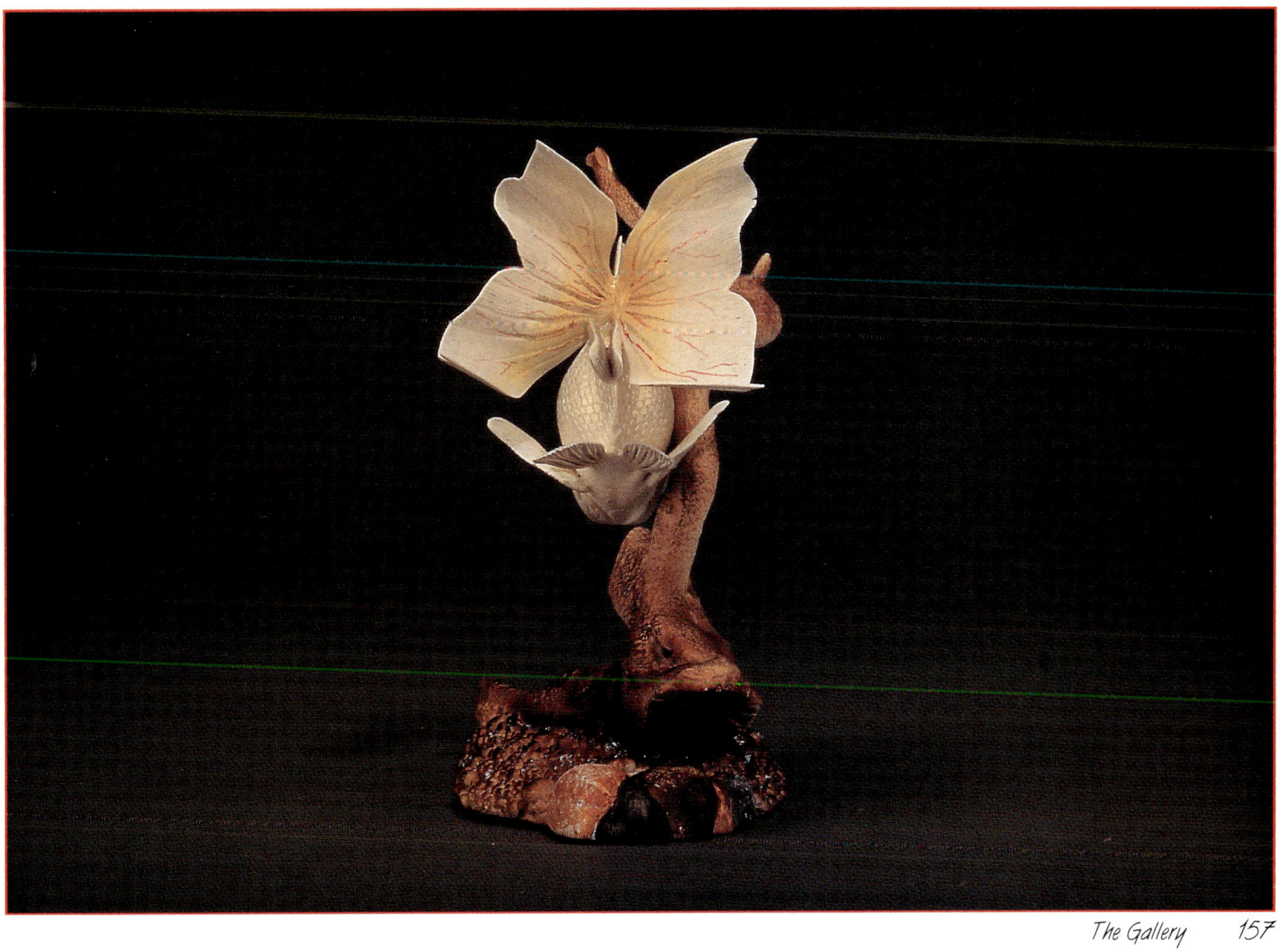

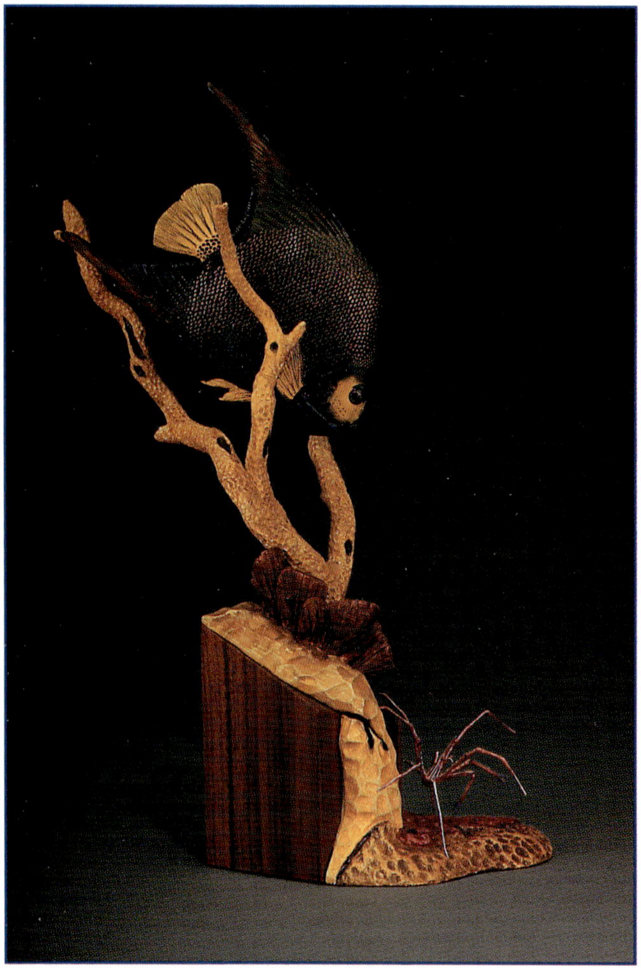

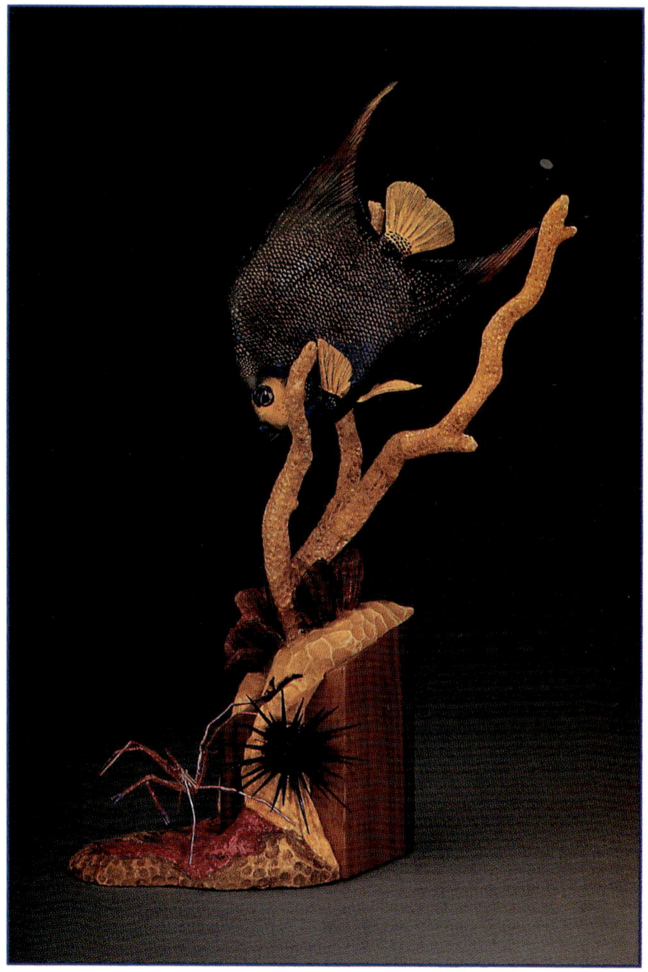

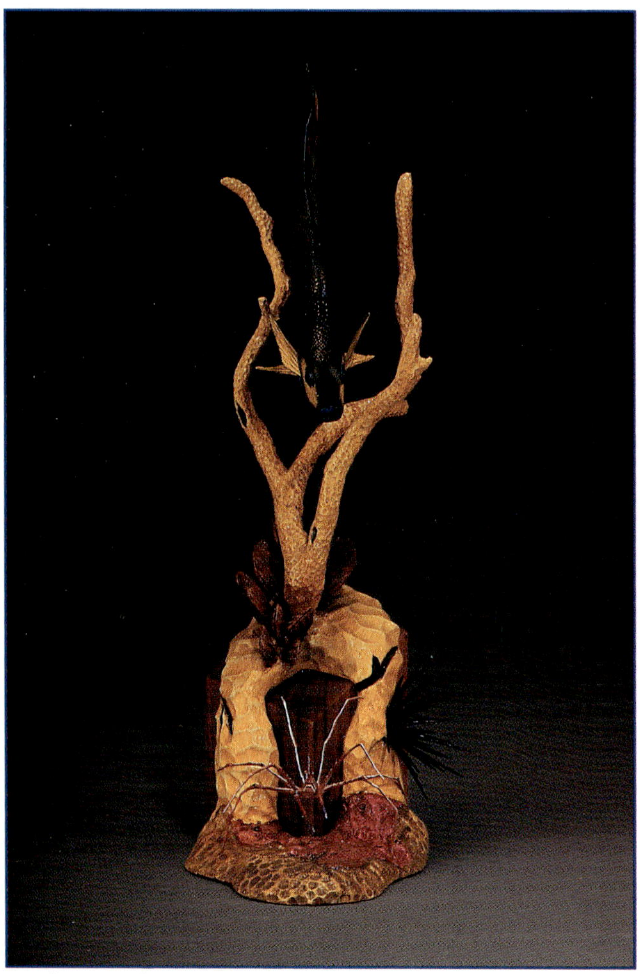

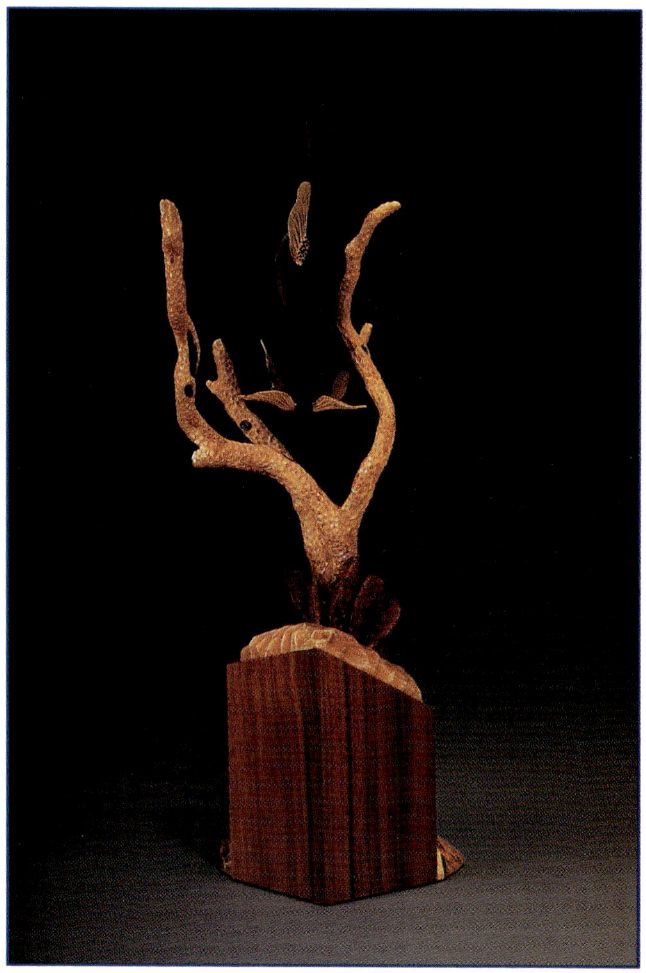

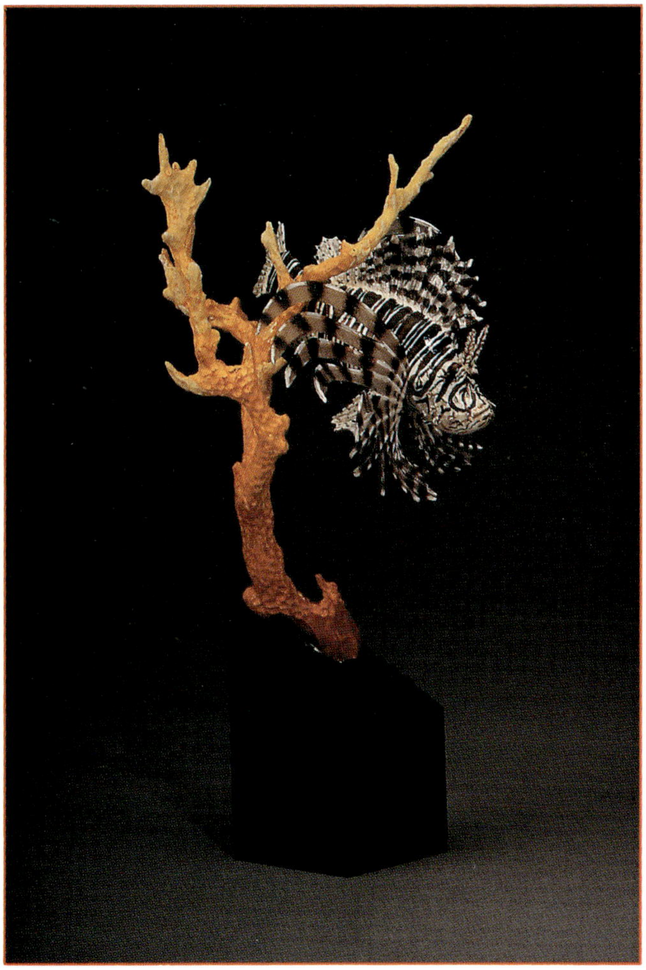

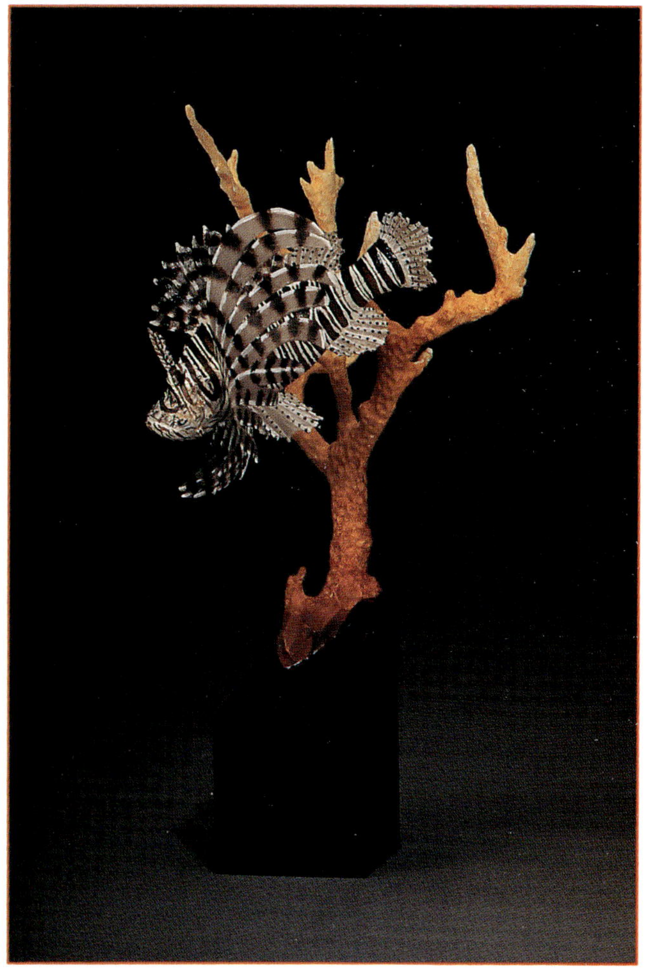

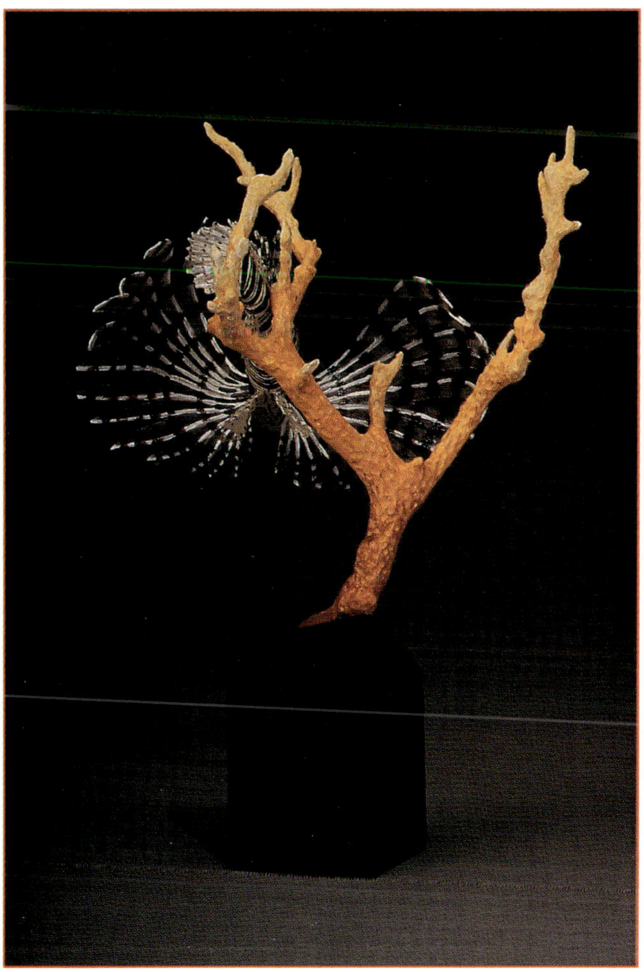

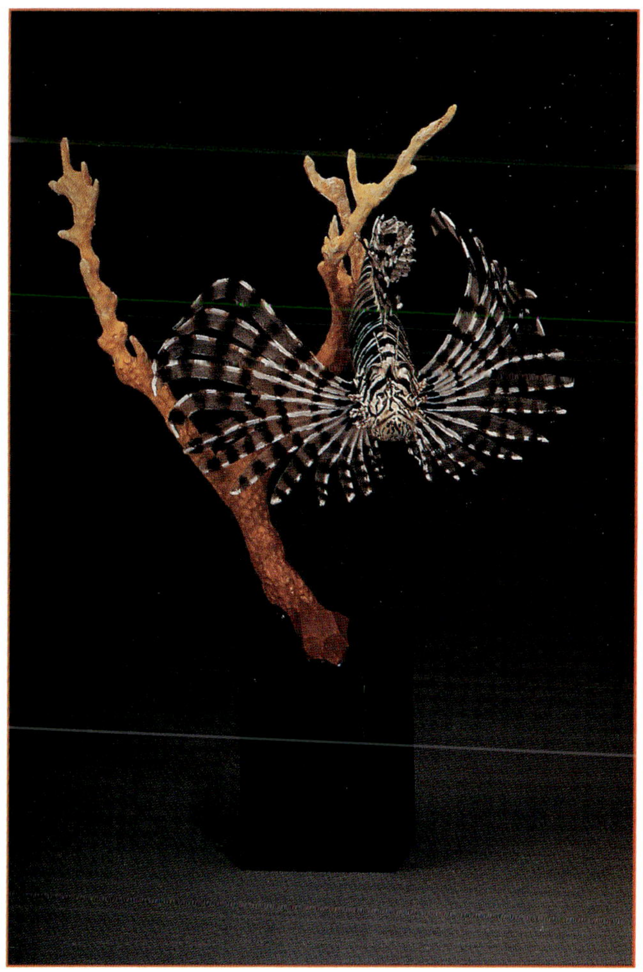

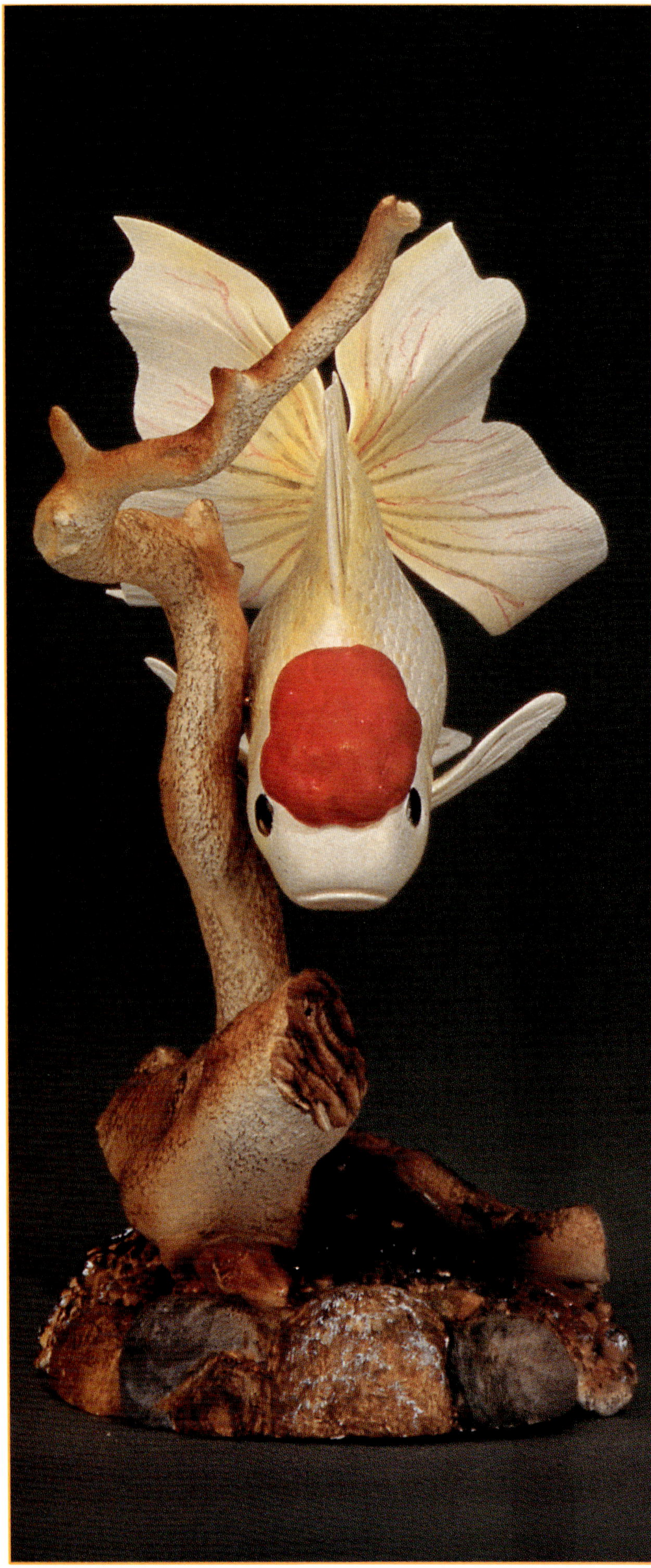

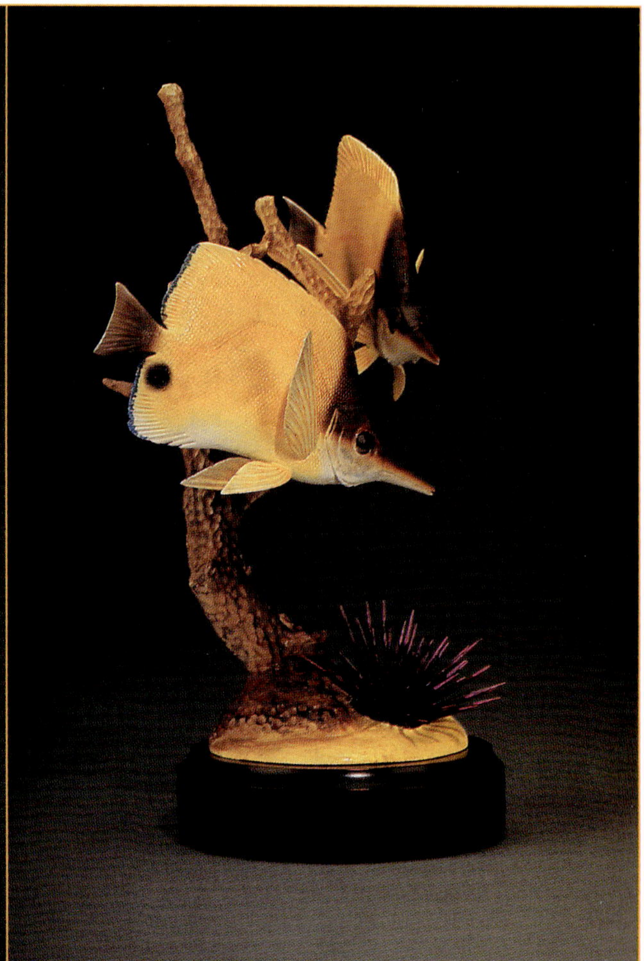

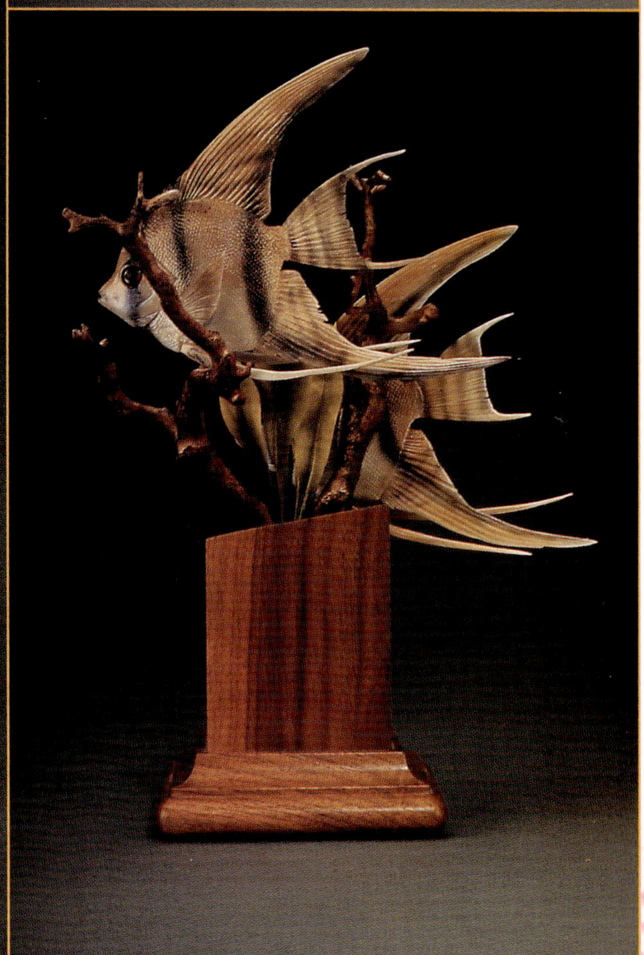